Spanish Golden Age Drama

El teatro del Siglo de Oro

Spanish Golden Age Drama

An Annotated Bibliography of United States Doctoral Dissertations 1899–1992 with a Supplement of Non-United States Dissertations

El teatro del Siglo de Oro

Bibliografía comentada de tesis doctorales estadounidenses 1899–1992 con una lista complementaria de tesis de varios otros países

John J. Reynolds
Szilvia E. Szmuk

The Modern Language Association of America

New York • 1998

Library of Congress Cataloging-in-Publication Data

Reynolds, John J., 1924–
Spanish Golden Age drama : an annotated bibliography of United States doctoral dissertations, 1899–1992 ; with a supplement of non-United States dissertations / John J. Reynolds, Szilvia E. Szmuk = El teatro del Siglo de Oro : bibliografía comentada de tesis doctorales estadounidenses, 1899–1992 ; con una lista complementaria de tesis de varios otros países / John J. Reynolds, Szilvia E. Szmuk.
p. cm.
Includes indexes.
ISBN 0-87352-570-1 (cloth)
1. Spanish drama—Classical period, 1500–1700—History and criticism—Bibliography. 2. Dissertations, Academic—United States —Bibliography. I. Szmuk, Szilvia E. II. Title.
Z2694.D7R6 1998
[PQ6105]
016.862'309—dc21 98-10630

Printed on recycled paper

Published by The Modern Language Association of America
10 Astor Place, New York, New York 10003-6981

Contents | Contenido

IN MEMORIAM

HANNAH E. BERGMAN

1925–1981

Preface

Some of us like to travel with maps. It comforts us to see which roads have been traveled, where densely populated areas are, where a dirt road may have been washed away by a storm. Others like to strike out and conquer the unknown. We offer you this bibliography as an inset in the collection of reference books that map Golden Age drama scholarship. The present work is a compilation of doctoral dissertations accepted in the United States from 1899 to 1992 on Spanish *Siglo de Oro* theater, supplemented with a listing of doctoral dissertations from Canada and several Western European countries, written on the subject between 1817 and 1992. We have covered only those foreign countries for which we have had adequate sources of current information.

In compiling this bibliography, we had the pleasure of discovering not only centers and periods of scholarly pursuit (e.g., at the University of Iowa under the tutelage of Edmund DeChasca) but also the possibility of following a line of scholarship, for example, from H. C. Heaton to E. W. Hesse to W. C. McCrary to D. H. Darst, who has directed a number of dissertations. It is hoped that Darst's students will direct dissertations in their turn. Readers may notice other trends, as well as the fact that United States and European dissertations seem to differ in tone and emphasis.

We hope that this bibliography will go beyond being appreciated as a simple reference tool in aiding scholars to choose, or to avoid, topics for dissertations or other projects. A doctoral candidate may wish to pursue a subject on which a previous dissertation has appeared, especially if the original work lacked substance or scope, but the existence of such a dissertation should be acknowledged, as well as the reason for which the new treatment is needed. By the same token, the discovery of a recently completed dissertation of high quality will rightfully deter someone from covering the same terrain.

We also wish to say a word about an unexpected finding in our research. Little did we suspect at the outset of this project what a psychological Pandora's box we would be opening. We learned that few personal or professional relationships seem to be as fraught with anxiety as those between student and director. If no dissertation has been written on this specific subject, psychologists and sociologists take heed!

Where *Dissertation Abstracts* (since 1951), *Dissertation Abstracts International* (from 1969), or other sources recorded the name of the director, we incorporated this information in our entry. Often our first notice about a dissertation came from *Hispania* (AATSP) with the mention of a director, but we could not be sure if that professor actually saw the dissertation through to completion. In a large percentage of cases we had no reference at all to a director. During the long process of compilation, we wrote directly to individuals, departments, libraries, and university archives asking them to supply the missing names of directors. The scope of answers was astounding. Not only did we learn about dissertations that have been lost forever (e.g., Rosenbach, Sears, Stephenson, etc.), but we also found dissertations on which the adviser's scrawl is so faded or illegible that even the archivist has lost hope of restoring a bit of university history. Also encountered were dissertations without any signatures, as well as many dissertations whose author's preface does not acknowledge intellectual indebtedness to anyone. Perhaps some of these practices reflect trends and fashions; others may bespeak strained relationships.

Even more telling were the answers to personal queries at the MLA and other gatherings. One of the compilers casually asked someone about his dissertation director and got an icy stare in reply, while the response of a second scholar was to regale the interviewer with intimate and touching details about the assistance this person's adviser had offered. Yet another colleague carefully explained that the person who gave her the most substantial and scholarly help was not on her "team," did not sign the dissertation, and, in fact, teaches on the other side of the Atlantic Ocean. Finally, one interviewee requested that we omit the director's name, since he was not deserving of that honor, never having taken an interest in or even having read the work. We have also read many introductions in which the director was acknowledged with profuse expressions of gratitude.

We would like to mention that we have experienced the truth of the warning in David J. Billick's foreword (see below): a large database of bibliographical citations *alone* does not meet the researcher's needs. We contacted the Fichier Central des Thèses (Nanterre, France) with a well-defined request for Spanish Golden Age drama dissertations. The reply was over two hundred items at a cost of $50. The results sent to us included anything and everything Spanish and Spanish American in the humanities and social sciences—all genres, all periods. Only about a dozen titles were relevant to our bibliography. Thus we learned at no small expense the wisdom of Billick's words: ". . . thorough use of bibliographic tools, in print or in machine-readable format, requires a combination of subject expertise, knowledge of the access tools, and research skills that few discipline specialists have, or can be expected to have."

We wish to emphasize that much of what we have compiled is secondhand information, and although we take responsibility for our own possible mistakes, some inaccuracies may have been transcribed from previous sources.

Because of restrictions on our time, finances, and, to a certain degree, available resources, we had to set limits on the scope of this work. Undoubtedly, an open-ended project of this type lends itself to updating as well as to expanding its geographical coverage. For example, we plan to include in our next edition the Italian *dottorato di ricerca* (established in 1980), regarded as the equivalent of the PhD and the Spanish *doctorado*. We would be happy to receive additions or corrections that will enhance future editions of this research tool.

Finally, for a look at the lighter (or perhaps darker) side of dissertations, we think the reader might enjoy "The Ghost Who Vanished by Degrees," an amusing short story, apropos the subject at hand, by Robertson Davies (1913–95) in his entertaining collection entitled *High Spirits.*

This authors' preface is followed by Karen Anderson's brief history of the American PhD, in which she shows the European, specifically

German, origin of the degree. There follows a foreword by Billick—the director (1989–92) of dissertations publishing at University Microfilms—in which he explains the need for a cumulative bibliography such as this one. Next, the introduction describes in detail the component parts of each bibliographical entry as well as the characteristics of the three indexes. The front matter concludes with acknowledgments, works consulted, a directory of institutions that identifies abbreviated institutional names, and a list of acronyms, abbreviations, and journal titles. The body of the work identifies pertinent doctoral dissertations from the United States, numbered 1 to 853, followed by doctoral dissertations from outside the United States, numbered 1001 to 1616. The back matter comprises an index of institutions, an index of dissertation writers and directors, and a subject and title index.

Prologue

The American PhD Rooted in European Tradition

Karen Anderson

Academic degrees have been awarded for more than eight hundred years. The first recorded was the doctorate conferred by the University of Bologna in the middle of the twelfth century. In the thirteenth century, the University of Paris conferred its first doctoral degree, and the academic model soon spread to Britain. By the sixteenth century, another variation of the doctorate had begun to develop in Germany. Three centuries later, the American PhD was born.

American higher education was founded on two European patterns: the English college and the German university. The English college system was the model for American undergraduate education; but in the early years, there was no graduate level in the American college. Scholars seeking graduate education during the nineteenth century traveled overseas to attend German universities.

The major German universities attended by American students were Göttingen, Berlin, Leipzig, Halle, Heidelberg, and Freiburg. Nearly ten thousand Americans made academic pilgrimages during the nineteenth century, and approximately half of that group matriculated at the University of Berlin. Outside Germany, sizable numbers of American students enrolled in the University of Vienna and in several Swiss universities—institutions influenced by the German tradition.

Studies at the German university were exciting—emphasizing freedom of teaching and learning, respect for logical arrangement of thought, the gathering of information, the classification and ordering of things, and the reporting of discoveries.

Equally compelling were German teaching methods, the most

important being the lecture, which differed from the American classroom recitation or the English tutorial system. The German method provided the student with an introduction to an entire field of study through a series of connected group lectures.

A second method was the seminar, or "seminary" as it was known. It provided training for independent study and investigation of a significant problem, equipping the student with the skills needed to conduct scientific work on their own.

American students were also attracted to the German university's library, museum, and laboratory. No contemporary American university had a comprehensive library, and, typically, the few volumes on the library shelves were not easily available for borrowing by students (Walters 9).

Graduate scholars returned to the United States with the German spirit of free thought, scholarly thoroughness, and hard work, providing the impetus for the university movement in America in the 1850s. The influence of these European-trained minds was considerable, and prominent scholars—many of whom returned from Germany to accept teaching posts at major eastern universities—expressed the desire to expand existing institutions or found new institutions that mirrored German universities.

As early as 1852, Bucknell University, in Lewisburg, Pennsylvania, awarded the honorary doctor of philosophy. However, not until 1860 did the earned PhD come to the United States. Stimulus for the American PhD came from the faculty of the then recently established Sheffield Scientific School at Yale University. At a meeting of the Yale Corporation held 24 July 1860, a proposal from the Scientific School recommended that

> . . . the degree of *Doctor of Philosophy* be instituted and in accordance with the usage of German Universities be conferred on those students who have successfully pursued the above-named higher course of scientific study . . . that the same degree of Doctor of Philosophy . . . be conferred for high attainments in Mathematics and Philology or such other branches as may be taught in the Department of Philosophy and the Arts.
>
> This degree . . . would remove a disadvantage under which our Department of Philosophy and the Arts labors in comparison with

> similar departments of German Universities. . . . Its establishment here would . . . enable us to retain in this country many young men, and especially students of Science, who now resort to German Universities. (Chittenden 1: 87–88)

Qualifications included

- studies in residence of at least one year before the PhD examination
- satisfactory examination in the specific course of study
- a written thesis containing original research and approved by faculty members.

America's first PhD recipients were James Morris Whiton, Arthur Williams Wright, and Eugene Schuyler, all of whom had previously earned their bachelor's degrees from Yale University. Whiton studied in the Yale department of philosophy and the arts from 1859 to 1861, continuing his Latin, Greek, and German without an instructor but passing examinations in each. In addition, he studied Sanskrit two hours a week for two years and turned in a six-page handwritten thesis in Latin, an essay on the proverb *Brevis vita, ars longa.* (Whiton's dissertation still exists and is available from UMI.) Wright's dissertation, Having Given the Velocity and Direction of Motion of a Meteor on Entering the Atmosphere of the Earth, to Determine Its Orbit about the Sun, Taking into Account the Attractions of Both These Bodies, has been lost over the years.

Schuyler submitted his study, Wedgewood on English Philology, which was printed the following year in *Bibliotheca Sacra* as a review article of twenty-four pages (Spurr 117).

Of the three men who first received the new degree at Yale in 1861, one became a minister and professor of ethics in a theological seminary, a second became a diplomat in the foreign service, and only one became a professor (of physics and chemistry).

Additional early degrees of doctor of philosophy were conferred by the University of Pennsylvania in 1871, by Harvard University in 1873, and by Columbia University in 1875. The first PhD awarded to a woman was earned by Helen Magill, at Boston University in 1877.

The founding of Johns Hopkins University—sometimes referred to as the first "real American university"—in 1876 brought commitment to graduate and advanced education. Johns Hopkins combined the worthiest elements of both the German university—the lecture, the seminar, the independent study—and the American college that had evolved in the 250 years since the founding of Harvard. Mirroring German methods, the new Baltimore institution nurtured freedom of teaching and learning, as well as freedom from traditional American instructional methods. Within a few years, Johns Hopkins had come to set the standards for graduate education, conferring its first PhD in 1878.

Following in the footsteps of Johns Hopkins, Clark University and Catholic University set up graduate programs in 1889, and the University of Chicago did so in 1890. In 1890 the Regents of the University of Nebraska recommended that the doctor of philosophy degree be granted on the condition that no extra expenses were incurred for instruction. Nebraska, which established the first graduate school in a state university, was followed in the same year by Harvard, Michigan, Wisconsin, and Kansas.

The evolution of American graduate study contributed two important new dimensions to higher education by the onset of the twentieth century. College teaching became recognized as a career for which a student specifically prepared, and the college curriculum became more sharply divided into disciplines similar to those in which the teachers had done their graduate work.

The development of the PhD at Johns Hopkins greatly influenced practices at other institutions. Standards established in 1876 were high but lenient by present-day standards. The required period between the bachelor's and doctoral degrees stretched from two to three years in 1881, and a graduate academic council controlled the program by 1883. In 1884 in-residence study requirements increased from one to two years, and by 1885 thesis requirements—including format, use of a typewriter, and the submission of a copy to the school's library—were outlined. Within two years French and German reading examinations and the appointments of an official adviser and two outside examiners to read the thesis were required.

Students played an important part in the development of standards for the PhD through affiliated graduate clubs on different university campuses. The first club was founded at Harvard in 1889. The first joint meeting of affiliated clubs was held by Harvard, Cornell, and Johns Hopkins in 1893. The Federation of Graduate Clubs, organized in 1896, held an annual convention for a number of years. At its 1896 convention the federation recommended that the minimum requirements for the doctor of philosophy degree should be

- the previous attainment of a bachelor's degree or equivalent
- the completion of at least two years of resident graduate study, one year of which should be on the campus of the institution conferring the degree
- an adequate examination
- a thesis covering the results of original research (Spurr 118–19).

By 1900, fourteen universities—Johns Hopkins, Columbia, Chicago, California, Harvard, Yale, Pennsylvania, Princeton, Clark, Cornell, Catholic University, Stanford, Michigan, and Wisconsin—actively engaged in graduate education. This group awarded nearly 90% of all doctoral degrees.

Efforts to standardize the PhD and promote scholarship at the institutional level began with the activities of the Association of American Universities (AAU), established in 1900, and the National Association of State Universities (NASU), dating from 1905. By 1908 an NASU committee recommended that the period of postgraduate study for the degree be at least three years, one of which should be in residence at the degree-granting institution. The AAU followed suit in 1916, so that the concept of a three-year rather than a two-year doctorate was generally accepted before World War I.

The evolution of the PhD in the twentieth century has been marked by a greater standardization of quality, the elimination of the PhD as an honorary degree, the extension of the PhD to applied fields and virtually all subject matters taught in the university, and a doctoral-study period lengthened to four or five years of enrollment and seven to eight years of total graduate work.

By 1935, present PhD practices had fully evolved. While the basic program has changed very little, the trend has been to microfilm rather than offset-print the dissertation, to add flexibility to (or even drop) the foreign language requirement, to add more course work at the graduate level, and to put increased emphasis on early "qualifying" examinations (Spurr 119).

In the United States the introduction of the doctorate was seen as a bold step, since American colleges were considered by most European and English scholars to be, at best, baccalaureate-level institutions. By the 1940s, however, the American universities had the capacity to train scholars at the highest level in every branch of modern knowledge, and their faculties were making contributions to learning that granted them worldwide prominence. Today the American doctorate has gained the respect of European scholars and is sought by students worldwide.

The years 1876 to 1900 were a period of educational revolution for colleges in the United States. In 1890 approximately 200 earned doctorates were conferred, increasing to 382 in 1899. At the same time, 150 universities offered graduate study while only about one-third of them conferred the prestigious doctoral degree. By 1925, earned PhDs totaled 1,200 annually, and by the early 1970s, the number ranged between 33,000 and 34,000.

Through 1988 more than 800,000 PhDs had been awarded in the United States. Today, nearly 36,000 earned doctoral degrees are conferred each year by more than 360 regionally accredited universities across the country (according to the National Research Council). Of that number, approximately 65% are awarded to men and 35% to women.

According to the Council of Graduate Schools in the United States, many students attend graduate school to earn master's degrees only; fewer go on to receive their doctorates. On the average, however, student enrollment in graduate schools in the United States increases at a rate of about 1% per year.

The nature of the doctorate has changed. The older European doctorate was an honor bestowed on those who had reached the peak of learning, but today the American doctorate has come to signify that the holder has acquired the tools and habits that will allow him or her to become a scholar or a teacher.

With the advent of micropublishing in 1938, UMI began publishing doctoral dissertations—not only helping students to meet the graduate school's publication requirements but also making individual research available worldwide.

A great deal has changed since UMI founder Eugene B. Power pioneered microphotography and economical, on-demand publishing of doctoral dissertations. Today, UMI offers access to the dissertations database through printed reference sources and online and ondisc searching.

Most major libraries offer and use UMI's printed reference tools, which cite more than one million dissertations worldwide. *Dissertation Abstracts International* and *Masters Abstracts International* are available by subscription—providing concise abstracts of the most current dissertations and theses published. The *Comprehensive Dissertation Index* provides citations of all American and Canadian dissertations, dating back to the first, in 1861.

Many libraries also provide access through electronic media. Individual researchers and librarians alike can perform specialized searches of UMI's database through online or CD-ROM services. Once relevant dissertations are identified, users can order full-text copies from UMI by mail, by phone, or as part of their online search. Dissertation copies are available in paper, on microfilm, or on microfiche.

Currently, UMI offers more than 700,000 dissertations from more than 550 graduate schools around the world. Approximately 35,000 new dissertations are added each year, further enhancing the world's most comprehensive collection of current and historical doctoral research.

Works Cited

Chittenden, Russell H. *History of the Sheffield Scientific School of Yale University, 1846–1922.* 2 vols. New Haven: Yale UP, 1928.

Spurr, Stephen H. *Academic Degree Structures: Innovative Approaches.* San Francisco: Carnegie Foundation for the Advancement of Teaching, 1970.

Walters, Everett. *Graduate Education Today.* Washington: American Council on Education, 1965.

Adapted with permission of University Microfilms, Incorporated, from *Research Update* (Spring-Summer 1989): 2, 42–44. University Microfilms Inc., 300 North Zeeb Road, Ann Arbor, MI 48106-1346

Foreword

The dissertation has formed an integral part of the doctoral degree process in the United States for over a century. Unfortunately, much of the valuable information contained in these studies remained largely untapped for many years because, in general, few titles were widely disseminated and the dissertations themselves were difficult to acquire in an easily readable form. Even after these problems were partially alleviated by the appearance of *Microform Abstracts* (1938) and *Dissertation Abstracts* (1951), followed by *Dissertation Abstracts International* (1969), many leading institutions initiated their participation in the system at relatively late dates—for example, Berkeley (1962), Yale (1963), Chicago (1974), and Harvard (1982). It should be noted that what we now know as *Dissertation Abstracts International (DAI),* although it had been in print for over half a century, really acquired the status of a comprehensive source of citation in the late 1960s and early 1970s. By this time the vast majority of doctoral-granting institutions were submitting records for inclusion in the database.

Part of the value of a fixed cumulation like this one—focusing on one genre and a well-defined literary period—results from the enormous effort put forth in examining scores of other printed bibliographies, card catalogs, automated catalogs, and even footnotes, to identify the material not included in *DAI.* The addition of pagination, directors' names, summaries of abstracts, and publications that derived from the dissertation, or are related to it, further enhances the worth of the Reynolds-Szmuk endeavor.

It may be argued that with the growth in coverage of *DAI* and with the availability of electronic access to dissertation citations, printed cumulations like this one are obsolete. I would argue quite the contrary. As databases become larger and more comprehensive, it becomes more difficult for the specialist to identify relevant material without the sort of classifying and indexing that John J. Reynolds and Szilvia E. Szmuk have done. *DAI* now includes in excess of one million citations. Even if the total domain is restricted to dissertations in the field of "literature," there are over seventy thousand titles to examine. The identification of the approximately seven hundred "hit records" on Spanish Golden Age drama, out of this vast universe of information, is *formidable* indeed. Furthermore, thorough use of bibliographic tools, in print or in machine-readable format, requires a combination of subject expertise, knowledge of the access tools, and research skills that few discipline specialists have, or can be expected to have.

In his book *Information Anxiety*, Richard Saul Wurman states that raw data, such as a large database of bibliographic citations, "must be imbued with form and applied to become meaningful information." Reynolds and Szmuk have made an invaluable contribution toward providing just such "form" to the continually expanding universe of Golden Age drama scholarship.

David J. Billick
Director, Dissertations Publishing, 1989-92
University Microfilms Inc. (UMI)

Introduction

This classified bibliography follows the same arrangement as the annual compilation on the *comedia* in the *Bulletin of the Comediantes.* The reasons are obvious: we have been compiling the annual bibliography for several years and the users of the volume at hand are likely to be the same public—hence already familiar with the categories used. For those who may not be acquainted with *BCom,* a brief sketch of the arrangement and our criteria for inclusion follows. The first section contains a broad category of general items related to Golden Age culture, history, art, and related subjects that may in some way shed light on themes discussed in the plays. The second section is also general, but more specifically focused on theater of the period. These sections are followed by an alphabetical list of playwrights, within which the individual entries are arranged alphabetically by dissertation writer under each dramatist. In addition, a few well-known themes in this field have been interfiled: Catalan theater, Don Juan theme, Inés de Castro theme, and Portuguese theater. As to the time span, we have focused on the theater of the sixteenth and seventeenth centuries, with an occasional look back to the beginnings (e.g., *Auto de los Reyes Magos*) and frequent looks forward to examine the influence of the Golden Age dramatists. The *Celestina* has been excluded (since a well-known bibliography on this work already exists) but not its dramatic continuations and imitations. With regard to such versatile authors as Lope de Vega, we have included their nondramatic works only when a dissertation writer has proposed a connection between them and the authors' theatrical works.

Several sources list dissertations annually, but we felt that no single reference tool gives an overview of all or most of the dissertations now available. Furthermore, none is annotated or leads scholars to the published results of the dissertations. Therefore we designed entries that meet what we believe to be the requirements of researchers interested in the field of Golden Age drama.

For each entry we have attempted to include the following information:

name of dissertation writer
title of dissertation
number of leaves or pages
institution (with specific campus that granted the degree)
name of director
date of submission or of awarding of degree
source reference
citation of the published version(s) of the dissertation
abstract or clarifying notation
resultant or related publication(s)

Little of the project was as straightforward as we had expected at the start. It soon became evident that each element of an entry could potentially present a problem all its own, beginning with the use of capitalization. We attempted to follow the rules of capitalization for each language. Thus in British and American titles all words (except articles and prepositions) are capitalized; in Spanish, only the first word; in French, an initial article and the noun that follows it; and in German, all nouns and verbs but not adjectives.

What follows is a breakdown of an entry into its component parts and an explanation of the problems we encountered, along with our solutions.

NAME: In each section, the names of the writers are listed and alphabetized using standard library practice: last name, first name, middle name or middle initial. Least problematic were simple (i.e., single) last names for males, because no change in the surname results from marriage or divorce (although some individuals use two forms of the first name—e.g., Louis and Luigi Imperiale). Somewhat more complicated were compound last names entered according to Spanish practice: father's surname followed by mother's (e.g., Carrasco Urgoiti, María Soledad). Portuguese rules, of course, differ from Spanish, and here we used the last element of the surname. Hispanics who live in the United States sometimes follow Anglo-American practice in signing publications; thus we noted variable forms for José Fernández Montesinos (José F. Montesinos), Diego Molina Marín (Diego Marín), and Alberto Sandoval Sánchez (Alberto Sánchez). Women scholars presented even further complications. Many completed their dissertation while still single, but all subsequent publications appeared under their married name (e.g., Hannah [Estermann] Bergman). Others did just the opposite, reverting to their parental name after a divorce (e.g., Doris L. Baum to Doris L. Meyer). Still others prefer to sign either or both names, depending on the publication (e.g., Alix Zuckerman/Alix Ingber). To complicate matters further, our bibliographic sources sometimes disagreed in the way they cited a name (e.g., Sirgado, Isabel M. Cid vs. Cid de Sirgado, Isabel Mercedes). Whenever possible, we have supplied cross-references and given as complete a form of the name as we knew (in spite of the confounding British habit of using only the initials of the first and middle names).

Title of Dissertation: We have tried to transcribe a complete and accurate title for each dissertation. Although we examined many dissertations at first hand, they still represent a relatively small percentage of all those we are including. Therefore we have had to rely on secondary sources. Where the dissertation title is nondescriptive or enigmatic, we have sought to clarify the matter in an editorial note.

Pagination: Our preferred way of indicating pagination is to report the front matter bearing roman numerals, followed by the text of the dissertation in arabic numbers. This method of paginating is most descriptive (and accurate), especially where an extensive introductory study was followed by text, such as an edition of a play (e.g., Kirk, C. F.: xcv+255 pp.). In these cases, we felt that the dissertation writer is given credit for the very substantial introduction, and the user immediately knows the exact length of the edition (i.e., the body of the dissertation). United States dissertations for which our only source was *DA* or *DAI,* as well as most European references, have a simple arabic numeral indicating the total number of leaves. UMI established this practice because at one time it charged a per-page fee for reproducing dissertations, combining front matter with the body of the text to calculate the payment. Bibliographic records found in OCLC and RLIN databases naturally follow Anglo-American cataloging rules, which reflect the number of leaves in a typescript or the number of pages in a printed book. We opted not to distinguish between pages and leaves; thus the abbreviation *pp.* is used in this book to refer not only to pages but also to leaves.

For a few United States dissertations and many more from outside the country, pagination is lacking. Some of these dissertations are no longer available (and we have noted that fact); therefore the length is unobtainable and ultimately irrelevant. In other cases, published versions exist, thereby making this element of data for the original dissertation less important.

INSTITUTION: In the index of institutions, in conjunction with the directory of institutions, we list the full and accurate name of each university included in this bibliography. To save space, we have shortened the names within the dissertation entries and used the name by which a school is best known. The choice was self-evident for the universities bearing distinctive names, such as Harvard, Johns Hopkins, and Yale. Most universities, however, take their name from the city in which they are located (which seems to give them a timeless quality) and are therefore listed thus, rather than by the specific name (e.g., Montpellier/III rather than Université Paul Valéry, or Münster rather than Westfälische Wilhelms Universität). As can be expected, this decision created the issue of which form of the city name to use. We decided to employ English equivalents for all cities: Copenhagen rather than København, Seville rather than Sevilla, Vienna rather than Wien. The matter becomes further complicated; because of the vagaries of war, politics, economics, and educational bureaucracy, universities have appeared, disappeared, or migrated from one country to another, changing their language, while standing in place (e.g., Strassburg and Strasbourg—German until 1681; French, 1681–1871; German, 1871–1918; French, 1918–40; German, 1940–45; and French again since the end of World War II). Many other universities have changed their name and accreditation status during their history.

The reader should bear in mind a noteworthy example of a changing name: for the Madrid institution historically known as Universidad Literaria, Universidad Central, and Universidad Complutense, we have used the simple form Complutense in the relevant entries.

The directory of institutions is divided into two sections: institutions in the United States and institutions outside the United States. In addition to complete name and town address, we have included the year of foundation. While it is generally assumed that only "universities" offer doctorates, there are exceptions: Bryn Mawr, Middlebury, and Boston College, to name just three. Wherever we noted a possible confusion (e.g., Boston University and Boston College), we were careful to differentiate. For universities with several locations, we have tried to identify the campus at which the PhD degree was awarded.

DIRECTOR: We decided to include the name of the director as one of the elements of the entry in the United States section. Our reason was to document the transmission of a line of scholarship and follow scholarly trends and relationships. The result of the dogged detective work is that we were able to ascertain the name of the director(s) in a high percentage of the cases. We hope that no one will feel slighted by our omissions in those instances in which we were unable to obtain the information. Perhaps the original intent of showing scholarly lineage has not been attained completely; nevertheless, we can see some clear lines of parentage. Unfortunately, this information was impossible to obtain for most dissertations outside the United States; therefore we opted not to include it in the few instances where we had personal contacts and learned the identity of the director.

DATE OF DEGREE: The year that appears in *DA* or *DAI* is the one most often accepted and quoted as the date the degree was granted. On occasion, the year on the title page of the dissertation is earlier (information that we ascertained from cataloging sources such as OCLC and RLIN). Our assumption is that there is frequently a lag between the submission of the dissertation and the granting of the degree. The inconsistency of dates seems more problematic with some of the European (especially early) dissertations.

SOURCE REFERENCE: Seventy percent of the dissertations listed in part 1 of this bibliography appear in *DA* or *DAI.* These are indicated by the *DA* or *DAI* volume and page reference. It is well-known that a number of universities historically did not participate in the UMI project. The number of noncontributing universities is diminishing in the United States; in fact, we are pleased to note that more and more European universities are starting to report to *DAI-C.*

Less well-known is the practice, at many institutions, of publishing summaries of the dissertations completed at their campuses: Harvard University *Summaries,* Iowa *Abstracts,* North Carolina *Record,* Stanford *Abstracts, Revista de la Universidad de Madrid,* and so on. Other universities included an abstract of the dissertation in the "Program of the Final Examination" (e.g., University of California, Berkeley) or "Announcement of the Final Examination" (e.g., University of California, Los Angeles). The diversity of the foregoing sources made it difficult to establish a uniform system of citation. Generally, quoted passages are from an abstract in a collection (Abs.). In the absence of such a source, we quoted directly from the dissertation (Diss.), the printed version of the dissertation (Prt. Diss.), the program, or the final examination announcement. In each instance we tried to give an accurate bibliographic citation of our source, so that any interested scholar may obtain the full text.

DISSERTATIONS SURVIVING IN PRINTED VERSION ONLY: This information appears in curly brackets {} as one element of some entries. In the 1920s and 1930s and even later, many universities in both the United States and Europe required dissertations to be published as a condition of acceptance. Many of these dissertations exist only in their printed form (e.g., L. Turkevich, Columbia University, 1950). It is not always clear whether the dissertations were simply printed at the expense of the doctoral candidate or had to pass rigorous editorial screening by the publisher. The concept of "published" is not easy to define; dissertations listed in *DA* or *DAI* are regarded by UMI as "published on demand." It is often especially difficult to determine whether a European title is in printed or other form.

Abstract or Other Annotation: Whenever possible, we quoted a few key sentences or a paragraph from the published abstract or from the writer's introduction to the dissertation. For critical editions—which are numerous—we indicate, wherever possible, the text(s) on which the edition is based. We supply ellipses where words or phrases were omitted at the beginning or middle of passages, and only in cases of typographical errors or embarrassing grammatical mistakes did we alter an author's words. We felt that the dissertation writers should speak for themselves. Of course, we do not attempt to pass judgment on these works. In the section on dissertations from outside the United States, we use square brackets to identify any commentary we provide.

Resultant or Related Publications: Dissertations have been a seminal force in the field of Golden Age drama. Frequently they are published in their entirety, or the most original parts are rewritten to appear as individual articles. We relied on MLA, OCLC, and RLIN searches, as well as our combined years of compiling the annual bibliography for the *Bulletin of the Comediantes*, to ferret out publications that we felt had their inception in a dissertation. These works are often more readily accessible than the original dissertation. Furthermore, books and articles that are an outgrowth of a dissertation may show a greater maturity and at times contain additional information. It should also be noted that a substantial number of related publications predate the granting of the degree.

The listing of resultant or related publications is introduced by the symbol ❖, and our findings are arranged in chronological order. For multiple publications, each citation is preceded by a capital letter in square brackets. We did not set a limit on the number of works we cited; therefore some scholars appear with one publication, others with as many as nine or ten publications. This list cannot be taken as a guide to a scholar's overall output. Our field is narrowly focused, and, while some academics choose to continue research in the area of their dissertation, others change intellectual direction completely or branch out into research concerning different Golden Age dramatists. Many dissertation writers have been honored with homage volumes that include a list of their publications. We have added all such references that have come to our attention.

Despite the rigorous guidelines we set for ourselves, not everyone will agree with all our choices. We know we have not been exhaustive; our intent was to point the researcher in the right direction. We were spared difficult editorial decisions in cases such as Robert Piluso's book *Amor, matrimonio y honra en Cervantes,* a verbatim printing of the dissertation typescript with the title changed. In other instances the relationships are less obvious. For example, we decided that doctoral candidates who chose to edit a play learned the methodology and the scholarly apparatus of this skill in the process of dissertation research. If one of their later publications treats the general topic of "editing," we see it as an outgrowth of something learned in the dissertation-writing process, even if the work relates to a different playwright. (See Cruickshank, Greer, Kirby, et al. in *Editing the* Comedia II. Ed. Michael McGaha and Frank P. Casa. Ann Arbor: Univ. of Michigan, Dept. of Romance Languages, 1991 [Michigan Romance Studies 11].) Where we perceived that the relationship between dissertation and later publication needed elaboration, we added clarification in square brackets.

For any one of a number of reasons, there may be no resultant or related publications in an entry: first, simply because none exists to date; second, we were unable to find one (perhaps because of a name change); third, after graduating, the doctoral candidate left the field of endeavor completely or developed scholarly interests in a different literary area; or, last, died shortly after the completion of the dissertation. Conversely, we would like to point out that there are many Hispanists currently active in Golden Age theater scholarship whose dissertations were not on that topic, among them John J. Allen, Frederick A. de Armas, Celsa Carmen García Valdés, and Joan Oleza Simó.

For European dissertations, our task was generally more difficult. Since firsthand access was well-nigh impossible, we had to forgo abstracts and summaries in most cases. Just to be able to clarify nondescriptive titles and to verify the relevance of ambiguous entries, we had to rely on the help of willing overseas contacts. So, in the absence of extensive information, we decided to include reviews of the dissertations (these appear on the dissertation title line separated by double slashes //) or, more frequently, reviews of the monographs that resulted from the dissertation. We felt that scholars in the United States might find the reviews more readily available and that these articles could shed some light on the work. A lowercase letter in parentheses separates one review from another. We collected these reviews from a wide variety of sources. The lack of standardization in the way these bibliographic entries appeared, including the use of differing acronyms, made this task particularly difficult.

DIRECTORY AND INDEXES: To make our reference work as useful as possible for researchers, we provide ease of access to all the information it contains, hence the one directory and three indexes:

Directory of institutions
Index of institutions
Index of dissertation writers and directors
Subject-title index

We opted not to assign separate numbering sequences to the two parts of this bibliography, yet we wanted users to distinguish easily between references to doctorates earned in the United States and doctorates earned abroad. Our solution was to number the foreign entries starting with 1001. As a result, in the combined indexes, users will immediately know that numbers 1-853 refer to United States entries, while those 1001 and higher represent non-United States items. Combining the indexes eliminates the need for searching in more than one index for any single element of information.

The total number of individual dissertations from the United States is 784. Multiple listings are included for such dissertations whose topic involves several playwrights; the full entry appears once in the most appropriate place; other entries have a *see* reference to the full listing (e.g., José A. Madrigal, La función del hombre salvaje en el teatro de Lope de Vega, Tirso de Molina y Calderón de la Barca). The total number of individual foreign dissertations is 577. More than one listing of such a dissertation also indicates that the topic involves more than one playwright. In addition, the reader will sometimes find more than one dissertation by the same writer, reflecting the complex French educational system. Historically in France there were four types of doctorates, with their corresponding dissertations: *Doctorat d'État, Nouveau Doctorat (régime de janvier 1984), Doctorat de 3e cycle,* and *Doctorat d'Université.* In earlier years there were also two types of French dissertations: *Thèse principale* and *Thèse complémentaire.* Because ours is a retrospective bibliography, we have recorded this information when it was available to us. Currently the French system consists of a *Doctorat* and an *Habilitation* (see Redondo 46, in works consulted). Except for the *Thèse d'État,* we have not included postdoctoral degrees that enable the candidate to aspire to a higher academic post, although we found an interesting reference to an 1843 *Pro venia docendi* dissertation by Carl Vilhelm Törnegren entitled Primordia artis scenicae Hispanorum adumbrans and completed at the University of Helsinki (founded in Turku). In Germany this type of dissertation is called a *Habilitationsschrift,* and we have had notice of several recent ones: Joachim Küpper, Sebastian Neumeister, and Christoph Strosetzki.

We would like to comment on two other foreign degrees that may be unfamiliar to our users. The Spanish *licenciatura* is granted at the end of five years of university studies and before the doctorate. The British "external degree" is conferred on a student who has not attended the university but has passed the qualifying examination.

We have attempted to make the subject-title index all-encompassing, thereby offering scholars entry points with either general (subject) or specific (title) information. We indexed only concepts and titles found in the dissertation title, or in the abstract or the printed version of the dissertation, but not in subsequent publications. Non-Spanish titles of literary works have been omitted from the subject-title index, because we felt that someone investigating a comparative literature topic would look under the headings Anglo-Spanish (Franco-Spanish, German-Spanish or Italo-Spanish, etc.) literary relations.

In the course of our work we came across several obscure references: little-known literary figures, unfamiliar themes and concepts. Since we cannot be certain that our audience will recognize them more readily than we did, we offer the result of our research in the form of a biographical or other editorial note to clarify or augment information. In view of the importance of chronology, we have indicated dates of even well-known literary figures. Our aim was to be helpful, and, if we err, we hope it is on the side of saying too much rather than too little.

Acknowledgments

We owe a particular debt of gratitude to James R. Chatham and his associates for their pioneering efforts listed in our works consulted. Their compilation of foreign dissertations—although different from ours in scope and detail—has been especially useful to us.

We are grateful to Hispanists from around the world; several dozen librarians, especially at St. John's University, the New York Public Library, and Arizona State University at Tempe; computer experts; mathematicians; musicians; and student assistants, for making a time-consuming and detailed project a little more manageable. Above all, we appreciate the many words and notes of encouragement we received from our colleagues who saw the value of this bibliography and expressed eagerness to use it.

The following individuals, many of them librarians and archivists, went out of their way to track down fugitive pieces of information in order to help us realize our project. We are grateful for their time and effort:

Robert D. Adamshick, Ofelia L. Alayeto, John J. Allen, Shyamala Balgopal, Susan Barribeau, Margarita Becedas González, John Beckham, Paul Belloni, Nuria Beltrán Grajera, Elizabeth Bigongiari, David J. Billick, D. Block, Robert W. Blue, Stewart Bodner, Kathleen Bourgeois, Robert Buckeye, James F. Burke, Richard A. Cardwell, María Soledad Carrasco Urgoiti, Joan Collette, Alice R. Cotten, Ana Cristan, Don W. Cruickshank, Halina Czarnocka, David H. Darst, Martin Davis, Stephen Davison, Frederick A. de Armas, Ángela B. Dellepiane, Chris

Densmore, Alan D. Deyermond, Virna R. Díaz, Jean Dickson, Teresa Divita, Victor F. Dixon, Elaine Engst, Henry Ettinghausen, Constance A. Fairchild, Marina Gálvez Acero, David M. Gitlitz, Debra Gitlitz, Nelly González, Miguel González Dengra, Agustín de la Granja, Jane Greenlaw, Lidia Gutiérrez Arranz, Jessica Hadlow, N. Sue Hanson, David Henn, Joseph Holub, Hugh Howard, William F. Hunter, Alix Ingber, Elizabeth Johnson, Lisa Johnston, Amy Kaminsky, Diane E. Kaplan, Catherine Larson, Joel Leftoff, Carol LeVine, María Luisa Lobato, Victoria M. Lord, Suzanne Lorimer, Rolf Lundelius, Gayle D. Lynch, Raymond R. MacCurdy, Nancy Macomber, Fiona Maguire, Francisco Márquez Villanueva, Julián Martín Abad, Donald McGrady, Melveena McKendrick, Janet Meek, Leslie A. Morris, Marjorie Murfin, Harriet Nelson, John Nolan, Kristina Nyman, David Oar, Yolanda Olivas, Mary Parker, James A. Parr, Mary Parr, C. George Peale, D. Pogue, Patrick M. Quinn, Richard C. Ramer, Glenn Read, Augustin Redondo, Cory Reed, Gail Reese, José M. Regueiro, Eva Reichenberger, Kurt Reichenberger, Roswitha Reichenberger, Caroline Rittenhouse, Susana Romanos de Tiratel, Máximo Rossi Jr., José María Ruano de la Haza, Enrique Ruiz-Fornells, Manuel Sánchez Mariana, Gregory Sherr, Diego Símini, Carolyn Smith, James Stimpert, Ronald E. Surtz, Barry Taylor, Woodman Taylor, Lorett Treese, Margaret Vigil, Amparo Viguer, Sharon D. Voros, Roger Walker, Aengus Ward, Bruce Wardropper, David Whitesell, Connie Koehler Widney, and Miguel Zugasti.

We wish to thank all the individuals who answered our form letter regarding the accuracy of their own dissertation entry and who supplied information about title, date, pagination, or the name of their director. We take responsibility for any errors in transcribing the information.

Finally, we must also say a word of appreciation for the free and virtually unlimited access to electronic information services such as RLIN's Eureka and OCLC's First Search, and the many CD-ROM products at St. John's University and the New York Public Library, which made this arduous task infinitely easier. A special note of gratitude to the forward-looking library administrators Sister Marie Melton, Julie Cunningham, Paul Fasana, Rodney Phillips, Elizabeth Diefendorf, and John Hawker, who see the value of making such databases available to researchers.

Palabras preliminares

A algunos de nosotros nos gusta viajar con mapas. Resulta agradable ver qué rutas han sido recorridas, qué áreas están densamente pobladas, dónde quedó el sendero que pudo haber borrado una tormenta. A otros les gusta salir y conquistar lo desconocido. Les ofrecemos esta bibliografía como una ampliación dentro de la colección de obras de referencia que dibujan los estudios de teatro del Siglo de Oro. Este trabajo es una compilación de tesis de doctorado presentadas en los Estados Unidos de 1899 a 1992 sobre este tema, con un suplemento de las tesis de Canadá y varios países del oeste de Europa, presentadas entre 1817 y 1992. Hemos incluido solamente los países extranjeros de los cuales tenemos información adecuada y puesta al día.

Al compilar esta bibliografía, resultó de gran interés descubrir no solamente centros y periodos de especialización, como es el caso de la Universidad de Iowa bajo la dirección de Edmund DeChasca, sino también seguir una línea de investigación, por ejemplo, la que marcan los directores de tesis: H. C. Heaton, E. W. Hesse, W. C. McCrary, y el más joven D. H. Darst quien ha dirigido varias tesis en los últimos años. Es de esperar que los alumnos de Darst, a su vez, dirijan nuevas tesis. Los lectores pueden enterarse de otras tendencias, tanto como del hecho de que las tesis de los Estados Unidos y de Europa parecen diferir en tono y acento.

Esperamos que esta bibliografía sea más que una simple obra de referencia y ayude a los estudiosos a seleccionar o rechazar temas para una tesis u otro trabajo de investigación. Un candidato al doctorado puede escribir sobre el mismo tema del cual ya apareció una tesis, sobre todo si la tesis previa puede ser mejorada, siempre que dé noticias de su existencia y de las razones por las cuales el tema merece un nuevo tratamiento. Del mismo modo, el descubrimiento de una tesis reciente de alta calidad hará quizá desistir a alguien de cubrir el mismo terreno.

También deseamos decir una palabra acerca de un hallazgo inesperado en nuestra investigación. No sospechábamos al inicio de este proyecto que abriríamos una caja de Pandora psicológica. Aprendimos que pocas relaciones personales y profesionales están tan llenas de ansiedad como aquellas que se establecen entre el doctorando y el director. Si todavía no se ha escrito ninguna tesis sobre este tema específico, valdría la pena que los psicólogos y sociólogos lo tuvieran en cuenta.

Cuando el nombre del director ha sido registrado en el *Dissertation Abstracts* (a partir de 1951), o en el *Dissertation Abstracts International* (desde 1969) u otra fuente, incorporamos esta información a nuestra entrada. A menudo nuestra primera información acerca de una tesis provino de *Hispania* (AATSP) con la mención de un director, pero no podíamos estar seguros de si ese profesor realmente siguió la tesis hasta que ésta se completó. Por otra parte, en muchos casos no teníamos ninguna referencia acerca del director. Durante el largo proceso de compilación, escribimos directamente a personas, departamentos, bibliotecas y archivos de universidades solicitándoles que nos completaran estos datos. El resultado de las respuestas fue sorprendente: no solamente nos enteramos de tesis perdidas para siempre, como las de Rosenbach, Sears, Stephenson y otras, sino que también encontramos tesis en las que la firma del director es tan borrosa e ilegible que se ha perdido la esperanza de recuperar una parte de la historia de la universidad. También nos enfrentamos con tesis sin firma del director, así como otras en las que los autores no reconocen ninguna deuda intelectual. Quizás algunas de estas prácticas reflejen tendencias o modas; otras pueden indicar relaciones no siempre satisfactorias.

Aun más reveladoras fueron las respuestas a preguntas directas hechas en los congresos de la MLA y en otras reuniones. Uno de los compiladores preguntó casualmente a alguien acerca de su director de tesis y recibió una gélida mirada como respuesta, mientras que la réplica de un segundo especialista fue un relato con detalles muy precisos de la asistencia que su director le había ofrecido. Otro colega más nos explicó cuidadosamente que la persona que más le ayudó enseñaba al otro lado del Océano Atlántico y no era ninguno de los que legalmente debían hacerlo, por lo que su nombre no apareció en la tesis. Finalmente, un entrevistado pidió que omitiéramos el nombre del director al que no quería rendir ese honor, ya que nunca se había interesado por la tesis y ni siquiera había leído el trabajo. También hemos visto muchas introducciones en las que se hacen referencias al director con expresiones llenas de gratitud.

Por otra parte, nos gustaría mencionar que hemos podido constatar personalmente las palabras de advertencia de David J. Billick (véase abajo). Una base de datos de citas bibliográficas *por sí misma* no satisface las necesidades del investigador. En este sentido, nos pusimos en contacto con el Fichier Central des Thèses (Nanterre, Francia) con una petición bien definida de tesis sobre el teatro español del Siglo de Oro. La respuesta fue de alrededor de doscientos títulos a un costo de $50. Los resultados que nos enviaron incluían absolutamente todo acerca de las humanidades y las ciencias sociales en España e Hispanoamérica, todos los géneros y todos los periodos, y apenas una docena de títulos eran relevantes para nuestra bibliografía. Así, llegamos a entender, con no poco gasto, la sabiduría de las palabras de Billick cuando indica que "... un verdadero uso metódico de los instrumentos bibliográficos, impresos o en formato legible por computadora, demanda una combinación de profunda pericia sobre el tema, conocimiento de los instrumentos de acceso, y dominio de la técnica de investigación que pocos especialistas en la disciplina poseen o puede esperarse que posean".

Queremos recalcar que gran parte de lo que hemos compilado son datos procedentes de fuentes secundarias, por lo que aunque nos responsabilizamos de posibles errores, pueden haberse transcrito algunas incorrecciones a partir de materiales de referencia anteriores.

Debido a la falta de tiempo, de medios económicos y hasta cierto punto a la carencia de recursos disponibles, tuvimos que limitar el alcance de este trabajo. Indudablemente, un proyecto de este tipo conduce por sí mismo a la continua actualización, tanto como a la ampliación de la cobertura geográfica. En este sentido, en la próxima edición desearíamos poder incluir el *dottorato di ricerca* italiano (establecido en 1980) que se considera, como es sabido, el equivalente del PhD y del doctorado español. Por todo ello, nos complacería recibir añadiduras o correcciones que contribuyeran a completar y corregir esta bibliografía en futuras ediciones.

Por último, si uno desea ver el lado más ameno —o tal vez más oscuro— de las tesis, creemos que disfrutaría leyendo "The Ghost Who Vanished by Degrees", un divertido cuento acerca del tema que tratamos, escrito por Robertson Davies (1913-95) en su muy entretenida colección titulada *High Spirits*.

Después de estas palabras preliminares se incluye una breve historia del doctorado norteamericano escrita por Karen Anderson en la cual ella demuestra el origen europeo, específicamente alemán, de este título universitario. A continuación, hay un apartado escrito por Billick, director (1989-92) de publicación de tesis de University Microfilms, en el cual explica la necesidad y la utilidad de una bibliografía acumulativa como la presente. Sigue una introducción en la que se describen detalladamente las partes que componen cada entrada bibliográfica, lo mismo que las características de los tres índices. Los preliminares del libro terminan con agradecimientos, obras consultadas, un directorio de instituciones que identifica los nombres institucionales abreviados, y un repertorio de siglas, abreviaturas y títulos de revistas. El cuerpo del libro consta de las tesis doctorales estadounidenses relacionadas con el tema, numeradas de 1 a 853, seguidas por las tesis doctorales de otros países, numeradas de 1001 a 1616. La parte final del libro incluye tres índices: de instituciones, de autores y directores de tesis, y de materias y títulos.

Traducción de Susana Romanos de Tiratel

Prólogo

El doctorado norteamericano y sus raíces en la tradición europea

Karen Anderson

Los títulos académicos se han venido confiriendo desde hace más de ocho siglos. El primero del que se tienen noticias fue el doctorado otorgado por la Universidad de Bolonia, a mediados del siglo XII. En el siglo XIII, la Universidad de París confirió su primer doctorado y el modelo académico fue prontamente seguido por Gran Bretaña. Ya para el siglo XVI, otra variación del doctorado había comenzado a desarrollarse en Alemania. Tres siglos más tarde, nacía el Doctorado en Filosofía (PhD) de las universidades estadounidenses.

La educación universitaria norteamericana fue establecida sobre la base de dos modelos europeos: el colegio (college) inglés y la universidad germánica. El sistema inglés fue el modelo adoptado para los cuatro primeros años de educación universitaria (undergraduate education). Pero, en los comienzos, no existía el nivel graduado en los colegios estadounidenses. Durante el siglo XIX los investigadores que deseaban proseguir estudios superiores solían viajar a Europa a fin de asistir a universidades alemanas.

Las principales universidades alemanas escogidas por los estudiosos norteamericanos fueron Gotinga, Berlín, Leipzig, Halle, Heidelberg y Friburgo. Un total de casi diez mil norteamericanos emprendió estos peregrinajes académicos durante el siglo XIX, y aproximadamente la mitad de ese grupo se matriculó en la Universidad de Berlín. Fuera de Alemania, gran número de estudiantes estadounidenses se matriculó en la Universidad de Viena y en varias universidades suizas, todas ellas instituciones influidas, naturalmente, por las tradiciones germánicas.

Los estudios en las universidades alemanas resultaban atrayentes puesto que enfatizaban la libertad en el enseñar y en el aprender, el respeto por la disposición lógica del pensamiento, la acumulación de información, la clasificación y organización de las ideas, y la difusión de los descubrimientos.

Igualmente atractiva era la metodología pedagógica alemana, siendo el método más importante el de la conferencia (lecture) que difería de la recitación norteamericana en el aula de clase, como asimismo del sistema inglés de clases individuales (tutorials). El método germano proporcionaba al alumno una introducción a un campo íntegro de estudio mediante una serie de clases magistrales relacionadas entre sí.

El segundo método era el seminario. Facilitaba el entrenamiento para la realización de estudios e investigaciones individuales de un problema significativo, suministrando, de este modo, al estudiante los conocimientos técnicos necesarios para realizar investigaciones científicas por su cuenta.

Las bibliotecas, museos y laboratorios de las universidades germanas representaban otro atractivo para los estudiantes norteamericanos. Ninguna universidad americana contemporánea disponía de una biblioteca bien dotada y además, como es habitual, los pocos volúmenes existentes en las estanterías no eran fácilmente prestados a los estudiantes (Walters 9).

Los investigadores universitarios regresaban a los Estados Unidos con el espíritu germano del libre pensamiento, de la exactitud en la investigación, del hábito de trabajo, todo lo cual propició el ímpetu para el desarrollo del movimiento universitario estadounidense en la década de 1850. La influencia de esos intelectuales entrenados en Europa fue considerable, e investigadores preeminentes —muchos de los cuales regresaron de Alemania para ocupar puestos académicos en las principales universidades del este—, expresaron el deseo de expandir las instituciones existentes y de fundar otras nuevas que se asemejaran a las germánicas.

Muy pronto, en 1852, la Universidad de Bucknell, en Lewisburg, Pensilvania, confirió el doctorado en filosofía *honoris causa*. Sin embargo, antes de 1860, no se otorgó en los Estados Unidos el título de doctor como culminación de los estudios universitarios. El estímulo para el establecimiento de un doctorado americano provino del cuerpo de profesores de la recién establecida Escuela Científica Sheffield

(Sheffield Scientific School) de la Universidad de Yale. Una propuesta presentada por dicha Escuela, en la reunión de la Corporación de Yale que tuvo lugar el 24 de julio de 1860, recomendaba que

> ... se otorgue el título de *Doctor en Filosofía* y, de acuerdo con la práctica de las universidades germanas, se confiera dicho título a aquellos estudiantes que hayan cursado con éxito los cursos científicos de Doctorado [...] que el mismo título de Doctor en Filosofía [...] sea conferido por alcanzar el más alto nivel en Matemáticas y Filología u otras disciplinas que se imparten en el Departamento de Filosofía y Artes.
>
> Este título [...] eliminará la desventaja bajo la cual trabaja nuestro Departamento de Filosofía y Artes, en comparación con Departamentos similares en las universidades germanas. [...] Su establecimiento entre nosotros [...] nos permitirá retener en nuestro país a numerosos jóvenes, y particularmente a estudiantes de Ciencias, que ahora se ven compelidos a estudiar en universidades alemanas. (Chittenden 1: 87-88.

Los requerimientos incluían:

- Permanecer estudiando en el recinto de la universidad por lo menos durante un año, antes de presentarse al examen de doctorado.
- Superar satisfactoriamente un examen relativo a la especialidad estudiada.
- Presentar una tesis escrita que desarrollara una investigación original y que debía ser aprobada por el cuerpo de profesores.

Los primeros estudiantes norteamericanos que recibieron un Doctorado en Filosofía fueron James Morris Whiton, Arthur Williams Wright y Eugene Schuyler, todos los cuales habían obtenido sus títulos de Bachiller en la Universidad de Yale. Whiton había estudiado en el Departamento de Filosofía y Artes, en Yale, de 1859 a 1861, continuando sus estudios de latín, griego y alemán de forma autodidacta y aprobando esas tres asignaturas. Además, había estudiado sánscrito dos horas semanales durante dos años y entregado una tesis de seis páginas manuscritas, en latín, consistente en un ensayo sobre el proverbio *Brevis vita, ars longa.* (La tesis de Whiton existe todavía y está disponible a través de University Microfilms [UMI]). La tesis de Wright titulada: Dadas la velocidad y dirección del movimiento de un meteoro al entrar en la atmósfera de la tierra, determinar su órbita alrededor del sol, tomando en consideración las atracciones sufridas por ambos cuerpos, se ha perdido con el transcurso de los años. El estudio de Schuyler en torno a Wedgewood y la filología inglesa, fue presentado y se publicó un año más tarde en la *Bibliotheca Sacra* como un artículo de veinticuatro páginas (Spurr 117).

De los tres alumnos que recibieron por primera vez el nuevo título en Yale en 1861, uno alcanzó el grado de pastor y fue profesor de ética en un seminario teológico; el segundo fue diplomático en el servicio exterior de su país; y solamente uno llegó a ser profesor universitario de física y química.

Otros tempranos títulos de Doctor en Filosofía fueron conferidos por la Universidad de Pensilvania en 1871, por la Universidad de Harvard en 1873, y por la Universidad de Columbia en 1875. El primer Doctorado en Filosofía conferido a una mujer fue obtenido por Helen Magill en la Universidad de Boston en 1877.

La fundación de la Universidad Johns Hopkins —a la que a veces se denomina la primera "verdadera universidad norteamericana"—, en 1876, estableció firmemente el compromiso de la educación universitaria avanzada y de posgrado. Johns Hopkins combinó los mejores elementos de las universidades germanas —las clases magistrales, los seminarios, los estudios independientes— y de las norteamericanas que se habían desarrollado en los 250 años transcurridos desde la fundación de Harvard. Siguiendo los modelos germanos, en la nueva institución de Baltimore se cultivó la libertad en la enseñanza y en el aprendizaje, y al mismo tiempo se liberalizaron los métodos docentes americanos rechazando el sistema tradicional. En muy pocos años, Johns Hopkins llegó a establecer las normas de la educación universitaria avanzada, confiriendo su primer doctorado en 1878.

Siguiendo el ejemplo de Johns Hopkins, se establecieron programas de doctorado en la Universidad de Clark y en la Universidad Católica [de Washington] en 1889, y en la Universidad de Chicago en 1890. En este mismo año, los Regentes de la Universidad de Nebraska recomendaron que se confiriera el grado de Doctor en Filosofía con la condición de que esto no supusiera una carga económica adicional. Nebraska estableció la primera escuela graduada en una universidad estatal, seguida, en el mismo año, por Harvard, Michigan, Wisconsin y Kansas.

La evolución de los estudios doctorales americanos contribuyó a conferir a la educación universitaria, a principios de siglo, dos nuevas dimensiones importantes. La de profesor universitario fue reconocida como una profesión para la cual se podía preparar a un estudiante. Además, el plan de estudios se dividía más específicamente en disciplinas similares a aquellas en las que los profesores se habían especializado.

El desarrollo del Doctorado en Filosofía en Johns Hopkins influyó de forma determinante en el sistema de otras instituciones. Las normas establecidas en 1876 eran estrictas, pero no en comparación con las actuales. El periodo requerido entre la obtención del título de Bachiller (bachelor's degree) y el de Doctor oscilaba entre dos y tres años en 1881, y un consejo de estudios superiores controlaba el programa ya en 1883. En 1884 las exigencias de residencia fueron incrementadas de uno a dos años, y para 1885 se habían estipulado las normas para las tesis —relativas a su formato, uso de máquina de escribir, y la presentación de un ejemplar a la biblioteca de la universidad—. Los exámenes de lectura de textos en francés y alemán, y la designación de un director oficial y de dos examinadores externos como lectores de la tesis, se establecieron ya en 1887.

Los estudiantes desempeñaron un importante papel en el desarrollo de los requisitos para el Doctorado en Filosofía, mediante círculos afiliados a los programas doctorales en diversos recintos universitarios. El primero de esos círculos se fundó en Harvard en 1889. La primera reunión conjunta de los círculos de estudiantes de doctorado fue llevada a cabo por Harvard, Cornell y Johns Hopkins en 1893. La Federación de Círculos de Estudiantes Doctorales (Federation of Graduate Clubs), organizada en 1896, se reunía anualmente durante varios años. En su encuentro de 1896, recomendó que las exigencias mínimas para la obtención del título de Doctor en Filosofía, deberían ser:

- La obtención previa del título de Bachiller (bachelor's degree) o su equivalente.
- Completar al menos dos años de residencia como estudiante doctoral, de los cuales un año debía transcurrir en el recinto de la institución que confiriera el título.
- Un examen adecuado.
- Una tesis que cubriera los resultados de una investigación original (Spurr 118-19).

En 1900, catorce universidades —Johns Hopkins, Columbia, Chicago, California, Harvard, Yale, Pensilvania, Princeton, Clark, Cornell, la Universidad Católica [Washington], Stanford, Michigan y Wisconsin— estaban activamente involucradas en estudios doctorales. Este grupo otorgaba casi el 90% de todos los títulos doctorales del país.

Los esfuerzos dirigidos a establecer los requisitos para el Doctorado en Filosofía y para promover la investigación a nivel institucional, se iniciaron con las actividades de la Asociación de Universidades Americanas (Association of American Universities, AAU), establecida en 1900 y de la Asociación Nacional de Universidades Estatales (National Association of State Universities, NASU), en 1905. Para 1908, un comité de NASU recomendó que el periodo de estudios de posgrado para el doctorado fuera al menos de tres años, uno de los cuales debía pasarse en residencia en la institución que confiriera el título. En 1916 la AAU sugirió lo mismo, de tal modo que el concepto de un doctorado de tres años de duración, en lugar de dos, fue generalmente aceptado con anterioridad a la primera guerra mundial.

El desarrollo de los estudios doctorales en el siglo XX ha estado marcado por una mayor uniformidad en cuanto a la calidad, la eliminación del Doctorado en Filosofía como título honorífico, la extensión de ese doctorado a campos de conocimiento aplicado, y a prácticamente todas las disciplinas impartidas en una universidad. Además, se amplió hasta cuatro o cinco años el periodo en que el alumno permanece matriculado en cursos específicos, lo cual extiende el tiempo total en que el título se obtiene a siete u ocho años.

Para 1935, el sistema actual de doctorado se había desarrollado ya completamente. Si bien el programa básico apenas ha variado, la tendencia ha sido la de microfilmar las tesis en vez de imprimirlas (en offset), flexibilizar o incluso suprimir el requisito de lengua(s) extranjera(s), aumentar la oferta de cursos a nivel de posgrado, y poner mayor énfasis en exámenes de "capacitación" previos a la obtención del título (Spurr 119).

La implantación de los estudios doctorales en los Estados Unidos fue percibida como un paso quizás algo temerario, puesto que las universidades americanas eran consideradas por la mayoría de los eruditos europeos e ingleses, en el mejor de los casos, como instituciones de nivel de bachillerato. No obstante, para la década de 1940, las universidades americanas tenían ya la capacidad necesaria para formar investigadores al más alto nivel en cada una de las ramas del saber moderno, y sus profesores hacían contribuciones al conocimiento que les conferían importancia universal. Hoy en día, los eruditos europeos valoran el PhD americano, y estudiantes de todas partes del mundo aspiran a obtenerlo.

Entre 1876 y 1900 se produjo una revolución educativa en las universidades estadounidenses. En 1890 se otorgaron, aproximadamente 200 doctorados, y en 1899 el número había aumentado hasta 382. Al mismo tiempo, 150 universidades ofrecían estudios graduados [de licenciatura], aunque solo una tercera parte de ellas conferían el prestigioso título de Doctor. Para 1925 el número de doctorados era de mil doscientos al año, y al llegar a la década de 1970, la cifra oscilaba entre treinta y tres, y treinta y cuatro mil.

Hasta finales de 1988 se habían conferido más de ocho mil títulos de Doctor en Filosofía en los Estados Unidos. En la actualidad, anualmente obtienen el PhD casi treinta y seis mil estudiantes en más de trescientas sesenta universidades acreditadas regionalmente a través de todo el país (según datos del Consejo Nacional de Investigaciones [National Research Council]). De ese total, aproximadamente el 65% se confiere a hombres, y un 35% a mujeres.

De acuerdo con el Consejo de Escuelas Graduadas de los Estados Unidos (Council of Graduate Schools), gran número de estudiantes asisten a escuelas graduadas con el fin de obtener tan solo la licenciatura o maestría (master's degree); son pocos los que continúan sus estudios hasta obtener el doctorado. Sin embargo, en general la matrícula en las escuelas graduadas de los Estados Unidos aumenta más o menos un 1% anual.

La naturaleza del doctorado ha cambiado. El antiguo doctorado europeo era un honor que se confería a aquellos que habían llegado al máximo del saber, pero en la actualidad el doctorado americano significa que quien lo obtiene ha llegado a adquirir los instrumentos y los hábitos que le permitirán convertirse en un investigador o en un educador.

Con el advenimiento de la micro-publicación en 1938, UMI comenzó a publicar tesis doctorales, ayudando así a los estudiantes no solo a cumplir con el requisito de publicación de las escuelas graduadas, sino también a poner a disposición del mundo entero su investigación personal.

Se han producido muchos cambios desde que el fundador de UMI, Eugene B. Power, promoviera el microfotografiado y la publicación económica y bajo pedido de las tesis doctorales. En la actualidad UMI ofrece acceso al banco de información de las tesis a través de fuentes de referencias impresas, "online" y en investigaciones en CD-ROM.

La mayor parte de las bibliotecas más importantes en los Estados Unidos ofrecen y usan los intrumentos de referencia impresos por UMI, que contienen información acerca de más de un millón de tesis doctorales de todo el mundo. *Dissertation Abstracts International* (Compendios internacionales de tesis doctorales) y *Masters Abstracts International* (Compendios internacionales de memorias de licenciatura) están disponibles mediante subscripción, y proporcionan resúmenes de las tesis doctorales y de maestría más recientes publicadas por UMI. El *Comprehensive Dissertation Index* (Índice global de tesis doctorales) ofrece mención de todas las tesis americanas y canadienses a partir de la primera defendida en 1861.

Muchas bibliotecas de los Estados Unidos permiten también el acceso mediante medios electrónicos. Investigadores individuales así como bibliotecarios pueden llevar a cabo búsquedas especializadas del banco de datos de UMI a través de servicios de "online" o de CD-ROM. Una vez que han identificado las tesis que les interesan, los usuarios pueden adquirir el texto completo dirigiéndose a UMI por correo, por teléfono, o bien como parte de su investigación "online." Los ejemplares de las tesis están disponibles en forma de libro, de microfilme o de microficha.

En la actualidad, UMI ofrece más de setecientas mil disertaciones provenientes de más de quinientas cincuenta universidades de todas partes del mundo. Se agregan, aproximadamente, treinta y cinco mil tesis al año, con lo que se acrecienta la colección de investigaciones doctorales actuales y del pasado más amplia del mundo.

Traducción de Ángela B. Dellepiane

Obras Citadas

Chittenden, Russell H. *History of the Sheffield Scientific School of Yale University, 1846–1922.* 2 vols. New Haven: Yale UP, 1928.

Spurr, Stephen H. *Academic Degree Structures: Innovative Approaches.* San Francisco: Carnegie Foundation for the Advancement of Teaching, 1970.

Walters, Everett. *Graduate Education Today.* Washington: American Council on Education, 1965.

Adaptado con el permiso de University Microfilms, Incorporated, de *Research Update* (Spring-Summer 1989): 2 y 42–44. University Microfilms Inc., 300 North Zeeb Road, Ann Arbor, MI 48106-1346

Advertencia

La tesis ha sido una parte integral del proceso de obtención del título de doctorado en los Estados Unidos durante más de un siglo. Lamentablemente, la mayor parte de la valiosa información contenida en esos estudios permaneció sin utilizarse durante muchos años porque, en general, se conocían solo unos pocos títulos, y también debido a que las tesis mismas eran difíciles de adquirir en un formato fácilmente accesible. Después de que tales problemas fueron en alguna medida resueltos con la aparición de los *Microform Abstracts* (Compendios en microforma) (1938) y con los *Dissertation Abstracts* (Compendios de disertaciones) (1951), seguidos por los *Dissertation Abstracts International* (Compendios internacionales de disertaciones) (1969), muchas instituciones importantes comenzaron a participar en el sistema en fechas relativamente tardías, como es el caso de Berkeley (1962), Yale (1963), Chicago (1974) y Harvard (1982). Debe destacarse que lo que conocemos por el título de *Dissertation Abstracts International (DAI),* aunque publicado durante más de medio siglo, solo empezó a considerarse como la más comprehensiva fuente de mención bibliográfica de tesis a fines de la década de 1960 y principios de la de 1970. En ese momento, la gran mayoría de las instituciones que conferían el título de doctorado estaban ya entregando información para su inclusión en el banco de datos.

En parte, el valor de una recopilación tal como la presentada en este libro —enfocada a un solo género y a un periodo literario bien definido—, es el resultado de un enorme esfuerzo realizado mediante el examen de una cantidad considerable de otras bibliografías impresas, ficheros, catálogos automatizados, y hasta la lectura de notas a pie de página para identificar material no incluido en el *DAI.* El haber agregado la paginación, los nombres de los directores de las tesis [en los Estados Unidos], un resumen del compendio, y las publicaciones derivadas de dichas tesis, o relacionadas con ellas, confiere todavía más valor a la tarea de Reynolds y Szmuk.

Se puede argüir que, con el crecimiento de lo cubierto por los *Dissertation Abstracts International (DAI)* y con el acceso a las referencias de tesis a través de medios electrónicos, los repertorios impresos como el presente están ya superados. Pienso exactamente lo contrario. A medida que los bancos de datos se vuelven más amplios y más comprehensivos, resulta más difícil para el especialista identificar material relevante sin la ayuda del tipo de clasificación e índices llevada a cabo por John J. Reynolds y Szilvia E. Szmuk. *DAI,* en la actualidad, incluye más de un millón de menciones. Aun si el campo total se restringe a tesis sobre temas literarios, hay que examinar más de setenta mil títulos. La identificación de aproximadamente setecientas "menciones exactas" sobre el teatro del Siglo de Oro español, sacadas de este vasto universo de información, resulta, pues, realmente *formidable.* Además, un verdadero uso metódico de los instrumentos bibliográficos, impresos o en formato legible por ordenador, demanda una combinación de profunda pericia sobre el tema, conocimiento de los instrumentos de acceso, y dominio de la técnica de investigación que pocos especialistas en la disciplina poseen o puede esperarse que posean.

Richard Saul Wurman, en su libro *Information Anxiety (Ansiedad acerca de la información),* afirma que un caudal de información tal como el de un enorme banco de datos bibliográficos "se debe estructurar de forma que se convierta en fuente de información significativa". Reynolds y Szmuk han realizado una inestimable contribución al conferir precisamante esa "forma" a la abrumadora proliferación de la bibliografía sobre el teatro del Siglo de Oro.

David. J. Billick
Director, Dissertations Publishing, 1989-1992
University Microfilms Inc. (UMI)

Traducción de Ángela B. Dellepiane

Introducción

Esta bibliografía clasificada sigue la misma organización que la que se incluye cada año sobre el teatro en el *Bulletin of the Comediantes*. Las razones son obvias: hemos estado compilando la bibliografía anual durante varios años y probablemente los usuarios de este volumen sean un público similar; por lo tanto, ya están familiarizados con las categorías utilizadas. Para aquellos que pueden no conocer el *BCom,* se da a continuación un pequeño resumen de los criterios allí utilizados. La primera sección contiene una amplia categoría de entradas generales relacionadas con la cultura, historia, arte y materias afines del Siglo de Oro, las cuales pueden de alguna manera ser útiles para la investigación teatral de este periodo. La segunda sección es también de índole general, pero se centra más específicamente en el teatro del periodo. A estas secciones sigue la lista alfabetizada de comediógrafos, dentro de la cual las entradas individuales se ordenan alfabéticamente por los autores de tesis bajo el nombre de cada dramaturgo. Además, se han incluido algunos temas bien conocidos en este campo, como los relativos al teatro catalán y portugués y a distintos personajes dramáticos, como es el de Don Juan. En cuanto al periodo de tiempo cubierto, nos hemos centrado en el teatro de los siglos XVI y XVII con ocasionales miradas retrospectivas hacia los orígenes: por ejemplo, *Auto de los Reyes Magos,* y frecuentes miradas hacia adelante para examinar la influencia del teatro del Siglo de Oro en épocas posteriores. La *Celestina* ha sido excluida, ya que existe una bibliografía específica de todos conocida, pero no sus continuaciones e imitaciones dramáticas. Teniendo en cuenta a polígrafos como Lope de Vega, hemos incluido sus obras no teatrales solo cuando se han presentado algunas conexiones con su teatro en la tesis.

Varias fuentes registran anualmente tesis, pero nos pareció que ningún instrumento de referencia individual proporciona un panorama de todas o de la mayoría de las tesis existentes. Además, ninguna está anotada o conduce a los eruditos hacia los resultados publicados a partir de la tesis. Por lo tanto, diseñamos entradas que satisfagan lo que creemos son los requerimientos de los investigadores interesados en el campo del teatro del Siglo de Oro.

Para cada entrada hemos intentado incluir la siguiente información:

nombre del autor de la tesis
título de la tesis
número de hojas o páginas
institución (especificando el recinto universitario donde se otorgó el grado)
nombre del director
fecha de presentación o fecha de otorgamiento del grado
cita de la fuente
cita de la(s) versión(es) publicada(s) de la tesis
resumen o anotación aclaratoria
publicaciones resultantes o relacionadas

Solo en parte el proyecto resultó tan sencillo como esperábamos al principio. Pronto se hizo evidente que cada elemento de una entrada podía presentar en sí mismo problemas, comenzando por el uso de mayúsculas. Intentamos seguir las reglas establecidas para las mayúsculas en cada lengua. Así, en los títulos en inglés todas las letras iniciales de palabras (excepto artículos y preposiciones) se ponen en mayúscula; en español solo la inicial de la primera palabra; en francés el primer artículo y el sustantivo que lo acompaña; y en alemán todos los sustantivos y verbos, pero no los adjetivos.

Lo que sigue es un análisis de una entrada con las partes que la componen y un intento de explicar los problemas y nuestras soluciones.

NOMBRE: En esta sección se alfabetiza usando la práctica bibliotecaria normalizada: apellidos, nombre, segundo nombre o inicial. Los menos problemáticos fueron los apellidos de los hombres porque no cambian al casarse o divorciarse si bien algunos usan dos formas del nombre, como es el caso de Louis y Luigi Imperiale. Citamos los apellidos paterno y materno según el uso español, por ejemplo Carrasco Urgoiti, María Soledad. Por supuesto, las reglas portuguesas difieren de las españolas y aquí usamos el último elemento del apellido. Los hispanos que viven en los Estados Unidos a veces modifican su apellido y siguen la práctica anglo-americana al firmar publicaciones, así destacamos formas variables para José Fernández Montesinos (José F. Montesinos), Diego Molina Marín (Diego Marín) y Alberto Sandoval Sánchez (Alberto Sánchez). Los apellidos de las mujeres presentan otra sistemática. Muchas completaron sus tesis mientras eran solteras, pero las publicaciones posteriores aparecen bajo su apellido de casada, por ejemplo Hannah [Estermann] Bergman. Otras hicieron precisamente lo contrario, retornando al apellido de soltera después de un divorcio como es el caso de Doris L. Baum a Doris L. Meyer, mientras que otras prefieren firmar con uno o con ambos apellidos, según sea la publicación, así lo hace Alix Zuckerman/Alix Ingber. Para complicar aun más las cosas, a veces nuestras fuentes bibliográficas no coinciden en la forma de presentar el nombre y apellido: Sirgado, Isabel M. Cid aparece también como Cid de Sirgado, Isabel Mercedes. En la medida de lo posible hemos incluido las variantes de un apellido mediante referencias adicionales, a pesar de los hábitos confusos de los británicos de usar solo las iniciales del primer y segundo nombres.

Título de la tesis: Hemos tratado de transcribir un título completo y preciso para cada tesis. Si bien examinamos muchas tesis de primera mano, éstas representan, sin embargo, un porcentaje relativamente pequeño del total de las incluidas; por lo tanto, hemos tenido que confiar en fuentes secundarias. En aquellos casos en que el título de la tesis no es descriptivo o no informa suficientemente de su sentido, hemos tratado de aclararlo en una nota explicativa.

Paginación: Nuestra forma preferida de mencionar la paginación es indicar las páginas preliminares con números romanos, seguidas por la numeración en arábigos del texto de la tesis. Este método de paginar es más descriptivo y preciso, especialmente en aquellos casos en los que un extenso estudio introductorio estaba seguido por el texto estudiado, así por ejemplo en la edición de una obra de teatro como la que hace Kirk, C. F.: xcv+255 pp. En esos casos pensamos que se daba importancia a una introducción amplia del autor de la tesis, y el usuario conocería inmediatamente la extensión exacta de la edición que constituía el cuerpo de la tesis. Las tesis sobre las cuales nuestra única fuente fue *DA* o *DAI*, además de la mayoría de las tesis europeas, presentan solo numerales arábigos que indican el número total de hojas. La razón que aduce UMI para esta práctica es que antes cobraban una tasa por página para reproducir tesis, combinando por ello las páginas preliminares con el cuerpo del texto para calcular el pago. Los registros bibliográficos encontrados en las bases de datos de OCLC y RLIN siguen naturalmente las reglas de catalogación anglo-americanas, que reflejan el número de hojas en un manuscrito, o el número de páginas en un libro impreso. Optamos por no distinguir entre páginas y hojas; por lo tanto, se usa la abreviatura *pp.* en este libro para referirse no sólo a páginas sino también a hojas.

Falta la paginación en algunas tesis de los Estados Unidos y en muchas más de los otros países. Algunas de esas tesis ya no están disponibles y hemos procurado señalarlo, por lo tanto la extensión no se puede saber y en última instancia es irrelevante. En otros casos, existen versiones publicadas, lo cual resta importancia a este elemento de la descripción de la tesis original.

INSTITUCIÓN: En el índice de instituciones y el directorio de las mismas registramos el nombre completo y exacto de cada universidad incluida en esta bibliografía. Con objeto de ahorrar espacio, hemos acortado los nombres en las entradas de las tesis y usamos el nombre por el que una institución es más conocida. Esto resulta evidente en el caso de las universidades con nombres distintivos como Harvard, Johns Hopkins, Yale entre otras. Pero la mayoría de las universidades toman su nombre de la ciudad donde se encuentran, lo que parece darles una cualidad intemporal, y así las registramos, aunque exista un nombre oficial; por ejemplo, usamos Montpellier/III en vez de Université Paul Valéry, y Münster antes que Westfälische Wilhelms Universität. Como podría esperarse, esta decisión originó el dilema de qué forma del nombre de la ciudad debía de usarse y, en consecuencia, hubo que adoptar un criterio uniforme respecto de los topónimos.

Decidimos utilizar la forma inglesa del nombre de la ciudad: Copenhagen antes que København, Seville antes que Sevilla, Vienna antes que Wien. El asunto se complica aun más; debido a los azares de la guerra, la política, la economía y la burocracia educativa, las universidades han aparecido, desaparecido, o se han trasladado de un país a otro, cambiando de lengua oficial aun permaneciendo en el mismo lugar, como es el caso de Strassburg y Strasbourg, alemán hasta 1681, francés de 1681 a 1871, alemán de 1871 a 1918, francés de 1918 a 1940, alemán de 1940 a 1945, y francés tras la guerra de 1945 hasta el presente. Muchas otras instituciones cambiaron su nombre y acreditación durante su historia.

El lector debe tener en cuenta un caso notable de nombre cambiante: para la institución madrileña conocida históricamente como Universidad Literaria, Universidad Central y Universidad Complutense, hemos usado simplemente Complutense en las entradas pertinentes.

El directorio de instituciones se dividió en dos secciones: instituciones en los EE.UU. e instituciones en otros países. Además de consignar el nombre y la dirección, incluimos el año de la fundación. Aunque generalmente se piensa que solo las "universidades" ofrecen doctorados, hay excepciones: Bryn Mawr, Middlebury y Boston College, por mencionar solamente tres. Donde vislumbramos una posible confusión, por ejemplo, entre Boston University y Boston College, hicimos lo posible por diferenciarlas. En el caso de las universidades con varios recintos, hemos procurado identificar el recinto exacto donde se otorgó el título.

DIRECTOR: Decidimos incluir el nombre del director de la tesis como uno de los elementos de la entrada en la sección de los EE.UU. Nos basamos en la necesidad de documentar la continuidad de una línea de investigación y en la conveniencia de seguir las tendencias y relaciones eruditas. Como resultado final de un no siempre fácil proceso, fuimos capaces de averiguar el nombre del director en un alto porcentaje de casos. Solo cabe esperar que nadie se sienta ofendido por nuestras omisiones en aquellos casos en los que no pudimos obtener esa información. Quizás el intento original de mostrar campos de especialización no se alcanzó plenamente; a pesar de ello, podemos ver algunas líneas claras de parentesco. Lamentablemente, fuera de los

EE.UU., tal información no estuvo a nuestro alcance en la mayoría de los casos. Por lo tanto, optamos por no incluirla en las pocas ocasiones en los que, a través de contactos personales, supimos la identidad del director.

FECHA DEL GRADO: El año que aparece en *DA/DAI* es la fecha más aceptada y más citada como aquella en la que se otorgó el grado. En ocasiones, el año que figura en la portada de la tesis es anterior, tal como supimos a través de fuentes catalográficas como OCLC y RLIN. Pensamos que frecuentemente existe un lapso de tiempo entre la defensa de la tesis y el otorgamiento del grado. La inconsistencia en las fechas es aun más problemática en las tesis europeas, especialmente en las más antiguas.

CITA DE LA FUENTE: El setenta por ciento de las tesis registradas en la primera parte de esta bibliografía aparecen en DA/DAI. Esto se indica mediante la cita del volumen y la página de DA/DAI. Es por todos conocido que históricamente cierto número de universidades no participaba en el proyecto de UMI. El número de universidades no contribuyentes en este país está disminuyendo; de hecho, es alentador destacar que cada día más universidades europeas están informando al DAI-C.

Una práctica menos conocida es que muchas instituciones tuvieron en el pasado sus propias publicaciones en las que aparecían los resúmenes de las tesis aprobadas en sus recintos: Harvard University *Summaries,* Iowa *Abstracts,* North Carolina *Record,* Stanford *Abstracts, Revista de la Universidad de Madrid,* etc. Otras incluían un resumen en el "Program of the Final Examination", por ejemplo University of California/Berkeley o "Announcement of the Final Examination", por ejemplo University of California/Los Angeles. La diversidad de las fuentes mencionadas hace difícil establecer un sistema uniforme de referencia. Generalmente los fragmentos citados proceden de colecciones de resúmenes como *DA/DAI,* con la indicación (Abs.). A falta de un resumen en tales fuentes, optamos por citar directamente a partir de la tesis (Diss.), de su versión impresa (Prt. Diss.), del programa, o del anuncio del examen final. En cada entrada tratamos de dar una cita bibliográfica exacta de nuestra fuente para que cualquier estudioso interesado pueda obtener el texto completo.

TESIS QUE SOLO EXISTEN EN VERSIÓN IMPRESA: Esta información aparece entre llaves {} como un elemento de algunas entradas. En las décadas de 1920 y 1930 y aun después, muchas universidades en los Estados Unidos, tanto como en Europa, exigían la publicación de la tesis como condición para otorgar el grado. Muchas de esas tesis existen solo en su forma impresa, por ejemplo L. Turkevich, Columbia University, 1950. No siempre queda claro si esas tesis simplemente fueron impresas a expensas del candidato al doctorado o tuvieron que pasar por un riguroso escrutinio editorial. El concepto de "publicada" no es fácil de definir; las tesis registradas en el *DA/DAI* se consideran por UMI como "publicadas a petición del usuario". A menudo es especialmente difícil determinar si un título europeo está impreso o existe en otra forma.

RESUMEN U OTRA ANOTACIÓN: Siempre que fue posible, transcribimos algunas frases clave o un párrafo del resumen publicado o de la introducción de la tesis. En el caso de ediciones críticas —que son numerosas— indicamos, siempre que pudimos, el(los) texto(s) en los que la edición se basó. Colocamos puntos suspensivos cuando se omitieron palabras o frases al principio o en medio del párrafo y solo en aquellos casos de errores tipográficos o faltas gramaticales graves alteramos las palabras del autor, ya que pensamos que los autores de tesis debían hablar por sí mismos. Desde luego quisiéramos dejar patente que en ningún caso hacemos una valoración personal de esos trabajos. En la sección de tesis extranjeras usamos corchetes [ ] para identificar cualquier comentario respecto a la tesis.

PUBLICACIONES RESULTANTES O RELACIONADAS: Las tesis han sido en la mayoría de los casos el germen de una línea de investigación en el campo del teatro del Siglo de Oro. Con frecuencia se publicaron ya sea en forma completa o reelaborada en artículos individuales. Confiamos en las búsquedas en MLA, OCLC y RLIN, tanto como en nuestros años conjuntos de compilación de la bibliografía anual para el *Bulletin of the Comediantes,* para descubrir publicaciones que pensamos que podrían tener relación con una determinada tesis. A menudo esos trabajos son más accesibles que la tesis original. Además, los libros y artículos que son el resultado de una tesis pueden mostrar una madurez mayor y, al mismo tiempo, contener información adicional. También cabe mencionar que en pocas ocasiones las publicaciones relacionadas anteceden al otorgamiento del grado.

La lista de publicaciones resultantes o relacionadas se introduce precedida del símbolo ❖ y nuestras entradas se ordenan cronológicamente. En los casos de publicaciones múltiples, cada cita va precedida por una letra mayúscula entre corchetes. No pusimos un límite al número de trabajos citados, por lo tanto algunos especialistas aparecen con uno, mientras que otros lo hacen con nueve o diez publicaciones. Esto no puede ser tomado como guía de la producción global del estudioso; nuestro campo tiene un enfoque especializado y si bien algunos académicos eligieron continuar la investigación en el área de su tesis, otros cambiaron su rumbo intelectual, o lo extendieron a diferentes dramaturgos del Siglo de Oro. Muchos autores de tesis han sido homenajeados en volúmenes que incluyen la lista de sus publicaciones. Añadimos todas las referencias de este tipo de las que nos hemos enterado.

A pesar de las rigurosas pautas establecidas por nosotros mismos, no todos estarán de acuerdo con nuestras elecciones; sabemos que no hemos sido exhaustivos, aunque intentamos orientar al investigador hacia la dirección correcta. En casos tales como el libro *Amor, matrimonio y honra en Cervantes* de Robert Piluso nos ahorramos tomar decisiones editoriales difíciles, dado que se trata de una impresión *verbatim* del manuscrito de la tesis con el título cambiado. En otros casos las relaciones fueron menos obvias. Por ejemplo, decidimos que los candidatos al doctorado que eligieron hacer una edición de una obra de teatro, habían aprendido la metodología y el aparato erudito de esa tarea en el proceso de investigación de la tesis. Si alguna de sus publicaciones posteriores se refiere al tema general de "editar una obra", lo consideramos como una derivación de algo aprendido en el proceso de redactar la tesis, aun cuando se tratara de un dramaturgo diferente, cf. Cruickshank, Greer, Kirby et al. en *Editing the* Comedia II. Ed. Michael McGaha and Frank P. Casa. Ann Arbor: Univ. of Michigan, Dept. of Romance Languages, 1991 (Michigan Romance Studies 11). En los casos en los que percibimos que la relación entre tesis y publicación posterior necesitaba una explicación más detallada agregamos una aclaración entre corchetes.

Por diversas razones puede no haber publicaciones resultantes o relacionadas con la tesis en una entrada. Primero, simplemente, porque no existe ninguna hasta la fecha de redacción del presente trabajo; segundo, porque no pudimos encontrarla (quizás debido a un cambio de apellido); tercero, porque al graduarse, el candidato al doctorado abandonó completamente ese campo de investigación o desarrolló otros intereses eruditos en un área literaria diferente; o, por último, porque murió poco después de completar la tesis. Por otra parte, hay muchos hispanistas muy activos en este campo de investigación cuyas tesis no tuvieron relación con el teatro del Siglo de Oro, entre ellos, John J. Allen, Frederick A. de Armas, Celsa Carmen García Valdés y Joan Oleza Simó.

En el caso de las tesis europeas, en general, nuestra tarea fue más difícil. Dado que el acceso de primera mano fue casi imposible, no pudimos consultar resúmenes y sumarios en la gran mayoría de los casos. Con objeto de poder clarificar títulos no descriptivos y verificar la relevancia de entradas ambiguas, contamos con la ayuda y la buena voluntad de colegas residentes en otros países. Así, ante la ausencia de información completa, decidimos incluir reseñas de las tesis (éstas aparecen en la línea del título de la tesis separadas por doble barra inclinada //) o, más frecuentemente, reseñas de las monografías que resultaron de la tesis. Pensamos que en los Estados Unidos algunos estudiosos encontrarían estas reseñas con más facilidad, las cuales podrían iluminar en algo el trabajo. Se usó una letra minúscula entre paréntesis para separar una reseña de otra. Reunimos esas reseñas a partir de una amplia variedad de fuentes. La falta de normalización en el modo en que aparecen esas entradas bibliográficas, incluyendo el uso de acrónimos diferentes, hizo esta tarea particularmente difícil.

DIRECTORIO E ÍNDICES: Con objeto de hacer nuestra obra de referencia lo más útil posible para los investigadores, quisimos proporcionar vías de acceso sencillas a toda la información que ella contiene. De ahí, un solo directorio y tres índices:

Directorio de instituciones
Índice de instituciones
Índice de autores y directores de tesis
Índice de materias y títulos

Optamos por no asignar secuencias numéricas separadas a las dos partes de esta bibliografía; sin embargo, quisimos que los usuarios distinguieran con facilidad entre las citas de los Estados Unidos y las no estadounidenses. Nuestra solución fue numerar las entradas extranjeras comenzando con 1001. Como resultado, en los índices combinados, los usuarios sabrán inmediatamente que los números 1-853 se refieren a entradas de los Estados Unidos, mientras que de 1001 en adelante las entradas representan trabajos no estadounidenses. Por supuesto, la idea de combinar los índices se hizo para eliminar el tener que buscar en más de un lugar cualquier información.

Hay un total de 784 tesis individuales de los Estados Unidos. Un registro múltiple de una tesis de los Estados Unidos significa que trata de varios dramaturgos —en cuyo caso la entrada completa aparece una sola vez en el lugar más adecuado— y las entradas subsecuentes remiten mediante la indicación "véase" al registro completo, por ejemplo la de José A. Madrigal: La función del hombre salvaje en el teatro de Lope de Vega, Tirso de Molina y Calderón de la Barca. Hay un total de 577 tesis individuales extranjeras. El hecho de registrar más de una vez una tesis extranjera también indica que el tema incluye más de un dramaturgo. Además, en la sección extranjera, el lector encontrará en ocasiones más de una tesis del mismo autor, reflejando esto el complejo sistema educativo de un país concreto. Por ejemplo, históricamente en Francia hubo cuatro tipos de doctorado con sus correspondientes tesis: *Doctorat d'État, Nouveau Doctorat (régime de janvier 1984), Doctorat de 3e cycle,* y *Doctorat d'Université.* En años anteriores hubo también dos tipos de tesis francesas: *Thèse principale* y *Thèse complémentaire.* A causa de que la nuestra es una bibliografía retrospectiva, tratamos naturalmente de registrar esta información cuando tuvimos acceso a ella. Actualmente el sistema francés consiste de un *Doctorat* y una *Habilitation* (véase Redondo 46, entre las obras consultadas). Con la excepción de la *Thèse d'État,* no hemos incluido grados posdoctorales que capacitan al candidato para aspirar a un puesto académico más alto, si bien encontramos una interesante cita a una tesis de 1843 *Pro venia docendi* por Carl Vilhelm Törnegren titulada "Primordia artis scenicae Hispanorum adumbrans" completada en la Universidad de Helsinki (fundada en Turku). En Alemania esta forma de tesis se llama una *Habilitationsschrift* y hemos tenido noticias de varias recientes, como las de Joachim Küpper, Sebastian Neumeister y Christoph Strosetzki.

Quisiéramos mencionar otros dos títulos extranjeros con los que pueden no estar familiarizados nuestros lectores. La *licenciatura* en España es un título que se recibe al finalizar los cinco primeros años de estudios universitarios y antes del doctorado. El "grado externo" (external degree) británico se le confiere al estudiante que haya pasado el examen eliminatorio aunque no haya asistido a la universidad.

Tratamos de hacer el índice de materias y títulos lo más amplio posible, con el objeto de ofrecer a los estudiosos puntos de acceso tanto a través de información general (materia) como específica (título). Solo incluimos en el índice conceptos y títulos que encontramos en el título o en el resumen de la tesis o en su versión impresa, pero no en las publicaciones subsecuentes. Se han omitido del índice temático general los títulos no españoles de obras literarias, porque pensamos que alguien que investigue un tema de literatura comparada buscará bajo los encabezamientos: Relaciones literarias anglo-españolas, franco-españolas, germano-españolas, ítalo-españolas, etc.

En el curso de nuestro trabajo nos hemos encontrado con varias referencias oscuras: figuras literarias poco conocidas, temas y conceptos no familiares. Puesto que no podemos tener la certeza de que nuestros lectores los reconocerán más fácilmente de lo que lo hemos hecho nosotros, allí donde lo creemos conveniente, ofrecemos el resultado de nuestra investigación como una nota aclaratoria para ampliar la información. Teniendo en cuenta la importancia de la cronología, hemos indicado las fechas aun de figuras literarias muy conocidas. Nuestro propósito fue ayudar, y si nos equivocamos, esperamos que haya sido por exceso antes que por defecto.

Traducción de Susana Romanos de Tiratel

Agradecimientos

Tenemos una particular deuda de gratitud con James R. Chatham y sus colaboradores por sus obras pioneras enumeradas en nuestras obras consultadas y citadas. Su compilación de tesis extranjeras —aunque diferente de la nuestra en alcance y detalle— ha sido especialmente útil para nosotros.

Agradecemos su colaboración a muchos hispanistas de todo el mundo; a varias docenas de bibliotecarios, especialmente de St. John's University, the New York Public Library y Arizona State University en Tempe; a expertos en informática, en matemática, en música, y a los estudiantes que nos ayudaron a transformar un proyecto detallado y prolijo en algo más manejable. Sobre todo, apreciamos las numerosas palabras de aliento que recibimos de nuestros colegas que vislumbraron el valor de esta bibliografía y expresaron sus deseos de utilizarla.

Las siguientes personas, muchas de ellas bibliotecarios y archiveros, fueron más allá de su tarea para localizar piezas de información fugitivas con el objeto de ayudarnos a completar nuestro proyecto. Les estamos agradecidos por su dedicación de tiempo y esfuerzo.

Robert D. Adamshick, Ofelia L. Alayeto, John J. Allen, Shyamala Balgopal, Susan Barribeau, Margarita Becedas González, John Beckham, Paul Belloni, Nuria Beltrán Grajera, Elizabeth Bigongiari, David J. Billick, D. Block, Robert W. Blue, Stewart Bodner, Kathleen Bourgeois, Robert Buckeye, James F. Burke, Richard A. Cardwell, María Soledad Carrasco Urgoiti, Joan Collette, Alice R. Cotten, Ana Cristan, Don W. Cruickshank, Halina Czarnocka, David H. Darst, Martin Davis,

Stephen Davison, Frederick A. de Armas, Ángela B. Dellepiane, Chris Densmore, Alan D. Deyermond, Virna R. Díaz, Jean Dickson, Teresa Divita, Victor F. Dixon, Elaine Engst, Henry Ettinghausen, Constance A. Fairchild, Marina Gálvez Acero, David M. Gitlitz, Debra Gitlitz, Nelly González, Miguel González Dengra, Agustín de la Granja, Jane Greenlaw, Lidia Gutiérrez Arranz, Jessica Hadlow, N. Sue Hanson, David Henn, Joseph Holub, Hugh Howard, William F. Hunter, Alix Ingber, Elizabeth Johnson, Lisa Johnston, Amy Kaminsky, Diane E. Kaplan, Catherine Larson, Joel Leftoff, Carol LeVine, María Luisa Lobato, Victoria M. Lord, Suzanne Lorimer, Rolf Lundelius, Gayle D. Lynch, Raymond R. MacCurdy, Nancy Macomber, Fiona Maguire, Francisco Márquez Villanueva, Julián Martín Abad, Donald McGrady, Melveena McKendrick, Janet Meek, Leslie A. Morris, Marjorie Murfin, Harriet Nelson, John Nolan, Kristina Nyman, David Oar, Yolanda Olivas, Mary Parker, James A. Parr, Mary Parr, C. George Peale, D. Pogue, Patrick M. Quinn, Richard C. Ramer, Glenn Read, Augustin Redondo, Cory Reed, Gail Reese, José M. Regueiro, Eva Reichenberger, Kurt Reichenberger, Roswitha Reichenberger, Caroline Rittenhouse, Susana Romanos de Tiratel, Máximo Rossi Jr., José María Ruano de la Haza, Enrique Ruiz-Fornells, Manuel Sánchez Mariana, Gregory Sherr, Diego Símini, Carolyn Smith, James Stimpert, Ronald E. Surtz, Barry Taylor, Woodman Taylor, Lorett Treese, Margaret Vigil, Amparo Viguer, Sharon D. Voros, Roger Walker, Aengus Ward, Bruce Wardropper, David Whitesell, Connie Koehler Widney y Miguel Zugasti.

Finalmente deseamos agradecer la colaboración prestada por todas las personas que contestaron a nuestras peticiones, aclarando sus propias entradas de la tesis y proporcionando información acerca del título, fecha, paginación, o el nombre de su director. Nos hacemos responsables de cualquier error en la transcripción de la información.

Por último también debemos expresar nuestra gratitud por el acceso gratuito y virtualmente sin límites a servicios electrónicos de información tales como Eureka (de RLIN) y First Search (de OCLC) y a los numerosos instrumentos bibliográficos en forma de CD-ROM existentes en St. John's University y the New York Public Library, los cuales facilitaron esta ardua tarea. Especial agradecimiento debemos a los funcionarios de las bibliotecas —Sor Marie Melton, Julie Cunningham, Paul Fasana, Rodney Phillips, Elizabeth Diefendorf y John Hawker— quienes, conscientes de las posibilidades futuras, comprendieron la importancia de poner en manos de los investigadores tales bases de datos.

Traducción de Ángela B. Dellepiane

Works Consulted and Cited
Obras consultadas y citadas

Abrams, Frederic. "Lope de Rueda: Una bibliografía analítica en el cuarto centenario de su muerte." *DHR* 4 (1965): 39-55.

"American Doctoral Degrees Granted in the Field of Modern Languages." *MLJ* 1922—. Title, compiler(s), and periodicity vary.

Arellano, Ignacio, and Agustín de la Granja. "Bibliografía esencial de estudios sobre el teatro de Mira de Amescua." *RILCE* 7.2 (1991): 267-79. Special issue entitled *Mira de Amescua: Un teatro en la penumbra.* Pamplona: Universidad de Navarra, 1991.

Asensio, Eugenio. *Itinerario del entremés desde Lope de Rueda a Quiñones de Benavente con cinco entremeses inéditos de D. Francisco de Quevedo.* Madrid: Gredos, 1965. 374 pp. (BRH. II. Estudios y ensayos 82.)

Bacchelli, Franco. *Per una bibliografia di A. Castillo Solórzano.* Verona: Università degli Studi, Facoltà di Economia e Commercio, Istituto di Lingue e Letterature Straniere, 1983. 102 pp.

Barrera y Leirado, Cayetano Alberto de la. *Catálogo bibliográfico y biográfico del teatro antiguo español desde sus orígenes hasta mediados del siglo XVIII.* Madrid: Rivadeneyra, 1860. Rpt. London: Tamesis, 1968.

Bibliografía española. Madrid (various imprints). 1959—.

Bibliographie Internationale de l'Humanisme et de la Renaissance. vol. 1— (1965)—.

"Bibliography of Publications on the Comedia" (title varies). *BCom* 1951—.

Blaney, Benjamin. "Spanish and German Literary Relations in U.S. and Canadian Dissertations: An Annotated Bibliography (1900-1976)." *REHb* 15 (1981): 459-71.

Boston University. *Abstracts of Dissertations,* 1941-56. Boston, 1945-57.

Cambridge. University. *Abstracts of Dissertations Approved for the Ph.D.,*

M.Sc., and M.Litt. Degrees in the University of Cambridge for the Academic Year, 1925-26—1956-57.

[Camón Aznar, José.] "Tesis [de licenciatura] sobre temas literarios presentados en la Facultad de Filosofía y Letras de Madrid [1954-61]." *RL* 19.37-38 (1961): 187-97.

———. "Tesis doctorales de interés literario de la Universidad de Madrid [1933-61]." *RL* 21.41-42 (1962): 107-16.

Castañeda, James A. *Agustín Moreto.* New York: Twayne, 1974. 200 pp. (TWAS 308.)

———. *Mira de Amescua.* Boston: Twayne, 1977. 217 pp. (TWAS 449.)

Catalogue des thèses de doctorat soutenues devant les universités françaises. Paris: (various imprints), 1959-80. Continued by *Inventaire des thèses de doctorat . . .*

Catalogue des thèses et écrits académiques. Paris: (various imprints), 1884-1958. Continued by *Catalogue des thèses de doctorat . . .*

Chatham, James R., and Carmen C. McClendon, with the collaboration of Enrique Ruiz-Fornells and Sara Matthews Scales. *Dissertations in Hispanic Languages and Literatures: An Index of Dissertations Completed in the United States and Canada. Vol. 2: 1967-1977.* Lexington: UP of Kentucky, 1981. 162 pp.

Chatham, James R., and Enrique Ruiz-Fornells. "La investigación doctoral cervantina en las universidades de los Estados Unidos, 1967-1973." *ACer* 15 (1976): 237-43.

Chatham, James R., and Enrique Ruiz-Fornells, with the collaboration of Sara Matthews Scales. *Dissertations in Hispanic Languages and Literatures: An Index of Dissertations Completed in the United States and Canada, 1876-1966.* Lexington: UP of Kentucky, 1970. 120 pp.

Chatham, James R., and Sara M. Scales, with the collaboration of Azzurra B. Givens, Benjamin Blaney, and William Edwin Ellis. *Western European Dissertations on the Hispanic and Luso-Brazilian Languages and Literatures: A Retrospective Index.* [Mississippi State]: Mississippi State Univ., Dept. of Foreign Languages, 1984. 145 pp.

Chicago. University of Chicago. Humanistic Series. *Abstracts of Theses, 1922-1932.* 9 vols. Chicago, 1925-34.

Coutu, Sister Albert Cécile. *Hispanism in France from Morel-Fatio to the Present (circa 1875-1950).* Washington: Catholic U of America P, 1954. 168 pp. (CUASRLL 49.) Rpt. New York: AMS, 1969.

Crosby, James O. *Guía bibliográfica para el estudio crítico de Quevedo.* London: Grant and Cutler, 1976. 140 pp. (Research Bibliographies and

Checklists 13.) This bibliography is updated in [A] Quevedo y Villegas, Francisco de. *Poesía varia* Ed. James O. Crosby. 2nd ed. Madrid: Cátedra, 1982. See "Bibliografia," pp. 27–40 and 579–86. [B] *Sueños y discursos*. Ed., introd., and notes by James O. Crosby. Madrid: Castalia, 1993. See "Bibliografia," pp. 87–96.

Delk, Lois Jo, and James Neal Greer. *Spanish Language and Literature in the Publications of American Universities: A Bibliography*. Austin: U of Texas P, 1952. 211 pp. (University of Texas Hispanic Studies 4.)

Díez de Revenga, Francisco Javier, and María del Pilar Díez de Revenga. *Los estudios literarios en Murcia (1927–1976)*. Murcia: Academia Alfonso X el Sabio, 1977. 216 pp. (Cuadernos bibliográficos 3.)

"Dissertations in the Hispanic Languages and Literatures" (title varies). *Hispania* [AATSP] 1935—. Always in the May issue.

"Doctoral Projects in Progress in Theatre Arts" (title and compilers vary). *TJ* 1952—. Formerly *Educational Theatre Journal* 1949—. Appears annually in the May issue, except for 1949.

Fernandes, Manuel Correia. *Literatura portuguesa em Espanha: Ensaio de uma bibliografia (1890–1985)*. Porto: Livraria Telos Editora, 1986. 339 pp.

Fichter, William L. "The Present State of Lope de Vega Studies." *H* [AATSP] 20.4 (1937): 327–52.

Flasche, Hans. *Die Sprachen und Literaturen der Romanen im Spiegel der deutschen Universitätsschriften 1885–1950: Ein Bibliographie*. Bonn: Bouvier, 1958. 299 pp. (Bonner Beiträge zur Bibliotheks -u. Bücherkunde 3.)

———. "Stand und Aufgaben der Calderónforschung (Ergebnisse der Jahre 1940–58)." *Deutsche Vierteljahrsschrift für Literaturwissenschaft und Geistesgeschichte* 32 (1958): 613–43.

Gabel, Gernot U. *Drama und Theater des deutschen Barock: Eine Handbibliographie der Sekundärliteratur*. Hamburg: Bönecke, 1974. 182 pp.

———. *Répertoire bibliographique des thèses françaises (1885–1975) concernant la littérature française des origines à nos jours*. Köln: Gemini, 1984. 336 pp. (Bibliographien zur Romanistik 3.)

Gabel, Gernot U., and Gisela R. Gabel. *La littérature française: Bibliographie des thèses de doctorat soutenues devant les universités autrichiennes et suisses, 1885–1975*. Köln: Gemini, 1981. 130 pp. (Bibliographien zur Romanistik 1.) *Supplément 1976–1985 et additions*. Hürth and Efferen: Gemini, 1991. 41 pp. (Bibliographien zur Romanistik 4.)

Gallego Morrell, Antonio. "La poesía lírica de Antonio Mira de Amescua y bibliografia del escritor." *BRAE* 64 (1984): 333–61.

Grismer, Raymond Leonard. *Bibliography of Lope de Vega*. 2 vols. (174, 154 pp.) Minneapolis: Burgess-Beckwith, 1965.

———. *Bibliography of the Drama of Spain and Spanish America*. 2 vols. (231, 231 pp.) Minneapolis: Burgess-Beckwith, 1967–69.

———. *Cervantes, a Bibliography: Books, Essays, Articles and Other Studies on the Life of Cervantes, His Works and His Imitators*. 2 vols. Millwood: Kraus, 1970, 1980. 183 pp.

Guittard, Jean-Michel. *Répertoire des thèses françaises relatives au monde ibérique et ibéro-américain des origines à 1980*. Paris: Sorbonne, 1993. 672 pp. (Mélanges de la Bibliothèque de la Sorbonne 23.)

Hanson, Carl A. "Dissertations on Luso-Brazilian Topics: A Bibliography of Dissertations Completed in the United States, Great Britain and Canada, 1892–1970." *Americas: A Quarterly Review of Inter-American Cultural History* 30.2 (1973): 251–67; 30.3 (1974): 373–403.

Harvard University. Graduate School of Arts and Sciences. *Summaries of Theses Accepted in Partial Fulfilment of the Requirements for the Degree of Doctor of Philosophy*. 1925–47. Cambridge: 1928–47.

Hauer, Mary Garrett. *Luis Vélez de Guevara: A Critical Bibliography*. Chapel Hill: Univ. of North Carolina, Dept. of Romance Languages, 1975. 183 pp. "An Addendum to *Luis Vélez de Guevara: A Critical Bibliography*." *Antigüedad y actualidad de Luis Vélez de Guevara: Estudios críticos*. Ed. C. G. Peale et al. Philadelphia: Benjamins, 1983. 254–98. (PUMRL 10.)

Hermann, André, and Gustav Siebenmann. "Verzeichnis der Spanien, Portugal und Lateinamerika betreffenden Schweizer Hochschulschriften aus dem Gebiet der Geistes- und Sozialwissenschaften (1897–1977)." *Ibero* 8 (1978): 118–39.

Hesse, Everett W. "Catálogo bibliográfico de Tirso de Molina." *Tirso de Molina*. Madrid: Revista "Estudios," 1949, pp. 781–889. Supplements by E. W. Hesse [1951, '52, '53, '54, '55, '56, '60, '71, '75] and by David H. Darst [1982, '85, '89, '93, '96] in the journal *EstM*.

Hoffmeister, Gerhart. *Spanien und Deutschland: Geschichte und Dokumentation der literarischen Beziehungen*. Berlin: Schmidt, 1976. 208 pp. (Grundlagen der Romanistik 9.) Spanish version by Isidro Gómez Romero. *España y Alemania: Historia y documentación de sus relaciones literarias*. Madrid: Gredos, 1980. 310 pp. (BHR. II. Estudios y ensayos 302.)

Index to Theses with Abstracts Accepted for Higher Degree by the Universities of Great Britain and Ireland and the Council for National Academic Awards (title varies). London: Aslib, 1950–51—.

Individual abstracts or summaries (in the Announcement of the Final Examination, or the Program of the Final Examination, or some other format), by the following institutions: CA/Berkeley, CA/Los Angeles, Cornell, Illinois, and Iowa.

Internationale Bibliographie der Festschriften von den Anfängen bis 1979. (IBF) Ed. Otto Leistner. 2nd enl. ed. 3 vols. (812, 967, 449 pp.) Osnabrück: Biblio, 1984, 1986, 1989.

Internationale Jahresbibliographie der Festschriften. (IJBF) 1 (1980)—. Osnabrück: Biblio (imprint varies).

Inventaire des thèses de doctorat soutenues devant les universités françaises. . . . Lettres . . . Nanterre: Université de Paris X, 1981—.

La investigación sobre temas hispánicos en Francia (1962–1984): España y América Latina. Actas del XX congreso, Madrid, 1984. Ed. Augustin Redondo. Madrid: Société des Hispanistes Français, 1985. 203 pp.

Iowa, The State University of. *Doctoral Dissertation Abstracts and References, 1900–1952.* 10 vols. Iowa City, 1937-52.

Jahresverzeichnis der Hochschulschriften (title and imprint vary). Leipzig: VEB Bibliographisches Institut, 1885-86—.

Litto, Frederic M. *American Dissertations on the Drama and the Theatre: A Bibliography.* Kent: Kent State UP, 1969. 519 pp.

MacCurdy, Raymond R. *Francisco de Rojas Zorrilla: Bibliografía crítica.* Madrid: CSIC, 1965. 47 pp. (Cuadernos bibliográficos 18.)

Madsen, John Kuhlmann. "El teatro clásico español en Dinamarca." *Tirsiana: Actas del coloquio sobre Tirso de Molina, Copenhague, 1984.* Ed. B. Pallares and J. K. Madsen. Madrid: Castalia; Copenhague: Instituto de Lenguas Románicas, 1990. 99–117.

Mäkelä-Henriksson, Eeva, and Tuovi Puupponen. *Helsingin yliopiston väitöskirjat 1828–1977 / Dissertationer vid Helsingfors universitet 1828–1977 / Dissertations at the University of Helsinki 1828–1977.* Helsinki: University, 1978. 222 pp. (Helsingfors. Universitet. Bibliotek. Skrifter 41.)

McCready, Warren T. *Bibliografía temática de estudios sobre el teatro antiguo español.* Toronto: U of Toronto P, 1966. 445 pp.

Merrill, Ray March. *American Doctoral Dissertations in the Romance Field, 1876–1926.* New York: Columbia UP, 1927. 87 pp.

Miazzi Chiari, Mariapaola, and Blanca Luca de Tena. *Don Agustín de Moreto: Bibliografía crítica.* Milano: Ricci, 1979. 64 pp.

Mills, Judy, and Irene Dombra. *University of Toronto Doctoral Theses, 1897–1967.* Toronto: U of Toronto P, 1968. 186 pp.

Morales, Francisco A. "Tesis doctorales de la Universidad de Madrid, años

1954-58." *BFE* 3.9 (1961): 30-32; "Tesis doctorales de la Univesidad de Madrid, años 1959-61." *BFE* 4.10 (1963): 45-46.

Moseley, William W., Glenroy Emmons, and Marilyn C. Emmons, comps. *Spanish Literature 1500-1700: A Bibliography of Golden Age Studies in Spanish and English, 1925-1980.* Westport: Greenwood, 1984. 765 pp.

Naaman, Antoine, with the collaboration of Léo A. Brodeur. *Répertoire des thèses littéraires canadiennes de 1921 à 1976.* Sherbrooke: Éditions Naaman, 1978. 453 pp.

National Library of Canada. *Canadiana. Canada's National Bibliography.* Ottawa: Natl. Lib. of Canada, 1976—.

North Carolina, University of. "Research in Progress." University of North Carolina *Record* no. 268 (Oct. 1930)—no. 590 (Oct. 1958).

Northwestern University. *Summaries of Doctoral Dissertations.* 20 vols. Evanston, 1933-52.

Ohio State University. *Abstracts of Dissertations Presented by Candidates for the Degree of Doctor of Philosophy.* Nos. 1-67. Columbus, 1929-57.

Parker, Jack H., and Arthur M. Fox. *Calderón de la Barca Studies, 1951-1969: A Critical Survey and Annotated Bibliography.* Toronto: U of Toronto P, 1971. 247 pp.

———. *Lope de Vega Studies, 1937-1962: A Critical Survey and Annotated Bibliography.* Toronto: U of Toronto P, 1964. 210 pp.

Poesse, Walter. "Disertaciones lopescas: Una compilación." *Hispanófila* 6.18 (1963): 77-89. "Disertaciones lopescas: Suplemento." *Hispanófila* 9.26 (1966): 1-6.

———. *Ensayo de una bibliografía de Juan Ruiz de Alarcón.* Valencia: Castalia, 1964. 85 pp. "Suplement." *Hispanófila* 9.27 (1966): 23-42.

Portuguese Literature from Its Origins to 1990: A Bibliography Based on the Collections of Indiana University. Comp. Hugo Kunoff. Metuchen: Scarecrow, 1994. 497 pp.

Positions des thèses de troisième cycle soutenues devant la Faculté des Lettres de Paris-Sorbonne. 10 vols. Paris: Presses Universitaires de France, 1962-72.

Profeti, Maria Grazia. *Per una bibliografia di Felipe Godínez.* Verona: Università degli Studi di Padova, 1982. 95 pp.

———. *Per una bibliografia di Juan Pérez de Montalbán.* Verona: Università degli Studi di Padova, 1976. 574 pp. Addenda et corrigenda. 1982. 94 pp.

Profeti, Maria Grazia, and Umile Maria Zancarini. *Per una bibliografia di Álvaro Cubillo de Aragón.* Verona: Università degli Studi di Padova, 1983. 174 pp.

Redondo, Augustin. "El hispanismo francés, de los años 60 a la actualidad: Organización y tendencias." *Actas del I encuentro franco-alemán de hispanistas, Mainz, 1989.* Ed. Christoph Strosetzki, Jean-François Botrel, and Manfred Tietz. Frankfurt: Vervuert, 1991. 40-50.

Reichenberger, Kurt, and Roswitha Reichenberger. *Bibliographisches Handbuch der Calderón-Forschung / Manual bibliográfico calderoniano.* Vol. 1. Kassel: Thiele und Schwarz, 1979. 831 pp. Vol. 3. 1981. 838 pp.

———. *Das spanische Drama im goldenen Zeitalter: Ein bibliographisches Handbuch.* Kassel: Reichenberger, 1989. 319 pp.

Reynolds, Michael M. *Guide to Theses and Dissertations: An International Bibliography of Bibliographies.* Rev. and enl. ed. Phoenix: Oryx, 1985. 263 pp.

Rodríquez Richart, José. "'Habilitationsschriften' y tesis de doctorado realizadas en las universidades de Austria, de la República Democrática Alemana y de la República Federal de Alemania, sobre temas de lengua y litertura española y portuguesa (1945-1974)." *Ibero* ns 3 (1975): 205-34.

Roig, Adrien. *Inesiana ou bibliografia geral sobre Inês de Castro.* Coimbra: Biblioteca Geral da Universidade, 1986. 369 pp.

Rojek, Hans Jürgen. *Bibliographie der deutschsprachigen Hochschulschriften zur Theaterwissenschaft von 1953 bis 1960.* Berlin: Gesellschaft für Theatergeschichte, 1962. 170 pp. (Schriften der Gesellschaft für Theatergeschichte 61.)

"Die romanistischen Dissertationen" (title varies). *RJ* 1951—.

Rubio San Román, Alejandro. "Aproximación a la bibliografía dramática de Luis Belmonte Bermúdez." *CILH* 9 (1988): 101-63.

———, "Inventario de la obra no dramática de Luis de Belmonte Bermúdez (1577?-1650?)." *CILH* 8 (1987): 193-209.

Schwanbeck, Gisela. *Bibliographie der deutschsprachigen Hochschulschriften zur Theaterwissenschaft von 1885 bis 1952.* Berlin: Gesellschaft für Theatergeschichte 1956. 563 pp. (Schriften der Gesellschaft für Theatergeschichte 58.)

Serialized abstracts or summaries are listed under the following institutions: Boston University, Chicago, Harvard, Iowa, North Carolina, Northwestern, Ohio State, Southern California, Stanford, Tulane, Virginia, Western Reserve, and Wisconsin.

Serís, Homero. *Manual de bibliografía de la literatura española.* Syracuse: Centro de Estudios Hispánicos, 1948-54. 1,086 pp. in 2 parts.

Simón Díaz, José, and Juana de José Prades. *Ensayo de una bibliografía de las obras y artículos sobre la vida y escritos de Lope de Vega Carpio.* Madrid: Centro de Estudios sobre Lope de Vega, 1955. 233 pp.

Singer, Armand E. *The Don Juan Theme: An Annotated Bibliography of Versions, Analogues, Uses, and Adaptations.* Morgantown: West Virginia UP, 1993. 415 pp. Enlargement of the 1965 edition.

Southern California, University of. *Abstracts of Dissertations, 1936–1958.* Los Angeles, 1938-59.

Stanford University. *Abstracts of Dissertations, 1924–1952.* Stanford, 1927-53.

Stathatos, Constantine Christopher. *A Gil Vicente Bibliography (1940–1975).* London: Grant and Cutler, 1980. 132 pp. + supplements. (See item 841 herein.)

Sullivan, Henry W. *Calderón in the German Lands and the Low Countries: His Reception and Influence, 1654–1980.Cambridge: Cambridge UP, 1983.* 510 pp.

Sutton, Donna. "The Cid: A Tentative Bibliography to January 1969." *BFC* 21 (1970): 21-173.

"Tesis de interés literario. [Tesis doctorales y de licenciatura de las Universidades de Barcelona, Murcia, Salamanca, Valladolid, y Zaragoza 1951-63]." *RL* 25.49-50 (1964): 197-205.

"Tesis doctorales recientes." *Revista Interamericana de Bibliografía* 29.2 (1979)—. Appears in each issue since that date.

"Theses in Hispanic Studies Approved for Higher Degree by British and Irish Universities" (title varies). *BHS* 49 (1972): 325-54; 52 (1975): 325-44; 56 (1979): 283-304; 61 (1984): 233-62; 66 (1989): 417-52.

Tiemann, Hermann. *Lope de Vega in Deutschland.* Hildesheim and New York: Olms, 1970. Rpt. of 1939 ed. 310 pp.

Torres, José Carlos de. "Tesis doctorales presentadas en la Universidad Complutense de Madrid (Cursos 1961-62 a 1968-69)." *BFE* 12.42-45 (1972): 115-21.

Torres Ramírez, Isabel de, and María Dolores Olvera Lobo, with the assistance of Antonio Lozano Palacios. *Diez años de tesis doctorales de la Universidad de Granada (1980–81/1989–90).* Granada: Universidad de Granada, 1993. 394 pp.

Tulane University. *Abstracts of Theses, 1938–1955.* New Orleans, 1938-55.

Tusón, Vicente. *Lope de Rueda: Bibliografía crítica.* Madrid: CSIC, 1965. 85 pp.

UMI Dissertation Abstracts: for details, see end of this list.

Universidad [Complutense] de Madrid. *Catálogo de las tesis doctorales ma-*

nuscritas existentes en la Universidad de Madrid. Madrid: González, 1952. 36 pp. See "Filosofía y Letras," pp. 3-21.

Valdivieso, Jorge H., and L. Teresa Valdivieso. "Acotaciones a la crítica cervantina a través del repertorio bibliográfico-analítico de las tesis doctorales norteamericanas." *ACer* 17 (1978): 191-233.

Vega García-Luengos, Germán. "Notas para una bibliografía de Felipe Godínez." *Castilla* 8 (1984): 127-39.

Virginia, University of. Dept. of Graduate Studies. *Abstracts of Dissertations Accepted in Partial Fulfillment of the Requirements for the Degree of Doctor of Philosophy, 1931-1952.* Charlottesville, 1931-52.

Western Reserve (later: Case Western Reserve) University. *Bibliography of Publications and Abstracts of Dissertations, 1950-1958.* Cleveland, 1952-58.

Williamsen, Vern G., and Walter Poesse. *An Annotated, Analytical Bibliography of Tirso de Molina Studies, 1627-1977.* Columbia: U Missouri P, 1979. 238 pp.

Wisconsin, University of. *Summaries of Doctoral Dissertations, 1935-1955.* Madison, 1937-55.

Zubatsky, David S. "An International Guide of Completed Theses and Dissertations in the Hispanic Languages and Literatures." *H* [AATSP] 55.2 (1972): 293-302.

UMI Dissertation Abstracts: The following brief chronology describes the various parts of this very valuable series:

Microfilm Abstracts vols. 1-11, 1938-51

Dissertation Abstracts vols. 12-26, 1951-June 1966

Dissertation Abstracts [divided into parts A + B] vols. 27-29, July 1966-June 1969

Dissertation Abstracts International vol. 30—, 1969—

Part C [=European dissertations] vol. 37—, Autumn 1976— (quarterly), online since 1988

The CD-ROM version of these printed indexes (known by the acronym *DAO*) includes all the bibliographic data in the various versions of *DA* and *DAI* since 1938. *DAO* also includes bibliographic citations for dissertations listed in the *Comprehensive Dissertation Index (CDI),* which has tried to reference all United States doctoral dissertations since 1861. The distinction is that *DAI* includes only materials that have passed through UMI's operation for filming, while *CDI* encompasses everything. Finally, *DAO* includes only abstracts beginning with the July 1980 issue of *DAI.*

In citing *DA* and *DAI,* we have included pagination plus volume numbers with the suffix A (designation for the humanities), but not the dates.

Directory of Institutions
Directorio de instituciones

Part 1 | Parte 1

Institutions in the United States
(Alphabetically by institution)

Instituciones en los Estados Unidos
(En orden alfabético por instituciones)

Alabama, University of
Tuscaloosa, Alabama 35487
Founded 1831

Arizona, University of
Tucson, Arizona 85721
Founded 1885

Arizona State University
Tempe, Arizona 85287-1003
Founded 1885

Arkansas, University of
Fayetteville, Arkansas 72701
Founded 1871

Boston College
Boston, Massachusetts 02167
Founded 1863

Boston University
Boston, Massachusetts 02215
Founded 1839

Brigham Young University
Provo, Utah 84602
Founded 1875

Brown University
Providence, Rhode Island 02912
Founded 1764

Bryn Mawr College
Bryn Mawr, Pennsylvania 19010
Founded 1880

CA/Berkeley SEE California, University of (Berkeley)

CA/Los Angeles SEE California, University of (Los Angeles)

CA/Riverside SEE California, University of (Riverside)

CA/San Diego SEE California, University of (San Diego)

CA/Santa Barbara SEE California, University of (Santa Barbara)

CA/Santa Cruz SEE California, University of (Santa Cruz)

California, University of (Berkeley)
Berkeley, California 94720
Founded 1868

California, University of (Los Angeles)
Los Angeles, California 90095
Founded 1881

California, University of (Riverside)
Riverside, California 92521
Founded 1907

California, University of (San Diego)
La Jolla, California 92093
Founded 1901

California, University of (Santa Barbara)
Santa Barbara, California 93106
Founded 1891

California, University of (Santa Cruz)
Santa Cruz, California 95064
Founded 1965

Case Western Reserve University
Cleveland, Ohio 44106
Founded 1826

Catholic University of America
Washington, D.C. 20064
Founded 1887

Chicago, University of
Chicago, Illinois 60637
Founded 1891

Cincinnati, University of
Cincinnati, Ohio 45221
Founded 1819

City University of New York [CUNY]
New York, New York 10036
Founded 1961

Colorado, University of
Boulder, Colorado 80309
Founded 1861

Columbia University
New York, New York 10027
Founded 1754

Connecticut, University of
Storrs, Connecticut 06269
Founded 1881

Cornell University
Ithaca, New York 14853
Founded 1865

CUNY SEE City University of New York

Denver, University of
Denver, Colorado 80208
Founded 1864

Duke University
Durham, North Carolina 27708
Founded 1838

Emory University
Atlanta, Georgia 30322
Founded 1836

Florida, University of
Gainesville, Florida 32611
Founded 1853

Florida State University
Tallahassee, Florida 32306
Founded 1857

George Peabody College for Teachers
[now part of Vanderbilt University]
Nashville, Tennessee 37235
Founded 1875

George Washington University
Washington, D.C. 20052
Founded 1821

Georgetown University
Washington, D.C. 20057
Founded 1789

Georgia, University of
Athens, Georgia 30602
Founded 1785

Harvard University
Cambridge, Massachusetts 02138
Founded 1636

Illinois, University of
Urbana-Champaign, Illinois 61801
Founded 1867

Indiana University
Bloomington, Indiana 47405
Founded 1820

Iowa, University of
Iowa City, Iowa 52242
Founded 1847

Johns Hopkins University
Baltimore, Maryland 21218
Founded 1876

Kansas, University of
Lawrence, Kansas 66045
Founded 1863

Kentucky, University of
Lexington, Kentucky 40506
Founded 1865

Louisiana State University and A. & M. College
Baton Rouge, Louisiana 70803
Founded 1860

Maryland, University of (College Park)
College Park, Maryland 20742
Founded 1807

Massachusetts, University of (Amherst)
Amherst, Massachusetts 01003
Founded 1863

Michigan, University of
Ann Arbor, Michigan 48109
Founded 1817

Michigan State University
East Lansing, Michigan 48824
Founded 1855

Middlebury College
Middlebury, Vermont 05753
Founded 1800

Minnesota, University of
Minneapolis, Minnesota 55455
Founded 1851

Missouri, University of (Columbia)
Columbia, Missouri 65211
Founded 1839

Missouri, University of (St. Louis)
St. Louis, Missouri 63121
Founded 1960

Nebraska, University of (Lincoln)
Lincoln, Nebraska 68588
Founded 1869

New Mexico, University of
Albuquerque, New Mexico 87131
Founded 1889

New York, State University of (Albany)
Albany, New York 12222
Founded 1844

New York, State University of (Buffalo)
Buffalo, New York 14260
Founded 1846

New York, State University of (Stony Brook)
Stony Brook, New York 11794
Founded 1957

New York University [NYU]
New York, New York 10003
Founded 1831

North Carolina, University of (Chapel Hill)
Chapel Hill, North Carolina 27599
Founded 1789

Northwestern University
Evanston, Illinois 60208
Founded 1851

NYU SEE New York University

Ohio State University
Columbus, Ohio 43210
Founded 1870

Ohio University
Athens, Ohio 45701
Founded 1804

Oklahoma, University of
Norman, Oklahoma 73019
Founded 1890

Oregon, University of
Eugene, Oregon 97403
Founded 1872

Pennsylvania, University of
Philadelphia, Pennsylvania 19104
Founded 1740

Pennsylvania State University
University Park, Pennsylvania 16802
Founded 1919

Pittsburgh, University of
Pittsburgh, Pennsylvania 15260
Founded 1787

Princeton University
Princeton, New Jersey 08544
Founded 1746

Radcliffe College
Cambridge, Massachusetts 02138
Founded 1879

Rochester, University of
Rochester, New York 14627
Founded 1850

Rutgers: The State University of New Jersey
New Brunswick, New Jersey 08903
Founded 1766

St. John's University
Jamaica, New York 11439
Founded 1870

St. Louis University
St. Louis, Missouri 63103
Founded 1818

South Carolina, University of
Columbia, South Carolina 29208
Founded 1801

South Florida, University of
Tampa, Florida 33620
Founded 1956

Southern California, University of [USC]
Los Angeles, California 90089
Founded 1879

Southern Illinois University
Carbondale, Illinois 62901
Founded 1874

Southern Mississippi, University of
Hattiesburg, Mississippi 39406
Founded 1910

Stanford University
Stanford, California 94305
Founded 1885

SUNY SEE New York, State University of

Syracuse University
Syracuse, New York 13244
Founded 1870

Temple University
Philadelphia, Pennsylvania 19122
Founded 1844

Texas, University of
Austin, Texas 78712
Founded 1881

Texas Tech University
Lubbock, Texas 79409
Founded 1923

Tulane University
New Orleans, Louisiana 70118
Founded 1852

USC SEE Southern California, University of

Utah, University of
Salt Lake City, Utah 84112
Founded 1850

Vanderbilt University
Nashville, Tennessee 37235
Founded 1872

Virginia, University of
Charlottesville, Virginia 22903-3196
Founded 1819

WA/Seattle SEE Washington, University of

Washington, University of
Seattle, Washington 98195
Founded 1861

Washington University
St. Louis, Missouri 63130
Founded 1853

Wayne State University
Detroit, Michigan 48202
Founded 1868

Western Reserve University SEE Case Western Reserve University

Wisconsin, University of (Madison)
Madison, Wisconsin 53706
Founded 1836

Yale University
New Haven, Connecticut 06520
Founded 1701

Part 2 | Parte 2

Institutions outside the United States

(Primary arrangement: alphabetical by country)

Instituciones en otros países

(En orden alfabético por país)

Austria

Graz: Karl-Franzens-Universität
Founded 1585

Innsbruck: Leopold-Franzens Universität
Founded 1669

Salzburg: Universität Salzburg
Founded 1622; closed 1810; reconstituted 1962

Vienna: Universität Wien
Founded 1365

Belgium

Brussels: Université Libre de Bruxelles
Founded 1834

Liège: Université de Liège
Founded 1817

Louvain-la-Neuve: Université Catholique de Louvain
Founded 1425; reorganized 1970

Canada

Alberta SEE Edmonton

British Columbia SEE Vancouver

Edmonton: University of Alberta
Founded 1906

Montreal: McGill University
Founded 1821

Ottawa: Université d'Ottawa/University of Ottawa
Founded 1848

Toronto: University of Toronto
Founded 1827

Vancouver: University of British Columbia
Founded 1890

Denmark

Copenhagen: Københavns Universitet
Founded 1479

England

Birmingham: University of Birmingham
Founded 1900

Cambridge: University of Cambridge
Founded 13th century

Exeter: University of Exeter
Founded 1955

London: University of London, Birkbeck College
Founded 1823

London: University of London, External Degree
Granted as of 1836

London: University of London, King's College
Founded 1829

London: University of London, University College
Founded 1826

London: University of London: Westfield College
Founded 1882
Nottingham: University of Nottingham
Founded 1881; University Charter 1948
Oxford: University of Oxford
Founded 13th century
Southampton: University of Southampton
Founded 1952

FRANCE

In the late 1960s and early 1970s, the French university system underwent a major reorganization that is reflected in the following list.
Aix-en-Provence: Université d'Aix-Marseille I (Université de Provence)
Founded 1413; 1970
Besançon: Université de Franche-Comté
Founded 1423; 1691; 1829; 1970
Bordeaux: Université de Bordeaux; Université de Bordeaux III
Founded 1423; 1970
During the early 1970s the university was divided into 3 sections: Université de Bordeaux I, II, III. Bordeaux III (at Talence) specializes in the liberal arts, humanities, and technology.
Clermont-Ferrand: Université de Clermont-Ferrand II (Université Blaise Pascal)
Founded 1810; 1854; 1970; 1976
Grenoble: Université de Grenoble III (Université Stendhal)
Founded 1339; 1810; 1970
Montpellier: Université de Montpellier; Université de Montpellier III (Université Paul Valéry)
Founded 1220; 1970
In 1970 the university was reorganized into Montpellier I, Montpellier II, and Montpellier III (Université Paul Valéry).
Nantes: Université de Nantes
Founded 1962; 1970
Nice: Université de Nice
Founded 1965; 1970; 1971
Paris: Sorbonne; Paris I (Panthéon-Sorbonne); Paris III (Sorbonne Nouvelle); Paris IV (Paris Sorbonne); Paris X (Paris Nanterre)
Founded c. 1170; 1970
In the late 1960s and early 1970s, the university was reorganized into 13 independent units, called Université de Paris I through Université de Paris XIII and located in, as well as near, Paris.
Perpignan: Université de Perpignan
Founded 1970
Poitiers: Université de Poitiers
Founded 1431; 1970
Rennes: Université de Rennes II (Université de Haute Bretagne)
Founded 1461; 1970
Strasbourg: Université de Strasbourg II (Sciences Humaines)
Founded 1537; 1538; 1970

[During its history it was at times part of Germany; SEE Introduction]

Toulouse: Université de Toulouse; Université de Toulouse II (Le Mirail)
Founded 1229; 1970
In 1970 the university was reorganized, and Toulouse II (Le Mirail) became the center for language and literary studies.

GERMANY

Berlin: Freie Universität Berlin
Founded 1948

Berlin: Humboldt-Universität zu Berlin
Founded 1810; 1946
The university when founded was called Friedrich-Wilhelms-Universität. It was reorganized in 1946, and in 1948 was renamed Humboldt-Universität zu Berlin.

Bonn: Rheinische Friedrich-Wilhelms-Universität
Founded 1786; refounded 1818

Breslau: Universität Breslau
German until 1945, when it became Uniwersytet Wroclawski, Wrocław, Poland.
Founded 1811

Cologne: Universität zu Köln
Founded: 1388; 1919

Erlangen: Friedrich-Alexander-Universität zu Erlangen-Nürnberg
Founded 1743

Frankfurt: Johann Wolfgang Goethe Universität
Founded 1901; 1914

Freiburg im Breisgau: Albert-Ludwigs-Universität
Founded 1457

Göttingen: Georg-August-Universität zu Göttingen
Founded 1737

Halle a. S.: Martin Luther-Universität, Halle-Wittenberg
Founded 1502 (Wittenberg), 1694 (Halle); merged with Univ. of Wittenberg in 1817

Hamburg: Universität Hamburg
Founded 1919

Heidelberg: Ruprecht-Karls-Universität
Founded 1386; 1803

Jena: Friedrich-Schiller-Universität
Founded 1554

Kiel: Christian-Albrechts Universität
Founded 1665

Leipzig: Universität Leipzig; renamed Karl-Marx-Universität from 1953 to 1990
Founded 1409

Mainz: Johannes-Gutenberg-Universität
Founded 1477; reopened 1946

Marburg: Philipps-Universität
Founded 1527; 1653

Munich: Ludwig-Maximilians-Universität
Founded 1472

Münster: Westfälische-Wilhelms-Universität
Founded 1780; regained university status in 1902

Paderborn: Universität-Gesamthochschule
Founded 1972
Rostock: Universität Rostock
Founded 1419
Strassburg: Universität Strassburg; now Université de Strasbourg, France; SEE Introduction
Founded 1537
Trier: Universität Trier
Founded 1970; 1975
Tübingen: Eberhard-Karls-Universität
Founded 1477
Würzburg: Bayerische-Julius-Maximilians-Universität
Founded 1582; 1945

Ireland [Republic of]

Dublin: National University of Ireland, University College
Charter granted in 1908

Israel

Jerusalem: Hebrew University of Jerusalem
Founded 1918; inaugurated 1925

Jamaica

Jamaica: University of the West Indies, Mona Campus
Founded 1948; granted university status 1962

Netherlands

Amsterdam: Universiteit van Amsterdam
Founded 1632
Groningen: Rijksuniversiteit te Groningen
Founded 1614
Leiden: Rijksuniversiteit te Leiden
Founded 1575
Utrecht: Rijksuniversiteit te Utrecht
Founded 1636

Portugal

Lisbon: Universidade de Lisboa
Founded 1288; restored 1911

Puerto Rico

San Juan: Universidad de Puerto Rico, Río Piedras Campus
Founded 1966

Scotland

Edinburgh: University of Edinburgh
Founded 1583
Glasgow: University of Glasgow
Founded 1451; reconstituted 1577
St. Andrews: University of St. Andrews
Founded 1411

Spain

Alicante: Universidad de Alicante
Founded 1979
Barcelona: Universitat Autònoma de Barcelona
Founded 1968
Barcelona: Universitat [Central] de Barcelona
Founded 1450
Bilbao: Universidad de Deusto
Founded 1886
Complutense SEE Madrid
Deusto SEE Bilbao
Granada: Universidad de Granada
Founded 1526

La Laguna: Universidad de La Laguna, Islas Canarias
Founded 1701; reorganized 1927
Madrid: Universidad Autónoma
Founded 1968
Madrid: Universidad Complutense
Originally in Alcalá de Henares: 1508–through the 18th century
Transferred to Madrid: 1836
1845, first named Universidad Literaria de Madrid
1857, renamed Universidad Central
1968, renamed Universidad Complutense de Madrid
Murcia: Universidad de Murcia
Founded 1915
Navarre: Universidad de Navarra
Founded 1952
Salamanca: Universidad de Salamanca
Founded 1218
Seville: Universidad de Sevilla
Founded 1502
Valencia: Universitat de València
Founded 1500
Valladolid: Universidad de Valladolid
Founded 1346
Zaragoza: Universidad de Zaragoza
Founded 1474

Sweden

Lund: Lunds Universitet
Founded 1668

Switzerland

Bern: Universität Bern
Founded 1528; 1834
Fribourg: Université de Fribourg
Founded 1889
Neuchâtel: Université de Neuchâtel
Founded 1909
Zürich: Universität Zürich
Founded 1833

Wales

Cardiff: University of Wales, University College
Founded 1893

Sources

Collier's Encyclopedia. New York: Collier's, 1996.
Doughty, Harold R. *Guide to American Graduate Schools*. 8th ed. rev. New York: Penguin, 1997.
International Handbook of Universities. 14th ed. New York: Stockton, 1996.
World List of Universities. 20th ed. New York: Stockton, 1995.
World of Learning. 48th ed. London: Europa, 1998.

Acronyms, Abbreviations, and Journal Titles

Siglas, abreviaturas y títulos de revistas

Certain journals known by single-word titles (e.g., *Criticón, Ínsula, Segismundo*) are listed by that title, with the exception of *Ibero,* for *Iberoromania*.

En el caso de las revistas conocidas por títulos de una sola voz (p.ej., *Criticón, Ínsula y Segismundo,* se usa únicamente esa palabra, con la excepción de *Ibero,* por *Iberoromania*.

{ } Encloses United States dissertations available only in printed form
Encierra tesis doctorales estadounidenses disponibles solo en forma impresa

// Precedes the review of a dissertation in its original form
Precede a la reseña de una tesis doctoral en su forma original

❖ Introduces publications that are a result of, or are related to, the dissertation
Precede a las publicaciones que son el resultado de la tesis doctoral, o están relacionadas con ella

[ ] Encloses capital letter that separates one publication from another
Encierra mayúscula que separa una publicación de otra

( ) Encloses lowercase letter that separates one review of a publication from another
Encierra minúscula que separa una reseña de otra

ABC (Madrid)
abs. *abstract*
ACCV *Anales del Centro de Cultura Valenciana*

ACer	*Anales Cervantinos*
AdUA	*Annales de l'Université d'Abidjan* (Série D: Lettres)
AEFil	*Anuario de Estudios Filológicos* (Cáceres)
AÉSC	*Annales: Économies, Sociétés, Civilisations*
AFE	Announcement of the Final Examination
AGald	*Anales Galdosianos*
AHR	*American Historical Review*
AHSI	*Archivum Historicum Societatis Iesu*
AHSoc	*Annales d'Histoire Sociale* (Paris)
AIEM	*Anales del Instituto de Estudios Madrileños*
AIHM	*Archivo Iberoamericano de Historia de la Medicina* (Madrid)
AION-SR	*Annali Istituto Universitario Orientale, Napoli-Sezione Romanza*
AISO	Asociación Internacional Siglo de Oro
ALE	*Anales de Literatura Española* (Alicante)
ALH	*Anales de la Literatura Hispanoamericana*
ALitASH	*Acta Litteraria Academiae Scientiarum Hungaricae*
ALM	*Anuario de Letras* (México)
Angélica	*Angélica: Revista de Literatura*
AnMal	*Analecta Malacitana*
ANRT	Atelier National de Reproduction des Thèses
AnST	*Analecta Sacra Tarraconensia*
AO	*Archivum* (Universidad de Oviedo)
APK	*Aufsätze zur portugiesischen Kulturgeschichte* (subseries of *Portugiesische Forschungen der Görresgesellschaft*)
Arbor	
Arcadia	*Zeitschrift für Vergleichende Literaturwissenschaft*
Archiv	*Archiv für das Studium der neueren Sprachen und Literaturen*
Argensola (Huesca)	
ArH	*Archivo Hispalense*
ARom	*Archivum Romanicum*
Arquivos	*Arquivos do Centro Cultural Português*
Asclepio	
Aslib	Association of Special Libraries and Information Bureaux
Atenea	*Revista de Ciencia, Arte y Literatura* (Chile)
Atenea (PR)	*Atenea* (Puerto Rico)
Ateneo (Madrid)	
Atlántida	
AUC	*Anales de la Universidad de Chile*
AUMad	*Anales de la Universidad de Madrid*

AUMLA	*Journal of the Australasian Universities Language and Literature Association*
AUMur	*Anales de la Universidad de Murcia*
Ausonia (Siena)	
BAbr	*Books Abroad*
BAE	Biblioteca de Autores Españoles (publisher series)
BAPLE	*Boletín de la Academia Puertorriqueña de la Lengua Española*
BB	*Bulletin of Bibliography*
BBGE	*Boletín Bibliográfico del Centro de Intercambio Intelectual Germano-Español*
BBMP	*Boletín de la Biblioteca de Menéndez Pelayo*
BCom	*Bulletin of the Comediantes*
BÉP	*Bulletin des Études Portugaises*
Berceo	
BFC	*Boletín del Instituto de Filología de la Universidad de Chile*
BFE	*Boletín de Filología Española*
BFFLS	*Bulletin of the Faculty of Foreign Languages and Studies* (Tokyo)
BH	*Bulletin Hispanique*
BHR	*Bibliothèque d'Humanisme et Renaissance*
BHS	*Bulletin of Hispanic Studies* (formerly: *Bulletin of Spanish Studies*)
BIE	*Boletín del Instituto de las Españas*
BIEA	*Boletín del Instituto de Estudios Asturianos*
BNM	Biblioteca Nacional, Madrid
BR	*Bucknell Review*
BRAE	*Boletín de la Real Academia Española*
BRAEH	*Boletín de la Real Academia Española de la Historia*
BRH	Biblioteca Románica Hispánica (publisher series)
Brotéria	
BSCC	*Boletín de la Sociedad Castellonense de Cultura*
BSEHM	*Boletín de la Sociedad Española de Historia de la Medicina*
BSS	*Bulletin of Spanish Studies* (later: *Bulletin of Hispanic Studies*)
BSVAP	*Boletín de la Sociedad Vascongada de Amigos del País*
BUG	*Boletín de la Universidad de Granada*
CA	*Cuadernos Americanos*
CAL	*Cuadernos de Arte y Literatura* (Universidad de Granada)
CAld	*Cuadernos de ALDEEU*
Canente, Revista Literaria	

Castilla	
Cauce (Sevilla)	
CB	*Cuadernos Bibliográficos*
CdD	*Ciudad de Dios*
CdF	*Cuadernos de Filología* (Valencia)
Celestinesca	
Centrum	
CÉR	*Cahiers d'Études Romanes* (Aix-en-Provence)
Cervantes	
ch.	chapter(s)
CH	*Crítica Hispánica*
CHA	*Cuadernos Hispanoamericanos*
CIH	*Cuadernos de Investigación Histórica*
CILH	*Cuadernos para Investigación de la Literatura Hispánica*
CL	*Cuadernos de Literatura* (Madrid)
Clavileño	
CLS	*Comparative Literature Studies*
CMHLB	*Caravelle/Cahiers du Monde Hispanique et Luso-Brésilien*
CN	*Cultura Neolatina*
CNRS	Centre National de la Recherche Scientifique
col.	column(s)
Colóquio	*Colóquio/Letras*
Confluencia	
Convivium	
Corónica	
CRCL	*Canadian Review of Comparative Literature*
Crisol	
Criticón	
Crotalón	
CRR	*Cincinnati Romance Review*
CSIC	Consejo Superior de Investigaciones Científicas
CSP	*Canadian Slavonic Papers*
CT	*La Ciencia Tomista* (Salamanca)
CTC	*Cuadernos de Teatro Clásico*
Cuadernos (Paris)	
CUASRLL	Catholic University of America Studies in Romance Languages and Literatures
Cultura (San Salvador)	
Cultura Española (Madrid)	

DA	*Dissertation Abstracts*
DAI	*Dissertation Abstracts International*
DAO	*Dissertation Abstracts* on CD-ROM
Diálogos Hispánicos de Amsterdam	
Dieciocho	*Dieciocho: Hispanic Enlightenment, Aesthetics and Literary Theory*
DHR	*Duquesne Hispanic Review*
Discurso	*Discurso: Revista de Estudios Iberoamericanos*
diss.	dissertation
DLit	*Discurso Literario*
DLZ	*Deutsche Literatur Zeitung*
DSS	*XVII*[e] *Siècle*
EA	*Estudios Americanos* (Sevilla)
ed.	edition; edited
EdO	*Edad de Oro*
Educadores	
EEsc	*Estudios Escénicos* (later: *Estudis Escènics*)
ÉG	*Études Germaniques*
EIA	*Estudos Ibero-Americanos* (Pôrto Alegre, Brazil)
Eidôlon	
EIRC	*Explorations in Renaissance Culture* (Memphis, TN)
EL	*Estafeta Literaria*
Emérita	
EnSt	*Englische Studien*
Erasmus	*Erasmus: Speculum Scientiarum* (Wiesbaden)
ErudIU	*Erudición Ibero-Ultramarina*
ES (Valladolid)	
Escorial	
EstM	*Estudios: Revista Trimestral Publicada por los Frailes de la Merced* (Madrid)
EstudB	*Estudio, revista mensual* (Barcelona)
Euphorion	
Euphrosyne	
ExTL	*Explicación de Textos Literarios*
Filología (Buenos Aires)	
FMLS	*Forum for Modern Language Studies*
FMod	*Filología Moderna* (Madrid)
Folio	
Foro Hispánico	

FS — *French Studies*
FUE — Fundación Universitaria Española

Gaceta — *La Gaceta Literaria* (Madrid)
GAKS — *Gesammelte Aufsätze zur Kulturgeschichte Spaniens* (subseries of *Spanische Forschungen der Görresgesellschaft*)
Gazette — *Gazette of the Grolier Club* (New York)
Gestos
Goya
GRM — *Germanische-Romanische Monatsschrift*
GSLI — *Giornale Storico della Letteratura Italiana*

H[AATSP] — *Hispania (USA)*
HAHR — *Hispanic American Historical Review*
HAR — *Hispanic American Report*
HisJ — *Hispanic Journal*
Hispanófila
HispM — *Hispania* (Madrid)
HISt — *Hispano-Italic Studies*
HR — *Hispanic Review*
HSA — Hispanic Society of America
HSNPL — *Harvard Studies and Notes in Philology and Literature*
HumC — *Humanitas* (Coimbra)
HumT — *Humanitas* (Tucumán)
HuRe — *Humanisme et Renaissance* (Paris)

IAL — *Índice de Artes y Letras*
Ibérica
Ibero — *Iberoromania*
Ideologies and Literature
IEA — *La Ilustración Española y Americana*
IJHL — *Indiana Journal of Hispanic Literatures*
illus. — illustration; illustrated
Incipit (Buenos Aires)
Ínsula: Revista Bibliográfica de Ciencias y Letras
Italica

JAPCS — *Journal of the American Portuguese Cultural Society* (New York)
JEGP — *Journal of English and Germanic Philology*
JEP — *Journal of Evolutionary Psychology*

JHP	*Journal of Hispanic Philology*
JJS	*Journal of Jewish Studies*
JNH	*Journal of Negro History*
Káñina	
KFLQ	*Kentucky Foreign Language Quarterly* (later: *Kentucky Romance Quarterly*)
KJrP	*Kritischer Jahresbericht über die Fortschritte der romanischen Philologie*
KN	*Kwartalnik Neofilologiczny*
KRQ	*Kentucky Romance Quarterly* (later: *Romance Quarterly*)
LanM	*Les Langues Modernes*
LangQ	*Language Quarterly* (formerly: *USF Language Quarterly*)
LATR	*Latin American Theater Review*
LBR	*Luso-Brazilian Review*
LdD	*Letras de Deusto*
L/F	*L/F (Hoja Informativa de Literatura y Filología)*
LFem	*Letras Femeninas*
LGRP	*Literaturblatt für germanische und romanische Philologie*
Library	
La Licorne	
LitEcho	*Literarische Echo* (Berlin)
Literature and Psychology	
Littératures (Toulouse)	
LitZent	*Literarisches Zentralblatt für Deutschland*
LJHum	*Lamar Journal of the Humanities*
LLNL	*Les Langues Néo-Latines*
LMex	*Literatura Mexicana*
LMS	*Littérature, Médicine, Société* (Nantes)
LR	*Lettres Romanes*
LRin	*La Rinascita* (Florence)
LSECL	*Libros de la Sociedad Española de Crítica de Libros*
Manresa	
MEC	Ministerio de Educación y Ciencias (Madrid)
Mediterráneo (Valencia)	
Mester	
MichA	*Michigan Academician*
MLJ	*Modern Language Journal*
MLN	*Modern Language Notes*

MLR *Modern Language Review*
Monteagudo (Murcia)
MP *Modern Philology*
MQ *Musical Quarterly*
MRRM *Monographic Review/Revista Monográfica*
MuK *Maske und Kothurn*

NBAE Nueva Biblioteca de Autores Españoles (series)
NE *Nueva Estafeta*
NEMLA Northeast Modern Language Association
Neophilologus *Neuphilologische Mitteilungen*
Notas
n.p., n.d. no page(s), no place, or no publisher, no date
NRFH *Nueva Revista de Filología Hispánica*
NRO *Nouvelle Revue d'Onomastique*
ns new series/nueva serie
NS *Neueren Sprachen*
NT *Nuestro Tiempo*
NUC National Union Catalog
NYPL New York Public Library

Ocidente (Lisbon)
OCLC Online Computer Library Center (bibliographic database)
OL *Orbis Litterarum*
Ottawa Hispánica

PCP *Pacific Coast Philology*
Pensamiento (Madrid)
PEsp *Poesía Española* (Madrid)
PEur *Punta Europa*
PFE Program of the Final Examination
pl plate(s)
PLL *Papers in Language and Literature*
PMLA *Publications of the Modern Language Association*
Polybiblion
PPU Promoción de Publicaciones Universitarias
PQ *Philological Quarterly*
Prohemio
prt. printed
PSA *Papeles de Son Armadans*

PSRL Purdue Studies in Romance Literatures
PUMML Purdue University. Monographs in Modern Languages
PUMRL Purdue University. Monographs in Romance Languages

QFEL *Quaderns de Filologia. Estudis Literaris*
QIA *Quaderni Ibero-Americani*
QL *La Quinzaine Littéraire*
QLL *Quaderni di Lingue e Letterature* (Padua)
QP *Quaderni Portoghesi*
Quadrant (Université Paul Valéry)
Quimera (Barcelona)

RABM *Revista de Archivos, Bibliotecas y Museos*
RAC *Revue d'Art Canadienne*
RAEPE *Revista de la Asociación Europea de Profesores de Español*
RB *Revue Bleue (Revue Politique et Littéraire)*
RBAM *Revista de la Biblioteca, Archivo y Museo del Ayuntamiento de Madrid*
RBD *Revista Bibliográfica y Documental*
RBN *Revista de Bibliografía Nacional*
RBPH *Revue Belge de Philologie et d'Histoire*
RC *Ruperto Carola* (Heidelberg)
RCEH *Revista Canadiense de Estudios Hispánicos*
RCHLP *Revue Critique d'Histoire et Littérature* (Paris)
RCLL *Revista de Crítica Literaria Latinoamericana*
RCont *Revista Contemporánea* (Madrid)
RdE *Revista de Educación* (Buenos Aires)
RdF *Revista de Filosofía* (Madrid)
RdHM *Revista de Historia Moderna*
RDM *Revue des Deux Mondes*
RDTP *Revista de Dialectología y Tradiciones Populares*
RE *Revista de Espiritualidad*
RECTR *Restoration and Eighteenth-Century Theatre Research*
REE *Revista de Estudios Extremeños*
Reflexión2
REHa *Revista de Estudios Hispánicos* (New York-Puerto Rico, 1928-29)
REHb *Revista de Estudios Hispánicos* (United States, 1967-)
REHc *Revista de Estudios Hispánicos* (Puerto Rico, 1971-)
REJ *Revue des Études Juives* (Paris)

Renaissance d'Occident (Brussels)
Ren&R *Renaissance & Reformation*
RenD *Renaissance Drama*
RenQ *Renaissance Quarterly*
REP *Revista de Estudios Políticos* (Madrid)
Revue (Paris)
RF *Romanische Forschungen*
RFE *Revista de Filología Española*
RFH *Revista de Filología Hispánica*
RFR *Revista de Filología Románica* (Univ. Complutense)
RG *Revue Germanique*
RH *Revue Hispanique*
RHist *Revue Historique* (Paris)
RHistM *Revue d'Histoire Moderne*
RHLP *Revista de História Literária de Portugal*
RHM *Revista Hispánica Moderna*
RHT *Revue d'Histoire du Théâtre*
RI *Revista Ibero-Americana*
RIber *Rassegna Iberistica*
RIE *Revista de Ideas Estéticas*
RILCE *Revista del Instituto de Lengua y Cultura Españolas*
RIS *Revista Internacional de Sociología*
RITL *Revista de Istorie si Teorie Literara*
RJ *Romanistisches Jahrbuch*
RL *Revista de Literatura*
RLAn *Romance Languages Annual*
RLC *Revue de Littérature Comparée*
RLIN Research Libraries Information Network (bibliographic database)
RLMC *Rivista di Letterature Moderne e Comparate*
RLR *Revue des Langues Romanes*
RLV *Revue des Langues Vivantes*
RM *Revista de Musicología*
RMed *Revue de la Méditerranée* (Algiers-Paris)
RO *Revista de Occidente*
Romania
RomN *Romance Notes*
RomQ *Romance Quarterly* (formerly: *Kentucky Romance Quarterly*)
RORD *Research Opportunities in Renaissance Drama*
RPh *Romance Philology*

rpt.	reprint
RR	*Romanic Review*
RSH	*Revue de Synthèse Historique*
RUBA	*Revista de la Universidad de Buenos Aires*
RUCM	*Revista de la Universidad Complutense de Madrid*
RUM	*Revista de la Universidad de Madrid*
Rumo (Lisbon)	
RVF	*Revista Valenciana de Filología*
RyF	*Razón y Fe*
SAB	*South Atlantic Bulletin* (later: *South Atlantic Review*)
SAR	*South Atlantic Review*
SCN	*Seventeenth-Century News*
SCSML	*Smith College Studies in Modern Languages*
Segismundo.	*Revista Hispánica de Teatro*
SFG	*Spanische Forschungen der Görresgesellschaft (see: GAKS)*
ShS	*Shakespeare Survey*
Sillages	
SN	*Studia Neophilologica*
SP	*Studies in Philology*
SpM	*Spicilegio Moderno*
StudFilMod	*Studi di Filologia Moderna*
SvglL	*Studien zur vergleichenden Literaturgeschichte*
Symposium	
TA	*Theatre Annual* (Florida)
TAH	*The American Hispanist*
Teatro	
Theatre Documentation	
Thesaurus. Boletín del Instituto Caro y Cuervo (Bogotá)	
ThR	*Theatre Research International* (formerly: *Theatre Research*)
ThS	*Theatre Survey: The American Journal of Theatre History*
TILAS	*Travaux de l'Institut d'Études Ibériques et Latino-Américaines de l'Université des Sciences Humaines de Strasbourg*
TL	*Textes et Langages* (Nantes)
TLL	*Travaux de Linguistique et de Littérature*
TLS	*Times Literary Supplement* (London)
Torre	*La Torre* (Puerto Rico)
TQ	*Texas Quarterly*

TR — *Theatre Research/Recherches Théâtrales* (later: *Theatre Research International*)
TS — *Théâtre et Société (Cahiers de l'Université Pau et des Pays de l'Adour)*
TWAS — Twayne's World Authors Series

UCM — Universidad Complutense, Madrid
UCPMP — University of California Publications in Modern Philology
UISSLL — University of Iowa Studies in Spanish Language and Literature
UMI — University Microfilms International
UNCSRLL — University of North Carolina Series/Studies in Romance Languages and Literature
UNED — Universidad Nacional de Educación a Distancia
Universidad (Universidad Nacional de Litoral, Argentina)
Universidad (Zaragoza)

Vórtice
VR — *Vox Romanica*

Wolfenbütteler Forschungen

YWMLS — *Year's Work in Modern Language Studies*

ZFSL — *Zeitschrift für französische Sprache und Literatur*
ZRP — *Zeitschrift für romanische Philologie*
ZVL — *Zeitschrift für vergleichende Literaturgeschichte*

United States Doctoral Dissertations with Annotations and Resultant or Related Publications

Tesis doctorales estadounidenses con anotaciones y publicaciones resultantes o relacionadas

General
Golden Age Culture, History, Art, and Related Subjects

1. Barnes, Gwendolyn. Sermons and the Discourse of Power: The Rhetoric of Religious Oratory in Spain (1550–1900). 408 pp. Minnesota, N. Spadaccini, 1988. *DAI* 50A: 455.

   "The first chapter draws upon theories of orality and literacy, speech-act theory, and semiotics of drama and the theater to provide a theoretical framework for subsequent chapters." (Abs.)

2. Barton, Erika Regina Seiberlich. Die spanische Literatur in Deutschland im Zeitalter des Barock: Ein Forschungsbericht. 286 pp. Nebraska, D. E. Allison, 1972. *DAI* 33A: 3573–74.

   ". . . the drama has been the subject of a great many investigations, especially those done earlier. Current scholarly endeavors devote little attention to the field because it has become obvious that the ties between the German and the Spanish stage were very superficial, although a number of Spanish plays found their way into the repertory of the 'Wanderbühne.'" (Abs.)

3. Biondi, Raymond Liberty. Hispanism in Italy: An Appraisal of the Contribution of Benedetto Croce to the Evaluation of Spanish Literature. 214 pp. Stanford, R. Juárez, 1955. *DA* 15: 1060.

   "It is precisely in Croce's Spanish studies that we can observe the transition from the old methodology [the historical method] to the new [the aesthetic method]." (Abs.)

   Among Croce's writings on Spanish topics are studies of Calderón, Lope, Tirso, and Torres Naharro.

4. Bourland, Caroline Brown. Boccaccio and the *Decameron* in Spain. Bryn Mawr, F. De Haan, 1902.

   ❖ [A] *"La comedia muy exemplar de la Marquesa de Saluzia llamada Griselda,* de Pedro Navarro." *RH* 9 (1902): 331–54. [B] *"Los moriscos de Hornachos." MP* 1 (1903–04): 547–62; 2 (1904–05): 77–96. [C] "Boccaccio and the *Decameron* in Castilian and Catalan Literature." *RH* 12 (1905): 1–232. The writer deals extensively with the influence of the *Decameron* on the theater, especially of Lope de Vega. (Prt. Diss.)

5. BRANCAFORTE, BENITO. Benedetto Croce as Critic of Spanish Literature: Theory and Practice. 227 pp. Illinois, M. A. Morínigo, 1965. *DA* 26A: 2744.

The writer proposes "to draw attention to the value and relevance of [Croce's] judgments on Spanish classic authors, from Cervantes to Lope, from *La Celestina* to popular ballads. . . . [The] main conclusion of this study stresses the validity and soundness of Croce's aesthetic premises and critical approach, and attempts at the same time to clarify some of Croce's views, such as those on genres, and on the role of philology." (Abs.)

❖ [A] "Benedetto Croce's Changing Attitude toward the Relevance of Spanish Influences in Italy." *Italica* 44.3 (1967): 326–43. [B] "Croce on Lope and Calderón: The Application of an Aesthetic Theory." *Symposium* 23 (1969): 101–15. [C] "Benedetto Croce and the Theory of Popularism in Spanish Literature." *HR* 38 (1970): 69–79. [D] *Benedetto Croce y su crítica de la literatura española*. Trans. J. Conde. Madrid: Gredos, 1972. 152 pp. (BRH II. Estudios y ensayos 172.)

6. BROOKS, LYNN MATLUCK. The Dance of the Processions of Seville in Spain's Golden Age. 499 pp. Temple, E. Ferdun, 1984. *DAI* 46A: 555–56.

"Drawing on a wide range of thematic material, and calling for spectacular costuming, these [dance] works blended traditional elements of Spanish theater and dance with new movement and clothing styles. . . . This [investigation] reveals new perspectives on Seville's history, on the city's spiritual traditions, and on the nature of religious, as well as theatrical, popular, and court dance in the Golden Age." (Abs.)

❖ [A] *The Dances of the Processions of Seville in Spain's Golden Age*. Kassel: Reichenberger, 1988. 411 pp. (Teatro del Siglo de Oro. Estudios de literatura 4.) [B] "Cosmic Imagery in the Religious Dances of Seville's Golden Age." *Choreography and Dance* 3.4 (1994): 17–27.

7. BROOKS, MARY ELIZABETH. Gabriel de Espinosa, "El Pastelero de Madrigal," in History and Literature. 374 pp. New Mexico, R. R. MacCurdy, 1960. *DA* 20: 4394.

❖ *A King for Portugal: The Madrigal Conspiracy, 1594–95.* Madison: U of Wisconsin P, 1964. 192 pp.

The titles of both the dissertation and the resulting book refer to a historical episode: "On August 1, 1595, Gabriel de Espinosa, pastry-maker of the Spanish town of Madrigal de las Altas Torres, was executed for impersonating the deceased King of Portugal, Sebastian I." (Prt. Diss.) In chapter 6, "The *Pastelero* in Spanish Literature," pp. 119–42 of the printed format, the writer describes, inter alia, the *comedia El Pastelero de Madrigal,* which has been attributed to José de Cañizares, and more frequently to Jerónimo de Cuéllar, who died sometime after 1665.

8. CAMAMIS, GEORGE. El tema del cautiverio en la narrativa del siglo XVII. 334 pp. CUNY, J. Casalduero, 1973. *DAI* 34A: 1896–97.

"Though [the theme of captivity] is quite prevalent in the *comedia* of Cervantes, Lope de Vega and other playwrights of that period, the most interesting manifestations of the captivity theme are found in the novel and non-fictional prose of the seventeenth century." (Abs.)

❖ *Estudios sobre el cautiverio en el Siglo de Oro.* Madrid: Gredos, 1977. 262 pp. (BRH II. Estudios y ensayos 264.)

9. CAMPA, PEDRO FRANCISCO. Lo medieval en la preceptiva literaria del Siglo de Oro. iv+254 pp. Illinois, A. Porqueras-Mayo, 1973. *DAI* 34A: 5901.

"La continuidad de los valores medievales en la teoría literaria la vemos expresada en una serie de 'topoi' que confirman el valor del tradicionalismo en nuestras letras." (Abs.)

❖ [A] "The Defense of Poetry in Spanish 16th and 17th Century Poetic Theory: The Platonic and Patristic Argument." *Studies in Language and Literature: Proceedings of the Twenty-Third Mountain Interstate Foreign Language Conference.* Ed. Charles Nelson. Richmond: Eastern Kentucky Univ., 1976. 91–94. ["Lope's victory over Torres Rámila and his Aristotelian mob, Fray Luis de León's use of biblical exegesis in his poetry, Gongoristic justifications of obscurity based on Platonic and Patristic tenets, and the theological nature of Spanish emblematic literature are but a few instances that show us the centrality of medieval values in the Siglo de Oro."] [B] Emblemata Hispanica: *An Annotated Bibliography of Spanish Emblem Literature to the Year 1700.* Durham: Duke UP, 1990. 248 pp.

10. Carey, Douglas MacArthur. Asides and Interiority in Spanish Literature of the Golden Age. ix+382 pp. Duke, B. W. Wardropper, 1970. *DAI* 31A: 6595–96.

   "Chapter IV treats specifically the Spanish Golden Age theater." The authors discussed include Juan del Encina, Torres Naharro, Gil Vicente, Lope de Rueda, Cervantes, Lope, Tirso, and Calderón. (Abs.)

11. Carrasco Urgoiti, María Soledad. The Moor of Granada in Spanish Literature of the Eighteenth and Nineteenth Centuries. ii+433 pp. Columbia, J. F. Shearer and Á. del Río, 1954.

   ❖ [A] *El moro de Granada en la literatura (del siglo XV al XX).* Madrid: Revista de Occidente, 1956. 499 pp. [498 + Fe de erratas.] ". . . precedí [mi tesis] de una parte introductoria de 150 páginas en que exponía el desarrollo previo del tema y su difusión en otras literaturas." Pp. 77–90 deal with Golden Age "comedias de moros y cristianos." (Prt. Diss.) [B] "Aspectos folclóricos y literarios de la fiesta de moros y cristianos en España." *PMLA* 78 (1963): 476–91. [C] "En torno a *La Luna africana,* comedia de nueve ingenios." *PSA* 96 (1964): 255–98. [D] *"El cerco de Santa Fe,* de Lope de Vega, ejemplo de comedia épica." *Homenaje a William L. Fichter: Estudios sobre el teatro antiguo hispánico y otros ensayos.* Ed. A. David Kossoff and José Amor y Vázquez. Madrid: Castalia, 1971. 115–25. [E] *"De buen moro, buen cristiano:* Notas sobre una comedia de Felipe Godínez." *NRFH* 30.2 (1981): 546–73. [F] "Notas sobre el romance morisco y la comedia de Lope de Vega." *RFE* 62 (1982): 51–76. [G] "La fiesta de moros y cristianos y la cuestión morisca en la España de los Austrias." *Actas de las jornadas sobre teatro popular en España.* Coord. Joaquín Álvarez Barrientos and Antonio Cea Gutiérrez. Madrid: CSIC, 1987. 65–84. [H] "La comedia hagiográfica *Los tres hermanos del cielo* (Godínez refundido por el actor Francisco de la Calle)." *RDTP* 43 (1988): 95–103. [I] Facsimile edition of publication A: Granada: Universidad de Granada, 1989. With a preliminary study by Juan Martínez Ruiz. (Colección Archivum 10.) [J] *El moro retador y el moro amigo: Estudio sobre fiestas y comedias de moros y cristianos.* Granada: Universidad de Granada, 1996. 320 pp.

12. Chinchilla, Rosa Helena. The Evolution of Classical Myth in Spain's Golden Age (1500–1680). viii+229 pp. SUNY/Stony Brook, E. L. Rivers, 1989. *DAI* 50A: 2510–11.

The writer discusses four authors: Garcilaso, Góngora, Quevedo, and Calderón. "Calderón's most important innovations in the use of myth are found in his *autos sacramentales*. In these, Cupid and Orpheus become symbolic of Christ. The rarely used legend of Ulysses and Circe is given Christian meaning. Calderón incorporates the Humanist tradition with Neo-Platonist ideals and Christian teachings to create a highly symbolic world." (Abs.)

13. CONTAG, KIMBERLY ELIZABETH. The Nature and Function of Burlesque: The Ideology of Mockery in Golden Age Spanish Literature. 293 pp. Minnesota, A. N. Zahareas and N. Spadaccini, 1989. *DAI* 50A: 2884.

The preface defines burlesque as "a mode of representing potentially alarming and highly sensitive issues in art and in life which, if treated in any way other than a well orchestrated burlesque, would either bring in the censors or be considered nonsense." Pages 127–54 of chapter 3 bear the heading "The Case of the Burlesque *Entremés*. A Blueprint for Burlesque Representation: Cervantes's *Retablo de las maravillas*." (Diss.)

❖ *Mockery in Spanish Golden Age Literature: Analysis of Burlesque Representation.* Lanham: UP of America, 1996. 214+[37] pp.

14. DARDÓN-TADLOCK, GISELA. *Lesedrama*: El género de *La Celestina*. 144 pp. Arizona, H. Iventosch and D. A. Nelson, 1976. *DAI* 37A: 1006.

"Chapter V argues that *La Celestina* is a *Lesedrama*. It compares its dramatic character with that of staged plays or 'comedias.' Some contemporaries of Rojas, like Torres Naharro, Lope de Rueda, and Juan Timoneda, adopted certain elements of *La Celestina* but rejected others that could not be adapted to the physical stage. Fernando de Rojas relied upon the imagination of his readers for the stage of *La Celestina*. Chapter VI studies imitations of *La Celestina (La comedia Thebaida, Comedia llamada Seraphina,* and *La Eufrosina)* as well as two sequels of Rojas' *Lesedrama (Segunda comedia de Celestina* and the *Tercera tragicomedia de Celestina)*. The analysis of these works shows the deliberate effort of these playwrights to imitate the technique of Rojas' *Lesedrama*. Ferreira de Vasconcelos, Gómez de Toledo, and Feliciano de Silva understood the advantages of the *Lesedrama* in the study of characters and environment. Chapter VII studies Lope de

Vega's *La Dorotea,* a play unanimously considered by the critics as a *Lesedrama*." (Abs.)

15. DE WENDLER-FUNARO, CARL. The *Gitano* in Spanish Literature. 322 pp. Columbia, Á. del Río, 1958. *DAI* 19A: 523–24.

"This study has been treated chronologically with a consideration of the role given the *Gitano* in the drama, novel, and poetry throughout the various literary periods and movements." The writer begins his investigation with the appearance of the *Gitano* in "the *autos* and *comedias* of the sixteenth century." (Abs.)

16. DEFERRARI, HARRY AUSTIN. The Sentimental Moor in Spanish Literature before 1600. Pennsylvania, J. P. W. Crawford, 1926.

❖ Title as is. Philadelphia: Univ. of Pennsylvania, 1927. 84 pp. (UPSRLL 17.)

Deals mainly with the Abencerraje story and Pérez de Hita's *Guerras civiles de Granada,* but there are some theater references: pp. 37, 51–52, and 56. (Prt. Diss.)

17. DOUDOROFF, MICHAEL JOHN. A Contribution to the Study of the Magi Theme in Hispanic Literature and Folklore. iv+402 pp. Stanford, J. B. Rael and A. M. Espinosa, 1969. *DAI* 30A: 1978–79.

"Brief discussions of the motifs which compose the Magi legend, and of the early religious theater in Spain, are followed by a chronological description of works dealing with the Magi theme in Spain and Spanish America." (Abs.)

❖ "Sobre la naturaleza del *Auto de los Reyes Magos* en época moderna." *RDTP* 29 (1973): 417–26.

18. DOUGLASS, RALPH THOMAS. The Evolution of Spanish Orthography from 1475 to 1726. 194 pp. Pennsylvania, E. B. Williams, 1964. *DA* 25: 4143–44.

"The purpose of this study is to describe the evolution of Spanish orthography from its first printed manifestation around 1475 to the date of the publication of the first volume of the *Diccionario de la Real Academia Española* in 1726. . . . The final chapter (Conclusions) contains not only conclusions, but also a summary and chronology of the important changes that took place, as well as comments on the outside influences that probably had an effect on spelling, such as the establishment of new printing presses, political upheavals or stability, and phonological changes in the language itself. It is hoped that the conclusions drawn from this study will have the corollary effect of helping to ascertain or confirm the approximate year of publication of undated printed documents. . . . However, even until 1726 spelling often depended on the dialect, age, and education of the typesetter." (Abs.)

❖ [A] "'Ph' for 'F' in Spanish." *H* [AATSP] 52.1 (1969): 81–82. [B] "More 'Ph' for 'F.'" *H* [AATSP] 53.2 (1970): 242–43.

19. FELKEL, ROBERT WILLIAM. The Theme of *Desengaño* in Spanish Dances of Death from the Fourteenth to the Seventeenth Century. 5+ii+353 pp. Michigan State, K. R. Scholberg, 1973. *DAI* 34A: 3388–89.

Included in this study are the following relevant works: Vicente's *Auto da Barca da Glória*, Diego Sánchez de Badajoz's *Farsa de la Muerte,* Juan de Pedraza's *Farsa llamada Danza de la Muerte,* and Calderón's *El gran teatro del mundo.* (Abs.)

❖ [A] "*El gran teatro del mundo* of Pedro Calderón de la Barca and the Centrality of Grace." *BCom* 31.2 (1979): 127–34. ["At this point the Dance of Death theme is introduced. Death in this play functions as a powerful agent of *desengaño.*"] [B] "El papel del pobre en *El gran teatro del mundo* y el *Grosse Salzburger Welttheater* de Hofmannsthal." *Calderón: Actas del congreso internacional sobre Calderón y el teatro español del Siglo de Oro, Madrid, 1981.* Ed. Luciano García Lorenzo. 3 vols. Madrid: CSIC, 1983. 1289–97.

20. FINCH, PATRICIA S. Magic and Witchcraft in the *Celestina* and Its Imitations. ii+221 pp. Catholic, B. M. Damiani, 1981. DAI 42A: 2699.

"This dissertation takes up the question of how magic functions in the *Celestina* and seven of its imitations: *Segunda Celestina* by Feliciano de Silva (1534), *Tercera Celestina* by Gaspar Gómez de Toledo (1536), *Lisandro y Roselia* by Sancho de Muñón (1542), *Tragedia Policiana* by Sebastián Fernández (1547), *Comedia Salvaje* by Romero de Cepeda (1554), *Lozana Andaluza* by Francisco Delicado (1528), and *La Dorotea* by Lope de Vega (1631)." (Abs.) Editorial note: Literary historians do not agree about the genre of a number of these works.

❖ "Gerarda como figura celestinesca." *Lope de Vega y los orígenes del teatro español: Actas del I congreso internacional sobre Lope de Vega.*

Ed. Manuel Criado de Val. Madrid: EDI-6, 1981. 617–21. [Apropos Gerarda in *La Dorotea.*]

21. Forcadas, Alberto Massó. El Siglo de Oro en las historias literarias norteamericanas recientes. 199 pp. Missouri, A. Porqueras-Mayo, 1966. *DA* 28A: 628.

"Thus we may conclude that there are no proper histories of Spanish literature written today, but rather, histories of civilization and thought. . . . The road is, then, left open for a more aesthetic treatment by historians of the Spanish literature in the XVI and XVII centuries." (Abs.)

❖ "El carácter subversivo del eroticismo [sic] y jocosidad de la 'inocua' *Comedia Seraphina* de Torres Naharro." *MRRM* 7 (1991): 38–57. [The writer concludes that earlier critics have misjudged this play.]

22. Fra Molinero, Baltasar. La imagen de los negros en la literatura española de los siglos XVI y XVII. 505 pp. Indiana, O. T. Impey, 1990. *DAI* 51A: 3426.

"But this ideal image in drama of Blacks who accept their role as slaves is frequently set against the thematic conflict of freedom and oppression. The conflict takes the form of Black men who woo or simply befriend white women, but find their relationship tested by a common oppressor: the master/husband. Spanish Golden Age writers, thus, were creating a stereotype about Blacks and at the same time undercutting it." (Abs.)

❖ [A] "La formación del estereotipo del negro en las letras hispanas: El caso de tres coplas en pliegos sueltos." *RLAn* 3 (1991): 438–43. [Cites from Cervantes, Lope de Rueda, Lope de Vega, and Gil Vicente.] [B] "El disfraz de Dorotea: Usos del cuerpo negro en la España de Cervantes." *IJHL* 2.2 (1994): 63–85. [C] "Cuestiones de limpieza étnica en *Juan Latino* de Diego Ximénez de Enciso." *Texto y espectáculo: Proceedings of the Thirteenth International Golden Age Spanish Theatre Symposium, El Paso, 1993.* Ed. José Luis Suárez García. York: Spanish Literature Publications, 1995. 19–31. [D] *La imagen de los negros en el teatro del Siglo de Oro.* Madrid: Siglo XXI de España, 1995. 222 pp.

23. Freyschlag, Elizabeth Kyle. A Consideration of Pelayo in Spanish Literature. 255 pp. Stanford, A. M. Espinosa, 1965. *DA* 26A: 5411–12.

This dissertation "has as its principal interest the evolution of the literary theme which concerns Pelayo, the initiator of the Reconquest of Spain from the Moors." The relevant play is Lope de Vega's *El último godo de España.* (Abs.)

24. GATES, EUNICE JOINER. The Metaphors of Luis de Góngora. Pennsylvania, J. P. W. Crawford, 1933. {Philadelphia: Univ. of Pennsylvania, 1933. 190 pp. (UPSRLL 25.)}

"The purpose of the present study is to show how extensively Góngora made use of metaphors, the spheres from which he derived them, what literary patterns he may have followed, the chronological development of the metaphors, and the reactions of his contemporaries to this aspect of his style." The writer does not deal specifically with Góngora's plays, but on pp. 169–82 she discusses Gongoristic influence in such playwrights as Lope, Tirso, A. Hurtado de Mendoza, and Calderón. (Prt. Diss.)

❖ "Góngora and Calderón." *HR* 5 (1937): 241–58. [Apropos Góngora's influence on Calderón.]

25. GIBSON, M. CARL. Xavier Lampillas: His Defense of Spanish Literature and His Contribution to Literary History. 255 pp. Oregon, P. J. Powers, 1960. *DA* 21: 2713–14.

". . . [Lampillas's] was the first scholarly treatise on all genres of Spanish literature and may therefore be considered the first literary history of Spain." (Abs.) [In his *Saggio storico-apologetico della letteratura spagnola* (6 vols., 1778–81), the Spanish-born Jesuit Francisco Javier Lampillas (1731–1810) praised the Spanish *comedia* and disputed the theory of the dramatic unities.]

26. GOODWYN, FRANK. An Interpretation of the Hispanic Folk Hero, Pedro Urdemalas. vii+199 pp. Texas, R. C. Stephenson, 1945.

"Although Juan del Encina, Miguel de Cervantes, Lope de Vega, Salas Barbadillo and other well-known authors have written about Pedro Urdemalas, no scholar has heretofore endeavored to study the character systematically, together with the social, economic and psychological implications of his widespread popularity. To do this, and to evaluate the character as a hero, as a symbol and as an expression of the spirit of the Spanish-speaking masses, is the purpose of this project." (Diss.)

27. HACTHOUN, AUGUSTO. Teoría literaria del Siglo de Oro: Los

teóricos puros. v+102 pp. Florida, J. J. Allen, 1978. *DAI* 39A: 4305.

"This study isolates and identifies treatises of literary theory whose *raison d'être* is legislation independent of any particular piece of creative writing, in so far as is possible, and it evaluates each work in the context in which it was presented to its contemporaries." (Abs.)

28. HATZANTONIS, EMMANUEL STAMATIOS. Circe nelle letterature classiche, medioevali e romanze: Da Omero a Calderón. 295 pp. CA/ Berkeley, M. De Filippis, 1958. PFE, 23 May 1958.

[For the complete entry, see no. 281.]

29. HILL, ARCHIBALD ANDERSON. English Translations from the Spanish and Their Influence on the English Drama, 1610–1630. 371+ 14+18+14+13+49+4 pp. Yale, 1927.

"This thesis is a study of the English translations made from the Spanish between 1610 and 1630, and the influence exerted by those translations on the dramas composed in the same period. The study of the translations themselves has shown that those of them that were of a literary character were made from one sort of composition; namely, the prose novel or romance." (Diss.)

[For a more complete list of this scholar's publications, see *Linguistic and Literary Studies in Honor of Archibald A. Hill,* ed. Mohammad Ali Jazayery, Edgar C. Polome, and Werner Winter (Lisse, Netherlands: De Ridder, 1979) 1: 19–32.]

30. HILLARD, ERNEST H. KILGORE. Spanish Imitations of the *Celestina.* v+474 pp. Illinois, R. P. Oliver, 1957. *DA* 18: 588–89.

This dissertation examines 25 works regarded as "the principal variations of the Celestina theme in Spanish literature" during the period between 1499 and 1650. The works studied are divided into three groups: "continuations" (8), "close imitations" (5), and "free imitations" (12). (Abs.) Editorial note: Not all the works studied were written for the stage.

31. HUTCHINGS, CHESLEY MARTIN. The Sentiment of Nationality in Spanish Literary Criticism (1400–1621). 297+ix pp. Harvard, R. L. Hawkins, 1922.

The two relevant chapters are entitled "The Spanish Drama in Relation to Classical Theory," pp. 171–230, and "Defenders of National Drama and National Meters," pp. 231–87. (Diss.)

32. JÁCOME, DOLORES W. The Conquistador Figure in Golden Age Letters. 319 pp. Kentucky, W. C. McCrary, 1973. *DAI* 35A: 456.

The dramatic works studied are Lope's *El Nuevo Mundo descubierto por Cristóbal Colón* and Tirso de Molina's Pizarro Trilogy. (Abs.)

33. KING, WILLARD FAHRENKAMP. Literary Academies and Prose Fiction in Seventeenth-Century Spain. 229 pp. Brown, Wm. L. Fichter, 1957. *DA* 18: 590.

"One of the major factors in the cultural environment of the Spanish seventeenth century is the private literary academy, which began its development in the first half of the sixteenth century and reached perhaps the summit of its popularity in the 1620's and 1630's, when the Academia de Madrid counted among its members almost all the famous writers (including Lope, Góngora, Quevedo, and Calderón) resident in the capital." (Abs.)

❖ [A] "The Academies and Seventeenth-Century Spanish Literature." *PMLA* 75 (1960): 367-76. ["Poetry, the drama, and prose fiction—all the major literary genres of the time—can, then, be shown to reveal some connection with the literary academy."] [B] *Prosa novelística y academias literarias en el siglo XVII.* Madrid: RAE, 1963. 248 pp. [C] "La ascendencia paterna de Juan Ruiz de Alarcón y Mendoza." *NRFH* 19 (1970): 49-86. [D] "*El caballero de Olmedo*: Poetic Justice or Destiny?" *Homenaje a William L. Fichter: Estudios sobre el teatro antiguo hispánico y otros ensayos.* Ed. A. David Kossoff and José Amor y Vázquez. Madrid: Castalia, 1971. 367-79. [E] "Dos citas bíblicas en Lope de Vega y su significado." *Poemas y ensayos para un homenaje* [a Phyllis B. Turnbull]. Madrid: Tecnos, 1976. 88-94. [F] *Juan Ruiz de Alarcón, letrado y dramaturgo: Su mundo mexicano y español.* Trans. Antonio Alatorre. México: Colegio de México, 1989. (Estudios de lingüística 17.) [Alarcón was an active participant in literary academies.]

34. KRUMMRICH, PHILIP EUGENE. The Interpolated Sonnet in Western Literature. 216 pp. Illinois, F. Jost, 1980. *DAI* 41A: 4705.

One of the "six contexts in which the interpolated sonnet appears with particular effect" is drama. Concerning Golden Age theater, the writer observes that "Spanish *comedias* regularly feature one or more sonnets, usually as monologues imparting impatience, wonder, confusion or resolve to the audience." (Abs.)

35. KURTZ, BARBARA ELLEN. With Human Aspect: Studies in European Personification Allegory with Special Reference to the Hispanic Contribution. 553 pp. Chicago, R. H. Webber and G. Haley, 1983. *DAI* 44A: 3378.

"Part II focuses exclusively on Spanish allegory of the Golden Age, particularly the *autos sacramentales* of Calderón de la Barca and *El Criticón* of Baltasar Gracián, as the culmination and zenith of the allegorical traditions of the European Middle Ages." (Abs.)

❖ [A] "'In Imagined Space': Allegory and the *Auto Sacramental* of Pedro Calderón de la Barca." *RR* 79 (1988): 647–64. [B] "'No Word without Mystery': Allegories of Sacred Truth in the *Autos Sacramentales* of Calderón de la Barca." *PMLA* 103.3 (1988): 262–73. [C] "Joining Forces: Allegory/History in the *Autos Sacramentales* of Pedro Calderón de la Barca." *Varia hispanica: Homenaje a Alberto Porqueras-Mayo*. Ed. Joseph L. Laurenti and Vern G. Williamsen. Kassel: Reichenberger, 1989. 137–45. (Teatro del Siglo de Oro. Estudios de literatura 5.) [D] "Defining Allegory, or Troping through Calderón's *Autos*." *HR* 58.2 (1990): 227–43. [E] *The Play of Allegory in the* Autos Sacramentales *of Pedro Calderón de la Barca*. Washington: Catholic U of America P, 1991. 250 pp.

36. LAPRADE, JOHN HARRY. Golden-Age Authors in Nineteenth-Century Spanish Plays. 289 pp. North Carolina, W. A. McKnight, 1963. *DA* 24: 3750.

"Quevedo, Cervantes, the Count of Villamediana, Calderón, and Lope de Vega proved to be the most popular subjects from the *Siglo de Oro,* but hardly any major writer from that period failed to find at least one interpreter." (Abs.)

37. LEÓN, ADOLFO FRANCISCO. The Cid as a Source of Literary Inspiration. 312 pp. South Carolina, M. Christopherson, 1970. *DAI* 31A: 3510.

Among the works studied are Guillén de Castro's *Las mocedades de Rodrigo [del Cid]* and Juan Bautista Diamante's *El honrador de su padre.* (Abs.)

38. LUCENTE, CARLA ELIZABETH. The Theme of Orpheus in Renaissance Europe. 211 pp. Pittsburgh, J. S. Herrero, 1979. *DAI* 40A: 2718.

"The Platonic ideas which envelop the myth of Orpheus in the

Renaissance fuse with Christian elements in the Baroque and culminate in the writings of Calderón." (Abs.)

39. LYTE, HERBERT O. Spanish Literature and Spain in Some of the Leading German Magazines of the Second Half of the Eighteenth Century. Wisconsin, 1930. {Madison, 1932. 117 pp. (University of Wisconsin Studies in Language and Literature 32.)}

 The dissertation includes material on the theater of Cervantes, Lope, and Calderón, among others; see pp. 67–73. (Prt. Diss.)

 ❖ *A Tentative Bibliography of Spanish-German Literary and Cultural Relations*. Minneapolis: Burgess, 1936. 98 pp.

40. MARTIN, JOHN WATSON. Objective Criteria of Syntax and the Determination of Authorship in Spanish Literature: A Study of the Method and Its Validity. [5]+141+[1] pp. WA/Seattle, W. E. Wilson, 1956. *DA* 17: 855.

 "The study of Ruth Davis on the authorship of the first act of the *Celestina* [UISSLL 3 (1928)]; that of Leavitt Olds Wright on the *-ra* verb in Spain [UCPMP 15.1 (1932)], in which are treated the authorship problems of the *Celestina, La estrella de Sevilla,* and *La tía fingida*; and that of M. Criado de Val on *La tía fingida,* are reviewed in terms of the criteria used and of linguistic considerations involved in those criteria. Through a diachronic study of the forms in *-ra* and *-se,* around which the aforementioned studies are centered, the functions of these forms at the level of evolution corresponding to each of the problems of authorship are established and the methodology of the proposed solutions is invalidated. The differences in the verbal system of prose as opposed to verse-drama of the Golden Age are established, and a contribution is made to historical syntax in the study of the mechanism of the shifts of the verbal system involving the forms in *-se* and *-ra*." (Abs.)

41. MATHEWS, ERNST GARLAND. Studies in Anglo-Spanish Cultural and Literary Relations, 1598–1700. iv+640 pp. Harvard, H. E. Rollins, 1938. Harvard *Summaries* (1938): 304–13.

 The writer focuses on the influence of Spanish poets and novelists on English literature. There are, however, some references to the Spanish dramatists—e.g., the writer speaks of the importance of Richard Fanshawe's paraphrase [London, 1671] of Antonio Hurtado de Mendoza's *comedia* entitled *Querer por sólo querer. (Summaries)*

❖ "English Translation from Spanish: A Review and a Contribution." *JEGP* 44 (1945): 387–424. [A review article of Remigio Ugo Pane's *English Translations from the Spanish, 1484–1943: A Bibliography*. New Brunswick: Rutgers UP, 1944. vi+218 pp. (Rutgers University Studies in Spanish 2.)]

42. McInnis, Judy B. Antecedents and Elements of Allegory in the *Siglo de Oro.* 533 pp. North Carolina, S. A. Stoudemire, 1974. *DAI* 36A: 279–80.

Included in this study is Calderón's use of allegory. (Abs.)

43. McSpadden, George Elbert. The Spanish Prologue before 1700. [4]+467 pp. Stanford, A. M. Espinosa, 1947. Stanford *Abstracts* 22 (1946–47): 45–49.

In chapter 3 the writer discusses the *loa* as a genre that is "distantly related" to the preface-prologue. In chapter 4 he deals extensively with the prefatory pieces of Tirso de Molina. (Diss.)

❖ Don Quijote *and the Spanish Prologues: Glimpses of the Genius of Cervantes at Work.* 2 vols. Potomac: Studia Humanitatis; Madrid: Porrúa Turanzas, 1978. [Deals exclusively with the prologues of *Don Quijote*.]

44. Morley, Sylvanus Griswold. Spanish Influence on Molière. 542 pp., partly in typescript, partly in manuscript. Harvard, 1902.

"And in fact Molière escaped Spanish *influence,* almost entirely, but the *material* which he drew from Spain is quite considerable. Most of it is in the shape of intrigue, plots, and situations. . . . There is a possibility also that the character of Molière's servants may have been affected somewhat by the Spanish *gracioso*." (Diss.)

❖ "Notes on Spanish Sources of Molière." *PMLA* 19 (1904): 270–90. [In this article the writer sees close resemblances between certain passages in Molière's plays and others in Spanish *novelas* and *entremeses*. But he cautions that "it is seldom possible to decide categorically whether or no these parallels are genuine instances of borrowing by Molière, or merely coincidences of thought and expression."] [For a more complete list of this scholar's publications, see Benjamin M. Woodbridge Jr., "An Analytical Bibliography of the Writings of Professor S. Griswold Morley," *RPh* 6.4 (1953): 215–30 and "Selective Supplement," 26.1 (1972): 213–14.]

45. Pavia, Mario N. Magic and Witchcraft in the Literature of the

Siglo de Oro, Especially in Drama. xiii+186 pp. Chicago, C. Castillo, 1947.

[For the complete entry, see no. 154.]

46. PEEBLES, WALDO CUTLER. Democratic Tendencies in the Spanish Literature of the Golden Age. 244 pp. Harvard, J. D. M. Ford, 1931. Harvard *Summaries* (1932): 313–15.

Three chapters deal specifically with the theater: chapter 5, "Democratic Feeling in Lope de Vega's Drama"; chapter 6, "Dramatists of Lope de Vega's School"; and chapter 7, "Democracy in Calderón's Drama." (Diss.)

❖ "Democratic Tendencies in the Spanish Literature of the Golden Age." *H* [AATSP] 15 (1932): 317–26.

47. PIQUÉ [ANGORDANS], JORDI. La fiesta de San Juan en la literatura española. vii+459 pp. Catholic, J. Solà-Solé, 1974. *DAI* 35A: 1667–68.

"Chapter III studies the use and function of the theme in the 'comedia' of the Golden Age. The stream of medievalism that stems from the popular and traditional lyrics is studied in the theatre of Gil Vicente, Cervantes, and, above all, Lope de Vega and his school of dramatists. The chapter also deals with the writers of the Calderón school and the short plays of Quiñones de Benavente." (Abs.)

❖ "Una fiesta barroca: Lope de Vega y las *Relaciones de fiestas.*" *CH* 12.1–2 (1990): 47–63. [The "fiesta barroca" of the title refers to "una fiesta cortesana de San Juan, de 1631."]

48. PITTS, RUTH ELEANOR LANDES. Don Juan Hidalgo, Seventeenth-Century Spanish Composer. 308 pp. George Peabody Coll. for Teachers, R. L. Weaver, 1968. *DAI* 29A: 1558–59.

"The dissertation provides a description and an analysis of the extant music of Don Juan Hidalgo [c. 1612–85]. A brief introductory chapter summarizes available biographical evidence. . . . His greatest fame derived from his dramatic compositions. Hidalgo wrote musical settings for at least five *comedias* and eight *autos sacramentales* (music not extant) by Calderón de la Barca. . . . Hidalgo set [to music] dramatic works by authors other than Calderón. Music by him exists for a solo, a duet, and a solo-choral number from *Triunfos de amor y fortuna* by Antonio de Solís. Two other solos by Hidalgo coincide with the texts of *El templo de Palas* by Francisco de

Avellaneda and *Alfeo y Aretusa* by Don Juan Bautista Diamante. More music by Hidalgo remains from the *zarzuela Los celos hacen estrellas* by Don Juan Vélez de Guevara than from any other dramatic work except the opera *Celos aun del aire matan* [by Calderón]." (Abs.)

49. PODOL, PETER LAUREN. The Evolution of the Honor Theme in Modern Spanish Literature. 305 pp. Pennsylvania, A. G. Reichenberger, 1968. *DAI* 30A: 1176–77.

"The object of this study is to consider how the approach to the theme of honor has changed during the nineteenth and twentieth centuries and to evaluate the significance of this change. In addition, the contrasting approaches of the two literary genres, theater and novel, are studied through four centuries of Spanish literature." (Abs.)

❖ [A] "The Evolution of the Honor Theme in Modern Spanish Drama." *HR* 40 (1972): 53–72. [B] "Non-conventional Treatment of the Honor Theme in the Theater of the Golden Age." *REHb* 7 (1973): 449–63.

50. RAMOS-SUÁREZ, JORGE. Narciso en la literatura española hasta el siglo XVII. 170 pp. Case Western Reserve, P. Marlay, 1972. *DAI* 33A: 1694.

The relevant works studied are Calderón's *comedia Eco y Narciso* and Sor Juana Inés de la Cruz's *auto El divino Narciso.* (Abs.)

51. RESNICK, SEYMOUR. The Jew as Portrayed in Early Spanish Literature (to the End of the Fifteenth Century). vi+247 pp. NYU, H. C. Heaton, 1950.

The author discusses the *Auto de los Reyes Magos* and the *Danza de la Muerte.* (Diss.)

❖ Abridgment: *H* [AATSP] 34.1 (1951): 54–58.

52. ROGERS-RODRÍGUEZ, JASON MARTIN. The Numantian Theme in Spanish Literature. 286 pp. New Mexico, R. R. MacCurdy, 1974. *DAI* 36A: 1563–64.

"This study first traces the transmission of the history of Numantia and its transformation into a literary theme. It then examines the moral, political and esthetic implications of the Numantian plays and poetry which have appeared in almost every Spanish literary movement from the sixteenth century down to the present time." (Abs.)

53. RUGGERIO, MICHAEL JOHN. The Evolution of the Go-Between: Eros and Witchcraft. 130 pp. Harvard, S. Gilman, 1964.

❖ *The Evolution of the Go-Between in Spanish Literature through the Sixteenth Century.* Berkeley: U of California P, 1966. 102 pp. Chapter 5 of the printed version ("Magic in the Imitations of *La Celestina*," pp. 64–71) deals specifically with Feliciano de Silva's *Segunda Celestina* and Sebastián Fernández's *Tragedia Policiana*. (Prt. Diss.)

54. St. Amour, Mary Paulina. A Study of the *Villancico* up to Lope de Vega: Its Evolution from Profane to Sacred Themes, and Specifically to the Christmas Carol. x+131 pp. Catholic, D. Rubio, 1940. {Washington: Catholic Univ. of America, 1940. 131 pp.}

"This investigation was based on the study of about one thousand *villancicos,* drawn from three main sources: the *cancioneros,* both general and individual, and *pliegos sueltos* of the fifteenth and sixteenth centuries; treatises on music . . . and the drama of the period, where the musical element often took the form of the *villancico*." (Prt. Diss.)

55. Sánchez, Ángel. Historia y representación: La ficción de Don Pedro I de Castilla (siglos XIV–XVII). 248 pp. Minnesota, N. Spadaccini, 1991. *DAI* 52A: 1861.

"Chapter Four concentrates on the King's [i.e., King Pedro's] portrayal in the theater of the 1600's which attempts to underscore the superiority of the monarchy over the nobles. My conclusion is that all such representations, whether 'historical' or fictional, contribute to the advancement of particular political goals." (Abs.)

56. Schuster, Edward James. "Yo el rey"—a Study of the Development of Monarchical Absolutism in the Spanish Golden Age, and Its Influence on the Literature of the Period. xvi+366 pp. Minnesota, R. L. Grismer, 1950.

In part 2, chapter 2, pp. 225–68, the writer deals specifically with the influence of monarchical absolutism on Golden Age drama. (Diss.)

57. Shepard, Sanford. López Pinciano and Aristotelian Literary Criticism in the Spanish Renaissance. 240 pp. NYU, R. J. Clements, 1960. *DA* 21: 903–04.

"This dissertation centers around the *Philosophía Antigua Poética* of López Pinciano which was published in 1596 and is the most elaborate treatment of Aristotelian literary theory in the Spanish Renaissance. . . . [The second part of the dissertation includes] a detailed analysis of Pinciano's dramatic theory in which there are sections devoted to tragedy, comedy, the dramatic unities, and the dramatic performance. . . . [In part 3] a section devoted to Lope de Vega, Juan de la Cueva, Bartolomé Leonardo de Argensola, Carrillo y Sotomayor and Cervantes assesses the influence of Aristotelian literary theory on the literary production of the Spanish Renaissance." (Abs.)

❖ [A] *El Pinciano y las teorías literarias del Siglo de Oro*. Madrid: Gredos, 1962; 2nd ed. 1970. [B] "Las huellas de Escalígero en la *Philosophía antigua poética* de Alonso López Pinciano." *RFE* 45 (1962; pub. 1964): 311–17. [C] "La teoría del *buen gusto* entre los humanistas." *RFE* 48 (1965): 415–21.

58. Stimson, Frederick Sparks. Spanish Themes in Early American Literature, in Novels, Drama, and Verse, 1770–1830. 243 pp. Michigan, I. A. Leonard, 1953. *DA* 13A: 394.

Chapter 8 (pp. 146–57), entitled "The *Comedia* [of the Golden Age]," begins with the following observation: "Second to the *Quijote* as a source of inspiration to American writers before 1831 was the *comedia,* the Spanish drama perfected and produced in quantity by Lope de Vega (1562–1635), Calderón de la Barca (1600–1681), and lesser figures of Spain's Golden Age of the sixteenth and seventeenth centuries." (Diss.)

❖ *Orígenes del hispanismo norteamericano.* México: Andrea, 1961. 131 pp. (Colección Studium 29.)

59. Stubbings, Hilda Rubena Uren. A Selective and Annotated Bibliography of Articles, Monographs, and Books Dealing with the Influence of Peninsular Spanish Literature of the Golden Age (c. 1560 to c. 1681) on the Literatures of England and France during the Sixteenth, Seventeenth, and Eighteenth Centuries. 176 pp. Vanderbilt, G. E. Wade, 1968. *DA* 29A: 2230–31.

"There are over 350 entries, with annotations giving necessary factual information and with commentaries or evaluations of the works." (Abs.)

❖ *Renaissance Spain in Its Literary Relations with England and France: A Critical Bibliography.* Nashville: Vanderbilt UP, 1969. 138 pp.

60. Taggard, Mindy Nancarrow. The Narrative Biblical Series in Seventeenth-Century Spanish Painting: Murillo's *Life of Jacob* and

The Prodigal Son. xii+374 pp. Kansas, L. Stone-Ferrier, 1985. *DAI* 47A: 5.

"This study analyzes two unusual late seventeeth-century series by the Sevillian painter Murillo, one based on the life of the Old Testament patriarch Jacob (Part I), and the other on Christ's Parable of the Prodigal Son (Part II). The visual sources for each series are discussed, as well as the relationship of each series to its original Biblical source, Church dogma, and seventeenth-century moralizing literature. Each series is then related to seventeenth-century Spanish drama, prose and poetry, as well as seventeenth-century Spanish culture and history." (Abs.)

❖ [A] "A Source for the Interpretation of Murillo's *Parable of the Prodigal Son:* The Golden Age Stage." *RAC* 14.1–2 (1987): 90–95. [B] *Murillo's Allegories of Salvation and Triumph:* The Parable of the Prodigal Son *and* The Life of Jacob. Columbia: U of Missouri P, 1992. 153 pp. 48 illus.

61. Trisler, Barbara Jean. A Comparative Study of the Character Portrayal of "Celestina" and Other Golden Age Celestinesque Protagonists. 104 pp. Oklahoma, P. Liria, 1977. *DAI* 38A: 2165.

"This study is a comparative analysis of the character portrayal techniques used by Fernando de Rojas to create the Celestina in *La tragicomedia de Calisto y Melibea* along with other Golden Age dramatic and novelesque presentations of this character type." Among the dramatic works treated are Gil Vicente's *Auto da Barca do Inferno, La comedia de Tidea* by Francisco de las Natas, *El infamador* by Juan de la Cueva, and the *Entremés famoso de la Celestina* by Juan Navarro de Espinosa. (Abs.)

62. Underhill, John Garrett. Spanish Literature in the England of the Tudors. Columbia, G. E. Woodberry, 1899. {*Spanish Literature in the England of the Tudors: A Study of the Growth of the Peninsular Influence North of the Channel.* New York: Pub. for Columbia UP by Macmillan, 1899. x+438 pp. (Columbia University Studies in Literature.)}

"The artistic literature of the peninsula . . . made its way across the channel, and was not without admirers in England. The heartiness of its reception did not always accord with its merit. The Spanish drama . . . was represented solely by the *Celestina,* a work that is pseudo-dramatic at best. . . . This, however, was not strange. The splendid maturity of the theatre of Lope de Vega and Calderon had just begun to unfold itself before the playgoers of Madrid at the time of Elizabeth's death [1603]. It developed too late to affect the writers of her reign." (Prt. Diss.)

❖ "Caracteres de la influencia española sobre la literatura inglesa." *Ateneo* (Madrid) 1 (1906): 489-99. [Trans. by Adolfo Bonilla y San Martín of ch. 10.]

63. VERY, FRANCIS GEORGE. The Corpus Christi Procession in Spain: A Literary and Folkloric Study. v+208 pp. + 20 plates. CA/Berkeley, E. Buceta, 1956.

❖ *The Spanish Corpus Christi Procession: A Literary and Folkloric Study.* Valencia: Tipografía Moderna, 1962. 160 pp.

"Occasionally, floats on which *autos* were to be performed took their place in the procession; in this respect I have included some details of their apparatus in Chapter II." (Prt. Diss.)

64. VILLALOBOS, MIGUEL ÁNGEL. El personaje de la pícara en la literatura española. 287 pp. Florida State, D. L. Hoffman, 1978. *DAI* 39A: 1627.

"En el capítulo quinto demostramos al estudiar comparativamente las manifestaciones picarescas en otros géneros (cuento, teatro) que la picardía es innata. No ocurre necesariamente en la mujer de baja condición social." (Abs.)

65. WAXMAN, SAMUEL MONTEFIORE. Chapters on Magic in Spanish Literature. v+208 pp. Harvard, J. D. M Ford, 1912.

❖ Title as is. *RH* 38 (1916): 325-463. Golden Age drama is included in this study—e.g., chapter 2 is entitled "Calderón's *Mágico prodigioso*" (pp. 367-86). (Prt. Diss.) [For a more complete list of this scholar's publications, see "Bibliography of the Writings of S. M. W.," *Studies in Honor of Samuel Montefiore Waxman,* ed. H. H. Golden (Boston: Boston UP, 1969) 15-18.]

66. WHYTE, FLORENCE. The Dance of Death in Spain and Catalonia. Bryn Mawr, J. E. Gillet, 1931. {Baltimore: Waverly, 1931. xi+175 pp. Rpt. New York: Arno, 1977.}

In part 2 of this dissertation the writer analyzes many dramatic works; among them, school plays and works by well-known authors such as Diego Sánchez de Badajoz, Quiñones de Benavente, and Calderón de la Barca. (Prt. Diss.)

Theater and Drama: Golden Age

67. Allen, Beverly Moulton. The Creation of the World in the Spanish Theater of the Sixteenth and Seventeenth Centuries. v+209 pp. Michigan, E. Glaser, 1973. *DAI* 34A: 1888.

The writer examines six *autos* in the Rouanet collection as well as works by Gil Vicente, Tirso de Molina, Lope de Vega, and Calderón. In the sixteenth century, the focus of the creation story is "the portrayal of sin and its effect on the human condition. . . . By the seventeenth century the story of creation has become one of several means of dramatizing the way of salvation." (Abs.)

68. Almasov, Alexey. El honor rústico en el teatro de Lope de Vega y en otros dramaturgos del Siglo de Oro. iv+348 pp. Iowa, E. DeChasca, 1968. *DA* 29A: 1888–89.

[For the complete entry, see no. 669.]

69. Álvarez, Miguel. El probabilismo y el teatro español del siglo XVII. 382 pp. NYU, A. Regalado, 1982. *DAI* 43A: 3613.

"The purpose of the thesis is to demonstrate how the concept of man and his existence elaborated by probabilism permeates the literary work and enriches the drama of the XVIIth century with new techniques, themes, problems and artistic structures." (Abs.) Editorial note: *Probabilism* is defined as "a theory that in disputed moral questions any solidly probable course may be followed even though an opposed course is or appears more probable."

70. Ballew, Hal Lackey. The Life and Works of Dionisio Solís. iv+217 pp. North Carolina, S. A. Stoudemire, 1957. North Carolina *Record,* no. 590, p. 264.

"Solís shows great skill in adapting the seventeenth-century plays of his own country into the nineteenth century—an era which demanded refinement in stage settings and more attention to scenic realism. This demanded revision on Solís' part. Many incidents of the older plays were discarded since they did not conform to the unity of time. Solís' skillful versification, his selection of plays to be reworked, and his appreciation for the values of the original, made him the greatest *refundidor* of his time. In number of works, and in the number of performances of these works, Solís outdistanced all of his contemporaries." (UNC *Record*) Editorial note: Dionisio Solís (Dionisio Villanueva y Ochoa, 1774–1834) was a writer, translator, and adapter of plays. He wrote adaptations of *comedias* by Lope, Calderón, Tirso, Rojas Zorrilla, and Moreto.

❖ "The Nineteenth Century Spanish *Refundiciones* as Literature." *RomN* 1.2 (1960): 117–21.

71. Barrett, Linton Lomas. The Supernatural in the Spanish Non-religious *Comedia* of the Golden Age. vii+276 pp. North Carolina, S. E. Leavitt, 1938. North Carolina *Record* no. 335, p. 126.

"This is a study of the supernatural devices used in one hundred and fifteen representative *comedias* of the *Siglo de Oro,* selected from over nine hundred printed plays from the time of Juan de la Cueva to the death of Calderón. Magic, a black art, and astrology, a science, are omitted, since they differ widely from other types of the supernatural and therefore should receive separate treatment. . . . In short, the supernatural improves tremendously from Cueva to Lope and Castro, appears at its best in Lope, and declines steadily to the death of Calderón." (UNC *Record*)

❖ [A] Title as is. New York: Wilson, 1938. 95 pp. [B] "The Omen in Guillén de Castro's Drama." *H* [AATSP] 22 (1939): 73–78. [C] "The Supernatural in Juan de la Cueva's Drama." *SP* 36 (1939): 147–68.

72. Beckmann, Frederick Ernst. Spanish Influence on Eichendorff. Chicago, 1900. Listed in *Comprehensive Dissertation Index 1861–1972,* vol. 33, author index, p. 299.

This dissertation is no longer available at the University of Chicago.

73. Betancourt, Helia Gloria. Teatro franciscano de evangelización en Nueva España. 210 pp. Pennsylvania, J. M. Regueiro, 1990. *DAI* 51A: 1627.

"El resultado del estudio demuestra cómo los autos del teatro religioso evangelizador en Nueva España adquieren características distintivas propias acordes a los fines proselitistas que los franciscanos perseguían." (Abs.)

74. Buchwalter, Grace May. The Don Carlos Theme in European Literature. iii+224+[4] pp. Northwestern, J. T. Hatfield, 1930–31.

A brief chapter entitled "The Don Carlos Theme in Spain" (pp. 187–89) refers to the following *comedias: El segundo Séneca de España [y príncipe don Carlos]* (Juan Pérez de Montalbán), *El príncipe don Carlos* (Diego Jiménez de Enciso), and the latter play as reworked by José de Cañizares. (Diss.) Editorial note: The actual dissertation, as well as the OCLC and RLIN entries, records the title as above. In *Comprehensive Dissertation Index 1861–1972* and the CD-ROM Proquest version, the title appears as "The Development and Relations of Characters in the Chief Don Carlos Dramas."

75. Buck, Donald Curtis. Theatrical Production in Madrid's Cruz and Príncipe Theaters during the Reign of Felipe V. xii+437 pp. Texas, L. Fontanella, 1980. *DAI* 41A: 3128.

After examining in detail various aspects of theatrical production in early eighteenth-century Spain, the writer analyzes two representative plays: *A cual mejor, confesada y confesor, San Juan de la Cruz y Santa Teresa* by José de Cañizares and *El mágico de Salerno* by Juan Salvo y Vela (d. 1770). (Abs.)

❖ [A] "Popular Theology, Miracles and Stagecraft in the *Comedia de santos:* Cañizares' *A cual mejor, confesada y confesor.*" *Dieciocho* 5.1 (1982): 3–17. [B] "Pedro Calderón de la Barca and Madrid's Theatrical Calendar, 1700–1750: A Question of Priorities." *ThS* 25.1 (1984): 69–81. [C] "Administrative Reform in Madrid's Theaters: The Montero Report of 1720." *Dieciocho* 9 (1986): 35–50. [D] "Juan Salvo y Vela and the Rise of the *Comedia de Magia:* The Magician as Anti-hero." *H* [AATSP] 69 (1986): 251–61. [E] Salvo y Vela, J. *El mágico de Salerno/Pedro de Vayalarde: Primera y segunda partes.* Critical ed. D. C. Buck. Miami: Universal, 1995. 207 pp.

76. Campbell, Dowling Gray. Background and Applications of the Honor Code in Dryden's Four Spanish-Oriented Heroic Plays. 191 pp. Missouri, D. K. Anderson, 1973. *DAI* 35A: 1041.

"Coupled with his ability to read the language, [the popularity of Peninsular themes during the Restoration] renders Dryden's treatment of honor in his four heroics *[The Indian Queen, The Indian Emperour,* and both parts of *The Conquest of Granada]* as all the more convincing evidence that he was strongly influenced by Spanish literature, and especially by *Siglo de Oro* playwrights." (Abs.)

77. CANTÚ, NORMA ELIA. The Offering and the Offerers: A Generic Illocution of a Laredo *Pastorela* in the Tradition of Shepherds' Plays. v+491 pp. Nebraska, P. Olson and R. Grajeda, 1982. *DAI* 43A: 3614.

"The *Pastorela,* a shepherds' play that originated in the Christmas cycle of medieval liturgical drama in Spain, survives as a folk play in various Spanish-speaking regions of Europe and America. This work traces the genre from that liturgical origin to its development in the sixteenth century in Mexico as a didactic colonizing vehicle, and to its eventual development as folk drama in the United States." (Abs.) Editorial note: Illocution is a communication, such as an order or a warning, expressed as a statement.

78. CASINES, GISELA PETRA. The Dramas of Restoration England and Golden Age Spain: Affinities and Correspondences. viii+188 pp. Florida, A. L. Williams, 1982. *DAI* 44A: 483.

"When Restoration British playwrights borrowed, either directly or indirectly, from the drama of Golden Age Spain, they adapted mostly the cape and sword plays because these dramas had exciting plots and, more importantly, presented a view of world order compatible with the British one. In addition, the dramatists of these two countries held similar assumptions about dramatic theory, poetic justice, and human conduct." (Abs.)

❖ [A] "Guardians in Restoration Plays with Direct Spanish Dramatic Sources." *LJHum* 14.1-2 (1988): 51-60. [B] "Private Sins, Public Penance: Poetic Justice in Some Restoration Plays with Spanish Sources." *SAR* 53.1 (1988): 27-39. [C] "The Concept of Poetic Justice in Spanish Golden Age Literary Theory." *Hispanófila* 32.96 (1989): 13-20. ["Writing, perhaps, less extensively than their European counterparts, the Golden Age commentators, nevertheless, recognize justice as a principle of drama that, although not strictly Aristotelian, ought to be practiced because it is so congenial to their Christian beliefs and to the Horatian dual aim of poetry."]

79. CAUVIN, [SISTER] MARY AUSTIN, O.P. The *Comedia de Privanza* in the Seventeenth Century. 505 pp. Pennsylvania, A. G. Reichenberger, 1957. *DA* 18: 229.

[For the complete entry, see no. 542.]

80. CAVE, MICHAEL ROBERT. La obra dramática de Luciano Francisco Comella. vii+202 pp. Connecticut, J. Romo-Arregui and G. Rosado, 1972. *DAI* 33A: 2926.

"Comella's . . . total production includes more than 150 works." According to the writer, "the longer works, of three acts, are obvious continuations of the traditional Spanish *Comedia*." He finds "a close structural and stylistic connection between the main body of Comella's works and the Spanish Golden Age *Comedia*." (Abs.)

81. CHECCA, PETER ANTHONY. The Role of the Devil in Golden Age Drama. 296 pp. Pennsylvania State, R. Lima, 1975. *DAI* 37A: 1004–05.

"This dissertation shows that in Golden Age drama the Devil is not a stereotyped character but a complex dramatic figure who varies with each playwright and drama." (Abs.)

82. CID SIRGADO, ISABEL M. Afrancesados y neoclásicos: Su deslinde en el teatro español del siglo XVIII. 237 pp. NYU, R. Bosch, 1971. *DAI* 32A: 4587.

"El siglo XVIII representa uno de esos períodos conflictivos durante el cual el español se debate entre lo conocido tradicional y lo novedoso y extranjerizante. En nuestro trabajo tratamos de establecer dos líneas paralelas dentro de la producción dramática española del dieciocho, atendiendo a estas dos modalidades, es decir: la que encarna la corriente grecolatina y la de influencia netamente francesa. Lo iniciamos con una breve consideración de las corrientes clasicistas que se desarrollan en España durante los siglos XVI y XVII, para adentrarnos después en sus manifestaciones principales en el transcurso del siglo de la Ilustración española." (Abs.)

❖ [A] Title as is. Madrid: Cultura Hispánica, 1973. 311 pp. [B] Cid de Sirgado, Isabel M. *Ignacio de Luzán: La poética o reglas de la poesía en general y de sus principales especies.* [Eds. of 1737 and 1789]. Introd. and notes by I. M. Cid de Sirgado. Madrid: Cátedra, 1974. 478 pp. [Book 3, pp. 286–425, "De la tragedia y comedia y otras poesías dramáticas."]

83. COHEN, WALTER ISAAC. Drama of a Nation: Public Theater in Renaissance England and Spain. i+811 pp. CA/Berkeley, L. G. Clubb, 1980. *DAI* 42A: 204.

"The plays of late sixteenth and early seventeenth-century England and Spain uniquely synthesize popular and learned elements. This synthesis in turn depended on the evolution of the neofeudal absolutist state. By its inherent dynamism and contradictions, absolutism first created and then destroyed the public theater." (Abs.) ❖ [A] Title as is. Ithaca: Cornell UP, 1985. 416 pp. [B] "The Politics of Golden Age Spanish Tragicomedy." *Renaissance Tragicomedy: Explorations in Genre and Politics.* Ed. Nancy Klein Maguire. New York: AMS, 1987. 155–76.

84. COLBERT, ROMAN. L'Influence de la *comedia* espagnole sur la comédie française de 1640 à 1660. 228 pp. CA/Los Angeles, M. Bensimon, 1970. *DAI* 31A: 1753–54.

The four authors studied are Antoine le Metel d'Ouville, his brother Boisrobert, Paul Scarron, and Thomas Corneille. (Abs.)

85. COUGHLIN, EDWARD VINCENT. Neo-classical *Refundiciones* of Golden Age *Comedias* (1772–1831). 154 pp. Michigan, C. N. Staubach, 1965. *DA* 26A: 2746.

"This study attempts to analyze representative eighteenth-century recasts of Golden Age *comedias* in order to examine and evaluate the qualities that characterized the dramatic theory and practices of the Spanish neo-classic period. . . . All too frequently the *comedias* were divested of their vitality and color at the hands of the *refundidores*. Consequently, after a brief period of success the neo-classical recasts were relegated to oblivion." (Abs.)

86. CZARNOCKA, HALINA. La figura del Rey Don Pedro en el teatro del Siglo de Oro. v+184 pp. Chicago, F. Ruiz-Ramón, 1992. *DAI* 53A: 170.

"The thesis analyzes the role of the character of king Pedro I of Castile in the Golden Age Spanish Theater. After discussing the historical background, the XVII c. theories of kingship and the ways in which the historical monarch is transformed into a mythical figure, the dramatic incarnations of the character of don Pedro within 18 dramas are analyzed according to its functions of *rey-tirano, rey-galán* and *rey-justiciero*. . . . The conclusions are that, contrary to the 'typical' functions of a king in Spanish Golden Age theater, the use of this specific monarch within the structure of a drama allows the authors to tackle the problems which the absolute rule of a flawed personality create for the kingdom and its people." (Abs.)

❖ "La figura del rey don Pedro el Cruel en *Deste agua no beberé* de Andrés de Claramonte." *RLAn* 4 (1992): 415–22.

87. Dale, George Irving. The Moors in the Spanish Drama of the Golden Age. 127 pp. Cornell, 1917. {Ithaca: Cornell UP, 1974. Microfilm.}

"The inborn hatred of all Moors by the Spanish has apparently made it impossible for them to depict the Moorish people as they really existed in Spain at the time the Comedias were written. Dramatic authors of the sixteenth and early seventeenth centuries have revealed to us but little more of the life, true customs and habits of the Moors than did the writers of the *romances*. Nevertheless they have introduced, unconsciously perhaps, certain realistic treatments which are unparalleled in any other literature. The mode of dress, the use of jargon, and the menial state of the oppressed and ridiculed Moor could be treated only by his Spanish contemporaries. . . . A more humane treatment of the hostile Moor is not forthcoming until Calderón's time when the feeling of the Spanish toward their former enemy had changed completely. The crowning play of all the *comedias de moros y cristianos,* in which the Moor comes into his own, is Calderón's *Amar Después de la Muerte,* written forty years after the final expulsion of the Moors from Spain." (Diss.)

❖ [A] "The Religious Element in the 'Comedias de moros y cristianos' of the Golden Age." *Washington University [St. Louis] Studies, Humanistic Studies* 7 (1919): 31–45. [B] "A Second Source of Lope de Vega's *El castigo del discreto*." *MLN* 43 (1928): 310–12. [The writer refers to an episode in the Moorish tale *El Abencerraje*.]

88. Dial, Eleanore Marjorie Maxwell. Critical Reaction to a Decade of Spanish Theater in Mexico, 1950–1959. 162 pp. Missouri, A. Brent, 1968. *DA* 29A: 3607–08.

". . . the revival of interest in classical theater was due largely to the tireless activity of one man, Álvaro Custodio, the founder of the Teatro Español de México. . . . critics continued throughout the decade to view with interest his productions of Lope, Calderón, Guillén de Castro, Vélez de Guevara, and [Rojas] Zorrilla." (Abs.)

❖ [A] "Spanish Classical Theatre in Mexico in the 1950's." *LATR* 4.2 (1971): 29-38. [B] "Álvaro Custodio and His Continuing Dream: The Teatro Clásico de México in the 1960's." *LATR* 7.2 (1974): 45-57. [C] "A Pleasure and a Source: The Publications of the Teatro Clásico de México." *LATR* 21.1 (1987): 53-64. [The writer deals with the years 1958-73.]

89. DIETZ, DONALD THADDEUS. The *Auto Sacramental* and the Parable in the Spanish Literature of the Sixteenth and Seventeenth Centuries. 319 pp. Arizona, H. R. Stone, 1968. *DA* 29A: 1205-06.

"The primary objective of this study is to examine those one-act allegorical dramas of sixteenth- and seventeenth-century Spain which have as their bases one of the New Testament parables." Thirty-two *autos* are discussed. (Abs.)

❖ [A] *The* Auto Sacramental *and the Parable in Spanish Golden Age Literature.* Chapel Hill: U of North Carolina P, 1973. 205 pp. (UNCSRLL 132.) [B] "Toward Understanding Calderón's Evolution as an *Auto* Dramatist." *Studies in Honor of Ruth Lee Kennedy.* Ed. Vern G. Williamsen and A. F. Michael Atlee. Chapel Hill: Estudios de Hispanófila, 1977. 51-55. (Estudios de Hispanófila 46.)[C] "Conflict in Calderón's *Autos Sacramentales.*" *Approaches to the Theater of Calderón.* Ed. Michael D. McGaha. Washington: UP of America, 1982. 175-86. [D] "Liturgical and Allegorical Drama: The Uniqueness of Calderón's *Auto Sacramental.*" *Calderón de la Barca at the Tercentenary: Comparative Views*. Ed. Wendell M. Aycock and Sydney P. Cravens. Lubbock: Texas Tech UP, 1982. 71-88. [E] "Theology and the Stage: The God Figure in Calderón's *Autos Sacramentales.*" *BCom* 34.1 (1982): 97-105. [F] "England's and Spain's Corpus Christi Theaters." *Parallel Lives: Spanish and English National Drama 1580-1680.* Ed. Louise Fothergill-Payne and Peter Fothergill-Payne. Lewisburg: Bucknell UP, 1991. 239-51.

90. DONOVAN, RICHARD BERTRAM. The Medieval Liturgical Drama in the Hispanic Peninsula and Its Relation with That of the Rest of Europe, Especially France. xiv+380 pp. Yale, 1956.

"[This study] is devoted chiefly to the publication of the dramatic texts themselves, the majority of which have not been previously edited. Texts previously edited are also included, in the hope that a convenient and relatively complete *corpus* of Spanish liturgical plays will thus be provided. There is an attempt, in addition, to focus these plays in their international setting, and to describe the liturgical background in Spain in which these plays grew, or could have grown; an understanding of the origins of Spanish drama, and of its relations with that of France, would be impossible without a knowledge of this element. We shall see that repeatedly the new Hispanic texts throw light on the drama of France and other countries, concerning such points as the manner in which certain liturgical plays were performed, the role conceded to the vernacular in the performance of these plays, etc.; in several instances the Spanish texts reveal new types of dramatic ceremonies which probably had a vogue throughout Europe." (Prt. Diss.)

❖ *The Liturgical Drama in Medieval Spain.* Toronto: Pontifical Inst. of Mediaeval Studies, 1958. 229 pp. (Studies and Texts 4.)

91. DREYFUSS, CECILIA ANNE STIBORIK. *Femina Sapiens* in Drama: Aeschylus to Grillparzer. 418 pp. Michigan, O. Graf, 1975. *DAI* 36A: 3676.

"... only three [male playwrights] have succeeded in recognizing and presenting *woman on stage* as a complete and multi-dimensional being, equal to man. The three are Aeschylus, Euripides and Shakespeare." Included in this study are Calderón and Lope de Vega. (Abs.)

92. DUGAN, JOHN THOMAS. The First Principles of Dramatic Composition. A Comparative Study of Selected Theories of Dramaturgy. ii+579 pp. Minnesota, D. W. Thompson, 1951.

Chapter 2 includes a discussion of Lope de Vega's *Arte nuevo de hacer comedias,* pp. 178–91. (Diss.)

93. DUNHAM, RICHARD ROY. The Birth of the Modern Theatre. [5]+ 349+2+6 pp. + illus. Cornell, A. M. Drummond and G. F. Purdy, 1944.

This study includes a brief discussion of staging in the early Spanish theater, pp. 113–18. (Diss.)

94. DUNZO, ANNETTE IVORY. Blacks of Sub-Saharan African Origin in Spain: Image in the Theater (1500–1700). x+227 pp. CA/Los Angeles, C. B. Johnson and J. Rodríguez-Puértolas, 1974. *DAI* 35A: 4426.

"The image in Spanish theater (1500–1700) of a Black ethnic group from sub-Saharan Africa has been presented through an analysis of more than thirty plays (light and serious in tone)." (Abs.)

❖ [A] "Black Heroes in the Theater of Early Spain." *Homenaje a Lydia Cabrera.* Ed. Reinaldo Sánchez, José Antonio Madrigal, and José Sánchez-Boudy. Miami: Universal, 1978. 267-73. [B] "*Juan Latino:* The Struggle of Blacks, Jews, and Moors in Golden Age Spain." *H* [AATSP] 62 (1979): 613-18 [Apropos Jiménez de Enciso's *La comedia de Juan Latino.*]

95. FALCONIERI, JOHN VINCENT. A History of Italian Comedians in Spain: A Chapter of the Spanish Renaissance. iv+139 pp. Michigan, F. Sánchez y Escribano, 1952. *DA* 12: 186.

"The purpose of this study is (a) to synthesize all known facts pertaining to the Italian theatrical companies that traveled and performed throughout Spain during the sixteenth century, (b) to prove that these companies and their actors contributed to the material growth of the Spanish theatre, and (c) to show that the visit of these Italian companies was a natural consequence of centuries of political, economic, and cultural contacts between Spain and Italy." (Abs.)

❖ [A] "Más noticias biográficas de Alberto Ganassa." *RABM* 60.1 (1954): 219-22. [Italian actor in Spain between 1574 and 1584.] [B] "Historia de la *commedia dell'arte* en España." *RL* 11 (1957): 3-37; 12 (1957): 69-90. [C] "La situación de Torres Naharro en la historia literaria." *Hispanófila* 1 (1957): 32-40. ["Sólo proyectando a Torres Naharro sobre el fondo del drama clásico italiano podrá ser exactamente entendido y valorado."] [D] "*Comedia* Manuscripts in Rome." *BCom* 33.1 (1981): 13-37; "*Comedia* Manuscripts in Rome, Part II." *BCom* 44.2 (1992): 243-51. [E] Prado y Tovar, D. *Hir buscando a quien me sigue.* Ed. J. V. Falconieri. Kassel: Reichenberger, 1992. 105 pp. [Based on MS in Biblioteca Casanatense, Roma.] [F] Mira de Amescua, A. *Callar en buena ocasión o Muerto vivo y enterrado.* Ed. J. V. Falconieri. Kassel: Reichenberger, 1993. 107 pp. [Based on MS in Biblioteca Nazionale, Roma.] [G] Sigler de la Huerta, A. *Las doncellas de Madrid.* Ed. J. V. Falconieri. Kassel: Reichenberger, 1993. 80 pp. [Based on MS in Bernini Collection, Vatican Library.]

96. FALLIS, GUADALUPE VALDÉS. Tragic Theory and Its Expression in Spanish Drama. 386 pp. Florida State, D. L. Hoffman, 1972. *DAI* 35A: 4513.

"This dissertation establishes that by its own nature tragedy demands many definitions." The writer says that if the limitations of definitions "which cannot ever be final" are left behind, "the doors are opened for the exploration of new aspects in the world of the Golden Age tragic masterpieces." (Abs.)

97. FISKE, JEFFREY THOMAS. The Parallel Phenomena of Societal Expansion and Dramatic Response to Ages of Self-Discovery. 253 pp. Ohio State, G. P. Crepeau, 1988. *DAI* 49A: 660.

 "This study investigates why great ages of theatre occur during periods of discovery and exploration." The ages examined include "The English, Spanish and French Renaissances." (Abs.)

98. FLEET, ANITA KANT. Prefiguration and Deliberate Anachronism in the Spanish Sacramental *Auto* Based on the Old Testament. 503 pp. Florida State, D. L. Hoffman, 1961. *DA* 22: 2787.

 "This study examines thirty-five Old Testament *autos sacramentales* written between 1525 . . . and 1695." (Abs.)

99. FLORES, RICHARD REYES. *Los Pastores:* Performance, Poetics, and Politics in Folk Drama. 254 pp. Texas, J. E. Limón and A. E. Burce, 1989. *DAI* 50A: 1712.

 "'Los Pastores' is a descendent of the Spanish *autos sacramentales* and morality plays which developed in conjunction with the popular humor of the middle ages. Today, this dramatic form is still performed in San Antonio, Texas, a tribute not only to its popularity, but more importantly, to the ability of this genre to represent the social world of those who perform it." (Abs.)

100. FREEMAN, SIDNEY LEE. The Forms of Nonproscenium Theatre: Their History and Theories. [5]+246 pp. Cornell, A. M. Drummond, 1951.

 This study includes a very brief description of staging in sixteenth-century Spain, pp. 33–34. (Diss.)

101. GARCÍA DÍEZ, VÍCTOR FERNANDO. La fabla en algunas comedias históricas del Siglo de Oro. v+134 pp. Iowa, R. Davis, 1967. *DA* 28A: 3166–67.

 "Las comedias disponibles donde se emplea la fabla son *Las hazañas del Cid,* de autor desconocido; *Las Batuecas del Duque de Alba* y *Las famosas asturianas* de Lope de Vega; *Nuestra Señora de Atocha* de Francisco de Rojas Zorrilla, y *Los jueces de Castilla* de

Lope de Vega, refundida por Agustín Moreto. . . . La fabla era un producto híbrido, que no se había usado nunca." (Abs.)

102. GILFORD, CHARLES BERNARD. A Critical Survey of the Morality Play. vii+379 pp. Denver, C. Bell, 1952.

Chapter 7, entitled "The Morality in Spain" (pp. 170–97), includes sections on sixteenth-century plays. (Diss.)

103. GITLITZ, DAVID MARTIN. The Jew in the Comedia of the Golden Age. iii+210 pp. Harvard, S. Gilman, 1968.

"In this study I shall concern myself with the portrayal of the Jews and *conversos* in the seventeenth-century theater. I shall attempt to show that there are certain commonplace anti-Jewish libels which are in use throughout Spanish Golden Age literature, and that there is a tendency toward simplification and a reduction of the number of these commonplaces as time passes and first-hand knowledge of the Jews is forgotten. I will demonstrate how in any play containing Jews there is a tendency toward polarization of character which in turn influences the style and dramatic techniques of the playwright. Moreover, the vehemence with which the Jews are libeled can be correlated with both the proximity to contemporary Spanish history of the setting of the play, and the proximity of the date of composition of the play to the date of the expulsion of the Jews." (Diss.)

❖ [A] "*Conversos* and the Fusion of Worlds in Micael de Carvajal's *Tragedia Josephina.*" HR 40 (1972): 260–70. [B] "La actitud cristiano-nueva en *Las cortes de la muerte* [by Carvajal]." *Segismundo* 9.17–18 (1973): 141–64. [C] "The New-Christian Dilemma in Two Plays by Lope de Vega." *BCom* 34.1 (1982): 63–81. [D] "Tirso's *Mari-Hernández* and the Red-Bearded Jew." *Hispanic Essays in Honor of Frank P. Casa*. Ed. A. Robert Lauer and Henry W. Sullivan. New York: Peter Lang, 1997. 146–55.

104. GLUCK, ROCHELLE LITA. The Fantastic Element as a Vehicle of Idealism in the Theater of Alejandro Casona. vi+225 pp. Rutgers, J. Vázquez-Amaral, 1981. *DAI* 42A: 1656.

"Chapter II is an analysis of the sources and influences of Casona's dramas. The inspiration of Spanish authors such as Alarcón, Calderón, Quevedo, Lope de Vega, and Cervantes is examined in regard to Casona's plays." (Abs.)

105. Golden, Bruce. Elizabethan Revenge and Spanish Honor: Analogues of Action in the Popular Drama of the Renaissance. iii+217 pp. Columbia, S. F. Johnson, 1966. *DAI* 30A: 1526.

"It is illuminating to the student of Renaissance drama to see such similar *topoi* lead to such different tragic effects in these two popular dramatic traditions, yet it is not surprising for conceptions of tragedy to differ in such diverse cultures as Reformation England and Catholic, Counter-Reformation Spain." (Abs.)

❖ [A] "Calderón's Tragedies of Honor: *Topoi,* Emblem, and Action in the Popular Theater of the *Siglo de Oro.*" *RenD* ns 3 (1970): 239–62. [B] "The Authority of Honor in Lope's *El castigo sin venganza.*" *Shakespeare and Dramatic Tradition: Essays in Honor of S. F. Johnson.* Ed. William R. Elton and W. B. Long. Newark: U of Delaware P, 1989. 264–75. [C] "*Hamlet* and *El médico de su honra*: The Significance of Intrigue." *BR* 33.1 (1989): 97–115. [The overall title of this volume of the *Bucknell Review* is Comedias del Siglo de Oro *and Shakespeare.* Ed. Susan L. Fischer. Lewisburg: Bucknell UP, 1989.]

106. Grismer, Raymond Leonard. The Influence of Titus Maccius Plautus on the Spanish Theatre through Juan de Timoneda. 301 pp. CA/Berkeley, R. Schevill, 1930.

[For the complete entry, see no. 655.]

107. Grupp, William John. Dramatic Theory and Criticism in Spain during the Sixteenth, Seventeenth and Eighteenth Centuries. [4]+303 pp. Cornell, G. I. Dale, 1949.

This dissertation is composed of the following chapters: 1. "The *Comedia*"; 2. "Dramatic Theory in the Sixteenth Century"; 3. "The Defenders of the 'Arte Nuevo' in the Seventeenth Century"; 4. "The Classical Argument in the Seventeenth Century"; 5. "Dramatic Theory and Criticism in the Eighteenth Century"; and 6. "Conclusion."

108. Gutiérrez, Jesús. La *Fortuna Bifrons* en el teatro del Siglo de Oro. 462 pp. CUNY, I. M. Gil, 1973. *DAI* 34A: 1911.

". . . this study concentrates on five *bilogías* or two-part plays, whose first part presents the *Fortuna Bona* or the prosperity of the protagonist and the second part dramatizes the *Fortuna Mala* or the adversity of the same character. The five *bilogías* are those of Salucio del Poyo's *Próspera y adversa fortuna de Ruy López de Ávalos;* Grajal's *Próspera y adversa fortuna del Caballero del Espíritu Santo;* Mira de Amescua's *Próspera y adversa fortuna de don Bernardo de Cabrera* and *Próspera y adversa fortuna de don Álvaro de Luna* (also attributed to Lope de Vega and Tirso de Molina, respectively); and Jacinto Cordero's *Próspera y adversa fortuna de Duarte Pacheco.*" (Abs.)

❖ [A] "El significado de 'fortuna bifrons': Su presencia en la literatura española del Siglo de Oro." *BBMP* 50 (1974): 3–88. [B] Title as is. Santander: Sociedad Menéndez Pelayo, 1975. 327 pp. [C] "El tema de *fortuna bifrons* en la comedia hasta 1630." *BBMP* 51 (1975): 283–411.

109. Hathaway, Robert Lawton. Love in the Early Spanish Secular Theatre [1490-ca. 1550]. iv+268 pp. Brown, A. S. Trueblood, 1969. *DAI* 31A: 389.

"By means of analysis of almost forty plays pertaining roughly to the first half of the sixteenth century, the declining use of courtly love as a dramatic ethic is illustrated, and the rise of a new construct with neoplatonic orientation is investigated." In an epilogue the writer studies Lope de Vega's *El verdadero amante.* (Abs.)

❖ [A] *Love in the Early Spanish Theatre [1490-ca. 1585].* Madrid: Playor, 1975. 308 pp. [B] "*La Égloga de Calixto y Melibea* de [Pedro Manuel] Ximénez de Urrea." *NRFH* 27 (1978): 314–30. [An annotated edition.] [C] "'Frustrated Lover' Farewells in the Early Iberian Theater." *From Dante to García Márquez: Studies in Romance Literatures and Linguistics Presented to Anson Conant Piper.* Ed. Gene H. Bell-Villada et al. Williamstown: Williams Coll., 1987. 12–23. [Includes Juan del Encina's *Égloga de tres pastores,* the *Égloga hecha por Salazar de Breno y otros tres pastores compañeros suyos,* the "Égloga de Torino" in the anonymous *Qüestión de amor,* and Gil Vicente's *Tragicomedia de Amadís de Gaula.*] [D] "Pedro Manuel Ximénez de Urrea, dramaturgo misántropo." *NRFH* 40.1 (1992): 131–42. [Jiménez de Urrea is one of the subjects of the writer's dissertation.]

110. Hayes, Francis Clement. The Use of Proverbs in the *Siglo de Oro* Drama: An Introductory Study. viii+227 pp. North Carolina,

S. E. Leavitt and R. S. Boggs, 1936. North Carolina *Record,* no. 311, p. 89.

"The purpose of this thesis is to determine the value and influence of proverb-lore in the *Siglo de Oro* drama. Preliminary chapters trace the increasing popularity of proverbs in Spain from the fourteenth century to 1700 and study the usage of proverb-lore in Spanish drama before Lope de Vega. The body of the work concerns the use of proverbs as titles and motives of plays. . . . The appendices contain two tentative lists: one of major and minor collections of proverbs made before the year 1700, and the other of some 230 Golden-Age dramas bearing proverbial titles." (UNC *Record)*

❖ [A] "The Collecting of Proverbs in Spain before 1650." *H* [AATSP] 20 (1937): 85–94. [B] "The Use of Proverbs as Titles and Motives in the *Siglo de Oro* Drama: Lope de Vega." *HR* 6 (1938): 305–23. [C] "The Use of Proverbs as Titles and Motives in the *Siglo de Oro* Drama: Tirso de Molina." *HR* 7 (1939): 310–23. [D] "The Use of Proverbs as Titles and Motives in the *Siglo de Oro* Drama: Calderón." *HR* 15 (1947): 453–63.

111. Heilman, Walter Ritter, Jr. The *Pastourelle* Theme in the Early Spanish Drama. iv+210 pp. North Carolina, S. E. Leavitt, 1953. North Carolina *Record,* no. 534, pp. 249–50.

The *pastourelle* "treats of a love adventure between a gallant and a shepherdess. . . . Beginning with the *Égloga representada en reqüesta de unos amores* by Juan del Encina, Spain's first real secular dramatist, the pre-Golden-Age drama makes wide use of the *pastourelle* theme and the songs and dances associated with it. Subsequent developments of *pastourelle* characters played a large part in producing the *gracioso* and the love affairs on two planes so characteristic of the Spanish *comedia.* After the middle of the sixteenth century, the appearance of the *pastourelle* theme as an integral part of the drama became rarer." (UNC *Record*)

112. Hendrix, William Samuel. Some Native Comic Types in the Early Spanish Drama. 113 pp. Chicago, G. T. Northup, 1922. Chicago *Abstracts* 1: 309–12.

"This study is an attempt to analyze the main comic characters in the Spanish drama from Juan del Encina to Juan de la Cueva." (Abs. and Prt. Diss.)

❖ [A] Title as is. Columbus: Ohio State Univ., 1925. 113 pp. Ohio State Univ. Studies, vol. 1, no. 3 (1925). (Contributions in Languages and Literatures 1.) [B] "Sancho Panza and the Comic Types of the Sixteenth Century." *Homenaje ofrecido a Menéndez Pidal: Miscelánea de estudios lingüísticos, literarios e históricos*. 3 vols. Madrid: Hernando, 1925. 2: 485–94. [For a more complete list of this scholar's publications, see Joanne Limber, "Publications by William S. Hendrix," *HR* 16 (1948): 246–49.]

113. HOBBS, EDNA EARLE. Spanish Influence on the Plays of Beaumont and Fletcher. 258 pp. Florida State, S. Herndon, 1963. *DA* 24: 283–84.

This dissertation "offers proof that Spanish drama also had a share in influencing the plays of these English playwrights." (Abs.)

114. HOGAN, FLORIANA TARANTINO. The Spanish *Comedia* and the English Comedy of Intrigue, with Special Reference to Aphra Behn. v+426+9 pp. Boston University, A. P. Bertocci, 1955.

"The purpose of this dissertation is to attempt to clarify somewhat the confusion and vagueness surrounding the question of the 'influence' of Spanish drama on the Restoration *comedy of intrigue* with special reference to Aphra Behn [1640–89]. The dissertation consists of two parts: Part I is a comparative study of the Restoration and Spanish *comedy of intrigue;* Part II is a study of Aphra Behn's *comedies of intrigue* and her debt to Spain." Editorial note: The Restoration is defined as "the period of the reign of Charles II (1660–1685), sometimes extended to include the reign of James II (1685–1688)."

❖ [A] "Notes on Thirty-One English Plays and Their Spanish Sources." *RECTR* 6.1 (1967): 56–59. [B] "Notes on Savage's *Love in a Veil* and Calderón's *Peor está que estaba*." *RECTR* 8.1 (1969): 23–29. [Richard Savage's play is dated 1718.] [C] "Elizabethan and Jacobean Dramas and Their Spanish Sources." *RORD* 19 (1976): 37–47.

115. HUDSON, HERMAN CLEOPHUS. The Development of Dramatic Criticism in England and Spain during the Elizabethan Period

and the Golden Age. 104 pp. Michigan, F. Sánchez y Escribano, 1962. *DA* 23: 235.

This investigation is made "with a view to comparing the coincident emergence of parallel aesthetic issues and attitudes in the two countries." (Abs.)

116. HVIZDALA, VLADIMIR. Alejandro Casona and the Literary Tradition of the Golden Age. 165 pp. Rutgers, E. Nagy, 1973. *DAI* 34A: 2564–65.

"This dissertation analyzes the impact of some themes found in the Spanish Golden Age literature on the works of Alejandro Casona." For example, chapter 1 "deals mainly with the relation between Casona's *La tercera palabra* and Calderón's *La vida es sueño*." In chapter 2 the writer compares Casona's *Corona de amor y muerte* and Luis Vélez de Guevara's *Reinar después de morir.* (Abs.)

117. IGLESIAS, LUIS GONZÁLEZ. Las primeras representaciones castellanas de la Pasión de Cristo: Estudio interpretativo. 2 vols. (vi+507 pp.) Tulane, D. W. McPheeters, 1977. *DAI* 38A: 7364.

"The third part [of the dissertation] is devoted to the analysis of nine Castilian 'representations' of the Passion, their stage settings, their relation to the liturgy, and their significance in the history of the medieval drama. It also takes into consideration the dramatic and liturgical qualities of the religious poems that, although probably written with no stage performance in mind, have many significant coincidences with the dramatization of the Passion. The general conclusion points out that these poems and plays are of special interest not only to the study of the history of Spanish theater, but also to that of European medieval drama." (Abs.)

118. JACK, WILLIAM SHAFFER. The Early *Entremés* in Spain: The Rise of a Dramatic Form. Pennsylvania, H. A. Rennert, 1923. {Philadelphia: Univ. of Pennsylvania, 1923. 136 pp. (UPSRLL 8.)}

"The aim of the present work has been to trace a history of both word and form from their earliest known appearances in Spain [up to the time of Cervantes, 1615]." (Prt. Diss.)

❖ "Development of the 'Entremés' before Lope de Rueda." *PMLA* 37 (1922): 187–207.

119. JOHNSON, HARVEY LEROY. An Edition of *Triunfo de los Santos,*

with a Consideration of Jesuit School Plays in Mexico before 1650. Pennsylvania, J. P. W. Crawford, 1940. {Philadelphia: Univ. of Pennsylvania, 1941. 179 pp. (UPSRLL 31.)}

The edition is based on the *princeps* (México: Antonio Ricardo, 1579). The probable authors were Padre Vicencio Lanuchi and Padre Juan Sánchez Baquero. (Prt. Diss.)

❖ [A] "Notas relativas a los corrales de la ciudad de México (1626-1641)." *RI* 3 (1941): 133-38. [B] "Nuevos datos para el teatro mexicano en la primera mitad del siglo XVII, referencias a dramaturgos, comediantes y representaciones dramáticas." *RFH* 4 (1942): 127-51. [C] "Noticias dadas por Tomás Gage a propósito del teatro en España, México y Guatemala (1624-1637): La representación de una comedia de Lope de Vega, habladurías relativas a la famosa actriz Amarilis y producciones de indios y criollos." *RI* 8 (1944): 257-73. [For a more complete list of this scholar's publications, see *Romance Literary Studies: Homage to Harvey L. Johnson,* ed. Marie A. Wellington and Marthe O'Nan (Potomac: Porrúa Turanzas, 1979) xvii-xxxvii.]

120. Joyce, Audrey B. The Dramas of Robert Bridges: A Critical Study. 271 pp. South Florida, E. E. Smith, 1980. *DAI* 41A: 1611.

"Using Spanish plays as a source, in his next three plays Bridges explores the relationship of earthly to heavenly love." The three dramas are *The Christian Captives, Achilles in Scyros,* and *The Humours of the Court.* (Abs.) Editorial note: Bridges (1844-1930) acknowledged the influence—whether major or minor—of Calderón in all three plays, and of Lope de Vega in the third one.

121. Kobbervig, Karl Irving. A System for Classifying Motif Elements in the Drama of the Golden Age and Its Application to the *Comedias* of Juan Ruiz de Alarcón y Mendoza. 171 pp. WA/Seattle, W. E. Wilson, 1955. *DA* 15: 2210.

[For the complete entry, see no. 577.]

122. Koros, Carole Marie Shaffer. The Image of the Woman in Nonfiction and the *Comedia* during the Golden Age in Spain. 221 pp. Pennsylvania, A. G. Reichenberger, 1973. *DAI* 34A: 1918-19.

"The purpose of this study is to investigate the interrelationships of Golden Age ideals for feminine behavior and the image of woman as presented in the Spanish drama of that period. . . . the very ideals for feminine behavior that were espoused by the moralists were supported by the dramatists." (Abs.)

123. LaGrone, Gregory Gough. The Imitations of *Don Quixote* in the Spanish Drama. Pennsylvania, M. Romera-Navarro, 1936. {Philadelphia: Univ. of Pennsylvania, 1937. vii+145 pp. (UPSRLL 27.)}

[For the complete entry, see no. 390.]

124. Larson, Sara Catherine. Act/Speech Act: Comic Manipulation in Selected Comedies of the Spanish Golden Age. 173 pp. Kansas, W. R. Blue, 1982. *DAI* 43A: 3931.

". . . Golden Age scholars have so far evidenced a certain reluctance toward applying post-Structuralist critical tools to the *comedia.* The purpose of this study is to fill part of that gap, specifically through the application of speech act theory to five Golden Age comedies. The works analyzed are *La verdad sospechosa* by Ruiz de Alarcón, *La dama boba* by Lope de Vega, *Entre bobos anda el juego* by Rojas Zorrilla, Calderón de la Barca's *La dama duende,* and Tirso de Molina's *Don Gil de las calzas verdes.*" (Abs.) ❖ [A] "Labels and Lies: Names and Don García's World in *La verdad sospechosa.*" *REHb* 20.2 (1986): 95–112. [The writer cites such studies as M. L. Pratt's "The Ideology of Speech Act Theory." *Centrum* 1.1 (1981): 361–68.] [B] "'Yo quiero hablar claro': Language as the Motivating Force of Lope's *La dama boba.*" *Things Done with Words.* Ed. Elias Rivers. Newark: Juan de la Cuesta, 1986. 29–38. [C] "Speech Act Theory and Linguistic Approaches to Teaching the *Comedia.*" *Approaches to Teaching Spanish Golden Age Drama.* Ed. Everett W. Hesse. York: Spanish Literature Publications, 1989. 43–55. [D] "*La dama duende* and the Shifting Characterization of Calderón's Diabolical Angel." *The Perception of Women in Spanish Theater of the Golden Age.* Ed. Anita K. Stoll and Dawn L. Smith. Lewisburg: Bucknell UP, 1991. 33–50. [E] *Language and the* Comedia: *Theory and Practice.* Lewisburg: Bucknell UP, 1991. [Includes revised editions of items A, B, and D. The writer states that A and B use "speech act theory as their point of departure."] [F] "The Visible and the Hidden: Speech Act Theory and Cervantes's *El retablo de las maravillas.*" *El arte nuevo de estudiar comedias: Literary Theory and Spanish Golden Age Drama*. Ed. Barbara Simerka. Lewisburg: Bucknell UP, 1996. 52–65.

125. LAUER, A. ROBERT. The Killing of the Tyrannical King in the Spanish Theater of the Golden Age (1582–1671). vi+391 pp. Michigan, F. P. Casa, 1983. *DAI* 44A: 500.

"[This dissertation] shows that the despotic monarch is not only opposed but frequently slain; this is evident throughout the period usually assigned to the *Comedia*." (Abs.)

❖ [A] *Tyrannicide and Drama.* Part 1: *The Tradition of Tyrannicide from Polybius to Suárez.* Part 2: *The Tyrannicide Drama in Spain from 1579 to 1698.* Stuttgart: Steiner, 1987. 182 pp. (Archivum Calderonianum 4.) [B] "The Use and Abuse of History in the Spanish Theater of the Golden Age: The Regicide of Sancho II as Treated by Juan de la Cueva, Guillén de Castro, and Lope de Vega." *HR* 56.1 (1988): 17–37.

126. LEARY, KATHERINE MARGARET. The Poetics of Mimesis. v+272 pp. Minnesota, W. Godzich, 1984. *DAI* 45A: 3632.

This study draws "upon various hermeneutical and semiotic practices rather than a single methodology" to analyze seventeenth-century drama in several European countries. "The notion of the availability of language investigated in *Iphigénie* [Racine] is explored further in *Le Menteur* [P. Corneille] and *La verdad sospechosa* [Ruiz de Alarcón] where the individual's appropriation of language becomes the problematic issue. . . . The Protestant-Catholic controversy surrounding the question of divine presence in the Eucharist proves an important one here, as the Catholic belief that the words of consecration are the mark of Christ's presence establishes a linguistic precedent upon which an entire discursive system is built and which is demonstrated in *El médico de su honra* [Calderón]." (Abs.)

127. LERZUNDI, PATRICIO CAVADA. La conquista de Chile en el teatro del Siglo de Oro. vi+394 pp. CUNY, H. E. Bergman, 1979. *DAI* 40A: 2717–18.

"The theme is studied in the following plays: *Arauco domado,* by Lope de Vega; *La Araucana,* a religious play attributed to Lope de Vega; *La Bellígera española,* by Ricardo de Turia; *Algunas hazañas*

de las muchas de don García Hurtado de Mendoza, Marqués de Cañete, by nine authors; *El Gobernador prudente,* by Gaspar de Ávila, and *Los Españoles en Chile,* by Francisco González de Bustos." (Abs.)
❖ [A] *Arauco en el teatro del Siglo de Oro.* Valencia: Albatros-Hispanófila, 1996. 165 pp. [B] Turia, R. de. *La Bellígera española.* Ed., introd., and notes by P. Lerzundi. Valencia: Albatros-Hispanófila, 1996. 128 pp.

128. Lifton, Paul Samuel. Thorton Wilder and "World Theatre." iii+770 pp. CA/Berkeley, T. M. Bogard, 1985. *DAI* 46A: 2486.
Chapter 7 ("Similarities between Wilder's Theatre and Miscellaneous Traditional and Historical Theatres") includes a section entitled "The Theatre of the Spanish Golden Age" (pp. 679–85). (Diss.)

129. Lovett, Gabriel H. The Churchman and Related Characters in the Spanish Drama before Lope de Vega. vi+297 pp. NYU, H. C. Heaton, 1950–51.
The body of this dissertation consists of the following four chapters: "The Churchman in Early Spanish Semi-dramatic Literature," "The Churchman as a Comic Character," "The Churchman as a Serious Character," and "The Hermit." (Diss.)
❖ [A] "The Churchman in the Spanish Drama before Lope de Vega." *BCom* 4.2 (1952): 10–13. [B] "The Hermit in the Spanish Drama before Lope de Vega." *MLJ* 35 (1952): 340–55.

130. Lundelius, Marguerite Ruth. The *Mujer Varonil* in the Theater of the Siglo de Oro. 310 pp. Pennsylvania, A. G. Reichenberger, 1969. *DAI* 31A: 1282.
"The present study traces [the *mujer varonil*'s] derivation from a multiplicity of antecedents and influences. . . . The antecedent elements provide nothing more than the framework, however, for the *mujer varonil* was clearly a product of the *comedia*." (Abs.)
❖ [A] "Tirso's View of Women in *El burlador de Sevilla*." *BCom* 27.1 (1975): 5–14. [In discussing Tisbea, the writer refers the reader to her dissertation.] [B] "Paradox and Role Reversal in *La serrana de la Vera*." *The Perception of Women in Spanish Theater of the Golden Age.* Ed. Anita K. Stoll and Dawn L. Smith. Lewisburg: Bucknell UP, 1991. 220–44.

131. Manson, William Rainey. Attitudes toward Authority as

Expressed in Typical Spanish Plays of the Golden Age. 288 pp. North Carolina, N. B. Adams, 1963. *DA* 25: 4703.

This investigation is based on plays of Lope de Vega, Vélez de Guevara, Tirso de Molina, Ruiz de Alarcón, Calderón, and Rojas Zorrilla. (Abs.)

132. MARTIN, CHARLES BASIL. The Survivals of Medieval Religious Drama in New Mexico. 193 pp. Missouri, H. Craig, 1959. *DA* 20A: 3298–99.

These performances "are a curious remnant of a very old form of religious drama which was transported from medieval Spain to colonial Mexico and finally up the Rio Grande valley to New Mexico. . . . Many farcical elements have crept into the plays, but the religious and devotional spirit has persisted through the centuries." (Abs.)

133. MARTÍNEZ, ENRIQUE JOSÉ. Tragedy in the Spanish Theater of the Golden Age. 326 pp. Pennsylvania, A. G. Reichenberger, 1970. *DAI* 31A: 2927–28.

"In the strictest sense, the only plays which are close to high tragedy are *El castigo sin venganza, Reinar después de morir,* and the closest, *La Estrella de Sevilla.* The Spanish dramatists continuously searched for a tragic formula. . . . Their failure to develop a high tragedy stemmed from the fact that they did not have a tragic view of life and the Universe." (Abs.)

134. MAURER, DAVID WARREN. The Spanish Intrigue Play on the Restoration Stage. 261 pp. Ohio State, J. H. Wilson, 1935. Ohio State *Abstracts* 18 (1936): 275–82.

This study of the Spanish intrigue play in England includes "a discussion of its sources both in pre-Restoration dramatic literature and on the Spanish stage." In chapter 2 the writer bases his analysis on "some fifty representative Spanish cape and sword plays." (Abs.)

135. MAZUR, OLEH. The Wild Man in Spanish Renaissance and Golden Age Theater: A Comparative Study. xxxiv+421 pp. Pennsylvania, A. G. Reichenberger, 1966. *DA* 27A: 1341.

This dissertation has two parts: "the wild man as an evolving concept in Europe and in Spain" and "the wild man as a dramatic device in Spain, 1530–1700." (Abs.)

❖ [A] "Various Folkloric Impacts upon the *Salvaje* in the Spanish *Comedia*." *HR* 36 (1968): 207–35. [B] "Different Aspects of Love in Lope de Vega's *Salvajes, Indios* and *Bárbaros*." *NEMLA Newsletter* 2 (1970): 67–73. [C] "Lope de Vega's *Salvajes, Indios* and *Bárbaros*." *Ibero* 2 (1970): 260–81. [D] *The Wild Man in the Spanish Renaissance and Golden Age Theater: A Comparative Study Including the 'Indio,' the 'Bárbaro' and Their Counterparts in European Lores*. Ann Arbor: UMI for Villanova Univ., 1980. 371 pp.

136. McCrary, William Carlton. The Classical Tradition in Spanish Dramatic Theory of the Sixteenth and Seventeenth Centuries. 217 pp. Wisconsin, E. W. Hesse, 1958. *DA* 19: 2092.

". . . the modernists felt that neither Lope nor the *comedia* represented a reaction against classical standards, but rather a new approach to drama quite compatible with the ancient masters. It may be asserted, therefore, that their work attempted to integrate authority with experience in order to accommodate traditional theory to a modern vision of the theater." (Abs.)

[For a complete list of this scholar's publications, see *Studies in Honor of William C. McCrary*, ed. Robert L. Fiore, Everett W. Hesse, John E. Keller, and José A. Madrigal (Lincoln: Univ. of Nebraska, Soc. of Spanish and Spanish-American Studies, 1986) 7–11.]

137. McCready, Warren Thomas. La heráldica en las obras de Lope de Vega y sus contemporáneos. 545 pp. Chicago, C. Castillo and B. Blanco-González, 1961.

[For the complete entry, see no. 734.]

138. McCrossan, [Sister] Joseph Marie, I.H.M. The Role of the Church and the Folk in the Development of the Early Drama in New Mexico. Pennsylvania, A. H. Quinn, 1948. {Philadelphia, 1948. viii+175 pp.}

"The plays in New Spain have been linked with the tradition in Old Spain through references to the religious drama of Manrique, Encina, Gil Vicente, and Torres Naharro, and of the later plays of the Golden Age of Spanish literature by Lope de Vega and Calderón de la Barca. The missionaries in New Spain merely continued the festal customs and religious dramatic traditions of Old Spain. The records and several of the extant plays in Mexico prove that many of the missionaries were authors of plays. . . . The synthesis here presented is intended to substantiate the claim that the [Franciscan] misssionaries in New Mexico are responsible for the deposit of the religious drama there, and possibly for its authorship. This is the contribution of the Church to the religious drama in the state. The contribution of the Folk is the preservation and survival of seventeenth century mystery plays in twentieth century America." (Prt. Diss.)

139. McHugh, Kathleen. The New Heroes of Renaissance Historical Drama on Religious Themes. 559 pp. NYU, R. Harrier, 1965. *DA* 27A: 750.

The writer deals with the following Iberian "new heroes": "Don Rodrig[o], Don Pelayo, El Cid, Fernando el Católico, Carlos V, Felipe II, Don Juan de Austria, Sebastian of Portugal, Thomas Stukeley," and others. (Abs.)

140. Meredith, Joseph Arthur. *Introito* and *Loa* in the Spanish Drama of the Sixteenth Century. 134 pp. Pennsylvania, J. P. W. Crawford, 1925. {Philadelphia: Univ. of Pennsylvania, 1928. 134 pp. (UPSRLL 16.)}

"It is the earlier period that is the concern of the present study, which attempts to trace the origins and development of the *introito, loa* and kindred forms, from the first *Églogas* of Juan del Encina up to the *Viaje entretenido* of Agustín de Rojas." (Prt. Diss.)

141. Middleton, Thomas. The Urban and Architectural Environment of the *Corrales* of Madrid: The Corral de la Cruz in 1600. 284 pp. CA/Los Angeles, R. H. Hethmon, 1976. *DAI* 37A: 1880.

"The dissertation culminates in a reconstruction, based on the only scaled floor plan of the theater, dated 1735, of ground-level and second-level floor plans as they probably appeared in 1600." (Abs.)

❖ "El urbanismo madrileño y la fundación del Corral de la Cruz." *V [Quintas] jornadas de teatro clásico español, Almagro, 1982.* Ed. Juan Antonio Hormigón. Madrid: Ministerio de Cultura, 1983. 139–67.

142. Mintz, Jacqueline Ann. A Comparative Study of Shame in Spanish and English Renaissance Drama. iii+143 pp. CA/Berkeley, H. M. Richmond, 1982. *DAI* 44A: 162.

This study is based on the comparison of the following pairs of plays: (1) *Measure for Measure* (Shakespeare) and *La Estrella de Sevilla* (Anon.), (2) *Peribáñez* (Lope) and *Much Ado about Nothing* (Shakespeare), (3) *La vida es sueño* (Calderón) and *King Lear* (Shakespeare). "With the significant exception of Calderón, mainstream Spanish culture chose not to recognize shame's potential for personal growth and moral awareness." (Abs.)

143. MOHLER, FRANKLIN CALVIN, II. Spectacular Effects on the Seventeenth-Century Continental Stage. 290 pp. Ohio State, A. L. Woods, 1976. *DAI* 37A: 699.

"These effects are classified in the dissertation as scene-shifting effects, water effects, effects from below the stage, and effects from above the stage. In each section, drawings of stage machinery are analyzed and the operation of the machinery is described." (Abs.)

144. MOORE, JAY EDWARD. Late Medieval Moral Drama: The Tradition of Personification Allegory in France and Spain. 249 pp. Pennsylvania State, A. E. Knight, 1991. *DAI* 52A: 4322.

"This study explores the essential elements of Spanish and French late-medieval moral theater [*autos sacramentales* and *moralités,* respectively] from a primarily socio-historical perspective and provides a reading theory for these plays that elucidates their didactic function. . . . [In chapters 4, 5, and 6, the writer] presents aspects of the form and content of the plays: personifications as *dramatis personae,* themes and motifs, and cross-generic subject matter." (Abs.)

145. MROCZKOWSKA-BRAND, KATARZYNA. Overt Theatricality and the "Theatrum Mundi" Metaphor in Spanish and English Drama, 1570–1640. xii+260 pp. Rochester, P. N. Dunn and A. N. Benston, 1985. *DAI* 46A: 3025.

"The similarities and differences in the use of overt theatricality are studied in a group of twenty Spanish and twenty English plays. The dramatization of the *theatrum mundi* metaphor is the focal point." Three Spanish plays are of special significance in this study: Lope de Vega's *Lo fingido verdadero* and Calderón's *La vida es sueño* and *En esta vida todo es verdad y todo mentira.* (Abs.)

❖ [A] "Overt Theatricality and the *Theatrum mundi* Metaphor in Spanish and English Drama, 1570–1640." *KN* 26 (1979): 201–14.

[B] *Lo fingido verdadero* de Lope de Vega como la interpretación más original y más moderna de la metáfora del Theatrum Mundi en el drama español del Siglo de Oro: Análisis comparado con *Le véritable Saint Genest* de Jean Rotrou." *Estudios hispánicos II: Actas del segundo simposio de hispanistas polacos, Wrocław y Karpacz, 1990.* Ed. Piotr Sawicki and Jerzy Slawomirski. Wrocław: Wydawnictwo Uniwersytetu Wroclawskiego, 1992. 213-30.

146. MURPHY, DONN BRIAN. Dramatic Portrayals of Christ. 303 pp. Wisconsin, R. E. Mitchell, 1964. *DA* 25A: 3746-47.

The writer examines some Spanish Golden Age examples on pp. 71-73 of chapter 3. In chapter 5 he elaborates on the following observation: "The first portrayals of Christ which appear in the New World reflect various stages of development as they have been seen in the plays of Europe." (Diss.)

147. MYERS, GABRIELA SANTONASTASIO. El *Gracioso* y la *Figura del Donaire:* Encuesta de estudios sobre su evolución genérica y léxico-etimológica. ii+250 pp. Southern California, J. D. Smith, 1972. *DAI* 33A: 4375-76.

"The purpose of this study is to demonstrate that the genesis of the *gracioso* and the *figura del donaire* in the Spanish theater occurred in pre-Hellenic times. . . . The conclusion is that although *el gracioso* and the *figura del donaire* may be defined with similar adjectives, they are never synonymous." (Abs.) Editorial note: It must be noted, however, that the *Academy Dictionary* (1992) treats the two terms as synonyms.

148. NEALE-SILVA, EDUARDO. The New World in the Spanish *Comedia:* A Preliminary Study. 2 vols. Wisconsin, J. Ortega, 1935.

". . . we intend to achieve three purposes: 1. To compare the dramatists' conception of New World events and conditions with historical truth, 2. To study the direct sources of information and the treatment accorded them by playwrights, 3. To study the linguistic contribution of America and other allied subjects. The materials used in this investigation are various types of dramatic productions of the seventeenth and eighteenth centuries." Most of the dramatic compositions date from the seventeenth century; only twelve from the eighteenth. (Diss.)

❖ "An Incident in the Life of Cortés: Its Possible Source." *HR*

6 (1938): 69–74. [The proposed source is a *romance* found in several *comedias*.]

149. OAKEY, VALERIE HEGSTROM. Conventions of the *Corral* Theater: Another Approach to *Comedias* Performed between 1610 and 1620. 257 pp. Kansas, W. R. Blue, 1992. *DAI* 54A: 1388.

"This study focuses on the non-illusory nature of plays performed in Spanish *corrales de comedias* in the 1610s. The chapters explore the use of effects produced by several conventions current in the *corrales* between 1610–20. Based on performance criticism, the interpretations go beyond more strictly literary approaches by replacing dramatic texts in their theatrical ambience, emphasizing the creative efforts of artists and spectators alike who participated in each play's full realization." (Abs.)

150. O'CONNELL, MARGARET ELLEN. The Motif of the Woman Disguised as a Man in Shakespeare and Some *Siglo de Oro* Spanish Dramatists: The Portia Figure. v+269 pp. Princeton, A. Forcione, E. Miner, and R. E. Surtz, 1983. *DAI* 44A: 1081.

". . . the Portia figure serves as a sort of litmus test for the playwright's attitudes toward women and the public sphere—attitudes which determine the drastically different presentations of this character type produced by different authors." (Abs.)

151. ORIEL, CHARLES MARC. Writing and Inscription in Golden Age Drama. 240 pp. George Washington, I. Azar, 1989. *DAI* 50A: 1676.

"The dramas examined in this study are Lope de Vega's *El villano en su rincón,* the anonymous *La Estrella de Sevilla,* Mira de Amescua's *El ejemplo mayor de la desdicha,* and Calderón's *La cisma de Inglaterra.* Each play enacts a preoccupation with the written word by insistently highlighting in different ways the various dimensions of textuality: reading, writing, and erasure." (Abs.)

❖ [A] Title as is. West Lafayette: Purdue UP, 1992. 189 pp. (PSRL 1). [B] "Reading the Writing on the Wall: Logocentrism and the Metaphysics of Presence in Calderón's *La cena del rey Baltasar.*" *Gestos* 7.13 (1992): 23–36. [C] "Text and Textile in *El caballero de Olmedo.*" *IJHL* 2.2 (1994): 131–56. [D] "Text and Textile in Lope's *El caballero de Olmedo.*" *Texto y espectáculo: Proceedings of the Thirteenth International Golden Age Spanish Theatre Symposium, El Paso, 1993.* Ed. José Luis Suárez García. York: Spanish Literature

Publications, 1995. 76–83. [E] "The Play of Presence and Absence: Writing and Supplementarity in the *Comedias de Privanza.*" *El arte nuevo de estudiar comedias: Literary Theory and Spanish Golden Age Drama.* Ed. Barbara Simerka. Lewisburg: Bucknell UP, 1996. 36–51. [F] "Shame, Writing, and Morality." *Heavenly Bodies: The Realms of* La Estrella de Sevilla. Ed. Frederick A. de Armas. Lewisburg: Bucknell UP, 1996. 245–57.

152. PASQUARIELLO, ANTHONY MICHAEL. The *Entremés, Sainete* and *Loa* in the Colonial Theater of Spanish America. vi+210 pp. Michigan, I. A. Leonard, 1950. *DA* 11: 466.

Among the authors treated are Fernán González de Eslava, Cristóbal de Llerena, Sor Juana Inés de la Cruz, and Juan del Valle y Caviedes. (Diss.)

❖ [A] "The *Entremés* in Sixteenth-Century Spanish America." *HAHR* 32 (1952): 44–58. [B] "The Seventeenth-Century Interlude in the New World Secular Theater." *Homage to I. A. Leonard: Essays on Hispanic Art, History and Literature.* Ed. Raquel Chang-Rodríguez and Donald A. Yates. East Lansing: Michigan State Univ., Latin American Studies Center, 1977. 105–13. [C] "Theater in Colonial Spanish America: Religious and Cultural Impact." *HisJ* 10.1 (1988): 27–38.

153. PATT, BEATRICE PENELOPE (SHAPIRO). The Development of the Christmas Play in Spain from the Origins to Lope de Vega. 340 pp. Bryn Mawr, J. E. Gillet, 1945. *DA* 8: 100–02.

"This dissertation constitutes a systematic study of the sources and characteristics of the available Christmas plays written in Spain from the twelfth century *[Auto de los Reyes Magos]* to the period of Lope de Vega. Some of the plays written in Spain and Spanish America in the seventeenth and eighteenth centuries are summarized briefly in an Appendix for the purpose of ascertaining the extent to which the traditions of the earlier presentations were followed; a second Appendix consists of a list of titles of lost Christmas plays." (Abs.)

154. PAVIA, MARIO N. Magic and Witchcraft in the Literature of the *Siglo de Oro,* Especially in Drama. xiii+186 pp. Chicago, C. Castillo, 1947.

❖ *Drama of the Siglo de Oro: A Study of Magic, Witchcraft, and Other*

Occult Beliefs. New York: Hispanic Inst., 1959. 166 pp. [copyright 1957.]

"This work is, with additional examples, a condensation of a revised doctoral dissertation, which was submitted at the University of Chicago in 1947. . . . In footnotes and sometimes in the text have been included also numerous examples from other *genres* of the *Siglo de Oro.*" (Prt. Diss.)

155. PETERS, HOWARD NEVIN. Sixteenth Century European Tragicomedy: A Critical Survey of the Genre in Italy, France, England, and Spain. 232 pp. Colorado, F. Sánchez y Escribano, 1966. *DA* 28A: 240.

"The full blend of the tragic and the comic, particularly evident in the dramas of England and Spain during the 16th and early 17th centuries, was presaged by the *Celestina.* The *Celestina,* whether called tragicomedy or not, was a tangible, precocious example for the drama of the whole of Europe of the blending of tragedy and comedy into one genre, whether called tragicomedy or not." (Abs.)

156. PORRATA, FRANCISCO EDUARDO. Asimilación del romance a la comedia prelopista. iii+193 pp. Iowa, J. Szertics, 1969. *DAI* 30A: 3917.

"Objetivo de este estudio: Es la incorporación de los romances, tesoro de leyenda e historia, al género dramático en España, como acontecimiento literario del siglo XVI." (Abs.)

❖ *Incorporación del romancero a la temática de la comedia española.* Madrid: Playor, 1973. 200 pp.

157. QUACKENBUSH, LOUIS HOWARD. The Latin American *Auto:* Themes and Forms. vi+371 pp. Illinois, M. H. Forster, 1970. *DAI* 31A: 6627.

"The Latin American *auto* dramatic structure has its origin in the European medieval liturgical theater, . . . and early renaissance works . . . and *autos* by Gómez Manrique, Juan del Encina, Lucas Fernández, and most important of all Gil Vicente. This was the *auto* technique transplanted to the New World in the early sixteenth century. . . . Therefore, the common assumption that the Latin American *auto* form is just a copy of the Spanish seventeenth century *auto sacramental* is an erroneous anachronism." (Abs.)

❖ "The *Auto* in the Contemporary Mexican Drama." *KRQ* 21 (1974): 15–30.

158. ROATEN, DARNELL HIGGINS. An Explanation of the Forms of Three Serious Spanish Baroque Dramas according to Wölfflin's *Principles of Art History*. 129 pp. Michigan, F. Sánchez y Escribano, 1951. *DA* 11: 687–88.

The three dramas studied are Lope's *Fuenteovejuna,* Calderón's *La vida es sueño* and Guillén de Castro's *Las mocedades del Cid*. (Abs.) Editorial note: Heinrich Wölfflin, 1864–1945, Swiss art historian.

❖ [A] "Wölfflin's Principles Applied to Lope's *Fuenteovejuna*." *BCom* 4.1 (1952): unpaged. [B] Roaten, D. H., and F. Sánchez y Escribano. *Wölfflin's Principles in Spanish Drama*: *1500–1700*. New York: Hispanic Inst. 1952. 200 pp. [The sixteenth-century plays analyzed are Hernán Pérez de Oliva, *La venganza de Agamenón;* Jerónimo Bermúdez, *Nise lastimosa;* Lupercio Leonardo de Argensola and Bartolomé Leonardo de Argensola, *Isabela*. The seventeenth-century plays analyzed are Lope, *Fuenteovejuna;* Guillén de Castro, *Las mocedades del Cid;* Calderón, *La vida es sueño*. (Prt. Diss.)]

159. ROBERTSON, SANDRA CARY. The Resurgence of the Theater of Popular Poetry: Federico García Lorca and Rafael Alberti, 1923–1935. xii+245 pp. CA/San Diego, D. D. Catalán, 1984. *DAI* 45A: 3141.

"Chapter 2 examines the lessons of Gil Vicente and Lope de Vega, two primary models for Lorca and Alberti, in their use of traditional poetry from the lullaby to the ballad. . . . Chapter 6 demonstrates Lorca's mastery of the theater of popular traditional poetry through his work with La Barraca." (Abs.)

❖ *Lorca, Alberti, and the Theater of Popular Poetry*. New York: Peter Lang, 1991. 267 pp. (American University Studies, ser. 2. Romance Languages and Literature 170.)

160. ROSENBACH, ABRAHAM SIMON WOLF. Spanish Influence in the English Drama before the Restoration. Pennsylvania, F. Schelling, 1901.

"The *nature* of the Spanish influence upon the English dramatists is considered by comparisons of the drama of Lope de Vega and his School and the Comedy of Manners. The comedies of *capa y espada* have their exact counterpart in the Jacobin [Jacobean] drama. A table has been added showing the similar methods of treatment in plays derived from common sources such as Fletcher's 'Maid in the Mill,' and Lope de Vega's *La Quinta de Florencia*." (Synopsis from Rosenbach Company Archive, IV:01: 03. Rosenbach Museum and Library, Philadelphia. The dissertation is no longer available.)

❖ "The Influence of the *Celestina* in the Early English Drama." *Jahrbuch der deutschen Shakespeare-Gesellschaft* 39 (1903): 43–61.

161. RUFFNER, SYDNEY JACKSON. The American Theme in Selected Dramas of the Golden Age. 508 pp. Southern California, D. E. McMahon, 1954. USC *Abstracts of Dissertations* (1954): 109–12.

"This investigation includes only those plays composed between 1600 and 1680 in which either the settings are in America or the principal character is in some way associated with the New World. Twenty-two works meet these qualifications. Six of these exist only in seventeenth century editions and were studied from microfilms secured from the British Museum. Four of equal rarity were found in single modern editions, while the remaining twelve were located among the collected works of their authors." (Abs.)

162. RUNDLE, JAMES URVIN. Restoration Comedy and the Spanish *Comedia:* A First Essay. [2]+242+xxviii pp. Cincinnati, W. S. Clark, 1947.

"For erratic, extreme generalizations unsupported by any considerable reading in the Spanish plays, the present study substitutes carefully weighed evidence which clearly indicates that the direct impact of the *comedia* on Restoration playwrights was much greater than there has been hitherto any considered reason to believe." (Diss.) Editorial note: The Restoration is defined as "the period of the reign of Charles II (1660–1685), sometimes extended to include the reign of James II (1685–1688)."

❖ [A] "More about Calderón, Boursault and Ravenscroft." *MLN* 62 (1947): 382–83. [B] "The Source of Dryden's 'Comic Plot' in *The Assignation* [1672]." *MP* 45 (1947–48): 104–11. [The source: Calderón's *Con quien vengo vengo.*] [C] "Footnote on Calderón, Ravenscroft and Boursault." *MLN* 63 (1948): 217–19. [In this note and in item A, the writer argues that the play *The Wrangling*

Lovers (1677), by Edward Ravenscroft (c.1650–c.1697), as well as three plays of Calderón, was influenced by a Spanish novel, now lost.] [D] "Wycherley and Calderón: A Source for *Love in a Wood*." *PMLA* 64 (1949): 701–07. [The source: Calderón's *Mañanas de abril y mayo*.] [E] "D'Avenant's *The Man's the Master* and the Spanish Source." *MLN* 65 (1950): 194–96. [The source: Rojas Zorrilla's *Donde hay agravios, no hay celos*.]

163. SCHONS, EMILY. New Material on the Dramatic Treatment of Peter the Cruel of Castile and the Diffusion of the Legend in France, Germany and England. 113 pp. Chicago, G. T. Northup, 1932.

"The author adds to the material on Pedro el Cruel published in José R. Lomba y Pedraja's 'El Rey Don Pedro en el teatro,' in *Homenaje a Menéndez y Pelayo* (Madrid, 1899), II, 257–339. The dissertation is divided into four parts dealing respectively with the treatment of Pedro el Cruel in Spanish, French, German, and English drama." (Benjamin Blaney, *REHb* 15 [1981]: 469.)

❖ Title as is. Chicago: [Author], 1936. iii+114 pp.

164. SEGALL, JACOB BERNARD. Corneille and the Spanish Drama. Columbia, 1902. {New York: Columbia UP; Macmillan, 1902. ix+147 pp. (Columbia University Studies in Romance Philology and Literature 3.)}

The principal chapters are devoted to the following comparisons: Pierre Corneille's *Le Cid* and Castro's *Las mocedades del Cid;* and Corneille's *Le Menteur* and Ruiz de Alarcón's *La verdad sospechosa.* (Prt. Diss.)

❖ Title as is. Rpt: New York: AMS, 1966, 1969. 147 pp. (Columbia University Studies in Romance Philology and Literature 3.)

165. SHERVILL, ROBERT NEWTON. The Old Testament Drama of the *Siglo de Oro*. vi+518 pp. North Carolina, S. E. Leavitt, 1958. *DA* 19: 2093.

"So far as can be determined, the Golden Age Old Testament theater consists of some twenty-seven full-length *comedias,* two of which are no longer extant." (Abs.)

❖ "Lope's Ways with Women." *BCom* 15.1 (1963): 10–13. [Study based on Lope's Old Testament heroines.]

166. SHIELDS, ROBERT LAWRENCE. A General Study of the Transition Period of Spanish Drama Following Juan de la Cueva.

vi+74 pp. Iowa, R. Davis, 1941. Iowa *Abstracts* 3, part 4, pp. 411–16.

The period under discussion is roughly the last quarter of the sixteenth century. The following are some of the writer's conclusions: (1) "With the presentation of the plays of Juan de la Cueva in 1579 the themes of Spanish drama become varied. After this date dramatists drew upon a wider range of material for their subject matter." (2) "In the last quarter of the sixteenth century the tendency toward flexibility in verse forms reappeared. Juan de la Cueva was the prime mover in this respect." (3) "The secular transition drama adheres in general to the Cueva formula of versification in the mingling of Spanish and Italian meters." (Abs.)

167. SHOEMAKER, WILLIAM HUTCHINSON. The Multiple Stage in Spain and Catalonia during the Fifteenth and Sixteenth Centuries. 212 pp. Princeton, J. E. Gillet, 1933.

❖ [A] "Windows on the Spanish Stage in the Sixteenth Century." *HR* 2 (1934): 303–18. [B] *The Multiple Stage in Spain during the Fifteenth and Sixteenth Centuries*. Princeton: Princeton UP, 1935. 150 pp. ["The chief aim of this study is to show the existence and extent of the multiple stage technique in Spain from its earliest manifestations to the latter part of the sixteenth century." (Prt. Diss.)] [Note that "and Catalonia" is not included in title of printed version, but Catalan material is included in the study.] [C] "The Llabrés Manuscript and Its Castilian Plays." *HR* 4 (1936): 239–55. [D] "Fernando de Basurto's 'Lost Play' on the Martyrdom of Santa Engracia." *HR* 6.1 (1938): 35–45. [The work "is of importance to our knowledge of the early Spanish theater."] [E] *Los escenarios múltiples en el teatro español de los siglos XV y XVI.* Barcelona: Diputación Provincial, 1957. 154 pp. (Estudios Escénicos–Cuadernos del Instituto del Teatro 2.) [F] Rpt. of item B, Westport: Greenwood, 1973. [For a more complete list of this scholar's publications, see "Publicaciones del Profesor William H. Shoemaker," *Estudios sobre Galdós: Homenaje ofrecido al Prof. W. H. Shoemaker* (Madrid: Castalia, 1970) 11–14.]

168. SIMERKA, BARBARA. Beyond "Clowns and Kings": Aesthetic and Ideological Subversion in Baroque Tragicomedy. iii+242 pp.

Southern California, J. A. Parr and N. Vickers, 1992. *DAI* 53A: 3205–06.

"[This dissertation] as a whole redefines tragicomedy in order to shed light on works that have often been called 'problem plays,' to demonstrate that this genre can most usefully be studied in conjunction with an analysis of the period complex in which it is situated, and to correct the critical impression that tragicomedy is an essentially escapist drama that provides facile wish-fulfillment." (Abs.) The writer discusses five Spanish plays: *La vida es sueño* (Calderón), *El médico de su honra* (Calderón), *El burlador de Sevilla* (Tirso), *Ganar amigos* (Alarcón), and *Lo fingido verdadero* (Lope).

❖ "The 'Efemination' of Flor: Satire and Sexuality in Ruiz de Alarcón's *Ganar amigos.*" *RLAn* 4 (1992): 580–83.

169. Sorkin, Max. Paul Scarron's Adaptations of Spanish *Comedias.* xxi+163 pp. NYU, 1936.

"The purpose of the present investigation is to study the comedies of Paul Scarron. As indicated by the title, the greater part of the work will consist of a detailed comparison of each play with its Spanish source or sources. In each case comparisons will be made from the points of view of: (1) plot, (2) structure, (3) characterization, and (4) comic technique." The following sources are studied: *Donde hay agravios, no hay celos, y amo criado, La traición busca el castigo, No hay amigo para amigo,* and *Obligados y ofendidos y gorrón de Salamanca* by Rojas Zorrilla; *No hay peor sordo* by Tirso; *El marqués del Cigarral* and *El mayorazgo figura* by Castillo Solórzano; *El alcaide de sí mismo* and *No siempre lo peor es cierto* by Calderón; and *Peor es hurgallo* by Coello. (Diss.)

❖ *Paul Scarron's Adaptations of the Comedia.* New York: Appellate Law Printers, 1938. 115 pp. "También se refiere [el autor] a fuentes dramáticas españolas de Corneille [Pierre y Thomas], Rotrou, d'Ouville y Boisrobert." (McCready, no. 1784.)

170. Sparks, Amy James. The Honor Code in Representative Spanish Romantic Dramas. 222 pp. Louisiana State, J. A. Thompson, 1964. *DA* 25A: 1220–21.

"The dramatic use of the *pundonor* in the nineteenth century romantic plays of Spain varies considerably from its use in the drama of Spain's Golden Age, where it is often the main source of action. In an attempt to note these variations this study examines the strict application of the code in the serious drama of the Golden Age as well as the distorted and sensational use of honor in selected plays by Victor Hugo and Alexandre Dumas (Père), two dramatists generally considered to have been important influences on the Spanish romantics. Against this background the code of honor as a way of life and as a dramatic *resorte* in representative nineteenth century romantic plays is studied in detail." (Abs.)

❖ [A] "Honor in Hartzenbusch's 'Refundición' of Calderón's *El médico de su honra*." *H* [AATSP] 49 (1966): 410–13. [B] "La refundición por Echegaray de *La hija del aire (Segunda parte)* de Calderón." *Calderón: Actas del congreso internacional sobre Calderón y el teatro español del Siglo de Oro, Madrid, 1981*. Ed. Luciano García Lorenzo. 3 vols. Madrid: CSIC, 1983. 1463–69. ["Elimina (Echegaray) el intrincado tratamiento de la fidelidad del sujeto a su soberano y sus inteligentes manipulaciones de las sutiles abstracciones del código de honor."]

171. Spikes, Judith Doolin. The Dramatization of History in Seventeenth-Century England and Spain: A Comparative Study of Selected Plays. iii+239 pp. Chicago, D. Bevington and G. Haley, 1970.

The dissertation includes the following seven chapters: "Introduction," "European Affairs," "Tudors on the English Stage," "The 'Spanish Match,'" "The Court of Henry VIII," "Tudors on the Spanish Stage," and "Historical Drama as Mirage."

172. Stafford, Lorna Lavery. The Soliloquy in the Spanish Drama before Lope de Vega. xiv+223 pp. Johns Hopkins, J. Robles, 1936.

"It is the aim of this study to trace, from its inception to the advent of Lope de Vega at the close of the sixteenth century, the evolution of one element in Spanish dramatic technique which bears a literary and artistic as well as structural relation to the body of the drama, *the soliloquy*." (Diss.)

173. Stein, Louise Kathrin Music in the Seventeenth-Century Spanish Secular Theater, 1598–1690. xi+674 pp. Chicago, H. M. Brown, 1987. *DAI* 48A: 510.

"This dissertation is a first step toward placing Spanish theatrical music and musical-theatrical genres in the context of the seventeenth-century European musical revolution. It is an interdisciplinary study in which both the musical and the literary sources have been given careful treatment and includes the identification of a large repertory of extant theatrical songs." (Abs.)

❖ [A] "Un manuscrito de música teatral reaparecido, *Veneno es de amor la envidia*." *RM* 5.2 (1982): 225–33. [Play by Antonio de Zamora, music by Sebastián Durón, first performed 1711.] [B] "Música existente para comedias de Calderón de la Barca." *Calderón: Actas del congreso internacional sobre Calderón y el teatro español del Siglo de Oro, Madrid, 1981.* Ed. Luciano García Lorenzo. 3 vols. Madrid: CSIC, 1983. 1161–72. [C] "La Plática de los Dioses: Music and the Calderonian Court Play, with a Transcription of the Songs from *La estatua de Prometeo* by L. K. Stein." *La estatua de Prometeo.* By Calderón de la Barca. Ed. Margaret R. Greer. Kassel: Reichenberger, 1986. 13–92. [This essay includes "Music and the *Comedia Nueva*" and "Music and Court Theater to c. 1650," in addition to specific treatment of Calderón.] [D] *Songs of Mortals, Dialogue of the Gods: Music and Theatre in Seventeenth-Century Spain.* Oxford: Clarendon P, 1993. 566 pp. [E] "Convenciones musicales en el legado de Juan Hidalgo: El aria declamatoria como tonada persuasiva." *F. Bances Candamo y el teatro musical de su tiempo (1662–1704).* Ed. José Antonio Gómez Rodríguez and Beatriz Martínez del Fresno. Avilés: Ayuntamiento; Oviedo: Universidad de Oviedo, 1994. 177–217.

174. Stern, Charlotte Daniels. Studies on the *Sayagués* in the Early Spanish Drama. 404 pp. Pennsylvania, J. E. Gillet and E. B. Williams, 1960. *DA* 21: 1195.

"Although the Sayagués was a literary jargon which became highly conventionalized in the Spanish *comedia,* it, nevertheless, contains valuable material for investigations in the fields of Spanish dialectology and lexicography." (Abs.)

❖ [A] "*Sayago* and *Sayagués* in Spanish History and Literature." *HR* 29 (1961): 217–37. [B] "Some New Thoughts on the Early Spanish Drama." *BCom* 18.1 (1966): 14–19. [C] "The Early Spanish Drama: From Medieval Ritual to Renaissance Art." *RenD* 6 (1973): 177–201.

175. STURN, SUZANNE. Federico García Lorca and La Barraca: The Influence of Classical Spanish Theatrical Form and the Puppet on the Repertory of La Barraca, and on Lorca's Approach to a Popular Stage. iii+228 pp. Minnesota, J. D. Hurrell, 1984. *DAI* 45A: 2307.

"During the last five years of his life, from 1931 to 1936, Lorca committed himself to creating a new people's theatre by founding an itinerant troupe of players who carried classical Spanish plays to remote regions of the country. Lorca founded La Barraca to carry out his long desired aim of establishing a theatre whose work was to be based on principles of stage poetry. At the same time he hoped to introduce ordinary Spanish people to their classical tradition. To achieve his purpose of returning to some of the fundamental truths in terms of acting and the whole process of theatrical communication he believed that it was necessary to go back to the beginning and reassert elements of style and stage poetry." (Abs.)

176. SUÁREZ GARCÍA, JOSÉ LUIS. La controversia sobre la licitud del teatro en el Siglo de Oro. Edición de un nuevo texto: Discurso segundo de "Noticias de los Juegos Antiguos, Comedias y Fiestas de Toros de Nuestros Tiempos" (Granada, 1642) del Licenciado Juan Herreros de Almansa. 245 pp. Illinois, A. Porqueras-Mayo, 1991. *DAI* 52A: 3955.

"El propósito de esta tesis doctoral es dar una revisión al tema de la controversia sobre la licitud del teatro en el Siglo de Oro con la aportación de un nuevo texto, hasta el momento presente, totalmente inédito y fechado en 1642. Se trata, por una parte, de recoger un material relativamente disperso, agruparlo y analizar su importancia en relación con el teatro del Siglo de Oro; por otra, de presentar un nuevo documento como elemento significativo de la importancia de la teoría dramática de carácter moral en la España de los Siglos XVI y XVII." (Abs.)

❖ [A] "La controversia sobre la licitud del teatro en el reinado de Carlos V." *Looking at the* Comedia *in the Year of the Quincentennial: Proceedings of the 1992 Symposium on Golden Age Drama, El Paso.* Ed. Barbara Mujica and Sharon D. Voros. Lanham: UP of America, 1993. 235–43. [B] "Un nuevo texto de la controversia sobre la licitud del teatro en el Siglo de Oro: Edición del discurso segundo de *Noticia de los juegos antiguos, comedias y fiestas de toros de nuestros tiempos* (Granada, 1642) del licenciado Juan Herreros de Almansa." *Criticón* 59 (1993): 127–59. [C] "Apologistas y detractores del teatro en la segunda mitad del siglo XVI." *Teatro, historia y sociedad. (Seminario internacional sobre teatro del Siglo de Oro español.) Asociación Internacional de Teatro Español y Novohispano del Siglo de Oro, Murcia, 1994.* Ed. Carmen Hernández Valcárcel. Murcia: Universidad de Murcia; Ciudad Juárez: Universidad Autónoma de Ciudad Juárez, 1996. 53–69.

177. Sumner, Gordon Heyward. Una bibliografía anotada de las comedias de santos del siglo diez y siete. ii+117 pp. Florida State, D. H. Darst, 1979. *DAI* 40A: 4079.

"Hagiographic plays, a sub-genre of the Spanish Golden Age theater, number around three-hundred." (Abs.)

❖ [A] "Lope de Vega's *Barlán y Josafá:* The Old World Reborn." *Looking at the* Comedia *in the Year of the Quincentennial: Proceedings of the 1992 Symposium on Golden Age Drama, El Paso.* Ed. Barbara Mujica and Sharon D. Voros. Lanham: UP of America, 1993. 213–18. [B] "Canonicity and the *Comedias de Santos*: Was Cervantes Correct?" *Texto y espectáculo: Proceedings of the Thirteenth International Golden Age Spanish Theatre Symposium, El Paso, 1993.* Ed. José Luis Suárez García. York: Spanish Literature Publications, 1995. 101–06.

178. Surtz, Ronald Edward. Dramatic Convention in the Early Peninsular Theater: Liturgy and Festivities, Time and Space. 306 pp. Harvard, S. Gilman, 1973.

The writer emphasizes "the prospering in Spain of a theater based largely on conventions derived, not from classical drama, but from the liturgy, festivities, and the early native dramatic tradition. The play does not seek to create illusion, to fool the spectators into believing that what they see is real. Rather, the conventions of direct address, the fluid and impressionistic handling of time and space, and topical relevance serve to destroy illusion, to link the action of the play to the present time and space of the audience." (Abs.)

❖ [A] *The Birth of a Theater: Dramatic Convention in the Spanish*

Theater from Juan del Encina to Lope de Vega. Princeton: Princeton Univ., Dept. of Romance Languages and Literatures; Madrid: Castalia, 1979. 205 pp. [B] "Spain: Catalan and Castilian Drama." *The Theater of Medieval Europe: New Research in Early Drama*. Ed. E. Simon. Cambridge: Cambridge UP, 1991. 189–206. [C] *Teatro castellano de la Edad Media*. Ed. R. E. Surtz. Madrid: Taurus, 1992. 203 pp. (Clásicos Taurus 13.)

179. Szmuk, Szilvia E. A Descriptive Catalog of a Collection of *Comedias Sueltas* in the Hispanic Society of America. 2 vols. (x+664 pp.) CUNY, I. Lerner, 1985. *DAI* 46A: 1296. // Rev.: Kurt Reichenberger and Roswitha Reichenberger. *CB* 47 (1987): 205–07.

"The impetus behind this dissertation was to bring to light 475 individual *comedias sueltas* bound in 26 volumes and entered under the single subject heading: 'Teatro español' in the library of the Hispanic Society of America. . . . The emphasis of the study is on *sueltas* as physical objects, i.e., the work constitutes a descriptive bibliography. The descriptions, averaging 3/4 of a page in length, are based on E. M. Wilson's adaptation of Fredson Bowers' rigorous standards for bibliographic description. Each entry begins with a quasi-facsimile transcription of the head-title and includes the following information: printer's serial number; first page or folio number; notes on the performance; author's name; dramatis personae; stage directions; format and collation; first and last two lines of the text; running headline; full colophon; quire catchwords; type measurements; and miscellaneous observations." (Abs.)

❖ [A] Bergman, Hannah E., and Szilvia E. Szmuk. *A Catalogue of* Comedias Sueltas *in the New York Public Library*. 2 vols. London: Grant and Cutler, 1980. (Research Bibliographies Checklists 32.1, 32.2) [B] "Why Collect *Comedias Sueltas*?" *Gazette* 46 (1994): 21–36.

180. Templin, Ernest Hall. The Carolingian Tradition in the Spanish Drama of the Golden Age (Excluding Lope de Vega). 358 pp. Stanford, A. M. Espinosa, 1926. Stanford *Abstracts* 2 (1926–27): 135–38.

"The object of this dissertation is to study the dramatic productions of the Golden Age of Spanish literature (with the exception of the works of Lope de Vega) in which some vestige or reminiscence of the Carolingian tradition appears, either in the development of the plot or in the form of allusions to characters associated with the name of Charlemagne. . . . Aside from [some] relatively sporadical instances of direct French influence, the Spanish drama limits itself to the versions of the ballads of the Carolingian cycle and to the immense body of heterogeneous material contained in the Italian poems and novels of chivalry dealing with Carolingian, or pseudo-Carolingian characters, the most important of which, from the point of view of the influence they exerted on the Spanish theatre, were Bojardo's *Orlando innamorato* and Ariosto's *Orlando furioso*." (Stanford *Abstracts*)

❖ [A] "Carolingian Titles in the Spanish Drama before 1800: Corrections and Additions." *RR* 26 (1935): 345–49. [Apropos A. Ludwig's Lope de Vegas Dramen aus dem karolingischen Sagenkreise—see non-United States dissertations, no. 1564.] [B] "Carolingian Heroes and Ballad Lines in Non-Carolingian Dramatic Literature." *HR* 7 (1939): 35–47.

181. Thomason, Phillip Brian. The *Coliseo de la Cruz*: Madrid's First Enclosed Municipal Playhouse (1737–1859). vi+351 pp. Kentucky, J. J. Allen, 1987. *DAI* 49A: 169.

"The *Coliseo de la Cruz,* the first enclosed public theatre in the city of Madrid, was constructed on the site of the city's first permanent public theatre—the *Corral de la Cruz,* continuing a theatrical tradition that began in 1579. The *corral,* an open air courtyard theatre, was soon surrounded by private boxes in neighboring houses which only intermittently contributed to the municipal coffers. As the management came to control some of these boxes, the loss of profits to private owners became more and more apparent. Recognizing this problem and the ill-repair of the two municipal *corrales,* the city government ordered the *Corral de la Cruz* replaced by a modern enclosed theatre building." (Abs.)

❖ "El Coliseo de la Cruz: Illustrations from the Archivo Municipal de Madrid." *BHS* 70.2 (1993): 237–47.

182. Torreyson, Dorothy. Woman in the Spanish *Comedia* of the Golden Age. 86 pp. Pittsburgh, M. A. DeVitis, 1934. Pittsburgh *Abstracts* 10: 372–76.

"The purpose of this study is to present a picture of woman in the Spanish *Comedia* of the Golden Age. Various investigations on the subject of woman in Spanish literature have been made within recent years: [namely, studies by Edith Cameron, Sadie E. Trachman, Sylvia M. Vollmer, E. H. Templin, Blanca de los Ríos, and Ruth Lansing]. I find, however, nothing definite in the way of a complete and scientific study of woman in the *Comedia* of the Golden Age." (Diss.) This study is based on more than 250 plays by some 30 authors.

183. TRAPIDO, JOEL. An Encyclopaedic Glossary of the Classical and Mediaeval Theatres and of the Commedia dell'Arte. xx+511 pp. Cornell, H. D. Albright, 1942.

❖ Trapido, Joel, et al. *An International Dictionary of Theatre Language.* Westport: Greenwood, 1985. 1,032 pp.

184. TROIANO, JAMES J. Literary Traditions and the Interplay of Illusion and Reality in the Work of Roberto Arlt. 148 pp. SUNY/Buffalo, L. Livingstone, 1973. *DAI* 34A: 3438.

All the plays of Roberto Arlt (1900–42), the Argentinian writer, show the influence of "three principal literary traditions: the Grotesque, Cervantinism, and Pirandellism. . . . Other literary traditions—the Dostoyevskyan theme of crime and punishment, the Calderonian vision of tyrannical despotism in relation to life and dream, the Shakespearian play-within-a-play . . .—occur in isolated plays." (Abs.)

185. TURK, JAMES FRANKLIN. Violence in Spanish Golden Age Drama. ii+264 pp. Maryland, P. Rovner, 1982. *DAI* 43A: 2362.

"Violence, then, as depicted on stage both overtly and covertly, is presented as a significant dramatic resource that when skillfully employed facilitates a work's continued vitality. These artistic violences are seen as creating a universal touchstone capable of eliciting empathy as much today as when these works were first performed. The study includes an appendix comprised of a compendium of acts of violence depicted in a representative selection of plays." (Abs.)

186. URBAIN, HENRI. La mode espagnole dans la comédie en France, de 1645 à 1656. 281 pp. CA/Berkeley, A. Calame, 1970. *DAI* 31A: 3567.

"With regard to the Spanish authors adapted, the end of the Fronde in 1653 is marked by a shift from the school of Lope de Vega to that of Calderón. Among the twenty-five authors used as sources, the most often imitated ones were the latter two major dramatists, as well as Rojas Zorrilla, Castillo Solórzano and Tirso de Molina." (Abs.)

187. Valency, Maurice Jacques. The Tragedies of Herod and Mariamne. Columbia, J. B. Fletcher, 1939. {New York: Columbia UP, 1940. ix+304 pp. (Columbia University Studies in English and Comparative Literature 145.)}

Three Golden Age *comedias* are treated: Lupercio Leonardo de Argensola, *La Alejandra;* Calderón, *El mayor monstruo los celos;* Tirso de Molina, *La vida y muerte de Herodes.*

❖ Rpt. New York: AMS, 1966.

188. Van Kerk, John William. The Figure of Don Carlos in Selected Plays of the Spanish Golden Age. vii+166 pp. Georgia, H. Ziomek, 1978. *DAI* 39A: 4312.

"The plays are *El águila del agua, El segundo Séneca [de España y príncipe don Carlos], El príncipe Don Carlos* written by Luis Vélez de Guevara, Juan Pérez de Montalbán and Diego Jiménez de Enciso respectively." (Abs.)

189. Vicente, Arie I. Lo judío en el teatro español contemporáneo: Mito, antimito e integración. xii+304 pp. Pennsylvania State, M. T. Halsey, 1988. *DAI* 49A: 2681.

"This study, written in Spanish, examines the various implications of the presence of Jewish elements in the Spanish theater since the Middle Ages, and until the institution of democracy in post-Franquist Spain. It contains three parts, developed around one specific theme: the myth which, in Western culture, represents the Jew as a grotesque character and equates this figure with immorality and Evil. The First Part examines the creation of the myth, beginning with the first Spanish drama, *Auto de los Reyes Magos.* Lope de Vega's *El Niño de la Guardia* represents the ritual crime attributed to the Jews and shows the infiltration of the myth into a collectivity through ritual behavior." (Abs.)

❖ *Lo judío en el teatro español contemporáneo.* Madrid: Pliegos, 1991. 200 pp.

190. WARDROPPER, BRUCE WEAR. The Growth of the *Auto Sacramental* before Calderón. xii+306 pp. Pennsylvania, O. H. Green, 1949. ❖ [A] "The Search for a Dramatic Formula for the *Auto Sacramental*." *PMLA* 65 (1950): 1196–1211. [B] "Honor in the Sacramental Plays of Valdivielso and Lope de Vega." *MLN* 66 (1951): 81–88. [C] Dissertation amended and translated as *Introducción al teatro religioso del Siglo de Oro (La evolución del auto sacramental: 1500–1648).* Madrid: Revista de Occidente, 1953. 329 pp.; 2nd ed., rev. Salamanca: Anaya, 1967. 339 pp. "Es nuestro propósito, pues, examinar los comienzos del teatro sacramental y su desarrollo en los siglos XVI y XVII hasta el momento en que Calderón lo hereda y lo convierte casi en monopolio suyo." (Prt. Diss., 1967 ed.) [For a more complete list of this scholar's publications, see *Studies in Honor of Bruce W. Wardropper,* ed. Dian Fox, Harry Sieber, and Robert ter Horst (Newark: Juan de la Cuesta, 1989) xiii–xvii.]

191. WARSHALL, JOAN. Miguel Hernández: From Golden Age Mystery Play to a Drama of Revolutionary Allegory. 170 pp. Columbia, P. W. Silver, 1983. *DAI* 44A: 3707.

"In writing his first drama, *Quién te ha visto y quién te ve y sombra de lo que eras,* Hernández relies heavily on the techniques of the Calderonian *auto sacramental. Los hijos de la piedra* is a transitional work in which Hernández incorporates different elements of the Calderonian *auto* and the honor plays of Calderón and Lope de Vega. As his political philosophy becomes a dominant theme in his theater, Hernández turns to the style of the Lopesque honor plays as he creates *El labrador de más aire*." (Abs.)

192. WEAVER, WILLIAM ROWE. An Introductory Study of Stage Devices in the *Siglo de Oro* Drama. 383 pp. North Carolina, S. E. Leavitt, 1937. North Carolina *Record* no. 323, p. 112.

"This thesis is an introductory study of the devices employed in over one thousand *comedias* of the *Siglo de Oro,* beginning with Cervantes and running through Calderón and his contemporaries. Private or court performances have not been considered, since they seemed unrepresentative of normal production methods. The study has been restricted, consequently, to plays clearly designed for commercial presentation. In these plays the stage directions were examined, and the appearance of equipment mentioned therein was listed. The devices noted have been divided into three major groups: those concerned with the physical features of the stage proper; those consisting of mobile accessories; and those utilizing general staging practises of a material or external nature. The text of the thesis presents a brief analysis of the individual devices, classified in subsections within the three primary divisions. *Appendix A* contains a list of these devices, alphabetically arranged by plays; and *Appendix B* is an index of the code symbols employed to identify the plays." (UNC *Record)*

193. WEBBER, EDWIN JACK. Origins of the Spanish Theater as Related to the Classical Latin Drama. 250 pp. CA/Berkeley, S. G. Morley, 1949. PFE, 6 May 1949.

"The Latin plays, in brief, were significant in this respect: it was in them, to a great extent, that the tradition of tragedy and comedy in dramatic form was preserved almost intact during the Middle Ages. It was through them and the 'dramatic' theory which accompanied them during the Middle Ages that the tradition of tragedy and comedy was transmitted to the Renaissance in the form of the drama. And in the fifteenth and sixteenth centuries it was the Latin plays largely which, still symbolizing and keeping alive the concepts of tragedy and comedy, finally perpetuated them in the modern drama by infusing their spirit and essence, directly and indirectly, into the *Celestina* and into the new comedies of Torres Naharro." (PFE)

❖ [A] "Plautine and Terentian *Cantares* in Fourteenth-Century Spain." *HR* 18 (1950): 93–107. [B] "Tragedy and Comedy in *La Celestina.*" *H* [AATSP] 35 (1952): 318–20. [On the influence of Plautus, Terence, and Seneca in *La Celestina.*] [C] "The Literary Reputation of Terence and Plautus in Medieval and Pre-Renaissance Spain." *HR* 24 (1956): 191–206. [D] "Manuscripts and Early Printed Editions of Terence and Plautus in Spain." *RPh* 11 (1957–58): 29–39. [E] "Comedy as Satire in Hispano-Arabic Spain." *HR* 26 (1958): 1–11. [On classical and nonclassical influences.]

194. WEIGER, JOHN GEORGE. The Relationship of Honor, *Fama,* and Death in the Valencian Drama of the Golden Age. 333 pp. Indiana, C. Ortigoza, 1966. *DA* 27A: 2165.

The playwrights studied are Rey de Artieda, Virués, Tárrega, Aguilar, Guillén de Castro, Beneyto, Boil, and Turia. "To judge by the concepts of honor, *fama* and death as presented in their works, the Valencian writers do not represent a school apart from that of the Golden Age *comedia* in general." (Abs.)

❖ [A] "Los silencios de *Las mocedades del Cid*." *Hispanófila* 23 (1965): 1-7. [B] "Nobility in the Theater of Virués." *RomN* 7.2 (1966): 180-82. [C] "Sobre la originalidad e independencia de Guillén de Castro." *Hispanófila* 31 (1967): 1-15. [D] *The Valencian Dramatists of Spain's Golden Age*. Boston: Twayne, 1976. 169 pp. [E] "Alpha and Omega: Structural Framework of Aguilar's *Comedias*." *BCom* 30.1 (1978): 26-36. [F] *Cristóbal de Virués*. Boston: Twayne, 1978. 166 pp. [G] *Hacia la comedia: De los valencianos a Lope*. Madrid: Cupsa, 1978. 246 pp. (Ensayos de lingüística y crítica literaria 59.) [H] "Initial and Extended Speech in the Theater of Guillén de Castro." *Studies in Honor of Gerald E. Wade*. Ed. Sylvia Bowman et al. Madrid: Porrúa Turanzas, 1979. 217-27. (Studia Humanitatis.) [I] "A Humanist Echo in Virués's *Monserrate*." *RomN* 20 (1979-80): 263-67. [J] "Guillén de Castro: Apostilla cronológica." *Segismundo* 14.27-32 (1980): 103-20. [K] "La conciencia de la nueva orientación teatral de fines del siglo XVI vista a través de la obra de Artieda." *H*[AATSP] 68.1 (1985): 15-21.

195. WEINER, JACK. The Spanish Golden Age Theater in Tsarist Russia (1672-1917). 286 pp. Indiana, J. Dowling and W. Barnstone, 1968. *DA* 29A: 3162-63.

"The role of Spain's Golden Age theater in Tsarist Russia, although very limited in the eighteenth century, became more and more important in the nineteenth century, and by 1917 it had played a significant role in the development of Russian realistic and symbolist theaters." (Abs.)

❖ [A] "Translations of Spanish Golden Age Plays in Tsarist Russia: A Bibliography." *Theatre Documentation* 1.1 (1968): 31-34. [B] "The Introduction of Spain's Golden Age Theater into Russia (1672-1800)." *AION-SR* 11 (1969): 193-223. [C] "Russian and Soviet Criticism of the Spanish *Comedia*." *Yearbook of General and Comparative Literature* 18 (1969): 48-69. [D] "The Death of Philip IV of Spain and the Early Russian Theatrical Repertoire." *TR*

10 (1970): 179–85. [E] *Mantillas in Muscovy: The Spanish Golden Age Theater in Tsarist Russia, 1672–1917.* Lawrence: Univ. of Kansas, 1970. 161 pp. (Humanistic Studies 41.) [F] "El teatro español del siglo de oro en Rusia durante la primera mitad del siglo XIX." *CHA* 241 (1970): 46–76. [G] "Lope de Vega's *Fuenteovejuna* under Tsars, Commissars, and the Second Spanish Republic (1931–1939)." *AION-SR* 24 (1982): 167–223. [H] Spanish version of publication E: *Mantillas en Moscovia: El teatro del Siglo de Oro español en la Rusia de los zares (1672–1917).* Trans. Sergio Pinero and Celia Pinero. Barcelona: PPU; Kassel: Reichenberger, 1988. 296 pp. (Colección ediciones y estudios. Estudios 3.) [I] Reichenberger, Kurt, and Juventino Caminero. *Calderón dramaturgo.* With a study by J. Weiner on Calderón in Russia. Kassel: Reichenberger, 1991. 247 pp. (Teatro del Siglo de Oro. Estudios de literatura 8.) [J. W.'s study is entitled "Calderón de la Barca in Russia (1672–1984)," pp. 191–247.]

196. Wertheimer, Elaine C. Honor, Love and Religion in the Theater before Lope de Vega. 351 pp. CUNY, A. A. Sicroff, 1975. *DAI* 35A: 7927.

The playwrights studied are Encina, Lucas Fernández, Torres Naharro, Vicente, and Sánchez de Badajoz. The writer, following Américo Castro's views, sees "the generative forces of this theater" in "the conflict between Old and New Christians, and the need to express this conflict." (Abs.)

❖ "Sánchez de Badajoz and the Reconciliation of the Two Testaments." *RF* 91.1–2 (1979): 24–42. "The concern with the problem of Old and New Christians is a common factor in the works of the pre-Lope dramatists Juan del Encina, Lucas Fernández, Gil Vicente, Bartolomé de Torres Naharro and Diego Sánchez de Badajoz."

197. White Navarro, Mary Gladys. The Imaginary Space of America in the Golden Age Drama. 228 pp. Stanford, A. Forcione and M. Predmore, 1989. *DAI* 50A: 3797–98.

"The aim of this dissertation is to examine the shift in the dramatic representation of the New World from the sixteenth to the seventeenth centuries in the Spanish Theater. . . . The first chapter on Micael de Carvajal's *Cortes de la Muerte* analyzes the early humanist vision of America. Subsequent chapters on the plays on America by Lope de Vega and Calderón de la Barca concentrate on the reassessment of this early vision." (Abs.)

198. WHITEHOUSE, VICTOR. The Theory of the Divine Right of Kings in the Spanish Drama of the Golden Age. 311 pp. Harvard, J. D. M. Ford, 1929. Harvard *Summaries* (1929): 192–95.

"Absolutism is shown in various plays by Lope de Vega, Tirso de Molina and Moreto y Cabaña, especially in plays dealing with feudal barons who attempt to mock the king's power and are brought to task for their presumption. The plays of the great dramatists of the seventeenth century present conflicting points of view." *(Summaries)*

199. WILLIAMS, JEROME. El teatro de evangelización en México durante el siglo XVI: Reseña histórico-literaria. 249 pp. Yale, M. Durán, 1980. *DAI* 41A: 5117.

"Described in Chapter I are the precedents that characterize peninsular drama before the sixteenth century and that made possible the rooting of the genre in Mexico." (Abs.)

❖ Williams, Jerry M. *El teatro del México colonial: época misionera.* New York: Peter Lang, 1992. 162 pp. (Ibérica 4.)

200. WILLIAMS, RONALD BOAL. The Staging of Plays in the Spanish Peninsula Prior to 1555. Iowa, R. E. House, 1930. {UISSLL, 1935, no. 5. 142 pp.}

The eight chapters that follow the introduction are entitled "Juan del Encina," "Lucas Fernández," "Gil Vicente," "Sánchez de Badajoz," "Other Followers of Juan del Encina," "Bartolomé de Torres Naharro," "Immediate Followers of Torres Naharro," and "Later Scenic Developments." In this "revision" of the author's doctoral thesis, "quotations, which comprised about one half of the original dissertation, have been greatly reduced in number. An effort has been made, then, to present significant findings and to suppress minor details." (Prt. Diss.)

201. WYNNE, CHARLES EDWARD. An Annotated Bibliography of the Biblical Theater of the *Siglo de Oro.* 284 pp. Cincinnati, J. O. Valencia, 1983. *DAI* 44A: 1811.

"Chapter I deals with Old Testament drama of the Siglo de

Oro. It is divided (as are all the chapters) into the following sections: manuscripts and editions, articles and doctoral dissertations. Chapter II deals with New Testament drama of the Siglo de Oro, and the last chapter treats the *autos sacramentales* exclusively. Our study concludes with an alphabetical index of the authors and a general bibliography." (Abs.)

202. YUDIN, FLORENCE LILLIAN. Genre Identity in the Golden Age: The Post-Cervantine *Novela Corta* and the *Comedia*. v+126 pp. Illinois, M. A. Morínigo, 1964. *DA* 25: 1223–24.

"The identification of the *novela corta* with dramatic function was demonstrated in an analysis of Lope's *Las fortunas de Diana,* Castillo's *La cautela sin efeto,* and Salas' *El pescador venturoso*." (Abs.)

❖ [A] The *Novela Corta* as *Comedia:* Lope's *Las fortunas de Diana*." *BHS* 45 (1968):181–88. [B] "Theory and Practice of the *Novela Comediesca*." *RF* 81 (1969): 585–94.

ACEVEDO, PEDRO PABLO DE (1522–1573)

203. SAA, ORLANDO EMMANUEL. El teatro escolar de los Jesuitas: La obra dramática de Pedro Pablo de Acevedo (1522–1573). 299 pp. Tulane, D. W. McPheeters, 1973. *DAI* 34A: 2807.

This study "includes Acevedo's complete dramatic output, a total of eight plays, under the title of 'Comoediae.' . . . Chapter III . . . studies the affinities with contemporary authors such as Erasmus, Lope de Rueda, Torres Naharro, Juan del Encina, Gil Vicente, and Garcilaso de la Vega." (Abs.)

❖ *El teatro escolar de los jesuitas en España.* New Brunswick: SLUSA, 1990. 218 pp.

AGUILAR, GASPAR DE (1561–1623)

204. LITTLEJOHN, DAVID HALLAM. The Dramatic Works of Gaspar de Aguilar. 328 pp. North Carolina, A. V. Ebersole, 1973. *DAI* 34A: 6648.

"It is concluded that, while the lack of a chronology of his plays makes impossible a definite statement concerning his influence on Lope, it is quite possible that Aguilar deserves credit as a contributor to the genesis of the *comedia* in Spain." (Abs.)

Anonymous

205. Asturias, [Sister] Rosario María, SNJM. A Critical Edition and Study of the Play *El rey don Pedro en Madrid y el Infanzón de Illescas.* vi+553 pp. Southern California, E. W. Hesse, 1963. *DA* 24: 5378–79.

The play has been attributed to Calderón, Claramonte, Tirso, and Lope de Vega. ". . . the division of opinion concerning the play's paternity continues to the present." The basic text is followed by the collation of variants, "and, in an appendix, the Calderón text, which differs so much that it is given in its entirety." (Abs.)

206. Babcock, James Chester. A Critical Edition of *La famosa comedia del çerco y libertad de Sebilla por el rey don Fernando el Santo* (MS of 1595). xix+170 pp. Iowa, R. E. House, 1935. Iowa *Program,* July 1934.

[For the complete entry, see no. 234.]

207. Barton, Donald K. A Diplomatic Edition of *La vida y muerte de San Gerónimo* from Manuscript 14767 in the Biblioteca Nacional, Madrid. vi+213 pp. Iowa, R. Davis, 1943. Iowa *Abstracts* 7: 939.

The play "deals with the life of Saint Jerome from the time of his last visit to Rome (381–385) until his death at Bethlehem about 420." (Abs.)

208. Buck, Vera Helen. Four *Autos Sacramentales* from Manuscript 14864, Biblioteca Nacional, Madrid, Edited with Preface, Introductions, and Notes. 98 pp. Iowa, R. E. House, 1933. {*Four autos sacramentales of 1590:* Sacramento de la Eucaristía, La conbersión de Sant Pablo, El Castillo de la Fee, El Testamento de Christo. UISSLL, 1937, no. 7. 98 pp.}

Some of the linguistic annotations found in the original dissertation have been eliminated in this publication. The edition is based on photostatic copies of the plays in BNM MS 14.864.

The first three plays were probably written between 1575 and 1590; the fourth one is dated 1582. (Prt. Diss.)

209. COOKE, WILLIAM PENDLETON. An Annotated Edition of the Play *Los Monteros de Espinosa.* 255 pp. Minnesota, R. Floripe(?), 1968. *DAI* 30A: 316.

The text of this anonymous *comedia* is based on a microfilm copy of the manuscript in the BN, Madrid, and a *suelta* owned by the University of Minnesota library. This *comedia* has been attributed to Lope de Vega and to others; its authorship remains uncertain. (Abs.)

❖ *Los Monteros de Espinosa: Comedia anónima del siglo XVIII.* Study and critical ed. by W. P. Cooke. Madrid: Playor, 1973. 207 pp. (Colección Plaza Mayor Scholar.) The writer states that "metrical chronology and paleography both deny Lope's authorship. . . . *Los Monteros de Espinosa* is constructed after the fashion of the Golden Age *capa y espada* type."

210. CORBATÓ, HERMENEGILDO. Los misterios del Corpus de Valencia: Edición diplomática, notas y estudio. 302 pp. CA/Berkeley, S. G. Morley, 1930.

This dissertation is no longer available at Berkeley.

❖ [A] *Los misterios del Corpus de Valencia.* Berkeley: Univ. of California, 1932. 172 pp. (UCPMP 16.1) The writer edits three mystery plays *(Misterio de San Cristóbal, Misterio de Adán y Eva,* and *Misterio de Herodes)* on the basis of a MS copy made in 1672 of an older MS now lost. The Valencian texts are written in language that, according to Corbató, is generally characteristic of the end of the fifteenth century. [J. E. Gillet, *HR* 1 (1933): 260–63.] [B] "Notas sobre *El Misterio de Elche* y otros dramas sagrados de Valencia." *H*[AATSP] 15 (1932): 103–08. [C] "Misterios y autos del teatro misionero en Méjico durante el siglo XVI y sus relaciones con los de Valencia." *ACCV*, Anejo 1 (1949). 23 pp.

211. DEVINE, MARY VIRGINIA. A Critical Edition of the Anonymous Play *El vandido más honrado, y que tuvo mejor fin, Matheo Vicente Benet, Primera Parte,* Together with a Study of the Figure of the *Bandido Generoso* in the *Comedia* of the Spanish Golden Age and the First Half of the Eighteenth Century. 323 pp. Wayne State, H. N. Bershas, 1972. *DAI* 33A: 6350.

"In order to produce the critical edition, the writer obtained and compared the four known surviving *sueltas* of this play. Due to its superiority to the other texts, the *suelta* published by the Viuda de Joseph de Orga at Valencia in 1769 was selected to serve as the basis of the writer's edition. The authorship of the play is uncertain, but the writer believes it to be the work of Gabriel Suárez, an obscure Valencian dramatist active during the late seventeenth and early eighteenth centuries." (Abs.)

212. DILLE, GLEN FRANK. A Critical Edition of the *Comedia Serafina.* 260 pp. Tulane, D. W. McPheeters, 1973. *DAI* 34A: 5164–65.

"... the text of the *Serafina* is based on photostats of the earliest known printing (1521). ... The important variants of the edition of 1546 are included in the notes to the text." (Abs.) ❖ [A] "The *Comedia Serafina* and Its Relationship to *La Celestina.*" *Celestinesca* 1.2 (1977): 15–20. [B] "Concerning the Authorship of the *Comedias Thebaida* and *Serafina.*" *JHP* 1 (1977): 187–93. [C] *La comedia llamada Serafina: An Anonymous Humanistic Comedy of 1521.* Ed. G. F. Dille. Carbondale: Southern Illinois UP, 1979. 114 pp.

213. DILLINGHAM, MARY JULIA WALL. *El martirio de Sant Lorençio, comedia y auto:* An Edition of a Sixteenth-Century Spanish Manuscript. v+199 pp. Chicago, G. T. Northup, 1932. Chicago *Abstracts* 9: 413–17.

The edition is based on BNM MS 14.684, dated 1590. The writer comments that the play "represents the flotsam and jetsam of a genre probably more prolific than meritorious." (Abs.)

214. DOUGLASS, PHILIP EARLE. The *Comedia Ypolita,* Edited with Introduction and Notes. Pennsylvania, J. P. W. Crawford, 1929. {Philadelphia: Univ. of Pennsylvania, 1929. 98 pp.}

"The text of the *Comedia Ypolita* is edited from a photostat copy of an edition preserved at the British Museum (A-H^6I^4)." (Prt. Diss.)

215. ENGERRAND, GABRIEL HORACE. A Diplomatic Edition of the *Comedia de la vida y muerte de San Agustín,* and the *Comedia de la vida y muerte del Santo Fray Diego.* 281 pp. Iowa, R. Davis, 1941. Iowa *Abstracts* 3, part 4, pp. 367–73.

The edition is based on BNM MS 14.767, written "in a clearly legible handwriting of the seventeenth century." Fray Diego is San Diego de Alcalá. (Abs.)

216. Gillespie, Ruth Caroline. A Study of the Authorship and Sources of *Nuestra Señora de la Peña de Francia* and Its Relation to *La Peña de Francia* of Tirso de Molina, with Texts, Notes and Commentary. 440 pp. Yale, 1929.

[For the complete entry, see no. 623.]

217. Hawley, Don Carlton. An Edition of *Las hazañas del Cid, y su muerte, con la tomada de Valencia.* vi+319 pp. Iowa, E. V. DeChasca, 1961. *DA* 22: 2793–94.

The printed edition of 1603 is collated with Hämel's Halle edition of 1910 and the Academy edition of 1929. "In the opinion of this writer, the attribution [to Lope de Vega] is erroneous. Lope himself rejected it explicitly. Moreover, the style and language of the play are not Lope's." (Abs.)

218. Horvath, Sabine. Königtum und Tyrannei, Rebellion und Verschwörung als Themen im europäischen Drama, von der Spät-Renaissance bis zum Ende des siebzehnten Jahrhunderts. 505 pp. CUNY, L. Bergel, 1975. *DAI* 36A: 882–83.

The relevant *comedias* are Anon., *El alcalde de Zalamea;* Calderón, *El alcalde de Zalamea;* Rojas Zorrilla, *Del rey abajo ninguno;* and Lope de Vega, *Fuenteovejuna* and *Los Tellos de Meneses.* "The survey of . . . plays from five countries allows the following conclusion: All of them are to a greater or lesser extent a reaction to Machiavelli's thought: His concept of reason of state and the tendency to separate politics and ethics in matters of statecraft." (Abs.)

219. Kemp, Alice Bowdoin. Critical Text and Study of Three *Autos Sacramentales* from Manuscript 14864, Biblioteca Nacional, Madrid. ix+217 pp. Iowa, R. E. House, 1933.

❖ *Three Autos Sacramentales of 1590* (La degollaçión de Sant Jhoan El rrescate del alma, Los amores del alma con el Prínçipe de la luz). Ed., with introd. and notes, by A. B. Kemp. Toronto: U of Toronto P, 1936. 134 pp.

"The three plays here edited are the first, second and fifth of a collection of eleven hitherto unpublished *autos sacramentales* of the late sixteenth century [BNM MS 14.864]." The first play exists also in another manuscript at the BNM, where it is cataloged as 3.672. "The present edition has been made from photostatic copies of the above-mentioned manuscripts, together with three unpublished Master's theses, in which helpful preliminary studies have been made." (Iowa, 1928 and 1929) In this printed version the linguistic annotation found in the original dissertation has been considerably reduced. (Prt. Diss.)

220. LAAS, ILSE GERTRUD PROBST. *Comedia yntitulada del tirano Rrey Corbanto,* Edited with Introduction and Notes. 111 pp. Iowa, R. E. House, 1928. {UISSLL, 1931, no. 2. 111 pp. (University of Iowa Studies, ns 210.)}

The edition is based on a photostatic reproduction of BNM MS 15.594, which includes a "carta de remisión," dated 4 May 1585.

❖ Microfiche ed. 1976.

221. LUENOW, PAUL FERDINAND, JR. An Edition of *Don Gil de la Mancha.* 366 pp. New Mexico, R. R. MacCurdy, 1955. *DA* 15: 1846–47.

The text is based on (1) a *suelta* edition, (2) a scribe's copy, and (3) an actor-adapter's version. The play has been attributed to Lope de Vega, Rojas Zorrilla, Castillo Solórzano, and Claramonte, but the writer concludes that "positive identification of author is impossible with the information presently at hand." (Abs.)

222. MOUSOLITE, PETER STANLEY. A Diplomatic Edition of the *Comedia de Nuestra Señora de Lapa y un milagro que hiço.* vi+127 pp. Iowa, R. Davis, 1948. Iowa *Abstracts* 7: 957–62.

The edition is based on BNM MS 14.767. ". . . the play was probably written in the 1580's or early 1590's." (Abs.)

223. STURDEVANT, WINIFRED. The *Misterio de los Reyes Magos:* Its Position in the Development of the Mediaeval Legend of the Three Kings. [4]+118 pp. Johns Hopkins, E. C. Armstrong, D. S. Blondheim, and H. C. Lancaster, 1920.

❖ [A] Title as is. Baltimore: Johns Hopkins UP, 1927. 130 pp. (Johns Hopkins Studies in Romance Literatures and Languages 10.) ["The similarities between the *Reyes Magos* and the whole tradition of French, English and German Three Kings plays places it unmistakably in that dramatic tradition."] [B] Rpt. New York: Johnson, 1973. 130 pp.

224. TYRE, CARL ALLEN. Three *Autos Sacramentales* from Manuscript

14864, Biblioteca Nacional, Madrid, Edited with Preface, Introduction, and Notes. Iowa, R. E. House, 1935. {*Religious Plays of 1590:* Comedia de la historia y adoración de los tres Rreyes magos, Comedia de buena y santa doctrina, Comedia del nacimiento y vida de Judas. UISSLL, 1938, no. 8. 112 pp.}

The edition is based on photostatic copies of the plays in BNM MS 14.864. They were written "between 1575 and 1590." According to the writer, "helpful preliminary studies of the three plays of the present edition have been made in unpublished Master's theses [Iowa, 1926, 1928, 1929]." In this publication the extensive linguistic annotation of the original dissertation has been reduced. (Prt. Diss.)

Arce, Pedro de (17th c.)

225. Lange, John Baptist. Pedro de Arce's *El príncipe incógnito:* A Historical and Paleographical Edition. 205 pp. St. Louis, R. Mazza, 1971. *DAI* 32A: 4616.

The text is based on "the only known extant version [a manuscript] in the National Library in Madrid." (Abs.)

Arguijo, Juan de (1567–1622)

226. Garzón-Blanco, Armando Ignacio Dionisio. The Inaugural Production of the Spanish Jesuit *Tragedia de San Hermenegildo,* Seville, 1590. xvi+232 pp. Louisiana State, G. L. Doty, 1976. *DAI* 37A: 6845–46.

[For the complete entry, see no. 227.] Juan de Arguijo was one of the three authors of this play.

Ávila, Hernando de (1558–after 1601)

227. Garzón-Blanco, Armando Ignacio Dionisio. The Inaugural Production of the Spanish Jesuit *Tragedia de San Hermenegildo,*

Seville, 1590. xvi+232 pp. Louisiana State, G. L. Doty, 1976. *DAI* 37A: 6845–46.

The writer concludes that this play, "considered the most important example of Spanish scholastic drama," was "the result of the collaborative efforts of Father Hernando Dávila, SJ, Father Melchor de la Cerda, SJ, and Don Juan de Arguijo." (Abs.) [For the form of this playwright's name, *Ávila* vs. *Dávila,* see Garzón-Blanco's 1979 article below as well as items 269 and 270 in *BCom* 46 (1994) annual bibliography on the *comedia*.]

❖ [A] "Note on the Authorship of the Spanish Jesuit Play of *San Hermenegildo,* 1580." *ThS* 15 (1974): 79–83. [B] "The Jesuit *Tragedia de San Hermenegildo*, Seville, 1590." *EIRC* 3 (1976): 1–19. [C] "La *Tragedia de San Hermenegildo* en el teatro y en el arte." *Estudios sobre literatura y arte dedicados al profesor Emilio Orozco Díaz.* Ed. Antonio Gallego Morell, Andrés Soria, and Nicolás Marín. 3 vols. Granada: Universidad de Granada, 1979. 2: 91–108. [Hernando de Ávila is the "escritor principal de la obra."] [D] "The Spanish Jesuit *Comedia de Sancta Catarina*, Córdoba, 1597." *LA CHISPA '82: Selected Proceedings of the Third Louisiana Conference on Hispanic Languages and Literatures.* Ed. Harry L. Kirby. Baton Rouge: Louisiana State Univ., 1984. 98–111.

Bances Candamo, Francisco Antonio de (1662–1709)

228. García-Castañón, Santiago. Estudio y edición crítica de *Sangre, valor y fortuna,* de Francisco Bances Candamo. 253 pp. Illinois, A. Porqueras-Mayo, 1992. *DAI* 53A: 2395.

"I offer my own edition of the text of *Sangre, valor y fortuna,* which is the first modern attempt to edit the [seventeenth-century] manuscript and correct the copyist's errors, thus presenting the play as close as possible to Bances Candamo's original intentions. Completing the edition is the critical apparatus, consisting of thorough explanatory footnotes and a bibliography—the most extensive about Bances Candamo up to date." (Abs.)

❖ [A] "Algunas consideraciones sobre la poesía de Bances

Candamo." *BIEA* 136 (1990): 707–15. [B] Bances Candamo, F. *Sangre, valor y fortuna*. Introducción y notas de S. García Castañón. Oviedo: Instituto de Estudios Asturianos, 1991. 196 pp. (Biblioteca literaria asturiana 5.) [C] "Corrientes del pensamiento maquiavélico en una obra inédita de Bances Candamo." *CAld* 17.1 (1991): 19–29. [Apropos *Sangre, valor y fortuna*.] [D] "La autoridad real en el teatro de Bances Candamo." *Looking at the* Comedia *in the Year of the Quincentennial: Proceedings of the 1992 Symposium on Golden Age Drama, El Paso.* Ed. Barbara Mujica and Sharon D. Voros. Lanham: UP of America, 1993. 229–34.

229. Herrera Oviedo, Antonio María. Edición crítica y anotada del manuscrito autógrafo *El sastre del campillo,* de Luis de Belmonte Bermúdez. x+336 pp. Oregon, P. J. Powers, 1973. DAI 34A: 5924.

[For the complete entry, see no. 232.] The writer provides a detailed study of Bances Candamo's adaptation of this play.

Barrios, Miguel de (1625?–1701)
(Daniel Leví de Barrios)

230. Peña, Ervie. *El español de Orán* by Miguel de Barrios: A Critical Edition and Study. vii+481 pp. Southern California, J. D. Smith, 1971. *DAI* 32A: 4574–75.

The edition of this *comedia de capa y espada* is based on the *princeps* (Bruselas, 1665) that has been collated with a *suelta* (Madrid, 1720?). (Abs.)

231. Rebollo Lieberman, Julia. El teatro alegórico-religioso de Miguel (Daniel Leví) de Barrios y la colonia de sefarditas de Amsterdam en el siglo XVII. 270 pp. Yale, M. Durán, 1989. *DAI* 51A: 177.

Chapter 4 includes "an introduction to Barrios' allegorical plays . . . ; a study of the allegorical comedy *Contra la verdad no hay fuerza,* which derives its technique from Calderón's *auto sacramental Los encantos de la culpa* . . . ; and a study of *Jonen Dalim,* a one-act play which also derives its technique from the Spanish *autos sacramentales.*" The dissertation contains, as well, an annotated edition of *Jonen Dalim*. (Abs.)

❖ [A] "*Contra la verdad no hay fuerza:* Comedia alegórica de

Miguel (Daniel Leví) de Barrios." *Actes del simposi internacional sobre cultura sefardita.* Ed. Joseph Ribera. Barcelona: Facultat de Filologia, 1993. 181–96. [B] Barrios, M. de. *El teatro alegórico de Miguel (Daniel Leví) de Barrios.* Study and ed. by J. Rebollo Lieberman. Newark: Juan de la Cuesta, 1996. 234 pp.

Belmonte Bermúdez, Luis de (1587?–1650?)

232. Herrera Oviedo, Antonio María. Edición crítica y anotada del manuscrito autógrafo *El sastre del campillo,* de Luis de Belmonte Bermúdez. x+336 pp. Oregon, P. J. Powers, 1973. *DAI* 34A: 5924.

"The text . . . is based on the only extant manuscript of this play ever signed by Belmonte Bermúdez [BNM MS 3220]." It is collated with printed editions of 1633 and 1930. Also studied in detail is the adaptation by Francisco de Bances Candamo. (Abs.)

233. Kincaid, William Abraham. The Life and Works of Luis de Belmonte Bermúdez. 307 pp. CA/Berkeley, S. G. Morley, 1928. PFE, December 1927.

"In this thesis a study has been made of all available works of Belmonte, in manuscript or in printed editions, special attention having been paid to the discussion of authorship in the doubtful plays. The candidate contests the attribution to Belmonte of the two plays . . . [*El diablo predicador* and *La renegada de Valladolid*]." (PFE)

❖ "The Life and Works of Luis de Belmonte Bermúdez (1587?–1650?)." *RH* 74 (1928): 1–258.

Benavides, Luis de (16th c.)

234. Babcock, James Chester. A Critical Edition of *La famosa comedia del çerco y libertad de Sebilla por el rey don Fernando el Santo* (MS of 1595). xix+170 pp. Iowa, R. E. House, 1935. Iowa *Program,* July 1934.

The edition is based on "a single MS in the Biblioteca Nacional in Madrid." It "bears a final note indicating that the play was presented in Valladolid, in the year 1595, by the famous actor-manager Villegas." (*Program*) Editorial note: The final note also states: "Es de Luis de Venabides este original."

Bermúdez, Jerónimo (1530?–1590?)

235. Miller, Gustavus Hindman. A Comparison of Late Renaissance and Early Baroque Aesthetics as Seen through Two Dramatic Interpretations of the Inés de Castro Story. 149 pp. Michigan, F. Sánchez y Escribano and C. N. Staubach, 1956. *DA* 17: 144–45.

[For the complete entry, see no. 478.] One of the plays is Jerónimo Bermúdez's *Nise lastimosa* (1577).

236. Triwedi, Mitchell David. The *Nise lastimosa* of Jerónimo Bermúdez: A Critical Edition Together with an Introductory Study and Notes. vi+468 pp. Southern California, D. E. McMahon, 1958. USC *Abstracts of Dissertations* (1958): 88–89.

The edition is based on the *princeps* (Madrid, 1577). ". . . significant variants have been recorded from editions published by López de Sedano (. . . 1772) and Eugenio de Ochoa (. . . 1838), as well as from a nineteenth-century manuscript copy now in the Biblioteca Nacional [Madrid]." (Abs.)

❖ [A] "Notes on Bermúdez's *Nise laureada* and Dolce's Paraphrase of Seneca's *Thyestes*." *PQ* 42 (1963): 97–102. [B] "Notas para una biografía de Jerónimo Bermúdez." *Hispanófila* 29 (1967): 1–9. [C] Bermúdez, J. *Primeras tragedias españolas*. Ed. M. D. Triwedi. Chapel Hill: Univ. of North Carolina, Dept. of Romance Languages; Madrid: Castalia, 1975. 223 pp. (Estudios de Hispanófila 34.)

Calderón de la Barca, Pedro (1600–1681)

237. Acker, Thomas Saunders. The Imagery of Baltasar Gracián

and Pedro Calderón de la Barca as Related to the Paintings of Diego Velázquez. xviii+237 pp. Temple, H. Galilea, 1992. *DAI* 53A: 4343.

"This dissertation discusses the imagery of the painter in the context of his times by relating it to the imagery in the literary works of two of his contemporaries: Pedro Calderón de la Barca and Baltasar Gracián. The syncretism of Christian and Classical symbols is a principal theme used to relate these three luminaries. Five chapters study topics in the works of the three which include realism, Habsburg glorification, religious themes and mythological subjects." (Abs.)

238. AMADEI DE PULICE, MARIA ALICIA. Hacia Calderón: Las bases teórico-artísticas del teatro barroco español. viii+262 pp. CA/Los Angeles, C. B. Johnson, 1981. *DAI* 42A: 1655.

"Este estudio trata de enmendar las deficiencias creadas con previos acercamientos 'literarios' al teatro calderoniano que han omitido el hecho importante que el teatro es un género politécnico, en el cual convergen juntamente con el texto poético, los sistemas fónicos y visuales que se perciben en la representación. El análisis confirma la presencia de estos dos sistemas de comunicación extratextuales con la aportación de datos históricos concluyentes que provienen de la preceptiva teatral que acompañaba al naciente género escénico, el *stile rappresentativo,* cuyas raíces se encuentran en Italia." (Abs.)

❖ [A] "El *stile rappresentativo* en la *comedia de teatro* de Calderón." *Approaches to the Theater of Calderón.* Ed. Michael D. McGaha. Washington: UP of America, 1982. 215-29. [B] "Realidad y apariencia: Valor político de la perspectiva escénica en el teatro cortesano." *Calderón: Actas del congreso internacional sobre Calderón y el teatro español del Siglo de Oro, Madrid, 1981.* Ed. Luciano García Lorenzo. 3 vols. Madrid: CSIC, 1983. 1519-31. [C] *Calderón y el Barroco: Exaltación y engaño de los sentidos.* Philadelphia: Benjamins, 1990. 221 pp.+illus. (PUMRL 31.)

239. ANDERSON, VERNON LOCKWOOD. Hugo von Hofmannsthal and Pedro Calderón de la Barca: A Comparative Study. vi+198 pp. Stanford, K. F. Reinhardt, 1953. *DA* 14: 523.

"It was Hofmannsthal's intention to establish Calderón in the permanent repertoire of the Austrian theater, and to this end he recast four of the Spaniard's dramas: a *comedia de capa y espada (La dama duende),* an *auto sacramental (El gran teatro del mundo),* a *comedia mitológica (La hija del aire),* and a *comedia filosófica (La vida es sueño).* The two-fold objective of this investigation was: first, to compare the plays of Hofmannsthal with Calderón's original dramas with respect to plot, characterization, theme, tributary ideas, dramatic structure, and language; and second, to evaluate and interpret the principal differences in terms of the distinctive temperament, artistic talent, literary taste, and philosophic viewpoint of each of the two poets." The Hofmannsthal recasts corresponding to the above-mentioned Calderonian dramas are *Dame Kobold, Das Salzburger Grosse Welttheater, Semiramis: Die beiden Götter,* and *Der Turm.* (Abs.)

240. ANDRIST, DEBRA DIANE. Love, Honor, and the Male-Female Relationship in Representative Authors of the Spanish *Comedia.* 265 pp. SUNY/Buffalo, C. Bandera, 1986. *DAI* 47A: 542–43.

"In short, using Girardian terminology, I will prove that deceit plus desire equals violence in the Comedia. And, violence is the key, structuring element of the created society." The writer bases her analysis on selected plays of Calderón and of Lope de Vega. (Abs.)

❖ *Deceit Plus Desire Equals Violence: A Girardian Study of the Spanish* Comedia. New York: Peter Lang, 1989. 229 pp. (American University Studies, ser. 2. Romance Languages and Literature 93.)

241. ASTURIAS, [SISTER] ROSARIO MARÍA, SNJM. A Critical Edition and Study of the Play *El rey don Pedro en Madrid y el Infanzón de Illescas.* vi+553 pp. Southern California, E. W. Hesse, 1963. *DA* 24: 5378–79.

[For the complete entry, see no. 205.]

242. BACALSKI, ROBERT RUDOLF. A Critical Edition of *El jardín de Falerina* by Francisco de Rojas Zorrilla, Antonio Coello y Ochoa, and Pedro Calderón de la Barca with Introduction and Notes. 351 pp. New Mexico, R. R. MacCurdy, 1972. *DAI* 33A: 5712.

The text is based on a microfilm of MS 17.320 in the BN, Madrid. This *comedia* was later recast by Calderón "as a *zarzuela* (1648) and an *auto sacramental* (1675), both with the same title." (Abs.)

243. BANDLER, JANE YANKOVIC. Comic Mechanisms in the Cape and

Sword Plays of Calderón de la Barca. 234 pp. Yale, M. Durán, 1975. *DAI* 36A: 2873–74.

"The essence of Calderón's success as a comic playwright was his ability to create a kind of balance in his use of comic devices. He was a master of intrigue who used physical comedy as a complement and wit as an embellishment." (Abs.)

244. BARRACHINA, RAYMOND. El libre albedrío en ocho dramas religiosos de Calderón. 297 pp. NYU, A. Regalado, 1986. *DAI* 47A: 1346.

The eight plays are *La cisma de Ingalaterra, El purgatorio de San Patricio, La devoción de la Cruz, Los dos amantes del cielo, El José de las mujeres, El mágico prodigioso, El gran príncipe de Fez, Las cadenas del demonio.*

245. BENEDETTI, THOMAS K. The Dramatic Components of Calderón's *Comedias Mitológicas.* vi+214 pp. Temple, A. Lewis Galanes, 1983. *DAI* 44A: 2157.

"Four plays . . . are discussed in light of the playwright's philosophical and theological perceptions and their relationship to the cultural canon of seventeenth-century Spain." (Abs.)

246. BERMÚDEZ, PEDRO PABLO. La imaginación escénica del teatro sacramental de Calderón. 224 pp. Virginia, A. L. Cilveti, 1969. *DAI* 31A: 1260.

"The purpose of this dissertation is not to work out a theory of the scenic imagination in Calderón's *autos,* but rather to discover such imagination 'at work' in four of his *autos sacramentales.*" The four *autos* are *Las órdenes militares, El pintor de su deshonra, El nuevo hospicio de pobres,* and *El año santo en Madrid.* (Abs.)

247. BIGELOW, GARY E. *De un castigo, tres venganzas* and the Relationship of Justice and Vengeance in the Theater of Calderón: A Critical and Historical Study. 122 pp. Pittsburgh, G. Sobejano, 1973. *DAI* 35A: 1086.

". . . the following plays have been studied in relation to *De un castigo, tres venganzas: Luis Pérez el Gallego, Amar después de la muerte, El alcalde de Zalamea, Las tres justicias en una,* and *La niña de Gómez Arias.*" The writer observes that "where both justice and vengeance occur together, Calderón usually prefers an exemplary public justice to a cruel, private vengeance." (Abs.)

❖ [A] "A Note on the Date and Editions of Calderón's *De un castigo, tres venganzas.*" *EIA* 1 (1975): 93–101. [B] "Analysis of Calderón's *De un castigo, tres venganzas:* Structure, Theme, Language." *Critical Perspectives on Calderón de la Barca.* Ed. Frederick A. de Armas, David M. Gitlitz, and José A. Madrigal. Lincoln: Univ. of Nebraska, 1981. 13–37. [C] "*De un castigo, tres venganzas* y la coincidencia de justicia y venganza en el teatro de Calderón." *Calderón: Actas del congreso internacional sobre Calderón y el teatro español del Siglo de Oro, Madrid, 1981.* Ed. Luciano García Lorenzo. 3 vols. Madrid: CSIC, 1983. 827–38.

248. BORING, OMEN KONN. Structural Balance in Calderón's Drama. iv+256 pp. Chicago, 1929. Chicago *Abstracts* 7: 369–73.

"All the plays of Calderón were read except the *autos sacramentales* and those written in collaboration. . . . The most interesting features of the study are the influence of the syllogism on Calderón's methods of workmanship and the existence of chiasmus, antithesis, and parallelism in plot as well as rhetoric, the former often being dependent upon or supplementary to the latter." (Abs.)

249. BREIDENTHAL, MARIANNE. The Legend of Hercules in Castilian Literature up to the Seventeenth Century. 250 pp. CA/Berkeley, C. B. Faulhaber, 1985. *DAI* 47A: 925–26.

The pertinent *comedia* examined is Calderón's *Los tres mayores prodigios.* (Abs.)

250. BUELOW, KENNETH DALE. A Semicritical and Annotated Edition of *El divino Orfeo, segunda parte.* 573 pp. Wisconsin, M. E. Brooks, 1976. *DAI* 37A: 1004.

There are four extant manuscripts of this *auto.* "A base text and variant readings from the remaining three extant manuscripts are presented." (Abs.)

251. CALVO-COSTA, JUAN ANTONIO. Estudio analítico de *El gran duque de Gandía:* Contribución al estudio de las comedias "de santo" de don Pedro Calderón de la Barca. [7]+209 pp. Michigan State, J. A. Ramsey, 1967. *DA* 28A: 2202–03.

"La obra en sí resulta una de las más perfectas comedias 'de santo' del autor centrada en la progresión a la santidad del protagonista, basada en el concepto del desengaño." (Abs.)

❖ "Aportación al estudio de la métrica de *El gran duque de Gandía.*" *BCom* 21.1 (1969): 12–15.

252. CASCARDI, ANTHONY JOSEPH. The Forms of a Theatre: The *Comedias* of Calderón de la Barca. 426(?) pp. Harvard, S. Gilman, 1979.

The writer emphasizes the need "to comprehend the dramatic text as a theatrical work of art, concrete, visible and representable, and not simply as a strange form of narrative poetry. . . . what I intend to do is provide an enlightened appreciation of the theatrical nature of Calderón's art, by examining in detail selected works from various points of Calderón's long career." (Diss.)

❖ *The Limits of Illusion: A Critical Study of Calderón.* Cambridge: Cambridge UP, 1984. xvii+181 pp. ["Roughly half the material here published was submitted, in a different form, at Harvard University, as part of a doctoral dissertation entitled 'The Forms of a Theatre.'"]

253. CASTILLO, CARLOS. *En la vida todo es verdad y todo mentira,* by D. Pedro Calderón de la Barca: An Edition from the Autograph, with Introduction and Notes. [237] pp. Chicago, G. T. Northup and K. Pietsch, 1923. Chicago *Abstracts* 1: 305–08.

"The study is based on photographs of the autograph kept in the Biblioteca Nacional de Madrid, described under number 1075 in the *Catálogo de las piezas de teatro,* by Paz y Melia, Madrid, 1899." (Abs.)

❖ "Acerca de la fecha y fuentes de *En la vida todo es verdad y todo mentira.*" *MP* 20 (1922–23): 391–401.

254. CHUTE, EDWARD JOSEPH. Comic Wrestling: A Comparative Analysis of the Comic Agon and Its Dramatic Idea and Form in Selected Comedies of Aristophanes, Shakespeare, Jonson, Shaw and Calderón. 301 pp. Minnesota, J. D. Hurrell, 1977. *DAI* 38A: 1367.

The Calderonian play analyzed in this study is *La vida es sueño.* ". . . the agon is revealed as a device of plot through which the comic action comes to metaphorically embody the thematic conflict." (Abs.)

255. CONNOR, PATRICIA JOSEPHINE. The Music in the Spanish Baroque Theater of Don Pedro Calderón de la Barca. 2 vols. (vol. 1:

240 pp.; vol. 2: [musical scores] 68 pp.) Boston University, J. Knapp, 1964.

". . . the first section of the present study will deal with the historical background of Spanish drama and the uses made of music in that theater. . . . The second section of the study is concerned with the literary aspects of the drama. A brief history of each type of drama is included. . . . In the final section of the study, Chapter IX concerns examples of the actual music from the theater of this period. . . . the principal source of theatrical music from Calderón's theater are the transcriptions which we have made from the voluminous manuscript in the possession of the Congregación de Nuestra Señora de la Novena de Actores Españoles." (Diss.)

256. CRAVEN, ALICE MIKAL. Doubting Consciousness: Theories of Characterization in Calderón and Other Seventeenth Century Dramatists. 293 pp. NYU, T. J. Reiss, 1992. *DAI* 53A: 800–01.

"This dissertation compares the Romantic reading of Calderón (as culmination of *comedia nueva*) to adaptations of the *comedia nueva* by French dramatists. Sight-oriented theatrical formulas are examined in order to show how theatrical practice of the French dramatists necessarily uses sight as the possibility for knowledge. I show Calderón's refutation of clear and distinct evidence as ground for proof, and his desire to elevate doubt or the fideistic argument, through his meticulous conversion of sight-oriented structures into 'spectatorial moments.' A spectatorial moment is when a character sees simultaneously in a conscious and textual manner. The present or the real cannot be privileged over the text or, illusion. I redirect the issue of whether or not the Spanish Golden Age produced any tragedies, to the question of how the tragic protagonist produces knowledge and how sight functions in the process. The *comedia nueva* comes into existence in the midst of this transformation. What does Calderón contribute to that transformation?" (Abs.)

257. CUESTA, ROGELIO. La figura de Cristo en los *autos sacramentales* de Calderón. 425 pp. NYU, A. Regalado, 1978. *DAI* 40A: 2715.

". . . some fifty *Autos Sacramentales* are analyzed." (Abs.)

258. CUMMINGS, DOROTHY PORTER. *El secreto a voces* of Don Pedro

Calderón de la Barca: An Edition with Introduction and Notes of the Autograph Manuscript of 1642. 256 pp. Ohio State, C. E. Anibal, 1933. Ohio State *Abstracts* 12 (1933): 41–47.

The text is based on a photostatic copy of the BNM MS under the signature R-117. "The variants of six printed editions—Hartzenbusch [1851], Keil [1829], Apontes [1762], Habana [La Habana, 1839], Vera Tassis [1683], and Salamanca [1881]—are given in the footnotes." (Abs.)

259. CUMMINS, WILLIAM ROBERT. Allegory and Language in the *Autos Sacramentales* of Calderón. 199 pp. SUNY/Albany, C. Nepaulsingh, 1988. *DAI* 49A: 1470–71.

"As multimedia works of dogmatic theater, the *autos sacramentales* of Calderón, combine the visual art of the stage with language. Given the criticism's attention to the plays' representation, the question of language's role in the presentation of the plays' allegories needs further consideration. This dissertation studies the presentation of these allegories through the language of Calderón's *autos sacramentales*." (Abs.)

260. DÍAZ-BALSERA, VIVIANA. Alegoría y resistencia en tres autos de Calderón de la Barca. 244 pp. Yale, R. O. González-Echevarría, 1989. *DAI* 51A: 518.

The three *autos* in question are *El jardín de Falerina, Los encantos de la culpa,* and *Lo que va del hombre a Dios*. "In the *Conclusion,* we compare the poetics of the *auto* with the official rhetoric of the Church and State about representation in order to show their differences, and how the *auto* yields a reading in which it turns away from the authority and meaning it is supposed to consolidate." (Abs.)

261. DILORENZO-KEARON, MARIA ANTONIA. Mythological, Literary and Philosophical Perspectives on *Amado y aborrecido* by Pedro Calderón de la Barca. 209 pp. CUNY, M. Nozick, 1982. *DAI* 43A: 1564.

"The present dissertation will focus on a study of the *comedia mitológica, Amado y aborrecido*. This play demonstrates a seriousness of intention previously denied by critics of Calderón's mythological theater, for in it Calderón presents man in his struggle to come to terms with himself and his nature through love. The theme of unrequited love which runs through the play is linked to the theme of physical, emotional and spiritual imprisonment." (Abs.)

262. DiPuccio, Denise Marie. Communicative Structures in Calderón de la Barca's Mythological *Comedias*. 243 pp. Kansas, W. R. Blue, 1982. *DAI* 43A: 2691.

"This dissertation includes detailed analyses of six *comedias*. . . . Three methods of criticism facilitated a study of communicative structures . . . : speech act theory, semiotics, and deconstruction. . . ." (Abs.)

❖ [A] "Ambiguous Voices and Beauties in Calderón's *Eco y Narciso* and Their Tragic Consequences." *BCom* 37.1 (1985): 129–44. [B] "The Enigma of Enchantment in *El mayor encanto, amor.*" *H*[AATSP] 70.4 (1987): 731–39. [C] "Deconstructing the *Comedia.*" *Approaches to Teaching Spanish Golden Age Drama*. Ed. Everett W. Hesse. York: Spanish Literature, 1989. 112–29.

263. Dorsey, Viola Marie. *Autos Sacramentales* de Calderón de la Barca: An Expression of the Culture of Spain's Golden Age. xiv+278 pp. Stanford, A. M. Espinosa, 1940. Stanford *Abstracts* 16 (1940–41): 105–08.

"Not only are the traits of the intellectual and social culture of the nation outlined in the *autos* but also the elements of the religious culture of seventeenth-century Spain as well." (Abs.)

264. Dreney, Sara Bernadine. Calderón, the Poet of the Eucharist. v+320 pp. Boston College, A. L. Mezzacappa, 1938.

". . . I have limited myself to the most representative of those *autos sacramentales* which concern themselves directly with the Eucharist and its powers of salvation and redemption." (Abs.)

265. Duncan-Irvin, Hayden Donelan. The "Beast/Monster" and Desire in Three of Calderón de la Barca's Mythological Plays: *Eco y Narciso, El monstruo de los jardines,* and *El mayor encanto, amor.* 198 pp. Wisconsin, M. E. Brooks, 1991. *DAI* 52A: 3952.

This study "presents Calderón as an artist who did not consciously anticipate modern psychoanalytic theory, but whose insights and understanding of human nature provided material that allows his texts to be read today from yet another perspective." (Abs.)

266. DUVERT, DOMINIQUE. The Tragedy of Language: An Application of Artaud's Criticism of the Dramatic Text to Shakespeare's *Coriolanus,* Molière's *Dom Juan,* and Calderón's *La vida es sueño.* 287 pp. North Carolina, J.-M. Heimonet, 1990. *DAI* 52A: 156.

"This study shows how *Coriolanus, Dom Juan,* and *La vida es sueño* illustrate what Artaud calls the limits of language. In these works language accounts for only one aspect of the tragic conflict. The tragic is created through the tension between language and action, and finds its expression in the hero's opposition to his community. The community coheres and exists as a result of rules and laws based on language, whereas the hero defines himself essentially through action. To fulfill a desire that language can neither express nor contain, the hero violates societal rules, ultimately going beyond language entirely. It is his transgression of language, perhaps more than his violation of his community's rules and laws, that condemns the hero. The dissertation demonstrates that dramatists as diverse as Shakespeare, Molière, and Calderón succeed in creating the tension that Artaud sought to generate in his Theater of Cruelty. By using the very limits of language, these dramatists create a powerful sense of the tragic." (Abs.)

267. EMIGH, JOHN STEWART. Love and Honor: A Comparative Study of Corneille's *Le Cid* and Calderón's Honor Plays. 231 pp. Tulane, R. Schechner, 1971. *DAI* 32A: 3949.

"In the 'honor plays,' Calderón inverts traditional tragicomic conventions in order to construct a form of Christian tragedy; the Christian values are affirmed by the disaster attending their negation. . . . Despite its theatrical brilliance, Corneille's adaptation of the 'Spanish plot' forms an important chapter in the trivialization of tragedy that was to plague dramatists through the Romantic period." (Abs.)

268. ERWIN, JOHN WALTER. *Narcissus Ludens:* Person and Performance in Baroque Drama. 613 pp. Yale, L. Nelson, 1970. *DAI* 31A: 2912.

"The major playwrights of the seventeenth century in Europe responded to a general shift in emphasis in the definition of authority from reference to traditional models to experimentation by self-conscious individuals by projecting the responsibility for reflexiveness upon their medium in plays which thoroughly exploit the conditions of theatrical performance." The relevant works examined are Calderón's *La vida es sueño* and his *autos sacramentales*. (Abs.)

269. ESTEVES, CARMEN C. The Dramatic Portrayal of Semíramis in Virués, Calderón and Voltaire. 179 pp. CUNY, F. J. Nichols, 1985. *DAI* 46A: 1271.

The two pertinent *comedias* analyzed are *La gran Semíramis* by Virués and *La hija del aire* by Calderón. (Abs.)

270. FIORE, ROBERT LOUIS. Neo-Scholasticism in Calderón's *Autos: No hay más fortuna que Dios, El gran teatro del mundo,* and *A Dios por razón de estado.* 136 pp. North Carolina, W. C. McCrary, 1967. *DA* 28A: 3180.

"The *auto sacramental* reaches its maturity as a genre in Calderón's theological synthesis which gives dramatic and plastic form to Neo-Scholastic doctrine. The sources from which Calderón derives the themes of his *autos* are the Church Fathers, the Bible, and Scholastic philosophy. The purpose of this study is to examine the philosophical content of three *autos: No hay más fortuna que Dios, El gran teatro del mundo,* and *A Dios por razón de estado,* stressing Thomistic-Aristotelian doctrines." (Abs.)

❖ [A] "Calderón's *El gran teatro del mundo:* An Ethical Interpretation." *HR* 40 (1972): 40–52. [B] *Drama and Ethos: Natural-Law Ethics in Spanish Golden Age Theater.* Lexington: UP of Kentucky, 1975. 120 pp. [C] "An Example of Resurgence of Natural Law in Golden Age Spain." *The Medieval Tradition of Natural Law.* Ed. Harold J. Johnson. Kalamazoo: Medieval Institute, 1987. 27–35. [Apropos Calderón's *A Dios por razón de estado.*]

271. FISCHER, SUSAN LEIBOWITZ. Psychological and Esthetic Implications of Role-Change in Selected Plays by Calderón. xv+252 pp. Duke, B. W. Wardropper, 1973. *DAI* 34A: 4197.

The selected plays include *El mayor monstruo del mundo, Los cabellos de Absalón, La cisma de Ingalaterra, La hija del aire, La devoción de la Cruz, A secreto agravio secreta venganza, El médico de su honra, El pintor de su deshonra, El alcalde de Zalamea, Los dos amantes del cielo, El mágico prodigioso, El príncipe constante,* and *La vida es sueño.* "The application to Calderón's drama of insights provided by twentieth-century psychological and esthetic thought shows that the *comedia,* as interpreted by him, is not so much unique as universal." (Abs.)

❖ [A] "The Function and Significance of the *Gracioso* in Calderón's *El pintor de su deshonra*." *RomN* 14 (1972–73): 334–40. [B] "The Art of Role-Change in Calderonian Drama." *BCom* 27 (1975): 73–79 [Apropos *El pintor de su deshonra.*] [C] "Calderón's *Los cabellos de Absalón:* A Metatheater of Unbridled Passion." *BCom* 28.2 (1976): 103–13. [D] "Reader-Response Criticism and the *Comedia:* Creation of Meaning in Calderón's *La cisma de Ingalaterra*." *BCom* 31.2 (1979): 109–25. [E] "Aspectos psicológicos de la clarividencia y del martirio en *El príncipe constante*." *Estudios sobre el Siglo de Oro en homenaje a Raymond R. MacCurdy*. Ed. Ángel González et al. Albuquerque: Univ. of New Mexico; Madrid: Cátedra, 1983. 135–49. [F] "Calderón and Jung: Unconscious Psychic Processes in *El mágico prodigioso*." *KRQ* 31.1 (1984): 71–87.

272. Fox, Dian. Kingship in the Drama of Don Pedro Calderón de la Barca. 212 pp. Duke, B. W. Wardropper, 1979. *DAI* 40A: 2089–90.

"Like most Spanish writers of the period, Calderón is shown to be anti-Machiavellian. His plays maintain a political stance in basic agreement with such theorists as Pedro de Rivadeneira, Juan de Mariana, and Diego de Saavedra Fajardo. . . ." (Abs.)

❖ [A] "Kingship and Community in *La vida es sueño*." *BHS* 58 (1981): 217–28. [B] *Kings in Calderón: A Study in Characterization and Political Theory*. London: Tamesis, 1986. 129 pp. (Colección Támesis, serie A. Monografías 121.) [C] "In Defense of Segismundo." *BCom* 41.1 (1989): 141–54.

273. Freund, Markéta Lily. Baroque Technique, Thought and Feeling in Certain Representative *Comedias* of Calderón. v+298 pp. Colorado, F. Sánchez y Escribano, 1966. *DA* 28A: 1433–34.

This study is based on Calderón's *La hija del aire, El médico de su honra,* and *El gran duque de Gandía.* (Abs.)

274. García, Juan José. Acercamiento semiótico a *El médico de su honra.* ii+236 pp. Southern California, J. A. Parr, 1980. *DAI* 40A: 5887.

"Todos los códigos se alían para crear la ambigüedad y la ironía de un médico que cura, deshaciéndose del paciente, una enfermedad inexistente, según él mismo." (Abs.)

275. Giacoman, Helmy Fuad. Estudio y edición crítica de la comedia *Los cabellos de Absalón* de Pedro Calderón de la Barca. 302 pp. Southern California, E. W. Hesse, 1967. *DA* 27A: 4251–52.

"The purpose of this dissertation has been threefold. First, to develop a detailed analysis of this *comedia,* including a discussion of the Biblical and literary sources of the theme; secondly, to present a thematic and stylistic comparison of Tirso de Molina's *comedia, La venganza de Tamar* and our play; and thirdly to compare systematically the later texts of the play with the *Princeps* edition [in *Comedias Nuevas,* Madrid, 1677]." (Abs.)

❖ [A] Calderón de la Barca, P. *Estudio y edición crítica de la comedia* Los cabellos de Absalón *de Pedro Calderón de la Barca.* Ed. H. F. Giacoman. Chapel Hill: Univ. of North Carolina, Dept. of Romance Languages; Madrid: Castalia, 1968. 183 pp. (Estudios de Hispanófila 9.) [B] "En torno a *Los cabellos de Absalón* de Pedro Calderón de la Barca." *RF* 80 (1968): 343–53. [C] "El rey David en *Los cabellos de Absalón* de Calderón." *BCom* 23.2 (1971): 39–43.

276. Gómez, Juan Manuel. A Critical Edition of Pedro Calderón de la Barca's *La gran Cenobia,* with Introduction and Notes. viii+229 pp. Oregon, P. J. Powers, 1981. *DAI* 42A: 3623–24.

The critical edition is based on the *princeps.* "The text of the *princeps* appeared in the *Primera parte de comedias de Don Pedro Calderón de la Barca,* printed in Madrid in 1636. This edition is given priority as a copy text due to the absence of the autograph or manuscript. Three other editions are consulted, two dated 1640 and the Vera Tassis edition of 1685. These later editions are used only when they correct obvious mistakes." (Abs.)

277. González [Echevarría], Roberto Oscar. Aproximación estructuralista a *La vida es sueño:* Ensayo de un método. v+251 pp. Yale, M. Durán, 1970. *DAI* 31A: 2916.

"The first [part of this study] traces the development of Calderón criticism in the Twentieth Century, focuses attention upon the concept of structure applied to his works, and develops a new approach to them. . . . Thus, *La vida es sueño* reveals a subtle twist: instead of obliterating time, its ritual structure makes the imminence of death more poignant. This is the meaning of the play's structure." (Abs.)

❖ [A] Manuel Durán and R. González Echevarría. *Calderón y la crítica: Historia y antología.* 2 vols. Madrid: Gredos, 1976. 786 pp. (BRH II: 238.) [B] "Calderón's *La vida es sueño:* Mixed-(up) Monsters" and "Threats in Calderón: *La vida es sueño* 1: 303–08." In the author's *Celestina's Brood: Continuities of the Baroque in Spanish and Latin American Literatures.* Durham: Duke UP, 1993. 81–113; 114–27.

278. Greer, Margaret Helen Rich. *La estatua de Prometeo* by Pedro Calderón de la Barca: A Critical Edition. 570 pp. Texas, S. Zimic, 1983. *DAI* 47A: 1742.

"The critical edition herein presented is based on the manuscript copy of the play of the Biblioteca Municipal of Madrid—which contains a much better text than that of the *Quinta Parte,* including a number of lines absent in the *princeps*—collated with the texts of the two 1677 editions of the *Quinta Parte* and the 1683 Vera Tassis *Sexta Parte.*" (Abs.)

❖ [A] Calderón de la Barca, P. *La estatua de Prometeo:* A Critical Edition by M. R. Greer, with a Study of the Music by L. K. Stein. Kassel: Reichenberger, 1986. 409 pp. [B] "The Play of Power: Calderón's *Fieras afemina Amor* and *La estatua de Prometeo.*" *HR* 55 (1988): 319–41. [C] "Art and Power in the Spectacle Plays of Calderón de la Barca." *PMLA* 104 (1989): 329–39. [D] "Bodies of Power in Calderón: *El nuevo palacio del Retiro* and *El mayor encanto, amor.*" *Conflicts of Discourse: Spanish Literature of the Golden Age.* Ed. Peter Evans. Manchester: Manchester UP, 1990. 145–65. [E] "'Authority' in *Comedia* Editions: Tirso de Molina's *Santa Juana.*" *Editing the* Comedia II. Ed. Michael McGaha and Frank P. Casa. Ann Arbor: Univ. of Michigan, Dept. of Romance Languages, 1991. 67–95. (Michigan Romance Studies 11.) [F] *The Play of Power: Mythological Court Dramas of Calderón de la Barca.* Princeton: Princeton UP, 1991. 256 pp.

279. Hamlett, Robert Curtis. An Investigation of Selected Colonial

Latin American Vocal/Choral Works, Including Practical Performance Editions. 294 pp. Southern Mississippi, J. Donovan, 1986. *DAI* 47A: 3902–03.

"This study was undertaken to examine music during the colonial era in the Latin American cultural centers of Lima, Peru, and Mexico City, Mexico, and to subsequently prepare practical performance editions of selected vocal/choral works by composers whose contributions to music of that epoch have been determined to be significant. The compositions under investigation included . . . the complimentary *Loa* from the opera *La púrpura de la rosa* by Tomás de Torrejón y Velasco (c. 1644–1728)." (Abs.) Editorial note: Torrejón's musical version of Calderón's play premiered in Lima in 1701. The Spanish-born composer lived in Peru from 1667 until his death.

280. HARWELL, MARGHERITA. Edizione, introduzione e note di *Le armi e gli amori,* melodramma di Giulio Rospigliosi tratto dalla commedia di Calderón de la Barca, *Los empeños de un acaso.* iii+306 pp. Chicago, P. Cherchi, 1972.

The edition is based on the MS of the play by Giulio Rospigliosi (1600–69), later Pope Clement IX.

281. HATZANTONIS, EMMANUEL STAMATIOS. Circe nelle letterature classiche, medioevali e romanze: Da Omero a Calderón. 295 pp. CA/Berkeley, M. De Filippis, 1958. PFE, 23 May 1958.

Chapter 7 includes discussion of the Circe theme in Spanish literature. The writer examines the following plays of Calderón: *El mayor encanto, amor; Los encantos de la culpa;* and *Polifemo y Circe* (Jornada 3). (PFE)

❖ "Lope de Vega's Non-Homeric Treatment of a Homeric Theme." *H*[AATSP] 48 (1965): 475–80. [The writer refers to Lope's poem *La Circe.*]

282. HERNÁNDEZ-ARAICO, SUSANA. El concepto de ironía en la tragicomedia calderoniana (del humor al determinismo). viii+246 pp. CA/Los Angeles, E. Rodríguez-Cepeda, 1976. *DAI* 37A: 6537.

"La parte de este trabajo dedicada al gracioso pretende . . . señalar el distanciamiento irónico del dramaturgo." In many Calderonian works, "el aleccionamiento moral de la obra se forja mediante el engaño que el dramaturgo perpetra contra sus personajes. Así lo demuestra la serie de comedias analizadas en torno al horóscopo nefasto que estimula una prevención contraproducente." (Abs.)

❖ *Ironía y tragedia en Calderón.* Potomac: Scripta Humanistica, 1986. 153 pp.

283. Herold, Bruce Walter. Precognition in Selected Dramas of Calderón de la Barca. vi+246 pp. Pennsylvania State, L. C. Pérez, 1977. *DAI* 38A: 7363-64.

"In *La cisma de Ingalaterra, El príncipe constante, El mayor monstruo del mundo, La vida es sueño, La hija del aire,* Parts I and II, and *Los cabellos de Absalón,* precognition always discloses eventual disorder, suffering or death." (Abs.)

284. Hesse, Everett Wesley. Vera Tassis' Text of Calderón's Plays (Parts I-IV). xx+348 pp. NYU, H. C. Heaton, 1941.

". . . in the future, scholars, in preparing new editions of the plays examined in this study, must utilize the text of the original first four *partes* of Calderón rather than that which has come down to us from the *pecadoras manos* of Vera Tassis." (Diss.)

❖ [A] Title as is. Mexico: n.p., 1941. 36 pp. Abridgment. [B] "The Two Versions of Calderón's *El laurel de Apolo.*" *HR* 14 (1946): 213-34. [Compares the Vera Tassis text of this *zarzuela* "with that of the first and second edition."] [C] "The First and Second Editions of Calderón's *Cuarta parte.*" *HR* 16 (1948): 209-37. [D] "The Publication of Calderón's Plays in the Seventeenth Century." *PQ* 27 (1948): 37-51. [Pp. 46-51 deal with the Vera Tassis edition (1682-91).] [For a more complete list of this scholar's publications, see *Studies in Honor of Everett W. Hesse,* ed. William C. McCrary and José A. Madrigal (Lincoln: Univ. of Nebraska, Soc. of Spanish and Spanish-American Studies, 1981) 15-21.]

285. Hildner, David Jonathan. The Role of Reason and the Passions in the *Comedias* of Calderón. 246 pp. Minnesota, N. Spadaccini, 1979. *DAI* 40A: 5073.

". . . Calderón shows how pragmatic reason can justify irrational stances and how even passions can help in realizing the characters' desired ends." (Abs.)

❖ [A] "Aristocracy and Reason: Behavior Patterns of Calderón's Secular Characters." *Ideologies and Literature* 3.13 (1980): 42-53.

[B] *Reason and the Passions in the Comedias of Calderón.* Philadelphia: Benjamins, 1982. 119 pp. (PUMRL 11.)

286. HILL, DEBORAH JOAN. The Elimination Motif in Selected Plays of Calderón de la Barca. viii+252 pp. Florida State, D. H. Darst, 1983. *DAI* 44A: 765.

"This study investigates the use in the *comedias* of Calderón de la Barca of a particular event which I have named the 'elimination motif.' This term refers to the excisement, whether physical or figurative, of one of the play's main characters from the dramatic events that usually, but not always, leads to the denouement, or final moments of the particular drama's action." The analysis is based on 35 dramas and includes a motif index of Calderón's "excision plays." (Abs.)

❖ "*El alcalde de Zalamea:* A Chronological Annotated Bibliography." *H*[AATSP] 66.1 (1983): 48–63. [The excised figure is Don Álvaro de Ataide, the captain who raped Pedro Crespo's daughter.]

287. HILL, [SISTER] JOAN MARY, S. N. D. DE N. Calderón's *La aurora en Copacabana:* A Figural Interpretation. iv+354 pp. Kentucky, W. C. McCrary, 1976. *DAI* 37A: 5816.

"In *La aurora en Copacabana* Calderón universalizes particular historic events from the conquest of Peru and the foundation of a local devotion to the Virgin Mary to provide a dramatic panorama of the whole scope of human history according to the Judeo-Christian tradition. Fittingly, the chief symbolic mode of the play is figuration or typology." (Abs.)

288. HIVNOR, MARY OTIS. Definitions of the Prince in Three Variants of the Baroque Dramatic Mode: Shakespeare's *The Tempest,* Corneille's *Héraclius,* and Calderón's *En la vida todo es verdad y todo mentira.* ii+149 pp. Columbia, M. Meisel, D. Fox, and N. Gross, 1983. *DAI* 44A: 2465.

"It is concluded that each playwright, addressing an elite generation during a period of political transition, makes use of romance themes and baroque theatricality, to offer his audience an inspiring and reassuring national image of perfection." (Abs.)

❖ "*En la vida todo es verdad y todo mentira:* Calderón's Prince Defined by Faith." *BCom* 37.2 (1985): 249–61.

289. HOLLMANN, HILDEGARD H. Calderón's Vision of the Tyrant. 304 pp. NYU, A. Regalado, 1973. *DAI* 34A: 7757.

The plays analyzed are *La gran Cenobia, La hija del aire,* Part 1 and Part 2, and *En la vida todo es verdad y todo mentira.* Dealt with "briefly" are *Yerros de naturaleza y aciertos de la fortuna* and *La vida es sueño.* (Abs.)

❖ "El retrato del tirano Aureliano en *La gran Cenobia.*" *Hacia Calderón: Cuarto coloquio anglogermano, Wolfenbüttel, 1975.* Ed. Hans Flasche, Karl-Hermann Körner, and Hans Mattauch. Berlin: de Gruyter, 1979. 46-55.

290. HORVATH, SABINE. Königtum und Tyrannei, Rebellion und Verschwörung als Themen im europäischen Drama, von der Spät-Renaissance bis zum Ende des siebzehnten Jahrhunderts. 505 pp. CUNY, L. Bergel, 1975. *DAI* 36A: 882-83.

[For the complete entry, see no. 218.]

291. HULSE, LLOYD KERMIT. Edición crítica y estudio de *La cena del Rey Baltasar* de Calderón de la Barca. v+284 pp. Cincinnati, J. O. Valencia, 1973. *DAI* 34A: 5177.

"The text of the *princeps* edition typed with neither changes in punctuation nor spelling comprises Part II." This text is collated with "the three extant manuscripts and a representative 20th-century edition, that of Clásicos Castellanos, 1967." (Abs.) Editorial note: The *princeps* is dated 1664.

292. HUNTER, WILLIAM ARTHUR. An Edition and Translation of a Nahuatl Version of the Calderonian *Auto Sacramental: El gran teatro del mundo.* 221 pp. Tulane, J. E. Englekirk, 1954. Tulane *Abstracts* 55, no. 14, pp. 94-99.

Calderón's *auto* "was adapted in Mexico by Father Bartolomé de Alva between the years 1640 and 1645. . . . The text used has been transcribed from the only copy known to be extant, now housed in the Bancroft Library of the University of California in Berkeley. . . . Bound with this version of *El gran teatro del mundo* in the same volume are two other *comedias* [Lope's (?) *El animal profeta y dichoso parricida* and his *La madre de la mejor*], also translated by Alva, plus a short anonymous *entremés.*" (Abs.)

❖ [A] "The Alva Manuscripts in the Bancroft Library." *KFLQ* 3.2 (1956): 76-81. [B] "The Seventeenth-Century Nahuatl

Entremés In Ilamatzin Ihuan in Piltontli." *KFLQ* 5 (1958): 26–34. [This is the anonymous *entremés* referenced in the above abstract.] [C] Calderón de la Barca, P. *The Calderonian Auto Sacramental* El gran teatro del mundo: *An Edition and Translation of a Nahuatl Version*. Ed. W. A. Hunter. *Middle American Research Institute* (Tulane Univ.) 27 (1960): 105–201. [D] "Toward a More Authentic Text of Calderón's *El gran teatro del mundo.*" *HR* 29 (1961): 240–44. [E] "Unas versiones aztecas de tres comedias del Siglo de Oro." *BH* 65 (1963): 319–21. [The three *comedias* are *El gran teatro del mundo* (Calderón), *El animal profeta y dichoso parricida* (Mira de Amescua [?]), *La madre de la mejor* (attributed to Lope)].

293. JIMÉNEZ, FERNANDO REINALDO. Edición crítica y estudio de una comedia de Calderón: *La sibila del Oriente y gran reyna de Sabá*. v+404 pp. Cincinnati, J. O. Valencia, 1982. *DAI* 43A: 1565.

The critical text is based on the *princeps* that is collated with later editions. "Le hemos dedicado un capítulo al problema de la paternidad de la obra, refutando la duda de Hartzenbusch. En otro capítulo comparamos la comedia con el auto sacramental calderoniano del mismo tema: *El árbol del mejor fruto.*" (Abs.)

294. KORNER, BARBARA OLIVER. The "Mystic Way" as an Analytical Tool Applied to Victoria's Requiem Mass (1605) and Calderón's *El día mayor de los días*. 249 pp. Ohio, J. H. Conover, 1983. *DAI* 44A: 3525.

"The analysis of the art works leads to the conclusion that the systematic approach of the religious mystical writers does seem to be borne out in the works of artists. Calderón and Victoria seem to share a common goal with St. Ignatius and St. Teresa; they desire to move religion from the realm of theology to the world of experience." (Abs.)

295. KRESSIN, HUGO MAXIMILIAN. Calderón as a Champion of Feminism: A Social and Philosophical Study in the Post-Renaissance in Spain. 687 pp. NYU, 1927.

"It was the 'pundonor' in connection with Love which became the basis of his 'comedias.' The conception of honor had to be revised, he felt, and this was done by his giving a different aspect to that word. By ridiculing the prevailing interpretation of Honor, the poet meant to raise the 'pundonor' from out of its current empty phraseology. Invariably, Calderón lets his female characters remind the men of the code of honor, thereby lending the former a prestige over male society which cannot be argued away by the strongest of his antagonists." (Diss.)

296. LaCaria, Nicola. Calderón's Treatments of the *Pastor Fido* Theme in Relation to the Spanish Translation of Guarini. 251 pp. Pittsburgh, J. S. Herrero, 1975. *DAI* 36A: 8096.

"Calderón, in collaboration with Antonio Solís and Antonio Coello, composed a *comedia palaciega* based on the Italian work [Gianbattista Guarini's *Pastor Fido*] and entitled *El Pastor Fido* (1656). In 1678, Calderón adopted the *Pastor Fido* theme in the religious, theological context with the composition of one of his maturer and subtler *autos sacramentales* with the same title." (Abs.)

297. Lekatis, Nikolaos E. The Motif of Prediction in the Drama of Calderón. 147 pp. CA/Berkeley, E. S. Morby, 1975.

The dissertation is divided into two main chapters: one deals with the devices of prediction (e.g., dreams, omens, etc.); the other examines the uses of prediction (e.g., in *La gran Cenobia, La cisma de Inglaterra,* etc.) (Diss.)

298. LeVan, John Richards, Jr. From Tradition to Masterpiece: Circe and Calderón. viii+366 pp. Texas, S. Zimic, 1981. *DAI* 42A: 4841.

The writer examines a number of seventeenth-century Spanish treatments of the Circe and Ulysses fable. He concludes that "*Los encantos de la Culpa* is the culminating work of Spain's Circe tradition, a powerful, poetic drama that exemplifies Calderón's unique mastery of the dramatic and allegorical arts." (Abs.)

❖ "Theme and Metaphor in the *Auto historial*: Calderón's *Los encantos de la culpa*." *Approaches to the Theater of Calderón*. Ed. Michael D. McGaha. Washington: UP of America, 1982. 187–97.

299. MacKinnon, David Norris. The Mythological Dramas of Pedro Calderón de la Barca. iv+317 pp. Kentucky, W. C. McCrary, 1977. *DAI* 39A: 1621–22.

"The present study first traces the development of critical attitudes toward [Calderón's thirteen] mythological plays. . . . The second part of this dissertation is an attempt to demonstrate a way of approaching one of Calderón's mythological *comedias* [*Ni amor se libra de amor*] in order to perceive many of the previously unrecognized qualities to be found there." (Abs.)

300. MADRIGAL, JOSÉ ANTONIO. La función del hombre salvaje en el teatro de Lope de Vega, Tirso de Molina y Calderón de la Barca. 375 pp. Kentucky, W. C. McCrary, 1973. *DAI* 35A: 2232.

"The main purpose of this dissertation is to analyze a selected number of plays that deal with the theme of the popular and profound figure of the Wild Man." (Abs.)

❖ [A] *El salvaje y la mitología, el arte y la religión*. Miami: Universal, 1975. 55 pp. [B] "La transmutación de Leonido: Un ensayo sobre la figura del hombre salvaje." *CH* 4.1 (1982): 37–46. [Leonido is the protagonist of Lope's *comedia El hijo de los leones*.] [C] "La transmutación de Aquiles, de salvaje a héroe: Tirso de Molina, *El Aquiles*." *Hispanófila* 26.2 (1983): 15–26. [D] "Las diferentes caras del hombre salvaje en el teatro del siglo XVI: Un ensayo sobre la génesis de su temática." *RL* 47 (1985): 65–80. [E] "Una revaloración del caballero salvaje en *La tragicomedia de don Duardos* (Gil Vicente)." *RomN* 26 (1985–86): 125–28.

301. MARANISS, JAMES ELLIOTT. The Theatre of Denial: A Study of Some Plays of Pedro Calderón de la Barca. 212 pp. Princeton, E. L. King and A. A. Alatorre, 1974. *DAI* 36A: 4545–46.

"Six of Calderón's plays *(La vida es sueño, El príncipe constante, La dama duende, El médico de su honra, El alcalde de Zalamea, Eco y Narciso)* and two *autos sacramentales (El gran teatro del mundo, Los encantos de la culpa)* are subjected to critical analysis in order to substantiate a new appraisal of Calderón's theater, which is here seen as a consecration of the values of a repressive and highly ordered idea of civilization—but not without its discontents." (Abs.)

❖ *On Calderón*. Columbia: U of Missouri P, 1978. 129 pp.

302. MARTÍN ACOSTA, [SISTER] MARÍA INÉS, CSJ. The Mythological *Autos* of Calderón de la Barca. ii+402 pp. Columbia, J. F. Shearer, 1969. *DAI* 30A: 4417–18.

This dissertation is a study of the ten *autos* of Calderón that were inspired by Greek mythology. (Abs.)

303. MCGARRY, [SISTER] FRANCIS DE SALES. The Allegorical and Metaphorical Language in the *Autos Sacramentales* of Calderón.

xxiii+157 pp. Catholic, D. Rubio, 1937. {Title as is. Washington: Catholic Univ. of America, 1937. xxiii+157 pp. (CUASRLL 16.)} ❖ Rpt. New York: AMS Press, 1969.

"The allegories and metaphors [of 50 plays] have been assembled, classified, and in some cases paraphrased and interpreted." (Prt. Diss.)

304. MÉNDEZ, ANTONIO, III. Eichendorff and Spain: Some Affinities. ix+241 pp. Texas, B. Becker-Cantarino, 1984. *DAI* 45A: 2120.

"Eichendorff's literary preoccupation with Spanish life and culture, particularly the achievements in the literature of Golden Age Spain are treated." The writer examines in detail Eichendorff's translations of Calderón's *autos sacramentales*. (Abs.)

305. MERRICK, CAROL ANN. Education and Art: Calderón's *La vida es sueño* and *Las fortunas de Andrómeda y Perseo.* 227 pp. Wisconsin, M. E. Brooks, 1972. *DAI* 33A: 3658–59.

These works "are two examples of didactic plays which both use art to instruct the audience and, simultaneously, explore the nature of education itself. *La vida es sueño* presents an inversion of the Renaissance ideal. . . . *Las fortunas* is a straightforward allegory analyzing the mind's ascent to God by means of the Perseus myth." (Abs.)

❖ [A] "Neoplatonic Allegory in Calderón's *Las fortunas de Andrómeda y Perseo.*" *MLR* 67 (1972): 319–27 ["Primarily the action of the play has explored man's inner constitution—the triumph of reason over passion, the love of truth and beauty which leads to noble deeds, marriage with the ideal, union with God, and the defeat of *discordia* within."] [B] "Clotaldo's Role in *La vida es sueño.*" *BHS* 50 (1973): 256–69 [". . . Clotaldo illustrates the way in which a father and a teacher . . . may pervert their proper rôles."]

306. MITCHELL, MARGARETE KOCH. Die Christliche Thematik im Drama Hugo von Hofmannsthals im Lichte Calderón de la Barcas. 224 pp. Indiana, N. Fuerst, 1965. *DA* 26: 3345–46.

"Chapters II through VIII analyze and compare those dramatic works by both authors relevant to our theme: Calderón's *El gran teatro del mundo* . . . and his three dramas entitled *La vida es sueño* . . . and Hofmannsthal's *Das Kleine Welttheater* (1897), *Das Salzburger*

Grosse Welttheater (1922), *Das Leben ein Traum* (about 1904) and the two versions of *Der Turm* (1925 and 1927)." (Abs.)

307. MOONEY, PAUL ARTHUR. A Reevaluation of Past and Current Critical Opinion on the *Comedias Mitológicas* of Pedro Calderón de la Barca. 230 pp. Pennsylvania State, L. C. Pérez, 1973. *DAI* 35A: 1630.

The writer analyzes the following plays: *El mayor encanto, amor; El hijo del sol, Faetón; El monstruo de los jardines; Ni amor se libra de amor;* and *La estatua de Prometeo.* "It has been demonstrated that the scholars who have condemned the myth theater have overlooked the importance of religious interpretation within the plays." (Abs.)

308. MROCZKOWSKA-BRAND, KATARZYNA. Overt Theatricality and the "Theatrum Mundi" Metaphor in Spanish and English Drama, 1570–1640. xii+260 pp. Rochester, P. N. Dunn and A. N. Benston, 1985. *DAI* 46A: 3025.

[For the complete entry, see no. 145.]

309. MUJICA, BARBARA LOUISE. Calderón's Characters: An Existential Point of View. 315 pp. NYU, A. Regalado, 1974. *DAI* 35A: 7318–19.

The characters in the following plays are analyzed: *La gran Cenobia, La dama duende, A secreto agravio, secreta venganza, La vida es sueño, El mágico prodigioso* and *La estatua de Prometeo.* (Abs.)

❖ [A] *Calderón's don Lope de Almeida: A Kafkian Character.* New York and Madrid: Plaza Mayor, 1971. 34 pp. [B] Title as is. Barcelona: Puvill, 1980. 350 pp. (Biblioteca universitaria Puvill. Ensayos 6.)

310. MUSTAFA, FAROUK ABDEL-WAHAB. Drama as Metaphor: Varieties of Theatrical Experience. 282 pp. Minnesota, J. D. Hurrell, 1977. *DAI* 38A: 7314.

"In this dissertation the theatre metaphor (that is, that the world is a stage) is discussed with particular emphasis on its ramifications as a dramaturgic principle. It is suggested that a play written from such a perspective would have to be a play-within-the-play. Varying degrees of awareness of this principle would determine the way an author conceives of his characters, the stage and the audience. In the first two chapters, the emphasis is on the theatre metaphor and how it could be used as a key principle for understanding the dramaturgy of Shakespeare and Calderón. . . . In the case of Calderón, it is shown that the theatrical metaphor is literalized in the attempt to depict explicitly the totality of the human condition in *El gran teatro del mundo* and that the literalization is carried over indirectly and less explicitly in the dramaturgy of *La vida es sueño,* at least as far as the author's role is conceived of." (Abs.)

311. NEWMAN, RICHARD WILLIAM. Calderón and Aquinas. xvi+194 pp. Boston University, J. O. Oñate, 1956. Boston University *Abstracts* 2 (1956): no pagination.

"Other critics have tried to discount the influence of Aquinas on Calderón, emphasizing his borrowing from Saint Augustine. While it is true that he reproduces many ideas of this great Doctor of the Church, they are largely confined to exegetical comments and do not constitute a fairly complete philosophical system, with theses in natural theology, cosmology, psychology, epistemology and ethics. Calderón, therefore, deserves the title of dramatist of Thomism, since he has so faithfully reflected in his plays the teachings of the great Scholastic." (Diss.)

312. NIELSEN, SANDRA LYNNE. A Critical Edition of Calderón's *El golfo de las sirenas.* vii+187 pp. Chicago, G. Haley, 1986. *DAI* 47A: 1743.

The work here edited is composed of *loa,* zarzuela, and *mojiganga.* "There are no extant manuscripts of this play. I have collated three editions of the *Quarta parte:* Fernández de Buendía, 1672; Bernardo de Hervada, 1674; and Vera Tassis, 1688. The first two were published during Calderón's lifetime. I have prepared an old-spelling edition, choosing the 1674 edition as my copy-text." (Abs.)

❖ [A] Calderón de la Barca, P. *El golfo de las sirenas: A Critical Edition, with Introduction and Notes.* Ed. S. L. Nielsen. Kassel: Reichenberger, 1989. 148 pp. (Teatro del Siglo de Oro. Ediciones críticas 22.) [B] "Editing *Polifemo y Circe*—A Preliminary Report." *Looking at the* Comedia *in the Year of the Quincentennial: Proceedings of the 1992 Symposium on Golden Age Drama, El Paso.* Ed. Barbara Mujica and Sharon D. Voros. Lanham: UP of America, 1993. 255–61.

313. Norton, Richard Whiteley. Causality in Calderón's *La vida es sueño.* v+577 pp. Illinois, R. P. Oliver, 1960. *DA* 21: 1569.

"It would appear, therefore, that Calderón gave preference in his own mind to the Molinist causal system, while not repudiating overtly the Thomist system or disregarding Stoicism in its ethical implications." (Abs.)

314. Oppenheimer, Max, Jr. Don Pedro Calderón de la Barca's *Comedia del astrólogo fingido:* An Edition. iii+309 pp. Southern California, M. Struble, 1947. USC *Abstracts of Dissertations* (1947): 30–31.

". . . the present edition, together with about one thousand collation notes, reproduces and combines the original texts of the 1632 and 1637 [printed] editions." In addition, there is "a thorough investigation of the sixteen French, English, Italian, Dutch, German, and Spanish adaptations" of the play. (Abs.)

❖ [A] "Addenda on the *'Segunda Parte'* of Calderón." *HR* 16 (1948): 335–40 [This *parte* includes *El astrólogo fingido.*] [B] "The *Burla* in Calderón's *El astrólogo fingido.*" *PQ* 27 (1948): 241–63. [C] "Supplementary Data on the French and English Adaptations of Calderón's *El astrólogo fingido.*" *RLC* 22 (1948): 547–60. [D] "A Note on Calderón's *El astrólogo fingido.*" *BCom* 2.1 (1950): 3–4. [E] "Bibliographical Note on the *Parte XXV de Comedias.*" *MLN* 66 (1951): 163–65 [This volume contains *El astrólogo fingido.*] [F] "A Spurious Edition of the *Segunda Parte* of the Vera Tassis Edition of Calderón's *Comedias.*" *HR* 19 (1951): 346–52. [G] "Two Stones and One Bird: A Bird Lore Allusion in Calderón." *MLN* 67 (1952): 253–54. [In *El astrólogo fingido.*] [H] "The German Adaptations of Calderón de la Barca's *El astrólogo fingido.*" *Geprägte Form-Festschrift für Robert Rie*. Wien: Europäischer, 1975. 67–70. [I] Calderón de la Barca, P. *The Fake Astrologer.* Ed. and trans. Max Oppenheimer Jr. Lawrence: Coronado, 1976. 177 pp. [Bilingual edition.] [J] *Pedro Calderón de la Barca's* The Fake Astrologer: *A Critical Spanish Text and English Translation.* Ed. and trans. Max Oppenheimer Jr. New York: Peter Lang, 1994. 258 pp. (Ibérica 9.) [K] "Arte nuevo de traducir *comedias* en este tiempo." *Texto y espectáculo: Proceedings of the Thirteenth International Golden Age Spanish Theatre Symposium, El Paso, 1993.* Ed. José

Luis Suárez García. York: Spanish Literature Publications, 1995. 69–75.

315. PETERSEN-WEINER, ANTJE-CHR. Hugo von Hofmannsthals *Turm*-Dichtungen: Trauerspiel, Politik, Lichtphänomene des Expressionismus. 230 pp. Stanford, R. A. Berman, 1985. *DAI* 46A: 2307.

"Chapter I investigates the genesis of the drama [Hofmannsthal's *Der Turm*] with respect to its changing relationship to its model, Calderón's *La vida es sueño,* and other dreamplays in the European tradition." (Abs.)

316. PONCE, JOAQUÍN. Metateatro: Su aplicación a tres dramas de honor de Calderón. iv+113 pp. Georgia, H. Ziomek, 1984. *DAI* 45A: 1772–73.

"En este estudio se analiza *El pintor de su deshonra, A secreto agravio, secreta venganza* y *El médico de su honra* como metadramas, utilizando como punto de referencia principal la teoría de Lionel Abel sobre el metateatro. Se da énfasis al concepto del personaje dramático como ente de ficción que actúa con cierto grado de independencia del autor, al uso de la imaginación en el proceso creativo del metadrama, a la participación del espectador en este proceso y al concepto del honor como dramaturgo invisible." (Abs.)

317. PORTERA, JOHN JACQUES. Estudio y edición crítica de la comedia *Darlo todo y no dar nada* de Pedro Calderón de la Barca. 383 pp. Southern California, R. G. Dodson, 1971. *DAI* 32A: 929.

The text is based on the *princeps* edition of 1657. "Immediately following the text is a collation of the variants of the first early editions of the play." (Abs.)

❖ [A] "Amor y lealtad en Lyly y Calderón." *BCom* 28.2 (1976): 96–100 [Apropos Lyly's *Campaspe* and Calderón's *Darlo todo y no dar nada.*] [B] "La temática de *Darlo todo y no dar nada,* de Calderón." *ExTL* 5 (1976): 75–83. [C] "El gracioso pícaro en Calderón." *La picaresca: Orígenes, textos y estructuras*. Ed. Manuel Criado de Val. Madrid: FUE, 1979. 841–47. [Apropos Clarín in *La vida es sueño.*]

318. PRINCE, ALVIN LAFAYETTE, III. The Role of the King in Selected Works of Calderón de la Barca. 276 pp. Georgia, H. Ziomek, 1974. *DAI* 35A: 5421.

The writer finds the works studied to be "Thomistic" and "anti-Machiavellian," and to be characterized by a "varying degree of historicity." (Abs.)

319. QUINN-MILLER, KATHLEEN MARY. Astrology: A Metaphor for Science in Five Plays by Pedro Calderón de la Barca. 256 p. NYU, A. Regalado, 1986. *DAI* 47A: 3062.

The five plays investigated are *El astrólogo fingido, La cisma de Ingalaterra, El mayor monstruo los celos, La vida es sueño,* and *La estatua de Prometeo.* "Calderón uses men's reactions to the prognostications of the old science, astrology, to warn against surrendering reason and free will to the dictates of any science. For Calderón the virtuous man utilizes science to triumph over fortune." (Abs.)

320. RAIMONDO, FRANCESCO. The Courtier's Ideal in Spanish Literature: Its Ascent and Decline. 269 pp. NYU, J. A. Coleman, 1983. *DAI* 44A: 2159–60.

". . . the fourth chapter analyzes, through the study of selected works of Calderón and Gracián, certain problems of self-perception, moral conscience, and outlook that distinguish the ideal man of the baroque age, as envisioned by these authors, from his renaissance counterpart." (Abs.)

321. REAVIS, SILKE AGNES. August Wilhelm Schlegels Auffassung der Tragödie im Zusammenhang mit seiner Poetik und ästhetischen Theorien seiner Zeit. 285 pp. WA/Seattle, E. Behler, 1975. *DAI* 37A: 999–1000.

Chapter 8 includes a discussion of Schlegel's views on Calderón de la Barca. (Abs.)

❖ Title as is. Bern: Peter Lang, 1978. 157 pp. (Europäische Hochschulschriften, Reihe 1. Deutsche Literatur und Germanistik 105, no. 1.)

322. RIPANDELLI, CAROL JANET. The Tropological Model of the Fall in *El divino Orfeo* and *El mágico prodigioso* by Calderón de la Barca. iv+223 pp. Florida State, D. L. Hoffman, 1979. *DAI* 40A: 5477.

"In this study, an application of St. Augustine's threefold process of the Fall in the doctrine of Original Sin (suggestion, delight, consent) is applied to two dramatic works by Calderón de la Barca (1600–1681). This process is defined as a psychological progression of the mind into sin through the will, toward *amor cupiditas. El divino Orfeo,* the myth of Orpheus and Eurydice, provides the framework of the concept of the Fall of Human Nature and its Redemption through marriage to Christ. Calderón's doctrine of love is to be found in this one act *auto sacramental* which affirms his adherence to the Augustinian doctrine of the Fall to his last years. An early religious drama, *El mágico prodigioso,* employs the Faustian theme to dramatize the concepts of Charity and the Fall against the background of cupidinous love. Through the analysis of these two works, representing two distinct periods in his dramatic production, a pattern emerges which testifies that Calderón viewed the salvation of man as a function of the dynamics of the movement of the will toward passion as opposed to rational contemplation of the Divine Truth alone. *El divino Orfeo* is the esthetic fulfillment of Calderón's dramatic logic starting with *El mágico prodigioso.*" (Abs.)

323. ROATEN, DARNELL HIGGINS. An Explanation of the Forms of Three Serious Spanish Baroque Dramas According to Wölfflin's *Principles of Art History*. 129 pp. Michigan, F. Sánchez y Escribano, 1951. *DA* 11: 687–88.

[For the complete entry, see no. 158.]

324. RODRÍGUEZ, SATURNINO G. La relación padrehijo en los dramas de Calderón de la Barca. 210 pp. Michigan State, J. A. Calvo-Costa, 1980. *DAI* 41A: 3133.

The writer bases his investigation on the following plays: *La vida es sueño; La devoción de la Cruz; Los cabellos de Absalón; El alcalde de Zalamea; Las tres justicias en una; Las armas de la hermosura; El hijo del sol, Faetón;* and *En esta vida todo es verdad y todo mentira.* (Abs.)

325. ROMÁN, DAVID. Constructing Comedy: Shakespeare and Calderón. 506 pp. Wisconsin, K. Cohen, 1990. *DAI* 51A: 3066.

"Chapter Four discusses Calderón's *comedias de capa y espada* and the function of dramatic comedy in Seventeenth Century Spain. Calderón constructs his comedy in direct response to the culture of crisis that exemplifies the rule of Philip IV. The formal designs of Spanish *capa y espada* are contextualized by a consideration of gender and politics during the period (1628–42). Plays such as

Mañanas de Abril y Mayo, No Hay Burlas Con El Amor, and *El Secreto a Voces* demonstrate Calderón's acute awareness of the limits of convention both as a literary device and a social practice. The comedies of Shakespeare and Calderón demonstrate the flexibility of a genre that dramatizes the discourses of patriarchy and absolutism, and its various and complex cultural responses." (Abs.)

❖ "Spectacular Women: Sites of Gender Strife and Negotiation in Calderón's *No hay burlas con el amor* and on the Early Modern Stage." *TJ* 43.4 (1991): 445-56.

326. ROSENBERG, SOLOMON LEOPOLD MILLARD. *La española de Florencia (O burlas veras, y amor invencionero), comedia famosa de Calderón de la Barca:* Edited with Introduction and Notes. Pennsylvania, H. A. Rennert, 1909. {Philadelphia: Univ. of Pennsylvania, 1911. xliv+132 pp. (UPSRLL 5.)}

"The edition is based on the first impression of 1658 and on the Leefdael and Padrino *sueltas*." (Prt. Diss.) The writer deals with *Las burlas veras* controversy here and in the following entries.

❖ [A] *Las burlas veras: Comedia famosa de Lope de Vega Carpio.* Ed. S. L. M. Rosenberg. Philadelphia: Univ. of Pennsylvania, 1912. 94 pp. (UPSRLL, extra ser. 2.) [B] *Comedia famosa de* Las burlas veras *de Ivlián de Armendárez.* Ed. S. L. M. Rosenberg. Philadelphia: Univ. of Pennsylvania, 1917. 206 pp. (UPSRLL, extra ser. 5.)

327. ROSSETTI, GUY. A Critical Edition, with Introduction and Notes of Pedro Calderón de la Barca's *El postrer duelo de España.* 372 pp. Pittsburgh, G. Sobejano, 1973. *DAI* 34A: 2652-53.

"The present edition . . . is based on the version found in the Bernardo de Hervada edition (Madrid, 1674) of Calderón's *Cuarta parte.*" (Abs.)

❖ [A] "Calderón's Use of History in *El postrer duelo de España.*" *EIA* 1 (1975): 275-83. [B] Calderón de la Barca, P. *El postrer duelo de España.* Ed., with introd. and notes, by G. Rossetti. London: Tamesis, 1977. 218 pp. (Colección Támesis, serie B. Textos 23.)

328. RUPP, STEPHEN JAMES. Articulate Illusions: Art and Authority in Jonson's Masques and Some *Autos sacramentales* of Calderón de la Barca. 327 pp. Princeton, A. Forcione, 1984. *DAI* 45A: 1392.

The writer examines the following pairs of "myth-plays": *Prince*

Henry's Barriers and *El maestrazgo del Toisón*; *Neptune's Triumph for the Return of Albion* and *El lirio y la azucena*; and *Love's Triumph through Callipolis* and *La segunda esposa y triunfar muriendo*. The principal aim of this analysis "is to elucidate the relationships between contemporary patterns and ideas of authority and the art of the two dramatists." (Abs.)

❖ [A] "Allegory and Diplomacy in Calderón's *El lirio y la azucena*." *BCom* 41.1 (1989): 107–25. [B] *Allegories of Kingship: Calderón and the Anti-Machiavellian Tradition*. University Park: Pennsylvania State UP, 1996. 187 pp. (Pennsylvania State Studies in Romance Literatures.) ["This book marks the end of a project that began with my doctoral dissertation in Comparative Literature."]

329. SÁEZ, RICHARD. The Redemptive Circe: Illusion and the Beneficence of Evil in Tasso, Milton, and Calderón. 237 pp. Yale, L. Nelson, 1967. *DA* 28A: 4608–09.

"I am interested in the theme and narrative material of the redemptive Circe myth, but I arrive at a definition of this myth through detailed analyses of prosody and epic and dramatic structure." (Abs.)

❖ *Theodicy in Baroque Literature*. New York: Garland, 1985. 190 pp. (Garland Publications in Comparative Literature.)

330. SALVIA, ANTHONY JOSEPH. The Theme of Time in Selected Plays by Calderón. iv+198 pp. Rutgers, E. Nagy, 1978. *DAI* 39A: 4309.

The following works are analyzed: *El día mayor de los días (auto), La nave del mercader (auto), El príncipe constante, Casa con dos puertas,* and *El pintor de su deshonra* (Abs.)

❖ "Time and *Heilsgeschichte* in the Theatrum Mundi: A Study of Calderón's *El día mayor de los días*." *BHS* 58.1 (1981): 31–45.

331. SANDONA, MARK. Patience and the Agents of Renaissance Drama. 320 pp. Harvard, W. J. Kaiser and W. Alfred, 1989. *DAI* 50A: 945.

"[The fourth chapter] focuses on kingship in Renaissance drama, not as a political semiotic, but as a demonstration of the mysterious conjunction of action and suffering. The discussion begins with Shakespeare's martyr-kings, Henry VI, Richard II,

Lear, and Pericles, and then considers later manifestations of the powerful become powerless (in Massinger, Calderón de la Barca, and Tourneur)." (Abs.)

332. Satake, Kenichi. Luz y oscuridad en el teatro de Calderón. v+313 pp. Illinois, A. Porqueras-Mayo, 1988. *DAI* 50A: 456.

The writer examines the function of the images of light and darkness in the *comedias de capa y espada,* the *dramas del honor,* the *dramas religiosos,* and in *La vida es sueño.* (Abs.)

❖ "Luz y oscuridad en los dramas religiosos de Calderón." *Hacia Calderón: Noveno coloquio anglogermano, Liverpool, 1990.* Ed. Hans Flasche. Stuttgart: Steiner, 1991. 81–91. (Archivum Calderonianum 6).

333. Silva, Claudio Ybarra. *Gustos y disgustos son no más que imaginación* by Pedro Calderón de la Barca: A Critical Edition and Study. v+388 pp. Southern California, R. G. Dodson, 1970. *DAI* 31A: 4136.

The edition is based on the first known printed text (1657) with variants from the edition of 1694. (Abs.)

❖ Calderón de la Barca, P. *Gustos y disgustos son no más que imaginación.* Estudio y edición crítica de C. Y. Silva. Madrid: Playor, 1974. 311 pp.

334. Silvero, Sylvia Hanzlik. Calderón en Checoslovaquia. 258 pp. Northwestern, D. Fernández-Morera, 1986. *DAI* 47A: 3063.

"Calderón entró en contacto con la literatura checa a principios del siglo diecinueve, y por ello comienzo analizando este período y continúo con las etapas literarias subsiguientes hasta llegar a la contemporánea." (Abs.)

❖ Fusek, Patricia A., and Sylvia Hanzlik-Silvero. "La influencia de Pedro Calderón de la Barca en el escritor checo Jaroslav Vrchlicky." *Calderón: Actas del congreso internacional sobre Calderón y el teatro español del Siglo de Oro, Madrid, 1981.* Ed. Luciano García Lorenzo. 3 vols. Madrid: CSIC, 1983. 1405–10.

335. Sloane, Robert Allerton. Character and Role: The Problem of Identity in Four Plays by Pedro Calderón de la Barca. iii+163 pp. Johns Hopkins, E. L. Rivers, 1972. *DAI* 33A: 6376.

The four plays are *La dama duende, El pintor de su deshonra, La devoción de la Cruz,* and *El príncipe constante.* "In intuiting the 'intimate realities' that lie beneath the formulae of roles, Calderón demonstrates his abiding modernity." (Abs.)

❖ [A] "Action and Role in *El príncipe constante*." *MLN* 85 (1970): 167-83. [B] "Diversion in Calderón's *El pintor de su deshonra*." *MLN* 91 (1976): 247-63. [C] "On Juanete's Final Story in *El pintor de su deshonra*." *BCom* 28.2 (1976): 100-03. [D] "The 'Strangeness' of *La devoción de la Cruz*." *BHS* 54 (1977): 297-310. [E] "Calderón's *No hay cosa como callar:* Character, Symbol and Comedic Context." *MLN* 99 (1984): 256-69. [F] "In the Labyrinth of Self: Character and Role in Calderón's *La dama duende*." *Studies in Honor of Elias Rivers*. Ed. Bruno M. Damiani and Ruth El Saffar. Potomac: Scripta Humanistica, 1989. 184-93.

336. Smith, Carolyn F. Imagination and Ritual in the Honor Tragedies of Calderón. iv+230 pp. Kentucky, W. C. McCrary, 1972. *DAI* 34A: 1295-96.

The honor tragedies analyzed are *El mayor monstruo los çelos, El médico de su honra, El pintor de su deshonra,* and *A secreto agravio secreta venganza.* "In all four tragedies the dialectics of love, honor, obedience and death symbolically manifest the spiritual ideal of the Christian community sharing in the glory of propitiatory sacrifice." (Abs.)

337. Socha, Donald Edward. The Garden Motif in Calderonian Drama. 283 pp. Virginia, J. S. Herrero, 1989. *DAI* 50A: 1303.

"The garden surfaces as a visual percept directly related to a character's moral and ethical circumstance and unifies concepts and images from all genres of Calderón's art." (Abs.)

❖ [A] "Calderón's Mythos of Paradise: A Hermeneutic Model." *RLAn* 1 (1989): 615-24. [B] "*El mágico prodigioso*: Cipriano's Genesis in Desire." *RLAn* 4 (1992): 584-88.

338. Soedjono, Soeprapto. Art as Medium of Propaganda: The Comparative Analysis of El Greco's Painting *The Burial of the Count of Orgaz* (1686) and Calderón's Drama *El gran teatro del mundo* (1645). 219 pp. Ohio, J. M. Haigney, 1992. *DAI* 53A: 3713.

"The main purpose of this study is to examine El Greco's *The Burial of the Count of Orgaz* and Calderón's *El gran teatro del mundo* for their propagandistic aspects. Both works chosen for analysis possess religious content. They represent a certain attitude of the Counter-Reformation propaganda which was based upon the Catholic doctrines and articulated in the Tridentine decrees." (Abs.)

339. SOUFAS, TERESA ANN SCOTT. Dreams, Nightmares, and Swoons: Calderón and Ancient Psychology. viii+306 pp. Duke, B. W. Wardropper, 1980. *DAI* 41A: 1631-32.

"The object of this study of five of Calderón's secular plays is to examine the symbiosis of psychology and dramaturgy through which the playwright depicts life as illusion." The five plays studied are *No hay cosa como callar, En la vida todo es verdad y todo mentira, Lances de amor y fortuna, El médico de su honra,* and *La vida es sueño.* (Abs.)

❖ [A] "Beyond Justice and Cruelty: Calderón's King Pedro." *JHP* 6 (1981): 57-65. [B] "Calderón's Joyless Jester: The Humanization of a Stock Character." *BCom* 34 (1982): 201-08. [C] "Calderón's Melancholy Wife-Murderers." *HR* 52 (1984): 180-203. [D] "Death and Sleep in *El médico de su honra:* Calderón's Startling Dramatization of a Poetic Tradition." *CH* 6.1 (1984): 61-67. [E] "'Happy Ending' as Irresolution in Calderón's *No hay cosa como callar.*" *FMLS* 24.2 (1988): 163-74.

340. STAAF, OSCAR EMIL. Classical Mythology in Calderón. xxiv+214 pp., handwritten. Yale, 1907.

"A great portion of the plays of Calderon contain mythological material, the collation and tabulation of which constitute the purpose of this thesis." It consists of "Introduction" (i-xviii), "Bibliography" (xix), "Titles of Plays Analyzed" (xx-xxiv), followed by an alphabetical arrangement of proper names, from Absyrtus to Vulcan, handwritten on lined paper in a bound notebook. (Diss.)

341. STEIN, LOUISE KATHRIN. Music in the Seventeenth-Century Spanish Secular Theater, 1598-1690. xi+674 pp. Chicago, H. M. Brown, 1987. *DAI* 48A: 510.

[For the complete entry, see no. 173.] The writer deals extensively with the role of music in the plays of Calderón.

342. SULLIVAN, HENRY WELLS. Two Hundred Years of Calderonian Criticism, 1681-1881. xiv+328 pp. Harvard, F. P. Casa, 1969.

"Taken as a whole, this study comprehends three broad phases:

the hostile reaction, on both moral and aesthetic grounds, to the dramatist in his native Spain (Chapters I–III), the rehabilitation of the playwright in Germany and the remarkable Calderonian furore to which it gave rise (Chapters IV–V), and finally the reactions in England and Spain to the massive influence of August Wilhelm Schlegel's epoch-making lectures on the drama in Europe down to 1881 (Chapters VI–VII)." (Diss.)

❖ [A] "*El alcalde de Zalamea* de Calderón en el teatro europeo de la segunda mitad del siglo XVIII." *LdD* 22 (1981): 15–21. [B] "Calderón, the German Idealist Philosophers, and the Question of Christian Tragedy." *CLS* 14 (1981): 51–70. [C] "A Select Bibliography of Calderón's Reception in Holland and Germany." *Ottawa Hispánica* 3 (1981): 91–101. [D] "Calderón's Reception in Spain during the Romantic Era, 1800–1850." *Ottawa Hispánica* 4 (1982): 27–54. [E] *Calderón in the German Lands and the Low Countries: His Reception and Influence, 1654–1980.* Cambridge: Cambridge UP, 1983. 510 pp. [F] "Calderón's Appeal to European Audiences during the Enlightenment and Romantic Eras: 1738–1838." *Ottawa Hispánica* 5 (1983): 41–58. [G] "La razón de los altibajos de la reputación póstuma de Calderón." *Hacia Calderón: Séptimo coloquio anglogermano, Cambridge, 1984.* Ed. Hans Flasche. Wiesbaden: Steiner, 1985. 204–11. (Archivum Calderonianum 3.) [H] "Calderón in Deutschland: Präsenz und Bedeutung." *Calderón: Fremdheit und Nähe eines spanischen Barockdramatikers: Akten des internationalen Kongresses anlässlich der Bamberger Calderón-Tage 1987.* Ed. Ángel San Miguel. Frankfurt: Vervuert, 1988. 17–33. [I] "Calderón en Inglaterra desde la restauración hasta el romanticismo." *Hacia Calderón: Noveno coloquio anglogermano, Liverpool, 1990.* Ed. Hans Flasche. Stuttgart: Steiner, 1991. 181–88. (Archivum Calderonianum 6.)

343. Suscavage, Charlene Evelyne. Calderón: Patterns of Tragedy. vi+244 pp. Pennsylvania State, L. C. Pérez, 1980. *DAI* 41A: 4415.

The writer bases her investigation on the following plays: *La gran Cenobia; La cisma de Ingalaterra; La hija del aire,* 1 and 2; *El mayor monstruo del mundo; El médico de su honra; El príncipe constante;* and *La vida es sueño.* "The Conclusion in its review of the results obtained through the analysis of Calderón's *comedias* reasserts the opinion that Golden Age dramatists did write tragedy, one that is to be found in the specific work through a careful reading, and not in some hypothetical biographical or philosophical idea of a writer's life and time." (Abs.)

❖ *Calderón: The Imagery of Tragedy.* New York: Peter Lang, 1991. 223 pp.

344. TER HORST, ROBERT MAX. *La vida es sueño:* The Rôle of Conflict. 161 pp. Johns Hopkins, C. Blanco Aguinaga, 1963.

"The thesis of the dissertation is that Calderón's Christian and Catholic idea of conflict is the key to a fuller understanding of the meaning and structure of *La vida es sueño.* . . . For Calderón, the whole struggle is between life and death. If man lives by his imperfections he dies. But if he dies to them he lives." (Diss.)

❖ *Calderón: The Secular Plays.* Lexington: UP of Kentucky, 1982. 254 pp. [Includes extensive commentary on *La vida es sueño (comedia):* pp. 51–58, 97–100, 215–33, and passim.]

345. TERRY, SUZANNE FREEMAN. A Tentative Orthoëpy of Calderón de la Barca. ii+140 pp. Virginia, D. McGrady, 1976. *DAI* 37A: 2928.

". . . Calderón was a considerably less careful craftsman of the verse than Lope and several of his contemporaries. The body of material here collected on the orthoëpic practices of Calderón provides a basis for future investigations on the authenticity of a number of plays." (Abs.)

346. THOMAS, MARY LORENE. A Critical Edition of Pedro Calderón de la Barca's *Tu prójimo como a ti* (Versions I and II). 321 pp. Michigan, L. López Grigera, 1984. *DAI* 46A: 165.

This critical edition of the two versions of Calderón's *auto sacramental* is based on the twelve early exemplars that are described as follows: "The first version, ca. 1654, exists in five manuscripts from the late seventeenth- and early eighteenth-centuries. The second version, ca. 1674, is found on an extensively emended autograph manuscript, in three additional manuscripts from the seventeenth- and eighteenth-centuries, and finally in three printed texts from the eighteenth-century." (Abs.)

❖ Calderón de la Barca, P. *Tu prójimo como a ti.* Ed. M. L. Thomas. Vol. 1, edition of the two versions; Vol. 2, paleographic ed. and concordance. Kassel: Reichenberger, 1989–94. (Teatro del Siglo de Oro. Ediciones críticas 20–21.)

347. TOMBE, SHEILA JOAN. Voice and Action: Women and Astraea in Seventeenth-Century European Drama. 156 pp. South Carolina, G. L. Geckle, 1992. *DAI* 53A: 3898.

"This dissertation focuses on the inability of women's voices to succeed in attaining justice in seventeenth-century European tragicomedy, no matter how effectively they speak, nor how much 'the law' is on their side. The Introduction examines how the static Petrarchan image of women is reconsidered in English and Spanish Renaissance literature. Using the concept of Justice embodied in the goddess Astraea and fictionalized by poets such as Spenser and Calderón de la Barca, the author shows that assertive women are to be found in plays such as Shakespeare's *The Merchant of Venice, Measure for Measure, Much Ado About Nothing,* and Calderón's *La vida es sueño (Life Is a Dream);* a chapter is devoted to each of these plays." (Abs.)

348. TOSCANO, FILIPPO MARIA. Stylistic, Structural, and Thematic Analysis of Luigi Sturzo's *Il Ciclo della Creazione.* 254 pp. Catholic, B. M. Damiani, 1989. *DAI* 50A: 973.

"This dissertation is a study based on a religious drama written by Don Luigi Sturzo (1871–1959) and entitled *Il Ciclo della Creazione* (1932). . . . In . . . chapter three, the parallel influence found in the *Ciclo* is studied, and it is possible that the source of inspiration is derived from two major catholic writers such as Dante Alighieri (1265–1321) and Pedro Calderón de la Barca (1600–1681)." (Abs.)

349. VALK, JEAN WRIGHT. Paradox as Technique in the Works of Luis de Góngora and Pedro Calderón de la Barca. v+207 pp. Kansas, A. Debicki, 1985. *DAI* 46A: 3050.

"This study asserts that there is a connection between the poetry of Luis de Góngora (1561–1627) and the plays of Pedro Calderón de la Barca (1600–1681) based on their use of paradox as a foundation for artistic technique and as an instrument for poetic mythmaking. . . . Chapter III proposes *La hija del aire,* Part I and Part II, as the key play for paradox in Calderón's theater. *La hija del aire* uses paradox and duality for the recreation of history and legend, but Chapter IV outlines the use of these same tools in other major divisions of Calderonian drama: *capa y espada (El astrólogo fingido, La dama duende,* and *Casa con dos puertas),* religious drama *(La devoción de la cruz* and *El mágico prodigioso),* and myth plays *(El mayor encanto, amor).*" (Abs.)

350. Vincent, Karen Dahlquist. A Critique of Concepts of Tragedy and *El príncipe constante* as Christian Tragedy. iii+471 pp. Southern California, J. A. Parr, 1976. *DAI* 37A: 5876–77.

"Tragedy does not involve morality; the concept of poetic justice does not apply. . . . The concepts of Christianity and tragedy are compatible. . . . The major Hispanic critics concerned with the tragedy in the Spanish Golden Age apply false concepts to the serious dramas they study. . . . Calderón's *El Príncipe Constante* contains all the necessary elements of tragedy. In a conflict of equivalent but opposite values Fernando dies as a result of a conscious decision to be true to his identity as a Christian Prince. . . ." (Abs.)

351. Voght, Geoffrey Michael. The Mythological *Autos* of Calderón de la Barca. vi+412 pp. Michigan, E. Glaser and M. Z. Hafter, 1974. *DAI* 35A: 3015–16.

Three *autos* are analyzed: *El divino Orfeo, Psiquis y Cupido,* and *El laberinto del mundo.* (Abs.)

352. Wang, I-Chun. Dream and Drama: In Late Sixteenth Century and Early Seventeenth Century—China, England, and Spain. iv+180 pp. Illinois, A. O. Aldridge, 1986. *DAI* 47A: 2575.

"The most representative and significant dream plays written during the late sixteenth and early seventeenth century in Europe and China came from the pens of William Shakespeare, Pedro Calderón de la Barca and Tang Hsien-Tzu. Their plays, *The Tempest, A Midsummer Night's Dream, La vida es sueño,* . . . share in common not only a play-within-a-play structure but also various important Baroque themes related to dream motifs: the problem of illusion and disillusion, or appearance and reality, the journey to the dream world and regenerative return; and the life-dream equation." (Abs.)

353. Warenreich, Edward David. The *Comedias de Capa y Espada* of Calderón. [3]+iii+341 pp. NYU, H. C. Heaton, 1933.

"It is hoped . . . that what will emerge from the present study will be a thorough and complete presentation of all the essential phases of Calderón's *comedias de capa y espada:* . . . their plots, their technique, their characters, the principles which motivate the action, the technical and conventional devices peculiar to them, their versification." (Diss.)

354. WATSON, JOHN ANDREW. The Metaphorical Procedure of Góngora and Calderón. vii+220 pp. Catholic, A. S. Crisafulli, 1976. *DAI* 37A: 5099.

"Góngora uses metaphorical language for purely esthetic effects; he takes delight in the object metaphorized for its own sake. Calderón's imagery has a double purpose. It is decorative in its rhetorical profusion; but primarily it serves dramatic functions; it reflects themes, foreshadows actions, is a means of characterization and is often symbolic." (Abs.)

355. WEXLER, SIDNEY FREDERICK. Comedia famosa de *La devoción de la Cruz* de D. Pedro Calderón de la Barca (Madrid, 1636). cdiii+507 pp. NYU, E. H. Hespelt, 1952.

The edition is based on the *editio princeps:* Calderón's *Primera parte,* Madrid, 1636. This text has been collated with seven *suelta* editions, the 1640 *Primera parte* of Calderón, the 1685 Vera Tassis *Primera parte* as well as the modern editions of Hartzenbusch and Valbuena Prat. (Diss.)

❖ Calderón de la Barca, P. *La devoción de la Cruz*. Ed. S. F. Wexler. Salamanca: Anaya, 1966. 156 pp.

356. WHITBY, WILLIAM MELCHER. Structural Symbolism in Two Plays of Pedro Calderón de la Barca. 211 pp. Yale, J. J. Arrom, 1954. *DAI* 32A: 989.

The plays studied are *El príncipe constante* and *La vida es sueño.* (Abs.)

❖ [A] "Calderón's *El príncipe constante:* Fénix's Role in the Ransom of Fernando's Body." *BCom* 8.1 (1956): 1–4. [B] "Rosaura's Role in the Structure of *La vida es sueño.*" *HR* 28 (1960): 16–27. Rpt. in *Critical Essays on the Theatre of Calderón*. Ed. Bruce W. Wardropper. New York: New York UP, 1965. 101–13.)

357. YOUNG, [SISTER] MARGARET PAULINE. The Liturgical Element in the *Autos Sacramentales* of Calderón. xxiii+146 pp. Boston

University, S. M. Waxman, 1947. Abstract: Boston Univ. Graduate School, 1947, no pagination.

"A close study of the complete corpus of the *Autos Sacramentales* of Calderón reveals the fact that they are constructed in accordance with a definite and original dramatic technique, and that each *Auto* is a carefully planned, logically developed exposition of a master thought. An examination of the *Autos* in conjunction with their liturgical sources serves to clarify many difficult passages, and brings out the fact that they are not unintelligible but profound." (Abs.)

Cañizares, José de (1676–1750)

358. Johns, Kim Lewis. José de Cañizares: Traditionalist and Innovator. 213 pp. North Carolina, A. V. Ebersole, 1976. *DAI* 38A: 2832.

This study is based on a detailed analysis of three plays: *Don Juan de Espina en su patria, Don Juan de Espina en Milán,* and *El pleyto de Hernán Cortés.* "The analysis . . . reveals that [Cañizares] was a dramatist who, because of his chronological position in literary history, was able to draw upon the dramatic aesthetics of both the seventeenth and the eighteenth centuries." (Abs.)

❖ Title as is. Valencia: Albatros-Hispanófila, n.d. (1981?). 131 pp. (Albatros-Hispanófila 17.)

Caramuel, Juan (1606–1682)

359. Hernández Nieto, Héctor Manuel. Las teorías dramáticas de Caramuel. 277 pp. Illinois, A. Porqueras-Mayo, 1975. *DAI* 36A: 273.

Caramuel's *Primus Calamus* (2nd ed., 1668) includes a commentary—favorable—on Lope de Vega's *Arte nuevo de hacer comedias.* (Abs.)

❖ [A] "La Epístola XXI de Juan Caramuel sobre el *Arte nuevo de hacer comedias,* de Lope de Vega." *Segismundo* 12.23–24 (1976):

203–88. [B] "Comparación entre Lope y Góngora según un manuscrito de Caramuel." *Perspectivas de la comedia 2: Ensayos sobre la comedia del Siglo de Oro español, de distintos autores, con una nota introductoria de Alva V. Ebersole.* Ed. Alva V. Ebersole. Valencia: Albatros-Hispanófila, 1979. 61–68. [C] "Los manuscritos inéditos de Caramuel." *Actas del sexto congreso internacional de hispanistas, Toronto, 1977.* Ed. Alan M. Gordon and Evelyn Rugg. Toronto: Univ. of Toronto, 1980. 381–82. [D] "Una traducción y compendio de Caramuel: Los apuntes sobre el 'Teatro' de José Alcázar." *KRQ* 27 (1980): 473–84. [E] "*La Epístola Octava* de Caramuel sobre la poesía de Quevedo." *ALM* 29 (1991): 245–77. [F] "Una senda singular: Las nuevas teorías poéticas de Caramuel." *RL* 53.106 (1991): 655–76. [G] *Ideas literarias de Caramuel.* Critical ed., trans., bibliog., and notes from "Las Epístolas preliminares" by H. Hernández Nieto. Prologue by Alberto Porqueras-Mayo. Barcelona: PPU, 1992. 238 pp.

Castillo Solórzano, Alonso de (1584–1648)

Editorial note: Following is a list of Castillo's dramatic works. Since most of them were inserted in the author's novels or novella collections, the latter titles are included in parentheses, where appropriate. A: Five *entremeses: El casamentero* (in *Tiempo de regocijo*); *El comisario de figuras* (in *Las harpías en Madrid*); *El barbador* (in *La niña de los embustes*); *La prueba de los doctores* (in *La niña de los embustes*); *Las castañeras* (in *Aventuras del bachiller Trapaza*). B: Seven *comedias: El agravio satisfecho* (in *Huerta de Valencia*); *Los encantos de Bretaña* (in *Fiestas del jardín*); *La fantasma de Valencia* (in *Fiestas del jardín*); *El marqués del Cigarral* (in *Fiestas del jardín*); *El mayorazgo figura* (in *Los alivios de Casandra*); *La torre de Florisbella* (in *Sala de recreación*); *La victoria de Nordlingen* (in *Parte veinte y ocho de comedias nuevas de los mejores ingenios,* 1667). C: One *auto sacramental: El fuego dado del cielo*. None of the dissertations below deals exclusively or extensively with Castillo's theater, but they do offer insights on this author, incidental information on the plays, and specific data about the works in which the plays were interpolated.

360. CUNNINGHAM, MALCOLM ANTHONY. Castillo Solórzano: A Reappraisal. 157 pp. Tulane, D. W. McPheeters, 1971. *DAI* 32A: 960.

"This dissertation, therefore, reexamines Castillo Solórzano from a more intensive perspective, by concentrating on some of the analytical tools of modern criticism. To this end, discussion has been limited to Castillo's three most popular picaresque works, *La niña de los embustes, Aventuras del bachiller Trapaza,* and *La garduña de Sevilla.*" (Abs.)

361. LONES, ROSEMARIE G. Alonso de Castillo Solórzano's *Novelas Cortas:* Meaning and Purpose. 295 pp. Oklahoma, J. P. Artman, 1974. *DAI* 36A: 322.

"This thesis demonstrates the meaning and purpose of Castillo's *novelas cortas* by a study of the function of their component elements. Literary theory of seventeenth-century Spain, the taste of the reading public and the pressures exerted by the Spanish censorship determined to a large extent the form and the tone an author employed." (Abs.) Castillo's *novelas cortas* are found in the following collections: *Tardes entretenidas, Jornadas alegres, Tiempo de regocijo, Huerta de Valencia, Noches de placer, Los alivios de Casandra, Sala de recreación, La quinta de Laura,* and *Fiestas del jardín.*

362. NEMTZOW, SARAH. Alonso de Castillo Solórzano: An Analysis of His Novelistic Production. 425 pp. CA/Los Angeles, C. Barja, 1952.

"The influence of the *comedia* of the period is noticeable in Castillo's technique of brief expositions, rapid action and somewhat brusque and illogical endings, and in such unrealistic devices as improbable encounters, disguises and coincidences." (AFE) This analysis includes the novellas as well as the novels.

363. SÁNCHEZ-DÍEZ, FRANCISCO JAVIER. La novela picaresca de protagonista femenino en España durante el siglo XVII. 255 pp. North Carolina, J. B. Avalle-Arce, 1972. *DAI* 34A: 286.

"Finally, Chapter six [pp. 200–28] deals with the treatment of the picaresque novel of female protagonist in the hands of Castillo Solórzano. His indebtedness to both López de Úbeda and Salas Barbadillo is shown. Castillo Solórzano, however, followed his own purposes quite independently, as can be seen especially in

[La niña de los embustes] Teresa de Manzanares, a novel which has usually been misunderstood by critics." (Abs.)

Castro y Bellvís, Guillén de (1569–1631)

364. Alpern, Hymen. *La tragedia por los celos,* comedia famosa de Don Guillén de Castro y Bellvís. 166 pp. NYU, H. C. Heaton, 1925.

The critical edition is based on a seventeenth-century *suelta* owned by E. B. Babcock, with variants from the Toledo MS, the Madrid MS as edited and printed in 1878, and the Madrid MS as transcribed by H. A. Rennert.

❖ [A] "Jealousy as a Dramatic Motive in the Spanish *Comedia.*" *RR* 14 (1923): 276–85. [B] Castro, G. de. La tragedia por los celos, *comedia famosa de Don Guillén de Castro y Bellvís.* Ed. after a seventeenth-century *suelta,* with introd., variants, and notes by H. Alpern. Paris: Champion, 1926. 150 pp. [C] Microfilm edition of typescript, 1990.

365. Crapotta, James Frank. Tyranny and the Abuse of Royal Power in the Theater of Guillén de Castro. iii+263 pp. Harvard, S. Gilman, 1979.

The following five plays are analyzed in detail: *El amor constante, El Conde Alarcos, El nacimiento de Montesinos, El perfecto caballero,* and *Las mocedades del Cid (Comedia segunda).* (Diss.)

❖ *Kingship and Tyranny in the Theatre of Guillén de Castro.* London: Tamesis, 1984. 188 pp. (Colección Támesis, serie A. Monografías C.)

366. Delgado Morales, Manuel. Tiranía y derecho de resistencia en el teatro de Guillén de Castro. 264 pp. Texas, S. Zimic, 1981. *DAI* 42A: 3175.

"The present study attempts to demonstrate that the doctrines of the right of resistance and of tyrannicide found expression in the works of one of the most important Spanish Golden Age dramatists, Guillén de Castro y Bellvís . . . These conclusions have been drawn from a careful study of the literary text of the following works of Guillén de Castro: *El Conde Alarcos, El amor constante, La piedad en la justicia, Cuánto se estima el honor, Las hazañas del Cid* and *El perfecto caballero*." (Abs.)

❖ [A] "Tiranía y derecho de resistencia en *Las mocedades del Cid*." *Segismundo* 15.33–34 (1981): 173–84. [B] "Guillén de Castro y las teorías políticas sobre el tiranicidio y el derecho de resistencia." *BH* 85 (1983): 65–82. [C] Title as is. Barcelona: Puvill, 1984. 155 pp. (Biblioteca universitaria Puvill. Ensayos 11.)

367. Escribano, Jean Schneider. The Function of Classical Myth in the Theater of Guillén de Castro. 161 pp. Emory, G. Umpierre, 1971. *DAI* 32A: 2683.

The writer examines *Los amores de Dido y Eneas, Progne y Filomena, La manzana de la discordia y robo de Elena,* and *El Narciso en su opinión.* (Abs.)

❖ "The Function of Classical Myth in the Theater of Guillén de Castro." *Studies in Language and Literature: Proceedings of the Twenty-Third Mountain Interstate Foreign Language Conference.* Ed. Charles Nelson. Richmond: Eastern Kentucky Univ., 1976. 147–51.

368. Krogh, Richard Neal. The Growth of Guillén de Castro's Dramatic Technique as Shown by Eight Selected Plays. 143 pp. WA/Seattle, W. E. Wilson, 1956. *DA* 16: 2166.

The eight plays are: *El amor constante, El Conde Alarcos, Los mal casados de Valencia, El curioso impertinente, Progne y Filomena, Las mocedades del Cid (Comedia segunda), La tragedia por los celos,* and *El pretender con pobreza.* (Abs.)

369. LaDu, Robert Richard. Honor in the Theater of Guillén de Castro. 157 pp. WA/Seattle, W. E. Wilson, 1960. *DA* 20: 4660–61.

"This study is based upon those plays attributed to Guillén de Castro by E. Juliá Martínez in his *Obras de Don Guillén de Castro y Bellvís* (3 vols., Madrid, 1925–1927)." (Abs.)

❖ "Honor and the King in the *Comedias* of Guillén de Castro." *H*[AATSP] 45 (1962): 211–17.

370. Mendicoa, John M. Los paralelos estructurales y estilísticos en la técnica dramática de Guillén de Castro. ii+384 pp. Catholic, J. M. Solà-Solé, 1973. *DAI* 34A: 5192–93. {CUASRLL 108; also no. 42 of its microfilm series.}

"The study begins with a summary of each of the 42 plays of Guillén de Castro published by Juliá Martínez, and a classification of them according to theme. And then it turns to an examination of structural and stylistic devices that characterize his dramatic technique. The principal structural device is the technique of parallel. These parallels can be classified as the *echoic, transferential* and *the rhythmic-parallelic structure of the theme.*" (Abs.)

371. PAPPANASTOS, GEORGIA. The Heroic Ideal in Five Plays of Guillén de Castro. 318 pp. Kentucky, W. C. McCrary, 1969. *DAI* 31A: 365–66.

The five plays are *El amor constante, El nacimiento de Montesinos, El Conde Alarcos, Progne y Filomena,* and *El mejor esposo.* (Abs.)
❖ [A] "The Heroic Ideal in Guillén de Castro's First Play." *KRQ* 23 (1976): 421–37 [The play is *El amor constante.*] [B] "Verbal Subtlety in Castro's *El amor constante.*" *BCom* 28.1 (1976): 17–22.

372. PÉREZ, ELISA. La influencia del *Romancero* en Guillén de Castro. [2]+209 pp. Wisconsin, A. García Solalinde, 1932.

"La importancia de la obra dramática de Guillén de Castro se deriva en gran parte del Romancero, a causa de su aprovechamiento del mismo. En este respecto podemos decir que él hizo revivir el Romancero, y el Romancero le dió la fama. Esto se puede afirmar (a) por la gran proporción de sus obras dramáticas debida a los romances; (b) por su arte especial que brilla más en las obras de esta fuente. No es extraño, pues, que el nombre de Guillén de Castro esté para siempre unido al Romancero." Two "Notas adicionales" are of special interest: "Apuntes sobre el Romancero en Juan de la Cueva," pp. 193–97, and "Apuntes sobre el Romancero en Tirso de Molina," pp. 198–206. (Diss.)
❖ "Algunos aspectos de la evolución del Romancero." *H* [AATSP] 18 (1935): 151–60. [On *romances* in the theater of Juan de la Cueva, Lope de Vega, and especially Guillén de Castro.]

373. POWERS, DOROTHEA THOMPSON. The Dramatic Art of Guillén de Castro. 410 pp. New Mexico, R. R. MacCurdy, 1958. *DA* 19: 1366.

"This work studies Castro's dramatic art as revealed in the twenty-seven plays which have been fully authenticated. The chronology determined by Courtney F. Bruerton has been followed. A new classification by structure has been developed to help determine the stages in Castro's development." (Abs.)

374. ROATEN, DARNELL HIGGINS. An Explanation of the Forms of Three Serious Spanish Baroque Dramas According to Wölfflin's *Principles of Art History*. 129 pp. Michigan, F. Sánchez y Escribano, 1951. *DA* 11: 687–88.

[For the complete entry, see no. 158.]

375. SEGALL, JACOB BERNARD. Corneille and the Spanish Drama. Columbia, 1902. {New York: Columbia UP; Macmillan, 1902. ix+147 pp. (Columbia University Studies in Romance Philology and Literature 3)}

[For the complete entry, see no. 164.]

CERDA, MELCHOR DE LA (1550–1615)

376. GARZÓN-BLANCO, ARMANDO IGNACIO DIONISIO. The Inaugural Production of the Spanish Jesuit *Tragedia de San Hermenegildo,* Seville, 1590. xvi+232 pp. Louisiana State, G. L. Doty, 1976. *DAI* 37A: 6845–46.

[For the complete entry, see no. 227.] M. de la Cerda was one of the three authors of this play.

CERVANTES, MIGUEL DE (1547–1616)

377. ALLEN, KENNETH PHILIP. Cervantes and the Pastoral Mode. v+180 pp. Columbia, G. S. Pathy and K.-L. Selig, 1977. *DAI* 40A: 3336.

Chapter 4 includes consideration of *Pedro de Urdemalas,* one of the *Ocho comedias*. (Abs.)

378. ARBOLEDA, CARLOS ARTURO. Teoría y formas del metateatro en la "Commedia dell'arte," "el Quijote" y algunas obras dramáticas de Cervantes. 216 pp. Syracuse, D. P. Testa, 1990. *DAI* 51A: 4141.

"El propósito de esta comunicación es explorar las ideas y técnicas dramáticas de Cervantes. Estas se hallan presentes no sólo en sus textos estrictamente dramáticos (comedias y entremeses), sino en el mismo *Quijote*. Su idea de teatro no hace referencia única y exclusivamente a la representación de un mundo fingido o imaginado en palabras. Su teatro es un teatro que se refiere mayormente a sí mismo, al proceso mismo de representación. Es un metateatro." (Abs.)

❖ [A] *Teoría y formas del metateatro en Cervantes*. Salamanca: Universidad de Salamanca, 1991. 103 pp. (Acta Salmanticensia. Estudios filológicos 244.) [B] "El concepto de distanciamiento en las dramaturgias de Cervantes y Brecht." *CAld* 8.1 (1992): 27-32.

379. Bates, Margaret J. *Discreción* in the Works of Cervantes: A Semantic Study. Catholic, D. Rubio, 1945. {Washington: Catholic Univ. of America, 1945. vii+86 pp. (Studies in Romance Languages and Literatures 31.)}

"The purpose of this dissertation is to analyze each occurrence of the word *discreción* and its cognates in the [dramatic and nondramatic] works of Cervantes and to classify its meanings." (Prt. Diss.)

380. Batlle, Margarita Caveda. A Critical Study of Cervantes' *Entremeses*. ix+152 pp. New Mexico, R. R. MacCurdy, 1980. *DAI* 41A: 2137-38.

"The purpose of this dissertation is two-fold. First, it summarizes all data pertaining to the *Entremeses,* including the etymology of the word itself, the development of the dramatic form, their chronology, and their sources. The plays are analyzed individually through an examination of each of their integral elements, namely, their themes, characters, language, style, and structure. The second objective of the dissertation is to define the humor of the *Entremeses*." (Abs.)

381. Cain, [Sister] Mariano. The Idea of a Theater in the *Entremeses* of Cervantes. iii+269 pp. Wisconsin, R. G. Sánchez, 1964. *DA* 25: 2507-08.

In this study, "the eight *entremeses* are considered as works conceived in terms of a *stage* to be projected by *actors* to an *audience*." (Abs.)

382. Chaves-García, José María. Intergroup Relations in the Works of Cervantes. [381 pp.] Columbia, R. K. Hall, 1953.

The writer studies intergroup relations in the dramatic as well as nondramatic works of Cervantes. (Diss.) Editorial note: The typescript contains many unnumbered leaves as well as many numbered leaves that are not in sequence. [In the Rare Book and Manuscript Room, Butler Library, 6th floor.]

❖ *Intergroup Relations in the Spain of Cervantes*. Staten Island: Mensaje, 1974. 396 pp.

383. CROOKS, ESTHER JOSEPHINE. The Influence of Cervantes in France during the First Half of the Seventeenth Century, with Special Reference to Guérin de Bouscal and a Critical Edition of His *Gouvernement de Sanche Pansa*. [389] pp. Johns Hopkins, H. C. Lancaster, 1923.

❖ *The Influence of Cervantes in France in the Seventeenth Century*. Baltimore: Johns Hopkins UP, 1931. 271 pp. (Johns Hopkins Studies in Romance Literatures and Languages, extra vol. 4.)

Chapter 6 is entitled "The Influence of Cervantes' Theater upon French Plays of the Seventeenth Century." (Prt. Diss.)

384. DISALVO, ANGELO J. Reflections of the Theological Tradition of St. Augustine in Cervantes. iii+238 pp. Florida State, W. P. Cooke, 1981. *DAI* 42A: 1172–73.

Pertinent works included in this analysis are "the captivity plays and the play *El rufián dichoso*." (Abs.)

❖ *Cervantes and the Augustinian Religious Tradition*. York: Spanish Literature Publications, 1989. 254 pp.

385. FRIEDMAN, EDWARD HERBERT. The Unifying Concept: An Approach to the Structure of Cervantes' *Comedias*. 269 pp. Johns Hopkins, H. Sieber, 1974. *DAI* 35A: 3678–79.

"Cervantes achieves unity not by developing complications around a single action as do Lope de Vega and his followers, but through parallel events (or episodes) which form a conceptual unity. The individual episodes, analogically related, reinforce or complement an idea rather than expand an action." (Abs.)

❖ [A] "Cervantes' Dramatic Development from *Los tratos de Argel* to *Los baños de Argel*." *REHb* 10 (1976): 31–55. [B] "Dramatic Structure in Cervantes and Lope: The Two *Pedro de Urdemalas* Plays." *H* [AATSP] 60 (1977): 486–97. [C] "*La Numancia* within Structural Patterns of Sixteenth-Century Spanish Tragedy." *Neophilologus* 61 (1977): 74–89. [D] "An Archetype and Its Modifications: Cervantes' Dramatic Theory and Practice." *TAH* 4.28 (1978): 9–11. [E] "Double Vision: Self and Society in *El laberinto de amor* and *La entretenida*." *Cervantes and the Renaissance.* Ed. Michael D. McGaha. Easton: Juan de la Cuesta, 1980. 157–66. [F] "Role and Reality: The Question of Identity in Cervantes' *Comedias*." *PCP* 15.1 (1980): 19–25. [G] *The Unifying Concept: Approaches to the Structure of Cervantes's Comedias.* York: Spanish Literature Publications, 1981. 185 pp.

386. GRIFFITHS, JANET. Las ideas literarias de Cervantes. 166 pp. Middlebury, 1949.

The writer deals with Cervantes's ideas on the theater in chapter 3, pp. 68–90. (Diss.)

387. HAWK MARKS, MORLEY JENNIFER. *La casa de los celos y las selvas de Ardenia* by Miguel de Cervantes (Critical Study with a Modernized Annotated Edition): An Examination of Cervantine Process toward the Conception of the *Quijote.* 296 pp. Temple, A. Lewis Galanes, 1981. *DAI* 42A: 5140.

"The first part of this dissertation examines past criticism of Cervantes' theater, sources, and mechanics of *La casa de los celos,* characterizations and literary topics shared by both the play and the *Quijote* of 1605 and their evolution in the *Quijote* of 1615. Part Two is a modernized text of the play followed by cultural and textual notes." (Abs.)

❖ "Deformación de la tradición pastoril en *La casa de los celos,* de Miguel de Cervantes." *Cervantes and the Pastoral (Proceedings).* Ed. José J. Labrador Herraiz and Juan Fernández Jiménez. Cleveland: Pennsylvania State Univ.–Cleveland State Univ., Behrend College, 1986. 129–38.

388. KANELLOS, NICHOLAS CHARLES. Cervantes and the *Comedia Nueva:* A Comprehensive Survey of His Dramatic Theory and Practice. vi+254 pp. Texas, S. Zimic, 1974. *DAI* 35A: 458.

"The plays [of the *Ocho comedias*] are studied in separate chapters in an order that indicates the progressive assimilation and accumulation of *comedia nueva* elements." (Abs.)

❖ "The Anti-Semitism of Cervantes' *Los baños de Argel* and *La gran sultana:* A Reappraisal." *BCom* 27.1 (1975): 48–52.

389. KENWORTHY, PATRICIA ANN. The *Entremeses* of Cervantes: The Dramaturgy of Illusion. vi+155 pp. Arizona, R. M. ter Horst, 1976. *DAI* 37A: 3674.

"This dissertation approaches Cervantes' comic interludes . . . from the perspective of their relationship to the Cervantine exploration of the boundaries of life and literature." (Abs.)

❖ [A] "Cervantes' Unrepentant Adulteress: The Birth of a Woman and Artist." *Women in the Literature of Medieval and Golden Age Spain*. Syracuse: Onondaga Community Coll., 1979. 90–95. [Apropos Lorenza in the *entremés El viejo celoso*.] [B] "The Character of Lorenza and the Moral of Cervantes' *El viejo celoso*." *BCom* 31.2 (1979): 103–08. [C] "La ilusión dramática en los entremeses de Cervantes." *Cervantes, su obra y su mundo: Actas del primer congreso internacional sobre Cervantes, Madrid, 1978*. Ed. Manuel Criado de Val. Madrid: EDI-6, 1981. 235–42.

390. LaGrone, Gregory Gough. The Imitations of *Don Quixote* in the Spanish Drama. Pennsylvania, M. Romera-Navarro, 1936. {Philadelphia: Univ. of Pennsylvania, 1937. vii+145 pp. (UPSRLL 27.)}

The writer discusses plays of the seventeenth, eighteenth, nineteenth, and early twentieth centuries. (Prt. Diss.)

391. Martín, Adrienne Laskier. Cervantes and the Burlesque Sonnet. 425 pp. Harvard, F. Márquez Villanueva, 1987.

❖ [A] "Un modelo para el humor poético cervantino: Los sonetos burlescos del *Quijote*." *Actas del primer coloquio internacional de la Asociación de Cervantistas, Alcalá de Henares, 1988*. Barcelona: Anthropos, 1990. 349–56. [B] "La 'sonetada,' o los problemas de una escondida poesía bufonesca." *La edición de textos: Actas del primer congreso internacional de hispanistas del Siglo de Oro, 1987*. Ed. Pablo Jauralde, Dolores Noguera, and Alfonso Rey. London: Tamesis, 1990. 271–77. (Colección Támesis, serie A. Monografías 139.) [C] Title as is. Berkeley: U of California P, 1991. 295 pp. [See pp. 114–22 of the 1991 edition on the burlesque sonnets in the *comedia La entretenida*. "The ultimate significance of all the *Entretenida* sonnets is to point to the senselessness of the type of theater produced by Lope." On other Cervantine sonnets that criticize Lope, see pp. 82–84, 129–30, 158–65, 206–07, and 229–33.]

392. Martínez y Quintana, Fernando. Cervantes, su teatro y sus críticos. 212 pp. Virginia, J. C. Bardin, 1930.

Following his discussion of the topic indicated in the title, the writer of this dissertation provides critical analyses of *La Numancia, La entretenida, El rufián viudo,* and *El retablo de las maravillas.* (Diss.)

393. ODDI, VICTOR L. The Interplay of Reality and Illusion in the Infrastructure of the Cervantine *Entremeses.* 317 pp. Pennsylvania State, L. C. Pérez, 1990. *DAI* 51A: 3097.

"In recapitulation, the objectives of the individual critical analyses are to accomplish the following: (a) reveal and define the infrastructure of the *entremés;* (b) identify the component parts of this infrastructure; (c) show the nature and functions performed by each component; (d) identify and describe the interplay of reality and illusion within the infrastucture; (e) explain, when appropriate and of particular interest, the source of humor resulting from this conflictive interplay." (Abs.)

394. ORGILL, DOUGLAS HAROLD. The Influence of Cervantes on the Plays of John Fletcher. iv+300 pp. Southern California, A. Arnold, 1960. *DA* 21: 625.

"This last play [Fletcher's *The Wild Goose Chase*] could also have been influenced by similar suggestions from *El Casamiento Engañoso* and *La Comedia Entretenida.*" (Abs.) Editorial note: *La entretenida* is the only Cervantine play cited by the writer.

395. PILUSO, ROBERT VINCENT. La actitud de Cervantes frente al problema del matrimonio según se desprende de sus obras. 236 pp. NYU, F. Ayala, 1965. *DA* 27A: 1792.

"This study presents in a systematized way the complex, though not contradictory, ideas on marriage which Cervantes incorporates into the situations and characters of his works. A necessary frame of reference for this study is the civil and canonical law before and after the Council of Trent." (Abs.)

❖ *Amor, matrimonio y honra en Cervantes.* New York: Las Americas, 1967. 168 pp. [Editorial note: This is the text of the dissertation with a title change.]

396. QUIÑONES-ROMÁN, DAVID L. Ventas cervantinas: La técnica dramática y el engaño de los sentidos. x+167 pp. Massachusetts, F. Fernández-Turienzo, 1988. *DAI* 49A: 3745.

"This dissertation concentrates upon the examination of the

country-inns as a stage in the *El ingenioso hidalgo don Quijote de la Mancha,* where Cervantes develops his dramatic technique and also the theme of the delusion of the senses." (Abs.)

397. RAMÍREZ, ALEJANDRO. Cervantes y la Biblia. [2]+175+1 pp. Washington/St. Louis, S. Eoff, 1951.

"El objeto de este estudio es el de plantear la cuestión de la utilización—directa o indirecta—de la Biblia por Cervantes. . . . El examen de los textos cervantinos . . . muestra que apenas hay libro en ambos Testamentos que no esté representado siquiera por una reminiscencia lejana." See especially "Comedias y entremeses," pp. 107-53. (Diss.)

❖ "Cervantes y la Inquisición." *Armas y Letras* (Universidad de Nuevo León), 2nd series, 2.2 (1959): 23-33. [A passage in the *Quijote,* condemned in the Portuguese Index of Bishop Mascareñas (1624), is examined in relation to similar ones in Ovid and in St. Jerome's translation of the Song of Songs.]

398. REED, CORY ARTHUR. Cervantes' Drama of Regeneration: Novelization and the Popular Tradition in the *Entremeses.* ix+243 pp. Princeton, A. Forcione, 1989. *DAI* 50A: 1677.

"This study examines the Cervantine interlude as a dramatic form which exhibits characteristics of both the lettered and popular traditions. Throughout, the plays are revealed to be highly complex and innovative satirical works, whose indeterminacy requires the thoughtful collaboration of the audience or reader, and whose social commentary and reconciliation of popular and elite cultures reflect the values of the Christian humanist movement and the consciousness of change in the late Renaissance." (Abs.)

❖ [A] "Cervantes and the Novelization of Drama: Tradition and Innovation in the *Entremeses.*" *Cervantes* 11.1 (1991): 60-84. [B] "Dirty Dancing: Salome, Herodias and *El retablo de las maravillas. BCom* 44.1 (1992): 7-20. [C] *The Novelist as Playwright: Cervantes and the "Entremés nuevo."* New York: Peter Lang, 1993. 212 pp. [D] "*Entremés* and Novel: Comic Theatricality in *Don Quijote.*" *Cervantes: Estudios en la víspera de su centenario*. Ed. Kurt Reichenberger. 2 vols. Kassel: Reichenberger, 1994. 1: 197-213.

399. ROTTA, JOHN BERNARD. The *Commedia dell'Arte* in the Theater

of Cervantes. ix+193 pp. SUNY/Stony Brook, V. Llorens(?), 1976. *DAI* 37A: 1598.

"It appears that the influence of the *commedia dell'arte* on the theater of Cervantes, although sporadic, is substantial. The similarities with the masks and the techniques, taken collectively, give hints of close dependence." (Abs.)

❖ "The Rebellious Woman in the *Entremeses* of Cervantes." *Women in the Literature of Medieval and Golden Age Spain*. Syracuse: Onondaga Community Coll., 1979. 86-69.

400. SEWELL, ROBERT GEORGE. The Theme of Suicide: A Study of Human Values in Japanese and Western Literature. iv+208 pp. Illinois, F. Jost, 1976. *DAI* 37A: 6467.

The relevant work discussed here is *El cerco de Numancia* of Cervantes. The writer concludes: "Suicides which express commitments to honor, love, and art reaffirm those transcendent values in human experience." (Abs.)

401. SYVERSON, JILL ANN. Theatrical Aspects of Cervantes' Prose: A Study of *Don Quijote*. 215 pp. Harvard, S. Gilman, 1980.

"We will indicate the striking proximity between techniques used in the drama—in Cervantes' own plays in particular—and methods employed in the novel, to bring scenes and characters to life." (Diss.)

❖ Syverson-Stork, J. A. *Theatrical Aspects of the Novel: A Study of* Don Quixote. Valencia: Albatros, 1986. 134 pp. (Albatros-Hispanófila 40.)

402. THOMPSON, EARL GLADSTONE, JR. Elements of Form: A Structural Analysis of Cervantes' Three- and Four-Act Dramas. iv+254 pp. Illinois, A. Porqueras-Mayo, 1974. *DAI* 35A: 482.

"The analysis itself consists of a schematic presentation of the play in which each segment is delineated, accompanied by commentary concerning the function of the segment as a part of the main or subplot, the source and nature of the dramatic conflict and its resolution, a brief quotation in Spanish from the turning point or moment of maximum tension in the segment, the verse forms utilized and their function, and the signals which indicate the conclusion of the segment." (Abs.)

❖ "Shepherds as Spanish Society: Cervantes' View in One

Comedia." *Varia hispanica: Homenaje a Alberto Porqueras-Mayo*. Ed. Joseph L. Laurenti and Vern G. Williamsen. Kassel: Reichenberger, 1989. 7–15. (Teatro del Siglo de Oro. Estudios de literatura 5.) [The *comedia* is *La casa de los celos*.]

403. TORBERT, EUGENE CHARLES. A Study of Place-Names in the Works of Cervantes. 291 pp. North Carolina, S. A. Stoudemire, 1974. *DAI* 36A: 289–90.

"This study comprises all of the place-names in the complete works of Miguel de Cervantes Saavedra." (Abs.)

❖ *Cervantes' Place-Names: A Lexicon*. Metuchen: Scarecrow, 1978. 181 pp.

404. TRACHMAN, SADIE EDITH. Cervantes' Women of Literary Tradition. 177 pp. Columbia, F. de Onís, 1932. {New York: Instituto de las Españas en los Estados Unidos, 1932. 177 pp.}

The women studied are found in dramatic as well as nondramatic works. (Diss.)

405. TURKEVICH, LUDMILLA BUKETOFF. Cervantes in Russia. 255 pp. Columbia, F. de Onís, 1950. {Princeton: Princeton UP, 1950. 255 pp.}

The dissertation deals with dramatic and nondramatic works. (Prt. Diss.)

❖ [A] *Spanish Literature in Russia*. Metuchen: Scarecrow, 1967. 273 pp. [B] Rpt. of diss. New York: Gordian, 1975.

406. ZIMIC, STANISLAV. Cervantes, lector de Aquiles Tacio y de Alonso Núñez de Reinoso. viii+212 pp. Duke, R. L. Predmore, 1964. *DA* 26: 379.

"One love intrigue used in *El trato de Argel*, and repeated in *Los baños de Argel*, . . . originates in the novel of Achilles Tatius." The novel *Leucippe and Clitophon* by the Greek Achilles Tatius (second century AD) was partially translated by Alonso Núñez de Reinoso, who, "after adding several chapters of his own, published it in Venice in 1552 as *Los amores de Clareo y Florisea*." (Abs.)

❖ [A] "El amante celestino y los amores entrecruzados en algunas obras cervantinas." *BBMP* 40 (1964): 361–87. [Apropos influence of Achilles Tatius on Cervantes.] [B] "Alonso Núñez de Reinoso, traductor de *Leucipe y Clitofonte*." *Symposium* 21 (1967): 166–75.

[C] "Sobre dos entremeses cervantinos: *La elección de los alcaldes de Daganzo* y *El rufián viudo*." *ACer* 19 (1981): 119-60. [D] *El teatro de Cervantes*. Madrid: Castalia, 1992. 422 pp. (Literatura y sociedad 53.)

Claramonte, Andrés de (died 1621 ?)

407. Asturias, [Sister] Rosario María, SNJM. A Critical Edition and Study of the Play *El rey don Pedro en Madrid y el Infanzón de Illescas.* vi+553 pp. Southern California, E. W. Hesse, 1963. *DA* 24: 5378-79.

[For the complete entry, see no. 205.]

408. Ganelin, Charles. A Critical Edition and Study of Andrés de Claramonte's *La infelice Dorotea.* v+298 pp. Chicago, G. Haley, 1983. *DAI* 44A: 3395.

The critical text is based on the manuscript. "The appendices include an alphabetical list of actors with whom Claramonte worked during his career and a detailed breakdown of plays in which Claramonte may have acted." (Abs.)

❖ [A] Claramonte, A. de. *La infelice Dorotea.* Ed., introd., and notes by C. Ganelin. London: Tamesis, 1987. 198 pp. (Colección Támesis, serie B. Textos 31.) [B] "Astrology, Poetic Justice and Providence in Andrés de Claramonte's *La infelice Dorotea*." *BCom* 39.2 (1987): 215-23. [C] "The MacIntosh Computer and the *Comedia* Text." *Editing the* Comedia II. Ed. Michael McGaha and Frank P. Casa. Ann Arbor: Univ. of Michigan, Dept. of Romance Languages, 1991. 139-55. (Michigan Romance Studies 11.)

409. Trejo, Alex Treviño. Edición crítica de *El valiente negro en Flandes* de Andrés de Claramonte. v+360 pp. Southern California, J. A. Parr, 1977. *DAI* 38A: 4873.

The critical text is based on "the first printed edition of Barcelona (1638) and the last printed edition of *B.A.E.* (1857)," which have been collated with five other printed versions as well as a manuscript regarded as "only a rough copy of the original MS." (Abs.)

Coello y Ochoa, Antonio (1611–1682)

410. Bacalski, Robert Rudolf. A Critical Edition of *El jardín de Falerina* by Francisco de Rojas Zorrilla, Antonio Coello y Ochoa, and Pedro Calderón de la Barca with Introduction and Notes. 351 pp. New Mexico, R. R. MacCurdy, 1972. *DAI* 33A: 5712.
  [For the complete entry, see no. 242.]
411. Gaw, Allison. Tuke's *Adventures of Five Hours,* in Relation to the "Spanish Plot" and to John Dryden. Pennsylvania, 1907.
  Tuke's play is an adaptation of *Los empeños de seis horas* by Antonio Coello.
  ❖ Title as is. *Studies in English Drama.* Ed. Allison Gaw. 1st ser. Philadelphia: Univ. of Pennsylvania, 1917. 1–61.
412. Schmiedel, Donald Emerson. *El conde de Sex* by Antonio Coello: A Critical Edition and Study. 340 pp. Southern California, E. W. Hesse, 1967. *DA* 28A: 2657–58.
  The text is "based on the first printed edition (1638) and [is] carefully collated with all seventeenth-century sources—two manuscripts and the edition of 1651." (Abs.)
  ❖ [A] Coello, A. El conde de Sex *de Antonio Coello: Study and Critical Edition.* Ed. by D. E. Schmiedel. Madrid: Playor, 1973. 214 pp. (Colección Plaza Mayor Scholar 14.) [B] "Coello's Debt to Góngora." *BCom* 25.2 (1973): 39–40. [This study is based on *El conde de Sex.*]

Cubillo de Aragón, Álvaro (1596?–1661)

413. Hwang, John Eun. Cubillo de Aragón's *La perfecta casada* and the Idea of Forgiveness in His Theater. ix+203 pp. Oregon, P. J. Powers, 1971. *DAI* 32A: 5230–31.
  "This thesis is a critical edition of . . . *La perfecta casada, prudente, sabia y honrada.*" The base text is "the first printed edition (1658)," which is collated with (1) two seventeenth-century MS copies, (2) two other seventeenth-century printings, (3) three *sueltas,* and (4) three nineteenth-century editions. "In many of his plays,

[Cubillo] criticized the code of honor and proposed instead the idea of forgiveness as the true basis of honor." (Abs.)

❖ Cubillo de Aragón, A. *La perfecta casada, prudente, sabia y honrada.* Critical ed. with introd. by J. E. Hwang. Barcelona: Núñez, 1978. 152 pp.

414. MACAS, WILLIAM. A Critical and Annotated Edition of Álvaro Cubillo de Aragón's *El vandolero de Flandes.* 479 pp. New Mexico, R. R. MacCurdy, 1967. *DA* 28A: 1439–40.

The text is based on a seventeenth-century manuscript ("probably a scribe's copy") and three *sueltas,* apparently of the eighteenth century. (Abs.)

415. SEEKAMP, JOHN HAROLD. The Dramatic Craftsmanship of Álvaro Cubillo de Aragón and the Sources for Some of His Plays. 155 pp. Rutgers, E. Nagy, 1974. *DAI* 35A: 3769.

Three plays are analyzed: *Ganar por la mano el juego, Añasco el de Talavera,* and *La perfecta casada.* (Abs.)

416. WHITAKER, SHIRLEY BLUE. The Dramatic Works of Álvaro Cubillo de Aragón. viii+382 pp. North Carolina, S. E. Leavitt, 1965. *DA* 27A: 217.

"Of the twenty-nine extant plays attributed to Cubillo with some foundation, twenty-eight were available to the present writer." (Abs.)

❖ Title as is. Chapel Hill: Univ. of North Carolina, Dept. of Romance Languages, 1975. 176 pp. (UNCSRLL 149.)

CUEVA, JUAN DE LA (1543–1610)

417. BATTLE, JOHN WAYNE. Dramatic Unity in the Plays of Juan de la Cueva. viii+217 pp. Duke, R. L. Predmore, 1970. *DAI* 31A: 5387.

"I analyze four of Cueva's most important plays to disprove the major accusations of lack of artistic structure and lack of moral implications." The four plays are *Comedia de la muerte del rey don Sancho, Tragedia de los Infantes de Lara, Comedia de la constancia de Arcelina,* and *Comedia del infamador.* (Abs.)

418. BURTON, DAVID GOODRICH. Juan de la Cueva's Dramatization of the Spanish Legend of Bernardo del Carpio. 160 pp. Kentucky, J. Lihani, 1983. *DAI* 45A: 1127.

This dissertation is a study of Juan de la Cueva's *Comedia de la libertad de España por Bernardo del Carpio* (1579). (Abs.)

❖ [A] *The Legend of Bernardo del Carpio from Chronicle to Drama.* Potomac: Scripta Humanistica, 1988. 82 pp. (Scripta Humanistica 47.) [B] "The Historical Dramas of Juan de la Cueva." *CH* 12.1-2 (1990): 5-13.

419. CIAVARELLI, MARIA ELISA. El tema de la fuerza de la sangre en el Siglo de Oro español y sus antecedentes en la literatura occidental. 330 pp. Pennsylvania, A. E. Foley, 1977. *DAI* 38A: 4864.

[For the complete entry, see no. 688.]

420. MORBY, EDWIN SETH. The Plays of Juan de la Cueva. 213 pp. CA/Berkeley, R. Schevill, 1936. PFE, 15 Apr. 1936.

"The one most significant characteristic of the *Comedias y tragedias* is their effort to exalt and dignify the drama, and the chief means taken to this end is the adaptation of classical features. Cueva must therefore lay claim to the position of first of the imitators of Seneca on the public stage, a position that has hitherto been assigned to his followers." (PFE)

❖ [A] "The Influence of Senecan Tragedy in the Plays of Juan de la Cueva." *SP* 34 (1937): 383-91. [B] "Notes on Juan de la Cueva: Versification and Dramatic Theory." *HR* 8 (1940): 213-18.

421. SHIELDS, ROBERT LAWRENCE. A General Study of the Transition Period of Spanish Drama Following Juan de la Cueva. vi+74 pp. Iowa, R. Davis, 1941. Iowa *Abstracts* 3, part 4, pp. 411-16.

[For the complete entry, see no. 166.]

DELICADO, FRANCISCO (FL. 1528)

422. IMPERIALE, LOUIS. The Dramatic Framework of Francisco Delicado's *El retrato de la Lozana andaluza:* A Semiological Reading. (El marco dramático del *Retrato de la Lozana andaluza:* Una lectura

semiológica.) [Spanish text.] 391 pp. Catholic, B. M. Damiani, 1990. *DAI* 52A: 175–76.

"The present thesis explores el *Retrato de la Lozana andaluza* from a perspective of dramaturgic technique, and attempts to point out all the authorial and textual effects which could facilitate the conversion of the dialogued novel into a performative text. Moreover, this study analyzes the correlation between dramatic resources and narrative discourse in Delicado's work through an integrated semiotic analysis of the theatrical signs found in *La Lozana*." (Abs.)

❖ [A] "Captación auditiva e imagen visual en la Roma de Francisco Delicado y Pietro Aretino." *Italo-Hispanic Literary Relations*. Ed. Jesús Helí Hernández. Potomac: Scripta Humanistica, 1989. 71–81. (Scripta Humanistica 49.) [B] *El contexto dramático de* La lozana andaluza. Potomac: Scripta Humanistica, 1991. 291 pp. (Scripta Humanistica 84). [C] Imperiale, Luigi. "Una realidad disfrazada en *La lozana andaluza*." *RFE* 72.1–2 (1992): 159–66.

Diamante, Juan Bautista (1625–1687)

423. Murray, Donald Alan. Mira de Amescua's *La desgraciada Raquel*. v+480 pp. Stanford, A. M. Espinosa, 1951. Stanford *Abstracts* 27 (1951–52): 372–74.

[For the complete entry, see no. 508.] This play has also been attributed to Diamante.

424. Parker, Mary. Los personajes femeninos en comedias de Juan Bautista Diamante. 575 pp. CUNY, H. E. Bergman and I. Lerner, 1986. *DAI* 47A: 1119.

"The systematic portrayal of heroic women draws attention towards Diamante's theatre because it is consistent with his treatment of the male protagonists." (Abs.)

❖ [A] "Don Juan Bautista Diamante: A Bibliography of Primary Sources." *BB* 49.3 (1992): 195–208. [B] *Santas, reinas, mártires y cortesansas: La mujer en el teatro de Juan Bautista Diamante*. [Potomac]: Scripta Humanistica, 1996 (?). 173 pp.

Don Juan Theme

425. Ackerman, Stephen Hamilton. Don Juan in the Generation of '98. iii+188 pp. Ohio State, C. Blanco Aguinaga, 1955. *DA* 16: 533.

The authors studied are Unamuno, Azorín, the Machados, Valle-Inclán, Baroja, and Maeztu. "In our study we have seen all but one of these authors completely reject the traditional concept of Don Juan, depriving him of the attributes which Tirso and Zorrilla had emphasized." (Abs.)

❖ "The Machados and Don Juan." *REH*b 1.2 (1967): 157–82.

426. Alder, Esther Romella. The Don Juan Theme in the Contemporary French Theatre. 184 pp. CA/Berkeley, C. D. Brenner, 1964. *DA* 25: 4139–40.

"Of eighteen French plays, contemporary interpretations of the Don Juan theme, almost all were unsuccessful theatrically as modernizations of the traditional legend. . . . Nevertheless, the plays afford an interesting study of the twentieth-century evolution of the Spanish myth." (Abs.)

427. Arias, Judith Hepler. Toward a Theory of the Don Juan Myth. 305 pp. North Carolina, J. B. Avalle-Arce, 1987. *DAI* 48A: 2351.

The writer analyzes Tirso's *El burlador,* Zorrilla's *Don Juan Tenorio,* and Valle-Inclán's *Las galas del difunto.* "Don Juan symbolizes a form of behavior which is linked to violence and is defined in Girardian terms as mimetic, or second-hand, desire. The hallucinatory madness of mimetic rivalry, rather than sexual instinct, motivates Don Juan's behavior, while his sexual attitude is important insofar as it stimulates social violence and provides the occasion for such violence to be released." (Abs.)

❖ [A] "Doubles in Hell: *El burlador de Sevilla y convidado de piedra.*" *HR* 58 (1990): 361–77. [B] "Don Juan, Cupid, the Devil." *H*[AATSP] 75.5 (1992): 1108–15. [C] "'The Devil at Heaven's Door': Metaphysical Desire in *Don Juan Tenorio.*" *HR* 61.1 (1993): 15–34.

428. Atwater, Régine Neveux. Don Juan, Eros et Thanatos: La

constitution d'un mythe et son évolution. 372 pp. CA/Los Angeles, H. El Nouty, 1991. *DAI* 52A: 3302–03.

"The myth of Don Juan has been probed by numerous writers of the Western world. We have tried here to go back to the origins of this myth and to see where it sprang from. We have traced it back to the young pagan hero and god associated with Eros and Thanatos, the rites of fertility and death, that is to say, the rites of passage between this world and the 'other world.' . . . [With Molière's transformation of Tirso de Molina's theme,] the myth moved . . . from a supernatural, religious plane to a social one. This social shift has become more and more predominant in our time to the point of occulting the religious aspect of the myth; however, the eroticism characterizing Don Juan, which is based on sexual transgression, death and sensuality, Eros and Thanatos, cannot be denied. Don Juan is a christian figuration of a pagan hero and god who has been damned. Death and Sensuality or *Thanatos* and *Eros* are deeply entwined in the myth of Don Juan as in our lives." (Abs.)

429. BROWNSTEIN, RACHEL MAYER. *Don Juan:* The Absurd Point of View. [8]+196 pp. Yale, F. A. Pottle, 1963.

"This study approaches the issues of Byron's modernity, the nature and meaning of his greatest poem, and that poem's relationship to his 'Romantic' works by analysing *Don Juan* with reference to Albert Camus' essay on the absurd, *Le Mythe de Sisyphe*. . . . The 'hero' of the poem is supposedly a familiar one. In his narrative and digressions, Byron refers to the legend of Don Juan which, with its hero, shares his favorite talent, mobility. He redefines the most human of famous heroes as a man very like one of Camus' heroes of the absurd, Don Juan *lucide*." (Diss.)

430. CONNELL, JAMES GOODMAN, JR. Freedom and the Don Juan Tradition in Selected Narrative Poetic Works and *The Stone Guest* of Alexander Pushkin. vi+193 pp. Ohio State, F. R. Silbajoris, 1973. *DAI* 34A: 2552–53.

"In Chapter I, the prototype Don Juan is constructed of relevant themes and motifs based solely on a close literary analysis of [Tirso de Molina's *El burlador de Sevilla*.]." (Abs.)

431. Denslow, Stewart. Don Juan and Faust: Their Parallel Development and Association in Germany, 1790–1850. ii+111 pp. Virginia, J. C. Bardin(?), 1941. Virginia *Abstracts* (1941): 23–27.

The principal sections of this dissertation are chapter 2, "The Origin of the Two Legends," and chapter 3, "Association of Don Juan and Faust in Germany (ca. 1800–1850)." In the latter chapter the writer discusses such works as the tragedy *Don Juan und Faust* (1822) by Christian D. Grabbe. (Diss.)

❖ "Don Juan and Faust." *HR* 10 (1942): 215–22.

432. Dominicis, María Canteli. Don Juan en el teatro español del siglo XX. 258 pp. NYU, J. B. Hughes, 1974. *DAI* 35A: 4512.

The plays studied range from Echegaray's *El hijo de Don Juan* to Ramón Sender's *Don Juan en la mancebía* (1972). (Abs.)

❖ Title as is. Miami: Universal, 1978. 181 pp. (Colección Polymita.)

433. Geffen, Amy Jill. Descendants of Don Juan in Eighteenth-Century France: Fact and Fiction. iii+413 pp. NYU, A. Vartanian, 1979. *DAI* 41A: 691–92.

". . . in the eighteenth century [the seducer] becomes a figure to be admired, imitated and rewarded by society." (Abs.)

434. Hook, John Ferguson. The Don Juan Theme in the Works of Valle-Inclán. 279 pp. NYU, H. Piñera, 1975. *DAI* 36A: 2243.

"Eleven works of Valle-Inclán include the Don Juan aspect as a major theme. . . . In addition, no less than thirteen works have the Don Juan aspect as a minor theme." The writer concludes that "Valle's relationship with his character [Don Juan] was psychic as well as aesthetic." (Abs.)

435. Kattán-Zablah, Jorge. Nacimiento, expansión y mitificación de un personaje teatral—Don Juan. 162 pp. CA/Santa Barbara, A. Serrano-Plaja, 1974.

❖ [A] *Don Juan: De Tirso de Molina a José Zorrilla*. San Salvador: Ministerio de Educación, Dirección de Cultura, Dirección de Publicaciones, 1972. 103 pp. ["El objetivo de este ensayo es presentar el enfoque que cada uno de los diferentes autores (Tirso, Molière, Shadwell, Mozart, Grabbe, Pushkin, Zorrilla) hace de Don Juan, de los otros personajes y del tema, como asimismo seguir la evolución de Don Juan, desde sus orígenes hasta llegar a su apoteosis consagrada en *Don Juan Tenorio,* de José Zorrilla.] [B] "Mito y mitificación de Don Juan: Su sentido." *Cultura* 65 (1979): 64–68. [C] "Mito y mitificación de Don Juan: Su sentido." *Káñina* 5.1 (1981): 99–101.

436. Knight, Eunice Edna. The Role of Women in Don Juan and Faust Literature. iii+216 pp. Florida State, J. Priest, 1973. *DAI* 35A: 1106.

"The dissertation attempts to define and interpret the role of women in Don Juan and Faust literature by examining the relationships between the heroes and the women in the Faust works of Marlowe, Goethe, Valéry, and Mann and the Don Juan works of Tirso de Molina, Molière, da Ponte, Zorrilla, Shaw, and Frisch." (Abs.)

437. Lahr-Well, Almeda Marie. The Don Juan and Feminist Myths in Unamuno: A Struggle toward Consciousness. v+168 pp. St. Louis, P. García, 1975. *DAI* 37A: 2221.

This study is centered on Unamuno's dramatic work *El hermano Juan o El mundo es teatro.* (Abs.)

438. Lensing, Arvella Hertje. José Zorrilla: A Critical, Annotated Bibliography, 1837–1985. vii+295 pp. Iowa, W. A. Dobrian 1986. *DAI* 47A: 3061–62.

"Despite the extensive number of entries dealing with the don Juan prototype (one source lists over 1200 titles), these are included; to exclude don Juan would have eliminated the theme for which Zorrilla is most known. However, works dealing with don Juan that are not specifically related to Zorrilla have been excluded, although they were consulted." (Abs.)

439. Little, William Thomas. Don Juanism in Modern European Literature. viii+433 pp. Washington/St. Louis, J. Schraibman, 1973. *DAI* 34A: 3410.

"In the first Chapter the origins of the Don Juan myth are traced to Spain's amalgamation of three cultures: Jewish, Islamic and Christian. . . . The gradual demise of the Don Juan myth is traced in the following four Chapters." The writer examines works by Clarín, Galdós, and Valle-Inclán, among others. (Abs.) ❖ "Varios aspectos de Don Juan y el donjuanismo." *Hispanófila* 80 (1984): 9–15.

440. LÓPEZ, IGNACIO JAVIER. *Donjuanismo* and Irony in the Modern Spanish Novel (1880–1930): An Historical Essay. [Spanish text.] 331 pp. Wisconsin, B. Ciplijauskaité, 1984. *DAI* 45A: 2126.

"This investigation analyzes the transformations undergone by the Don Juan figure in the Spanish novel during the period 1880–1930. They are studied in the light of the general evolution of the novel as a genre during this period." (Abs.)

❖ [A] "Ortega Munilla y la doble génesis de *La desheredada*." *AGald* 20.2 (1985): 7–17. [The writer deals with the influence of the novel *Don Juan Solo* (1880) by José Ortega Munilla on Galdós's novel *La desheredada* (1881); both of these works contain Don Juan figures.] [B] *Caballero de novela: Ensayo sobre el donjuanismo en la novela española moderna, 1880–1930.* Barcelona: Puvill, 1986. 249 pp. (Biblioteca universitaria Puvill 2. Ensayos 13.)

441. LOWTHER, LEO MARLEY. Don Juan and Comparative Literary Criticism: Four Approaches. xii+329 pp. Utah, D. K. Barton, 1971. *DAI* 32A: 2060.

"This dissertation isolates the evolution of the seducer-hero Don Juan; it explains the development of the relationship between Don Juan and his *gracioso;* it studies the development and interdependence of a select number of the Don Juan plays through a motive and theme analysis; and finally, it studies the poetic genre of the Don Juan *Stoff* during the Romantic Period." The four approaches are archetypal, literary history, motive and theme analysis, and the Zeitgeist. (Abs.)

442. MANDRELL, JAMES BENNETT. Don Juan and Revision: Myth, Textuality, and *Don Juan Tenorio.* v+238 pp. Johns Hopkins, P. R. Olson, 1984. *DAI* 46A: 164.

". . . I focus on José de Zorrilla's *Don Juan Tenorio,* a *refundición* of Tirso de Molina's *El burlador de Sevilla y convidado de piedra,* in order to demonstrate the thematization of the issue of writing and rewriting." (Abs.)

❖ [A] "*Don Juan Tenorio* as *Refundición:* The Question of Repetition and Doubling." *H*[AATSP] 70.1 (1987): 22–30. [B] "Language and Seduction in *El burlador de Sevilla.*" *BCom* 40.2 (1988): 165–80. [C] *Don Juan and the Point of Honor: Seduction, Patriarchal*

Society, and Literary Tradition. University Park: Pennsylvania State UP, 1992. 310 pp.

443. MANSOUR, GEORGE PHILLIP. The *Don Juan Tenorio, Zarzuela* of Zorrilla: The Progression and Modulation of a Theme. 301 pp. Michigan State, J. A. Ramsey, 1965. *DA* 26: 4666–67.

"In the *zarzuela* Zorrilla distinguished between the concept of the *burlador* and that of *donjuanismo*—the former being the tradition of Tirso's protagonist, and the latter, the emergence of the *homme fatal.*" The dissertation includes a critical edition of the MS of the zarzuela. (Abs.)

❖ [A] "*El convidado de piedra, a Zarzuela* by Rafael del Castillo." *H*[AATSP] 48 (1965): 811–15. In chapter 1 of the dissertation, the writer discusses the four Don Juan zarzuelas that preceded Zorrilla's (1877); among them is Castillo's. [B] "Algunos don Juanes olvidados del siglo XIX." *REHb* 2.2 (1968): 251–63.

444. MARTIN, KENNETH JOSEPH. A Portfolio of Three Papers in Literature, Language, and Curriculum Development in Spanish and French. (1) A Comparative Study of *El burlador de Sevilla y convidado de piedra* of Tirso de Molina and Molière's *Dom Juan: ou, Le festin de pierre,* with Special Attention to the Female Characters in Each Work. (2) A Comparative Study of the French and Spanish Verb. (3) An Alternative Approach to Level III Foreign Language Study in the Private Secondary School. 162 pp. [Only part 1 is relevant.] Catholic, D. Lagmanovich, 1976. *DAI* 37A: 2153.

[For the complete entry, see no. 635.]

445. NEGGERS, GLADYS CRESCIONI. Don Juan: Innovación y tradición en el teatro y el ensayo del siglo XX en España. iv+168 pp. Alabama, E. Ruiz-Fornells, 1975. *DAI* 37A: 1009–10.

"There are thirteen important dramatizations by the following authors: Dionisio Ridruejo, Ramón Sender, Juan Ignacio Luca de Tena, Gregorio Martínez Sierra, Salvador de Madariaga, Jacinto Grau, Miguel de Unamuno, Jacinto Benavente, Eduardo Marquina, los hermanos Álvarez Quintero and los Machado. We have studied these plays in order to determine the ways in which they conform to the traditional conception of the legend and in what ways they innovate. We have also established the relationships—or lack of them—that exist between plays and the most controversial topics treated in the essays." (Abs.)

❖ *Don Juan (Hoy)*. Madrid: Turner, 1977. 150 pp.

446. NOZICK, MARTIN. The Don Juan Theme in the Twentieth Century. iii+278+iii+xx pp. Columbia, M. J. Valency, 1953. *DA* 14: 1417–18.

"The primary objective of this dissertation is to bring Georges Gendarme de Bévotte's book *La Légende de Don Juan* up to date. This two-volume scholarly work traces the evolution of the Don Juan theme in literature from Tirso de Molina's *El Burlador de Sevilla,* published in 1630, to the beginning of the twentieth century." (Abs.) Editorial note: Georges Gendarme de Bévotte, French Hispanist, appears among the non-United States dissertations (no. 1385). His dissertation on the Don Juan legend was completed in 1907.

447. PARLATO, LOUIS JOSEPH. La Floraison du thème Don Juan dans le théâtre français au XXe siècle, avec un historique. xxii+454 pp. Middlebury, 1968.

"Nous ferons précéder la principale partie de notre ouvrage d'un historique. . . . Nous prêterons . . . une attention particulière aux deux principales pièces anciennes, *El Burlador de Sevilla y convidado de piedra* de Tirso de Molina et *Dom Juan* de Molière." (Diss.)

448. PRICE, ELISABETH. Don Juan: A Chronicle of His Literary Adventures in Germanic Territory. 408 pp. Washington/St. Louis, E. Schwarz, 1974. *DAI* 35A: 2291.

This dissertation summarizes "the use of the theme in German literature from its first appearance until the mid-nineteenth century." (Abs.)

449. SAAD, YOUSSEF SOBHI. Don Juanism in Arabic Literature. 175 pp. Utah, A. S. Atiya, 1970. *DAI* 31A: 2354.

"Although it becomes clear beyond a shadow of doubt that sensuality in numerous specimens of Arab poetry are identical with Tirso de Molina's conception of his Don Juan, it must be admitted that the character he had woven in his immortal play must be regarded as a joint product of Arabic as well as Hispanic ways of life." (Abs.)

❖ "The Don Juan of Classical Arabia." *CLS* 13 (1976): 304–14.

450. SCHULZ, ROSTILAW. Pushkin and the Cnidus Myth. [Russian text.] v+246 pp. NYU, A. L. Kodjak, 1984. *DAI* 45A: 1774.

"This study compares eight works of Pushkin—. . . [including] the drama *The Stone Guest* . . .—with the Cnidus Myth. This myth denotes a recurrent construct: the separation of man and woman by a supernatural force." In other versions "other statues and other supernatural forces like statues of men (the Legend of Don Juan), other demons and even skeletons play the role of the antagonist, while the plot kernel itself remains unchanged." (Abs.)

451. SMITH, ANNA LAURA. Twentieth-Century Interpretations of the Don Juan Theme. 155 pp. Oklahoma, J. H. Abbott, 1973. *DAI* 34A: 5932.

"The treatment of the Don Juan theme in works by Azorín, Valle-Inclán, Unamuno, [Pérez de] Ayala, Grau, and Torrente Ballester shows the individuality of their interpretations." (Abs.)

452. TOWNSEL, AURELIE SYLVIANE. Teoría comparativa del donjuanismo en Zorrilla y en Valle-Inclán. 160 pp. Emory, C. Rojas, 1987. *DAI* 48A: 3123.

"Both writers not only reject the final punishment,—by so doing, they discard the didactic principle of the drama of Tirso *El burlador de Sevilla*—but make their heroes undergo a metamorphosis caused by the true love of a woman." (Abs.)

453. WEINSTEIN, LEO. A Critical Study of the Don-Juan Legend. x+272 pp. Stanford, F. Anderson, 1951.

"The purpose of this dissertation is two-fold: (1) since a modern author, who wishes to treat the Don-Juan legend, cannot be expected to read the innumerable versions which have appeared on the subject, he will be able to obtain a general picture of the development and of the present state of the legend from this study; (2) it is my hope that this dissertation will enable the reader to judge more intelligently the value of any new Don-Juan version." (Diss.)

❖ *The Metamorphoses of Don Juan*. Stanford: Stanford UP, 1959. 223 pp.

454. WORTHINGTON, MABEL PARKER [SOKEL]. Don Juan: Theme and Development in the Nineteenth Century. vii+239 pp. Columbia, S. H. Nobbe(?), 1953. *DA* 13: 399.

"From defier of God to defier of nature to defier of society to defier of the reality principle: that is the progress of Don Juan. And as he passed through these stages, he gradually shed his original glory and significance. Said Shaw, 'Mozart's is the last of the true Don Juans'. Another historical epoch will find a new variation of the Rebel Son archetype." (Abs.)

❖ "Don Juan as Myth." *Literature and Psychology* 12 (1962): 113–24.

Encina, Juan del (1468?–1529?)

455. Anderson, James Anthony. Juan del Encina: Aesthetics of His Poetry. 338 pp. CA/Berkeley, L. Monguió, 1967. *DA* 28A: 1363–64.

"Traditionally discussed aspects of his work (his use of several levels of language, his several poetic styles, his theater and his translations) and certain rhetorical elements of his poetry . . . without regard to generic, linguistic or thematic divisions are studied." (Abs.)

❖ [A] "Juan del Encina: An Abuse of Form?" *RomN* 10.2 (1968–69): 353–58. ["Common sense dictates that these technical transgressions be labelled slips of the pen; but a knowledge of the whole of Encina's work shows this kind of playing to be within the realm of his use of subtle and personal devices in his poetry." [B] *Encina and Virgil.* University: Romance Monographs, 1974. 84 pp. (Romance Monographs M8.) ["In the following pages I will study aspects of Juan del Encina's poetic aesthetics as they are seen in his translation of Virgil's eclogues (called the *Bucólicas* by Encina)." The writer analyzes Encina's first, second, and fourth eclogues.]

456. Gimeno, Rosalie Helen. Juan del Encina: Teatro del primer *Cancionero,* composición y significado. v+107 pp. Case Western Reserve, J. Casalduero and D. M. Carey, 1972. *DAI* 33A: 311.

"Las ocho representaciones que coloca Juan del Encina en los catorce últimos folios de su *Cancionero* de 1496 son el primer grupo conservado de obras dramáticas castellanas." These works are "la expresión artística de un nuevo acercamiento a la vida humana, acercamiento que nos permite entender mejor el proceso gradual que lleva del mundo de la Edad Media al del Renacimiento." (Abs.)

❖ [A] "Juan del Encina: Teatro del primer *Cancionero*." *Segismundo* 9.17–18 (1973): 75–140. [B] Encina, J. del. *Obras dramáticas 1 (Cancionero de 1496)*. Ed. R. Gimeno. Madrid: Istmo, 1975. 228 pp. [C] Encina, J. del. *Teatro (Segunda producción dramática)*. Ed. R. Gimeno. Madrid: Alhambra, 1977, 1982. 437 pp.

457. McGinniss, Cheryl Folkins. La danza literaria como símbolo de metamorfosis: Empleo y sentido en el teatro de Juan del Encina y Gil Vicente. 119 pp. Case Western Reserve, D. M. Carey, 1977. *DAI* 38A: 1437.

[For the complete entry, see no. 835.]

458. Myers, Oliver Tomlinson. Phonology, Morphology and Vocabulary in the Language of Juan del Encina. xxxiii+239 pp. Columbia, F. H. Jungemann, 1961. *DA* 22: 569–70.

Along with his detailed description of phonology, morphology, and vocabulary, the writer observes that "the orthography of the 1496 Salamanca edition of Encina's *Cancionero* is remarkable for its modernity and consistency." (Abs.)

❖ [A] "Church Latin Elements in *Sayagués*." *RomN* 4.2 (1963): 166–68. [In Encina and others.] [B] "Juan del Encina and the *Auto del repelón*." *HR* 32 (1964): 189–201. [The writer indicates that the phonology, morphology, vocabulary, orthography, and similar elements in the *Auto* differ from Encina's usual practices, and concludes that the work should "be removed from the list of the works of Juan del Encina."] [C] "*Señor* in *Sayagués*." *MLN* 80 (1965): 271–73. [D] "Lexical Notes on Encina: Some Revisions for Recent Additions to the *DCELC*." *RomN* 8.1 (1966): 143–46. [The acronym refers to the *Diccionario crítico etimológico de la lengua castellana*, by Joan Corominas.]

459. Rambaldo, Ana María. El *Cancionero* de Juan del Encina dentro de su ámbito histórico y literario. clviii+[5]+371 pp. NYU, R. Bosch, 1971. *DAI* 32A: 4018.

"Creo que, teniendo en cuenta las consideraciones aquí apuntadas, no puede descartarse la posibilidad de que el verdadero Juan del Encina esconda su frialdad religiosa detrás de un barniz formal y conformista, o su resentimiento detrás de una apariencia jocosa. Tampoco podemos negar la posibilidad de que el tema de la expulsión de los judíos le resultara arriesgado por su asociación personal con él, o que proyectara su resentimiento sobre el elemento social [los rústicos] que, para el converso, representaba un pedantesco alarde de superioridad." (Abs.)

❖ Title as is. Santa Fe, Argentina: Castellví, 1972. 123 pp.

460. SCHERR, ELLIOTT BROWN. A Study of the 1496 *Cancionero* of Juan del Encina. ix+81 pp. Iowa, R. E. House, 1934. Iowa *Program,* August 1934.

"An examination was made of the phonology, morphology, and various syntactical phenomena of the *Cancionero*. . . . A study of the *Aucto del repelón,* attributed to Encina, has been added in the hope that some light might be thrown on the question of authorship." (*Program*)

461. TEMPRANO, JUAN CARLOS. Móviles poéticos en el *Cancionero* de 1496 de Juan del Encina: Lo pastoril y lo popularizante (con una edición anotada de su *Arte de poesía castellana*). 259 pp. Princeton, R. S. Willis, 1972. *DAI* 33A: 1182–83.

"Encina, convinced that the rustic-pastoral mode was finally being accepted as a legitimate form of poetic expression, brings to his theatrical eclogues all the lyric expressions that he had incorporated earlier in his poems of fixed form." (Abs.)

❖ [A] "El *Arte de poesía castellana* de Juan del Encina (edición y notas)." *BRAE* 53 (1973): 321–50. [B] "Cronología de las ocho primeras églogas de Juan del Encina." *HR* 43 (1975): 141–51. [C] *Móviles y metas en la poesía pastoril de Juan del Encina*. Oviedo: Universidad de Oviedo, 1975. 210 pp. [D] *Cancionero de las obras de Juan del Enzina, Salamanca, 1496*. Ed. J. C. Temprano. Madison: Hispanic Seminary of Medieval Studies, 1983. 21 pp. + 5 microfiches.

462. TURK, LAUREL HERBERT. Juan del Encina and the Spanish Renaissance. iii+419 pp. Stanford, A. M. Espinosa, 1933. Stanford *Abstracts* (1933–34): 69–72.

"Encina is frequently called the patriarch of the Spanish theater. Although he was not the first Spanish author to compose works containing dramatic elements, he was the first to write plays which were produced on a regular stage. His plays included the unfinished sketches of the principal dramatic types which have since been cultivated in Spain. His inspiration, save in the three Italianate dramas, is popular and therefore realistic and national. The introduction of the Italian influence into the Spanish drama is all-important. The elements which Encina borrowed from the Italian plays were the theme itself, the suicide and resurrection of a given character, the larger number of characters, the prologue, and mythological matter. Juan del Encina exemplified, in his life and work, the human and pure spirit of the Spanish Renaissance. He gave expression to his personal feelings and his individualism; he attempted to portray the life of the people; he was a Humanist, a devotee of the classics; he helped to formulate the Renaissance pastoral eclogue in Spain; and he had a prominent part in the development of Spanish national music." (Abs.)

Enríquez Gómez, Antonio (1600/02–1663?)
(Fernando de Zárate y Castronovo)

463. Porras-Landeo, Juan. Una edición crítica del manuscrito *El noble siempre es valiente,* comedia de don Fernando de Zárate y Castronovo. iii+395 pp. Wayne State, H. N. Bershas, 1976. *DAI* 37A: 2924.

[For the complete entry, see no. 850.] Editorial note: For a discussion of the polemic as to whether Zárate was a pseudonym of Enríquez Gómez, see Glen F. Dille, "Antonio Enríquez Gómez Alias Fernando de Zárate," *PLL* 14.1 (1978): 11–21.

Fernández, Lucas (1474?–1542)

464. Bryant, William C. Lucas Fernández and the Early Spanish Drama. 254 pp. CA/Berkeley, D. C. Shadi, 1964. *DA* 25: 6616.

". . . Fernández emerges as less medieval than modern, less an imitator than a creator." (Abs.)

465. Lihani, John. Glossary of the *Farsas y églogas* of Lucas Fernández.

xxxvi+413 pp. Texas, M. Romera-Navarro and R. H. Williams, 1954.

Glossary-dictionary of words in Lucas Fernández's *farsas* and *églogas,* especially those in *sayagués* dialect.

❖ [A] "The Preclassical Meaning of Spanish *Tempero.*" *RR* 47 (1956): 161-65. [In Lucas Fernández and others.] [B] "Lucas Fernández and the Evolution of the Shepherd's Family Pride in Early Spanish Drama." *HR* 25 (1957): 252-63. [C] "Quevedo's *Romance sayagués burlesco.*" *Symposium* 12 (1958): 94-102. [D] "Some Notes on *sayagués.*" *H*[AATSP] 41 (1958): 165-69. [E] "The Question of Authorship of the *Coplas* Attributed to Lucas Fernández." *KFLQ* 12 (1965): 238-45. [*Coplas* is an anonymous one-act play.] [F] *El lenguaje de Lucas Fernández: Estudio del dialecto sayagués.* Bogotá: Instituto Caro y Cuervo, 1973. 653 pp. [G] *Lucas Fernández.* New York: Twayne, 1973. 179 pp. [H] "A Literary Jargon of Early Spanish Drama: The Sayagués Dialect." *Linguistic Approaches to the Romance Lexicon.* Ed. Frank H. Nuessel Jr. Washington: Georgetown UP, 1978. 39-44.

Figueroa y Córdova, Diego (1619?-1673?)
Figueroa y Córdova, Josep (1625?-1678)

466. Rivas, Aída Harriet. A Critical Edition of *Mentir y mudarse a un tiempo,* by Diego and José de Figueroa y Córdoba. 327 pp. Wayne State, H. N. Bershas, 1978. *DAI* 39A: 1625-26.

This dissertation includes a biography of the playwrights, summaries of the plots of all their plays except the one here edited, and a comparison of this play with Ruiz de Alarcón's *La verdad sospechosa,* "with which it has some points in common." (Abs.)

Godínez, Felipe (1588-1639?)

467. Goldberg, Alice. Felipe Godínez, dos comedias: Edición anotada de *La Reyna Ester* y *Amán y Mardocheo,* con introducción. 321 pp. Brown, A. D. Kossoff, 1981. *DAI* 43A: 461.

The first of the two plays is edited on the basis of a 1613 actor's copy, whereas the text of the second play is based on the printed versions that appeared in the *Comedias escogidas de los mejores ingenios de España.* (Abs.)

❖ "Felipe Godínez's Queen Esther Play." *BCom* 35.1 (1983): 47–50.

468. RAUCHWARGER, JUDITH. The Theme of Job in Four Spanish Golden Age Authors. 230 pp. Michigan, E. Glaser and M. Z. Hafter, 1973. *DAI* 34A: 1931.

The writer studies one dramatic work: *Los trabajos de Job* by Felipe Godínez. (Abs.)

❖ "Comedic Transformation of Biblical and Legendary Sources in Felipe Godínez *Los trabajos de Job.*" *RJ* 29 (1978): 303–21.

469. TURNER, THOMAS CHARLES. A Critical Edition of *La traición contra su dueño* by Felipe Godínez, Together with an Introductory Study. 277 pp. Missouri, V. G. Williamsen, 1970. *DAI* 31A: 5431.

The critical edition is based on a "previously unedited manuscript." (Abs.)

❖ Godínez, F. La traición contra su dueño *by Felipe Godínez.* With introd. and notes by T. C. Turner. Chapel Hill: Estudios de Hispanófila, 1976. 130 pp. (Estudios de Hispanófila 35.)

GÓMEZ DE TOLEDO, GASPAR (16TH C.)

470. BARRICK, MAC EUGENE. A Critical Edition of Gaspar Gómez de Toledo's *Tercera Parte de La Tragicomedia de Celestina.* 743 pp. Pennsylvania, O. H. Green and A. G. Reichenberger, 1965. *DA* 26A: 7308.

❖ [A] "Sancho's Trip to El Toboso: A Possible Source." *MLN* 81 (1966): 222–25. [A possible source proposed by the writer is Gómez de Toledo's *La tercera Celestina.*] [B] Gómez de Toledo, G. *Tercera Parte de la Tragicomedia de Celestina.* Critical ed., introd., and notes by M. E. Barrick. Philadelphia: U of Pennsylvania P, 1973. 597 pp. "It must be observed that Gómez showed no intention of writing a performance work. His *Tercera Celestina,* despite its dramatic nature, was intended only for reading. . . . The present edition is based on the Leyden copy of the Medina, 1536, edition, with variants appearing in the Toledo, 1539, text indicated in footnotes." (Prt. Diss.)

Góngora, Luis de (1561–1627)

471. Quintero, María Cristina. Poetry as Play: Luis de Góngora's Dramatic Experiment. vi+166 pp. Stanford, A. Forcione, 1984. *DAI* 45A: 1773.

"*Las firmezas de Isabela* enacts the theatrical possibilities of Góngora's use of metaphor and intensification of figurative language. The play becomes not just a meditation on the *comedia,* but also a commentary on Gongorine language itself." (Abs.)

❖ [A] "Dramatic Convention and Poetic Discourse: Dialogue, Monologue, and Aside in Luis de Góngora's *Las firmezas de Isabela.*" *BCom* 37.2 (1985): 225–48. [B] "Luis de Góngora and the *Comedia de Enredo.*" *Symposium* 39.4 (1985–86): 268–83. [C] "The Cervantine Subtext in Góngora's *Las firmezas de Isabela.*" *Cervantes* 11.2 (1991): 43–58. [D] *Poetry as Play:* Gongorismo *and the* Comedia. Philadelphia: Benjamins, 1991. 260 pp. (PUMRL 38.)

472. Valk, Jean Wright. Paradox as Technique in the Works of Luis de Góngora and Pedro Calderón de la Barca. v+207 pp. Kansas, A. Debicki, 1985. *DAI* 46A: 3050.

[For the complete entry, see no. 349.]

473. Watson, John Andrew. The Metaphorical Procedure of Góngora and Calderón. vii+220 pp. Catholic, A. S. Crisafulli, 1976. *DAI* 37A: 5099.

[For the complete entry, see no. 354.]

González de Eslava, Fernán (Mexico. 1534?–1601?)

474. Arce, Roberto Matthew. A Reappraisal of the Evolution of the *Auto Sacramental,* with Special Reference to the *Coloquios*

Sacramentales of Fernán González de Eslava. ix+230 pp. CA/ Santa Barbara, E. Martínez-López, 1976. *DAI* 37A: 6524–25.

"Patterned in many respects after the Spanish sacramental drama of the period, Eslava's *coloquios sacramentales* were undeniably influenced by the culture of Spain. However, literary trends unique to Mexico are revealed in Eslava's works." (Abs.)

Hurtado de Mendoza, Antonio (1586–1644)

475. Ramos, Noemí E. A Critical Edition of Antonio Hurtado de Mendoza: *Cada loco con su tema.* 230 pp. Tulane, D. L. Heiple, 1980. *DAI* 41A: 2632.

"The basis of the text is a microfilm copy of the autograph manuscript (signed and dated August 29, 1630), located in the Biblioteca Nacional in Madrid. This manuscript was collated with two other early manuscripts and the three printed editions." (Abs.)

476. Vogt, Eric William. A Critical Edition of *Ni callarlo ni decirlo* by Antonio Hurtado de Mendoza. 437 pp. Missouri, V. G. Williamsen, 1988. *DAI* 49A: 2654.

"The basis of the text is a microfilm copy obtained from the Library of the Vatican (Barb. Lat. 3481 XLIII.29). It is the only known manuscript of this play, one which has remained unedited until now." (Abs.)

❖ Hurtado de Mendoza, A. *Ni callarlo ni decirlo*. Introd., notes, and bibliog. by E. W. Vogt. Ciudad Juárez: Universidad Autónoma de Ciudad Juárez, 1992. 202 pp.

Inés de Castro (1320?–1355) Theme

477. Anderson, Carleton Q. The Evolution of the Inés de Castro Story in Drama. iii+174 pp. Brigham Young, M. C. Gibson, 1970. *DAI* 31A: 2333.

". . . I conclude that . . . [the theme] has undergone a movement away from historical fact toward fictitious characters, events and interpretation." (Abs.)

478. MILLER, GUSTAVUS HINDMAN. A Comparison of Late Renaissance and Early Baroque Aesthetics as Seen through Two Dramatic Interpretations of the Inés de Castro Story. 149 pp. Michigan, F. Sánchez y Escribano and C. N. Staubach, 1956. *DA* 17: 144–45.

The two plays are *Nise lastimosa* (1577) by Jerónimo Bermúdez and *Doña Inés de Castro, Reina de Portugal* (1612) by Mejía de la Cerda. (Abs.)

479. TRIWEDI, MITCHELL DAVID. The *Nise lastimosa* of Jerónimo Bermúdez: A Critical Edition, Together with an Introductory Study and Notes. vi+468 pp. Southern California, D. E. McMahon, 1958. USC *Abstracts of Dissertations* (1958): 88–89.

[For the complete entry, see no. 236.]

JIMÉNEZ DE ENCISO, DIEGO (1585–1634)

480. BAS, JOE. Una edición crítica y anotada de la comedia de don Diego Ximénez de Enciso, *El príncipe don Carlos.* v+473 pp. Southern California, E. W. Hesse, 1967. *DA* 27A: 4242.

"The First Part . . . traces the literary chronology of the theme, from 1581 to 1910, sketching 105 treatments, which range from melodramas to burlesques, in prose as well as in verse. . . . The Second Part consists of the annotated text of the 1773 printed version of the *comedia,* and the Third Part collates two seventeenth-century manuscripts to this 1773 printed version." (Abs.)

481. PLATT, FRANK THOMAS. *El príncipe don Carlos* of Diego Ximénez de Enciso: A Critical Edition with Introduction and Notes (Parts I and II). 472 pp. Ohio State, R. C. Rozzell, 1956. *DA* 17: 138–39.

"In the preparation of the present critical edition the following manuscripts and editions of *El príncipe don Carlos* have been consulted and collated: MSS 15.554, 17.407, and 16.684 in the Biblioteca Nacional (Madrid); MSS CC*, IV, 28.033, vol. LXXXI and CC*, IV, 28.033, vol. LXXI at the Biblioteca Palatina (Parma); a manuscript copy made by the German scholar Adolph Schaeffer at the Universitätsbibliothek (Freiburg); the editions of Huesca, 1634; Madrid, 1667; Valencia, 1773; an undated *suelta;* and a modern edition by Juan Hurtado y Jiménez de la Serna (Madrid, 1925). We have based our text on MS 15.554, justifying our emendations and recording variants." (Abs.)

❖ "'Era el remedio olvidar.'" *BCom* 9.1 (1957): 10 [In discussing this verse, the writer cites his unpublished dissertation].

482. SPRATLIN, VALAUREZ BURWELL. Juan Latino: Un estudio sobre el ébano humano. 196 pp. Middlebury, S. Gili-Gaya, 1931.

The dissertation includes a discussion of *La comedia de Juan Latino* by Jiménez de Enciso.

❖ [A] "The Negro in Spanish Literature." *JNH* (Jan. 1934): 62–71. [B] *Juan Latino, Slave and Humanist.* New York: Spinner, 1938. 216 pp. Includes an English translation of Jiménez de Enciso's *Comedia de Juan Latino.* [C] Rpt. of publication A in *Blacks in Hispanic Literature: Critical Essays*. Ed. Miriam DeCosta. Port Washington: Kennikat, 1977. 47–52.

483. VAN KERK, JOHN WILLIAM. The Figure of Don Carlos in Selected Plays of the Spanish Golden Age. vii+166 pp. Georgia, H. Ziomek, 1978. *DAI* 39A: 4312.

[For the complete entry, see no. 188.] One of the works analyzed is *El príncipe don Carlos* by Diego Jiménez de Enciso. (Abs.)

JUANA INÉS DE LA CRUZ (MEXICO. 1648/51–1695)

484. BEAUPIED, AÍDA MARÍA. Narciso hermético: Sor Juana Inés de la Cruz y José Lezama Lima. v+294 pp. Yale, R. González Echevarría, 1988. *DAI* 51A: 174.

"This dissertation will argue that both writers use the myth of Narcissus in order to conceal and to transmit to their readers an esoteric message that is at the root of their heterodox conception of the Christian mystery of the Holy Trinity. It is possible to conclude that both writers subscribe to the ancient conception of God as an androgynous Being, in what today could be interpreted as a feminist reading of the Trinity. The chapters about Sor Juana analyze two of her major works, *Primero sueño* and *El divino Narciso*. This dissertation proposes a comparative analysis of both works in order to show how the myth of Narcissus—as it appears in the ancient treatises of the *Corpus hermeticum*—is the key that answers affirmatively the question of whether or not there is a revelation. This revelation can be found through the syncretic treatment of the Trinitarian mystery as it is presented in *El divino Narciso*." (Abs.)

❖ [A] "Revelación velada pero rebelde en la *Respuesta* de Sor Juana Inés de la Cruz." *HisJ* 14.2 (1993): 117-30. [". . . las implicaciones de esta comparación con Cristo (en la *Respuesta*) eran demasiado revolucionarias para que su época pudiera asimilarlas y mucho menos aceptarlas, ya que corresponden al concepto de una divinidad andrógina. El desarrollo de dicho concepto se puede ver mejor en *El divino Narciso*."] [B] *Narciso hermético: Sor Juana Inés de la Cruz and José Lezama Lima*. Liverpool: Liverpool UP, 1996. 241 pp.

485. Carullo, Sylvia Graciela. El retrato literario en Sor Juana Inés de la Cruz. 296 pp. SUNY/Buffalo, M. Camurati, 1988. *DAI* 49A: 3374.

"In this dissertation I study Sor Juana's use of the portrait and the self-portrait in a selection of poems and in one of her plays, *Los empeños de una casa*." (Abs.)

❖ [A] "El retrato literario en algunos poemas de Sor Juana Inés de la Cruz." *Sor Juana Inés de la Cruz: Selected Studies*. Ed. Luis Cortest. New York-Buenos Aires-Asunción: CEDES, 1989. 65-77. [B] "Sor Juana y Velázquez: Modos de representación." *La Palabra y el Hombre* 71 (1989): 13-29. [C] Title as is. New York: Peter Lang, 1991. 232 pp. (American University Studies, ser. 2. Romance Languages and Literature 164.)

486. Daniel, Lee Alton. A *"Terra Incognita":* Sor Juana's Theatre. iii+236 pp. Texas Tech, R. J. Morris, 1979. *DAI* 40A: 1494.

". . . a major objective of this study has been to call attention to all of the Sorjuanian drama [26 extant pieces] and in doing so, for the first time ever, provide an overview of it." (Abs.)

❖ [A] "The *Loa:* One Aspect of the Sorjuanian Mask." *LATR* 16.2 (1983): 43-50. [B] "The Use of Echo in the Plays of Sor Juana." *LA CHISPA '83: Selected Proceedings of the Fourth Louisiana Conference on Hispanic Languages and Literatures.* Ed. Gilbert Paolini. New Orleans: Tulane UP, 1983. 71–78. [C] "The *Loas* of Sor Juana Inés de la Cruz." *LFem* 11 (1985): 42–48. [D] "Satan as Character in Sor Juana's Joseph *Auto*." *Confluencia* 3.2 (1988): 79–83 [Apropos *El cetro de San José*, 1692.] [E] "Sor Juana's Pentad of Carlosian *Loas*." *Sor Juana Inés de la Cruz: Selected Studies*. Ed. Luis Cortest. New York-Buenos Aires-Asunción: CEDES, 1989. 78–87. [F] *The* Loa of *Sor Juana Inés de la Cruz*. Fredericton: York, 1994. 44 pp.

487. FLYNN, GERARD COX. A Revision of the Criticism of Sor Juana Inés de la Cruz. 428 pp. NYU, F. R. Thompson, 1958. *DA* 25: 3568–69.

"The profane theatre of Sor Juana is Spanish, not only in its style, but even in its themes. . . . The *auto El divino Narciso* is the masterpiece of Sor Juana." (Abs.)

❖ [A] *Sor Juana Inés de la Cruz*. New York: Twayne, 1971. 123 pp. (TWAS 144.) ["I have discussed the criticism of several authors and have attempted to set the critical house in order."] [B] "Sor Juana Inés de la Cruz: Las trampas de la crítica." *Sor Juana Inés de la Cruz: Selected Studies*. Ed. Luis Cortest. New York-Buenos Aires-Asunción: CEDES, 1989. 44–52.

488. PÉREZ, MARÍA ESTHER. Lo americano en el teatro de Sor Juana Inés de la Cruz. 419 pp. NYU, H. Piñera, 1972. *DAI* 33A: 762.

"Hopefully, this study will emphasize those unique and distinguishing aspects of her work which suggest the pervasive American influences that were inspired by her cultural background." (Abs.)

❖ Title as is. New York: Torres, 1975. 257 pp.

LASSO DE LA VEGA, GABRIEL LOBO (1559–1615)

489. ISAR, HERBERT EUGENE. The Tragedies of Gabriel Lobo Lasso de la Vega (1587). 253 pp. Pennsylvania, J. E. Gillet, 1955. *DA* 15: 1854.

This dissertation is an edition and study of the author's two tragedies, *Honra de Dido restaurada* and *Destrvyción de Constantinopla*. The edition is based on the *princeps:* Alcalá de Henares, 1587. (Abs.)

❖ "La cuestión del llamado 'senequismo' español." *Hispanófila* 2 (1958): 11–30. [Article examines the complex question of Senequism in connection with the *Destrucción de Constantinopla.*]

Leonardo de Argensola, Lupercio (1559?–1613)

490. Green, Otis Howard. The Life and Works of Lupercio Leonardo de Argensola. Pennsylvania, J. P. W. Crawford, 1927. {Philadelphia: Univ. of Pennsylvania, 1927. 203 pp. (UPSRLL 21.)}

Argensola's two extant plays, *Isabela* and *Alejandra,* are discussed in chapter 3, "The Saragossa Stage," pp. 23–27, and chapter 13, "The Tragedies," pp. 104–25. See also pp. 146–49 on his essay entitled "Memorial contra la representación de las comedias." (Prt. Diss.)

❖ [A] "Notes on the Lucianesque Dialogues of Bartolomé Leonardo de Argensola." *HR* 3 (1935): 275–94. [B] *Vida y obras de Lupercio Leonardo de Argensola.* Trans. Francisco Ynduráin. Zaragoza: Institución Fernando el Católico, 1945. 194 pp. [For a more complete list of this scholar's publications, see P. M. Lloyd and U. J. De Winter, "Publications of Otis H. Green," *HR* 37 (1969): 12–22.]

Mejía de la Cerda, Licenciado Juan María (fl. 1612)

491. Miller, Gustavus Hindman. A Comparison of Late Renaissance and Early Baroque Aesthetics as Seen through Two Dramatic Interpretations of the Inés de Castro Story. 149 pp. Michigan, F. Sánchez y Escribano and C. N. Staubach, 1956. *DA* 17: 144–45.

[For the complete entry, see no. 478.] The play by Mejía de la Cerda is *Doña Inés de Castro, Reina de Portugal* (1612). (Abs.)

Mesa, Gaspar de (15?–16?)

492. Basemann, Max L. A Critical Text of the Dramatic Works Known or Reputed to Be by Gaspar de Mesa. vi+265 pp. Iowa,

R. Davis, 1940. Iowa *Abstracts* 3, part 4, pp. 361–66.

The three plays edited are "*El Bruto ateniense,* 1602, and the *Auto del nacimiento,* 1607, both autograph plays of Gaspar de Mesa, together with the *Nínive y su conversión,* a *comedia y auto sacramental* attributed by some to the same author." (Abs.)

Mira de Amescua, Antonio (1574?–1644)

493. Anibal, Claude E. A Critical Text, with Introduction, of *El arpa de David* by Mira de Amescua, Together with a Dissertation on Lisardo, His Pseudonym. Indiana, 1922.

This dissertation is no longer available at Indiana University.

❖ [A] 1. El arpa de David: *Introduction and Critical Text.* 2. *Lisardo—His Pseudonym.* Columbus: Ohio State Univ., 1925. 201 pp. (Contributions in Language and Literature 2.) The edition is based on BNM MS 15.516, which has been collated with BNM MS 16.326. Neither is an *autógrafo.* (Prt. Diss.) [B] "*Voces del cielo:* A Note on Mira de Amescua." *RR* 16 (1925): 57–70. [Apropos a dramatic device found in *El arpa de David* and other plays by Mira.] [C] "Another Note on the *Voces del cielo.*" *RR* 18 (1927): 246–52. [D] "Mira de Amescua and *La ventura de la fea.*" *MLN* 42 (1927): 106. [To the arguments advanced in his printed dissertation, the writer adds another one in favor of Mira's authorship of *La ventura de la fea.*] [For a more complete list of this scholar's publications, see Arnold G. Reichenberger, "Claude E. Anibal (1888–1955)," *HR* 23.4 (1955): 298–302, esp. 300–02.]

494. Brown, Sandra Lou. Tirso de Molina: His Treatment of Medieval Spanish History. 327 pp. North Carolina, S. E. Leavitt, 1969. *DAI* 30A: 3450.

This dissertation deals with the Don Álvaro plays, sometimes attributed to Mira de Amescua.[For the complete entry, see no. 608.]

495. Buchanan, Milton Alexander. Comedia famosa del esclavo del demonio *compvesta por el doctor Mira de Mesqua* (Barcelona, 1612): Edited with an Introduction and Notes. 144 pp. Chicago, 1906.

❖ Mira de Amescua, A. Comedia famosa del esclavo del demonio, *compvesta por el doctor Mira de Mesqua.* With introd. and notes by M. A. Buchanan. Baltimore: Furst, 1905. 144 pp. [per HSA catalog.] [This printing, with a new title page, served as a PhD dissertation, Univ. of Chicago, 1906. Information from Castañeda, *Mira de Amescua* 196.] "The present edition is a reprint of . . . [the text in Lope de Vega's *Tercera parte,* Barcelona, 1612], with such emendations as are suggested by the other editions [Barcelona, 1614; Madrid, 1613; *Parte sexta de comedias varias,* 1649 and four *sueltas* (3 of the 18th century and 1 of the 17th)]." (Prt. Diss.) [For a more complete list of this scholar's publications, see J. H. Parker, "Publications of Milton Alexander Buchanan," *HR* 20.4 (1952): 325–32.]

496. Cooper, Al LeRoy. A Critical Edition of Antonio Mira de Amescua's *Obligar contra su sangre.* ix+179 pp. Arizona, K. C. Gregg, 1974. *DAI* 35A: 5394.

"The base text . . . is from the Biblioteca Nacional (Madrid), MS 18.142. The manuscript is not an 'autograph' but rather a copy dated 1636." Variants are provided from four eighteenth-century *sueltas* and from the nineteenth-century BAE edition. (Abs.)

497. Darst, David High. A Structural Analysis of the *Próspera* and *Adversa fortuna de don Álvaro de Luna* Attributed to Tirso de Molina. iv+223 pp. Kentucky, W. C. McCrary, 1970. *DAI* 31A: 4155.

"The favorite's tragic demise acts to direct the attention of the dramatic personages—and the audience—to the characteristic ambivalence of nature and the limits of sin and innocence, thus giving purpose to the downfall of Álvaro de Luna. Moreover, the playwright has established throughout the two pieces a clear analogy between the Castilian Constable and Jesus Christ." (Abs.) Editorial note: For a discussion of the controversy concerning the authorship of these plays, see Castañeda, *Mira de Amescua* 51–52.

498. Fameli, John Carmelo. *La casa del tahur* de Antonio Mira de Amescua, edición paleográfica anotada. v+294 pp. Southern California, J. R. Araluce-Cuenca, 1970. *DAI* 31A: 4711.

The text is "transcribed, with few exceptions, as it appears in Mira's mostly holographic manuscript, which is found in the

Biblioteca Nacional of Madrid under the call number *Reservado 118*." (Abs.)

499. FAVAZZO, [SISTER] M. CARMEL THERESE, CSAC. An Edition and Study of Mira de Amescua's *Nuestra Señora de los Remedios*. v+306 pp. St. John's, J. J. Reynolds, 1970. *DAI* 31A: 5397–98.

"This critical edition is based on a seventeenth-century manuscript which is collated with a second manuscript of the same century." The play is an *auto mariano*. (Abs.)

500. FORBES, FRANCIS WILLIAM. A Critical Edition of Antonio Mira de Amescua's *Galán, valiente y discreto*. 278 pp. Arizona, H. R. Stone and K. C. Gregg, 1971. *DAI* 32A: 2684.

"The base text presented is from the Biblioteca Nacional (Madrid), MS. R-17.025. Verification of Act I as 'autograph' was inconclusive. Unique lines from a second manuscript at the same location (R-15.323) and other *sueltas*, have been intercalated. . . . The listing of variants is the result of the collation of the two manuscripts, as well as eleven printed editions which span the period 1636–1969." (Abs.)

❖ [A] Mira de Amescua, A. Galán valiente y discreto: *Estudio y edición crítica*. Ed. F. W. Forbes. Madrid: Playor, 1973. 240 pp. [B] "*El más feliz cautiverio y los sueños de Josef* de Mira de Amescua: Uso de los textos bíblicos en la comedia." *Looking at the* Comedia *in the Year of the Quincentennial: Proceedings of the 1992 Symposium on Golden Age Drama, El Paso*. Ed. Barbara Mujica and Sharon D. Voros. Lanham: UP of America, 1993. 187–94. [C] "Uso y abuso de la historia: El caso de *Nardo Antonio, bandolero* de Mira de Amescua." *En torno al teatro del Siglo de Oro: Actas de las jornadas IX-X celebradas en Almería*. Ed. Heraclia Castellón, Agustín de la Granja, and Antonio Serrano. Almería: Instituto de Estudios Almerienses, 1995. 113–23. (Colección Actas 17.)

501. GARCÍA, LINO, JR. Una edición crítica de *La confusión de Hungría* de Antonio Mira de Amescua. iii+213 pp. Tulane, W. J. Smither, 1981. *DAI* 42A: 1173.

"The basis for this text is a microfilm of the printed copy [*Escogidas, Parte 35*, 1671, pp. 274–316] found in the Biblioteca Nacional in Madrid." (Abs.)

502. GREGG, KARL CURTISS. A Critical Edition of Antonio Mira de

Amescua's *La mesonera del cielo.* iii+290 pp. Syracuse, D. W. McPheeters and D. P. Testa, 1968. *DA* 29A: 4487–88.

"The text of the play presented here is that of the earliest known version with minimal (and justifiable) emendations. A total of six different printed editions were compared with the base version." (Abs.)

❖ "A Brief Biography of Antonio Mira de Amescua." *BCom* 26.1 (1974): 14–22.

503. Hopper, Edward Warren. A Critical and Annotated Edition of Mira de Amescua's *La rueda de la fortuna.* 384 pp. Missouri, V. G. Williamsen, 1972. *DAI* 34A: 2563–64.

"By examining all of the extant editions of the play, the editor has reconstructed what he believes to be a fairly accurate edition of the play." (Abs.)

504. Huck, George Ann. A Critical Edition of Mira de Amescua's *La tercera de sí misma.* 274 pp. Tulane, D. W. McPheeters, 1968. *DA* 29A: 1897–98.

"The purpose of this study is to present a fresh appraisal of the dramatic art of Antonio Mira de Amescua by a re-evaluation of his work in general, and a concentration on the comedy *La tercera de sí misma.*" The edition is based on an unpublished manuscript in the BN, Madrid, and a printed edition in the *Comedias Escogidas* collection. (Abs.)

❖ [A] Mira de Amescua, A. *La tercera de sí misma.* Critical ed. G. A. Huck. Valencia: Albatros, n.d. (1981?). 184 pp. (Hispanófila 19.) [B] "Antonio Mira de Amescua, Forgotten Playwright—Facts, Not Fiction." *National Symposium on Hispanic Theatre, 1982.* Ed. Adolfo M. Franco. Cedar Falls: Univ. of Northern Iowa, 1985. 249–55. [C] "New Data: Mira de Amescua, Royal Chaplain." *Renaissance and Golden Age Essays in Honor of D. W. McPheeters.* Ed. Bruno Damiani. Potomac: Scripta Humanistica, 1986. 130–33. [D] "Lo que puede una mujer." *Mira de Amescua en candelero: Actas del congreso internacional sobre Mira de Amescua y el teatro español del siglo XVII, Granada, 1994.* Ed. Agustín de la Granja and Juan Antonio Martínez Berbel. 2 vols. Granada: Universidad de Granada, 1996. 1: 281–90.

505. Linares, Henry Amaya. A Paleographic Edition of Mira de

Amescua's *El mártir de Madrid.* 249 pp. Missouri, V. G. Williamsen, 1974. *DAI* 35A: 6100.

The edition is based on "the partially holograph manuscript" with variants from "a second manuscript copy." (Abs.)

506. MALONEY, JAMES CHARLES. A Critical Edition of Antonio Mira de Amescua's *El monte de la piedad, La fe de Hungría,* and *La jura del príncipe.* 302 pp. Arizona, R. M. ter Horst, 1973. *DAI* 34A: 3412–13.

"The base texts for the three *autos* are, respectively: MSS 15490, 15318 and 17098. MS 15305 *(El Monte de la piedad)* was the only alternate text available. All manuscripts were obtained from the Biblioteca Nacional at Madrid." (Abs.)

❖ *A Critical Edition of Antonio Mira de Amescua's* La fe de Hungría *and* El monte de la piedad. Ed. J. C. Maloney. New Orleans: Tulane Univ., 1975. 151 pp. (Tulane Studies in Romance Languages and Literature 7.)

507. MITCHELL, PHYLLIS IRENE PATTESON. The *Autos Sacramentales* of Mira de Amescua. x+210 pp. Johns Hopkins, E. L. Rivers, 1971. *DAI* 34A: 281.

[In a number of Mira's *autos*] Spain is seen "as the defender of the faith against some type of heresy which threatens belief in the Eucharist. This approach demonstrates that heresy was considered a problem long after the immediate Protestant threat in Spain had been eradicated, and that the concern it caused may have had some effect on the development of the *auto*." (Abs.)

508. MURRAY, DONALD ALAN. Mira de Amescua's *La desgraciada Raquel.* v+480 pp. Stanford, A. M. Espinosa, 1951. Stanford *Abstracts* 27 (1951–52): 372–74.

"The purpose of this dissertation is twofold: first, to study the growth and development of the legend of the Jewess of Toledo in Spanish literature, and, second, to provide a critical edition of the most popular version of this theme in the dramatic literature of the *Siglo de Oro,* attributing its authorship, moreover, to Mira de Amescua, rather than to Juan Bautista Diamante." The critical edition is based on George Ticknor's manuscript of the play "entitled *La desgraciada Raquel,* attributed to Mira de Amescua and bearing the date of 1625." This text has been collated with the printed versions of the play as it appeared under the title of *La judía de Toledo* and attributed to Juan Bautista Diamante. In the latter form, "the play was published once in the seventeenth century [1667], five times in the eighteenth, and ultimately, in the nineteenth, in the *Biblioteca de Autores Españoles*." (Abs.)

509. PICKERING, ADRIAN TIMOTHY. Mira de Amescua, *El conde Alarcos:* A Critical Edition with Introduction and Notes. cxliv+175 pp. Ohio State, C. E. Anibal and R. Lida, 1952. Ohio State *Abstracts* 67: 521–27.

"Thirteen seventeenth- and eighteenth-century printed editions of *El Conde Alarcos* are described in the dissertation. The earliest, the *Escogidas* of 1653, . . . is a good text, with only two missing lines, and is incomparably superior to the others in adherence to what Mira's practice is known to have been." (Abs.) ❖ "A Note on the *Comedia Serafina* and *El conde Alarcos*." *MLN* 71 (1956): 109–14.

510. RAMBO, JAMES STONE. An Annotated Critical Edition of *También tiene el sol menguante,* by Luis Vélez de Guevara and Francisco de Rojas Zorrilla. viii+424 pp. New Mexico, R. R. MacCurdy, 1972. *DAI* 33A: 2948.

[For the complete entry, see no. 555.] This play "is a *refundición* of Mira de Amescua's two-part drama, *La próspera y la adversa fortuna de don Bernardo de Cabrera*."

511. SÁNCHEZ, ROBERTO. Luis Vélez de Guevara: *El negro del Seraphin:* A Critical and Annotated Edition with Introduction. vii+309 pp. Florida State, D. L. Hoffman, 1979. *DAI* 40A: 3345.

[For the complete entry, see no. 824.] This play was also published as *El negro del mejor amo* and attributed to Mira de Amescua.

512. STEVENS, CHARLES HENRY. Lope de Vega's *El palacio confuso,* Together with a Study of the Menaechmi Theme in Spanish Literature. xcii+138 pp. NYU, H. C. Heaton, 1938. {New York: Instituto de las Españas en los Estados Unidos, 1939. xcii+138 pp.}

[For the complete entry, see no. 787.] Editorial note: This play has been attributed to Mira de Amescua and to Lope de Vega. For a discussion, see Castañeda, *Mira de Amescua* 103–05.

513. Taracido, Jorge Ezequiel. The Poetry of Antonio Mira de Amescua. ix+731 pp. Missouri, V. G. Williamsen, 1984. *DAI* 45A: 3359.

"Although they are relatively few in number, an in-depth analysis of his poems casts some light on his abilities as a lyric poet. In spite of this sparse production Mira was well-known and frequently praised during his lifetime for having written beautiful poetry including some of the most lyrical passages in the Golden Age theater." (Abs.)

514. Tock, Shirley Anne. A Critical Edition of Mira de Amescua's *El animal profeta,* with an Introductory Study. xv+323 pp. Missouri, V. G. Williamsen, 1973. *DAI* 34A: 7249.

"The text presented is based on a study of three manuscripts and thirteen printed versions." According to the writer, "it has been necessary to establish plausible proof that Mira de Amescua is the author." (Abs.)

515. Wilds, Bonnie. A Critical Edition of *El animal profeta,* with an Introduction and Notes. iii+168 pp. Pittsburgh, J. S. Herrero, 1973. *DAI* 35A: 1069.

The critical edition is based on three manuscripts of the play in the BN (Madrid). The writer, in agreement with S. G. Morley and C. Bruerton that the play was not written by Lope de Vega, concludes that it belongs to Mira de Amescua. (Abs.)

❖ Mira de Amescua, A. El animal profeta: Critical ed., introd., and notes by B. Wilds. Barcelona: Borrás, 1979. 201 pp. (Colección Tirant lo Blanch 3.)

516. Williamsen, Vern G. A Critical Edition of Mira de Amescua's *No hay dicha ni desdicha hasta la muerte,* Together with an Introductory Study. 370 pp. Missouri, A. Porqueras-Mayo, 1968. *DA* 29A: 3163.

The critical edition is based on "an almost completely autograph manuscript dated in 1628, a manuscript copy of 1685, and three imperfect editions, one each from the seventeenth, eighteenth, and nineteenth centuries." (Abs.)

❖ [A] "The Development of a *Décima* in Mira de Amescua's Theater." *BCom* 22.2 (1970): 32–36. [B] Mira de Amescua, A. No hay dicha ni desdicha hasta la muerte, *with Introduction and*

Notes. Ed. V. G. Williamsen. Columbia: U of Missouri P, 1970. 145 pp. (University of Missouri Studies 52.) [C] "The Dramatic Function of 'Cuentecillos' in Some Plays by Mira de Amescua." *H*[AATSP] 54 (1971): 62–67. [D] "The Versification of Antonio Mira de Amescua's *Comedias* and of Some *Comedias* Attributed to Him." *Studies in Honor of Ruth Lee Kennedy*. Ed. Vern G. Williamsen and A. F. Michael Atlee. Chapel Hill: Estudios de Hispanófila, 1977. 151–67. (Estudios de Hispanófila 46.) [E] "A Commentary on 'The Uses of Polymetry' and the Editing of the Multistrophic Texts of the Spanish *Comedia*." *Editing the* Comedia. Ed. Frank P. Casa and Michael D. McGaha. Ann Arbor: Univ. of Michigan, Dept. of Romance Languages, 1985. 126–45. (Michigan Romance Studies 5.)

Monroy y Silva, Cristóbal de (1612–1649)

517. Kromayer, Astrid Bottis. Some Aspects of the Theater of Cristóbal de Monroy y Silva: *Refundiciones* and the Comic Element. vii+154 pp. Rutgers, E. Nagy, 1978. *DAI* 39A: 4306.

The writer compares Monroy's *El caballero dama* with Tirso's *El Aquiles* and Monroy's *Los tres soles de Madrid* with Lope's *Los mártires de Madrid* and concludes that Monroy's *refundiciones* have "a greater dramatic impact" than their source plays. (Abs.)

❖ "Tirso de Molina's *El Aquiles* and Monroy y Silva's *El caballero dama:* A Comparison." *Tirso de Molina: Vida y obra. Actas del primer simposio internacional sobre Tirso, Washington, 1984* (error for 1985). Ed. Josep M. Solà-Solé and Luis Vázquez Fernández. Madrid: Revista "Estudios," 1987. 167–74.

518. Peters, John William. The Dramatic Works of Cristóbal de Monroy y Silva: A Preliminary Survey. v+491 pp. Ohio State, C. E. Anibal, 1954.

"The purpose of this study has been to present the dramatic works of Cristóbal de Monroy y Silva so as to give a preliminary idea of their content and verse form. So far as I am aware, this is the first time that summaries of all the works of a single Spanish dramatist have been attempted in accordance with the strophic structure of the plays concerned. I believe this method to be more just to an author in conveying what he wrote, for significant details may easily be missed from a summary that does not take cognizance of the fact that there is a significant reason for every change in verse form." (Diss.)

MONTEMAYOR, JORGE DE (1520?–1561)

519. VIDAL, CARMEN. Aspectos dramáticos en *Los Siete Libros de la Diana* de Jorge de Montemayor. 251 pp. Catholic, B. M. Damiani, 1990. *DAI* 51A: 1600.

"The purpose of this study was to examine Jorge de Montemayor's use of dramatic devices and structures that inject the novel with operatic and dramatic effects in the action. Montemayor employed dramatic devices frequently through his career as poet and court musician. Such devices are first seen in the *Cancionero* and *Three Autos.* . . . Montemayor's 1554 Antwerp edition of his poetry comes complete with three *autos* ('one act plays') which were actually enacted Christmas Eve of that year. *La Diana* itself is replete with theatrical elements, a fact underscored by the fact that the principal episodes of the novel were set to dramatic representations (e.g., *La Grande Pastorelle* by Nicholas Chretien de Croix, 1613; *Felismena,* by Alexandre Hardy, 1613; *Les enchantments de Felicia,* by Jacob Pousset, 1653). I conclude that in *La Diana,* Montemayor achieves a complete dramatic effect." (Abs.)

MORETO, AGUSTÍN (1618–1669)

520. BRITT, CLAUDE HENRY, JR. A Variorum Edition of Moreto's *El valiente justiciero.* xix+156 pp. Northwestern, J. G. Fucilla, 1966. *DA* 27A: 3036.

". . . the oldest known copy, bearing the date 1657, has been considered to be the most reliable text, and has been compared with fifteen other editions and non-autograph manuscripts." (Abs.)

521. CARNER, ROBERT JORDAN. The *Loas, Entremeses* and *Bailes* of D. Agustín Moreto. iv+[333] pp. Harvard, J. D. M. Ford, 1940. Harvard *Summaries* (1940): 399–400.

The writer has edited thirty-one of the thirty-six shorter plays listed by E. Cotarelo y Mori in his *La bibliografía de Moreto* (Madrid, 1927). *(Summaries)*

❖ "*El vestuario*: An Unpublished *Entremés* of Moreto." *HSNPL* 14 (1932): 187–96. [An edition.]

522. CASA, FRANK PAUL. The Dramatic Craftsmanship of Moreto. 253 pp. Michigan, E. Glaser, 1962. *DA* 24: 1611–12.

"The purpose of this study is to analyze in detail the relationship between five *comedias* of Moreto and their sources in order to arrive at a deeper understanding of the dramatic craftsmanship of the playwright." The five plays are *San Franco de Sena, El licenciado Vidriera, Antíoco y Seleuco, El valiente justiciero,* and *El lindo don Diego*. "The conclusion that is drawn from this study is that . . . Moreto was capable of great individuality, and by introducing substantial modifications to the *comedias* he borrowed, he expressed his own themes with great effectiveness." (Abs.)

❖ [A] Title as is. Cambridge: Harvard UP, 1966. 187 pp. (Harvard Studies in Romance Languages 29.) [B] "Diana's Challenge in [Moreto's] *El desdén con el desdén*." *RJ* 23 (1972): 307–18.

523. DEDRICK, DWAIN EDWARD. A Critical Edition of Moreto's *El poder de la amistad*. xxviii+176 pp. Northwestern, J. G. Fucilla and F. G. Very, 1964. *DA* 25: 3567.

"This critical edition is based on a comparison of the autograph copy, dated April 29, 1652, and [six printed editions: 1654, 1677, a *suelta* dated 1751, an undated *suelta* printed in Salamanca, an undated *suelta* printed in Seville, and the *BAE* edition, edited by Fernández-Guerra]." (Abs.)

❖ Title as is. Valencia: Castalia, 1968. xxvii+122 pp. (Estudios de Hispanófila 8.)

524. KENNEDY, RUTH LEE. The Dramatic Art of Moreto. ix+316 pp. Pennsylvania, J. P. W. Crawford, 1931.

"In making my investigation I have limited myself to a consideration of his longer comedies . . . [i.e., the *entremeses* are not studied]." (Prt. Diss.)

❖ [A] Title as is. *SCSML* 13 (1931-32). 221 pp. [B] Rpt. Philadelphia: Banta, 1932. 221 pp. [C] "Concerning Seven Manuscripts Linked with Moreto's Name." *HR* 3 (1935): 295-316. [D] "Manuscripts Attributed to Moreto in the Biblioteca Nacional." *HR* 4 (1936): 312-32. [E] *"La milagrosa elección de San Pío V."* *MLR* 31 (1936): 405-08. [The attribution of this play to Moreto is rejected.] [F] "The Sources of *La fuerza del natural* [by Moreto]." *MLN* 51 (1936): 369-72. [G] "*Los engaños de un engaño y confusión de un papel:* A Play by Don Rodrigo de Herrera y Ribera." *MLR* 32 (1937): 593-95. [The attribution of this play to Moreto is rejected.] [H] "Moreto's Span of Dramatic Activity." *HR* 5 (1937): 170-72. [I] *"La renegada de Valladolid."* *RR* 28 (1937): 123-34. [This play, dated 1637, "should be attributed to (Luis de) Belmonte, Moreto, and (Don Antonio) Martínez (de Meneses)."] [J] "*La gala del nadar*—Date and Authorship." *MLN* 54 (1939): 514-17. [The attribution of this play to Moreto is rejected.] [K] "Moretiana." *HR* 7 (1939): 225-36. [L] *"Sin honra no hay valentía."* *SCSML* 21 (1939-40): 110-21. [The attribution of this play to Moreto is rejected.] [M] "The Theme of 'Stratonice' in the Drama of the Spanish Peninsula." *PMLA* 55 (1940): 1010-32. [Includes a detailed study of Moreto's *Antíoco y Seleuco.*] [For a more complete list of this scholar's publications, see *Studies in Honor of Ruth Lee Kennedy,* ed. Vern G. Williamsen and A. F. Michael Atlee (Chapel Hill: Estudios de Hispanófila, 1977) 19-21. (Estudios de Hispanófila 46.)]

525. Lottmann, Anna Marie. The Comic Elements in Moreto's *Comedias.* 255 pp. Colorado, C. Ortigoza, 1958. *DA* 19: 2953-54.

"... [Moreto] had a gaiety and a comic grace superior to that of any dramatist of the age." (Abs.)

526. Park, Philip Mortimer. *Tarugo's Wiles:* or, *The Coffee House* by Thomas St. Serfe: A Facsimile Edition with Notes and an Introduction. xvi+269 pp. Pennsylvania, P. B. Murray, 1968. *DA* 29A: 2272-73.

The play is an adaptation of the *comedia No puede ser* by Moreto. The original edition of St. Serfe's play is dated 1668. (Abs.)

527. Rissel, Hildegard. Three Plays by Moreto and Their

Adaptation in France. 361 pp. Georgetown, B. L. Mujica, 1990. *DAI* 51A: 3769.

"This study analyzes three plays by Agustín Moreto y Cabaña: *El desdén con el desdén, De fuera vendrá quien de casa nos echará* and *Lo que puede la aprehensión.* It will focus on the expression of feminine passion in these three comedies. Also, the paper will give a contrasting analysis between the three Spanish plays and their adaptations in French theater, i.e., Molière's *La Princesse d'Élide,* Thomas Corneille's *Le Baron d'Albikrac* and his *Le Charme de la Voix.*" (Abs.)

❖ [A] "Agustín Moreto y Cabaña: A Transitional Playwright and His Heroines." *BCom* 46.2 (1994): 219–28. [B] Title as is. New York: Peter Lang, 1995. 164 pp. (Ibérica 11.)

528. White, Ralph Eugene. *La Comedia de Figurón* of Rojas Zorrilla and Moreto. v+121 pp. Texas, E. R. Sims, 1949.

The writer discusses the social types and conventions of the *figurón* in the theater of Moreto and of Rojas Zorrilla.

❖ "The Social and Economic Background of the *Comedia Figurón*." [*Comedia de Figurón.*] *Centenary Review* (Centenary Coll., Shreveport) 1 (1949): 46–51.

529. Wofsy, Samuel Abraham. A Critical Edition of Nine Farces of Moreto. [3]+ii+225 pp. Wisconsin, A. García Solalinde, 1927.

The nine plays are *La loa de Juan Rana, Las brujas fingidas, Los órganos y el reloj, La reliquia, El hijo del vecino, La Mariquita, Doña Esquina, Los galanes,* and *El cortacaras.* Editorial note: Nine plays are listed in Castañeda, *Agustín Moreto* 176.

Mota, Henrique da (Portugal. 16th c.)

530. Miller, Neil Ted. Henrique da Mota and the Origins of Iberian Drama. 573 pp. CUNY, E. G. DaCal, 1972. *DAI* 32A: 6939.

"This relatively ignored contemporary of Gil Vicente was the author of various poems and dramatic dialogues. . . . In fact, such is the value of Henrique da Mota's contribution to the evolution of the Portuguese theatre, that we are led to call him one of its true founders." (Abs.)

❖ *Obras de Henrique da Mota: As origens do teatro ibérico.* Trans. João

Caiado Campos. Lisboa: Livraria Sá da Costa-Instituto Português do Livro, 1982. 472 pp. (Clássicos Sá da Costa, nova série.)

Ortiz, Agustín (16th c.)

531. House, Ralph Emerson. The *Comedia Radiana* of Agustín Ortiz, with Introduction and Notes. 50 pp. Chicago, K. Pietsch, 1909.

❖ "The *Comedia Radiana* of Agustín Ortiz." *MP* 7 (1909-10): 507-56. Rpt. Chicago: Univ. of Chicago, 1910.

The edition is based on a sixteenth-century printed text in the Biblioteca Nacional, Madrid, "where it is now catalogued as R-5006." (Prt. Diss.)

[For a more complete list of this scholar's publications, see E. K. Mapes, Foreword to "Hispanic Studies in Memory of R. E. House," *PQ* 21.1 (1942): 3-7.]

Palau, Bartolomé (1525?-?)

532. Sweeney, Mary S. *Victoria de Cristo* by Bartholomé Palau. ccix+ 205 pp. Bryn Mawr, J. E. Gillet, 1947.

The base text of this critical edition is the *princeps:* Zaragoza, 1569.

Pantaleón de Ribera, Anastasio (1580-1629)
(1600-1629 according to K. Brown)

533. Brown, Kenneth. Anastasio Pantaleón de Ribera (1600-1629): Witty Member of the Spanish Literary Republic. x+486 pp. Pennsylvania State, A. A. Triolo, 1975. *DAI* 37A: 1003-04.

"De suma importancia para el estudio de la literatura son [las] relaciones del poeta [Pantaleón de Ribera] con Pellicer, Lope, Alarcón, Paravicino, Castillo Solórzano, Gabriel de Corral y otros." (Abs.)

❖ *Anastasio Pantaleón de Ribera (1600–1629): Ingenioso miembro de la república literaria española.* Potomac: Studia Humanitatis; Madrid: Porrúa Turanzas, 1980. 426 pp.

Pastor, Juan (fl. 1528)

534. Goldman, Rachel Margaret. The Lucretia Legend from Livy to Rojas Zorrilla. 251 pp. CUNY, L. Feder, 1976. *DAI* 37A: 1531.

[For the complete entry, see no. 550.] The relevant play by Juan Pastor is *Farsa de Lucrecia.* (Abs.)

Pérez de Montalbán, Juan (1602–1638)

535. Bacon, George William. Life and Dramatic Works of Dr. Juan Pérez de Montalbán. Pennsylvania, H. A. Rennert, 1903. {*An Essay upon the Life and Dramatic Works of Dr. Juan Pérez de Montalván*. Philadelphia: [Univ. of Pennsylvania], 1903. v+46 pp.} (Extract from diss.)

❖ [A] "The *Comedias* of Dr. Juan Pérez de Montalván." *RH* 17 (1907): 46–65. [A footnote explains that this article was "condensed from the author's *Life and Dramatic Works of Doctor Juan Pérez de Montalván* . . . now in course of preparation."] [B] "The *comedia El segundo Séneca de España,* of Dr. Juan Pérez de Montalbán." *RR* 1 (1910): 64–86. [C] "The Life and Dramatic Works of Dr. Juan Pérez de Montalván, 1602–1638." *RH* 26 (1912): 1–474. ["The object of the present volume is to supply . . . minute analyses of all the (50) *comedias* which appear genuine, together with whatever data regarding their source, performance, etc., I have been able to collect."]

536. Hershey, Phares Robert. *Pedro de Vrdemalas,* comedia famosa de Ivan Pérez de Montalván: Edited with Introduction and Notes. xl+162 pp. Northwestern, T. R. Palfrey, 1932.

The edition is based on an undated *suelta* (owned by M. A. Buchanan), which has been collated with three other versions:

(1) a partially handwritten text in the Palatine Library of Parma, (2) a *suelta* in the BNM, and (3) Emilio Cotarelo's redaction in the Spanish Academy's edition of Lope's works *(Nueva edición).* The play has been attributed to Cervantes, to Lope, and to Pérez de Montalbán. The writer argues in favor of the last named. He adds that "until additional facts of a more convincing nature are discovered, we cannot attribute the play either to Lope or Cervantes." (Diss.)

537. Morales de Rodríguez, Hilda Angélica. Philip II in the Historical Comedies of Juan Pérez de Montalbán. vii+133 pp. Pennsylvania State, L. C. Pérez, 1984. *DAI* 45A: 3358.

"The purpose of this dissertation is to study the literary-artistic figure of Philip II as he appears in the plays of Juan Pérez de Montalbán: *Comedia Famosa De El Gran Séneca de España, Felipe Segundo; Segunda parte del Séneca de España, don Felipe Segundo;* and *El señor don Juan de Austria en Madrid.*" (Abs.)

538. Parker, Gary Wallace. The Dramatic Art of Juan Pérez de Montalbán. viii+282 pp. CA/Riverside, C. Ayllón, 1977. *DAI* 38A: 3547.

"Some of the weaknesses which are evident in Montalbán's drama were shared by the *comedia* in general as a result of the tastes and demands of the public at that time. While his action-oriented plays were consistently popular, his style could have been of better quality if perhaps he had taken more care in writing." (Abs.)

539. Van Kerk, John William. The Figure of Don Carlos in Selected Plays of the Spanish Golden Age. vii+166 pp. Georgia, H. Ziomek, 1978. *DAI* 39A: 4312.

[For the complete entry, see no. 188.] One of the works analyzed is *El segundo Séneca* by Juan Pérez de Montalbán. (Abs.)

Pérez de Toledo, Juan (1512?–1545)

540. Bibb, Elizabeth Sterrett. The Published Comedies of Juan Pérez de Toledo. iii+247 pp. Illinois, R. P. Oliver, 1959. *DA* 20: 295.

All the works of this author are in Latin. His four comedies are *Necromanticus, Lena, Decepti,* and *Suppositi,* "and were published posthumously by the author's brother in 1574. Written for performance by students, all are adaptations of Italian comedies." (Abs.)

QUEVEDO, FRANCISCO (1580–1645)

541. BAUM, DORIS L. Traditionalism in the Works of Don Francisco de Quevedo y Villegas. 318 pp. Virginia, F. de Toro-Garland, 1967. *DA* 28A: 2641–42.

"Within the dramatic genre, Quevedo wrote several plays, entremeses, dialogues, loas, bailes and jácaras, many of which have since been lost. . . . These dramatic compositions are based on themes which Quevedo had treated previously in his prose, many of them being social satires of types such as students, pícaros, doctors and drunkards. . . . If one is to single out the most traditional aspects of [*Cómo ha de ser el privado*], they are to be found in the content of the play's moral message. . . . [In his *entremeses*] Quevedo, like Lope, followed a national literary tradition of close contact with the spirit of the people. It is significant that he returns to this popular style in every genre of his work." (Prt. Diss.)

❖ Title as is. Chapel Hill: U of North Carolina P, 1970. 210 pp. (UNCSRLL 91.)

542. CAUVIN, [SISTER] MARY AUSTIN, O.P. The *Comedia de Privanza* in the Seventeenth Century. 505 pp. Pennsylvania, A. G. Reichenberger, 1957. *DA* 18: 229.

"For this study a large number of the dramas of the period were consulted, some fifty of which were selected." (Abs.) On pp. 372–87 the writer deals with Quevedo's only *comedia, Cómo ha de ser el privado.*

Editorial note: James Crosby's Quevedo bibliographies (1976, 1982, and 1993) include some 35 other U.S. dissertations on Don Francisco. Although several make sporadic references to his plays and all contribute to our knowledge of the great *polígrafo,* none of them deals exclusively or extensively with his theater and therefore they have not been listed here. One example of an insightful and valuable contribution that does not deal substantively with Quevedo's theater is the dissertation of James Iffland: Quevedo and the Grotesque, Brown University, 1977. A printed version with the same title was published by Tamesis of London in two volumes: 1, 1979, 174 pp.; 2, 1982, 283 pp. In part 3 (The Genesis of the Grotesque in Quevedo), the writer includes a chapter entitled "The Environmental Influences," in which he discusses at some length several aspects of "popular-festive grotesquery" that may have influenced Quevedo. One of the aspects described is the *entremés* as a genre, with its "gestic nature" and "less-than-human" characters. Two other facets treated are the commedia dell'arte and puppet theater.

Quiñones de Benavente, Luis (1589?–1651)

543. Estermann, Hannah. Luis Quiñones de Benavente: His Technique of the Interlude. 587 pp. CA/Berkeley, J. F. Montesinos, 1953. PFE, June 1953.

The seven chapters of this dissertation are as follows: "The Interlude," "Benavente," "Bibliography of Benavente's Works," "Subject Matter of the Interludes," "Elements of Comedy in the Interludes," "Versification," and "Chronology." (Diss.)

❖ [A] Bergman, Hannah E. "El Romancero en Quiñones de Benavente." *NRFH* 15 (1961): 229–46. [B] Bergman, Hannah E. *Luis Quiñones de Benavente y sus entremeses: Con un catálogo biográfico de los actores citados en sus obras.* Madrid: Castalia, 1965. 571 pp. (Biblioteca de erudición y crítica 7). [C] Bergman, Hannah E. "Algunos entremeses desconocidos de Luis Quiñones de Benavente." *Homenaje a Casalduero: Crítica y poesía. Ofrecido por sus amigos y discípulos*. Ed. Rizel Pincus Sigele and Gonzalo Sobejano. Madrid: Gredos, 1972. 85–94. [D] Bergman, Hannah E. *Quiñones de Benavente.* New York: Twayne, 1972. 171 pp. [For a complete list of this scholar's publications, see Sz. Szmuk, "Hannah E. Bergman: Publications and Presentations," *BCom* 49.2 (1997): 407–12.]

Remón, Fray Alonso (1561–1632)

544. Kaatz, Gerda Ruth. A Diplomatic Edition of the *Comedia del católico español* and the *Comedia del glorioso San Martín*. v+348 pp. Iowa, R. Davis, 1945. Iowa *Abstracts* 7: 947–54.

The edition is based on BNM MS 14.767. The *Comedia del católico español* is attributed to Fray Alonso Remón. "Whether the play *[Comedia del glorioso San Martín]* is to be ascribed to Lope or to an anonymous playwright, the strophes employed do not provide a very definitive clue as to the date of composition. From the rather meager evidence it may be conjectured that it was written in the 1580's or early 1590's." (Abs.)

545. Serna López, Ven. A Critical Edition of Alonso Remón's *Las tres mujeres en una* (Estudio de la obra teatral de Alonso Remón, seguido de una edición de *Las tres mujeres en una*). xiii+484 pp. CA/Los Angeles, J. H. Silverman, 1966. *DA* 27A: 3018.

❖ [A] "Observaciones sobre el arte de Alonso Remón, dramaturgo lopista." *Actas del segundo congreso internacional de hispanistas, Nijmegen, 1965*. Ed. Jaime Sánchez Romeralo and Norbert Poulussen. Nijmegen, Netherlands: Univ. Nijmegen, 1967. 591–97. [B] *El teatro de Alonso Remón:* Tres mujeres en una. Madrid: Pliegos, 1983. 299 pp. "Of the two hundred plays which Remón is supposed to have written, some fifteen have been examined along with others purported to be his." The edition is based on BNM MS 14.896—a nonautograph seventeenth-century manuscript—which has been collated with a printed version in *Parte treinta y dos con doze de diferentes* (Zaragoza, 1640). (Prt. Diss.)

Roa, Gabriel de (17th c.)

546. Ewing, Boyd Ross. *El villano gran señor y gran Tamorlán de Persia* by Rojas, Villanueva and Roa: Edited with an Introduction and Notes. cviii+151 pp. Cornell, 1932. Abstract. Ithaca: Cornell Univ., 1932. 6 pp.

The purpose of this dissertation "is to present the play by Rojas, Villanueva and Roa according to the Manuscript [14997] of the Biblioteca Nacional [Madrid]; to show the source from which the poets received their inspiration for its composition; and to assemble and present the known data concerning the Tamorlan material as it appears in Spanish [dramatic] literature." (Diss.)

Rojas Villandrando, Agustín de (1572–after 1618)

547. Crowell, James White. Description and Abstract of *El natural desdichado* by Agustín de Rojas Villandrando: Edited, from an Autograph in the Biblioteca Nacional at Madrid, with an Introduction and Notes. 216 pp. Cornell, G. I. Dale, 1929.
❖ *Agustín de Rojas'* El Natural desdichado: *Edited from an Autograph in the Biblioteca Nacional at Madrid, with an Introduction and Notes.* Ed. J. W. Crowell. New York: Instituto de las Españas en los Estados Unidos, 1939. lxxi+201 pp. This edition of Rojas Villandrando's only extant play is based on BNM MS R-104. (Prt. Diss.)

Rojas Zorrillla, Francisco de (1607–1648)

548. Bacalski, Robert Rudolf. A Critical Edition of *El jardín de Falerina* by Francisco de Rojas Zorrilla, Antonio Coello y Ochoa, and Pedro Calderón de la Barca, with Introduction and Notes. 351 pp. New Mexico, R. R. MacCurdy, 1972. *DAI* 33A: 5712.
[For the complete entry, see no. 242.]

549. Ewing, Boyd Ross. *El villano gran señor y gran Tamorlán de Persia* by Rojas, Villanueva and Roa: Edited with an Introduction and Notes. cviii+151 pp. Cornell, 1932.
[For the complete entry, see no. 546.]

550. Goldman, Rachel Margaret. The Lucretia Legend from Livy to Rojas Zorrilla. 251 pp. CUNY, L. Feder, 1976. *DAI* 37A: 1531.
The writer examines two pertinent plays: Juan Pastor's *Farsa de Lucrecia* and Rojas Zorrilla's *Lucrecia y Tarquino*. (Abs.)

551. Horvath, Sabine. Königtum und Tyrannei, Rebellion und Verschwörung als Themen im europäischen Drama, von der

Spät-Renaissance bis zum Ende des siebzehnten Jahrhunderts. 505 pp. CUNY, L. Bergel, 1975. *DAI* 36A: 882–83.

[For the complete entry, see no. 218.] One of the plays examined is *Del rey abajo ninguno* by Rojas Zorrilla.

552. Jeans, Fred Wilson. An Annotated Critical Edition of Rojas Zorrilla's *Peligrar en los remedios.* 630 pp. Brown, W. L. Fichter, 1957. *DA* 18: 589–90.

The critical edition is based on the MS version dated 1634, "a stage copy shown by its handwriting to have been emended by Rojas and at least four other persons." This text has been collated with "eight editions, including seven of the seventeenth century." (Abs.)

553. Leyte-Vidal, Nocidia Joel. El personaje "gracioso" en la dramaturgia de Francisco de Rojas Zorrilla. xii+286 pp. Catholic, J. M. Solà-Solé, 1977. *DAI* 38A: 5511–12.

"This dissertation studies the character and role of the *gracioso* in the 36 dramas of Rojas Zorrilla. . . . The conclusions show that Rojas Zorrilla's *gracioso* is more closely related to Lope's type than to Calderón's." (Abs.)

554. Powers, Harriet Boyer. A Critical Edition of Francisco de Rojas Zorrilla's *Los trabajos de Tobías.* 392 pp. New Mexico, R. R. MacCurdy, 1967. *DAI* 28A: 3680.

The edition is based on the one "published by Rojas himself" in 1645, together with "variant readings of the six unauthorized texts known today." (Abs.)

❖ "The Grotesque Vision of Rojas Zorrilla." *BCom* 23.1 (1971): 1–6 [Study based on *Los trabajos de Tobías.*]

555. Rambo, James Stone. An Annotated Critical Edition of *También tiene el sol menguante,* by Luis Vélez de Guevara and Francisco de Rojas Zorrilla. viii+424 pp. New Mexico, R. R. MacCurdy, 1972. *DAI* 33A: 2948.

This play "is a *refundición* of Mira de Amescua's two-part drama, *La próspera y la adversa fortuna de don Bernardo de Cabrera.*" The text is based on a manuscript containing *censuras* that are dated 1655, with textual variants from (1) a printed edition of 1666, (2) an eighteenth-century manuscript, and (3) an eighteenth-century *suelta.* (Abs.)

556. Rodríguez, Luz María. Women in Twenty-Five Plays of Rojas Zorrilla. viii+262 pp. New Mexico, R. R. MacCurdy, 1981.

"One concludes after studying the female characterization in twenty-five of his plays, that Rojas' work reflects a sympathetic appreciation of women that goes well beyond the norm of his day." (Diss.)

557. Schmelter, Kevin Thomas. An Annotated Critical Edition of Francisco de Rojas Zorrilla's *Nuestra Señora de Atocha.* 325 pp. New Mexico, R. R. MacCurdy, 1969. *DAI* 31A: 1770.

The edition is based on "a partly autograph, signed manuscript" and is collated with other manuscript copies and the first printed edition (1645). (Abs.)

558. White, Ralph Eugene. *La Comedia de Figurón* of Rojas Zorrilla and Moreto. v+121 pp. Texas, E. R. Sims, 1949.

[For the complete entry, see no. 528.]

Rueda, Lope de (?–1565)

559. Abrams, Frederic. A Critical Edition of Lope de Rueda's *Comedia Eufemia.* iv+207 pp. Iowa, E. DeChasca, 1960. *DA* 21: 1559.

The critical text is based on the *princeps* (1567), which is collated with the second edition (1576) and the "eight modern" editions. (Abs.)

❖ [A] "The Date of Composition of Lope de Rueda's *Comedia Eufemia.*" *MLN* 76 (1961): 766–70. [B] "Lope de Rueda: Una bibliografía analítica en el cuarto centenario de su muerte." *DHR* 4 (1965): 39–55.

560. DeChasca, Edmund Villela. Lope de Rueda's *Comedia de los engañados:* An Edition. Chicago, H. Keniston, 1941. {Chicago: Private ed., distributed by Univ. of Chicago Libraries, 1941. iv+192 pp.}

"I have used the *Princeps* [Valencia, 1567] as my basic text and have collated it with the second, 1576 Seville edition and with the four modern editions [1830, 1832, 1895, 1908]." (Prt. Diss.)

❖ [A] "The Phonology of the Speech of the Negroes in Early Spanish Drama." *HR* 14 (1946): 322–29. [Rueda's *Los engañados* is one of the plays on which this study is based.] [B] "Early Editions of *Gl'Ingannati:* The Problem of Overlapping Dates." *MP* 50 (1952): 79–87. [The anonymous Italian play was Rueda's model for *Los engañados.*] [For a more complete list of this scholar's publications, see "Edmund de Chasca: List of Publications," *Hispanic Studies in Honor of Edmund de Chasca,* ed. C. A. Zimansky, *PQ* 51.1 (1972): 343–44.]

561. Geib, Kathleen Louise. Lope de Rueda's *Pasos:* An Edition of *El deleitoso* and the *Registro de representantes.* xiii+283 pp. Iowa, E. DeChasca, 1970. *DAI* 31A: 1275.

"The present edition is based on that of Cotarelo y Mori, 1908. . . . The 100 closely packed pages of notes that follow the text and that are intended to clarify textual problems constitute the bulk of the original contribution of the thesis." (Abs.)

562. Jablon, Kenneth. A Critical Edition of Lope de Rueda's Pastoral Colloquies *Camila* and *Tymbria.* iv+236 pp. Iowa, E. DeChasca, 1962. *DA* 23: 2905.

"The text [of the *colloquies*] is a copy of the *Princeps* (Valencia, 1567) with variants from the following subsequent editions: Seville, 1576, the edition of the Marqués de la Fuensanta del Valle, 1895, and the Cotarelo edition of 1908." (Abs.)

❖ "The Dates of Composition of Lope de Rueda's Pastoral Colloquies *Camila* and *Tymbria.*" *RomN* 11 (1969–70): 156–59.

563. Listerman, Randall Wayne. The *Pasos* of Lope de Rueda and the *Fastnachtsspiele* of Hans Sachs: A Comparative Study. 163 pp. Missouri, V. G. Williamsen, 1971. *DAI* 33A: 278.

". . . the two dramatists, . . . in spite of differences, to a large degree shared a similar heritage; and therefore, reflected artistically their relationship to their times and to each other." (Abs.)

❖ [A] "Lope de Rueda's *La tierra de Jauja:* Boccaccio Inspired?" *LangQ* 14 (1975): 1–22. [B] "Some Material Contributions of the Commedia dell'Arte to the Spanish Theater." *RomN* 18 (1976): 1–5. [C] "Lope de Vega's Formula for Success: Practiced Previously by Lope de Rueda." *LangQ* 15 (1977): 23–24. [D] "La commedia dell'arte: Fuente técnica y artística en la dramaturgia de Lope de Rueda." *Actas del sexto congreso internacional de hispanistas, Toronto, 1977.* Ed. Alan M. Gordon and Evelyn Rugg.

Toronto: Univ. of Toronto, 1980. 464–66. [E] Rueda, L. de. *The Interludes*. Trans., with an introd. and notes, by R. W. Listerman. Ottawa: Dovehouse, 1988. 118 pp.

Ruiz de Alarcón y Mendoza, Juan (Mexico. 1581?–1639)

564. Anderson, Carl Dixon. A Critical Edition of Juan Ruiz de Alarcón's *Examen de maridos.* vii+278 pp. Texas, R. W. Tyler, 1965. *DA* 26: 1035.

"The text of the present critical edition . . . is based on that of the author's *Parte segunda* (Barcelona, 1634). . . . Of the ten editions whose variants are listed, only the spurious version of 1633 is useful for establishing the text and for the study of the author's revisions." (Abs.)

565. Brenes, Carmen Olga. El sentimiento democrático en el teatro de Juan Ruiz de Alarcón. vi+343 pp. Southern California, D. E. McMahon, 1955. USC *Abstracts of Dissertations* (1955): 96–98.

❖ Title as is. Valencia: Castalia, 1960. 278 pp. (La lupa y el escalpelo 3.)

"El propósito de esta obra ha sido analizar el sentimiento democrático en la obra de Alarcón, y colocarlo dentro de la tradición democrática de la literatura española." (Prt. Diss.)

566. Byrnes, Joseph Alfred. Four Plays of Samuel Foote: *The Knights, The Minor, The Lyar, The Mayor of Garratt.* An Edition with Commentary. 2 vols. (v+495 pp.) NYU, G. W. Stone, 1963. *DA* 24: 2011.

The Lyar (1761–62, published 1764) was derived from Pierre Corneille's *Le Menteur.* (Abs.) Editorial note: In turn, *Le Menteur* was derived from Ruiz de Alarcón's *La verdad sospechosa.*

567. Ciavarelli, Maria Elisa. El tema de la fuerza de la sangre en el Siglo de Oro español y sus antecedentes en la literatura occidental. 330 pp. Pennsylvania, A. E. Foley, 1977. *DAI* 38A: 4864.

[For the complete entry, see no. 688.]

568. Claydon, Ellen Easton. Juan Ruiz de Alarcón: Baroque

Dramatist. 260 pp. Colorado, F. Sánchez y Escribano, 1965. *DA* 28A: 2203.

"Thirteen of the twenty plays known to be written by Alarcón have been examined in the light of seventeenth-century ideology and aesthetics." (Abs.)

❖ [A] Title as is. Chapel Hill: Univ. of North Carolina, Dept. of Romance Languages; Madrid: Castalia, 1970. 175 pp. (Estudios de Hispanófila 12). [B] "Some Observations on Alarcón's Position in the Development of the Seventeenth-Century Theater." *Hispanófila* 42 (1971): 7–19.

569. De Benchoff, María del Carmen Soto. El teatro de Juan Ruiz de Alarcón y las preceptivas dramáticas. 216 pp. CA/Riverside, E. Carilla, 1982. *DAI* 43A: 3310.

"Alarcón does not conform with the classic theories or with the theories of his contemporaries. His theatre is different. It is the product of a complex personality." (Abs.)

570. DiLillo, Leonard Michael. Characterization and Ethics in the Plays of Juan Ruiz de Alarcón. iii+158 pp. Rutgers, E. Nagy, 1970. *DAI* 31A: 4115.

The writer analyzes the leading figures in *La verdad sospechosa, Las paredes oyen, Ganar amigos, Mudarse por mejorarse,* and *No hay mal que por bien no venga.* (Abs.)

❖ [A] "Moral Purpose in Ruiz de Alarcón's *La verdad sospechosa.*" *H*[AATSP] 56 (1973): 254–59. [B] "Characterization and Ethics in Ruiz de Alarcón's *Las paredes oyen.*" *Hispanófila* 65 (1979): 31–41.

571. Ebersole, Alva Vernon, Jr. El ambiente español visto por Juan Ruiz de Alarcón. iv+301 pp. Kansas, J. M. de Osma, 1957.

❖ [A] Title as is. [Valencia]: Castalia, 1959. 191 pp. "Esta obra es una revisión (con el mismo título) de la disertación doctoral presentada en la Universidad de Kansas en 1957. . . . Las páginas que siguen serán, pues, una exposición o enfoque de la obra de Juan Ruiz de Alarcón hacia una fase menos explorada de su producción teatral: el reflejo del ambiente español tal como él lo conoció y observó o criticó durante sus años de residencia en Salamanca, Sevilla y Madrid, en las primeras décadas del siglo XVII en España." (Prt. Diss.) [B] Ruiz de Alarcón y Mendoza,

J. *Obras completas*. Introd. and new preliminary study by A. V. Ebersole. 2 vols. Facsimile. Valencia: Albatros-Hispanófila, 1990. (Siglo de Oro 5 and 6.) [For a more complete list of this scholar's publications, see "Alva V. Ebersole: Publications," *Hispanófila* 100 (1990): 5–6.]

572. Espantoso Foley, Augusta María. The Use of the Occult Arts in the *Comedias* of Juan Ruiz de Alarcón, Together with a Preliminary Survey of the Occult Arts in Dramatic Literature. 188 pp. Pennsylvania, O. H. Green, 1962. *DA* 23: 1363–64.

"The *comedias* pertinent to this study are: *La cueva de Salamanca, Quien mal anda en mal acaba, La manganilla de Melilla, La prueba de las promesas,* [and] *El dueño de las estrellas*. . . . once [Alarcón] presents his orthodox position relative to the occult, he proceeds to make use of it in the manner that best suits his dramatic purposes." (Abs.)

❖ [A] "The Problem of Astrology and Its Use in Ruiz de Alarcón's *El dueño de las estrellas*." *HR* 32 (1964): 1–11. Also in *Critical Essays on the Life and Work of Juan Ruiz de Alarcón*. Ed. James A. Parr. Madrid: Dos Continentes, 1972. 213–22. [B] "Las ciencias ocultas, la teología y la técnica dramática en algunas comedias de Juan Ruiz de Alarcón." *Actas del segundo congreso internacional de hispanistas, Nijmegen, 1965*. Ed. Jaime Sánchez Romeralo and Norbert Poulussen. Nijmegen, Netherlands: Univ. Nijmegen, 1967. 319–26. [Apropos *Quien mal anda en mal acaba* and *La prueba de las promesas*.] [C] *Occult Arts and Doctrine in the Theater of Juan Ruiz de Alarcón*. Genève: Droz, 1972. 108 pp.

573. González, Mariano. El galán en el teatro de Juan Ruiz de Alarcón. ii+214 pp. Southern California, J. D. Smith, 1971. *DAI* 32A: 4563.

"Why is Alarcón's treatment of the *galán* so extensive when compared to the other characters of his plays? None of his contemporary playwrights insisted so upon developing only one character. This unilateral perspective may be explained by viewing Alarcón's works as a self-portrait resulting from his experiences and goals—goals based on his observations of daily life, and his idealization and desire for moral betterment of that life, yet balancing all with the stoicism he needed in his own existence as *homo deformis et parvus*." (Abs.)

574. HALPERN, CYNTHIA LEONE. The Political Theater of Early Seventeenth-Century Spain, with Special Reference to Juan Ruiz de Alarcón. 225 pp. Bryn Mawr, W. F. King, 1990. *DAI* 52A: 175.

"This study deals with a number of political dramas written during the reign of Philip III and Philip IV. Primary attention is given to the work of Juan Ruiz de Alarcón, whose theater displays an interest in statecraft and politics much more constant than that of his contemporaries. . . . Chapter IV analyzes several of the plays of Lope de Vega, Tirso de Molina, and Francisco de Quevedo which reveal concern about the state of the nation. None of these writers, however, deals as systematically and thoughtfully as does Alarcón with the issues of divine-right monarchy and possible social and political reform under it. Chapters V and VI provide a detailed analysis of seven plays by Alarcón, from which a body of consistent political thought may be gleaned." (Abs.)

❖ Title as is. New York: Peter Lang, 1993. 179 pp. (Ibérica 6.)

575. HAMILTON, THOMAS EARLE. The Structure of the Alarconian *Comedia*. vii+178 p. Texas, C. M. Montgomery(?), 1940.

The principal topics discussed by the writer are plot, characters, humor, relationship to the dramatic unities, and Alarcón's universality in theme and scope.

❖ [A] "Spoken Letters in the *Comedias* of Alarcón, Tirso, and Lope." *PMLA* 62 (1947): 62–75. [B] "*Comedias* Attributed to Alarcón Examined in the Light of His Known Epistolary Practices." *HR* 17 (1949): 124–32. [Rpt. in *Critical Essays on the Life and Work of Juan Ruiz de Alarcón*. Ed. James A. Parr. Madrid: Dos Continentes, 1972. 151–61, 295–97.] [C] "The Aside in the *Comedias* of Alarcón." *H* [AATSP] 46 (1963): 536–39.

576. KING, SAMUEL CARL, JR. Love as a Theme in the Theatre of Juan Ruiz de Alarcón. 192 pp. Louisiana State, F. A. de Armas, 1971. *DAI* 32A: 6933.

"Thus, whatever the type of love, the lovers are constantly aware of the fact that they do not operate in a vacuum but in society. There is, then, a restraint on the personal freedom to act of the lovers." (Abs.)

577. KOBBERVIG, KARL IRVING. A System for Classifying Motif Ele-

ments in the Drama of the Golden Age and Its Application to the *Comedias* of Juan Ruiz de Alarcón y Mendoza. 171 pp. WA/Seattle, W. E. Wilson, 1955. *DA* 15: 2210.

"In this study, a system for classifying motif elements in the Spanish drama of the Golden Age has been evolved along the lines of the *Motif-Index of Folk Literature* of Stith Thompson, but completely independent of that system in its arrangement and application. The twenty-six *comedias* of Juan Ruiz de Alarcón y Mendoza contained in volume XX of the *Biblioteca de autores españoles* have been analyzed according to the classification." (Abs.)

578. MELVIN, MIRIAM VIRGINIA. Juan Ruiz de Alarcón: Classical and Spanish Influences. xiii+120 pp. Kansas, J. M. de Osma, 1941.

After quoting Ermilo Abreu Gómez's comment that "habrá de verse a Lope, para explicar a Alarcón," the writer goes on to say: "Such is the conclusion offered by this study. From the Classics, Alarcón transferred no more than a tendency to restrict and simplify his action, and an attention to character study. Beyond this, the Classics cannot claim him. His is a seventeenth century *comedia,* his characters are seventeenth century Spaniards, his dialogue a more serious edition of Lope de Vega, his morals a challenge to his enemies and a defense of his misfortune. . . . Juan Ruiz de Alarcón, like other writers of the Spanish *comedia,* is deeply indebted to that great master Lope de Vega." (Diss.)

❖ Title as is. Ann Arbor: Edwards, 1942. v+111 pp. "Reproduced from type-written copy." (*NUC*)

579. NEUMANN, DWIGHT KEITH. The Inferiority Complex in the Characters of Juan Ruiz de Alarcón. xi+247 pp. CA/Los Angeles, C. B. Johnson, 1980. *DAI* 41A: 1625.

The writer bases his investigation on the following *comedias: La industria y la suerte, Las paredes oyen, La prueba de las promesas, La verdad sospechosa, Ganar amigos, Los pechos privilegiados, La crueldad por el honor,* and *No hay mal que por bien no venga.* "In the production of the dramatist's best characters, it is the inferiority complex and the goal of superiority that form the very foundation of [his creative] process." (Abs.)

580. OLIVER-PREFASI, CATALINA M. La figura femenina en el teatro

de Juan Ruiz de Alarcón. 391 pp. NYU, A. Pollin, 1982. *DAI* 43A: 2361.

". . . we dedicate our work to an in-depth, ample and specific study of the feminine figure in the [twenty] *comedias* of this playwright." (Abs.)

581. PARR, JAMES ALLAN. Moral Philosophy in the Plays of Juan Ruiz de Alarcón. iv+135 pp. Pittsburgh, R. Cardona, 1967. *DA* 28A: 1443–44.

"Alarcón is possibly the first Spanish writer to present a man-centered moral philosophy which is independent of theological considerations and supernatural sanctions." (Abs.)

❖ [A] "*¿Todo es ventura?:* Alarcón's Fortune Plays." *BCom* 24.2 (1972): 36–40. [B] "Honor-Virtue in *La verdad sospechosa* and *Las paredes oyen*." *REHb* 8 (1974): 173–88. [C] "On Fate, Suicide and Free Will in *El dueño de las estrellas*." *HR* 42 (1974): 199–207. [D] "Ruiz de Alarcón: Marginal Meditations on Manners." *Proceedings of the Fourth Annual Golden Age Spanish Drama Symposium (Texto y espectáculo), El Paso, 1984*. El Paso: Univ. of Texas, 1984. 107–21.

582. PASTO, DAVID JOSEPH. A Translation and Critical Study of Two Plays by Juan Ruiz de Alarcón. 290 pp. Michigan, M. Pilkinton, 1984. *DAI* 45A: 348.

The two plays are *Las paredes oyen (The Walls Have Ears)* and *La prueba de las promesas (The Test of Promises)*. "Each text appears in a rough form of iambic pentameter to transfer Alarcón's poetic style into English." (Abs.)

❖ "The Independent Heroines in Ruiz de Alarcón's Major *Comedias*." *BCom* 40.2 (1988): 227–35 [The *comedias* in question are *La verdad sospechosa, Las paredes oyen,* and *La prueba de las promesas*.]

583. PERRY, CHARLES ELLIOTT. Role-Playing in the Theater of Juan Ruiz de Alarcón. xii+161 pp. Oregon, P. J. Powers, 1971. *DAI* 32A: 5196–97.

"The study of role-playing in Alarcón's theater provides both an analytic tool and a fresh approach to this dramatist's *obra,* of which ten plays were selected for this purpose: *La industria y la suerte, Las paredes oyen, El semejante a sí mismo, Mudarse por mejorarse, El desdichado en fingir, La verdad sospechosa, El Anticristo, El tejedor de Segovia, La prueba de las promesas* and *El examen de maridos*. The conclusion to the study of role-playing supports the thesis that Ruiz de Alarcón was more interested in the dramatic possibilities of the interplay of role and identity than with either the moral edification of his audience or with the projection of his own personality onto his dramatic creations. The notion of *extrañeza,* or uniqueness, long applied to the theater of Ruiz de Alarcón, is shown to be without foundation." (Abs.)

❖ [A] "Comedy and Common Sense in Alarcón's *El semejante a sí mismo*." *RomN* 16.3 (1974–75): 734–41. [On the function of role-playing.] [B] "The Question of Means and Magic in Alarcón's *La prueba de las promesas*." *BCom* 27.1 (1975): 14–19.

584. Pollin, Alice M. The *Gracioso* of Significant Name in the Theatre of Juan Ruiz de Alarcón y Mendoza. iii+241 pp. NYU, J. Casalduero, 1955. *DA* 16: 340–41.

"A detailed analysis is . . . made of the functions and significance of the symbolically-named *graciosos* in nine plays of Ruiz de Alarcón." The plays are *La crueldad por el honor, La industria y la suerte, La manganilla de Melilla, Ganar amigos, El examen de maridos, Los empeños de un engaño, Mudarse por mejorarse, Los pechos privilegiados,* and *El tejedor de Segovia*. (Abs.)

❖ Paulin [sic], Alice. "The Religious Motive in the Plays of Juan Ruiz de Alarcón." *HR* 29.1 (1961): 33–44.

585. Sandoval Sánchez, Alberto. Estructura e ideología en las comedias de Juan Ruiz de Alarcón (Hacia la determinación de una cronología). ii+286 pp. Minnesota, N. Spadaccini, 1983. *DAI* 44A: 2786.

"This thesis examines the *comedias* of Juan Ruiz de Alarcón . . . from a sociohistorical perspective while relying at the same time on a thematic-structural approach. The focus is on the structural and ideological evolution of the plays in order to establish a chronology. . . . this study shows that his plays are both a metaphorical defense and exegesis of his own social interaction, and a critique of the socioeconomic and political crises of Spain in the early 1600s." (Abs.)

❖ [A] "Aportes para una canonización de Juan Ruiz de Alarcón en la literatura latinoamericana." *RCLL* 14.28 (1988): 281–90. [B] "Moros por indios: Ensayando una lectura excéntrica del discurso colonial en *La manganilla de Melilla* de Juan Ruiz de Alarcón." *RIber* 172–73 (1995): 535–53.

586. SCHONS, DOROTHY. Apuntes y documentos nuevos para la biografía de Juan Ruiz de Alarcón y Mendoza. 95 p. Chicago, G. T. Northup(?), 1929.

The dissertation is based on documents discovered by the writer in the Archivo de Indias in Seville. On p. 4 of the reprint she points out: "Este estudio ha sido aceptado como tesis doctoral por la Universidad de Chicago, y se me ha dado permiso para publicarlo antes de recibir el grado correspondiente."

❖ [A] Title as is. *BRAEH* 95.3 (1929): 59–151. [B] Title as is. Madrid: Tipografía de Archivos, 1929. [C] Rpt. Private ed., distributed by Univ. of Chicago Libraries, 1932(?). [D] *Notes from Spanish Archives.* Austin: n.p., 1946. 40 pp. (New World Studies 1.) [From unpublished letters and petitions relating to Juan Ruiz de Alarcón, Mateo Alemán, Bernardo de Balbuena, Gutierre de Cetina, et al.]

587. SCOTT, ANTOINETTE ESTÉVEZ. Estudiantes y letrados en las obras dramáticas de Lope de Vega, Tirso de Molina, y Juan Ruiz de Alarcón. vii+231 pp. Florida State, D. L. Hoffman, 1974. *DAI* 35A: 3008.

"Altogether, students and *letrados* of some forty-two plays were analyzed." (Abs.)

588. SEGALL, JACOB BERNARD. Corneille and the Spanish Drama. Columbia, 1902. {New York: Columbia UP; Macmillan, 1902. ix+147 pp. (Columbia University Studies in Romance Philology and Literature 3.)}

[For the complete entry, see no. 164.] The writer compares Pierre Corneille's *Le Menteur* and Alarcón's *La verdad sospechosa*.

589. SMYTHE DE URQUIETA, KATHLEEN CECILIA. The Seventeenth-Century Image of the Spanish Dramatist Juan Ruiz de Alarcón. iii+181 pp. Harvard, S. Gilman, 1984. *DAI* 45A: 2128.

"In this dissertation we re-examine the seventeenth-century image of the dramatist that appears in the works of contemporaries and in Alarcón's own *comedias*. Our investigation points to an image that is at odds with modern-day speculation. The real-life Alarcón apparently was not the cowering outcast that he has been made out to be; rather, he was a disarming 'chocarrero' who was quick to humorously capitalize on his own shortcomings." (Abs.)

Salas Barbadillo, Alonso Jerónimo de (1581–1635)

590. Andrade, Marcel Charles. Una nueva edición de *El subtil cordovés Pedro de Urdemalas* de Salas Barbadillo, que incluye la comedia *El gallardo Escarramán*. lx+426 pp. Louisiana State, F. A. de Armas, 1970. *DAI* 31A: 4753.

This annotated edition is based on the *editio princeps* of 1620. "La comedia *El gallardo Escarramán* forma parte intrínseca de la obra." (Abs.)

❖ Salas Barbadillo, A. J. de. El subtil cordovés Pedro de Urdemalas *y* 'El gallardo Escarramán' de Salas Barbadillo. Ed., introd., and notes by M. C. Andrade. Chapel Hill: Estudios de Hispanófila, 1974. 312 pp. (Estudios de Hispanófila 30.)

591. Hamlett, Alan Auguste. An Annotated Edition of *El sutil cordobés Pedro de Urdemalas* by Alonso Jerónimo de Salas Barbadillo, Based on the *Princeps* of 1620 with Introduction. lvii+299 pp. Texas, E. R. Sims and L. Casís, 1940.

The edition includes the *comedia* entitled *El gallardo Escarramán*.

592. Marshall, Pauline Maude. An Edition of Alonso de Salas Barbadillo's *El caballero perfecto* (1620), Together with a Study of Previous Spanish Literary Portrayals of the Ideal Gentleman. xcvi+197 pp. Northwestern, E. B. Place, 1943. *Summaries of Doctoral Diss., Northwestern University* 11 (1943): 19–23.

Among other Spanish literary portrayals discussed by the writer are four *comedias* of Lope as well as Ruiz de Alarcón's *Las paredes oyen. (Summaries)* Editorial note: The edited work is a novel.

❖ Salas Barbadillo, A. J. de. El caballero perfecto *de Alonso Jerónimo de Salas Barbadillo: An Edition with Introduction and Notes*. Ed. P. M. Marshall. Boulder: U of Colorado P, 1949. lii+95 pp. (University of Colorado Studies. Ser. in Language and Literature 2.)

593. Place, Edwin Bray. A Study of the Works of Salas Barbadillo and María de Zayas. iv+415 pp. Harvard, J. D. M. Ford, 1919.

". . . it is the object of this essay to give adequate descriptions of the several works of Salas and Doña María . . . ; to furnish as complete a bibliography as possible of these works . . . ; and to set forth . . . their sources of inspiration and their influence upon the productions of subsequent novelists and playwrights." (Diss.) ❖ [A] "Salas Barbadillo, Satirist." *RR* 17 (1926): 230–42. [B] Salas Barbadillo, A. J. de. La casa del placer honesto, *de Alonso Jerónimo de Salas Barbadillo, Together with an Introduction in Which His Life and Works Are Studied.* Ed. E. B. Place. Boulder: Univ. of Colorado, 1927. 263–466. (University of Colorado Studies 15.4)

594. SCHERER, SHERINDA IDYLL. The Literary Vision of Alonso Jerónimo de Salas Barbadillo. 330 p. CA/Riverside, C. Ayllón, 1981. *DAI* 42A: 2159.

This dissertation offers "a broad perspective . . . by reviewing Salas' life and literary production." At the same time, "a narrower perspective is achieved through the close analyses of a number of Salas' books"—for example, *El caballero puntual,* parts 1 and 2. "The Appendix offers a guide to Salas' works (dates, description, length, plot, literary units included), and the Selected Bibliography includes an annotated list of principal studies on the author's life and works." (Abs.) Editorial note: Intercalated in part 2 of *El caballero puntual* are the *comedia Los prodigios de amor* and the *entremés Las gradas de San Felipe.*

SALAZAR Y TORRES, AGUSTÍN DE (1642–1675)

595. O'CONNOR, THOMAS AUSTIN. Structure and Dramatic Techniques in the Works of Agustín de Salazar y Torres. 461 pp. SUNY/Albany, G. Torrente Ballester, 1971. *DAI* 32A: 2099.

"As a result of this stylistic investigation it is clearly demonstrable that Salazar y Torres is a dramatic disciple of Calderón and poetic disciple of Góngora. Salazar represents the will to combine cultism and conceptism in a hyperbolicized dramatic form which becomes the spectacular and illusionist diversion and entertainment of the Court. While he pertains to Calderón's dramatic school, the unique and acute musical sensitivity of Salazar's versification gives him a principal role in the evolution of the *zarzuela*. To summarize his poetic style only four words are necessary—imaginative and intellectual, or aristocratic and lyrical." (Abs.)

❖ [A] "A Lost Play of Salazar y Torres." *BCom* 25 (1973): 40–42. *[Más triunfa el amor rendido.]* [B] "A Bibliographical Note on Salazar y Torres' *Cytara de Apolo*." *RomN* 15 (1973–74): 129–31. [C] "The Curious Ending of *Elegir al enemigo*." *RomN* 15 (1973–74): 318–22. [D] "On the Authorship of *El encanto es la hermosura:* A Curious Case of Dramatic Collaboration." *BCom* 26 (1974): 31–34. [Salazar y Torres and Vera Tassis.] [E] "Don Agustín de Salazar y Torres: A Bibliography of Primary Sources." *BB* 32 (1975): 158–61, 167, 180. [F] "Dramatic Use of *Letras cantadas* in *El amor más desgraciado, Céfalo y Pocris*." *BCom* 27 (1975): 35–40. [G] "An Allusion to Agustín de Salazar y Torres' *Los juegos olímpicos* by Count Harrach." *RomN* 17 (1976–77): 82–83. [Count Harrach = Ferdinand Bonaventura.] [H] "La desmitificación de Celestina en *El encanto es la hermosura* de Salazar y Torres." La Celestina *y su contorno social: Actas del primer congreso internacional sobre* La Celestina. Ed. Manuel Criado de Val. Barcelona: HISPAM (Borrás), 1977. 339–45. [I] "Dramatic Use of a *Letra cantada irregular* in *Elegir al enemigo:* A Structural Approach." *REH*b 11 (1977): 119–32. [J] "The Mythological World of Agustín de Salazar y Torres: Is *El amor más desgraciado, Céfalo y Pocris* a Tragedy?" *RomN* 18 (1977–78): 221–29. [K] "Language, Irony and Death: The Poetry of Salazar y Torres' *El encanto es la hermosura*." *RF* 90 (1978): 60–69. [L] "On Dating the *Comedias* of Agustín de Salazar y Torres: A Provisional Study." *Hispanófila* 67 (1979): 73–81. [M] "Los enredos de una pieza: El contexto histórico teatral de *El encanto es la hermosura; o, La segunda Celestina* de Salazar y Torres, Vera Tassis y Sor Juana." *LMex* 3.2 (1992): 283–303. [N] Salazar y Torres, A. de. *El encanto es la hermosura y el hechizo sin hechizo; La segunda Celestina.* Ed. T. A. O'Connor. Binghamton: Medieval and Renaissance Texts and Studies, 1994. 224 pp. (Pegasus Paperbooks 24.)

Salucio del Poyo, Damián (1550?–1614)

596. Jewell, James J. The Plays of Damián Salucio del Poyo. vii+224 pp. New Mexico, R. R. MacCurdy, 1974. *DAI* 35A: 6142.

"Of the many *comedias* that he supposedly wrote, only six have been preserved. . . . The influence of Salucio del Poyo on the Spanish *comedia* in general and on Antonio Mira de Amescua in particular is quite profound. Poyo is the originator of the *comedia de privanza*." (Abs.)

Sánchez, Miguel (1545–1630)

597. Stephenson, Robert Clarence. Miguel Sánchez: A Contemporary Terentian Influence upon Lope de Vega. iv+373 pp. Texas, 1930.

This dissertation is no longer available at the University of Texas.

Sánchez de Badajoz, Diego (16th c.)

598. Gustafson, Donna Jean. Tradition and Originality in the *Farsas* of Diego Sánchez de Badajoz. 285 pp. Stanford, A. M. Espinosa, 1967. *DA* 27A: 4253.

This is a study of the twenty-eight dramatic pieces called *farsas* in the author's *Recopilación en metro,* 1554. (Abs.)

❖ [A] "The Role of the Shepherd in the Pre-Lopean Drama of Diego Sánchez de Badajoz." *BCom* 25 (1973): 5–13. [B] "Towards the *Auto Sacramental:* Eucharistic Prefiguration in the *Farsas* of Diego Sánchez de Badajoz." *Hispanófila,* special no. 2 (1975): 79–93.

599. Kelz, Rochelle Kanter. Four *Farsas* of Diego Sánchez de Badajoz and the Old Testament: A Critical Edition with Notes. xxiii+512 pp. Northwestern, F. G. Very, 1971. *DAI* 32A: 4616.

The edited plays are the *Farsa de Tamar, Farsa de la fortuna o hado, Farsa del rey David,* and *Farsa de Abraham*. The writer "also attempts to show the importance of the Old Testament in the works of Sánchez." (Abs.)

600. WILTROUT, ANN ELIZABETH. Erasmismo y angustia vital en el teatro de un converso. v+242 pp. Indiana, M. Enguídanos, 1968. *DA* 29A: 4028–29.

"Like many other new Christians of his day, Diego Sánchez clung to the idealism of Erasmian thought to which he added his own social protest and unending requests for just treatment for the converts." (Abs.)

❖ [A] "Antisemitism and Christian Reconciliation in the Theater of Diego Sánchez de Badajoz." *TAH* 3.20 (1977): 11–13. [B] *A Patron and a Playwright in Renaissance Spain: The House of Feria and Diego Sánchez de Badajoz.* London: Tamesis, 1987. 179 pp. (Colección Támesis, serie A. Monografías 126.) ["Earlier versions of two chapters have been published previously, and three others read at conferences." (Those five titles have been omitted from the present list.)]

SOLÍS Y RIVADENEYRA, ANTONIO DE (1610–1686)

601. MARTELL, DANIEL ERNEST. The Dramas of Don Antonio de Solís y Rivadeneyra. Pennsylvania, H. A. Rennert, 1902.

❖ Title as is. Philadelphia: International, 1902. 57 pp.

"I shall, in the succeeding pages, devote myself to a study of his dramas, nine in number." (Prt. Diss.)

SUÁREZ DE FIGUEROA, CRISTÓBAL (1571?–1639?)

602. CRAWFORD, JAMES PYLE WICKERSHAM. The Life and Works of Cristóbal Suárez de Figueroa. Pennsylvania, H. A. Rennert, 1906. {Philadelphia: [Univ. of Pennsylvania], 1907. 159 pp. (UPSRLL 1.)}

Concerning theatrical matters, see especially chapter 5, which is entitled "*El Passagero;* Opposition to the National Theatre; Relations with Alarcón and Cervantes." (Prt. Diss.)

❖ [A] "Some Notes on *La Constante Amarilis* of Cristóbal Suárez de Figueroa." *MLN* 21 (1906): 8–11. [B] *Vida y obras de Cristóbal Suárez de Figueroa.* Trans. N. Alonso Cortés. Valladolid: Imprenta del Colegio Santiago, 1911. [C] "Suárez de Figueroa's *España Defendida* and Tasso's *Gerusalemme Liberata.*" *RR* 4 (1913): 207–20. [For a more comprehensive listing of publications by this scholar, consult M. Romera-Navarro, "J. P. Wickersham Crawford," *HR* 8 (1940): 1–8.]

603. Puerta, Manuel. La trayectoria ideológica de Cristóbal Suárez de Figueroa. viii+226 pp. Illinois, D. Hershberg, 1975. *DAI* 36A: 6140.

"En el Teatro Suárez de Figueroa es el principal instigador de la *Spongia* (1617), dirigida contra Lope de Vega, al que dedica también en *El Pasajero* (1617) durísimos ataques, censurándole su desprecio de las reglas del arte." (Abs.)

Tárrega, Agustín Francisco (1554?–1602)

604. González-Quevedo, Benito Ramón. Vida y obra dramática del canónigo Francisco Agustín Tárrega. iv+264 pp. North Carolina, A. V. Ebersole, 1971. *DAI* 32A: 2641–42.

"In his own *comedias* this priest offers a type of scenic spectacle which embodies the fundamental characteristics of the Spanish *comedia,* a form which appears to have been initiated by him." (Abs.)

❖ "Francisco Agustín Tárrega: Biografía y reputación." *Hispanófila* 59 (1977): 1–7.

Téllez, Fray Gabriel (1583?–1648)
(Tirso de Molina)

605. Agheana, Ion Tudor. The Situational Drama of Tirso de Molina. xii+179 pp. Harvard, S. Gilman, 1970.

❖ Title as is. Madrid: Playor, 1973. 135 pp. (Colección Plaza Mayor Scholar 10.)

"This work . . . aims at contributing to the delineation of Tirso's artistic individuality. Three aspects indicating a situational approach to the drama have required our attention: the presence of singularly intelligent characters, the experimental utilization of dialogues, and a metaphorical system underlying traits of human behavior." (Prt. Diss.)

606. ALBRECHT, JANE WHITE. Ironic Form, Technique and Effect in Seven Plays by Tirso de Molina. vi+128 pp. Indiana, J. L. Alborg, 1985. *DAI* 46A: 2707.

The seven plays are *El burlador de Sevilla, La venganza de Tamar, Marta la piadosa, El Aquiles, El vergonzoso en palacio, Don Gil de las calzas verdes,* and *La celosa de sí misma.*

❖ [A] "The Satiric Irony of *Marta la piadosa.*" *BCom* 39.1 (1987): 37–45. [B] "Formas y funciones de ironía en cinco obras de Tirso de Molina." *Neophilologus* 72.4 (1988): 546–55. [Plays discussed: *El burlador de Sevilla, La venganza de Tamar, Marta la piadosa, El vergonzoso en palacio, La celosa de sí misma.*] [C] "Divine Providence and Human Morality: The Ironic Perspective of *La venganza de Tamar.*" *BCom* 43.2 (1991): 215–24. [D] "Irony in Four Comedies by Tirso de Molina." *H*[AATSP] 75.2 (1992): 260–65. [The four comedies are *El Aquiles, El vergonzoso en palacio, Don Gil de las calzas verdes, La celosa de sí misma.*] [E] "The Statistical Analysis of Verse Form as a Tool for Assigning Authorship and the Case of Tirso de Molina." *Looking at the* Comedia *in the Year of the Quincentennial: Proceedings of the 1992 Symposium on Golden Age Drama, El Paso.* Ed. Barbara Mujica and Sharon D. Voros. Lanham: UP of America, 1993. 247–53. [F] *Irony and Theatricality in Tirso de Molina.* Ottawa: Dovehouse, 1994. 201 pp. (Ottawa Hispanic Studies 16.)

607. ASTURIAS, [SISTER] ROSARIO MARÍA, SNJM. A Critical Edition and Study of the Play *El rey don Pedro en Madrid y el Infanzón de Illescas.* vi+553 pp. Southern California, E. W. Hesse, 1963. *DA* 24: 5378–79.

[For the complete entry, see no. 205.]

608. BROWN, SANDRA LOU. Tirso de Molina: His Treatment of Medieval Spanish History. 327 pp. North Carolina, S. E. Leavitt, 1969. *DAI* 30A: 3450.

"It is the primary purpose of this study to establish the probable sources of these plays and to consider the dramatist's manipulation of history." After listing Tirso's main sources, the writer states: "Except for *Próspera fortuna de Don Álvaro de Luna,* wherein there is considerable borrowing from plays of another dramatist (a practice in which Tirso was not inclined to indulge), the same sources were apparently used in connection with the plays of disputed authorship." (Abs.) Editorial note: For a discussion of the controversy concerning the authorship of these plays, see Castañeda, *Mira de Amescua* 51–52.

❖ [A] "The Hero's Tragic Fall in *La adversa fortuna de don Álvaro de Luna.*" *Hispanófila,* special issue no. 1 (1974): 63–69. [B] "A Reconsideration of the Authorship of the *Don Álvaro de Luna* Plays." *H* [AATSP] 57 (1974): 422–27. [Concludes that "at the present time, any categorical attribution of the *Don Álvaro de Luna* plays to Mira de Amescua is inaccurate. . . . In short, if not accepted by critics, Tirso's claim still cannot be completely ruled out."]

609. Brown, Sherman William. *La villana de Vallecas* of Tirso de Molina: An Edition with Introduction and Notes. iii+79 pp. Chicago, G. T. Northup, 1933.

"The present study is based upon photostatic copies of the *princeps* edition (Seville, 1627), of the second issue of the play (Valencia, 1631), and of the eighteenth-century manuscript (No. 18081) belonging to the Biblioteca Nacional. . . . Additions to the original text, such as those made by Hartzenbusch, are included in the Notes." (Prt. Diss.)

❖ [A] "The Seville and the Valencia Editions of the *Primera parte* of Tirso de Molina's Plays." *MP* 30 (1932): 97–98. [The *Primera parte* includes *La villana de Vallecas.*] [B] Title as is. Chicago: Private ed., distributed by Univ. of Chicago Libraries, 1934. 79 pp., lithographed. [C] Molina, T. de. La villana de Vallecas, *comedia famosa del maestro Tirso de Molina.* Ed., with introd., notes, and vocabulary, by S. W. Brown. Boston: Heath, 1948. 238 pp.

610. Chittenden, Margaret Jean Stahl. Los nombres de personajes en las comedias de Tirso de Molina. xxxiv+310 pp. Texas, R. W. Tyler, 1964. *DA* 25: 7263.

"This dissertation is a study of the character names in the sixty-one plays known to have been written by Tirso de Molina. Not only will it consider the correlation of name with social status, but it will compare the names used by Tirso with those used by Lope de Vega and with those apparently in vogue during the time when Tirso was writing." (Abs.)

611. CONLON, RAYMOND EDWARD. A Study and Translation of Two Plays by Tirso de Molina. 267 pp. Massachusetts, F. Will, 1977. *DAI* 38A: 241.

The two plays are *El condenado por desconfiado* and *El vergonzoso en palacio.* "In my view, the use of prose lines and the concentration on the poetic character of Tirso's language, strikes the best possible balance between fidelity to the poetic form of Golden Age drama and its literal meaning." (Abs.)

❖ [A] "Enrico in *El condenado por desconfiado:* A Psychoanalytical View." *RCEH* 10 (1985): 173–82. [B] "Sexual Passion and Marriage—Chaos and Order in Tirso de Molina's *El vergonzoso en palacio.*" *H*[AATSP] 71.1 (1988): 8–13.

612. COUTO, MANUEL S. *El amor médico:* Introducción, edición y notas al texto de la edición príncipe de la cuarta parte de las comedias del maestro Tirso de Molina, 1635. viii+179 pp. Florida, F. C. Hayes, 1971. *DAI* 32A: 6370.

The play's "protagonist is a champion of 'women's rights.' . . . Tirso de Molina, in twenty-four of his plays, portrays spirited female characters who try to free themselves from restrictive social traditions and rules which seemed to assign women numerous duties but few 'rights.'" (Abs.)

613. DARST, DAVID HIGH. A Structural Analysis of the *Próspera* and *Adversa fortuna de don Álvaro de Luna* Attributed to Tirso de Molina. iv+223 pp. Kentucky, W. C. McCrary, 1970. *DAI* 31A: 4155.

"The favorite's tragic demise acts to direct the attention of the dramatic personages—and the audience—to the characteristic ambivalence of nature and the limits of sin and innocence, thus giving purpose to the downfall of Álvaro de Luna. Moreover, the playwright has established throughout the two pieces a clear analogy between the Castilian Constable and Jesus Christ." (Abs.)

Editorial note: For a discussion of the controversy concerning the authorship of these plays, see Castañeda, *Mira de Amescua* 51–52.

614. DODSON, ROBERT GEORGE. The Marian Legend in the Religious Theater of Tirso de Molina. 778 pp. Southern California, E. W. Hesse, 1969. *DAI* 30A: 1559–60.

The following seven *comedias* and one *auto* are studied: *La Santa Juana* (parts 1 and 3), *La dama del Olivar, Los lagos de San Vicente, Doña Beatriz de Silva, La Reina de los reyes, La Peña de Francia,* and *La Madrina del cielo.* (Abs.)

615. DOMEIER, MARY CATHERINE (SISTER RENÉE, OSB). The Parable of the Prodigal Son in the Theater of Tirso de Molina. 310 pp. Michigan, E. Glaser, 1970. *DAI* 31A: 2381.

The four plays studied are *Tanto es lo de más como lo de menos, La Ninfa del cielo, Quien no cae no se levanta,* and *La venganza de Tamar.* (Abs.)

616. EUBANKS, MELVIN OLIVER. The Use of Music in the Dramatic Works of Tirso de Molina. iv+537 pp. Florida State, D. L. Hoffman, 1969. *DAI* 30A: 4941.

The writer proposes "to make the reader aware of the wealth of musical elements embodied within [Tirso's] plays, to demonstrate the varied ways in which the musical elements are employed, and to convince the reader that there is value in investigating further this nearly virgin area." (Abs.)

617. FORNOFF, FREDERICK HOWELL. Tirso de Molina's *Vida y muerte de Herodes:* A Study of the Ritual Forms in Tragedy. iv+366 pp. Kentucky, W. C. McCrary, 1971. *DAI* 33A: 751.

"All that transpires on the stage is a sign, a sacrament, through which one must look to the signified. In Tirso's universe, as in God's, one looks through the creation to the creator. . . . In the *Herodes,* the priest and the dramatist in Tirso are utterly united and ultimately fulfilled." (Abs.)

❖ [A] *Tirso's Christmas Tragedy,* La vida y muerte de Herodes: *A Study of Ritual Form in Drama.* Chapel Hill: Hispanófila, 1977. 199 pp. (Estudios de Hispanófila 42.) [B] Molina, T. de. *La vida y muerte de Herodes/The Life and Death of Herod: A Christmas Tragedy and Epiphany.* Ed. and trans. F. H. Fornoff. New York: Peter Lang, 1991. 365 pp.

618. Fox, John Francis. Tirso's *Los amantes de Teruel* as Christomimesis. iv+227 pp. Kentucky, W. C. McCrary, 1981. *DAI* 42A: 3176.

"My hypothesis is that Tirso sought to present legendary (perhaps historical) events in such a way that the play functioned as an instrument by which the dramatist could imitate events known to his audience and yet expand the scope of these events to represent an ideal. Thus Tirso sought to refer the legend of the *amantes* to something greater, specifically the cosmological epic which recounts fallen man's unending search for Salvation. When seen from within this referential/figural mode of interpretation the internal cohesiveness of the play becomes clear." (Abs.)

❖ "Tirso's *Los amantes de Teruel* as Christomimesis." *Tirso de Molina: Vida y obra. Actas del primer simposio internacional sobre Tirso, Washington, 1984* (error for 1985). Ed. Josep M. Solà-Solé and Luis Vázquez Fernández. Madrid: Revista "Estudios," 1987. 105–10.

619. Franquiz-Trujillo, Evelyn. La presencia de la Virgen en las obras dramáticas de Tirso de Molina. 225 pp. Florida State, D. H. Darst, 1991. *DAI* 52A: 4347.

"The purpose of this study is to investigate the presence of the Virgin in the dramatic works of Tirso de Molina based on two premises: the sources utilized, and the presence, images and miracles of the Virgin." The plays studied are *La Santa Juana* (1, 2, 3), *Los lagos de San Vicente, La dama del Olivar, La Reina de los reyes* (Tirso's *refundición* of Vergara's play, according to E. Franquiz-Trujillo), *Doña Beatriz de Silva, La Peña de Francia,* and *La Madrina del cielo*. (Abs.)

620. Fuertes-Díaz, Covadonga M. Edición crítica y estudio de *Los lagos de San Vicente* de Tirso de Molina. 251 pp. Catholic, J. Solà-Solé, 1990. *DAI* 51A: 1600.

"This text is based on the 'princeps' edition and on the comparison of that edition to the six 'sueltas' of the XVIII century which we have been able to identify, and which originated in printing workshops in Sevilla. In conclusion, based on previously researched material of preceding writers, we have been able to improve the text of this play which dramatizes the life of Casilda, the Moorish princess who converted to Christ's faith." (Abs.)

621. GALASSI, BATTISTA JOHN. A Critical Edition and Study of the Play *Privar contra su gusto.* 239 pp. Southern California, E. W. Hesse, 1967. *DA* 28A: 3141.

The edition is "based on a seventeenth-century manuscript of the play [apparently an actor's copy], the *princeps* edition published in 1635, and an eighteenth-century *suelta*." (Abs.)

❖ Molina, T. de. *Privar contra su gusto*. Ed., prologue, and notes by B. J. Galassi. Madrid: Playor, 1971, 1973. 151 pp. (Colección Plaza Mayor Scholar 5.)

622. GARCÍA, ELVIRA ELENA BRYNICKI. A Critical Edition of Tirso de Molina's *Marta la piadosa.* 156 pp. Nebraska, R. W. Tyler, 1976. *DAI* 37A: 4332.

The edition is based on the *princeps* of 1636, which is collated with Hartzenbusch's text in the BAE (Abs.)

❖ Title as is. Salzburg: Universität Salzburg, 1978. 177 pp. (Elizabethan and Renaissance Studies 78.)

623. GILLESPIE, RUTH CAROLINE. A Study of the Authorship and Sources of *Nuestra Señora de la Peña de Francia* and Its Relation to *La Peña de Francia* of Tirso de Molina, with Texts, Notes and Commentary. 440 pp. Yale, 1929.

"Gillespie presents an edited text of *Nuestra Señora de la Peña de Francia,* first published under the name of Lope de Vega. It is, barring minor changes, the same as *La Peña de Francia* that Tirso published in the *Cuarta parte* of his plays. Tirso's source was undoubtedly the *Historia y milagros de nuestra señora de la Peña de Francia* (1567), from which Gillespie quotes in full all pertinent passages. Tirso also must have been acquainted with the various chronicles relating the history of the reign of Juan II (1404-1454). The four longest chapters compare the text of *La Peña de Francia* with other plays by Tirso. Then follows the text of both plays, printed side by side." (Williamsen and Poesse 62)

624. GONZÁLEZ, JAIME JOSÉ. Estudios genealógicos de varias comedias de Tirso de Molina. iii+137 pp. Vanderbilt, G. E. Wade, 1969. *DAI* 30A: 4410.

"The genealogical study of the names appearing in the casts, as well as in the texts of the comedies studied *(La villana de Vallecas; La villana de la Sagra; Quien da luego da dos veces; Ventura te dé Dios, hijo; La huerta de Juan Fernández; Amar por señas; No hay peor sordo;* and *Por el sótano y el torno),* has shown that many of them were actually names of living persons who belonged to the Spanish gentility or nobility." (Abs.)

❖ Wade, Gerald E., and Jaime J. González. "Tirso de Molina and the Gonzagas." *H*[AATSP] 65 (1972): 264–77. [The *comedias* examined are *Del enemigo el primer consejo, Quien da luego da dos veces,* and *Ventura te dé Dios, hijo.*]

625. HAUGHTON, LINDA ELIZABETH. The Comic Craft of Tirso de Molina. ix+209 pp. Arizona, R. M. ter Horst, 1976. *DAI* 37A: 3673.

The writer examines in detail *El vergonzoso en palacio, Por el sótano y el torno, Don Gil de las calzas verdes,* and *El amor médico.* (Abs.)

626. HERNÁNDEZ-GARCÍA, CARMELA. El tópico del "mundo al revés" en Tirso de Molina. 214 pp. NYU, H. Piñera, 1976. *DAI* 37A: 1592.

The writer examines in detail Tirso's *La república al revés* and *El pretendiente al revés.* "The third Chapter will show the extent to which Tirso is imbued in [sic] the concept of the world upside down, . . . by tracing it through some of his most representative plays." (Abs.)

❖ "El tópico del mundo al revés en Tirso de Molina." *EstM* 163 (1988): 5–35.

627. HUGHES, ANN NICKERSON. Religious Imagery in the Theater of Tirso de Molina. 322 pp. Georgia, H. Ziomek, 1973. *DAI* 34A: 5972.

"Some of the specific plays studied are: *El condenado por desconfiado, El burlador de Sevilla,* the *Santa Juana* trilogy, *Santo y sastre, Las quinas de Portugal, La romera de Santiago, La vida y muerte de Herodes, La venganza de Tamar,* and the *autos, El Colmenero divino* and *Tanto es lo de más como lo de menos.*" (Abs.) Editorial note: The last-named play is a *comedia.*

❖ Title as is. Macon: Mercer UP, 1984. 151 pp. (Mercer's sesquicentennial series.)

628. ISCLA ROVIRA, LUIS, SJ. Una edición crítica de *La Virgen de los reyes* de Hipólito de Vergara cotejada con *La Reina de los reyes* de Tirso de Molina. 299 pp. Northwestern, F. G. Very, 1973. *DAI* 34A: 5927–28.

[For the complete entry, see no. 827.]

629. JARDINI, ORLANDO. A Critical Edition with Introduction and Notes of Tirso de Molina's *La celosa de sí misma.* 391 pp. Pittsburgh, J. Lihani, 1968. *DA* 29A: 900.

"The text of the present edition of *La celosa de sí misma* is based (as are all other editions and manuscripts) on the earliest surviving version of the play, which is found in Tirso's *Primera parte* (Seville, 1627)." (Abs.)

630. KENNINGTON, NANCY LOU. A Structural Analysis of the Extant Trilogies of Tirso de Molina. 257 pp. North Carolina, W. C. McCrary, 1966. *DA* 27A: 2532.

"This study attempts to determine the motivations and dramatic conceptions which led to Tirso's use of the trilogic form in *La Santa Juana, trilogía hagiográfica* and *Las hazañas de los Pizarros.*" (Abs.)

631. KIRBY, CAROL L. BINGHAM. The Transformation of History into Poetry: The Treatment of Pedro I de Castilla in *El Rey Don Pedro en Madrid y el Infanzón de Illescas.* iv+242 pp. Kentucky, W. C. McCrary, 1977. *DAI* 38A: 826.

"Scholars continue to debate whether Lope or Tirso wrote the play. Investigators have used the debatable criterion of thematic similarities between *El Rey Don Pedro en Madrid* and other plays by Lope and Tirso to argue this question, but the *comedia* as a whole was so repetitive that it is almost impossible to assess thematic or stylistic originality within the entire genre. According to the most scientific criterion available, that of versification, it is doubtful that either Lope or Tirso wrote the drama. I conclude in Chapter I that it is not possible to state definitely who penned *El Rey Don Pedro en Madrid;* consequently, I refer only to 'the dramatist' in my analysis of the play." (Abs.)

❖ [A] "Observaciones preliminares sobre el teatro histórico de Lope de Vega." *Lope de Vega y los orígenes del teatro español: Actas del primer congreso internacional sobre Lope de Vega.* Ed. Manuel Criado de Val. Madrid: EDI-6, 1981. 329-37. [B] "Theater and the Quest for Anointment in *El Rey Don Pedro en Madrid.*" *BCom* 33 (1981): 149-60. [C] "Los problemas bibliográficos en torno a *El Rey Don Pedro en Madrid.*" *Actas del octavo congreso internacional de hispanistas, Providence, 1983.* Ed. A. David Kossoff, José Amor y Vázquez, Ruth H. Kossoff, and Geoffrey W. Ribbans. 2 vols. Madrid: Istmo, 1986. 2: 77–82. [D] "La verdadera edición crítica de un texto dramático del Siglo de Oro: Teoría, metodología y aplicación." *Incipit* 6 (1986): 71–98. [The analysis is based on *El rey don Pedro en Madrid.*] [E] "*'El personaje del rey'*: King Pedro as Dramatic Personage in the *Comedia.*" *Proceedings of the Fifth Annual Golden Age Drama Symposium (Texto y espectáculo), El Paso, 1985.* Ed. Jean S. Chittenden, Richard Ford, and Arturo Pérez-Pisonero. San Antonio: Trinity Univ., Dept. of Foreign Languages (1987 for 1985). 10–18. [F] "Performance, Text and Standard Edition: Critical Divergences and Questions of Methodology." *Texto y espectáculo: Nuevas dimensiones críticas de la* comedia. *[Eighth Annual Golden Age Spanish Drama Symposium, El Paso, 1988.]* Ed. Arturo Pérez-Pisonero. New Brunswick: SLUSA, 1990. 93–100. [G] "The Preparation of a Genuine Critical Edition of Golden-Age Dramatic Texts: Theory, Methodology, and Application." *Editing the* Comedia II. Ed. Michael McGaha and Frank P. Casa. Ann Arbor: Univ. of Michigan, Dept. of Romance Languages, 1991. 1–38. (Michigan Romance Studies 11.) [H] "Hacia una definición precisa del término refundición en el teatro clásico español." *Actas del décimo congreso de la Asociación Internacional de Hispanistas, Barcelona, 1989.* Ed. Antonio Vilanova. 4 vols. Barcelona: PPU, 1992. 2: 1005–11.

632. KNIGHT, EUNICE EDNA. The Role of Women in Don Juan and Faust Literature. iii+216 pp. Florida State, J. Priest, 1973. *DAI* 35A: 1106.

[For the complete entry, see no. 436.]

633. LOUD, MARY BETH. A Study of Selected Comedies of Tirso de Molina. iv+294 pp. Kentucky, W. C. McCrary, 1970. *DAI* 32A: 974–75.

"The comedies of Tirso de Molina . . . have been divided into three groups corresponding to the comic perspective provided in each." The three groups are represented by *El castigo del penséque, Marta la piadosa,* and *El vergonzoso en palacio.* The writer concludes that "mutual tolerance and forgiveness in an imperfect world is Tirso's 'message.'" (Abs.)

❖ "Tirso's Comic Masterpiece *Marta la piadosa.*" *Hispanófila,* special issue no. 1 (1974): 81–94.

634. MADRIGAL, JOSÉ ANTONIO. La función del hombre salvaje en el teatro de Lope de Vega, Tirso de Molina y Calderón de la Barca. 375 pp. Kentucky, W. C. McCrary, 1973. *DAI* 35A: 2232.

[For the complete entry, see no. 300.]

635. MARTIN, KENNETH JOSEPH. A Portfolio of Three Papers in Literature, Language, and Curriculum Development in Spanish and French. (1) A Comparative Study of *El burlador de Sevilla y convidado de piedra* of Tirso de Molina and Molière's *Dom Juan: ou, Le festin de pierre,* with Special Attention to the Female Characters in Each Work. (2) A Comparative Study of the French and Spanish Verb. (3) An Alternative Approach to Level III Foreign Language Study in the Private Secondary School. 162 pp. [Only part 1 is relevant.] Catholic, D. Lagmanovich, 1976. *DAI* 37A: 2153.

". . . Molière expands on the Tirso model of *burlador* and *creyente,* and thus the French *Dom Juan* presents the character as *hypocrite* and *athée.*" The writer observes that "the female characters in Molière's play serve rather as vehicles to highlight don Juan's hypocrisy, and in the case of the peasant women, to mock provincial attitudes, speech, and *mores.*" (Abs.)

636. MEKEMSON, MARY J. A Critical Modern-Spelling Edition of James Shirley's *The Opportunity.* 366 pp. Wisconsin, S. Henning, 1988. *DAI* 49A: 2232.

"A. L. Stiefel identified Tirso de Molina's *El castigo del penséque* as the source for the main plot of *The Opportunity.* Roughly half of Shirley's play is based on Tirso's. Shirley's additions to and compression and modification of Tirso's play create a more complicated comedy, structured by means of analogy and contrast, that is focused on social concerns, most importantly the relationship between social hierarchy and social stability and on the proper grounds for choosing a mate." (Abs.)

637. MINELLI, FIORIGIO. Tirso de Molina's *La fingida Arcadia:* A Critical and Annotated Edition. iv+206 pp. Brown, A. S. Trueblood, 1978. *DAI* 39A: 6162.

". . . the text of this play has been determined by collating nine of the fourteen extant copies of the *Parte tercera,* as well as the three modern editions by Cotarelo y Mori, Blanca de los Ríos and María del Pilar Palomo." (Abs.)

❖ [A] "Estructura y tema de *La fingida Arcadia* de Tirso de Molina." *EstM* 34.122 (1978): 399–418. [B] Molina, T. de. *La fingida Arcadia*. Ed., critical study, and notes by F. Minelli. Madrid: Revista "Estudios," 1980. 158 pp. [C] Publication B also in *EstM* 36.130–31 (1980): 5–158.

638. Miranda, Rafael Joseph. Iberian Geography in the Plays of Tirso de Molina. 274 pp. North Carolina, S. E. Leavitt, 1954. North Carolina *Record* no. 548, pp. 277–78.

"It is not possible to determine with absolute certainty just where the settings of Tirso de Molina's plays are located. In thirty-six of his plays the action takes place entirely in Spain and Portugal, and in six the greater part of the action takes place in the peninsula. In the rest of his plays that have been examined, the scenes are located wholly or mainly outside the Iberian Peninsula." (UNC *Record*)

639. Morton, John Gillespie. Aspects of Evil and Death in Eight Plays by Tirso de Molina. iv+263 pp. Vanderbilt, J. R. Andrews, 1972. *DAI* 33A: 4427–28.

The writer bases his analysis on the following *comedias: La mujer que manda en casa, La venganza de Tamar, La vida y muerte de Herodes, Escarmientos para el cuerdo, El burlador de Sevilla, El condenado por desconfiado, Los amantes de Teruel,* and *Amazonas en las Indias.* (Abs.)

640. Ortuño, Marian Mikaylo. The *Autos Sacramentales* of Tirso de Molina. iv+247 pp. Michigan, E. Glaser, 1973. *DAI* 34A: 1926–27.

The writer studies four *autos: El colmenero divino, No le arriendo la ganancia, Los hermanos parecidos,* and *El laberinto de Creta.* (Abs.)

❖ [A] "Pagan Myth and African Legend in Tirso's *Auto, El laberinto de Creta.*" *RF* 88 (1976): 361–75. [B] "From Theology to Drama: The Artistic Evolution of Tirso de Molina's *Auto, Los hermanos parecidos.*" *Neophilologus* 63 (1979): 59–73. [C] "The Bee as the Soul: Apicultural Allegory in Tirso de Molina's *Auto Sacramental, El colmenero divino.*" *KRQ* 29 (1982): 93–105.

641. Reynolds, John Joseph. A Study and Critical Edition of Tirso de Molina's *El condenado por desconfiado.* 310 pp. CA/Berkeley, J. F. Montesinos, 1956. PFE, 20 January 1956.

"In the emendation of the *princeps* . . . , Madrid, 1635, the writer has utilized for the first time the very rare, somewhat shorter, contemporary version, dated 1640(?) by Adolf Schaeffer . . . as well as the two emended versions based on the text of 1635, viz., the editions of Hartzenbusch . . . (1848) and A. Castro . . . (1919)." (PFE)

❖ [A] "An Anecdote in *El condenado por desconfiado*." *BCom* 8.1 (1956): 13–14. [B] "'Como un padre': A Note on *El condenado por desconfiado*." *RomN* 16 (1974–75): 505–08. [C] "*El condenado por desconfiado:* Tres siglos y medio de ediciones." *Homenaje a Tirso.* Madrid: Revista "Estudios," 1981. 733–50.

642. Santomauro, María. El gracioso en el teatro de Tirso de Molina. 259 pp. CUNY, I. M. Gil, 1975. *DAI* 36A: 1564–65.

This study includes an appendix "compuesto de un índice de los graciosos tirsianos." (Abs.)

❖ [A] "Tres estudios sobre el gracioso en Tirso. (1. El gracioso tirsiano como elemento activo en la comedia; 2. El gracioso y los cuentecillos en Tirso; 3. Índice de los graciosos de Tirso de Molina)." *EstM* 31.110 (1975): 373–402. [B] "Notas cómicas sobre el gracioso tirsiano." *EstM* 32.114 (1976): 391–98. [C] "El gracioso tirsiano, contrafigura del galán." *EstM* 34.123 (1978): 563–75. [D] *El gracioso en el teatro de Tirso de Molina.* Madrid: Revista "Estudios," 1984. 203 pp. [Offprint of the *Revista Estudios* 40.144–45.]

643. Sarre, Dolores. La mujer en el teatro de Tirso de Molina. 249 pp. Stanford, A. M. Espinosa and A. González Palencia, 1940. Stanford *Abstracts* 15 (1939–40): 88–90.

"Competent critics had previously pointed out both the diversity of feminine characters in Tirso, and their human psychology. Here it has been attempted to reconcile the idea of uniformity and variety in his characterization of women and to prove that the stimulus experienced by the human will before an obstacle is the key to Tirso's feminine psychology. However, the most interesting conclusion arrived at is to point out with certainty that fidelity and constancy are distinguishing features of woman in the theater of Tirso de Molina." (Abs.)

644. Scott, Antoinette Estévez. Estudiantes y letrados en las obras

dramáticas de Lope de Vega, Tirso de Molina, y Juan Ruiz de Alarcón. vii+231 pp. Florida State, D. L. Hoffman, 1974. *DAI* 35A: 3008.

[For the complete entry, see no. 587.]

645. SEDWICK, FRANK. Spanish Themes in Italian Opera. 336 pp. Southern California, L. Moreno, 1953. USC *Abstracts of Dissertations* (1953): 65–67.

"Tirso de Molina's Don Juan *(El burlador de Sevilla)* and Mozart's Don Giovanni are compared in detail with each other and with the other Don Juans in between in order to trace Mozart's sources and to resolve ultimately the extent to which Tirso's conception of the *burlador* is reflected in Mozart. . . . A hypothesis is developed that Tirso intended Don Juan to be an allegorical character typifying early Protestantism, finally eradicated by Catholicism. Nothing of this flavor survives in any of the interim versions of the legend or in Mozart's opera." (Abs.)

❖ [A] "Mozart's Sources for *Don Giovanni*." *H* [AATSP] 37 (1954): 269–73. [Includes a detailed comparison of *El burlador* and Mozart's opera.] [B] "*El burlador, Don Giovanni* and the Popular Concept of Don Juan." *H* [AATSP] 38 (1955): 173–77. [C] *A History of the "Useless Precaution" Plot in Spanish and French Literature.* Chapel Hill: U of North Carolina P, 1964. 84 pp. (UNCSRLL 49.) [The writer examines, inter alia, two Cervantine *entremeses,* three plays of Molière, Beaumarchais's *Le Barbier de Séville* (originally as opéra comique), and Rossini's *Il barbiere di Siviglia.* He concludes: "With the fame of (Beaumarchais' *Barbier de Séville*), enhanced and even perpetuated by Rossini's operatic version, the useless-precaution theme reaches its apogee."]

646. SHECKTOR, NINA MARÍA. The Achillean Hero in the Plays of Tirso de Molina. 180 pp. Temple, A. Lewis Galanes, 1983. *DAI* 44A: 186.

"The purpose of the present dissertation is to demonstrate the continuity of thought, theme, characterization and technique between *El Aquiles* and the rest of Tirso's drama." From this perspective the writer examines *La vida y muerte de Herodes; La venganza de Tamar; Ventura te dé Dios, hijo; La república al revés; La prudencia en la mujer;* and *El burlador de Sevilla.* (Abs.)

647. SORENSEN, JORGE E. El uso de temas histórico-tradicionales en Tirso de Molina: Las tres comedias del Viejo Testamento. 189 pp. Michigan State, R. L. Fiore, 1978. *DAI* 39A: 6164.

The three plays studied are *La mejor espigadera, La mujer que manda en casa,* and *La venganza de Tamar.* (Abs.)

❖ [A] "*La mejor espigadera:* Una glosa dramática del Libro de Rut." *RF* 90 (1978): 70–77. [B] Sorensen, Jorge E., and Robert L. Fiore. "La Jezabel de Tirso: Reina astuta, mujer que manda en casa." *CH* 8.1 (1986): 73–88.

648. SPRANGLE, IRMA IRIS. The Figure of the Mother in Selected Works of Spanish Literature from the Medieval Period to the Seventeenth Century. iii+176 pp. Catholic, J. Solà-Solé, 1984. *DAI* 45A: 1417.

"Chapter V centers upon the analysis of the mother in the theatrical genre. After briefly reviewing the representative mother figures throughout the history of the Spanish theater," the chapter analyzes this figure "in detail in the Golden Age *comedias* of Tirso de Molina. Ten figures are found which can be classified into four categories: the unwed mother, the persecuted or wronged mother, the mother-in-law and the queen mother type." (Abs.)

649. STOLL, ANITA KAY. Thematic Development in the Biblical Plays of Tirso de Molina. vi+171 pp. Case Western Reserve, D. M. Carey, 1972. *DAI* 33A: 2396.

The five plays studied are *La mejor espigadera, La venganza de Tamar, La mujer que manda en casa, La vida y muerte de Herodes,* and *Tanto es lo de más como lo de menos.* (Abs.)

❖ [A] "The Sacred and Profane in Tirso's *La vida y muerte de Herodes.*" *BCom* 28.1 (1976): 22–27. [B] "Time: Temporal and Eternal in Tirso's *La vida y muerte de Herodes.*" *Studies in Language and Literature: Proceedings of the Twenty-Third Mountain Interstate Foreign Language Conference.* Ed. Charles Nelson. Richmond: Eastern Kentucky Univ., 1976. 539–44.

650. TRUBIANO, MARIO F. El hombre y su destino: La teología de la gracia en el teatro de Tirso de Molina. 398 pp. Massachusetts, F. Fernández-Turienzo, 1979. *DAI* 40A: 1505.

The works studied are *Los lagos de San Vicente, La Santa Juana (partes 1, 2, 3), El mayor desengaño, La Madrina del cielo* (auto), *La*

Ninfa del cielo (auto), *El condenado por desconfiado,* and *El burlador de Sevilla.* The author affirms Tirso's "adhesión a la escuela teológica de Francisco Zumel." (Abs.)

❖ [A] *Libertad, gracia y destino en el teatro de Tirso de Molina.* Madrid: Alcalá, 1985. 227 pp. [B] "The Theological Disputes and the Guzmán Affair in *El burlador* and *El condenado:* Theological Preoccupation or Satirical Intention?" *Tirso's Don Juan: The Metamorphosis of a Theme.* Ed. Josep M. Solà-Solé and George E. Gingras. Washington: Catholic U of America P, 1988. 95–105.

651. Urtiaga, Alfonso. El indiano en la dramática de Tirso de Molina. 299 pp. Louisiana State, A. Berumen, 1963. *DA* 24: 4201–02.

"This dissertation is primarily intended as a study of the role of the 'indiano' character in the dramatic works of Tirso de Molina. It is ultimately intended as a contribution to the study of that character in Spanish literature." (Abs.) Editorial note: The writer defines the "indiano" as "el español que había marchado a América y vuelto a la patria."

❖ [A] Title as is. Madrid: Revista "Estudios," 1965. 256 pp. [B] Also *EstM* 21.71 (1965): 529–774 (special issue). [C] "La formulación del ideal humano en Tirso de Molina: El 'discreto' indiano." *Homenaje a Tirso.* Madrid: Revista "Estudios," 1981. 447–60.

652. Valencia, Juan Octavio. Edición crítica y estudio de la comedia de Tirso, *La venganza de Tamar.* v+295 pp. Southern California, E. W. Hesse, 1967. *DA* 28A: 1451–52.

The edition is based on the *princeps* of 1634, which is compared with an anonymous manuscript entitled *La fuerza de Tamar* and with Hartzenbusch's edition. (Abs.)

❖ [A] "La función del símbolo en una comedia de Tirso *(La venganza de Tamar).*" *BCom* 26.1 (1974): 1–5. [B] *Pathos y tabú en el teatro bíblico del Siglo de Oro.* Madrid: Isla, 1977. 137 pp. [One of the five biblical plays on the theme of incest discussed in this study is Tirso's *La venganza de Tamar.*]

653. Wade, Gerald Edward. Tirso de Molina, *La Sancta Juanna, primera parte:* An Edition with Introduction and Notes. xciii+396 pp. Ohio State, C. E. Anibal, 1937. Ohio State *Abstracts* 22 (1937): 305–12.

"The text of the first part of the trilogy as given in our edition is of course taken from the surviving manuscript, except at those points where its mutilation made necessary the use of the *Quinta Parte* version." (Abs.)

❖ [A] "The Orthoepy of the Holographic *Comedias* of Tirso de Molina." *PMLA* 55 (1940): 993–1009. [Tirso's two extant holographic *comedias* are *La Santa Juana, primera parte* and *La Santa Juana, tercera parte.*] [B] "Tirsiana." *RomN* 9.1 (1967–68): 95–101. [Study of a 19th-century play about Tirso by Luis de Eguílaz.] [For a more complete list of this scholar's publications, see *Studies in Honor of Gerald E. Wade,* ed. Sylvia Bowman et al. (Madrid: Porrúa Turanzas, 1979) 5–10.]

654. Wolfe, Jacqueline Fisher. A Study of the *Cigarrales de Toledo* as a Satire. [6]+176 pp. Johns Hopkins, E. L. Rivers and H. Sieber, 1976. *DAI* 37A: 6543.

"Considered without the *novela* bias, the *Cigarrales* emerges as an integrated structure in which prose, poetry, and drama contribute equally to a unified whole. The mixture of genres characteristic of satire reflects the ethos of a novelty-seeking, pleasure-oriented society." (Abs.)

Timoneda, Juan (?–1583)

655. Grismer, Raymond Leonard. The Influence of Titus Maccius Plautus on the Spanish Theatre through Juan de Timoneda. 301 pp. CA/Berkeley, R. Schevill, 1930.

"Throughout the first three quarters of the sixteenth century the influence of Plautus is clearly shown in the plays of the Spanish dramatists." The authors discussed include Encina, Lucas Fernández, Diego Sánchez de Badajoz, Torres Naharro, Rueda, and Timoneda. (Prt. Diss.)

❖ [A] "Another Reminiscence of Plautus in the *Comedias* of Torres Naharro." *HR* 8 (1940): 57–58. [B] *The Influence of Plautus in Spain before Lope de Vega, Together with Chapters on the Dramatic Technique of Plautus and the Revival of Plautus in Italy.* New York: Hispanic Inst., 1944. 210 pp. [C] "Introduction to the Classical

Influence on the Literatures of Spain and Spanish America." *Thesaurus* 5 (1949): 433–46.

656. JOHNSON, MILDRED EDITH. A Critical Edition of Juan de Timoneda, *Auto del castillo de Emaús* and *Auto de la Iglesia.* 83 pp. Iowa, R. E. House, 1929. {*The* Aucto del castillo de Emaús *and the* Aucto de la iglesia *of Juan Timoneda: Edited with Introduction, Notes, and Translation into English.* UISSLL, 1933, no. 4. 83 pp.}

The edition is based on a photostatic reproduction of the two plays in the BNM copy of Timoneda's *Ternario sacramental* (Valencia, 1575). "The present publication differs from the original thesis in several respects. Prefatory material and annotations have been materially reduced." In addition, "it has seemed appropriate to add a translation into English of both *autos*." (Prt. Diss.)

657. REGUEIRO, JOSÉ MIGUEL. Juan Timoneda y la tradición dramática española. 316 pp. Pennsylvania, A. G. Reichenberger, 1972. *DAI* 33A: 6881–82.

"We view the formation of the *comedia* and the *auto sacramental,* the two dramatic genres peculiar to the Spanish soil, rather than as the result of the creative genius of one single dramatist, as the product of the cumulative achievement of many dramatists who shaped a multisecular tradition, religious and profane, to adapt it to the popular taste of the mid-sixteenth century audience. Timoneda is an important member of this generation of dramatists who in this period bring old and new themes to the stage, making them appealing to the *vulgo,* whose dictates will dominate the Spanish theater for the next hundred years." (Abs.)

❖ "Rito y popularismo en el teatro antiguo español." *RF* 89 (1977): 1–17.

TORQUEMADA, ANTONIO DE (1530?–1590)

658. CROW, GEORGE DAVIS, JR. *Los colloquios satíricos, con un colloquio pastoril,* por Antonio de Torquemada: A Critical Edition. xxviii+330 pp. Texas, E. R. Sims, 1953.

The dissertaton discusses Torquemada's *colloquios* in light of the chivalric romance, Erasmian colloquies, and classical antecedents. Editorial note: La Barrera describes Torquemada's "coloquio pastoril" as "de formas dramáticas y propio para ser representado." (*Catálogo* 397)

❖ "Antonio de Torquemada: Spanish Dialogue Writer of the Sixteenth Century." *H* [AATSP] 38 (1955): 265–71.

659. Elsdon, James Harold. Aspects of a Study of the Life and Works of Antonio de Torquemada. 272 pp. CA/Berkeley, R. Schevill, 1934. PFE, May 1934.

This dissertation is no longer available at Berkeley. "The dissertation . . . is devoted chiefly to an intensive study of the *Jardin de flores curiosas*. . . . Biographical material about Torquemada is practically nonexistent." (PFE)

❖ *On the Life and Works of the Spanish Humanist Antonio de Torquemada.* Berkeley: UCPMP 20, no. 3 (1937): 127–86.

The principal chapters of the printed version are "Biographical Sketch" (pp. 127–31), "Torquemada and the Counterreformation in Spain" (pp. 132–39), "Folklore in the *Jardín de flores curiosas*" (pp. 140–67). There is nothing specific on the "dramatic" *coloquio pastoril*. (Prt. Diss.)

Torres Naharro, Bartolomé de (?–1524?)

660. García-Varela, Jesús M. El discurso del marginado en la obra dramática de Torres Naharro. 223 pp. Indiana, L. Beltrán, 1989. *DAI* 50A: 3972.

"This dissertation discusses the systematic use of the 'loco' (the fool), as a vehicle of linguistic and ideological estrangement, within the dramatic work of the Spanish playwright Bartolomé Torres Naharro (XVI century). The discourse of Torres Naharro is shaped into a system of meanings whose origin and function come from the Carnival tradition, and also from the discourse of the buffoon; it establishes a lucid vision of an upside down world that points out the defects and contradictions of a given society." (Abs.)

❖ [A] "*Soldadesca* o la derogación de la épica." *RLAn* 2 (1990):

414–18. [B] "*Calamita:* La parodia del amor cortés." *CAld* 8.1 (1992): 33–41. [C] "*Tinellaria:* Una corte degradada." *CAld* 9.2 (1993): 205–11. [D] "Los discursos de marginación en la comedia." *Texto y espectáculo: Proceedings of the Thirteenth International Golden Age Spanish Theatre Symposium, El Paso, 1993.* Ed. José Luis Suárez García. York: Spanish Literature Publications, 1995. 32–36. [E] "Para una ideología de la exclusión: El discurso del 'moro' en Sánchez de Badajoz." *Criticón* 66–67 (1996): 171–78.

661. MALINAK, EDWARD MICHAEL. The Dramaturgy of Bartolomé de Torres Naharro. v+252 pp. Kentucky, J. Lihani, 1977. *DAI* 39A: 1622.

"The dissertation examines the methods and techniques of the dramatic art of Torres Naharro in three chapters, each of which is devoted respectively to the author's *comedias a fantasía:* the *Comedia Ymenea, Comedia Calamita* and *Comedia Aquilana.*" (Abs.)

❖ "Torres Naharro's Innovative Contributions to the Spanish Theater." *Estudios alfonsinos y otros escritos en homenaje a John Esten Keller y a Aníbal A. Biglieri.* Ed. and prologue by Nicolás Toscano. New York: Natl. Endowment for the Humanities, Natl. Hispanic Foundation for the Humanities, 1991. 140–48.

662. WEINERTH, NORA. The Experimental Theatre of Bartolomé de Torres Naharro. v+332 pp. Harvard, S. Gilman, 1977.

The dissertation "examines the following plays: *Diálogo del Nascimiento, Soldadesca, Tinellaria, Jacinta,* and *Trophea.*" The writer concludes that "this study underscores the dramatist's highly original idea of the drama, born of his practical experience with performance, and of a critical, keen intelligence at odds with the chaotic, vertiginously changing world around him." (Personal communication from N. Weinerth)

❖ [A] "Bartolomé de Torres Naharro's *Diálogo del nascimiento:* A *Converso* Christmas Play." *REHc* 9 (1982): 249–54. [B] "Torres Naharro's Anti-war Play." [Apropos the *comedia* entitled *Soldadesca.*] *Creation and Re-creation: Experiments in Literary Form in Early Modern Spain: Studies in Honor of Stephen Gilman.* Ed. Ronald E. Surtz and N. Weinerth. Newark: Juan de la Cuesta, 1983. 29–39. [C] (With Ronald E. Surtz.) "'Algún diabro de fiesta': La *comedia Trophea* de Bartolomé de Torres Naharro." *Torre* ns 1.3–4 (1987): 575–83.

Valdivielso, José de (1560?–1638)

663. González, Mauricio René. A Critical Edition of José de Valdivielso's *El Ángel de la guarda.* iii+297 pp. Tulane, W. J. Smither and T. A. Montgomery, 1982. *DAI* 43A: 1989–90.

The critical text is based on the printed version of Toledo, 1622, which was collated with the printed text of Braga, 1624, and MS 15277 in the Biblioteca Nacional in Madrid. (Abs.)

664. Nachtigall, Wilbur G. A Critical Edition of José de Valdivielso's *El villano en su rincón,* with a Study of the Play's Biblical Sources. vii+424 pp. Iowa, E. DeChasca, 1969. *DAI* 30A: 732–33.

The text of this play is based on the 1622 Toledo *princeps,* with variants from the edition of Braga, 1624, and from the undated, unsigned MS 15.664 of the BN, Madrid. (Abs.)

665. Oberlander, Barbara Joyce. The *Autos Sacramentales* of José de Valdivielso: Their Dramatic Theory. 684 pp. Louisiana State, W. A. Pickens, 1969. *DAI* 30A: 2976.

"Before Calderón, however, this study seeks to prove . . . that the dramatist José de Valdivielso . . . developed a dramatic formula which produced true Eucharistic *autos.*" (Abs.)

Vasconcelos, Jorge Ferreira de (Portugal. 1527?–1584/85)

666. Piper, Anson Conant. The Portuguese Court of the Sixteenth Century as Reflected in the Dramatic Novels of Jorge Ferreira de Vasconcellos [sic]. iv+269 pp. Wisconsin, L. Kasten, 1953. Wisconsin *Summaries* 15(1953–54): 629.

"Jorge Ferreira de Vasconcellos, through his dialogued or 'dramatic' novels composed between the years 1537 and 1555, furnishes modern readers with a unique and invaluable key to an understanding of the Portuguese court during the height of its maritime and mercantile splendor. . . . Of even greater importance, perhaps, than this detailed picture of his external surroundings is the author's concern with the intellectual and moral tone of the Portuguese capital. . . . It is in his subtle blending of the two main currents of sixteenth-century letters, the Peninsular and the Classical, that his originality is to be found." (Diss.) Editorial note: Three works of Vasconcelos (*Eufrosina, Ulisipo,* and *Aulegrafia*), often called "dialogued novels," belong to the history of Portuguese theater; see Adrien Roig, *O teatro clássico em Portugal no século XVI* (Lisboa: Instituto de Cultura e Língua Portuguesa, 1983) 57–77.

❖ [A] "Jorge Ferreira de Vasconcellos, Defender of the Portuguese Vernacular." *H* [AATSP] 37 (1954): 400–05. [B] "Jorge Ferreira de Vasconcellos and the Spirit of Empire." *H* [AATSP] 50 (1967): 44–48. [C] "The Lisbon of Jorge Ferreira de Vasconcellos." *LBR* 4.1 (1967): 17–26. [D] "Courtly Love in the Works of Jorge Ferreira de Vasconcellos." *SAB* 34.4 (1969): 7–9. [For a more complete list of this scholar's publications, see "Biography and Bibliography," *From Dante to García Márquez: Studies in Romance Literatures and Linguistics. Presented to Anson C. Piper by Former Students, Colleagues and Friends,* ed. Gene H. Bell-Villada, Antonio Giménez, and George Pistorius (Williamstown: Williams Coll., 1987) xxx–xxxi.]

Vega Carpio, Lope Félix de (1562–1635)

667. Adam, Francis Osborne, Jr. Some Aspects of Lope de Vega's Dramatic Technique as Observed in His Autograph Plays. xix+393 pp. Illinois, J. Van Horne, 1936. Abstract. Urbana, 1936. 19 pp.

"The present thesis is an examination of certain aspects of the dramatic technique of Lope de Vega as observed in his [38] autograph plays." The writer examines "in succession the exposition of the plays, the body of the action, the conclusion, the influence of character types upon the action, and such miscellaneous devices as symmetrical effects, the use of dramatically extraneous material for the purpose of padding a play, [and] the use of the moving stage." (Abs.)

668. Adams, Charles Lindsey. Traditional and Novelesque Elements in the Development of Plot in the Dated Plays of Lope de Vega. ii+247 pp. Stanford, A. M. Espinosa, 1954. *DA* 14: 1706.

"The general conclusion to be drawn is that Lope de Vega was a 'popular' dramatist throughout his career, although he became more interested in moralizing and in artistic form in his later years. In addition, the 115 plays studied indicate that Lope deserves to be called one of the most fertile inventors of plots in world literature—not so much because of his originality in the invention of detail, as because of the original and varied manner in which he used and combined them." (Abs.)

❖ [A] "The Problem of the Motif-Index, with Special Reference to Lope de Vega." *BCom* 7 (1955): 1–3. [B] "Motivos folklóricos en las comedias de Lope de Vega." *CHA* 67 (1966): 577–93.

669. ALMASOV, ALEXEY. El honor rústico en el teatro de Lope de Vega y en otros dramaturgos del Siglo de Oro. iv+348 pp. Iowa, E. DeChasca, 1968. *DA* 29A: 1888–89.

"The central problem of the plays of rustic honor is not class struggle but universal justice. In his handling of this problem, Lope starts from concrete facts of social injustice prevalent in his own time. He does not, however, call for a reorganization of society." (Abs.)

❖ [A] "*Fuenteovejuna* y el honor villanesco en el teatro de Lope de Vega. *CHA* 54.161–62 (1963): 701–55. [B] "Die Bauernehre im Theater Lope de Vegas." *Lope de Vega*. Ed. Eberhard Müller-Bochat. Darmstadt: Wissenschaftliche, 1975. 91–128.

670. AMES, DEBRA COLLINS. The Function of Classical Allusions in the Theater of Lope de Vega. ii+299 pp. Virginia, D. McGrady, 1987. *DAI* 48A: 2763–64.

"Classical allusions in Lope's theater frequently serve to characterize someone, add a humorous touch, or emphasize a theme, but their most interesting function is the prefiguration of impending events." The writer bases her study on fifty *comedias* and concludes her examination "with in-depth analyses of two plays containing noteworthy classical references: *La villana de Getafe* and *La quinta de Florencia*." (Abs.)

❖ [A] "Phaeton's Second Fall: Lope's Burlesque Treatment of the Myth in *La villana de Getafe*." *RLAn* 1 (1989): 361–65. [B] "'Sacred and Profane Love': Venus Figures in Lope de Vega's *Comedia*." *CRR* 8 (1989): 78–85. [C] "*La quinta de Florencia:*

Lope's Debt to Belleforest." *Hispanófila* 98 (1990): 1–16. [D] "Love Melancholy in *La quinta de Florencia.*" *BCom* 44.1 (1992): 45–58. [E] Vega, L. de. *La quinta de Florencia: A Critical, Annotated Edition.* Ed. D. C. Ames. Kassel: Reichenberger, 1995. 225 pp. (Teatro del Siglo de Oro. Ediciones críticas 65.)

671. ANDRIST, DEBRA DIANE. Love, Honor, and the Male-Female Relationship in Representative Authors of the Spanish *Comedia.* 265 pp. SUNY/Buffalo, C. Bandera, 1986. *DAI* 47A: 542–43.

[For the complete entry, see no. 240.]

672. ARJONA, JAIME HOMERO. *Las bizarrías de Belisa:* Edición crítica precedida de un estudio del "disfraz varonil" en su teatro. iv+145 pp. Brown, W. L. Fichter, 1932.

The critical text is based on the autograph.

❖ [A] "Apunte cronológico sobre *El Arenal de Sevilla* de Lope de Vega." *HR* 5 (1937): 344–46. [B] "El disfraz varonil en Lope de Vega." *BH* 39.2 (1937): 120–45. ["De cuatrocientas sesenta comedias suyas que hemos examinado, ciento trece revelan el uso del *disfraz varonil;* es decir, casi la cuarta parte de su obra."] [C] "Dos errores de cronología lopesca." *RR* 28 (1937): 311–17. [D] "La fecha de *La francesilla.*" *HR* 5 (1937): 73–76. [E] "Un dato sobre la fecha de *El anzuelo de Fenisa* de Lope de Vega." *MLN* 53 (1938): 190–92. [F] "La introducción del gracioso en el teatro de Lope de Vega." *HR* 7 (1939): 1–21. [G] "Another Sonnet in Lope de Vega's *Los tres diamantes.*" *HR* 20 (1952): 313–15. [H] "The Case of Lope de Vega's *Amar, servir y esperar* (A Problem of Literary Relationships)." *RR* 44 (1953): 257–62. [I] "Defective Rhymes and Rhyming Techniques in Lope de Vega's Autograph *Comedias.*" *HR* 23 (1955): 108–28. [J] "Did Lope de Vega Write the Extant *El Príncipe melancólico*?" *HR* 24 (1956): 42–49. [K] "False Andalusian Rhymes in Lope de Vega and Their Bearing on the Authorship of Doubtful *Comedias.*" *HR* 24 (1956): 290–305. [L] "Ten Plays Attributed to Lope de Vega." *HR* 28 (1960): 319–40. [M] "Improper Use of Consonantal Rhyme in Lope de Vega and Its Significance Concerning the Authorship of Doubtful Plays." *Hispanófila* 6.16 (1962): 7–39. [N] "Two Plays Attributed to Lope de Vega and Guillén de Castro." *HR* 33 (1965): 387–94. [O] Vega, L. de. *La desdichada*

Estefanía. Paleographic ed. by J. H. Arjona. Valencia: Castalia, 1967. 114 pp. (Estudios de Hispanófila 6.)

673. ARTIGAS, MARÍA DEL CARMEN. Una edición crítica y anotada de *La buena guarda*, de Lope de Vega. iv+523 pp. Virginia, J. S. Herrero, 1990. *DAI* 51A: 874.

The text is based on the autograph MS, which has been collated with six printed versions: 1621 (Madrid: F. Correa Montenegro), 1621 (Madrid: Viuda de Alonso Martín), 1873 (Hartzenbusch), 1895 (Menéndez Pelayo), 1934 (Juliá Martínez), and 1936 (Pilar Díez). (Abs.)

❖ [A] "El mito del paraíso en *La buena guarda* (1610) de Lope de Vega." *ExTL* 19.2 (1990–91): 29–36. [B] "'La mancha en la sangre *versus* la mancha en el alma' en *La buena guarda* de Lope de Vega." *RomN* 32.2 (1991): 127–32.

674. ARTMAN, JIM PAINE. The Soldier in the Dramatic Works of Lope de Vega. iv+497 pp. CA/Los Angeles, E. H. Templin, 1958.

"Using as a point of departure the Spanish soldier as dramatically interpreted by Lope, this study presents an analysis of the diverse aspects of military life and customs as they are revealed in the *comedias*. Its principal objectives are to effect a greater understanding of and appreciation for the figure of the Spanish *infante* as Lope chose to create him for the stage, and to determine the poet's attitude toward the profession of arms as symbolized by the soldier. Over one hundred and fifty of Lope's plays were selected as suitable for study because of their military theme and the nature of their characters. In these plays all references to the soldier or to military life, customs, terminology, practices and procedures were carefully examined." (AFE, 26 April 1958.)

675. ASTURIAS, [SISTER] ROSARIO MARÍA, SNJM. A Critical Edition and Study of the Play *El rey don Pedro en Madrid y el Infanzón de Illescas.* vi+553 pp. Southern California, E. W. Hesse, 1963. *DA* 24: 5378–79.

[For the complete entry, see no. 205.]

676. BADENDYCK, CYNTHIA RODRIGUEZ. The Lovers of Verona in Lope de Vega and Shakespeare: Problems in Comparison. 290 pp. CUNY, F. J. Nichols, 1990. *DAI* 51A: 1602.

"Lope de Vega's three-act *tragicomedia Castelvines y Monteses,* written between 1606 and 1612, is the most important contemporary analogue extant of Shakespeare's *Romeo and Juliet*. Yet *Castelvines y Monteses* is a play that has received very little attention and virtually no serious study. The present essay argues that political and cultural prejudices dating back to the century in which Lope and Shakespeare were born have rendered *Castelvines y Monteses* invisible. Therefore, the first part of the essay is devoted to examining the most conspicuous of those prejudicial elements. . . . The rest of the essay studies how these prejudices have both restricted and distorted what we allow ourselves to see in the two plays, and argues that by a number of traditional standards regularly applied to *Romeo and Juliet, Castelvines y Monteses* is in fact a better play—more plausible, more controlled, more resonant, more complex, more aesthetically satisfying, less specious. Chapters discuss issues of genre, pederastic subtext vectored by the prepubescent boy actress of Shakespeare's stage, the relationship of love to feud, and the implications of death and reconciliation." (Abs.)

❖ Rodriguez-Badendyck, C. "The Neglected Alternative: Shakespeare's *Romeo and Juliet* and Lope de Vega's *Castelvines y Monteses*." *Parallel Lives: Spanish and English National Drama 1580–1680*. Ed. Louise Fothergill-Payne and Peter Fothergill-Payne. Lewisburg: Bucknell UP, 1991. 91–107.

677. Blázquez Rodrigo, Marcelo. Estudios sobre *La Gatomaquia* de Lope de Vega. 1041 pp. SUNY/Albany, M. Alvar, 1985. *DAI* 47A: 884.

"Finally, we should add that Lope in this burlesque epic poem has not belied his genius as a playwright. He follows in it the same techniques he employs in his plays; one could classify the *Gatomaquia* as a theatre piece." (Abs.)

678. Blue, William Robert. A Reevaluation of the Ideas of Marcelino Menéndez Pelayo in the *Estudios sobre el teatro de Lope de Vega* in Light of Current Critical Opinion on the Baroque. 178 pp. Pennsylvania State, L. C. Pérez, 1971. *DAI* 32A: 5219.

"We have demonstrated that while Pelayo may provide valid historical information on Lope's plays and while at times he may be quite sensitive to the techniques used, he did not fully comprehend the Baroque and, as a result, misinterpreted stylistic and structural elements of many of the plays that he analyzed." (Abs.)

679. BRADFORD, MARJORIE ESTHER CAMPBELL. The *Gracioso* of Lope de Vega. vii+204 pp. Radcliffe, J. D. M. Ford, 1929.

This dissertation is composed of the following chapters: "Representative Examples of the *Gracioso* of Lope de Vega," "The Composite *Gracioso,*" "Origins of the *Gracioso,*" and "The Survival of the *Gracioso.*" (Diss.)

680. BRODY, ERVIN CONSTANTIN. Events of the Russian Time of Troubles in Two Baroque Dramas: Lope de Vega's *El Gran Duque de Moscovia* and John Fletcher's *The Loyal Subject.* xvii+224 pp. Columbia, W. E. Harkins and H. B. Segel, 1967. *DA* 28A: 1388.

"The dissertation attempts to analyze the use in two baroque dramas of the theme of the Demetrius legend which grew out of the extraordinary events known in Russian historiography as the Time of Troubles (1598–1613)." (Abs.)

❖ *The Demetrius Legend and Its Literary Treatment in the Age of the Baroque.* Cranbury: Associated U Presses, 1971; Rutherford: Fairleigh Dickinson UP, 1972. 323 pp.

681. BROOKS, JOHN. *La gran comedia del mayor imposible* de Lope de Vega Carpio. 430 pp. Wisconsin, H. A. Smith, 1924.

❖ El mayor imposible *of Lope de Vega Carpio, with an Introduction and Notes by J. Brooks.* Univ. of Arizona Bulletin 5, no. 7 (Humanities Bulletin 2) October 1, 1934. Tucson, Arizona. 209 pp.

The present edition is "a revision" of the writer's doctoral dissertation (1924). "Although it has been entirely rewritten, the conclusions remain substantially unchanged." The text is based on the *princeps:* Lope's *Parte veinticinco* (1647). (Prt. Diss.)

682. BUNN, ELAINE ANN. The Early History Plays of Lope de Vega: Classification and Analysis. xxx+337 pp. Pennsylvania, A. G. Reichenberger, 1976. *DAI* 37A: 7154.

"Lope's unique contribution to the dramatization of history is best understood through the consideration of his plays as communal drama. Lope recognized the needs, assumptions, and interests of his audiences and was able to respond to and to satisfy them in his history plays. The separate analysis of five history plays, which concludes this investigation, applies the results of the earlier chapters on background and composition to individual examples." (Abs.)

683. BURKORT, HAYDEE MACERA. Typology in the Biblical Plays of Lope de Vega. xi+310 pp. Florida State, D. H. Darst, 1983. *DAI* 44A: 1808.

"Typology is the science that establishes the relationships between figures and events of the Old Testament, called types, and their counterparts in the New, called antitypes." The writer studies typological matter in the following plays: *La creación del mundo y primera culpa del hombre, El robo de Dina, Los trabajos de Jacob, La corona derribada y vara de Moisés, David perseguido y montes de Gelboe, Historia de Tobías, La hermosa Ester,* and *El inobediente: o, La ciudad sin Dios*. (Abs.)

684. CAMPIGLIA, JEANNETTE. Some Aspects of Nature in the *Comedia* of Lope de Vega. iv+446 pp. CA/Los Angeles, E. H. Templin, 1958.

"In this study, we have traced the functions of nature in those plays whose plots unfold in a natural retreat, in a sylvan hideout, in Arcadia, or in the country. We have scrutinized his pastoral, mythological, and rural plays, examining them from the point of view of their use of nature and natural phenomena. We have likewise sampled the other types of plays in which the action is principally localized in an urban area or which make use of the sea, exotic lands, or the tame nature of the cultivated garden." (AFE, 13 February 1959)

685. CASE, THOMAS EDWARD. A Critical Edition of Lope de Vega's *Las almenas de Toro.* 320 pp. Iowa, E. DeChasca, 1962. *DA* 23: 4673–74.

The text is based on a nonautograph MS in the Biblioteca Nacional (Madrid), which has been collated with the following printed editions: 1620 (Lope's *Parte catorce*), 1890 (Spanish Academy), and 1956 (Aguilar). (Abs.)

❖ [A] "The Early Date of Composition of Lope's *Las almenas de Toro.*" *RomN* 6.2 (1965): 156–59. [B] "Some Observations on the References to the Goths in the Dramas of Lope de Vega." *REHb* 3 (1969): 67–89. [Among the *comedias* cited is *Las almenas de Toro.*] [C] "Lope's *Las almenas de Toro:* An Example of the Poetic

Interpretation of History." *RomN* 11.2 (1969-70): 333-38. [D] *A Critical and Annotated Edition of Lope de Vega's* Las almenas de Toro. Ed. T. E. Case. Chapel Hill: U of North Carolina P, 1971. 217 pp. (UNCSRLL 104.) [E] "The Significance of Morisco Speech in Lope's Plays." *H* [AATSP] 65 (1982): 594-600. [F] Vega, L. de. *San Diego de Alcalá.* Ed. T. E. Case. Kassel: Reichenberger, 1988. 177 pp. (Teatro del Siglo de Oro. Ediciones críticas 14.) [G] *Lope and Islam: Islamic Personages in His* Comedias. Newark: Juan de la Cuesta, 1993. 187 pp.

686. Castañeda, James Agustín. A Critical Edition of Lope de Vega's *Las paces de los reyes y judía de Toledo.* 315 pp. Yale, F. S. Reckert, 1958.

❖ [A] Vega, L. de. *A Critical Edition of Lope de Vega's* Las paces de los reyes y judía de Toledo. Ed. J. A. Castañeda. Chapel Hill: U of North Carolina P, 1962. 265 pp. (UNCSRLL 40.) [B] Vega, Lope de. *Las paces de los reyes y judía de Toledo.* Ed., introd., and notes by J. A. Castañeda. Salamanca: Anaya, 1971. 166 pp. (Biblioteca Anaya. Autores españoles 2.) "The present work was a dissertation presented for the degree of Doctor of Philosophy in Yale University in April, 1958." As the writer explains, "the Madrid edition of the *Séptima parte* [1617] is . . . the basis of our edition. The three other printings used for our collation [are] that of Barcelona [1617], Hartzenbusch's [BAE 41] and Menéndez Pelayo's Academy edition." (Prt. Diss.)

687. Cherry, Charles Maurice. The Nature of Comedy in the Early Drama of Lope de Vega. 232 pp. Northwestern, F. G. Very, 1980. *DAI* 41A: 2628.

"This study investigates the nature of comedy in what, according to the Morley-Bruerton chronology, appear to be the dramatist's first thirty-six *comedias,* those works probably composed before 1595, the final year of Lope's residency in Alba de Tormes." (Abs.)

688. Ciavarelli, Maria Elisa. El tema de la fuerza de la sangre en el Siglo de Oro español y sus antecedentes en la literatura occidental. 330 pp. Pennsylvania, A. E. Foley, 1977. *DAI* 38A: 4864.

The writer examines the following pertinent works: *Los Infantes de Lara* (Juan de la Cueva), *El tejedor de Segovia* (Juan Ruiz de Alarcón), and *Los Prados de León, Los Tellos de Meneses, El bastardo*

Mudarra, El primero Benavides, La moza de cántaro (Lope de Vega). (Abs.)

❖ *El tema de la fuerza de la sangre: Antecedentes europeos. Siglo de Oro español: Juan de la Cueva, Cervantes, Lope, Alarcón.* Potomac: Studia Humanitatis; Madrid: Porrúa Turanzas, 1980. 278 pp.

689. CLARK, FREDDIE MACARTHUR. Evidence for the Rejection of Certain *Comedias* Attributed to Lope de Vega. v+213 pp. Florida, F. C. Hayes, 1968. *DAI* 30A: 314–15.

"The conclusions reached were that the non-Lopean elements in the following ten plays provide sufficient evidence for rejecting them from a canon of Lope's authentic works: *Alejandro el segundo, Los contrarios de amor, El prodigioso príncipe transilvano, Santo Angelo, El rey fingido y amores de Sancha, El rey por trueque, El toledano vengado, El valiente Juan de Heredia, La venganza piadosa, Bernardo del Carpio*." (Abs.)

❖ [A] "A Note on the Authorship of a *Comedia* Attributed to Lope: *Alejandro el segundo*." *RomN* 11.1 (1969–70): 144–47. [B] "Objective Tests of Authenticity and the Attribution of *El toledano vengado* to Lope de Vega." *Hispanófila* 13.38 (1970): 13–18. [C] *Objective Methods for Testing Authenticity and the Study of Ten Doubtful* Comedias *Attributed to Lope de Vega.* Chapel Hill: U of North Carolina P, 1971. 186 pp. (UNCSRLL 106.)

690. COHEN, LOUISE GALE. The *Gatomaquia* within the Context of Lope's Life and Times. iii+151 pp. Harvard, R. Lida, 1969.

The study includes references to Lope's plays.

691. COMPTE-BACKUS, DEBORAH ELENA. The Pastoral Drama of Lope de Vega. v+352 pp. Princeton, A. Forcione and R. E. Surtz, 1980. *DAI* 41A: 3128–29.

"This study examines the ways in which the dramatist exploited, transformed, and subverted the themes and formal conventions of bucolic literature in his theater." (Abs.)

❖ [A] "*La fingida Arcadia:* Tirso's Disenchantment with the Pastoral." *BCom* 36.2 (1984): 155–66. ["Tirso de Molina's play *La fingida Arcadia* (1622), is a work which draws its inspiration from Lope de Vega's pastoral romance *La Arcadia* (1598)."] [B] "Lope de Vega's Pastoral Drama: Remythification." *CRR* 5 (1986): 16–25. [C] "Lope de Vega's Stormy Pastoral: Transforming the

Genre." *CRR* 11 (1992): 26–33. [D] "The Sojourn in the Garden: The Pastoral Tradition in Lope de Vega's *Novelas a Marcia Leonarda*." *H*[AATSP] 76.4 (1993): 656–63.

692. COOKE, WILLIAM PENDLETON. An Annotated Edition of the Play *Los Monteros de Espinosa*. 255 pp. Minnesota, R. Floripe(?), 1968. *DAI* 30A: 316.

[For the complete entry, see no. 209.] The play has been attributed to Lope.

693. CRAIG, VIRGINIA WALLACE ROBERTSON. The Brother-Sister Theme in Lope de Vega's Plays. 267 pp. Missouri, A. Porqueras-Mayo, 1968. *DA* 29A: 3607.

The author finds that 127 of Lope's plays "contain at least one brother-sister relationship." According to the writer, "two themes emerge as the most fruitful for study: the honor code and incestuous attractions." The third area of this work "considers the dramatist's use of the sibling relationship in his subplots." (Abs.)

694. D'ANTUONO, NANCY LINDA. The Italian *Novella* and Lope de Vega's Comedies. vii+375 pp. Michigan, E. Glaser and M. Z. Hafter, 1975. *DAI* 36A: 1552.

"This study centers on four of Lope's plays which offer varying degrees of indebtedness to Boccaccio and Bandello and which present a contrastive treatment of two themes: honor and prudence. The detailed analyses of *El llegar en ocasión* (Boccaccio II, 2); *La discreta enamorada* (Boccaccio III, 3); *El genovés liberal* (Bandello II, 26) and *El mayordomo de la Duquesa de Amalfi* (Bandello I, 26) point up the translation of the themes to a contemporary milieu and Lope's technique of adapting *novella* to drama." Discussed in less detail are Lope's *El castigo sin venganza* and *El castigo del discreto*. (Abs.)

❖ [A] "*Discreción* as a Remedy against Adverse Fortune: Boccaccio's Third Story of the Third Day and Lope's *La discreta enamorada*." *BCom* 27.1 (1975): 26–35. [B] "Genoese History and Lope's *El genovés liberal*: Sources and Implications." *AION-SR* 18 (1976): 5–13. [The play's action is from Bandello; however, for the historical background, "Lope's principal (but not exclusive) source of information" was Francesco Guicciardini's *Historia d'Italia*.] [C] "*Letteratura amena* to *Literatura docente:* The Techniques of Adaptation in Lope de Vega's Boccaccio Plays." *HISt* 2 (1979): 93–112. [D] "La configuración ambivalente de *El mayordomo de la Duquesa de Amalfi* de Lope de Vega." *Actas del coloquio (Roma, 1978): Teoría y realidad en el teatro español del siglo XVII. La influencia italiana.* Roma: Instituto Español de Cultura y de Literatura, 1981. 325–45. [A Bandello-based *comedia.*] [E] "Lope de Vega y la commedia dell'arte: Temas y figuras." *CdF* 3 (1981): 261–78. [F] "The Spanish *Comedia* in Italy: Lope's *La discreta enamorada* and Its Commedia dell'Arte Counterpart." *LA CHISPA '81: Selected Proceedings of the Second Louisiana Conference on Hispanic Languages and Literatures.* Ed. Gilbert Paolini. New Orleans: Tulane UP, 1981. 69–81. [G] "Bandello, Lope de Vega, and an Unedited Commedia dell'Arte Scenario: *Il castico della disonesta moglie.*" *LA CHISPA '83: Selected Proceedings of the Fourth Louisiana Conference on Hispanic Languages and Literatures.* Ed. Gilbert Paolini. New Orleans: Tulane UP, 1983. 79–87. [Apropos *El castigo del discreto.*] [H] *Boccaccio's* Novelle *in the Theater of Lope de Vega.* Potomac: Studia Humanitatis; Madrid: Porrúa Turanzas, 1983. 190 pp. [I] "Pantalone Hispanicized: The Comic Father Figure in Lope de Vega's *La francesilla.*" *Italo-Hispanic Literary Relations.* Ed. Jesús Helí Hernández. Potomac: Scripta Humanistica, 1989. 41–55. (Scripta Humanistica 49.) [J] "The Evolution of *Il cavaliere perseguitato:* Literary Interdependence in Bandello, Lope de Vega and the Commedia dell'Arte." *BCom* 44.1 (1992): 103–12.

695. Delano, Lucile Kathryn. A Critical Index of the Sonnets in the Plays of Lope de Vega. x+68 pp. Iowa, R. E. House, 1934. Iowa *Program*, May 1934.

The dissertation "is divided into three parts: an introduction explanatory of the use of the sonnet in the Spanish theater and in the plays of Lope de Vega in particular; an alphabetical index of the first lines of the sonnets in all plays known to be by Lope or assigned to him with some degree of probability; a second index, also alphabetical, of the plays in which sonnets are found." (*Program*)

❖ [A] "The Relation of Lope de Vega's Separate Sonnets to Those in His *Comedias.*" *H* [AATSP] 10.5 (1927): 307–20. [B] "The

Sonnet in the Golden Age Drama of Spain." *H*[AATSP] 11.1 (1928): 25–28. [C] "An Analysis of the Sonnets in Lope de Vega's *Comedias.*" *H*[AATSP] 12.1 (1929): 119–40. [D] "Lope de Vega's *Gracioso* Ridicules the Sonnet." *H*[AATSP], 1st special issue (1934): 19–34. [E] Title as is. Toronto: U of Toronto P, 1935. 70 pp. [F] "The *Gracioso* Continues to Ridicule the Sonnet." *H* [AATSP] 18.4 (1935): 383–400.

696. Duarte, Julio M. Estudio y edición crítica de *La creación del mundo y primera culpa del hombre,* de Lope de Vega. 240 pp. Emory, G. Umpierre, 1968. *DAI* 30A: 719.

"... se da el texto de *La creación del mundo* con las variantes de más interés en cuanto a cuatro de las más antiguas ediciones sueltas." (Abs.)

❖ Vega, L. de. *La creación del mundo y primera culpa del hombre.* Ed., critical study, and notes by J. M. Duarte. Zaragoza: Ebro, 1972. 206 pp. (Biblioteca clásica Ebro 118–19. Serie teatro 58.)

697. Eason, Elizabeth Auvert. Del sentimiento trágico de la vida en el teatromundo de Lope de Vega y Shakespeare. ix+652 pp. Arkansas, B. D. Kimpel, 1967. *DA* 28A: 625.

"To back those extremely tentative conclusions sketched above, the work of Lope de Vega was reviewed within the limitations of time and space: two novels and some aspects of *La Dorotea,* several samples of his popular, *culta,* elegiac and religious poetry and some 67 plays." (Abs.)

❖ *Lope de Vega. El Duque de Viseo: Observaciones preliminares.* Valencia: Albatros, 1969. 279 pp. ["... el simbolismo mesiánico es en *El Duque de Viseo* ... el tema de fondo y el verdaderamente importante. ... Cuando quien esto escribe componía su tesis doctoral en 1966 adelantó entonces la teoría que tanto *El Duque de Viseo* como *El caballero de Olmedo* ... podrían ser interpretadas ... como alegorías mesiánicas."]

698. Elizondo, Sergio Danilo. A Critical Edition of Lope de Vega's *¡Si no vieran las mujeres!* lxx+160 pp. North Carolina, J. A. Castañeda, 1963. *DA* 28A: 626.

The dissertation includes a critical edition of the *princeps* (1637) and a study of this and the four other plays by Lope that have a theme similar to Bandello's *novella* 1: 18. The other four plays are

El hombre de bien, Obras son amores, La mayor victoria, and *El poder en el discreto.* (Abs.)

699. ELLIS, MIRIAM. Lope de Vega's *La francesilla:* A Critical, Annotated Edition Together with a Metric Translation of the Gálvez Manuscript. 412 pp. CA/Santa Cruz, J. H. Silverman, 1979. *DAI* 40A: 2716–17.

In the preparation of this edition, the writer has used the three printed texts of 1620 and 1621 as well as the eighteenth-century Gálvez MS. (Abs.)

700. ESTENOZ, OSVALDO A. Retórica en los autos sacramentales de Lope de Vega. 299 pp. SUNY/Buffalo, C. Bandera, 1977. *DAI* 38A: 1434.

"[Lope's] audience is one of believers, who do not have to be convinced intellectually, but rather persuaded emotionally to practice what they already know and believe. This rhetorical perspective thus becomes an integrating principle in the analysis of Lope's *autos.*" (Abs.)

701. EXUM, FRANCES BELL. The Treatment of Pedro I de Castilla in the Drama of Lope de Vega. 424 pp. Florida State, D. L. Hoffman, 1970. *DAI* 31A: 4767.

"The eight plays attributed to Lope in which King Pedro appears range from historical and legendary treatments of the character in *Audiencias del rey don Pedro, Ya anda la de Mazagatos, El médico de su honra, La carbonera, El rey don Pedro en Madrid* and *Los Ramírez de Arellano* to *comedias de enredo* such as *La niña de plata* and *Lo cierto por lo dudoso,* in which Pedro appears as a more conventional protagonist." (Abs.)

❖ [A] "Lope's King Pedro: The Divine Right of Kings vs. the Right of Resistance." *H* [AATSP] 57.3 (1974): 428–33. [B] *The Metamorphosis of Lope de Vega's King Pedro: The Treatment of Pedro I de Castilla in the Drama of Lope de Vega.* Madrid: Playor, 1974. 212 pp. (Colección Plaza Mayor Scholar.)

702. FEIT, RONNA SPRING. A Critical and Annotated Edition of Lope de Vega's *Viuda, casada y doncella.* 551 pp. Virginia, D. McGrady, 1990. *DAI* 51A: 3095–96.

The critical edition is based on the eighteenth-century Gálvez MS, which has been collated with the following printed versions:

(1) *Parte* 7, Madrid, 1617 and Barcelona, 1617, (2) a *suelta,* Barcelona, no date, and (3) the text in volume 10 of the Spanish Academy edition of Lope's works (*Nueva edición*). (Abs.)

❖ McGrady, Donald, and Ronna Feit. "Recollections of Juan de Mena in Lope de Vega's *Viuda, casada y doncella*." *BCom* 45.1 (1993): 7–11.

703. FERNÁNDEZ CERRA, CARMEN PILAR. El lirismo en los argumentos históricos de Lope de Vega. [7]+310 pp. Johns Hopkins, P. Salinas, 1952.

"The aim of this work is to determine the function of the lyrical passages in the plots of Lope de Vega's national-historical plays, explaining the co-existence of the different poetic and non-poetic tensions in his theater." (Diss.)

704. FICHTER, WILLIAM LEOPOLD. Lope de Vega's *El castigo del discreto,* Together with a Study of Conjugal Honor in His Theater. Columbia, F. de Onís, 1925. {New York: Instituto de las Españas [en los Estados Unidos] 1925. 283 pp.}

The text is based on the Madrid edition of Lope's *Parte* 7 (1617), which has been collated with the *Parte* 7 of Barcelona (1617) and Cotarelo's Academy edition (1917). (Diss.)

❖ "The Source of Lope de Vega's *El castigo del discreto.*" *RR* 16 (1925): 185–86. [For a more complete list of this scholar's publications, see *Homenaje a William L. Fichter: Estudios sobre el teatro antiguo hispánico y otros ensayos,* ed. A. David Kossoff and José Amor y Vázquez (Madrid: Castalia, 1971) 5–9.]

705. FLINT, WESTON. The Figure of Christopher Columbus in French, Italian and Spanish Dramas. xi+279 pp. North Carolina, S. A. Stoudemire, 1957. North Carolina *Record,* no. 590, p. 266.

The relevant play examined (pp. 24–37) is Lope de Vega's *El Nuevo Mundo descubierto por Cristóbal Colón.* The writer states that "from his first appearance in a play by Spain's immortal Lope de Vega until his most recent portrayal in 1951, the discoverer of America has been used as the crux of almost all conceivable dramatic forms." He also observes that "the inevitable conclusion is that the life of Columbus cannot be easily adapted into effective dramatic form." (Abs.)

❖ "Colón en el teatro español." *EA* 22.111 (1961): 165–86.

706. FRICK, PATSY RUTH. The Role of the Spanish King in Plays of Lope Félix de Vega Carpio. 227 pp. Georgia, H. Ziomek, 1972. *DAI* 33A: 3644.

"Twenty-five kings are studied in this work, beginning with Mauregato, who ruled in the eighth century, and concluding with Felipe II." (Abs.)

707. FRIESNER, ESTHER MONA. The Mirror of Queens: The Queen in the Theatre of Lope de Vega. vi+302 pp. Yale, M. Durán, 1977. *DAI* 38A: 3540.

"This dissertation examines thirty-three plays of Lope de Vega in which queens appear." (Abs.)

708. GLENN, RICHARD FOSTER. The Genesis of Lope de Vega's Dramatic Art. xvi+283 pp. Duke, B. W. Wardropper, 1967. *DA* 28A: 4173.

"This investigation is undertaken to examine, in the light of dramatic tradition and Lope's innovations, the plays he composed before 1590. . . . Lope's unexcelled eminence as the greatest dramatist of his age is largely the consequence of his recognition of the pastoral romances as a fertile source for dramatic themes and motifs." (Abs.)

❖ [A] "The Impact of the Spanish Pastoral Romance on Lope de Vega's Dramatic Art." *AION-SR* 13 (1971): 5–25. [B] "The Loss of Identity: Towards a Definition of the Dialectic in Lope's Early Drama." *HR* 41 (1973): 609–26. [C] "The Evolution of a Dramatic Style: Lope de Vega's First Urban Plays." *AION-SR* 22.2 (1980): 397–410.

709. GONZÁLEZ, ANTONIO. Análisis e interpretación de *Don Juan de Castro* de Lope de Vega. vi+296 pp. Louisiana State, F. A. de Armas, 1976. *DAI* 37A: 3672.

". . . el tema central de la obra es el amor de amistad en aras de la lealtad y el sacrificio." (Abs.)

❖ Title as is. Miami: Universal, 1981. 241 pp.

710. HALSTEAD, FRANK GEDNEY. The Attitude of Lope de Vega toward Astrology. 199 pp. Virginia, 1937. Virginia *Abstracts* (1937): 19–21.

Along with the subject indicated in the title of this dissertation, the writer discusses the relationship between astronomy and astrology in Golden Age Spain, as well as the sources and extent of Lope's knowledge of those two "sister sciences." (Diss.) On the basis of his study of 450 *comedias,* the writer shows that Lope did not believe in astrological predestination.

❖ [A] "The Attitude of Lope de Vega toward Astrology and Astronomy." *HR* 7 (1939): 205–19. [B] "The Attitude of Tirso de Molina toward Astrology." *HR* 9.4 (1941): 417–39.

711. HARLAN, MABEL MARGARET. A Critical Edition of Lope de Vega's *El desdén vengado.* xlix+196 pp. Indiana, J. M. Hill, 1927.

❖ [A] *Lope de Vega's* El desdén vengado. Ed. with introd. and notes. New York: Instituto de las Españas en los Estados Unidos, 1930. 196 pp. "The present edition . . . is based on the autograph found in the Biblioteca Nacional in Madrid. The relation of the first known edition of the play [1662] to the manuscript is also discussed." Collated, as well, are MS 15680 of the BNM, an eighteenth-century copy of the original; the nineteenth-century Ortega edition; and the 1913 Academy edition. (Prt. Diss.) [B] Vega, L. de. *Cuatro comedias.* Ed., with notes and vocabulary, by John M. Hill and Mabel M. Harlan. New York: Norton, 1941. 699 pp. [The four plays are *Peribáñez* (Lope), *No hay mal que por bien no venga* (Alarcón), *El burlador de Sevilla* (Tirso), and *No siempre lo peor es cierto* (Calderón).]

712. HEALD, WILLIAM FRANK. A Comparison of the Plot Patterns in the Plays of Shakespeare and Lope de Vega. 152 pp. North Carolina, S. E. Leavitt and R. B. Sharpe, 1954. North Carolina *Record* no. 548, p. 51.

In his comparative analysis the writer makes use of the following plays of Lope de Vega: *El castigo del discreto, Castelvines y Monteses, La dama boba, El mejor alcalde el rey, El perro del hortelano, El castigo sin venganza, El remedio en la desdicha, Fuenteovejuna,* and *El caballero de Olmedo.* (Abs.)

713. HICKS, MARGARET RUTH. Honor Conflicts and the Role of the Imagination in Selected Plays by John Fletcher and Lope de Vega. 161 pp. North Carolina, A. Dessen, 1980. *DAI* 41A: 3565–66.

"If there is indeed an answer to the problems raised by the honor conflicts in these plays, that answer seems to lie in the creative potential of the imagination represented by the intriguer figures." (Abs.)

❖ "Strategies of Ambiguity: The Honor Conflict in *La batalla del honor*." *Things Done with Words: Speech Acts in Hispanic Drama. Proceedings of the 1984 Stony Brook Seminar.* Ed. Elias L. Rivers. Newark: Juan de la Cuesta, 1986. 15–27.

714. HOGE, HENRY WILLIAM. A Critical, Annotated Edition of Lope de Vega's *El príncipe despeñado.* xlvi+282 pp. Wisconsin, E. W. Hesse, 1949. Wisconsin *Summaries* 10 (1950): 638.

"This edition is based on the autograph manuscript . . . at present located in the library of the Real Academia Española in Madrid. . . . Variants have been taken from three seventeenth-century printed versions of the play: [the Madrid and Barcelona *Séptima parte* editions and a *suelta* located in the Library of Parma, Italy]." (Summaries)

❖ [A] "Notes on the Sources and the Autograph Manuscript of Lope de Vega's *El príncipe despeñado*." *PMLA* 65 (1950): 824–40. [B] Vega, L. de. El príncipe despeñado: *A Critical and Annotated Edition of the Autograph Manuscript.* Ed. H. W. Hoge. Bloomington: Indiana UP, 1955. 188 pp. (Indiana University Publications. Humanities ser. 33.)

715. HORNE, RUTH NUTT. Lope de Vega's *Peregrino en su patria* and the Romance of Adventure in Spain before 1604. viii+290 pp. Brown, W. L. Fichter, 1946.

Part 1, chapter 9, of this dissertation is entitled "Interpolated Poetry and Plays" (pp. 79–99). (Diss.)

716. HORVATH, SABINE. Königtum und Tyrannei, Rebellion und Verschwörung als Themen im europäischen Drama, von der Spät-Renaissance bis zum Ende des siebzehnten Jahrhunderts. 505 pp. CUNY, L. Bergel, 1975. *DAI* 36A: 882–83.

[For the complete entry, see no. 218.] Included in this analysis are Lope's *Fuenteovejuna* and *Los Tellos de Meneses.*

717. JONES, SONIA HARRISON. The Devices of Foreshadowing in Lope de Vega's *Comedia.* iv+233 pp. Harvard, S. Gilman, 1971.

Part 1 analyzes the following devices: vocal *sombras,* omens, dreams, kledonomancy, and prophecies. Parts 2 and 3 are respectively entitled "The Triumph of Free Will" and "Passion and Foreshadowing." (Diss.)

❖ [A] "The Tragedy of Passion: Lope's *El caballero de Olmedo*."

Reflexión2 3-4 (1974-75): 138-45. [B] "Lope's Use of Foreshadowing in *La imperial de Otón.*" *Ren&R* 11 (1975): 79-84.

718. KAATZ, GERDA RUTH. A Diplomatic Edition of the *Comedia del católico español* and the *Comedia del glorioso San Martín.* v+348 pp. Iowa, R. Davis, 1945. Iowa *Abstracts* 7: 947-54.

[For the complete entry, see no. 544.] The second play is sometimes ascribed to Lope.

719. KAISER, GUNDA SABINA. A Critical and Annotated Edition of Lope de Vega's *La villana de Getafe.* cxxxix+399 pp. Wisconsin, E. W. Hesse, 1958. *DA* 19: 2614.

The critical text is based on the *princeps* of 1620, which has been collated with another seventeenth-century edition and three texts of the twentieth century. (Abs.)

720. KECK, RAY MARVIN, III. Lope's Hybrid Romance: Mimesis and Allegory in *El peregrino en su patria.* 273 pp. Princeton, A. Forcione, 1978. *DAI* 39A: 2319.

"The purpose of this study is to establish a literary-historical context for the classification of the *Peregrino*'s structural features, and then to elucidate the thematic unity which binds the adventure story to the [four] *autos* into a coherent, highly original example of Spanish romance of the Golden Age. . . . Lope thus creates a unique, original form of romance, in which human action (Pánfilo and Nise's love story) and moral commentary (interpolated *autos*) are structurally and thematically fused." (Abs.)

721. KENNEDY, HUGH W. Lope de Vega's *La desdichada Estefanía:* A Critical, Annotated Edition of the Autograph Manuscript. 226 pp. CA/Los Angeles, J. H. Silverman, 1964. *DA* 25: 3575-76.

The autograph is collated with six other versions: two editions dated 1619; Barcelona, 1630; the Gálvez MS; the Academy edition by Menéndez y Pelayo; and J. H. Arjona's edition of 1967. (Prt. Diss.) The Estefanía theme in Spanish literature is discussed, including a comparison between this play and that of Luis Vélez de Guevara: *Los zelos hasta los cielos y desdichada Estefanía.* (Abs.)

❖ Vega, L. de. *Lope de Vega's* La desdichada Estefanía: *A Critical, Annotated Edition of the Autograph Manuscript.* Ed. H. W. Kennedy. University: Romance Monographs, 1975. 265 pp. (Romance Monographs 13.)

722. KIRBY, CAROL L. BINGHAM. The Transformation of History into Poetry: The Treatment of Pedro I de Castilla in *El Rey Don Pedro en Madrid y el Infanzón de Illescas.* iv+242 pp. Kentucky, W. C. McCrary, 1977. *DAI* 38A: 826.

[For the complete entry, see no. 631.]

723. KIRSCHNER, TERESA J. El protagonista colectivo en *Fuenteovejuna* de Lope de Vega. iii+139 pp. Chicago, 1973.

"El próposito de nuestra tesis es estudiar el papel del personaje colectivo en *Fuenteovejuna* de Lope de Vega. Es nuestra intención el mostrar que tanto la concepción como la elaboración de la comedia a la vez que su difusión y evaluación han sido grandemente afectadas por la presencia del héroe colectivo." (Diss.)

❖ [A] "Sobrevivencia de una comedia: Historia de la difusión de *Fuenteovejuna.*" *RCEH* 1 (1977): 255–71. [B] *El protagonista colectivo en* Fuenteovejuna. Salamanca: Univ. de Salamanca, 1979. 157 pp. (Acta Salmanticensia. Studia Philologica Salmanticensia. Anejos. Estudios 1.) [C] "La importancia de la tradición oral y el héroe unanimista en *Fuenteovejuna* de Lope de Vega." *Actas del sexto congreso internacional de hispanistas, Toronto, 1977.* Ed. Alan M. Gordon and Evelyn Rugg. Toronto: Univ. of Toronto, 1980. 419–22. [D] "La masa airada en Shakespeare y Lope de Vega." *Vidas paralelas: El teatro español y el teatro isabelino, 1580–1680.* Ed. Anita K. Stoll. London: Tamesis, 1993. 25–35. (Colección Támesis, serie A. Monografías 153.)

724. LARSON, DONALD ROY. The Development of the "Honor Plays" of Lope de Vega. ix+315 pp. Harvard, S. Gilman, 1967.

❖ [A] *The Honor Plays of Lope de Vega.* Cambridge: Harvard UP, 1977. 217 pp. [This book] "differs from other investigations of the same subject in that it attempts to comprehend the entire corpus of Lope's honor plays while at the same time respecting the integrity of the individual work. . . . there is within the group of Lope's honor plays a development of some sort. It is my aim to chart, and try to understand, that development." (Prt. Diss.) [B] "*Los comendadores de Córdoba:* An Early Honor Play." *Homenaje a William L. Fichter: Estudios sobre el teatro antiguo hispánico y otros ensayos.* Ed. A. David Kossoff and José Amor y Vázquez. Madrid: Castalia, 1971. 399–412.

725. LAVINE, ROBERTA ZIMMERMAN. The Jew and the *Converso* in the Dramatic Works of Lope de Vega. vii+262 pp. Catholic, J. M. Solà-Solé, 1983. *DAI* 44A: 185.

"In spite of Lope's occasional 'sympathetic' portrayals of the Jew and the *converso,* the dramatist always affirms the fundamental values of society. Whatever atypical depictions of these characters are offered by the playwright stem from the aesthetic demands of individual dramas, and do not signify Lope's advocacy of the Jewish or *converso* cause. Lope's works testify to his ability to satisfy the anti-Jewish demands of his audience, without blindly overemphasizing the harsh anti-Semitic feelings of his age." (Abs.)

726. LEFORT PEÑA, EMILIO CARLOS. Edición paleográfica de la comedia *Del monte sale (quien el monte quema)* de Lope Félix de Vega Carpio, con un estudio de la misma. x+220 pp. Minnesota, E. W. Olmsted, 1935.

❖ Del monte sale (quien el monte quema): *Comedia de Lope de Vega.* Paleographic ed., with critical study and notes by E. LeFort Peña. Buenos Aires: Impresora de Argentina, 1939. 220 pp.

The writer bases this paleographic edition on a photostatic copy of the autograph manuscript owned by the Biblioteca Nacional in Madrid. The text has been collated with Cotarelo y Mori's Academy edition. (Prt. Diss.)

727. LEVITAN, AIDA TOMÁS. Lope de Vega y su tragedia "al estilo español." iii+323 pp. Emory, E. Navarro Kelley, 1977. *DAI* 38A: 4870.

This study is based on "un análisis de la concepción lopesca según se revela en algunas comedias de amor *(El caballero de Olmedo, La desdichada Estefanía, El mayordomo de la Duquesa de Amalfi,* y *El castigo sin venganza)* y en otras de temática histórica y sociopolítica *(La inocente sangre* y *El Duque de Viseo)*." (Abs.)

728. LIONETTI, HAROLD E. Ariosto's Influence on the Plays of Lope de Vega. 170 pp. Northwestern, J. G. Fucilla, 1955. *DA* 15: 1855.

"Ariosto's influence is reflected in 103 plays, approximately one-third of Lope's [authentic] dramatic works." (Abs.)

729. MADRIGAL, JOSÉ ANTONIO. La función del hombre salvaje en el

teatro de Lope de Vega, Tirso de Molina y Calderón de la Barca. 375 pp. Kentucky, W. C. McCrary, 1973. *DAI* 35A: 2232.

[For the complete entry, see no. 300.]

730. MARTIN, PHILIP HOWARD. Los autos sacramentales de Lope de Vega. 133 pp. North Carolina, A. V. Ebersole, 1981. *DAI* 42A: 2702–03.

The writer bases his analysis on thirty *autos* of Lope. His conclusion is as follows: "The sacramental theater of Lope is an important link in the evolution of the *auto sacramental*. It paved the way for the blossoming of this genre which occurred in the second half of the 17th century." (Abs.)

731. MARTÍNEZ, CHRISTINE DZIWURA. The Literary Function of the *Cuento* in the Plays of Lope de Vega. 197 pp. Pennsylvania State, L. C. Pérez, 1987. *DAI* 48A: 934.

"The interpolated *cuento* in Lope's plays functions in relation to elements significant for the course of dramatic action, namely, didacticism, theme, dramatic structure, motif, and characterization. The *cuento* is not mere ornamentation but, indeed, contributes to and forms an integral part of a play." (Abs.)

❖ "Alejandro y Diógenes: Inversión e ironía en *El villano en su rincón* de Lope de Vega." *BCom* 43.1 (1991): 21–30. [Apropos an interpolated anecdote.]

732. MARTÍNEZ, JOSÉ RAMÓN. Estudio de la mujer en las comedias novelescas auténticas y de fecha conocida de Lope de Vega entre 1600 y 1620. xiv+444 pp. Florida State, D. L. Hoffman, 1971. *DAI* 32A: 5190.

"A group of twenty-eight plays classified by Menéndez y Pelayo as novelesque has been selected for this study. . . . the findings confirm Lope's ability to create characters, the fertility of his imagination in their depiction and in the embodiment of the ideals of Spanish womanhood." (Abs.)

733. MAZZARA, RICHARD A. Italian and Spanish Influences and Parallels in the Life and Works of Saint-Amant, 1594–1661. 200 pp. Kansas, J. N. Carman, 1959. *DAI* 20A: 1365–66.

"Comparisons of Lope de Vega's and Saint-Amant's with Ovid's version of *Andromeda* show that Lope's piece is an important source of *L'Andromède*. Lope's influence as a dramatist is at least indirectly as significant as his influence as a poet." (Abs.) Editorial note: Marc Antoine Girard de Saint-Amant, French writer; Lope's *La Andrómeda* is a mythological poem.

❖ "Saint-Amant's *L'Andromède* and Lope de Vega's *La Andrómeda*." *KFLQ* 8 (1961): 7-14.

734. McCready, Warren Thomas. La heráldica en las obras de Lope de Vega y sus contemporáneos. 545 pp. Chicago, C. Castillo and B. Blanco-González, 1961.

"En fin, pensamos estudiar el tema de la heráldica en la comedia del *Siglo de Oro* desde los puntos de vista histórico, literario, artístico, psicológico, cronológico y comparativo, para averiguar lo posible con respecto a su función dramática, su valor artístico, su significación en la vida y en la ideología de Lope de Vega y su utilidad como medio de confirmar la autenticidad de algunas comedias que se han atribuído a Lope de Vega." (Diss.)

❖ [A] Title as is. Toronto: n.p., 1962. 470 pp. [B] Photocopy. Univ. of Chicago Library, Dept. of Photoduplication, 1968. 2 vols.

735. McMillan, Véronique Brunet. Complicité en conflit entre la poésie et la prose dans *La Dorotea* de Lope de Vega. [8]+159 pp. Case Western Reserve, D. M. Carey, 1977. *DAI* 38A: 2833.

"L'interaction entre la littérature et la vie est caractéristique à la fois de Lope et des personnages de *La Dorotea*." (Abs.)

736. Michels, Ralph John. Las unidades dramáticas en el teatro de Lope de Vega. vii+351 pp. Stanford, A. M. Espinosa, 1938. Stanford *Abstracts* 13 (1937-38): 58-59.

"The purpose of this dissertation is to study the practice of Lope de Vega, with regard to the dramatic unities of action, time and place, in one hundred fifteen of his plays; that is, in about one-fourth of his total extant dramatic production. The plays studied are of several different types, excluding plays treating the lives of saints, with one or two exceptions, because this latter type of play presents a very special time problem." (Abs.)

737. Miller, William Irvin. A Critical Edition of Lope de Vega's *La boba para los otros y discreta para sí*. vi+239 pp. Florida, F. C. Hayes, 1970. *DAI* 32A: 446.

"The text of the play is based on the 1635 edition, prepared for publication by Lope himself. This edition is accepted as authoritative; corrections are made sparingly and variants found in subsequent editions are given in footnotes." (Abs.)

738. MOORE, CHARLES ISAAC. A Brief Analysis of the Rhetorical Practices of Lope de Vega. 208 pp. Ohio State, G. L. Lewis, 1975. *DAI* 36A: 4852.

"Vega was not restrained by classical rhetoric. He was an original thinker, experimenter, and innovator." (Abs.)

739. MOORE, JEROME AARON. The *Romancero* in the Chronicle-Legend Plays of Lope de Vega. viii+162 pp. Pennsylvania, M. Romera-Navarro, 1937. {Philadelphia: Univ. of Pennsylvania, 1940. (UPSRLL 30.)}

"The purpose of the following study is to determine how and to what extent Lope de Vega drew directly upon the *romancero* in the plays which Menéndez y Pelayo classified as *Crónicas y leyendas dramáticas de España*." (Prt. Diss.)

740. MORRISON, ROBERT REID. Sainthood in the Theater of Lope de Vega. iv+598 pp. Florida, F. C. Hayes, 1963. *DA* 25: 481–82.

The 25 plays on which this study is based "contain a total of 108 roles for saints." (Abs.)

❖ [A] "*Graciosos con breviarios:* The Comic Element in the *Comedia de santos* of Lope de Vega." *CH* 12.1–2 (1990): 33–45. [B] "Lope's Padre Roxas and Niño Inocente Are Authentic Saints." *BCom* 44.1 (1992): 181–83.

741. MORROW, CAROLYN ROBERTS. Popular Lyric Tradition in the *Autos* of Lope de Vega. iii+100 pp. Tulane, D. W. McPheeters, 1969. *DAI* 30A: 2542–43.

"The purpose of this study is to indicate the folk background of many of the songs in the *autos* of Lope de Vega and, secondarily, to consider the dramatic function of some of these." (Abs.)

❖ "Another Aspect of the Fénix: Lope as a Writer of *Autos*." *Reflexión2* 1.1 (1972): 93–97.

742. MOYER, HELEN IDA TILL. A Study of the Authenticity of Eight Plays Attributed to Lope de Vega. viii+382 pp. Virginia, D. McGrady, 1976. *DAI* 37A: 2223.

"In the present study, we utilize only objective criteria to test the authenticity of eight plays for which Morley and Bruerton's versification analysis proved inconclusive: *Las pérdidas del que juega* (1596–1603), *Las hazañas del Cid* (1597–1603), *Los mártires de Madrid* (1602–06), *La paloma de Toledo* (1610–15), *El Antecristo* (1613–15), *Acertar errando* (1630–35), *Satisfacer callando* (not datable), and *La tercera orden de San Francisco,* a play which Lope supposedly wrote in collaboration with Juan Pérez de Montalván. An examination of their internal line-structure, rhyme patterns, vocabulary, and use of character names leads us to deny the authenticity of all eight plays." (Abs.)

743. MROCZKOWSKA-BRAND, KATARZYNA. Overt Theatricality and the "Theatrum Mundi" Metaphor in Spanish and English Drama, 1570–1640. xii+260 pp. Rochester, P. N. Dunn and A. N. Benston, 1985. *DAI* 46A: 3025.

[For the complete entry, see no. 145.] Includes an analysis of Lope's *Lo fingido verdadero.*

744. NARKINSKY, JOHNNY MCNEIL. Lope de Vega's Chivalric Plays: The Technique of Handling the Chivalric Themes and a Study of the Plays. v+340 pp. Florida State, D. L. Hoffman, 1969. *DAI* 30A: 5453.

"The study was based on the thirteen plays classified by Menéndez y Pelayo as *novelescas,* which are based on chivalric literature, the eight plays based on the Spanish epic themes, and three miscellaneous works: *Melisendra,* a chivalric *entremés; La puente del mundo,* a chivalric *auto sacramental;* and the *suelta* edition of *La puente de Mantible,* reputed to have been written by Lope, a copy of which is now in the Austrian National Library." (Abs.)

745. NEUVILLE, H. RICHMOND, JR. The Scepter and the Soul: The Nature and Education of a Prince in Renaissance Literature. 297 pp. NYU, R. J. Clements, 1968. *DAI* 30A: 692.

Among the treatises and creative works discussed is Lope de Vega's *comedia El príncipe despeñado.* (Abs.)

746. NIEHOFF, SUSAN CAROL. Figural Art in Lope de Vega's Epico-historical Play *El último godo.* iv+219 pp. Kentucky, J. E. Keller, 1978. *DAI* 39A: 3621.

"The play is typologically arranged in that Lope assigns the characteristics of an Adam-figure to Rodrigo and those of a Christ-figure to Pelayo." (Abs.)

❖ [A] "The Unity of Lope's *El último godo.*" *RomQ* 29.3 (1982): 261-72. [B] McCrary, Susan Niehoff. El último godo *and the Dynamics of Urdrama.* Potomac: Scripta Humanistica, 1987. 116 pp. (Scripta Humanistica 31.) ["Rodrigo, then, is a figure of Adam; Pelayo, of Christ."] [C] McCrary, Susan N. "'La noche de San Juan,' as the Temporal Coordinate in *El último godo.*" *Discurso* 11.1 (1993): 113-26.

747. NOBLE, BETH WILSON. The Function of the Rustic in the Dramatic Technique of Lope de Vega. iv+416 pp. Yale, 1948.

"This is not a study of the *gracioso,* but of rustic scenes and the rustic character in 96 plays. These are considered chronologically in three divisions: to 1604; 1604-18; and 1619-35. In the earlier plays, the 'rustic' material often seems to be crude and extraneous, but becomes more essential to the plot and is better integrated in later plays." (Parker, *Lope de Vega Studies* 94)

748. OLIVER, WILLIAM IRVIN. Spanish Theatre: A Study in Dramatic Discipline. vi+615 pp. Cornell, A. M. Drummond, 1959. *DA* 20: 2434.

"This dissertation examines important differences in content, style, and form between Spanish drama and contemporary American drama. It recommends the study of Spanish plays as a valuable discipline for American theatre artists and student playwrights. . . . The dissertation includes actable translations of plays by three of the greatest playwrights in Spanish literature." The relevant translated play is Lope's *The Lady Nit-Wit* (*La dama boba*). (Abs.)

749. O'NEAL, ROBERT DAWSON. An Interpretation and Extension of the *Gracioso* Idea in the Plays of Lope de Vega. x+219 pp. Florida State, D. L. Hoffman, 1966. *DA* 27A: 3058.

"Part I treats of the definition of the term *gracioso.* . . . Part II presents a catalogue and an analysis of the *gracioso* characters of one hundred thirty *comedias.*" (Abs.)

750. OSUNA, RAFAEL. *La Arcadia* de Lope de Vega: Génesis, estructura y originalidad. x+328 pp. Brown, A. S. Trueblood, 1966.

❖ [A] El *Dictionarium* de Stephanus y la *Arcadia* de Lope." *BHS* 45 (1968): 265-69. [B] "La forma interior de la *Arcadia* de Lope de Vega." *BBMP* 45 (1969): 255-69. [C] Title as is. Madrid: BRAE. Anejo 26 (1972; on cover, 1973). 268 pp. [On pp. 83-94, the writer compares the pastoral novel *La Arcadia* with three related *comedias* of Lope: *La Arcadia, Los amores de Albanio y* [sic] *Ismenia,* and *La pastoral de Jacinto.* (Prt. Diss.)]

751. PATT, BEATRICE PENELOPE (SHAPIRO). The Development of the Christmas Play in Spain from the Origins to Lope de Vega. 340 pp. Bryn Mawr, J. E. Gillet, 1945. *DA* 8: 100–02.

[For the complete entry, see no. 153.]

752. PÉREZ, LOUIS CELESTINO. Afirmaciones de Lope de Vega sobre preceptiva dramática a base de cien comedias. iv+256 pp. Michigan, F. Sánchez y Escribano, 1957. *DA* 18: 1438–39.

"We can also conclude that his precepts were not, in many respects, very different from those of the mainstays of classical dramatic theory—Aristotle and Horace. He kept in mind these precepts and discovered others suitable to his times." (Abs.)

❖ [A] Pérez, Louis C., and Federico Sánchez Escribano. Title as is. Madrid: CSIC, 1961. 218 pp. [B] "Preceptiva dramática en *El gran teatro del mundo.*" *Hispanófila* 30 (1967): 1–6.

753. PHILLIPS, ROY CLEVELAND. A Critical Edition of *La francesilla,* a Drama by Lope de Vega. 339 pp. Wisconsin, F. O. Reed, 1924.

The critical edition is based on Lope's *Parte 13* (Madrid, 1620, in BNM) with variants from a *suelta* (Madrid, 1620, in British Library) and from *Parte 13* (Barcelona, 1620, in BNM). (According to D. McGrady's edition, Lope de Vega, *La francesilla* [Charlottesville: Biblioteca Siglo de Oro, 1981] 60.)

754. PIANCA, ALVIN HUGO. A Paleographic and Annotated Edition of Lope de Vega's *Don Lope de Cardona.* iv+517 pp. Wisconsin, M. Singleton, 1961. *DA* 21: 3790.

The text is based on MS 17417 in the Biblioteca Nacional (Madrid), which has been collated with Cotarelo y Mori's version (1917), published by the Spanish Academy. (Abs.)

755. PICERNO, RICHARD ANGELO. Lope de Vega's *Lo que pasa en una tarde:* A Critical, Annotated Edition of the Autograph Manuscript. vii+265 pp. Connecticut, J. Romo-Arregui, 1969. *DAI* 30A: 3473.

The writer has collated his reading of the autograph with the four known printed editions—namely, those of D. K. Petrov, E. Cotarelo y Mori, E. Juliá Martínez, and Madre Merrill. (Abs.)

❖ Title as is. Chapel Hill: U of North Carolina P, 1971. 190 pp. (UNCSRLL 105.)

756. PLONKEY, KENNETH DALE. Translations of Three Plays by Lope de Vega: *La moza de cántaro, El acero de Madrid,* and *Por la puente, Juana,* with an Investigation of Their Dramatic Form. 431 pp. Southern Illinois, C. H. Moe, 1968. *DA* 29A: 3715.

The translator classifies "these plays as *comedias de capa y espada* and clarifies the form of this genre for better understanding by English language audiences." (Abs.)

757. POESSE, WALTER. The Internal Line-Structure of Twenty-Seven Autograph Plays of Lope de Vega. 223 pp. CA/Berkeley, S. G. Morley, 1940. PFE, 7 May 1940.

"The immediate object of the dissertation is to present in as convenient a form as possible a rather detailed analysis of Lope de Vega's practice with regard to the inner structure of Spanish verse, i.e., diphthongization and bisyllabism within the word and synalepha and hiatus between words." (PFE)

❖ [A] *The Internal Line-Structure of Thirty Autograph Plays of Lope de Vega.* Bloomington: Indiana UP, 1949. 106 pp. (Indiana University Publications. Humanities ser. 18.) [B] Rpt. New York: Haskell, 1973. 106 pp.

758. PORTUONDO, AUGUSTO A. Diez comedias atribuidas a Lope de Vega: Estudio de su autenticidad. 229 pp. Virginia, D. McGrady, 1974. *DAI* 35A: 3763.

"The present dissertation examines the authenticity of ten plays attributed to Lope. Nine of these works are considered by S. G. Morley and C. Bruerton *(Cronología de las comedias de Lope de Vega)* to be doubtful, and one *(¿De cuándo acá nos vino?)* they regard as authentic. We conclude that seven of these plays *(La aldehuela y el gran prior, Los cautivos de Argel, La ilustre fregona, El jardín de Vargas, Los milagros del desprecio, El príncipe don Carlos* and *La selva confusa)* are not by Lope. Furthermore, we reject the attribution to him of the second act of *¿De cuándo acá?* We ratify the ascription to Lope of *La esclava de su galán* and *Porfiar hasta morir.* In our study we use principally the objective criteria enumerated above, although some subjective judgments are also offered. The most useful criteria were found to be orthoepy and rhyme, although some use was made of vocabulary, verb forms and names." (Abs.)

❖ Title as is. Charlottesville: Biblioteca Siglo de Oro, 1980. 191 pp. (Biblioteca Siglo de Oro 3.)

759. POTEET-BUSSARD, LAVONNE C. The Impostor-Braggart Archetype in the Early Theater of Lope de Vega. 559 pp. Bryn Mawr, W. F. King, 1977.

"The present study examines a total of thirty-one impostor-braggarts within the context of the thirteen plays in which they appear. An even clearer understanding of Lope's versatility and creativity in using this type is achieved by a detailed analysis of the impostor-braggarts in two specific plays—*La ingratitud vengada* and *El rufián Castrucho*." (Diss.)

❖ [A] "*La ingratitud vengada* and *La Dorotea:* Cervantes and *La ingratitud*." *HR* 48 (1980): 347–60. [B] "Algunas perspectivas sobre la primera época del teatro de Lope de Vega." *Lope de Vega y los orígenes del teatro español: Actas del primer congreso internacional sobre Lope de Vega.* Ed. Manuel Criado de Val. Madrid: EDI-6, 1981. 341–54. [C] "Deconstructing Traditional Types: Creative Characterization in Lope de Vega's Early Theater: The Case of *El rufián Castrucho*." *Proceedings of the Fifth Annual Golden Age Drama Symposium (Texto y espectáculo), El Paso, 1985.* Ed. Jean S. Chittenden, Richard Ford, and Arturo Pérez-Pisonero. San Antonio: Trinity Univ., Dept. of Foreign Languages (1987 for 1985). 36–46.

760. POWERS, PERRY JOHN. The Concept of the City-State in the Dramas of Lope de Vega. 337 pp. Johns Hopkins, L. Spitzer, 1947.

The concept of the city "as an entity which possesses a distinct personality and which acts with one will" is examined in "the major historical plays of Lope de Vega and one play attributed to him *(Estrella de Sevilla)*." (Diss.)

761. PRIMORAC, BERISLAV. An Annotated Edition of *El Antecristo* Attributed to Lope de Vega. iii+247 pp. Michigan, E. Glaser and J. Durand, 1974. *DAI* 35A: 2952.

The text is based on the Parma manuscript and Menéndez y Pelayo's Academy edition. The present edition "does not pretend to resolve the problem of authorship, but rather examines the play as part of a long series of artistic works on one of the most intriguing subjects in the Judeo-Christian tradition." (Abs.)

❖ [A] "Lope de Vega's *El Antecristo*." *RJ* 33 (1983): 293–310. [See p. 293, n. 1 for a discussion of the spellings *Anticristo* and *Antecristo*.] [B] "Las luchas literarias y el estreno de *El Anticristo* de Alarcón." *El escritor y la escena: Actas del primer congreso de la Asociación Internacional de Teatro Español y Novohispano de los Siglos de Oro, Ciudad Juárez, 1992.* Ed. Ysla Campbell. Ciudad Juárez: Universidad Autónoma de Ciudad Juárez, 1993. 167–75.

762. QUIROGA, ALEX ROLANDO. *Los comendadores de Córdoba* de Lope de Vega Carpio: A Critical Edition with Introductory Study. xii+ 188 pp. Boston Univ., J. H. Hoddie, 1976. *DAI* 36A: 7463–64.

This text is based on the *princeps* of 1609. (Abs.)

❖ Vega, L. de. Los comendadores de Córdoba *de Lope de Vega Carpio.* Critical ed. and introd. study by A. R. Quiroga. La Paz: Urquizo, 1985. 209 pp.

763. REESE, LOWELL GRANT. Lope de Vega and Shakespeare: A Comparative Study of Tragicomic Style. 186 pp. WA/Seattle, F. W. Jones, 1962. *DA* 24: 285–86.

The writer bases his investigation on a comedy, a tragedy, and a tragicomedy of each dramatist. The Shakespearean works are *As You Like It, Othello,* and *The Winter's Tale;* the Lopean plays are *La dama boba, El castigo sin venganza,* and *Peribáñez.* (Abs.)

❖ "Cervantes and Shakespeare: A Comparative Study." *Proceedings of the Pacific Northwest Conference on Foreign Languages: Fifteenth Annual Meeting, Montana State University, 1964.* Bozeman: Montana State Univ., 1964. 67–73.

764. REID, CHARLES GORDON, JR. The Problem of Social Inequality in Love and Marriage as Presented in the Theater of Lope de Vega. 149 pp. Virginia, 1941. Virginia *Abstracts* (1941): 32–34.

The principal topics discussed are indicated by the chapter titles: "Equality of Rank Considered as Preferable for Love," "Equality of Rank Considered as Irrelevant in Love," "Love versus Marriage," and "The Attitude toward Social Inequality in Marriage." (Diss.)

765. RETZ, MYRA ESTHER. The Sources of Jean Rotrou's Plays from

L'Hercule mourant to *Les Sosies* (1634–1635 or 1637). xii+354 pp. Southern California, L. M. Riddle, 1931.

Lope de Vega's *La fuerza lastimosa* is an important source of Rotrou's *L'Innocente infidélité*.

766. Reynolds, Kay Bissell. The Dramatic Function of the Supernatural in Non-religious *Comedias* by Lope de Vega. iv+181 pp. Connecticut, G. Rosado, 1971. *DAI* 32A: 452.

"In this dissertation an analysis of non-religious *comedias* by Lope is undertaken with a view to interpreting the dramatic function of the supernatural in them. To achieve this end, a thematic framework consisting of the distinctions of historical, novelesque, mythological and legendary *comedias* is used. In the historical category are: *Las Paces de los Reyes, El Marqués de las Navas, El Príncipe Perfecto I, La Imperial de Otón, La Santa Liga, Los Españoles en Flandes, La Nueva Victoria del Marqués de Santa Cruz,* and *El Duque de Viseo*. Novelesque *comedias* studied are *Don Juan de Castro I* and *II, El Ganso de Oro, El Premio de la Hermosura* and *Castelvines y Monteses*. There is one mythological *comedia* examined, *Las Justas de Tebas,* and one legendary play, *El Caballero de Olmedo*. The prevalent supernatural manifestation in the plays is the ghostly figure, frequently depicted by Lope as a *sombra* or as a *difunto,* with *sombra* the more popular choice of the two." (Abs.)

767. Roaten, Darnell Higgins. An Explanation of the Forms of Three Serious Spanish Baroque Dramas according to Wölfflin's *Principles of Art History*. 129 pp. Michigan, F. Sánchez y Escribano, 1951. *DA* 11: 687–88.

[For the complete entry, see no. 158.] One of the dramas studied is Lope's *Fuenteovejuna*.

768. Roselló, Carlos Gabriel. The Form and Meaning of Lope de Vega's Prose Fiction. iv+444 pp. Columbia, K.-L. Selig, 1981. *DAI* 42A: 241.

"Viewed as 'novelle,' Lope's novelistic production emerges as highly imaginative renditions of autobiographical experiences. Considering that the historically factual substratum of these works engenders the substance of tragi-comedy, and further attendant to the extant relationship of the Lopean 'comedia' to the 'novelle,' the author's prose fiction compositions are shown to be directly linked to his drama. Lope's novelistic writings, it is hence demonstrated, are typically governed by the same precepts that preside over his 'comedia.'" (Abs.)

769. ROSS, CECILIA. Lope de Vega, *La hermosa Ester:* An Edition with an Introduction and Notes. 295 pp. CA/Berkeley, J. F. Montesinos, 1952. PFE, 11 June 1952.

"There is only one manuscript of our play. It is the Lopean autograph, now in the British Museum dated at Madrid, April 5, 1610, of which the Library of the University of California possesses a photostat copy." The latter copy has been the base text for this dissertation. (Diss.)

770. ROVNER, PHILIP. Lope de Vega on Kingship. v+329 pp. Maryland, F. Goodwyn, 1958. *DA* 20: 307.

"Lope de Vega's political precepts as found in more than one hundred plays form an *ars gubernandi* which is analyzed in connection with piety, justice, evidence, *razón de estado,* punishments, rewards, largess, the royal word, the *corte,* the *campo,* the natural analogy, depersonalization, political origins, secular and spiritual powers, and divine right." (Abs.)

771. RUIZ-ASCARZA, MANUEL. Edición crítica y anotada de *El trato de la corte y ferias de Madrid* de Lope de Vega. viii+524 pp. Virginia, D. McGrady, 1974. *DAI* 34A: 7720.

The writer sees this play, "popularly known as *Las ferias de Madrid,*" as a parody of conjugal honor. The edition is based on an unedited manuscript copy dated in Granada, 1589, which is collated with Cotarelo's Spanish Academy edition. (Abs.)

772. RUIZ-ASCARZA, MARILYN MARIE. An Examination of Objective Methods for Determining *Comedia* Authorship, Together with Case Studies of Eight Plays Attributed to Lope de Vega. iii+334 pp. Virginia, D. McGrady, 1975. *DAI* 36A: 2203.

"As a step towards establishing a definitive canon of Lope's theater, we apply the criteria of orthoepy, vocabulary and rhyme to eight plays of doubtful attribution. We expose numerous deviations from Lope's norm in *La estrella de Sevilla,* previously rejected by Morley and Bruerton on the basis of strophic patterns. We repudiate the legitimacy of six plays for which the versification analysis alone proved inconclusive: *Las dos bandoleras, La fianza satisfecha, La honra por la mujer, El ingrato, La mejor enamorada* and *Ver y no creer.* Finally, we dismiss the attribution to Lope of *El sastre del campillo,* a play omitted from the Morley-Bruerton study." (Abs.)

773. SACKS, DIANE. Breaking the Silence: An Archetypal and Feminist Analysis of *La hermosa Ester, Fuente Ovejuna,* and *La mal casada.* 158 pp. Utah, C. R. Morrow, 1989. *DAI* 50A: 1677.

"In the three plays of Lope de Vega chosen for analysis, the female protagonist acts in a manner that is congruent with the powerful female archetype, and can be termed a female hero. Each female hero takes risks, is aggressive, and negotiates or fights her way to a victorious conclusion. In contrast with the codes of conduct for women of the seventeenth century that proclaimed that a woman's proper course was service to her husband or service to her God, Laurencia of *Fuente Ovejuna* and Ester of *La hermosa Ester* courageously decide to risk their lives to save their people from destruction. . . . In contrast, the quest of Lucrecia, the protagonist of *La mal casada,* is purely personal." (Abs.)

774. SCORDILIS, MARINA. Adaptation as Literary Creation: The Poetics of Adaptation in Lope de Vega's *Comedias* Based on Bandellian Models. v+233 pp. Princeton, A. Forcione and R. E. Surtz, 1978. *DAI* 38A: 7368–69.

The writer examines in detail the following *comedias: El castigo sin venganza, El mayordomo de la Duquesa de Amalfi, Castelvines y Monteses, Si no vieran las mujeres,* and *La mayor victoria.* In addition, she studies Lope's concepts of the *novella* and the *comedia* as he explains them in his *Novelas a Marcia Leonarda.* (Abs.)

❖ [A] Brownlee, Marina S. "Belleforest's *Histoire Tragique II,* 19 as Model for Lope's *El mayordomo de la Duquesa de Amalfi:* A Note on the Poetics of Adaptation." CH 3 (1981): 17–20. [B] Brownlee, Marina S. *The Poetics of Literary Theory: Lope de Vega's* Novelas a Marcia Leonarda *and Their Cervantine Context.* Potomac: Studia Humanitatis; Madrid: Porrúa Turanzas, 1981. 182 pp. [Sec. 2 of ch. 1 is entitled "*Novella* and *Comedia,*" and sec. 1 of ch. 4 bears the title "Generic Interpretation of *Novela* and *Comedia:* Their Cervantine Context."] [C] Brownlee, Marina S. "Lope's Conception of Literary Theory: The Example of the *Novelas.*" *KRQ* 30.2 (1983): 149–57.

775. SCOTT, ANTOINETTE ESTÉVEZ. Estudiantes y letrados en las obras dramáticas de Lope de Vega, Tirso de Molina, y Juan Ruiz de Alarcón. vii+239 pp. Florida State, D. L. Hoffman, 1974. *DAI* 35A: 3008.

[For the complete entry, see no. 587.]

776. SCUNGIO, RAYMOND LEWIS. A Study of Lope de Vega's Use of Italian *Novelle* as Source Material for His Plays, Together with a Critical Edition of the Autograph Manuscript of *La discordia en los casados.* viii+370 pp. Brown, W. L. Fichter, 1961. *DA* 27A: 186.

". . . it has been definitely demonstrated that Lope used *novelle* by Boccaccio, Bandello, and Giraldi Cintio as source material for as many as twenty-seven of his plays. An examination was made of these plays, considering their relationship to their sources." (Abs.)

777. SEARS, HELEN L. The Concepts of Fortune and Fate in the *Comedia* of Lope de Vega. 505 pp. CA/Los Angeles, E. H. Templin, 1950. This dissertation is no longer available at UCLA.

"Lope proclaims the doctrine of free will in all stages of his dramatic career, even when his practice seems to deny it. The fatalistic element in the plays can be theoretically reconciled with orthodoxy in various manners, but, in reality, a number of Lope's characters cannot act freely because of inevitable predestinations. In the latter part of his life, the dramatist seems to show a greater preoccupation with free will; and, in the last extant prophecy plays, he not only proclaims the doctrine, but consciously emphasizes the exercise of the will in practice." (AFE, 12 September 1949)

❖ Title as is. *BCom* 2.1 (1950): 1–3.

778. SEMINARIO, LEE ANNE DURHAM. The Black, the Moor and the Jew in the *Comedia* of Lope de Vega (1609–c. 1625). viii+245 pp. Florida State, D. L. Hoffman, 1974. *DAI* 35A: 3008–09.

"[Lope] adds the spice of his rollicking sense of humor with which he entices the audience into joining in the laughter with the personages on the scene, thereby mollifying ancient prejudices in the cleansing and purifying act of laughing." (Abs.)

❖ *The History of the Blacks, the Jews, and the Moors in Spain.* Madrid: Playor, 1975. 112 pp.

779. Seymour, Consuelo Willard. Popular Elements and the Idea of Justice in the *Comedias* of Lope de Vega. xvi+309 pp. Stanford, A. M. Espinosa, 1953. *DA* 13: 813–14.

"Lope de Vega champions the ideals of the Spanish people, and reveals his complete accord with their sentiments, desires, prejudices, and outlook on life; his work shows the blending of Lope's personality and the tastes of the Spanish people." (Abs.)

780. Shannon, Robert M. Visions of the New World in the Drama of Lope de Vega. 369 pp. Bryn Mawr, W. F. King, 1984. *DAI* 46A: 439.

The writer examines Lope's *comedias El Nuevo Mundo descubierto por Cristóbal Colón, Arauco domado,* and *El Brasil restituido.* "I have appended plot summaries of all known Golden Age plays which treat the discovery of America." (Abs.)

❖ [A] Title as is. New York: Peter Lang, 1989. 204 pp. [B] "The Staging of America in Golden Age Theater: Scenery, Costumes, Special Effects." *Looking at the* Comedia *in the Year of the Quincentennial: Proceedings of the 1992 Symposium on Golden Age Drama, El Paso.* Ed. Barbara Mujica and Sharon D. Voros. Lanham: UP of America, 1993. 53–66. [Apropos *El Nuevo Mundo descubierto por Cristóbal Colón* by Lope and *La aurora en Copacabana* by Calderón.] [C] "Historicity and Universal Truth: Lope de Vega's American and Flemish Plays." *Texto y espectáculo: Proceedings of the Thirteenth International Golden Age Spanish Theatre Symposium, El Paso, 1993.* Ed. José Luis Suárez García. York: Spanish Literature Publications, 1995. 84–90.

781. Sheppard, Douglas Claire. A Critical and Annotated Edition of Lope de Vega's *El villano en su rincón.* lxxv+196 pp. Wisconsin, E. W. Hesse, 1955. *DA* 16: 341–42.

The text is based on the *princeps* (1617), which has been collated with eight later editions. (Abs.)

782. Shopmaker, Stanton Neuhart. An Analysis and Edition of Lope de Vega's *Porfiar hasta morir.* iv+236 pp. Southern California, J. D. Smith, 1973. *DAI* 34A: 740.

The text is based on the *princeps* of 1638. "Macías, the hero, is studied as a historical, literary and legendary figure." (Abs.)

783. Silverman, Joseph H. Lope de Vega's *Figura del Donaire:* Defini-

tion and Description. xxviii+748 pp. Southern California, M. A. Morínigo, 1955. USC *Abstracts of Dissertations* (1955): 102–03.

"Using Lope de Vega's 314 authentic *comedias* as a basis, this dissertation seeks to present a working definition of the *figura del donaire* and an analysis of his role. . . . He is defined as a servant who is often, but not always, on stage with a gentleman master, usually the *comedia's* protagonist. . . . The present study, which provides a complete catalogue of Lope's *figuras del donaire,* prepares the way for hermeneutical and comparative analyses of the character." (Abs.)

❖ [A] "El gracioso de Juan Ruiz de Alarcón y el concepto de la figura del donaire tradicional." *H* [AATSP] 35 (1952): 64–69. [B] "Lope de Vega's Last Years and His Final Play: The Greatest Virtue of a King." *TQ* 6 (1963): 174–87. [For a more complete list of this scholar's publications, see *Hispanic Studies in Honor of Joseph H. Silverman,* ed. Joseph V. Ricapito (Newark: Juan de la Cuesta, 1988) xv–xxxiv.]

784. SOLENNI, GINO DE. Lope de Vega's *El Brasil restituido,* Together with a Study of Patriotism in His Theater. cxli+161 pp. Columbia, F. de Onís, 1929. {New York: Instituto de las Españas en los Estados Unidos, 1929. 303 pp.}

The edition is based on the autograph MS (1625), at the New York Public Library, which has been collated with the Academy edition (1902). (Diss.)

❖ "The Source of Lope de Vega's *El Brasil restituído.*" *REHa* 1 (1928): 168–69.

785. STALEY, GRANT B. The Eucharist in Its Symbolic Manifestations in Selected *Autos Sacramentales* of Lope de Vega. 221 pp. Utah, C. R. Morrow, 1980. *DAI* 41A: 2632–33.

"Although some critics maintain that Lope treats the Sacrament very lightly, if at all, in his *autos,* this study has as its object to prove that they are abundant in Eucharistic imagery and symbolism. Biblical, historical and mythological references often relate to events or ideas which have Eucharistic connotations within the context of the *auto.*" (Abs.)

❖ "Pagan Mythology as Eucharistic Vehicle in an *Auto Sacramental* of Lope de Vega." *Selected Proceedings of the Thirty-Ninth Annual*

Mountain Interstate Foreign Language Conference, 1989. Ed. Sixto E. Torres and S. Carl King. Clemson: Clemson UP, 1991. 83–89.

786. STEPHENSON, ROBERT CLARENCE. Miguel Sánchez: A Contemporary Terentian Influence upon Lope de Vega. iv+373 pp. Texas, 1930.

[For the complete entry, see no. 597.]

787. STEVENS, CHARLES HENRY. Lope de Vega's *El palacio confuso,* Together with a Study of the Menaechmi Theme in Spanish Literature. xcii+138 pp. NYU, H. C. Heaton, 1938. {New York: Instituto de las Españas en los Estados Unidos, 1939. xcii+138 pp.}

"The play has come down to us with its authorship in question and its date of composition undetermined. The purpose of this study, therefore, is (1) to present a critical edition of the play, . . . (2) to discuss the matter of authorship and date of composition, and (3) to show the relationship of the play to the Menaechmi theme as it descended in Spanish literature." (Prt. Diss.) Editorial note: This play has been attributed to Mira de Amescua and to Lope de Vega. For a discussion, see Castañeda, *Mira de Amescua* 103–05.

788. STROUD, MATTHEW DAVID. A Phenomenological Study of *Anagnorisis* in Selected Theatrical Works of Lope de Vega. vi+200 pp. Southern California, J. A. Parr, 1977. *DAI* 38A: 6160–61.

"Eleven plays were selected because of their variety of subject matter and uses of recognition, divided for convenience into the traditional categories of tragedy *(Peribáñez y el comendador de Ocaña, El castigo sin venganza, El médico de su honra,* and *El caballero de Olmedo),* comedy *(El castigo del discreto, El perro del hortelano, La dama boba,* and *El villano en su rincón),* and religious drama including two *autos (El viaje del alma* and *La Maya)* and a martyr play which also contains a play within a play *(Lo fingido verdadero).*" (Abs.)

❖ "Social-Comic *Anagnorisis* in [Calderón's] *La dama duende.*" *BCom* 29.2 (1977): 96–102.

789. STROUT, LILIA DAPAZ. Psicomaquia y hierogamia en *Las paces de los reyes y judía de Toledo* de Lope de Vega. v+332 pp. Kentucky, W. C. McCrary, 1973. *DAI* 34A: 5205–06.

"This dissertation contradicts the traditional interpretation about *Las paces de los reyes y judía de Toledo* of Lope de Vega. A profound analysis of this play was achieved by using modern theories about psychoanalysis, archetypes and myths. It is our opinion that this play exemplifies a very personal artistic creation, in which the author offers his version of the archetype of the Great Mother and an intimate intuition of several myths, particularly those of Orpheus and Narcissus. . . . The soul of Lope can be perceived through the character of Alfonso, who acts as a mask or *persona* for the author." (Abs.)

❖ [A] "Alfonso VIII como *persona* de Lope en *Las paces de los reyes y judía de Toledo*." *Studies in Language and Literature: Proceedings of the Twenty-Third Mountain Interstate Foreign Language Conference.* Ed. Charles Nelson. Richmond: Eastern Kentucky Univ., 1976. 481-88. [B] Dapaz Strout, Lilia. "El proceso de individuación en *Las paces de los reyes y judía de Toledo:* El amor y el rol de lo femenino." *Lope de Vega y los orígenes del teatro español: Actas del primer congreso internacional sobre Lope de Vega.* Ed. Manuel Criado de Val. Madrid: EDI-6, 1981. 485-90. [C] Dapaz Strout, Lilia. "Psicomaquia o el conflicto de Eros y Logos en *Las paces de los reyes y judía de Toledo*." *Studies in Honor of William C. McCrary.* Ed. Robert L. Fiore, Everett W. Hesse, John E. Keller, and José A. Madrigal. Lincoln: Univ. of Nebraska, Soc. of Spanish and Spanish-American Studies, 1986. 77-90.

790. SWISLOCKI, MARSHA HELENE. Lope, the *Romancero* and the *Comedia.* vi+239 pp. Harvard, S. Gilman, 1976.

"In the following pages I will, for the most part, be concerned with the dramatic function of the *romances* in several different types of plays, and with the relationship between the two genres—ballad and play—as it is perceived by Lope and expressed in the context of the *comedia*." (Diss.)

❖ [A] "Ballad Formation in the Plays of Lope de Vega." *El romancero hoy: Historia, comparatismo, bibliografía crítica.* Ed. Antonio Sánchez Romeralo, Diego Catalán, and Samuel Armistead. Madrid: Gredos, 1979. 63-73. [B] "On the *Romancero* in *Peribáñez: La esposa fiel* and *La adúltera*." *REHc* 9 (1982): 233-40. [C] "El romance de *La adúltera* en algunas obras dramáticas de Lope de

Vega: Pretextos, intertextos y contextos." *BHS* 63 (1986): 213-23. [D] "Oralidad y recepción: La comedia lopesca." *EdO* 12 (1993): 321-31. [E] "Romancero y comedia lopesca: Formación de una consciencia histórica en la España áurea." *Estado actual de los estudios sobre el Siglo de Oro: Actas del segundo congreso internacional de hispanistas del Siglo de Oro, Salamanca y Valladolid, 1990.* Ed. Manuel García Martín, Ignacio Arellano, Javier Blasco, and Marc Vitse. 2 vols. Salamanca: Universidad de Salamanca, 1993. 2: 977-85. [F] "Lope de Vega entre romancero y comedia: *El conde Fernán González.*" *Mira de Amescua en candelero: Actas del congreso internacional sobre Mira de Amescua y el teatro español del siglo XVII, Granada, 1994.* Ed. Agustín de la Granja and Juan Antonio Martínez Berbel. 2 vols. Granada: Universidad de Granada, 1996. 2: 497-506.

791. TAYLOR, KAREN LYNN. Lope de Vega's Persona in *La hermosura de Angélica, La Dragontea* and *El Isidro.* iii+220 pp. Harvard, S. Gilman, 1981.

"... in these poetic narratives, a center of focus is produced by the presence of the author's persona, who recounts and emotes over incidents in Lope's biography and who participates in some of the great artistic debates of the day." (Diss.)

792. TREACY, MARY JANE. An Approach to the Structure of Lope de Vega's Comedies (1585-1610). xiii+445 pp. Boston Univ., J. H. Hoddie, 1979. *DAI* 39A: 7372.

"The twenty-two comedies included in this study seem to be quite similar; however, an examination of their plots reveals notable changes in Lope's concept of comedy: from farce to ritual which leads to social renewal." (Abs.)

793. TRUEBLOOD, ALAN STUBBS. Substance and Form in *La Dorotea:* A Study in Lope's Artistic Use of Personal Experience. vi+355 pp. Harvard, A. Alonso and J. Marichal, 1951.

"My aim is to reach a fuller understanding of Lope's creative processes, and signally of the meaning of *La Dorotea,* by examining the interaction of substance with form, *historia* or *Erlebnis* with *poiesis,* in the artistic products of the experience. . . . [The underlying assumption of such a study is] an unusual proximity between the spheres of personal history and artistic creation in

Lope, and unusual ease in the passage from experience to art. I shall seek . . . to explore the character and consequences of this intimate symbiosis." (1974 ed.) Both versions, 1951 and 1974, contain specifically dramatic material—e.g., in both formats the writer deals with Lope's *comedia Belardo el furioso* in chapter 5.

❖ [A] "The Case for an Early *Dorotea:* A Reexamination." *PMLA* 71 (1956): 755-98. [B] "Espacio, tiempo y género en la *Dorotea.*" *NRFH* 11 (1957): 189-93. [C] "The *Officina* of Ravisius Textor in Lope de Vega's *Dorotea.*" *HR* 26 (1958): 135-41. [D] "Plato's *Symposium* and Ficino's Commentary in Lope de Vega's *Dorotea.*" *MLN* 73 (1958): 506-14. [E] "Role-Playing and the Sense of Illusion in Lope de Vega." *HR* 32 (1964): 305-18. [In *La Dorotea* and elsewhere.] [F] "'Al son de los arroyuelos': Texture and Context in a Lyric of *La Dorotea.*" *Homenaje a Rodríguez-Moñino: Estudios de erudición que le ofrecen sus amigos o discípulos hispanistas norteamericanos.* 2 vols. Madrid: Castalia, 1966. 2: 277-87. [G] "Masters and Servants: *La Dorotea* vis-à-vis the *Comedia.*" *KRQ* 16 (1969): 55-61. [H] "Lope's *A mis soledades voy* Reconsidered." *Homenaje a William L. Fichter: Estudios sobre el teatro antiguo hispánico y otros ensayos.* Ed. A. David Kossoff and José Amor y Vázquez. Madrid: Castalia, 1971. 713-24. [In *La Dorotea.*] [I] *Experience and Artistic Expression in Lope de Vega: The Making of* La Dorotea. Cambridge: Harvard UP, 1974. 785 pp. [J] Vega, L. de. *La Dorotea.* Trans. and ed. A. S. Trueblood and E. Honig. Cambridge: Harvard UP, 1985. 343 pp.

794. Tyler, Richard Willis. Lope de Vega's *La corona de Hungría:* A Critical Edition, with an Introductory Study of the Treatments of the *Reina Sevilla* Legend in the Theatre of Lope de Vega. 198 pp. Brown, W. L. Fichter, 1946.

"The text that I followed was a photostat of the autograph MS (Madrid, 1623). . . . I also compared the autograph with the printed text in the 'new' Spanish Academy edition (*Acad. N.*), vol. II, and with *Los pleitos de Ingalaterra* (*Acad. N.,* VIII), from which Lope took many lines and the basic plot of *La corona.*" (Personal letter from R. W. Tyler)

❖ [A] "Otra mirada a dos comedias de Lope de Vega: *La corona de Hungría* y *Los pleitos de Inglaterra.*" *Hispanófila* 18 (1963): 21-

75. [B] "False Accusation of Women in 'Plays Probably by Lope' de Vega." *BCom* 17.2 (1965): 13–15. [Apropos the *Reina Sevilla* theme.] [C] "Algunas versiones de la leyenda de la 'Reina Sevilla' en la primera mitad del Siglo de Oro." *Actas del segundo congreso internacional de hispanistas, Nijmegen, 1965.* Ed. Jaime Sánchez Romeralo and Norbert Poulussen. Nijmegen, Netherlands: Univ. Nijmegen, 1967. 635–41. [D] "False Accusation of Women in the Plays of Tirso de Molina." *KRQ* 16 (1969): 119–23. [E] "Algunos aspectos técnicos de la acusación falsa en Lope de Vega." *Homenaje a William L. Fichter: Estudios sobre el teatro antiguo hispánico y otros ensayos.* Ed. A. David Kossoff and José Amor y Vázquez. Madrid: Castalia, 1971. 725–33. [Apropos the *Reina Sevilla* theme.] [F] Vega, L. de. *A Critical Edition of Lope de Vega's* La corona de Hungría. Ed. R. W. Tyler. Chapel Hill: Univ. of North Carolina, Dept. of Romance Languages; Madrid: Castalia, 1972. 311 pp. (Estudios de Hispanófila 20.)

795. UMPIERRE, GUSTAVO. The Dramatic Function of the Songs in the Plays of Lope de Vega. iii+152 pp. NYU, F. Ayala, 1966. *DA* 27A: 3884.

"More than one hundred of Lope's plays with songs are examined and the diverse dramatic functions of each song have been grouped into nine related categories dealing with author, characters, plot, themes, dramatic action, mood, atmosphere, time, and place." (Abs.)

❖ *Songs in the Plays of Lope de Vega: A Study of Their Dramatic Function.* London: Tamesis, 1975. 110 pp.

796. VÉLEZ-QUIÑONES, HARRY. La celestinesca, la comedia y *La Dorotea:* Huellas de un intertexto. 338 pp. Harvard, F. Márquez Villanueva, 1990. *DAI* 51A: 4143.

"Throughout Lope de Vega's very prolific literary career celestinesque traits are a constant presence. This influence and the trail of 'anxieties' it left behind in Lope's works constitute a unique case in the history of Spanish letters. My dissertation examines the development and significance of this unusual intertextual relationship in a corpus of approximately one hundred of Lope de Vega's *comedias,* or plays, and his *acción en prosa, La Dorotea.* I show that in 'misreading' Rojas' work and its tradition, the *celestinesca,* Lope exploits in an original manner all the different possibilities of imitation. In *La Dorotea,* his final and most elaborate celestinesque work, Lope moves closer to the model and in so doing transcends it." (Abs.)

❖ "Cruel and Pathetic Dissonance: The Grotesque and the Celestinas." *REHb* 29.1 (1995): 51-72. [Discusses *Tragedia Policiana* by Sebastián Fernández, *Tercera parte de la Celestina* by Gaspar Gómez de Toledo, and *Segunda Celestina* by Feliciano de Silva.]

797. VILLAREJO, OSCAR MILTON. Lope de Vega and the Elizabethan and Jacobean Drama. ix+406 pp. Columbia, M. J. Valency, 1953. *DA* 13: 816-17.

The writer points out resemblances between certain Lopean plays and certain Elizabethan and Jacobean plays that appear to have been written later. He is usually cautious, however, about claiming that a given Spanish play in necessarily the direct source of a given English play. For example, he states that "Marlowe might have seen Lope's *El Gran Tamorlán* of 1583 in print when the former composed his *Tamburlaine the Great, Part 1* (limits, 1587-1588)." (Abs.)

❖ [A] "Revisión de las listas de *El Peregrino* de Lope de Vega." *RFE* 46 (1963; publ. 1965): 343-99. [The writer suggests that Shakespeare, at the time of writing *Romeo and Juliet,* could have known Lope's *Castelvines y Monteses.*] [B] "Shakespeare's *Romeo and Juliet:* Its Spanish Source." *ShS* 20 (1967): 95-105. [Lope's *Castelvines y Monteses* is proposed.] [C] "Shakespeare y los dramaturgos compañeros suyos: Las fuentes españolas de varias de sus obras." *RABM* 78 (1975): 829-67.

798. WADLEY, DONALD RAY. Lope de Vega and the Elizabethans. 219 pp. Colorado, M. T. Cobin, 1977. *DAI* 38A: 3811.

"Lope de Vega was a lauded dramatist around the world when Elizabethan drama was still in its infancy. This research strongly suggests that mere coincidence does not account for the similarity between Elizabethan and Spanish Golden Age drama. On the contrary, it suggests the need to explore quite seriously the possibility that Spanish playwrights, Lope de Vega specifically, had an influence on the nature of English drama during the Age of Elizabeth." (Abs.)

❖ "Lope and Shakespeare." *TAH* 4.32–33 (1979): 13–19.

799. WATTS, LECLAIRE BARNETT. The Clown: A Comparison of the Comic Figures of Lope de Vega and William Shakespeare. iv+377 pp. Connecticut, J. H. Arjona, 1966. *DA* 27A: 4270.

This study is based on "the Shakespearian characters listed as 'Clown' and the *graciosos* from twenty-five of the Lopista *comedias*." (Abs.)

800. WHALEN, EDNA SOFÍA. Edición crítica del *Arauco domado* de Lope de Vega. vii+288 pp. Iowa, O. Fernández, 1972. *DAI* 33A: 6888.

"La edición de Juan González de 1625, cotejada con otro ejemplar del mismo año, con cinco reimpresiones del siglo diez y siete y dos ediciones modernas, se usó como base de comparación y verificación del texto." (Abs.)

801. WHATLEY, FRANCES. The Life of the *Dama* in Lope de Vega. xiii+272 pp. Illinois, H. R. Kahane and A. Hamilton, 1947. Abstract: Urbana, 1947. 10 pp.

"The purpose of this thesis is to portray the life of the Spanish woman of the Golden Age of Spanish literature as it is depicted in the plays of Lope Félix de Vega Carpio. The discussion is centered on the life of the *dama,* the name applied to a woman of the noble class and the *haute bourgeoisie,* for the action of the plays, generally speaking, centers on these two classes of society." The writer bases her analysis exclusively on the autograph *comedias* of Lope. (Abs.)

802. WILDS, BONNIE. A Critical Edition of *El animal profeta,* with an Introduction and Notes. iii+168 pp. Pittsburgh, J. S. Herrero, 1973. *DAI* 35A: 1069.

[For the complete entry, see no. 515.] The writer ascribes this play to Mira de Amescua, not to Lope de Vega.

803. WILLIAMS, JEANELLE SHIVAR. *The Bastard Mudarra:* An English Translation. 136 pp. South Carolina, I. J. Levy, 1976. *DAI* 37A: 4341.

"[This translation] is as nearly a literal rendition of the Spanish play as penned by the dramatist as can be achieved while attempting at the same time to capture the spirit and intuitive meaning of its language." (Abs.)

804. WOOLDRIDGE, JOHN BEVERLY, JR. A Study and Critical Edition of Lope de Vega's *El amor enamorado.* 400 pp. Maryland, E. W. Hesse, 1974. *DAI* 35A: 3779.

The basis for this edition is the *princeps* (1637), which has been collated with the texts of 1669, 1777, and 1895. (Abs.)

❖ [A] "The Theme of Love in Lope de Vega's *El amor enamorado.*" *BCom* 27.2 (1975): 101–08. [B] Title as is. Madrid: Porrúa Turanzas, 1978. 236 pp. (Studia Humanitatis 4.) [C] "Toward a Bibliography of Publications on Editing *Comedia* Texts." *Editing the* Comedia II: Ed. Michael McGaha and Frank P. Casa. Ann Arbor: Univ. of Michigan, Dept. of Romance Languages, 1991. 157–62. (Michigan Romance Studies 11.)

805. WRIGHT, LELAND DUANE, JR. Lope de Vega's *Amor, pleito y desafío:* A Critical, Annotated Edition of the Autograph Manuscript. xi+286 pp. Washington/St. Louis, A. Ramírez, 1970. *DAI* 31A: 6078.

"Recorded in separate footnotes are the variant readings found in the two previous printings of the play in the *Colección de libros españoles raros o curiosos* (1873), and in the new Royal Academy edition of Lope de Vega's works (volume X, 1931)." (Abs.)

806. ZIOMEK, HENRYK. A Paleographic Edition of Lope de Vega's Autograph Play *La nueua victoria de D. Gonzalo de Córdoua.* 260 pp. Minnesota, R. L. Grismer, 1961. *DA* 22: 568.

The MS (dated 1622) has been collated with the following printed versions: 1637 (ed. Joseph de Villena), 1641 (ed. Pedro Verges), 1777 (ed. Antonio de Sancha), and 1902 (ed. Menéndez Pelayo). (Abs.)

❖ Vega, L. de. *A Paleographic Edition of Lope de Vega's Autograph Play* La nueua victoria de D. Gonzalo de Córdoua. Ed. H. Ziomek. New York: Hispanic Inst. in the United States, 1962. 211 pp.

807. ZUCKERMAN, ALIX SARA. Honor Reconsidered: Lope de Vega's Treatment of Honor in His Conjugal Honor Plays. 313 pp. CUNY, A. A. Sicroff, 1979. *DAI* 40A: 893.

"Careful examination of these plays thus reveals that Lope's conjugal honor plays are far more complex and far less conventional in their treatment of honor than they are generally thought to be." (Abs.)

❖ [A] "Honor Reconsidered: *Los comendadores de Córdoba.*" *JHP* 4 (1979): 59-75. [B] Zuckerman-Ingber, A. El bien más alto: *A Reconsideration of Lope de Vega's Honor Plays.* Gainesville: UP of Florida, 1984. 203 pp. (University of Florida Monographs. Humanities 56.)

Vélez de Guevara, Luis (1579-1644)

808. Ashcom, Benjamin Bowles. Luis Vélez de Guevara's *El gran Iorge Castrioto y Príncipe Escanderbey:* A Critical Edition, with Introduction and Notes. iv+312 pp. Michigan, 1937.

The only copy listed in OCLC is a carbon copy at Wayne State University Library. According to an OCLC annotation, the critical text is based on the 1634 edition (*Parte veinte y ocho de comedias de varios autores,* Huesca: Blusón), "with revisions from the 1679 printing" *(Comedias nuevas, escogidas . . . Parte quarenta y cinco).* For a commentary, see Hauer, *Vélez de Guevara* no. 18.

❖ *A Descriptive Catalogue of the Spanish* Comedias Sueltas *in the Wayne State University Library and the Private Library of Professor B. B. Ashcom.* Detroit: Wayne State Univ. Library, 1965. 103 pp.

809. Berndt, Robert John. A Qualitative Analysis of the Versification of Selected *Comedias* of Luis Vélez de Guevara. 305 pp. Case Western Reserve, R. Cardona, 1956. Western Reserve *Abstracts* (1954-56): 99-100.

The plays analyzed are *La serrana de la Vera, El conde don Pero Vélez, El rey en su imaginación, El águila del agua, Reinar después de morir, El caballero del sol,* and *El príncipe viñador.* The writer observes that Vélez "made a conscious effort to adapt the verse form to the subject matter or the thought expressed in specific scenes." (Abs.)

810. Bianco, Frank J. A Critical Edition with Notes and Analysis of Luis Vélez de Guevara's *Más pesa el rey que la sangre.* ii+225 pp. Pittsburgh, G. Sobejano, 1973. *DAI* 34A: 6625.

"In presenting the text, every attempt has been made to preserve the Sedó *suelta,* considered to be the oldest extant text." (Abs.)

❖ Vélez de Guevara, L. *Más pesa el rey que la sangre.* Critical ed., with notes and analysis, by F. J. Bianco. Barcelona: Puvill, 1979. 180 pp. (Biblioteca universitaria Puvill 3. Textos literarios 4.)

811. BININGER, ROBERT JEFFERS. A Critical Edition, with Introduction and Notes, of Vélez de Guevara's *El conde don Sancho Niño.* lxxxv+167 pp. Ohio State, C. E. Anibal and R. C. Rozzell, 1955. *DA* 16: 533–34.

"The text . . . is based upon a photostatic copy of a single *suelta* printing preserved in the Palatinate Library of Parma, a copy of which also exists in the Bibliothèque Nationale in Paris." (Abs.)

❖ Vélez de Guevara, L. El conde don Sancho Niño*: Edición con introducción y notas.* Ed. R. J. Bininger and Ricardo L. Landeira. Vigo: Faro de Vigo, 1970. 145 pp.

812. ENDRES, VALERIE FLORENCE. The Aesthetic Treatment of *Romancero* Material in the *Comedias* of Luis Vélez de Guevara. 188 pp. Arizona, W. M. Whitby, 1966. *DA* 27A: 2150–51.

"In this study a chapter is devoted to each of the twelve *comedias* of Vélez that incorporate the greatest amount of *Romancero* material." (Abs.)

813. ESPINOSA, HILMA MARÍA. Personajes femeninos en veinticinco comedias de Luis Vélez de Guevara. viii+262 pp. New Mexico, A. Rodríguez, 1990.

"Each play studied is provided with a short historical bibliography, a brief summary of the plot and the analysis of its feminine characters. . . . the conclusion reveals that the dramatist was indeed interested in the plight of the women in a predominantly masculine society." (Abs.)

814. HAUER, MARY GARRETT. Luis Vélez de Guevara: A Critical Bibliography. 217 pp. Louisiana State, F. A. de Armas, 1971. *DAI* 32A: 6929–30.

"Baena, Pellicer, and Vélez himself state that the dramatist composed four hundred *comedias.* Less than one hundred are known today and they have not been assembled to provide a collection of the *obras* of Luis Vélez de Guevara. . . . The bibliography . . . contains two hundred eighty-three entries listed in alphabetical order under the name of the critic." (Abs.)

❖ [A] Title as is. Chapel Hill: Univ. of North Carolina, Dept. of Romance Languages, 1975. 183 pp. (UNCSRLL. Texts, Textual Studies, and Translations 5.) [B] "An Addendum to *Luis Vélez de Guevara: A Critical Bibliography*." *Antigüedad y actualidad de Luis Vélez de Guevara: Estudios críticos*. Ed. C. G. Peale et al. Philadelphia: Benjamins, 1983. 254–98. (PUMRL 10.)

815. Hernández-Chiroldes, Rita Denise Cobián. Nueva interpretación de los problemas políticos y sociales en el teatro de Luis Vélez de Guevara. vi+387 pp. Texas, S. Zimic, 1981. *DAI* 42A: 4841.

This study centers on the following five *comedias: La serrana de la Vera, Más pesa el rey que la sangre, La niña de Gómez Arias, La luna de la sierra,* and *Reinar después de morir.* "Contrary to the conclusions of other critics, our analysis shows that Vélez de Guevara does not follow the prevailing conventions of the Baroque theater with respect to the monarchical system and the social establishment. . . . A similar critical attitude toward society and monarchical absolutism can be evidenced in our brief study of more than forty other plays written by Vélez de Guevara at different periods of his life." (Abs.)

816. Iglesias, Diane Margaret. Edición crítica y análisis de *Atila, azote de Dios,* de Luis Vélez de Guevara. vi+405 pp. CUNY, H. E. Bergman, 1979. *DAI* 40A: 2717.

The edition is based on three eighteenth-century *sueltas*. (Abs.)

817. Kirk, Charles Frederick. A Critical Edition, with Introduction and Notes, of Luis Vélez de Guevara's *Virtudes vencen señales*. xcv+255 pp. Ohio State, R. C. Rozzell, 1957. *DA* 17: 2268.

"The text of *Virtudes* which is offered is a collation of the two extant texts: [a *suelta* (n.p., n.d.) and the edition printed in *Parte treinta y dos, con doze comedias de diferentes autores* (Zaragoza: Diego Dormer, 1640)]." (Abs.)

818. Olmsted, Richard Hubbell. A Critical Study of the Autographed Manuscript of the Play *El conde don Pero Vélez y don Sancho el deseado* of Luis Vélez de Guevara. v+289 pp. Minnesota, R. L. Grismer, 1934.

The edition is based on a photostatic copy of the autograph manuscript owned by the Biblioteca Nacional in Madrid. (Diss.)

❖ Vélez de Guevara, L. El conde don Pero Vélez y don Sancho el deseado: *Comedia en tres actos.* Critical ed. by R. H. Olmsted. Minneapolis: U of Minnesota P, 1944. 189 pp.

819. Rambo, James Stone. An Annotated Critical Edition of *También tiene el sol menguante,* by Luis Vélez de Guevara and Francisco de Rojas Zorrilla. viii+424 pp. New Mexico, R. R. MacCurdy, 1972. *DAI* 33A: 2948.

[For the complete entry, see no. 555.]

820. Reas, Marjorie Virginia. Three Thematically Similar Plays Attributed to Luis Vélez de Guevara, Together with a Critical Annotated Edition of *La obligación a las mvgeres.* iii+324 pp. Wayne State, B. B. Ashcom, 1968. *DAI* 32A: 452.

The three plays are *La obligación a las mujeres, Cumplir dos obligaciones,* and *Cumplir dos obligaciones y Duquesa de Saxonia.* The writer concludes that "all three plays are by the hand of Luis Vélez de Guevara." The critical edition is based on the text in the seventeenth-century collection known as *Escogidas.* (Abs.)

821. Reichenberger, Arnold Gottfried. Luis Vélez de Guevara, *El embuste acreditado y el disparate creído:* A Critical Edition with Introduction and Notes. 289 pp. Ohio State, C. E. Anibal, 1947. Ohio State *Abstracts* 52 (1947): 249–54.

"This edition is on the whole based on the two texts incorporated in the great drama collection known as the *Comedias Escogidas.* . . . In addition to the two *Escogidas* texts, there have been used two copies of the *suelta* edition . . . [found in the British Library]." (Abs.) Editorial note: For an attribution of this play to Juan de Zabaleta, see M. G. Profeti, "L. Vélez de Guevara e l'esercizio ecdotico," *QLL* 5 (1980): 49–94 (esp. pp. 60–63).

❖ [A] Vélez de Guevara, L. *El embuste acreditado.* Ed. A. G. Reichenberger. Granada: Universidad de Granada, 1956. 364 pp. (Colección filológica 12.) [B] "Currency Inflation Reflected in Luis Vélez de Guevara's *El embuste acreditado.*" *MLN* 76 (1961): 34–35. [C] "Editing Spanish *Comedias* of the XVIIth Century: History and Present-Day Practice." *Editing the* Comedia. Ed. Frank P. Casa and Michael D. McGaha. Ann Arbor: Univ. of Michigan, Dept. of Romance Languages, 1985. 1–23. (Michigan Romance Studies 5.) [Originally published in *Editing Renaissance*

Dramatic Texts: English, Italian and Spanish. Ed. Anne Lancashire. New York: Garland, 1976.] [For a more complete list of this scholar's publications, see José Regueiro and Gail Geiver, "Publications of Arnold G. Reichenberger," *HR* 41 (1973): 143–50.]

822. ROSEN, HAROLD EARL. A Critical Edition, with Introduction and Notes, of Vélez de Guevara's *El amor en vizcaíno, los celos en francés y torneos de Navarra*. lxxi+175 pp. Oregon, P. J. Powers, 1966. *DA* 27A: 3062.

"The text of the play has been based on a microfilm copy of the printed edition of 1662. . . . Xerox copies of eighteenth-century *sueltas* have been compared and variations in text indicated in the notes; the same procedure was used with the manuscript copy of the play, in the Biblioteca Nacional in Madrid." (Abs.)

823. ROZZELL, RAMON CONRAD. Luis Vélez de Guevara, *La niña de Gómez Arias:* A Critical Edition with Introduction and Notes. 286 pp. Ohio State, W. S. Hendrix, 1947. Ohio State *Abstracts* 54 (1948): 313–18.

The edition is based on the British Library *suelta* with the call number 1728.h.7. (14), which has been collated with another British Library *suelta* with the call number 11728.g.3. (Abs.)

❖ [A] "The Song and Legend of Gómez Arias." *HR* 20 (1952): 91–107. [B] Vélez de Guevara, L. La niña de Gómez Arias: *Edición, introducción y notas*. Ed. R. Rozzell. Granada: Universidad de Granada, 1959. 289 pp. (Colección filológica 16.)

824. SÁNCHEZ, ROBERTO. Luis Vélez de Guevara: *El negro del Seraphin:* A Critical and Annotated Edition with Introduction. vii+309 pp. Florida State, D. L. Hoffman, 1979. *DAI* 40A: 3345.

The text is based on MS 17317 in the BN, Madrid. "Ten published variants of *El negro del Seraphin,* published as *El negro del mejor amo* and attributed to Antonio Mira de Amescua, were minutely examined." (Abs.)

825. SPENCER, FORREST EUGENE. Luis Vélez de Guevara: A Study in His Life and Dramatic Art. CA/Berkeley, R. Schevill, 1919.

There is a 60-page typed abstract of the dissertation in the Berkeley library; however, the original dissertation is no longer available.

❖ Spencer, Forrest E., and Rudolph Schevill. *The Dramatic Works of Luis Vélez de Guevara: Their Plots, Sources, and Bibliography.* Berkeley: U of California P, 1937. xxvi+387 pp. (UCPMP 19.) [Ninety-four *comedias* are included.]

826. Van Kerk, John William. The Figure of Don Carlos in Selected Plays of the Spanish Golden Age. vii+166 pp. Georgia, H. Ziomek, 1978. *DAI* 39A: 4312.

[For the complete entry, see no. 188.] One of the works analyzed is *El águila del agua* by Luis Vélez de Guevara. (Abs.)

Vergara, Hipólito de (fl. late 16th c. to early 17th c.)

827. Iscla Rovira, Luis, SJ. Una edición crítica de *La Virgen de los reyes* de Hipólito de Vergara cotejada con *La Reina de los reyes* de Tirso de Molina. 299 pp. Northwestern, F. G. Very, 1973. *DAI* 34A: 5927-28.

The edition of the *La Virgen de los reyes* is based on the *princeps* (Osuna, 1629), which is collated with *La Reina de los reyes* in Tirso's *Segunda parte* (Madrid, 1635) and in Cotarelo's edition in the NBAE. (Prt. Diss.)

❖ [A] *Hipólito de Vergara, autor de* La Reina de los reyes *de Tirso de Molina: Estudio y edición crítica anotada de* La Virgen de los reyes. Madrid: CSIC, Instituto Enrique Flórez, 1975. 281 pp. [B] "Contribución al esclarecimiento bibliográfico de la *Segunda parte* de Tirso de Molina." *BCom* 27.2 (1975): 108-17; also *Segismundo* 14.27-32 (1980): 145-62.

Vicente, Gil (Portugal. 1460?-1536?)

828. Andrews, James Richard. The Artistry of the Plays of Gil Vicente. vi+205 pp. Princeton, A. Castro and R. S. Willis, 1953. *DA* 14: 116-17.

"Throughout his theater his preoccupation with 'pacíficas concordanças' constantly directs the expressive impulse, creating lyrical dialogue devoid of conflictive tensions. By constantly avoiding a clash of opposing forces, his adramatic intent presents animated lyrical narratives, in which a chronological progression of events, without teleological, dynamic action, develops within an integrating coalescing structure." (Abs.)

❖ "The Harmonizing Perspective of Gil Vicente." *BCom* 11.2 (1959): 1–5.

829. Carvalho, Ilka Valle de. Estrutura e "Mensagem" de *Inês Pereira.* xii+194 pp. CA/Santa Barbara, E. Martínez-López, 1981. *DAI* 43A: 2360.

"In general, this investigation proposes to demonstrate the structural regularity and formal design that makes *Inês Pereira* the greatest of Gil Vicente's technical achievements, without neglecting, on the other hand, the play's ironic underlying significance or 'message.'" (Abs.)

❖ "A linguagem sólida de *Inês Pereira.*" *QP* 9–10 (1981): 109–43.

830. Clemente, Alice Rodrigues. The Allegories of Gil Vicente. 188 pp. Brown, A. S. Trueblood, 1967. *DA* 28A: 3138.

"After considering the basic themes and techniques of Vicente's allegories, this thesis studies the *autos* as theater." (Abs.)

❖ "*Comédia sobre a Divisa da Cidade de Coimbra:* Fantasía caballeresca." *Homenaje a William L. Fichter: Estudios sobre el teatro antiguo hispánico y otros ensayos.* Ed. A. David Kossoff and José Amor y Vázquez. Madrid: Castalia, 1971. 161–74.

831. Garay, René Pedro. Concept and Structure of the Vicentine Comedy. xiii+331 pp. Vanderbilt, J. R. Andrews, 1984. *DAI* 45A: 3633–34.

"In his *Comédia de Rubena* (1521) and *Comédia do Viúvo* (1524?), Vicente withdraws from the dramatic techniques of the medieval past and formulates a new dramatic genre which will contribute to other subsequent perspectives on drama in the Iberian Peninsula. *Mestre* Gil evolves a concept of *comédia* which is structurally more significant to later manifestations of comic forms than his earlier *autos.* A careful analysis of the two *comédias* will help uncover Vicente's contribution to the *comédia* form as well as to the enrichment of the Iberian theatrical tradition." (Abs.)

❖ *Gil Vicente and the Development of the* Comedia. Chapel Hill: U of North Carolina P, 1988. 220 pp. (UNCSRLL 232.)

832. HAMILTON, HOPE. The Farces of Gil Vicente: A Study in the Stylistics of Satire. 187 pp. Colorado, R. B. Kite, 1974. *DAI* 35A: 7866.

The writer's analysis is based on *Farsa dos Físicos, Quem Tem Farelos?, Auto de Inês Pereira, O Juiz da Beira,* and *Romagem de Agravados.* (Abs.)

❖ Faria, Hope Hamilton. Title as is. Madrid: Playor, 1976. 138 pp.

833. JOINER, IDA VIRGINIA. The Dramatic Art of Gil Vicente. v+241 pp. Texas, L. Casís, 1940.

The writer presents a general analysis of Vicente's plays and of his contributions to the development of Spanish drama. She discusses the dramatist's life as well as the structure, language, styles, versification, and themes of his plays. (Diss.)

❖ Joiner, I. V., and Eunice Joiner Gates. "Proverbs in the Works of Gil Vicente." *PMLA* 57 (1942): 57–73.

834. LUNARDINI, PETER JOHN. The Poetic Technique of Gil Vicente. 151 pp. New Mexico, A. R. Lopes, 1953.

The dissertation is divided into two parts: part 1, "Versification of Gil Vicente" and part 2, "Lyricism of Gil Vicente." (Diss.)

835. MCGINNISS, CHERYL FOLKINS. La danza literaria como símbolo de metamorfosis: Empleo y sentido en el teatro de Juan del Encina y Gil Vicente. 119 pp. Case Western Reserve, D. M. Carey, 1977. *DAI* 38A: 1437.

"[The literary dance] repeatedly defines and clarifies those metamorphoses of characterization, scene, or of inner experience which otherwise would not be readily apparent." (Abs.)

❖ "The Dance, a Metamorphic Symbol in Gil Vicente's *Auto de la sibila Casandra.*" *HR* 52.2 (1984): 163–68.

836. MOSELEY, WILLIAM WHATLEY. An Etymological Vocabulary of the Spanish in the Works of Gil Vicente. xxx+655 pp. New Mexico, R. M. Duncan, 1954. *DA* 15: 119–20.

"The primary purpose of this dissertation is to provide . . . a complete Spanish-English vocabulary, with etyma, embracing the drama and lesser works of Gil Vicente. . . . The vocabulary contains some five thousand entries." (Abs.)

❖ [A] "Portugal and the Vision of Empire in Gil Vicente."

Interdisciplinary Essays 3 (1973): 21–23. [B] "'O Rei do Mar': Portugal, the Sea, and Gil Vicente." *LBR* 11.1 (1974): 98–104. [C] *A Concordance to the Spanish in the Complete Works of Gil Vicente.* Ann Arbor: Monograph Ser., Xerox Univ. Microfilms, 1977. 2 vols. (1,001 pp.)

837. RAMSAY, EIZABETH GRACE. A Computer-Assisted Literary Analysis of the *Barcas* of Gil Vicente. ix+264 pp. Catholic, J. M. Solà-Solé, 1984. *DAI* 45A: 3655.

"The analysis undertaken in this study has made it possible to express in quantitative terms much of what is already known about Vicente's style in Spanish and Portuguese. The Portuguese plays, the *Barca do Inferno* and the *Barca do Purgatório,* are written in a highly colloquial style as evidenced by a high frequency of words generally associated with conversational speech; a large proportion of concrete and domestic terms; a high use of verbs and adverbs; an insistence on short sentences; and, rapid exchanges between characters. On the other hand, the Spanish play, the *Barca da Glória,* reflects a more elevated and literary tone. Here, there is an abundance of abstract, psychological terms; an emphasis on nouns and, especially, adjectives; and, a general tendency for longer sentences with frequent coordination." (Abs.)

838. RANGEL-GUERRERO, DANIEL. Gil Vicente, *Comédia sobre a Divisa da Cidade de Coimbra,* con una introducción y notas. vi+129 pp. Oregon, P. J. Powers, 1967. *DA* 28A: 2219–20.

The base text is that of the *princeps,* 1562. "This 'comédia' is a court masque that reveals the author's indisputable comic genius and his ability to produce satire." (Abs.)

❖ [A] "Gil Vicente, *Comédia sobre a Divisa da Cidade de Coimbra:* Una interpretación." *Proceedings of the Pacific Northwest Conference on Foreign Languages.* Ed. Walker C. Kraft. Corvallis: Oregon State Univ., 1974. 40–44. [B] "La responsabilidad en la *Comédia de Rubena* [de Gil Vicente]." *Proceedings of the Pacific Northwest Conference on Foreign Languages.* Pullman: Washington State Univ., 1975. 154–58. [C] Vicente, G. *Comédia sobre a Divisa da Cidade de Coimbra.* Introd. and notes by D. Rangel-Guerrero. University: Romance Monographs, 1980. 82 pp. (Romance Monographs 38.)

839. RIGGIO, EDWARD ANTHONY. The Place of the Comic in the Theater of Gil Vicente. xvi+661 pp. Pittsburgh, R. Cardona, 1969. *DAI* 30A: 1572.

"Vicente is essentially a dramatic satirist: in nearly thirty of his plays the comic-satiric overshadows the lyric and devotional aspects of his art." (Abs.)

❖ "The Originality of Gil Vicente's *Maria Parda*." *JAPCS* 3.1–2 (1969): 44–55.

840. SMOLEN, MARIAN LEANNA. Bilingualism as Semiotic Code in the Theatrical Code Systems of the Theater of Gil Vicente. 173 pp. Arizona State, E. H. Friedman, 1990. *DAI* 51A: 2740.

"The works of Gil Vicente offer an unusual opportunity to study how a bilingual dramatist has integrated the use of two languages into a complex system of linguistic and nonlinguistic theatrical codes. . . . In each of the seven plays studied, the balance among these codes shifts to another configuration, so that as a group they offer a greater appreciation of the sophistication of this playwright's understanding of the possible modes of communication inherent to his chosen medium. In addition, in the study of these code systems one is led to many markers which offer clues to the form the performance text would be most likely to assume, clues which may otherwise be difficult to discover in texts nearly five hundred years old." (Abs.)

841. STATHATOS, CONSTANTINE CHRISTOPHER. A Critical Edition, with Introduction and Notes, of Gil Vicente's *Floresta de Enganos.* 193 pp. Oregon, T. R. Hart, 1970. *DAI* 31A: 3521.

"The present text of the play is based on that of the *Copilaçam de todalas obras de Gil Vicente* (Lisbon, 1562), as reproduced in the facsimile edition of the Biblioteca Nacional (Lisbon, 1928), and with a few modifications necessary to ensure better readability." (Abs.)

❖ [A] "Antecedents of Gil Vicente's *Floresta de Enganos.*" *LBR* 9.2 (1972): 87–95. [B] *A Critical Edition with Introduction and Notes of Gil Vicente's* Floresta de Enganos. Chapel Hill: U of North Carolina P, 1972. 138 pp. (UNCSRLL 125.) [C] "A Bibliography of Translations of Gil Vicente's Works since 1940." *Vórtice* 1.3 (1975): 83–88. [D] "Editions and Adaptations of Gil Vicente's Works (1942–1975)." *Segismundo* 12.23–24 (1976): 87–110. [E] "Anglo-

American Contributions to the Study of Gil Vicente: A Bibliography (1940–1975)." *Sillages* 5 (1977): 127–56. [F] "French Contributions to the Study of Gil Vicente: A Bibliography (1942–1975)." *LBR* 15 (1978): 105–16. [G] *A Gil Vicente Bibliography (1940–1975)*. London: Grant and Cutler, 1980. 132 pp. [H] "Supplement to *A Gil Vicente Bibliography (1940–1975)*." *Segismundo* 16.35–36 (1982): 2–25. [I] "Gil Vicente Studies [1976–1980]." *LBR* 20 (1983): 119–38. [J] "Gil Vicente Studies (1985–1990)." *LBR* 29.2 (1992): 99–111. [K] *A Gil Vicente Bibliography (1975–1995), with a Supplement for 1940–1975*. Bethlehem: Lehigh UP, 1997. 187 pp.

842. SUÁREZ, JOSÉ IGNACIO. Bakhtinian Theory and the Codification of Gil Vicente's Comic Modes. viii+245 pp. New Mexico, J. E. Tomlins, 1981.

"... the application of Bakhtin's critical theories to Gil Vicente has helped us to understand the genre and plot-compositional traits and sources of his drama." (Diss.)

❖ [A] "The 'Journey through Time and Space' in Gil Vicente's Drama." *DLit* 2.1 (1984): 31–39. [B] "A Menippean Continuator: The Tri-leveled Structure of Gil Vicente's *Trilogia das Barcas*." *MichA* 16.2 (1984): 179–85. [C] "The 'Scandalous' and the 'Eccentric' in Vicentine Playlets." *LangQ* 23.1–2 (1984): 42–44. [D] "Master Gil's 'Experimental Fantasticality': The Traditional Supernatural." *LangQ* 25.1–2 (1986): 28–30. [E] "The Variance of the Comic Element in Vicentine Drama." *Selected Proceedings of the Thirty-Fourth Annual Mountain Interstate Foreign Language Conference*. Ed. Eduardo Zayas-Bazán and Christa I. Hungate. [Johnson City]: East Tennessee State Univ., 1986. 157–68. [F] "The Vicentine Oxymoron within the Seriocomic Mode." *RomN* 28.2 (1987): 101–07. [G] "Moral-Psychological Abnormalities in Gil Vicente." *JEP* 9.1–2 (1988): 11–16. [H] *The Carnival Stage: Vicentine Comedy within the Serio-comic Mode*. Rutherford: Fairleigh Dickinson UP, 1993. 172 pp.

843. TOMLINS, JACK EDWARD. The Nature of Gil Vicente's Dramatic Artistry. x+127 pp. Princeton, R. S. Willis, 1957. *DA* 18: 238.

"This classification of the Vicentine drama as sacred, profane, and fantastic derives from the poet's view of the condition of conflictive man and augments the significance of [Vicente's] 1531 *Carta*. Gil Vicente is thereby viewed as thinker and playwright, organically united like the plays." (Abs.)

❖ [A] "Una nota sobre la clasificación de los dramas de Gil Vicente." *DHR* 3 (1964): 115–31; 4 (1965): 1–16. ["Este emplazamiento de la cosmogonía Vicentina al lado de los dramas pudiera también proporcionarnos una visión de unidad orgánica con relación a Gil Vicente, el hombre y el comediógrafo"—vol. 4 (1965): 16.] [B] "Toward an Aesthetic of Gil Vicente's Drama." *JAPCS* 2 (1968): 42–64.

VILLANUEVA, JERÓNIMO DE (17TH C.)

844. EWING, BOYD ROSS. *El villano gran señor y gran Tamorlán de Persia* by Rojas, Villanueva and Roa: Edited with an Introduction and Notes. cviii+151 pp. Cornell, 1932.

[For the complete entry, see no. 546.]

VIRUÉS, CRISTÓBAL DE (1550–1609)

845. ESTEVES, CARMEN C. The Dramatic Portrayal of Semíramis in Virués, Calderón and Voltaire. 179 pp. CUNY, F. J. Nichols, 1985. *DAI* 46A: 1271.

[For the complete entry, see no. 269.] The *comedia* by Virués is *La gran Semíramis*. (Abs.)

846. SARGENT, CECILIA VENNARD. A Study of the Dramatic Works of Cristóbal de Virués. 162 pp. Columbia, F. de Onís, 1930. {New York: Instituto de las Españas en los Estados Unidos, 1930. 162 pp.}

This dissertation consists of the following chapters: "Virués' Life and Works," "The Plays of Virués," and "Virués' Dramatic Art," plus an appendix. (Diss.)

847. VALLVÉ, GRACIELA. Los personajes femeninos en los dramas de Cristóbal de Virués. xi+187 pp. Emory, E. Navarro Kelley, 1978. *DAI* 39A: 2324.

"Sin mirar su sexo [Virués] les da [a las mujeres] el mismo

enfoque y presentación que a sus personajes masculinos, destacándose así entre los autores responsables de la introducción del tema feminista dentro del teatro español." (Abs.)

Zabaleta, Juan de (1610?-1670?)

848. Doty, George Lewis. Juan de Zabaleta, *El día de fiesta por la mañana:* A Critical Annotated Edition. xii+226 pp. Illinois, J. D. FitzGerald, 1925.

The edition is based on the *princeps* (1654).

❖ [A] "Juan de Zabaleta's *Día de fiesta por la mañana:* A Critical Annotated Edition." *RF* 41-42 (1928): 147-400. The introduction in the article includes a list of Zabaleta's dramatic works, pp. 151-52. (Prt. Diss.) [B] El día de fiesta por la tarde: *A Collated Annotated Edition.* Jena: Romanische Literatur, 1938. 182 pp. (Gesellschaft für romanische Literatur 50.) [This work includes the frequently quoted section entitled "La comedia." See J. M. Díez Borque's edition, Madrid: Cupsa, 1977. 13-36.]

Zamora, Antonio de (1664?-1728?)

849. González-Quevedo, Arnhilda Badía. Las comedias de Antonio de Zamora. iv+427 pp. North Carolina, S. A. Stoudemire, 1971. *DAI* 32A: 2641.

". . . in his plays [Zamora] continued the same structure of the Golden Age *Comedia,* influenced mainly by Lope de Vega, Tirso de Molina, Agustín Moreto as well as Calderón." (Abs.)

❖ "Antonio de Zamora: Su vida y sus obras." *Hispanófila* 57 (1976): 35-46.

Zárate y Castronovo, Fernando de (?-1660?)

(Antonio Enríquez Gómez)

850. Porras-Landeo, Juan. Una edición crítica del manuscrito *El noble siempre es valiente,* comedia de don Fernando de Zárate y

Castronovo. iii+395 pp. Wayne State, H. N. Bershas, 1976. *DAI* 37A: 2924.

"Until now no detailed study has been made of the poet and playwright Fernando de Zárate y Castronovo. In fact, his historicity has been questioned by a number of literary critics, such as I. S. Révah, who contended that Zárate did not exist and that the plays attributed to him were written by Antonio Enríquez Gómez under the pseudonym Fernando de Zárate. This writer has found substantial historical and bibliographical information on Fernando de Zárate y Castronovo, proving his existence and his authorship of the thirty-two plays attributed to him. Indeed, a comparative study of the plays of Zárate and Enríquez, emphasizing themes, historical and literary sources, style and characters, shows that the two authors are opposed in their religious, philosophical and political ideas. . . . The essential source of our critical edition is the holograph manuscript in the Biblioteca Nacional de Madrid, entitled *El noble siempre es valiente* (1660). However, we also discuss the typographic and orthographic irregularities in the variant texts of the play, those printed by Orga in 1774, by Quiroga in 1792, and by Serra y Centené in 1807, as well as the eighteenth-century manuscript called 'Holandesa.'" (Abs.) Editorial note: For a discussion of the polemic as to whether Zárate was a pseudonym of Enríquez Gómez, see Glen F. Dille, "Antonio Enríquez Gómez Alias Fernando de Zárate," *PLL* 14.1 (1978): 11–21.

Zayas y Sotomayor, María de (1590–1661?)

851. De García, Susan Paun. Love and Deceit in the Works of Doña María de Zayas y Sotomayor. 282 pp. Michigan, C. Fraker, 1987. *DAI* 48A: 406–07.

"The obsession with the portrayal of deceit is what sets Zayas apart from her peers. Love and deceit are fundamental to her work. The themes are present in her early poetry, her *comedia*, the *Novelas amorosas* and the *Desengaños amorosos*." (Abs.) Editorial note: Her *comedia* is entitled *La traición en la amistad*.

852. PLACE, EDWIN BRAY. A Study of the Works of Salas Barbadillo and María de Zayas. iv+415 pp. Harvard, J. D. M. Ford, 1919.

[For the complete entry, see no. 593.]

❖ *María de Zayas: An Outstanding Woman Short-Story Writer of Seventeenth-Century Spain*. Boulder: Univ. of Colorado, 1923. 65 pp. (University of Colorado Studies 13.1.)

853. SYLVANIA, LENA EVELYN VINCENT. Doña María de Zayas y Sotomayor: A Contribution to the Study of Her Works. Columbia, F. de Onís, 1922. {New York: Columbia UP, 1922. 52 pp. (Columbia University Studies in Romance Philology and Literature 31.)}

"On a subject as extensive as this, it has not been feasible to compress into these few pages more than the discovered facts about the author's life, her salient ideas as exposed in her works, a sketch of the general framework of her short stories, and a study of two of them in particular—*El jardín engañoso* and *El castigo de la miseria*." (Diss.)

❖ [A] Title as is. *RR* 13 (1922): 197–213; 14 (1923): 199–232. [B] Rpt. New York: AMS, 1966. [See pp. 46–50 on Juan de la Hoz y Mota's "dramatization" of María de Zayas's *novela El castigo de la miseria* in his *comedia* of the same title.]

NOTE

There are no numbers between 854 and 1000. The sequence of non-United States entries begins with number 1001 in order that United States and non-United States references can be differentiated with ease in the combined indexes.

NOTA

No hay números entre 854 y 1000. La numeración de las tesis fuera de los EE.UU. empieza con 1001 para facilitar la diferenciación entre las dos partes en los índices combinados.

Supplement

A Classified Checklist of Non-United States Doctoral Dissertations

Suplemento

Lista clasificada de tesis doctorales de varios otros países

General
Golden Age Culture, History, Art, and Related Subjects

1001. Abouaf, Sylvain. Contribution au vocabulaire du Siècle d'Or: Étude critique des *Phrases de hablar difíciles de la lengua española* de Jerónimo de Techeda (1629). lxx+635 pp. Paris/IV, 1982. (Thèse de 3e cycle)

1002. Alonso Cortés, Narciso. La Corte de Felipe III en Valladolid. 162 pp. Complutense, 1908.
❖ [A] *Noticias de una Corte literaria.* Valladolid: Nueva Pincia, 1906. 168 pp. [B] Title as is. Valladolid: Castellana, 1908. 68 pp. [Ch. 4, pp. 53–64, deals briefly with literary, artistic, and theatrical activities in Valladolid during the period 1600–06, in which Felipe III held court in that city. The writer comments: "En otro lugar he bosquejado el movimiento de las letras en este período (see publication A), y lo que aún tengo que decir será materia, según pienso, de una obra más extensa (see publication C.)" Among the writers who resided at that time in Valladolid were Quevedo, Cervantes, Góngora, Vélez de Guevara, and Salas Barbadillo.] [C] *El teatro en Valladolid.* Madrid: Revista Archivos, 1923. 428 pp. [Includes "Lista de comedias representadas en los siglos XVII y XVIII," pp. 284–413.] The volume had appeared earlier in serialized version in *BRAE* 4–10 (1917–23).

1003. Alonso Hernández, José Luis. Contribución al estudio del léxico de las clases marginales de la sociedad española del siglo XVI al XVIII. 487 pp. Salamanca, 1972.
❖ [A] "La sinonimia en el lenguaje marginal de los siglos XVI y XVII españoles (Los sinónimos de *delator, cornudo* y *ojo*)." *AO* 22 (1972): 305–49. [B] *Léxico del marginalismo del Siglo de Oro. (Lenguaje de las prostitutas, rufianes, valentones, tahures, fulleros, ladrones, estafadores y embusteros.)* Salamanca: Universidad de Salamanca, 1976. 801 pp. (Acta Salmanticensia 99.) [C] *El lenguaje de los maleantes españoles de los siglos XVI y XVII: La germanía. (Introducción al léxico del marginalismo español.)* Salamanca: Universidad

de Salamanca, 1979. 319 pp. (Acta Salmanticensia 108.) [D] "Símbolo, léxico y psicocrítica en la literatura clásica española." *Actas del sexto congreso internacional de hispanistas, Toronto, 1977*. Ed. Alan M. Gordon and Evelyn Rugg. Toronto: Univ. of Toronto, 1980. 44–50.

1004. BACAICOA SANZ, FRANCISCO. Lo vizcaíno en la literatura castellana. Complutense, 1952. Abstract in *RUM* 1.3 (1952): 447.

❖ [A] "Primera frase vasca impresa conocida en Torres Naharro." *BSVAP* 7 (1951): 41–48. [B] Anselmo de Legarda, Fray. Title as is. San Sebastián: Biblioteca Vascongada de los Amigos del País, 1953. 589 pp. Rev.: (a) R. Ricard. *BH* 56 (1954): 454–55; (b) F. Arocena. *BSVAP* 10 (1954): 109–10; (c) J. Simón Díaz. *RL* 8.16 (1955): 350.

1005. BARBAZZA, MARIE-CATHERINE. La Part du paysan: La Famille rurale en Nouvelle Castille aux seizième et dix-septième siècles. Montpellier/III, 1992. (Thèse d'État)

❖ [A] "Le Corps vêtu: Le Vêtement de la paysanne en Nouvelle Castille au tournant du XVIe et XVIIe siècles." *Le Corps dans la société espagnole des XVIe et XVIIe siècles: Colloque international, Sorbonne, 1988*. Ed. Augustin Redondo. Paris: Publications de la Sorbonne, 1990. 73–82. [B] Title as is. Lille: ANRT, 1992.

1006. BATAILLON, MARCEL. Érasme et l'Espagne: Recherches sur l'histoire spirituelle du XVIe siècle. Paris, 1937.

❖ [A] Title as is. Paris: Droz, 1937. 903 pp. "La question de l'influence d'Érasme sur le théâtre espagnol du temps de Charles-Quint [1516–58] comporte, à notre avis, la même solution négative." The writer argues against the supposed Erasmian influence on Gil Vicente, Torres Naharro, Diego Sánchez de Badajoz, and Sebastián de Horozco. However, in an addendum, Bataillon seems to accept the possibility of Erasmian influence in *Las cortes de la muerte* by Miguel de Carvajal and Luis Hurtado de Toledo. Concerning Cervantes, he says: "Nous voulions seulement replacer l'œuvre du plus grand écrivain de l'Espagne dans la perspective de l'érasmisme, montrer qu'elle y devient plus intelligible, et jouir une dernière fois du spectacle des idées érasmiennes à la faveur de cette apparition suprême, inespérée, qu'elles font dans les lettres espagnoles, tandis que le nom d'Érasme rentre dans l'obscurité." (1991 ed.) Rev.: (a) M. Delcourt. *HuRe* (1937): 326–31; (b) M. Bonnard. *BH* 40 (1938): 5–32; (c) V. Beltrán de Heredia. *CT* 57 (1938): 544–82; (d) I. S. Révah. *REJ* 103 (1938): 97–101; (e) A. Renaudet. *RHist* 182 (1938): 97–104; (f) L. Febvre. *AHSoc* 1 (1939): 28–42; (g) W. Krauss. *Archiv* 175 (1939): 76–89; (h) G. M. Bertini. *Convivium* 17 (1939): 79–93; (i) R. Schevill. *HR* 7 (1939): 93–116; (j) E. Garin. *LRin* 2 (1939): 737–45; (k) P. Mesnard. *RMed* 11 (1946): 57–77. [B] "Essai d'explication de l'*auto sacramental.*" *BH* 42 (1940): 193–212. [C] *Erasmo y España: Estudios sobre la historia espiritual del siglo XVI.* Trans. Antonio Alatorre. 2nd Spanish ed., rev. and enl. México and Buenos Aires: Fondo de Cultura Económica, 1966. 923 pp.+32 pl. Rev.: (a) V. Bozal. "Bataillon: Erasmo y España." *CHA* 215 (1967): 429–34; (b) M. Batllori. *AHSI* 37 (1968): 169–71; (c) F. Márquez Villanueva. *HR* 36 (1968): 264–70; (d) E. Asensio. *RO* 63 (1968): 302–19 [article entitled: "Los estudios sobre Erasmo, de Marcel Bataillon"]; (e) A. Redondo. *BH* 72 (1970): 190–94. [D] "Le *Torres Naharro* de Joseph E. Gillet." *RPh* 21 (1967): 143–70. [E] *Érasme et l'Espagne.* Text established by Daniel Devoto. Ed. Charles Amiel. New ed. Genève: Droz, 1991. 3 vols. (928+544+568 pp.) (Travaux d'Humanisme et Renaissance 250.) Vol. 1: Note préliminaire, Texte revu de l'édition de 1937. Vol. 2: Prologues, Notes additionnelles, Bibliographie. Vol. 3: Annexes (Études diverses de Marcel Bataillon sur Érasme et l'érasmisme), Bibliographie des travaux de Marcel Bataillon. Rev.: L. E. F. de Orduna. *Incipit* 12 (1992): 273–75. [F] Rpt. of publication C. Madrid: Fondo de Cultura Económica, 1995. [For a more complete list of this scholar's publications, see *Érasme et l'Espagne,* 1991 ed., 3: 517–61.]

1007. Baubeta, Patricia Anne Odber de. Church Discipline and Social Satire in Medieval Portugal. [8]+380 pp. Glasgow, 1989. *Aslib* 41.5 (1992): 1925. [Ch. 1 includes the works of Gil Vicente.]

❖ *Anticlerical Satire in Medieval Portuguese Literature.* Lewiston: Mellen P, 1992. 346 pp. [For some 24 references to Gil Vicente's *autos,* see the book's index under Gil Vicente (not Vicente, Gil). Several more such references are missing from the index.] Rev.: S. Parkinson. *BHS* 72.4 (1995): 422–23.

1008. BENNASSAR, BARTOLOMÉ. Valladolid au Siècle d'Or: Une Ville de Castille et sa campagne au XVIe siècle. Paris, 1967.

❖ [A] Title as is. Paris and La Haye: Mouton, 1967. 635 pp. [See esp. book 3, ch. 5, "Le spectacle permanent" (pp. 473–92) and ch. 7, "Les comportements" (pp. 531–55).] Rev.: J. Pérez. *BH* 70 (1968): 151–59. [B] *L'Homme espagnol: Attitudes et mentalités du XVIe au XIXe siècle.* Paris: Hachette, 1975. 252 pp. [C] *Los españoles: Actitud y mentalidad.* Barcelona: Argos, 1976. 286 pp. [D] *The Spanish Character: Attitudes and Mentalities from the 16th to the 19th Centuries.* Trans. and introd. Benjamin Keen. Berkeley: U of California P, 1979. 325 pp. [E] *Un Siècle d'Or espagnol: Vers 1525-vers 1648.* Paris: Laffont, 1982. 331 pp. [F] *Valladolid en el Siglo de Oro: Una ciudad de Castilla y su entorno agrario en el siglo XVI.* Trans. Francisca Aramburu Riera et al. Valladolid: Ayuntamiento, 1983. 586 pp. 2nd ed. Valladolid: Ámbito, 1989. 584 pp. [G] *La España del Siglo de Oro.* Trans. Pablo Bordonava. Barcelona: Crítica, 1983. 347 pp.

1009. BERGER, PHILIPPE. Livre et lecture à Valence à l'époque de la Renaissance. Bordeaux/III, 1983. (Thèse d'État)

❖ *Libro y lectura en la Valencia del Renacimiento.* Trans. Amparo Balanza Pérez. 2 vols. Valencia: Institució Alfons el Magnànim, 1987. 588 pp. Rev.: L. Rodríguez Cacho. *EdO* 7 (1988): 253–58. [". . . una gran parte del trabajo de Berger responde sencillamente a la cuestión de 'cómo se hacía un libro en el Siglo de Oro español.'"]

1010. BIGEARD, MARTINE. La Folie dans les lettres espagnoles (1500–1650). 361 pp. Paris, 1970. (Thèse de 3e cycle)

❖ *La Folie et les fous littéraires en Espagne 1500–1650.* Paris: Centre de Recherches Hispaniques, Institut d'Études Hispaniques, 1972. 188 pp. (Thèses, mémoires et travaux 18.) [Works cited include *comedias* by Calderón, Cervantes, Lope, Ruiz de Alarcón, and Valdivielso, as well as anonymous plays.]

1011. BLANCO UNZUÉ, RICARDO. Die Aufnahme der spanischen Literatur bei Friedrich Schlegel. Köln, 1981.

❖ Title as is. Frankfurt: Peter Lang, 1981. 557 pp. (Europäische Hochschulschriften 1. Deutsche Sprache und Literatur 430.)

1012. BOLZ, GUSTAV. Die spanischen Vorbilder P. Corneille's. Rostock, 1878.

❖ Title as is. Greifswald: Kunike, 1878. 40 pp. [The writer discusses, inter alia, Lope's *Amar sin saber a quién* and *El palacio confuso,* which has been attributed to Lope and to Mira de Amescua.]

1013. Bomli, Petronella Wilhelmina. La Femme dans l'Espagne du Siècle d'Or. Amsterdam, 1950.

❖ Title as is. 's Gravenhage: Nijhoff, 1950. 390 pp. Rev.: (a) G. Larrieu. *BH* 52.4 (1950): 408–09; (b) A. A. Parker. *BHS* 28.109 (1951): 62–64; (c) G.B. *Clavileño* 2.8 (1951): 70–71; (d) O. H. Green. *HR* 20 (1952): 255–57; (e) E. F. Jareño. *RIS* 10 (1952): 512–14; (f) K. L. Selig *H* [AATSP] 36 (1953): 127.

1014. Bravo Villasante, Carmen. La mujer vestida de hombre en la literatura española. 177 pp. Complutense, 1954.

❖ [A] *La mujer vestida de hombre en el teatro español, siglos XVI–XVII.* Madrid: Revista de Occidente, 1955. Rev.: (a) A. Carballo Picazo. *RFE* 39.1–4 (1955): 403–08; (b) M. Wilson. *BHS* 33.4 (1956): 235–36; (c) J. L. Cano. *Clavileño* 7.38 (1956): 75–76; (d) E. S. Speratti Piñero. *NRFH* 10.3–4 (1956): 441–42; (e) G. E. Wade. *BCom* 9.2 (1957): 19–20; (f) M. Alfaro. *IAL* 11 (1957): 28; (g) J. Campos. *Ínsula* 12.131 (1957): 8; (h) B. B. Ashcom. *HR* 28 (1960): 43–62; (i) M. Vanderstraeten. *LR* 16 (1962): 278–79. [B] 2nd ed. Madrid: Sociedad General Española de Librería, 1976. 191 pp. Rev.: M. Peña Muñoz. *EL* 624 (1977): 2998. [C] 3rd ed. Madrid: Mayo de Oro, 1988. 188 pp. [For a more complete list of this scholar's publications, see Manuel Peña Muñoz, *Bibliografía de Carmen Bravo-Villasante* (Madrid: Artes General Minerva, 1985) 67 pp.]

1015. Brisset Martín, Demetrio E. Representaciones rituales hispánicas de conquista. iv+893 pp. Complutense, 1988. (Colección tesis doctorales, no. 443/88.)

❖ *Fiestas de moros y cristianos en Granada.* Granada: Diputación Provincial, 1988. 193 pp. Rev.: M. S. Carrasco Urgoiti. *RDTP* 44 (1989): 349–50.

1016. Burchardt, Ursula. Die Formen des Sonetts in Spanien von den Anfängen bis zum Ende des *Siglo de Oro.* 128 pp. Berlin, 1948.

1017. Cabañas Martín, Pablo. El mito de Orfeo en la literatura española. 466 pp. Complutense, 1947.

❖ Title as is. Madrid: CSIC, Instituto Miguel de Cervantes, 1948. [Included in this study is an edition of Calderón's *auto* entitled *El divino Orfeo*.] Rev.: (a) J. M. Martínez Cachero. *AO* 9.53-54 (1948): 139-41; (b) J. García Nieto. *CL* 3 (1948): 317-19; (c) N. de L[iñán y] H[eredia] *RBD* 2 (1948): 449-53; (d) E. Pardo Canalís. *RIE* 6 (1948): 402-03; (e) J. Campos. *BBMP* 25 (1949): 384-87; (f) Ch. V. Aubrun *BH* 51.4 (1949): 447; (g) J. Delgado. *CHA* 8 (1949): 458-60; (h) D. Castro Villacañas. *Escorial* 58 (1949): 729-31; (i) P. O'Connor. *HR* 17 (1949): 182; (j) S. Gili Gaya. *NRFH* 3 (1949): 307-08; (k) M. S. Carrasco Urgoiti. *RHM* 16 (1950): 166; (l) A. Maniet. *LR* 5 (1951): 157-58.

1018. Caramés-Martínez, Xesús. La imagen de Galicia y los gallegos en la literatura castellana. Trier, 1990.

❖ Caramés Martínez, Xesús. *A imaxe de Galicia e os galegos na literatura castelá*. Vigo: Galaxia, 1993. 268 pp. (Coleccion ensaio e investigacion 19.)

1019. Cardaillac, Louis. Morisques et chrétiens: Un Affrontement polémique (1492-1640). Montpellier/III, 1973. (Thèse d'État)

❖ [A] Title as is. Paris: Klincksieck, 1977. 543 pp. [For theater references, see the book's index under the following names: Calderón, Cervantes, Pacheco (Don Rodrigo), Sánchez de Badajoz, Tirso, Vega.] Rev.: (a) A. Roig. *Arquivos* 11 (1977): 744-46; (b) J.-P. Galibert. *LLNL* 71.221 (1977): 126-27; (c) J. M. Laspéras. *CILH* 2-3 (1980): 504-05. [B] *Moriscos y cristianos: Un enfrentamiento polémico (1492-1640)*. Trans. Mercedes García Arenal. Madrid and México: Fondo de Cultura Económica, 1979. 567 pp. [C] "Les Morisques et leur langue." *CÉR* 16 (1990): 1-25. [D] "Le Vêtement des morisques." *Signes et marques du "convers" (Espagne XV*[ème]*-XVI*[ème] *siècles)*. Aix-en-Provence: Université de Provence, 1993. 15-30. (Études hispaniques 20.)

1020. Carrasco, Raphaël. État, sociétés et religion en Espagne au Siècle d'Or: Recherches sur les mécanismes du pouvoir. Montpellier/III, 1986. (Thèse d'État)

❖ *L'Espagne classique 1474-1814*. Paris: Hachette, 1992. 223 pp.

1021. Carreres [Carreras] y de Calatayud, Francisco de A. Las fiestas valencianas y su expresión poética en los siglos XVI-XVIII. 740 pp. Complutense, 1945.

❖ [A] "Lope de Rueda y Valencia." *ACCV* 7 (1946): 128–38. [B] "Notas para la biografía de Lorenzo Palmireno." *RBN* 7 (1946): 362–64. [C] Title as is. Madrid: CSIC, 1949. 495 pp.+17 pl. ["Desde el punto de vista literario, aparece en este siglo [XVII] la justa poética . . . y con las justas también solían representarse comedias." Among other theater references are lengthy quotations from Gaspar de Aguilar's *Comedia de la vida y muerte de San Luis Bertrán* (pp. 141–44). The plates include pictures of 24 seventeenth-century *carros triunfales (rocas)* of the type used in the staging of *autos sacramentales.*]

1022. Chauchadis, Claude. L'Honneur chez les moralistes du temps de Philippe II: Recherches sur le lexique, la morale et la société. 340 pp. Toulouse/II, 1980. (Thèse de 3e cycle)

❖ [A] "El honor, la religión y el mercader. Estudio comparativo de dos comedias de santos: *Fray diablo y el diablo predicador,* y el *Diablo predicador y mayor contrario amigo.*" *Criticón* 2 (1978): 1–17. [The first play is attributed to Lope de Vega; the second, to Luis Belmonte Bermúdez.] [B] "Risa y honra conyugal en los entremeses." *Risa y sociedad en el teatro español del Siglo de Oro: Actes du troisième colloque du GESTE, Toulouse, 1980.* Ed. Yves-René Fonquerne. Paris: CNRS, 1980. 165–85. [C] "'Honor' y 'Honra', o cómo se comete un error en lexicología." *Criticón* 17 (1982): 67–87. [D] *Honneur, morale et société dans l'Espagne de Philippe II.* Paris and Toulouse: CNRS, 1984. 249 pp. Rev.: (a) A. Gallego Barnés. *Criticón* 28 (1984): 181–87; (b) S. Gerhard and B. M. Damiani. *QIA* 8.59–60 (1985–86): 133–36; (c) J. A. Jones. *BHS* 64.2 (1987): 152–53. [E] "La moral del honor: El choque de las ortodoxias." *RAEPE* 36–37 (1989): 129–37.

1023. Chauchadis, Claude. La Loi du duel: Le Code du point d'honneur dans la société et la littérature espagnoles des XVI–XVII siècles. 702 pp. Toulouse/II, 1991. (Thèse d'État)

❖ [A] "Libro y leyes del duelo en el Siglo de Oro." *Criticón* 39 (1987): 77–113. [B] "Duel sémantique au Siècle d'Or: Desafío et Duelo." *Mélanges offerts à Maurice Molho.* Ed. Jean Claude Chevalier and M.-F. Delport. 3 vols. Paris: Éditions Hispaniques, [1987]–1988. 3: 69–82. [C] "Un Champ d'honneur: Le Champ clos." *Espaces.* Toulouse: Presses Universitaires du Mirail, 1988.

159–72. [D] "'La Loi du duel' et le savoir-vivre de l'homme d'honneur en Espagne au XVIIe siècle." *Savoir Vivre 1*. Ed. Alain Montandon. Meyzieu: Lyon Édition, 1990. 41–62. [E] "Las denuncias de la ley de duelo en *El postrer duelo de España:* Nuevo examen." *La comedia: Seminario hispano-francés organizado por la Casa de Velázquez, Madrid, 1991–1992*. Ed. Jean Canavaggio. Madrid: Casa de Velázquez, 1995. 381–96. (Collection de la Casa de Velázquez 48.) [F] *La Loi du duel. Le code du point d'honneur dans l'Espagne des XVIe–XVIIe siècles.* Toulouse: Presses Universitaires du Mirail, 1997. 520 pp. (Anejos de *Criticón* 8.)

1024. CHEVALIER, MAXIME. L'Arioste en Espagne (1530–1650): Recherches sur l'influence du *Roland furieux*. Bordeaux, 1966. (Thèse d'État)

❖ [A] Title as is. Bordeaux: Institut d'Études Ibériques et Ibéro-Américaines; Féret, [1966]. 539 pp. (Bibliothèque de l'École des Hautes Études Hispaniques 39.) [Pp. 405–38 are devoted to the *comedia*.] Rev.: F. Pierce. *BHS* 45 (1968): 52–55. [B] *Los temas ariostescos en el Romancero y en la poesía española del Siglo de Oro*. Madrid: Castalia, 1968. Rev.: J. G. Fucilla. *HR* 39 (1971): 448–50. [For a more complete list of this scholar's publications, see "Bibliographie des travaux de Maxime Chevalier," *BH* 92.1 (1990): i–x. Special issue entitled *Hommage à Maxime Chevalier.*]

1025. CLARE, LUCIEN. La Quintaine, la course de bague et le jeu des têtes: Étude historique et ethno-linguistique d'une famille de jeux équestres. Paris/IV, 1979. (Thèse d'État)

❖ [A] Title as is. Paris: CNRS, 1983. 266 pp. [On Spanish theater, see pp. 142–48, 153–54, 155–56.] Rev.: (a) P. J. Guinard. *BBMP* 61 (1985): 355–60; (b) P. Heugas. *BH* 87.1-2 (1985): 195–99. (c) M. S. Carrasco Urgoiti. *RFE* 65 (1985): 331–33. [B] "Les Courses de bague en Espagne au dix-septième siècle." *Problèmes, interférences des genres au théâtre et les fêtes en Europe*. Ed. Irène Mamczarz. Paris: Presses Universitaires de France, 1985. 27–62. [Apropos the spectacle known as *correr sortija,* references to which are found in Lope, Vélez de Guevara, Ruiz de Alarcón, Tirso, Moreto, and Calderón.] [C] "Trois compétitions sportives dans le Portugal ancien, d'aprés la *Comédia da pastora Alfea* de Simâo Machado (1601)." *Arquivos* 23 (1987): 611–33. Special issue entitled *Homenagem à Paul Teyssier.*

[D] "Une Fête dynastique à Grenade en 1658." *La fiesta, la ceremonia, el rito: Coloquio internacional, Granada, 1987*. Ed. Pierre Cordoba and Jean-Pierre Étienvre. Granada: Universidad de Granada-Casa de Velázquez, 1990. 21-42.

1026. CLEMENTE SAN ROMÁN, YOLANDA. Impresos madrileños de 1566 a 1625. Complutense, 1991.

❖ Title as is. Madrid: Editorial de la Universidad Complutense, 1992. 1,248+6 pp. (Colección tesis doctorales, no. 224/92.)

1027. DAVID-PEYRE, YVONNE. Le Personnage du médecin et la relation médecin-malade dans la littérature ibérique, XVIe et XVIIe siècles. 680 pp. Paris, 1970. (Thèse d'État)

❖ [A] Title as is. Lille: Université de Lille, Service de Reproduction des Thèses; Paris: Ediciones Hispano-Americanas, 1971. 515 pp. Rev.: A. Roig. *LLNL* 204 (1973): 96-99. [B] "Lope de Vega ante la mujer enferma." *PSA* 61 (1971): 117-39. [C] "*El amor médico:* Comedia documentée de Tirso de Molina." *Hommage des hispanistes français à Noël Salomon: Publié par les soins de la Société des Hispanistes Français*. Barcelona: Laia, 1979. 209-23. [D] "Coimbre dans *L'Amour médecin* de Tirso de Molina." *Les Cultures ibériques en devenir: Essais publiés en hommage à la mémoire de Marcel Bataillon, 1895-1977*. Paris: Fondation Singer-Polignac, 1979. 381-89. [E] "Les Remèdes et leur influence sur les esprits, ou du mauvais usage des médicaments." *LMS* 2 (1980): 117-41. [F] "Rêves, sommeil et insomnie dans la littérature ibérique du Siècle d'Or." *LMS* 3 (1981): 82-110. [G] *Medicinalia*. Nantes: Univ. de Nantes, 1983. 274 pp. [H] "Quelques maux féminins dans la littérature ibérique du Siècle d'Or." *TL* 14 (1987): 49-65.

1028. DAVID-PEYRE, YVONNE. La Peste et le mal vénérien dans la littérature ibérique du XVIe et du XVIIe siècle. 425 pp. Poitiers, 1967. (Thèse de 3e cycle)

❖ [A] "Un caso de observación clínica en Tirso de Molina." *Asclepio* 20 (1968): 221-33. [B] "La Peste et le mal vénérien dans la littérature portugaise du XVIe et du XVIIe siècles." *Arquivos* 1 (1969): 195-207; part 2. *Arquivos* 2 (1970): 404-33. [C] "Un Cas d'observation clinique chez Tirso de Molina." *LLNL* 4.199 (1971): 9-22.

1029. DELEITO Y PIÑUELA, JOSÉ. Estado de la sociedad española en tiempos de Felipe IV. Complutense, 1900.

❖ [A] Title as is. *RCont* 123 (1901): 275–92, 437–53, 713–33; 124 (1902): 27–52. [B] *La España de Felipe IV.* (Later entitled *La vida española en tiempos de Felipe IV.*) 7 vols. Vol. 1: *El declinar de la Monarquía española.* Madrid: Voluntad, 1928. Vols. 2–7, Madrid: Espasa Calpe. Vol. 2: *El Rey se divierte.* 1935. Vol. 3: *Sólo Madrid es Corte.* 1942. Vol. 4: *También se divierte el pueblo.* 1944. Vol. 5: *La mujer, la casa y la moda.* 1946. Vol. 6: *La mala vida en la España de Felipe IV.* 1948. Vol. 7: *La vida religiosa española bajo el cuarto Felipe: Santos y pecadores.* 1952. [There are many later editions and printings.] Rev.: M. Núñez de Arenas. *BH* 53.4 (1951): 433–46.

1030. Elizalde Armendáriz, Ignacio. La figura de San Francisco Javier en la literatura española. 315 pp. Complutense, 1956.

❖ [A] *San Francisco Xavier en la literatura española.* Madrid: CSIC, 1961. 324 pp. [In part 2 "se persigue la figura de Francisco como personaje de nuestro teatro, haciendo hincapié en el teatro jesuítico del Siglo de Oro."] Rev.: (a) J.A. *BSVAP* 17 (1961): 355; (b) J. L. C[ano]. *Ínsula* 173 (1961): 9; (c) J. M. Granero. *Manresa* 33 (1961): 287; (d) C.M. *Punta Europa* 66–67 (1961): 130–32; (e) J.A.J.C. *RE* 20 (1961): 578; (f) B. Sánchez Alonso. *RFE* 44 (1961): 461–64; (g) J.L.M.B. *RyF* 164 (1961): 130; (h) J. M. Rozas. *RL* 22.43–44 (1962): 259–60. [B] "El antiguo teatro de los colegios de la Compañía de Jesús." *Educadores* 4 (1962): 667–84. [For a more complete list of this scholar's publications, see Roberto Pérez, "Bibliografía," *LdD* 19.44 (1989): 8–16. Special issue entitled *Homenaje al profesor Ignacio Elizalde: Estudios literarios.*]

1031. Étienvre, Jean-Pierre. Le Jeu de cartes en Espagne, 16ème–18ème siècles: Recherches ethnolinguistiques. Paris/IV, 1987. (Thèse d'État)

❖ [A] *Figures de jeu: Études lexico-sémantiques sur le jeu de cartes en Espagne, XVIe–XVIIIe siècle.* Madrid: Casa de Velázquez, 1987. 384 pp. (Bibliothèque de la Casa de Velázquez 4.) Rev.: (a) A. Egido. *Ínsula* 491 (1987): 5–6; (b) P. Heugas. *BH* 90.3–4 (1988): 448–52; (c) G. Carnero. *HR* 57.1 (1989): 73–76; (d) M. S. Carrasco Urgoiti. *RFE* 69.3–4 (1989): 355–58; (e) I. Arellano. *RL* 51.102 (1989): 611–13. [B] *Márgenes literarios del juego: Una poética del naipe, siglos XVI–XVIII.* London: Tamesis, 1990. 344 pp. (Colección Támesis, serie A. Monografías 142.) Rev.: I.

Arellano. *Ínsula* 546 (1992): 4–5. [Review discusses both publications A and B.]

1032. ETREROS MENA, MERCEDES. Sátira política en el siglo XVII español. Complutense, 1977. Abstract in *UCM. Tesis doctorales* 2 (1977–78): 95–96; *MEC. Tesis doctorales* 258 (1977–78): 135.
❖ [A] "Poesías satíricas contra el Conde-Duque de Olivares." *Primeras jornadas de bibliografía.* Madrid: FUE, 1977. 173–96, 691–92. [See p. 691 for commentary by Manuel Penedo on relationship to Tirso de Molina.] [B] *La sátira política en el siglo XVII.* Madrid: FUE, 1983. 473 pp. [On the use of theatrical elements in political satire, see pp. 173–74, 181–82, 187–88, 468–69, and passim.] Rev.: (a) V. Roncero López. *El Crotalón* 1 (1984): 857–60; (b) I. Arellano Ayuso. *RL* 47.93 (1985): 179–81.

1033. FARINELLI, ARTURO. Die Beziehungen zwischen Spanien und Deutschland in der Litteratur der beiden Länder. 1. Teil bis zum 18. Jahrhundert. 2 vols. (1–72, 73–128 pp.) Zürich, 1890.
❖ [A] Title as is. Berlin: Haack, 1892. 72 pp. Chapter 6 is entitled "Das spanische Theater in Deutschland im 17. Jahrh.—Die Jesuiten.—Die Wandertruppen" (pp. 51–61 in Prt. Diss.). Rev.: (a) A. Morel-Fatio. *RCHLP* 34 (1892): 111–12; (b) Anon. *Romania* 22 (1893): 174. [B] *Spanien und die spanische Litteratur im Lichte der deutschen Kritik und Poesie.* 1 und 2 Teil. Berlin: Haack, 1892. 128 pp. [Part 1 is the same as publication A.] [C] Same title as item B, in *ZVL* ns 5 (1892): 135–206, 276–332. [D] *Grillparzer und Lope de Vega.* Berlin: Felber, 1894. 333 pp. [E] "Deutschlands und Spaniens litterarische Beziehungen (Spanien und die spanische Litteratur im Lichte der deutschen Kritik und Poesie. III. und IV. Teil.)" *ZVL* 8 (1895): 318–407. [F] "Apuntes sobre Calderón y la música en Alemania." *Cultura Española* (Madrid) 1 (1907): 119–60. [G] *Lope de Vega en Alemania.* Trans. by A. Massaguer of item D; Barcelona: Bosch, 1936. 324 pp. [For a more complete list of this scholar's publications, see *Relaciones literarias entre España e Italia: Ensayo de una bibliografía de literatura comparada,* comp. Joseph Siracusa and Joseph L. Laurenti, (Boston: Hall, 1972) 67–72.]

1034. FRANCO RODRÍGUEZ, ÁNGEL. El tema de América en los autores del Siglo de Oro español. 526 pp. Complutense, 1954. Abstract in *RUM* 3.10 (1954): 263–64.

❖ *El tema de América en los autores españoles del Siglo de Oro.* Madrid: Nueva Imprenta Radio, 1954. 576 pp.

1035. García de Enterría, María Cruz. El pliego suelto poético en los siglos XVI y XVII. Vol. 1 (estudio crítico) 539 pp.; vol. 2 (parte 1 documental) 203 pp.; vol. 3 (parte 2 documental) 380 pp. Barcelona, 1970.

❖ [A] *Sociedad y poesía de cordel en el Barroco.* Madrid: Taurus, 1973. 402 pp. [See esp. pp. 336-74, "El teatro y las 'relaciones de comedias' en la poesía de cordel del siglo XVII."] [B] *Catálogo de los pliegos sueltos poéticos del siglo XVII en el British Museum.* Pisa: Giardini, 1977. [C] *Literaturas marginadas.* Madrid: Playor, 1983. 146 pp. (Lectura crítica de la literatura española 22.) [D] "Literatura de cordel en tiempo de Carlos II: Géneros parateatrales." *Diálogos Hispánicos de Amsterdam* 8.1 (1989): 137-54.

1036. García Gómez, Ángel María. The Theme of "Democritus ridens" in Sixteenth and Seventeenth Century Spanish Literature: A Study of Its Sources and an Appraisal of Its Significance. 705 pp. London/University College, 1983.

❖ *The Legend of the Laughing Philosopher and Its Presence in Spanish Literature (1500-1700).* Córdoba: Universidad de Córdoba, 1984. 292 pp. (Monografías 7.) Deals with the theme of the tears of Heraclitus and the laughter of Democritus. Includes an analysis of the *comedia* entitled *Los filósofos de Grecia* by Fernando de Zárate/Antonio Enríquez Gómez (pp. 206-20 and 223, notes 17-21, of the printed version). Rev.: A. Soons. *Criticón* 49 (1990): 104-06.

1037. García Lorenzo, Luciano Enrique. El tema del Conde Alarcos a través de la literatura. 308 pp. Complutense, 1969.

❖ [A] Castro, G. de. *Don Quijote de la Mancha.* Ed. and critical study by L. García Lorenzo. Salamanca: Anaya, 1971. 186 pp. [B] *El tema del Conde Alarcos: Del Romancero a Jacinto Grau.* Madrid: CSIC, 1972. 229 pp. [Ch. 2 discusses plays by Torres Naharro, Guillén de Castro, Lope de Vega, Mira de Amescua, and Pérez de Montalbán.] [C] "*Entremés del Conde Alarcos.*" *Prohemio* 5.1 (1974): 119-35. [D] Castro, G. de. *Los malcasados de Valencia.* Ed., introd., and notes by L. García Lorenzo. Madrid: Castalia, 1976. 303 pp. (Clásicos Castalia 76.) [E] *El teatro de Guillén de Castro.* Barcelona:

Planeta, 1976. 211 pp. (Ensayos-Planeta 52.) ["El capítulo de mi libro *El tema del Conde Alarcos: Del Romancero a Jacinto Grau,* en que desarrollo el trágico tema, y mis ediciones de *Don Quijote de la Mancha* y *Los malcasados de Valencia* son antecedentes directos del presente libro."] [F] Castro, G. de. *Las mocedades del Cid.* Ed. L. García Lorenzo. Madrid: Cátedra, 1978. 188 pp.

1038. García Solalinde, Antonio La primera versión española de *El purgatorio de San Patricio* y la difusión de esta leyenda en España. 41 pp. Complutense, 1924.

❖ Title as is. *Homenaje ofrecido a Menéndez Pidal.* 2 vols. Madrid: Sucesores de Hernando, 1925. 2: 219–57.

1039. Gerhardt, Mia Irene. Essai d'analyse littéraire de la pastorale dans les littératures italienne, espagnole et française. 318 pp. Leiden, 1950.

❖ [A] *La Pastorale: Essai d'analyse littéraire.* Assen: Van Gorcum, 1950. 317 pp. [Ch. 4 deals with the pastoral plays of Juan del Encina and Gil Vicente.] Rev.: (a) A. Micha. *BHR* 13 (1951): 117–20; (b) A. Lytton Sells. *FS* 5 (1951): 161–63; (c) C. Serrurier. *Neophilologus* 35 (1951): 171–72. [B] Rpt. of Van Gorcum edition, but with dissertation title. Utrecht: H&S, 1975. 317 pp.

1040. Gimber, Arno. Der Zuhälter als komische Figur in der Literatur der spanischen Renaissance und des beginnenden Barockzeitalters. Köln, 1991.

❖ Title as is. Genève: Droz, 1995. 245 pp. (Kölner romanistische Arbeiten 69.)

1041. Gómez Sacristán, M. María. Enigmas y jeroglíficos del Siglo de Oro. 2 vols. Complutense, 1989.

1042. Goyri de Menéndez Pidal, María. El tema de la difunta pleiteada en la literatura española. 60 pp. Complutense, 1909.

❖ [A] *La difunta pleiteada: Estudio de literatura comparada.* Madrid: Suárez, 1909. 70 pp. [In the words of the writer, this theme deals with "una mujer que, después de sepultada, recobra la vida, y luego disputan, sobre su posesión, dos o más hombres que se creen con derecho a ella."] [B] Rpt. in *De Lope de Vega y del Romancero.* Zaragoza: Librería General, 1953. 7–59. Rev.: (a) E. Mérimée. *BH* 12.2 (1910): 230–32; (b) J. D. M. Ford. *RR* 1 (1910): 440–43; (c) R. *GSLI* 57 (1911): 118–20.

1043. GRAHAM, ROBERT HARRY SNOWDEN. The Sequels of *Celestina,* 1534-54: A Reconsideration of Form, Means, and Effect in Relation to Questions of Imitation and Genre. 419+1 pp. Oxford, 1987. Abstract in *Aslib* 38.2 (1988): 540.

1044. GUTIÉRREZ, ASENSIO. La France et les français dans la littérature espagnole: Un aspect de la xénophobie en Espagne, 1598-1665. Montpellier/III, 1974. (Thèse d'État)

❖ [A] Title as is. Saint-Étienne: Publications de l'Université de Saint-Étienne, 1977. 581 pp. [See pp. 476-79 for "Localisation des principales *comedias* consultées" and pp. 480-93 for "Ébauche d'un repertoire des personnages français des principales œuvres dramatiques consultées."] [B] Title as is. Lille: ANRT, 1982. 581 pp.

1045. HAUN, HERTA. Semiramis in den romanischen Literaturen. 124 pp. Vienna, 1949.

1046. HERMANN, CHRISTIAN. L'Église d'Espagne sous le patronage royal (1476-1834). Paris/IV, 1984.

❖ *L'Église d'Espagne sous le patronage royal: Essai d'ecclésiologie politique.* Madrid: Casa de Velázquez, 1988. 342 pp. (Bibliothèque de la Casa de Velázquez 3.) Rev.: J.-P. Dedieu. *BH* 94.1 (1992): 364-66.

1047. HERRERO GARCÍA, MIGUEL. Estimaciones literarias del siglo XVII. [1]+92 pp. Complutense, 1929.

❖ [A] Title as is. Madrid: Voluntad, 1930. 423 pp. [Of particular interest is ch. 3, pp. 107-37, on the theater of Lope de Vega. Also, ch. 4, pp. 139-352, on Góngora, includes many quotations from contemporary plays. "Mi intento en este trabajo es reconstruir la prehistoria de la crítica literaria. Hoy, que tan maduros juicios poseemos, tras largas elaboraciones, del arte de Cervantes, del arte de Lope, del arte de Góngora, etc., encontraremos un indudable placer, y una enseñanza también indudable, en examinar el juicio que esos grandes ingenios formaron unos de otros, la estimación que merecieron a sus contemporáneos, las contradicciones de que tal vez fueron objeto; esto será, en suma, conocer la ideología del siglo XVII en materias literarias."] [B] *Madrid en el teatro.* Madrid: CSIC, 1963. 450 pp. [Annotated short plays chiefly of the seventeenth century] [For a more complete list of this scholar's publications, see *El Libro Español* 3.27 (1960): 82–84.]

1048. HEUGAS, PIERRE. *La Célestine* et sa déscendance directe. 613 pp. Bordeaux/III, 1972. (Thèse d'État)

❖ [A] Title as is. Bordeaux: Université de Bordeaux, Institut d'Études Ibériques et Ibéro-Américaines; Bière, 1973. 612 pp. Rev.: (a) A. K. G. Paterson. *YWMLS* 36 (1974): 271–72; (b) J. Savoye. *CHA* 296 (1975): 452–56; (c) K. Whinnom. *BHS* 53 (1976): 139–41; (d) K. Kish. *HR* 44 (1976): 284–86; (e) D. E. Eisenberg. *NRFH* 25 (1976): 407–12; (f) A. Castro Díaz. *CHA* 322–23 (1977): 285–305. [B] "Sur une scène censurée: Encina et *La Célestine*." *Les Cultures ibériques en devenir: Essais publiés en hommage à la mémoire de Marcel Bataillon, 1895–1977*. Paris: Fondation Singer-Polignac, 1979. 397–403. [C] "¿*La Celestina,* novela dialogada?" *Seis lecciones sobre la España de los Siglos de Oro (Homenaje a M. Bataillon).* Ed. Pedro Manuel Piñero Ramírez and Rogelio Reyes Cano. Sevilla: Universidad de Sevilla, Facultad de Filosofía y Letras, 1981. 161–77.

1049. IGLESIAS-OVEJERO, ÁNGEL. Onomastique: Motivation et typification du nom propre (proverbial et populaire) en espagnol. Paris/IV, 1987. (Thèse d'État)

❖ [A] "Eponimia: Motivación y personificación en el español marginal y hablado." *BRAE* 61 (1981): 304–08. [B] "Iconocidad y parodia: Los santos del panteón burlesco en la literatura clásica y el folklore." *Criticón* 20 (1982): 6–83. [C] "Nominación marginante en el picarismo literario y el folklore." *RFR* 1 (1983): 137–81. [D] "Figuración proverbial y nivelación en los nombres propios del refranero antiguo: Figuras vulgarizadas del registro culto." *Criticón* 28 (1984): 5–95. [E] "El estatuto del nombre proverbial en el refranero antiguo." *RFR* 4 (1986): 11–50. [F] "Figuración proverbial e inversión en los nombres propios del refranero antiguo: Figurillas populares." *Criticón* 35 (1986): 5–98. [G] "El relato oral en la época clásica y el folklore moderno: El caso del blasón popular." *La edición de textos: Actas del primer congreso internacional de hispanistas del Siglo de Oro, 1987*. Ed. Pablo Jauralde, Dolores Noguera, and Alfonso Rey. London: Tamesis, 1990. 245–52. (Colección Támesis, serie A. Monografías 139.) [H] "Inventario parcial de términos españoles de referencia onomástica (Para un metalenguaje onomástico)" and "Nombres propios: Para una tentativa de clasificación." *Dictionnaire historique des noms de famille romans: Actes del tercer Colloqui, Barcelona, 1989*. Ed. Antoni M. Badia i Margarit. Tübingen: Niemeyer, 1991. 229-41 and 227-28. [I] "Onomastique rurale: Surnoms collectifs actuels dans la region du Ciudad Rodrigo et autres lieux de la province de Salamanque (Espagne)." *NRO* 19-20 (1992): 111-25. [J] "La figura etimológica en la paremiología clásica." *Estado actual de los estudios sobre el Siglo de Oro: Actas del segundo congreso internacional de hispanistas del Siglo de Oro, Salamanca y Valladolid, 1990.* Ed. Manuel García Martín, Ignacio Arellano, Javier Blasco, and Marc Vitse. 2 vols. Salamanca: Universidad de Salamanca, 1993. 2: 519-27. [K] "Nombres de personajes y figuras tradicionales o tradicionalizadas en la *Recopilación* (1554) de Diego Sánchez de Badajoz." *Criticón* 66-67 (1996): 57-74.

1050. Infantes de Miguel, Víctor. Estudio de las Danzas de la Muerte. 2 vols. Complutense, 1987. Abstract in *Resumen de tesis doctorales,* Complutense (1988): 85-86.

The dissertation is divided into two parts: "La Danza de la Muerte como grupo genérico: Origen y desarrollo en Europa" and "Las Danzas de la Muerte en España." Part 1 includes a section entitled "Teatralidad y representación," pp. 126-42; part 2 includes "La dramaturgia de las Danzas," pp. 538-48.

❖ [A] *Dança general de la Muerte (siglo XV-1520)*. Ed. V. Infantes. Madrid: Visor, 1982. 211 pp. illus. (Colección Visor de Poesía 127.) [B] "La Muerte como personaje literario en los siglos XVI y XVII." *Le Personnage dans la littérature du Siècle d'Or: Statut et fonction (Tableronde, 1979). Colloque de la Casa de Velázquez*. Ed. Yves-René Fonquerne. Paris: Recherche sur les Civilisations, 1984. 89-102. [C] "Litertura e iconografía macabra en la España de los Siglos de Oro: Los jeroglíficos de la Muerte." *Arte funerario: Coloquio internacional sobre historia del arte [1980]*. Ed. Louise Noelle. México: Universidad Nacional Autónoma de México, 1987. 1: 105-12.

1051. Ingunza Santodomingo, Miguel. La cueva de Salamanca en la literatura española. Complutense, 1946.

1052. Isaza Calderón, Baltasar. El retorno a la naturaleza: Los orígenes del tema y sus direcciones fundamentales en la literatura española. 216 pp. Complutense, 1933.

❖ [A] Title as is. Madrid: Bolaños y Aguilar, 1934. 260 pp. Rev.: (a) M. J. Benardete. *BIE* 3 (1934): 106; (b) A. Baig Baños. *RBAM* 11 (1934): 241–43; (c) G. Cirot. *BH* 37 (1935): 251–53; (d) R. Schevill. *HR* 4 (1936): 73–74; (e) M. Bataillon. *RLC* 16 (1936): 250–53. [B] 2nd ed. Madrid: Gráficas España, 1966. [The *autos* of Gil Vicente are included in this study.]

1053. KEIGHTLEY, RONALD GEORGE. Hercules in Spanish Literature before 1700: The Middle Ages, Mythographers and the Emblem-Books. Cambridge, 1963.

1054. KONG, DEBORAH A. A Study of the Medical Theory of the Humours and Its Application in Selected Spanish Literature of the Golden Age. iv+290 pp. Edinburgh, 1981.

The thesis studies in detail the characters of don Domingo de Don Blas in *No hay mal que por bien no venga* (Alarcón) and Diana in *El desdén con el desdén* (Moreto). It also includes plays by Tirso, Rojas Zorrilla, and Calderón. (Diss.)

1055. LABERTIT, ANDRÉ. Études philologiques et stylistiques de littérature espagnole. Bordeaux/III, 1979. (Thèse d'État)

❖ [A] "L'Ordre du héros dans *La vie est un songe* (étude dramaturgique)." *TILAS* 16–17 (1976–77): 133–55. [B] "Note philologique au *Burlador de Sevilla:* La bourle du souper escamoté." *Hommage des hispanistes français à Noël Salomon: Publié par les soins de la Société des Hispanistes Français.* Barcelona: Laia, 1979. 447–53. [C] "El enredo amoroso (La Burla) en el *Retablo de las maravillas:* Apuntes estilísticos." *Actas del coloquio (Roma, 1978): Teoría y realidad en el teatro español del siglo XVII. La influencia italiana.* Roma: Instituto Español de Cultura y de Literatura, 1981. 55-67. [D] "Note philologique au texte du *Burlador de Sevilla:* La bourle du souper escamoté." *Don Juan: Actes du colloque de Treyvaux, 1981.* Fribourg: Éditions Universitaires, 1982. 151–59. [Cf. publication B.] [E] "L'Intermittence de l'illusion au théâtre: Le cas des clignements du texte dans la *comedia* d'intrigue." *TLL* 25.2 (1987): 247–62. [Based on Calderón's *La dama duende.*]

1056. LATOUR, JEANNE. La Légende de Bernardo del Carpio, depuis les origines jusqu'à la décadence de la littérature espagnole. Brussels, 1933–34.

1057. Leblon, Bernard. Les Gitans d'Espagne: Recherches sur les divers aspects du problème gitan du XVe au XVIIIe siècle. 3 vols. (xlv+1973+257 pp.) Montpellier/III, 1980.

❖ [A] *Les Gitans dans la littérature espagnole.* Toulouse: France-Ibérie Recherche, 1982. 247 pp. (Thèses et recherches 11.) [B] "Amours et mariage chez les gitans au Siècle d'Or." *Amours légitimes, amours illégitimes en Espagne (XVIe–XVIIe siècles): Colloque international, Sorbonne, 1984.* Ed. Augustin Redondo. Paris: Publications de la Sorbonne, 1985. 151–58. [C] *Les Gitans d'Espagne: Le prix de la différence.* Paris: PUF, 1985. 256 pp.

1058. Lessig, Doris. Ursprung und Entwicklung der spanischen Ekloge bis 1650 (mit Anhang eines Eklogenkataloges). Cologne, 1962.

❖ Title as is. Genève: Droz; Paris: Minard, 1962. 289 pp. (Kölner romanistische Arbeiten ns 22.) [See esp. ch. 5, section A (a), pp. 81–95 of the printed version, entitled "Dramatische Ekloge."]

1059. López Abadía Arroita, Isabel Sara. Le Diable dans la littérature européenne: Rapports entre l'Espagne, la France et l'Angleterre. 328 pp. Rennes/II, 1979.

1060. López y González, Agustín. Examen crítico de D. Álvaro de Luna. 201 pp., handwritten. Complutense, 1905.

1061. Loupias, Bernard. L'Image du Maroc dans la littérature espagnole des origines au terme des lumières. Paris/X, 1987. (Thèse d'État)

1062. Lucero Ontiveros, Dolly María. El Escorial y su significado a través de la literatura española. 61+2+10+85[unpublished texts]+2 pp. Complutense, 1953.

❖ *El Escorial en el Barroco.* Bahía Blanca [Arg.]: Instituto de Humanidades, Universidad Nacional del Sur, 1958. 26 pp. (Cuadernos del Sur 2.) ["La enorme fábrica siempre estaba en labios del pueblo y se le citaba en las obras teatrales de la época donde brillaban los mejores ingenios. Agustín Moreto . . . en una de ellas *De fuera vendrá* le nombra encareciendo su riqueza."]

1063. Malaquilla, Sofía. Costumbres en Madrid durante el reinado de Felipe IV. 172 pp. Complutense, 1920.

1064. MAS, ALBERT. Les Turcs dans la littérature espagnole du Siècle d'Or: Recherches sur l'évolution d'un thème littéraire. Paris, 1968. (Thèse d'État)

❖ Title as is. Flers: Folloppe; Paris: Centre de Recherches Hispaniques, Institut d'Études Hispaniques, 1967. 2 vols. (565, 527 pp.) (Thèses, mémoires et travaux 9.) [For a more complete list of this scholar's publications, see P.-J. Guinard, "Publications d'Albert Mas," *Ibérica: Cahiers Ibériques et Ibéro-Américains de l'Université de Paris-Sorbonne* 4 (1983): 208-09.]

1065. MÉCHOULAN, HENRY. Le Thème de l'altérité dans la pensée espagnole (1550-1650), ou les responsabilités morales et politiques d'une ontologie de l'absence. Paris/I, 1977. (Thèse d'État)

❖ [A] *Le Sang de l'autre, ou l'honneur de Dieu: Indiens, juifs, morisques dans l'Espagne du Siècle d'Or.* Paris: Fayard, 1979. 302 pp. [B] *El honor de Dios: Indios, judíos y moriscos en el Siglo de Oro.* Barcelona: Argos-Vergara, 1980. Rev.: (a) C. Aguilera. *CIH* 4 (1980): 282-83; (b) M. C. Bianchini. *RI* 14 (1982): 38-40.

1066. MILLÉ Y GIMÉNEZ, ISABEL. Guzmán el Bueno en la historia y en la literatura. 315 pp. Complutense, 1928.

❖ Title as is. *RH* 78 (1930): 311-488.

1067. MOLINARO, JULIUS A. R. Angélica and Medoro: The Development of a Motif from the Renaissance to the Baroque. 181 pp. Toronto, 1954.

❖ Angélica y Medoro: *Zarzuela inédita de José de Cañizares, con su loa y entremés.* Critical ed. J. A. Molinaro and W. T. McCready. Torino: Quaderni Ibero-Americani, 1958. 84 pp. (Collana di testi e studi 3.) Rev.: (a) W. K. Jones. *BAbr* 33 (1959): 447; (b) D. C. Shepperd. *H* [AATSP] 42 (1959): 439; (c) I. L. McClelland. *BHS* 37 (1960): 65-66; (d) N. Glendinning. *MLR* 55 (1960): 125-26.

1068. MONTILLE, RÉGINE DE. Vocabulaire du vêtement au Siècle d'Or. 265 pp. Toulouse/II, 1978. (Thèse de 3e cycle)

1069. MOORE, PETER. La Flandre dans la littérature espagnole. Brussels, 1947-48.

1070. MORILLOT, ANDRÉ-LOUIS-PAUL. Scarron: Étude biographique et littéraire. Paris, 1887-88.

❖ [A] Title as is. Paris: Lecène et Oudin, 1888. 432 pp. [B] Rpt. Genève: Slatkine, 1970. [C] *Scarron et le genre burlesque.* Paris:

Lecène et Oudin, 1888. 432 pp. [Publications A and C are identical except for the title page. Ch. 5, pp. 268–312, "Le Théâtre," describes Scarron's borrowings from plays by Rojas Zorrilla, Calderón, and Castillo Solórzano.]

1071. NAVAS MORMONEO, ÁNGEL. Lenguaje de locura y tradición bufonesca en la España de los siglos XVI y XVII. Barcelona, 1981.

1072. OOSTENDORP, HENRICUS THEODORUS. El conflicto entre el honor y el amor en la literatura española hasta el siglo XVII. Utrecht, 1962.

❖ [A] Title as is. Den Haag: Van Goor Zonen, 1962. 215 pp. (Publicaciones del Instituto de Estudios Hispánicos, Portugueses e Iberoamericanos de la Universidad Estatal de Utrecht 4.) Rev.: (a) V. Ruiz Ortiz. *BFE* 4 (1963): 39–40; (b) G. Correa. *HR* 31 (1963): 164–66; (c) P. Heugas. *BH* 67 (1965): 392–93. [B] *Het motief van de huwelijkseer in de Spaanse Comedias.* Groningen: Wolters-Noordhoff, 1968. 17 pp. [C] "El sentido del tema de la honra matrimonial en las tragedias de honor." *Neophilologus* 53 (1969): 14–29. [Spanish version of publication B.] [For a more complete list of this scholar's publications, see "Lista de publicaciones de H. Th. Oostendorp," *España, teatro y mujeres: Estudios dedicados a Henk Oostendorp,* ed. Martin Gosman and Hub. Hermans (Amsterdam: Rodopi, 1989) vi–viii.]

1073. ORTIZ DE MENDÍVIL DAÑOBEITIA, JUAN JOSÉ. San Lorenzo en la literatura. 3 vols. (1,290 pp.) Complutense, 1980.

❖ "Datación de un *Mystère* del siglo XV sobre el mártir San Lorenzo." *Actas do XIX congreso internacional de lingüística e filoloxía románicas 7: Sección IX. Filoloxía medieval e renacentista. A: Crítica textual e edición de textos. B: Historia e crítica literarias.* Ed. Ramón Lorenzo. Coruña: Fundación Pedro Barrié de la Maza, 1992–94. 463–69.

1074. PAETZ, BERNHARD. Kirke und Odysseus. Überlieferung und Deutung von Homer bis Calderón. Hamburg, 1968. [Apropos Circe and Odysseus.]

❖ Title as is. Berlin: de Gruyter, 1970. 160 pp. (Hamburger romanistische Studien B. Ibero-amerikanische Reihe 33. Calderoniana 4.) Rev.: (a) J. Vives. *AnST* 42 (1969): 391–92; (b) A.

Salas. *CdD* 183 (1970): 625; (c) P. B. Bell. *BCom* 23.1 (1971): 19; (d) J. S. Lasso de la Vega. *Emérita* 40 (1972): 231–33.

1075. PALLARÉS GARZÓN, MARÍA BERTA. La Danza de la Muerte española y su lugar y caracteres en relación con las europeas: Vocabulario. 267+[1] pp. Salamanca, 1956.

1076. PELORSON, JEAN-MARC. Les *Letrados* juristes castillans sous Philippe III: Recherches sur leur place dans la société, la culture et l'état. Bordeaux/III, 1978. (Thèse d'État)
❖ Title as is. Poitiers: Université de Poitiers, 1980. 549 pp. [In ch. 8, "*Letras* et Littérature," pp. 367–90, the writer discusses the role of the *letrado* in the *entremés* and in plays by Tirso, Ruiz de Alarcón, and Lope de Vega. Also of interest is ch. 9, "Le Cas particulier de Cristóbal Suárez de Figueroa," pp. 391–443. (Prt. Diss.)]

1077. PITOLLET, LÉON-ALEXANDRE-CAMILLE. Contributions à l'étude de l'hispanisme de G. E. Lessing. Toulouse, 1909. (Thèse d'État)
[G. E. Lessing's writings on Spanish Golden Age theater include an analysis and translation of Antonio Coello's *El conde de Sex*.]
❖ [A] Title as is. Paris: Alcan, 1909. 342 p. Rev.: R. Schevill. *MLN* 26 (1911): 21–28. [B] *L'Hispanisme de Lessing*. [Signed: Camille Pitollet.] N.p.: n.d. 54 pp. [Rept. from *Vragen en Mededeelingen op het gebied der geschiedenis, taal en letterkunde*.] [C] "A propos de 'l'hispanisme allemand.'" *BH* 37 (1935): 489–97. [A commentary on J. J. A. Bertrand's publication B (see no. 1112).]

1078. PORQUERAS MAYO, ALBERTO. El prólogo como género literario: Su estudio en el Siglo de Oro español. 329 pp. Complutense, 1954. Abstract in *RUM* 4.15 (1955): 414–15.
❖ [A] Title as is. Madrid: CSIC, 1957. 199 pp. [Dramatic prologues are included in this study.] Rev.: (a) E. Náñez. *ACer* 6 (1957): 303–05; (b) M. Baquero Goyanes. *RL* 12 (1957): 122–24; (c) J. Montero Padilla. *BBMP* 34 (1958): 80–82; (d) M. de Riquer. *RFE* 42 (1958–59): 298–300; (e) H. Weinrich. *Archiv* 110.195 (1959): 370; (f) A. I. Watson. *BHS* 36 (1959): 167–68; (g) L. C. de Morelos. *RHM* 25 (1959): 247; (h) A. G. Reichenberger. *RPh* 13 (1959): 107–08; (i) G. E. McSpadden. *HR* 28 (1960): 92–93; (j) H. R. Jauss. *ZRP* 76 (1960): 252–55; (k) N. Kerremans. *LR* 15 (1961): 96–97. [B] *El prólogo en el Renacimiento español*. Madrid: CSIC,

1965. 224 pp. [Antología.] Rev.: (a) J. M. Lope Blanch. *ALM* 5 (1965): 236–38; (b) J. Cano Ballesta. *RF* 78 (1966): 175–77; (c) F. Caravaca. *RJ* 17 (1966): 355–57; (d) R. Esquer Torres. *RL* 29 (1966): 240; (e) H. Janner. *Archiv* 204 (1967): 70; (f) G. A. Davies. *BHS* 44 (1967): 127–28; (g) J. L. Laurenti. *H* [AATSP] 50 (1967): 183–84; (h) P. Groult. *LR* 21 (1967): 276–78; (i) A. Ebersole. *REH*b 2 (1968): 309–10. [C] *El prólogo en el Manierismo y Barroco españoles.* Madrid: CSIC, 1968. 297 pp. [Antología.] Rev.: (a) F. Pierce. *BHS* 46.3 (1969): 276; (b) S. A. Stoudemire. *H* [AATSP] 52 (1969): 326–27; (c) A. Sarmiento. *MLN* 84.2 (1969): 352–53; (d) J. Artiles. *REH*b 4.1 (1970): 172–74; (e) W. Hirdt. *RLMC* 23.2 (1970): 156–58. [D] Laurenti, Joseph L., and A. Porqueras-Mayo. *Ensayo bibliográfico del prólogo en la literatura.* Madrid: CSIC, 1971. 72 pp. (Cuadernos bibliográficos 26.) [For a more complete list of this scholar's publications, see *Varia hispanica: Homenaje a Alberto Porqueras-Mayo,* ed. Joseph L. Laurenti and Vern G. Williamsen (Kassel: Reichenberger, 1989) 489–505. (Teatro del Siglo de Oro. Estudios de literatura 5.) See also J. L. Laurenti and A. Porqueras-Mayo, *Nuevos estudios bibliográficos sobre la Edad de Oro: Más fondos raros y colecciones en la biblioteca de la Universidad de Illinois* (Barcelona: PPU, 1994) 468–69.]

1079. Poveda, Françoise. L'Espagne de Montherlant. 251 pp. Toulouse/II, 1985. (Thèse de 3e cycle)

1080. Ravillard Nicol, Martine. Bibliographie commentée des morisques: Documents imprimés de leur origine à 1982. Montpellier/III, 1982.

1081. Requejo y Avedillo, Miguel. Influencia de la literatura española en la francesa durante los siglos XVI y XVII. Complutense, 1879.

1082. Rull Fernández, Enrique. El mito de Psique en la literatura española y sus relaciones con la universal. 624 pp. Complutense, 1969. Abstract in *RUM* 18.72 (1969): 47–48.

[The dissertation includes discussion of an *auto* by Valdivielso as well as two *autos* and a *comedia* by Calderón.]

❖ [A] "*Psiques y Cupido:* Auto sacramental de Valdivielso." *Segismundo* 2.3 (1966): 135–95. [B] Extracto de tesis. Madrid: Rolando, 1969. 22 pp. ["El presente estudio tiene por origen, en parte al menos, el interés que suscitaron en nosotros los temas mitológicos en la literatura, interés que surgió al realizar nuestra Memoria de Licenciatura sobre unos autos de Valdivielso y Calderón que versaban precisamente acerca del mito de Psique. Allí esbozamos la línea de un estudio que abarcase la materia temática de forma global."] [C] Rull Fernández, E., and J. C. de Torres Martínez. "Manuscritos calderonianos de autos sacramentales [1]." *BFE* 10.34-35 (1970): 29-72; 2: *Segismundo* 8.15-16 (1972): 91-134; 3: *Segismundo* 9.17-18 (1973): 197-214; 4: *Segismundo* 13.25-26 (1977): 147-86. [D] *Calderón y Nördlingen: El auto* El primer blasón del Austria *de don Pedro Calderón de la Barca.* Critical study and ed. by E. Rull and José Carlos de Torres. Madrid: CSIC, 1981. 204 pp. (Clásicos hispánicos, serie 3. Vol. 6.) [E] Rull, E., and J. C. de Torres. "Manuscritos calderonianos de autos sacramentales (5)." *Segismundo* 18.39-40 (1984): 73-114. [The five lists include one or both of the Psyche *autos.*] [F] *Autos sacramentales del Siglo de Oro.* Ed. E. Rull Fernández. Esplugues de Llobregat (Barcelona): Plaza y Janés, 1986. 400 pp. [G] "*Auto de la Montañesa,* de Don Pedro Calderón de la Barca." Ed. E. Rull and J. C. de Torres. *RL* 53.105 (1991): 181-210. [H] Rull, E., and José Carlos de Torres. "La escenografía del auto sacramental de Calderón *Psiquis y Cupido* (versión de Madrid)." *CTC* 8 (1995): 201-12.

1083. SANTOS DOMÍNGUEZ, LUIS ANTONIO. Las hablas marginales en la literatura española: Morisco, guineo y vizcaíno. Madrid/ Autónoma, 1983.

❖ "El lenguaje teatral del morisco." *BBMP* 63 (1987): 5-16.

1084. SCHULTE, HANSGERD. *El desengaño:* Wort und Thema in der spanischen Literatur des goldenen Zeitalters. Freiburg, 1968.

❖ Title as is. München: Fink, 1969. 236 pp. (Freiburger Schriften zur romanischen Philologie 17.) [The analysis is based mainly on prose texts, but see the following relevant sections of the printed dissertation: "Das Leben ein Traum" (Life Is a Dream theme), pp. 132-34; "Die Schauspielmetapher" (*theatrum mundi* theme), pp. 197-208; on *desengaño* in the *auto sacramental,* pp. 211-12.] Rev.: F. Schalk. *RF* 83 (1971): 649-54.

1085. SCHWARTZ, [JAKOB] WILHELM. August Wilhelm Schlegels Verhältnis zur spanischen und portugiesischen Literatur. Halle, 1913.

❖ [A] Title as is. Halle: Karras, 1913. 67 pp. Rev.: L. R. *Revue* (Paris) 49 (1915): 170–72. [B] Title as is. Halle: Niemeyer, 1914. 144 pp. (Romanistiche Arbeiten 3.)

1086. SECO SANTOS, ESPERANZA. Historia de las traducciones literarias del italiano al español durante el Siglo de Oro: Influencias. 760 pp. Complutense, 1983.

❖ [A] Title as is. Madrid: Editorial de la Universidad Complutense, 1985. [B] "1. Influencia de la literatura italiana del Quattrocento en el Siglo de Oro español. 2. Un ejemplo de esta influencia en la obra dramática *Los celos de Rodamonte* y el problema de su atribución." *CILH* 10 (1988): 145–72. [C] "Historia de las traducciones literarias del italiano al español durante el Siglo de Oro: Influencias (Breve introducción)." *CILH* 13 (1990): 41–97.

1087. SERRANO MARTÍNEZ, MARÍA DE LA ENCARNACIÓN IRENE. "Honneur" y "Honor": Su significación a través de las literaturas francesa y española. 471 pp. Complutense, 1955.

❖ [A] Title as is. *AUMur. Filosofía y Letras* 14.1–2 (1955–56): 47–191, 279–451. [B] Title as is with subtitle: *Desde los orígenes hasta el siglo XVI.* Murcia: Universidad de Murcia, 1956. 327 pp. Rev.: G. Correa. *HR* 26 (1958): 305–07.

1088. SICROFF, ALBERT ABRAHAM. Les Statuts de pureté de sang en Espagne aux XVIe et XVIIe siècles. 586 pp. Paris, 1955. (Doctorat d'Université) // Rev. Ch. V. Aubrun. *BH* 59.1 (1957): 78.

❖ [A] *Les Controverses des statuts de "pureté de sang" en Espagne du XVe au XVIIe siècle.* Paris: Didier, 1960. 318 pp. (Études de littérature étrangère et comparée 39.) Rev.: (a) J. Elliott. *BHS* 38 (1961): 249–50; (b) E. Glaser. *HR* 30 (1962): 156–60. [B] "Notas equívocas en dos dramatizaciones de Lope del problema judaico: *El niño inocente de La Guardia* y *La hermosa Ester.*" *Actas del sexto congreso internacional de hispanistas, Toronto, 1977.* Ed. Alan M. Gordon and Evelyn Rugg. Toronto: Univ. of Toronto, 1980. 701–05. [C] *Los estatutos de limpieza de sangre: Controversias entre los siglos XV y XVII.* Trans. by Mauro Armiño and rev. by the author. Madrid: Taurus, 1985. 377 pp. Rev.: Anon. *LSECL* 39 (1985): 25.

1089. SKOVRON, ESTRELLA. Statut juridique de la femme en Espagne: Une Étude sur le mariage faite d'après l'épitome de Diego de

Covarrubias y Leyva [1512–77]—la législation royale et les moralistes. Paris/IV, 1983. (Thèse de 3e cycle)

1090. SOLER PASTOR, TERESA. Las palabras *Gloria* y *Gloire:* Sus distintos significados en las literaturas francesa y española. 294 pp. Complutense, 1955.

[Among the playwrights cited are Torres Naharro, Gil Vicente, Micael de Carvajal, Juan de Pedraza, and Juan de la Cueva.]

❖ [A] Title as is. *AUMur. Filosofía y Letras* 15.2–3 (1956–57): 176–284, 309–423. [B] Title as is with subtitle: *Desde los orígenes hasta el siglo XVI.* Murcia: Universidad de Murcia, 1957. 227 pp. Rev.: J. González Muela. *HR* 28 (1960): 180–81.

1091. STAUBWASSER, GABRIELE. Schiller und Spanien. 328 pp. Jena, 1965.

❖ [A] Koch, Herbert, and Gabriele Staubwasser de Mohorn. Title as is. München: Hueber, 1973. 214 pp. (Münchener romanistische Arbeiten 31.) [B] Koch, Herbert, and Gabriele Staubwasser de Mohorn. *Schiller y España.* Madrid: Cultura Hispánica del Centro Iberoamericano de Cooperación, 1978. [See pp. 106–14, "Schiller y el calderonianismo."]

1092. STUMFALL, BALTHASAR. Das Märchen von Amor und Psyche in seinem Fortleben in der französischen, italienischen und spanischen Literatur bis zum 18. Jahrhundert. Munich, 1907.

❖ [A] Title as is. Naumburg: Lippert, 1907. 36 pp. [B] Title as is. Leipzig: Deichert Nachf. 1907. 205 pp. (Münchener Beiträge zur romanischen und englischen Philologie 39.) [See pp. 102–34 on Calderón's *comedia* entitled *Ni amor se libra de amor* and his two *autos* entitled *Psiquis y Cupido;* see pp. 168–84 on Antonio de Solís y Rivadeneyra's *comedia Triunfos de Amor y Fortuna.*]

1093. TAMA BENA, VITAL. Les Noirs en Espagne aux seizième et dix-septième siècles. Perpignan, 1990. (Doctorat de Nouveau Régime)

1094. TARDIEU, GUY JEAN-PIERRE. Le Noir dans la littérature espagnole des XVIème et XVIIème siècles. Bordeaux/III, 1977. (Thèse de 3e cycle)

❖ [A] "Les Noirs en Espagne aux XVe, XVIe, XVIIe siècles (Brève synthèse)." *LLNL* 77.247 (1983): 27–44. [B] Title as is. Ussel (Corrèze): Lombarteix, n.d., 311 pp. [C] *Le Destin des noirs aux*

Indes de Castille: XVIe-XVIIIe siècles. Paris: L'Harmattan, 1984. 350 pp.

1095. TERLINGEN, JUAN (JOHANNES HERMANUS). Los italianismos en español desde la formación del idioma hasta principios del siglo XVII. Utrecht, 1943.

❖ Title as is. Amsterdam: Noord-hollandsche uitgevers maatschappij, 1943. 400 pp.

1096. TORRES MARTÍNEZ, JOSÉ CARLOS DE. Contribución al estudio diacrónico del léxico taurino en España: Fuentes y clasificación del mismo (siglos XVI-XX). Complutense, 1970. Resumen, 1971, 29 pp.

❖ [A] "El léxico taurino en el ciclo celestinesco." La Celestina *y su contorno social: Actas del primer congreso internacional sobre* La Celestina. Ed. Manuel Criado de Val. Barcelona: HISPAM (Borrás), 1977. 433-68. [Includes quotations from such sixteenth-century dramatic works as *Florinea* (1554), *Policiana* (1547), *Selvagia* (1554), *Serafina* (1521), and *Tebaida* (1521).] [B] "El léxico taurino en la obra cervantina." *RDTP* 34 (1978): 79-107. [Includes theater.] [C] "El léxico taurino en España (siglos XVI-XX)." *Actas del cuarto congreso internacional de hispanistas, Salamanca, 1971.* Ed. Eugenio de Bustos Tovar. Salamanca: AIH, Consejo General de Castilla y León, Universidad de Salamanca, 1982. 707-25. [D] "El léxico taurino en el ciclo de Calderón." *Calderón: Actas del congreso internacional sobre Calderón y el teatro español del Siglo de Oro, Madrid, 1981.* Ed. Luciano García Lorenzo. 3 vols. Madrid: CSIC, 1983. 1173-1219. [E] *Léxico español de los toros: Contribución a su estudio.* Madrid: CSIC, 1989. 542 pp. [For coauthored publications, see under Rull Fernández, Enrique, no. 1082.]

1097. TROUSSON, RAYMOND. Le Mythe de Prométhée dans la littérature de l'Europe occidentale, des origines à la fin du Romantisme. Brussels, 1962-63.

❖ [A] *Le Thème de Prométhée dans la littérature européenne.* 2 vols. Genève: Droz, 1964. [Dissertation includes discussion of Calderón's *La estatua de Prometeo.* See pp. 167-78.] [B] "Feijoo, crítico de la exégesis mitológica." *NRFH* 18 (1965-66): 453-61 [the writer cites his 1964 book on p. 460, n. 21]; also published in *Beiträge zur romanischen Philologie* 7 (1968): 286-94. [C] 2nd ed. of *Le Thème de Prométhée* . . . 1976. 561 pp. Rev.: (a) Gh. Ceausescu. *RITL* 17 (1968): 375–78; (b) P. Moreau. *RLC* 42 (1968): 291–96.

1098. UNGERER, GUSTAV. Anglo-Spanish Relations in Tudor Literature. Bern, 1956.

❖ [A] Title as is. Madrid: Clavileño, 1956. Rev.: E. B. Knowles. *HR* 25 (1957): 305–06. [B] Title as is. Bern: Francke, 1956. 231 pp. (Schweizer anglistische Arbeiten 38.) [C] "The Printing of Spanish Books in Elizabethan England." *Library,* 5th ser. 20 (1965): 177–229. [D] Title as is. Rpt. New York: AMS, 1972. 231 pp. [The writer comments: "The general conclusions reached by Underhill"—United States dissertations no. 62, Spanish Literature in the England of the Tudors (1899)—"are still valid, yet it is true that his presentation of literary facts is spoiled by many a mistake of detail" (5). Like Underhill, Ungerer deals with the influence of only one Spanish "dramatic" work: *La Celestina* (which he describes as a "dramatic novel").]

1099. VILLAR CASTEJÓN, CARIDAD. La teoría de la historia en el siglo XVII y su proyección en la literatura barroca. Complutense, 1975. Abstract in *RUCM* 24.100–2 (Nov.–Dec. 1975): 133–34.

[In Golden Age drama from Lope to Bances Candamo.]

1100. VINGE, LOUISE. The Narcissus Theme in Western European Literature up to the Early 19th Century. Lund, 1967.

❖ Title as is. Trans. Robert Dewsnap, L. Grönlund, N. Reeves, and I. S. Reeves. Lund: Gleerups, 1967. 448 pp. [Includes Calderón's *Eco y Narciso,* pp. 237–44; Juana Inés de la Cruz's *El divino Narciso,* pp. 244–48; also discusses section "El Narciso" of Lope's *Laurel de Apolo,* pp. 202–04.] Rev.: (a) D. Briesemeister. *Archiv* 205 (1968): 202–04; (b) R. O. Jones. *BHS* 45 (1968): 254–55; (c) J. Donovan. *MLR* 63 (1968): 924–25; (d) E. Köhler. *RF* 80 (1968): 444–48; (e) M. Beller. *OL* 24 (1969): 315–20. (f) Rev. article: Frederick Goldin. "The Narcissus Theme in Western European Literature (and Some Problems in Thematology)." *RPh* 23.2 (1969): 220–27.

1101. WALTER, FÉLIX. La Littérature portugaise en Angleterre à l'époque romantique. Paris, 1927(?). (Doctorat d'Université)

❖ Title as is. Paris: Ancienne Honoré Champion, 1927. 150 pp. Rpt. Genève: Slatkine, 1980. (Bibliothèque de la Revue de

Littérature Comparée 36.) [On Thomas Moore Musgrave, translator of António Ferreira's *Castro,* see pp. 97–99. On Edward Quillinan, commentator of Gil Vicente, see pp. 117–18.]

1102. WANNENMACHER, FRANZ XAVER. Die Griseldissage auf der iberischen Halbinsel. Strassburg, 1894.

❖ Title as is. Strassburg: Müh, 1894. 110 pp. [The writer discusses, inter alia, Lope's *El ejemplo de casadas y prueba de la paciencia.*] Rev.: (a) A. L. Stiefel. *LGRP* 16 (1895): cols. 415–17; (b) W. von Biedermann. *ZVL* 9 (1896): 142–43.

1103. WHITE, ALISON. The Continuity and Development of Traditional Themes and Imagery: Miguel Hernández's *El rayo que no cesa* [1936]. 375 pp. Nottingham, 1985. Abstract in *Aslib* 35.1 (1986): 61.

[The writer indicates Hernández's "reliance upon well-established Spanish poets and dramatists, such as Góngora, Quevedo, Calderón and Lope de Vega." (Abs.)]

1104. WIETZOREK, MARGARETA. Die Legenden der Thais und der Maria Aegyptiaca in den romanischen Literaturen vornehmlich des Mittelalters. Münster, 1941.

❖ Title as is. Lengerich: Lengericher, 1939. 139 pp. [The writer refers briefly to three *comedias: Santa Taez* (Zárate y Castronovo), *Santa Taez* (Rojas Zorrilla), and *La gitana de Menfis* (Pérez de Montalbán).]

1105. YARNALL, JUDITH H. The Transformations of Circe: The History of an Archetypal Character. xi+336 pp. Montreal/McGill, 1989. *DAI* 50A: 943.

[Includes references to Calderón.]

❖ *Transformations of Circe: The History of an Enchantress.* Champaign: U of Illinois P, 1994. 245 pp.

THEATER AND DRAMA: GOLDEN AGE

1106. ÁLVAREZ BARRIENTOS, JOAQUÍN. La *comedia de magia* (Estudio de su estructura y recepción popular). xii+ 489 p. Complutense, 1986.

❖ [A] Anon. *Brancanelo el Herrero.* Ed., introd., and notes by

J. Álvarez Barrientos Roma: Bulzoni, 1987. [This eighteenth-century play with the alternate title *El mágico Brancanelo* was based on a seventeenth-century model.] [B] "Desarrollo del teatro popular a finales del siglo XVIII." *Actas de las jornadas sobre teatro popular en España.* Coord. J. Álvarez Barrientos and A. Cea Gutiérrez. Madrid: CSIC, 1987. 215–25. [The *comedia de magia* was among the elements that played a role in the development of the *teatro popular.*] [C] "Problemas de género en la comedia de magia." *Teatro español a fines del siglo XVII: Historia, cultura y teatro en la España de Carlos II.* Ed. Javier Huerta Calvo, Harm den Boer, and Fermín Sierra Martínez. 3 vols. Amsterdam: Rodopi, 1989. 2: 301–10.

1107. ANDIOC, RENÉ. Sur la querelle du théâtre au temps de Leandro Fernández de Moratín. 2 vols. (1,075 pp.+28 pl.) Toulouse, 1969. (Thèse d'État)

❖ [A] Title as is. Tarbes: Saint-Joseph, 1970. 721 pp. Rev.: I. L. McClelland. *BHS* 49 (1972): 408–10. [B] *Teatro y sociedad en el Madrid del siglo XVIII.* [Madrid]: Fundación Juan March; Editorial Castalia, 1976. 571 pp. Rev.: (a) J. M. Díez Borque. *EL* 609 (1977): 2782–84; (b) J. S. P. *Ínsula* 368–69 (1977): 20; (c) J. Huerta Calvo. *CILH* 1 (1978): 226–29; (d) D. T. Gies. *HR* 47 (1979): 118–20; (e) G. E. Mazzeo. *HisJ* 2.2 (1981): 149–51. [C] *Teatro y sociedad en el Madrid del siglo XVIII.* 2nd ed., corrected and expanded. Madrid: Castalia, 1988. 571 pp. [Of particular interest are ch. 1, "El teatro del Siglo de Oro en el XVIII: Leyenda y realidad," pp. 13–26, and ch. 3, "El teatro del Siglo de Oro en su nuevo contexto," pp. 123–82.]

1108. ARRÓNIZ BÁEZ, OTHÓN. La influencia italiana en el nacimiento de la comedia española. Complutense, 1967.

❖ [A] Title as is. Madrid: Gredos, 1969. 339 pp. (BRH. II. Estudios y ensayos 133.) Rev.: (a) B. W. Wardropper. *BHS* 47 (1970): 353–55; (b) G. L. Reyes. *Filología* 14 (1970): 196–200; (c) G. C. Rossi. *Ibero* 2 (1970): 247–48; (d) R. Kersten. *NRFH* 21 (1972): 114–15; (e) F. Meregalli. *Arcadia* 9 (1974): 76–77. [B] 2nd ed. of publication A, 1971. [C] *Teatros y escenarios del Siglo de Oro.* Madrid: Gredos, 1977. 272 pp. [In ch. 3 ("El teatro mediterráneo," pp. 100–27) the writer examines the question of Italian influence on theater architecture in Valencia.] [For a more complete list of this scholar's publications, see Rosalina Reyes Nicolat, "Bibliografía de O. Arróniz," *LMex* 4.2 (1993): 293. Special issue entitled *Homenaje a Othón Arróniz*.]

1109. BADENHAUSEN, ROLF. Das spanische Kostüm und seine Bedeutung für die Bühne. Munich, 1936.

❖ Title as is. Kallmünz: Lassleben, 1936. 85 pp. [On Spanish costumes in the sixteenth, seventeenth, and eighteenth centuries, inside and outside Spain.]

1110. BARCLAY, THOMAS BRIAN. The Role of the Dance and Dance Lyrics in the Spanish *Comedia* to the Early 18th Century. 342 pp. Toronto, 1957.

❖ [A] "The Importance of the Dance in the Spanish *Comedia* before the Eighteenth Century." *BCom* 10.2 (1958): 21-23. [B] "Dos 'Maestros de danzar.'" *Homenaje a William L. Fichter: Estudios sobre el teatro antiguo hispánico y otros ensayos*. Ed. A. David Kossoff and José Amor y Vázquez. Madrid: Castalia, 1971. 71-80. [Apropos two plays of that title: one by Lope, the other by Calderón.]

1111. BARKLEY, PILAR. Main Themes in the Spanish Drama of Franco's Rule: 1940-1975. 2 vols. (ix+422; 423-600 pp.) Toronto, 1982. *DAI* 44A: 183.

". . . amongst the themes surveyed there [is] . . . the development—during the period studied—of two classic themes: 'honour' and 'donjuanismo.'" (Abs.)

1112. BERTRAND, JEAN-JACQUES-ACHILLE. Ludwig Tieck et le théâtre espagnol. Paris, 1914. (Thèse complémentaire)

❖ [A] Title as is. Paris: Colin à Mayenne, for F. Rieder, 1914. 182 pp. (Bibliothèque de Littérature Comparée.) Rev.: (a) W. von Wurzbach. *Euphorion* 22 (1915): 164-66; (b) L. Mensch. *Polybiblion* 2nd ser. 82 (July-Dec. 1915): 195-96; (c) L. Roustan. *RCHLP* ns 79 (1915): 171-72; (d) L. P. *Revue* (Paris) 49 (1915): 170-72; (e) A. Hämel. *RFE* 2 (1915): 181-83; (f) A. Hämel. *LGRP* 37 (1916): col. 387-88; (g) H. Albert. *Mercure de France* (Paris) 115 (1916): 336-42; (h) A. Hämel. *NS* 28 (1920): 188-89. [B] "L'Hispanisme allemand (XIXe et XXe siècles)." *BH* 37 (1935): 220-35. [For a more complete list of this scholar's publications, see R. Pageard, "Bibliographie annotée des œuvres de Jean Achille Bertrand (1884-1960)," *SFG* 23 (1967): 370-80.]

1113. Beysterveldt, Antonie Adrianus van. Répercussions du souci de la pureté de sang sur la conception de l'honneur dans la *Comedia nueva* espagnole. Amsterdam, 1966.
❖ Title as is. Leiden: Brill, 1966. 247 pp. Rev.: (a) A. Gloesener. *RBPH* 46 (1968): 667-68; (b) L. V. Aracil. *REP* 158 (1968): 300-02.

1114. Brieva y Salvatierra, Fernando Segundo. Semejanzas y diferencias entre la tragedia antigua y la moderna. Complutense, 1867.

1115. Brotherton, John Thomas. The *Pastor-Bobo* in the Spanish Theatre before the Time of Lope de Vega. [4]+308 pp. Birmingham, 1974.
❖ Title as is. London: Tamesis, 1975. 210 pp. (Colección Támesis, serie A. Monografías 51.) Rev.: (a) V. Dixon. *BHS* 54 (1977): 150-51; (b) C. Stern. *RPh* 31 (1977-78): 702-04; (c) R. Hess. *RJ* 29 (1978): 369-70.

1116. Bückmann-de Villegas López, Sabine Ulrike. Erfahrungen der Rache im englischen und spanischen Drama der Blütezeit. Münster, 1990.
❖ Title as is. Frankfurt: Peter Lang, 1991. 383 pp. (Münsteraner Monographien zur englischen Literatur 4.) Rev.: A. Gérard. *RLC* 67.4 (1993): 556-58.

1117. Buezo Canalejo, Catalina. La mojiganga dramática: Historia y teoría. 2 vols. (1239 pp.) Complutense, 1990.
❖ [A] "Del entremés burlesco a la mojiganga." *Teatro español a fines del siglo XVII: Historia, cultura y teatro en la España de Carlos II.* Ed. Javier Huerta Calvo, Harm den Boer, and Fermín Sierra Martínez. 3 vols. Amsterdam: Rodopi, 1989. 2: 553-68. [B] "*El que busca la mojiganga:* Estudio y edición de una pieza anónima de posible atribución a Calderón." *RL* 51.101 (1989): 157-88. [C] "*El sacristán fariseo:* Edición de un entremés inédito y apuntes sobre la figura del fariseo." *Criticón* 50 (1990): 93-112. [D] "*El triunfo de Don Quijote:* Una máscara estudiantil burlesca de 1610 y otras invenciones." *ACer* 28 (1990): 87-98. [E] "Problemas que plantea la edición crítica del género 'mojiganga dramática.'" *Teatros y vida teatral en el Siglo de Oro a través de las fuentes documentales.* Ed. Luciano García Lorenzo and John E. Varey. London: Tamesis, 1991. 237-44. (Colección Támesis, serie A. Monografías 145.) [F] *La mojiganga*

dramática: De la fiesta al teatro. Kassel: Reichenberger, 1993. 550 pp. (Teatro del Siglo de Oro. Estudios de literatura 19.) Rev: (a) J. Caminero. *LdD* 24.65 (1994): 235–37: (b) C. de Lucas. *Teatro* 6–7 (1994–95): 312–13. [G] "El rey de los reyes en la mojiganga dramática." *Estado actual de los estudios sobre el Siglo de Oro: Actas del segundo congreso internacional de hispanistas del Siglo de Oro, Salamanca y Valladolid, 1990.* Ed. Manuel García Martín, Ignacio Arellano, Javier Blasco, and Marc Vitse. 2 vols. Salamanca: Universidad de Salamanca, 1993. 1: 203–07. [H] "El arca del Nuevo Mundo: Un artificio escénico del teatro breve barroco." *Teatro* 6–7 (1994–95): 81–91. [I] "El niño en el teatro cómico breve del siglo XVII." *Studia aurea: Actas del tercer congreso de la AISO, Toulouse, 1993.* 3 vols. Toulouse-Pamplona: GRISO-LEMSO, 1996. Vol 2. *Teatro.* Ed. Ignacio Arellano, María del Carmen Pinillos, Frédéric Serralta, and Marc Vitse. 2: 97–107.

1118. Canalejas y Méndez, José. Consideraciones generales acerca de los orígenes del teatro moderno. iv+196 pp., handwritten. Complutense, 1873.

1119. Couper, Mary Morrison. The Evolution of the Spanish *Comedia* from the Close of the Seventeenth Century to the Present Day, with Special Reference to the Period 1835–1898. [3]+316 pp. Edinburgh, 1936.

1120. Cuenca Cabeza, Manuel. El tema de los Infantes de Lara en el teatro español. 2 vols. Navarre, 1980.

❖ [A] *Córdoba y la leyenda de los Infantes de Lara.* Córdoba: Monte de Piedad y Caja de Ahorros, 1988. 103 pp. (Colección de bolsillo Cajasur 16.) [B] *La leyenda de los Infantes de Lara en el teatro español.* Córdoba: Monte de Piedad y Caja de Ahorros; Bilbao: Universidad de Deusto, 1990. 171 pp.

1121. Díaz Regañón López, José María. Influencia de la tragedia griega en la literatura española. 453 pp. Valencia, 1955.

❖ *Los trágicos griegos en España.* Valencia: Universitat de València, 1955. 374 pp. (Anales de la Universidad de Valencia 29.3.) Filosofía y Letras [1955–56].) [Of some interest are ch. 1 (pp. 7–109) and ch. 2 (pp. 111–52), which deal with the sixteenth and seventeenth centuries, respectively.] Rev.: (a) M. Dolç. *Argensola* 8 (1957): 268–69; (b) A. Hermenegildo. *RL* 15.29–30 (1959): 132.

1122. DUQUE, PEDRO J. Presencia de España y lo español en Shakespeare y su obra. Deusto, 1978.
❖ [A] "*The Taming of the Shrew* [by Shakespeare] y sus antecedentes españoles." *ES* 8 (1978): 199-221. [B] "Lope de Vega y Shakespeare." *Lope de Vega y los orígenes del teatro español: Actas del primer congreso internacional sobre Lope de Vega*. Ed. Manuel Criado de Val. Madrid: EDI-6, 1981. 851-69. [C] "Calderón-Shakespeare: Algunas similitudes y diferencias." *Calderón: Actas del congreso internacional sobre Calderón y el teatro español del Siglo de Oro, Madrid, 1981*. Ed. Luciano García Lorenzo. 3 vols. Madrid: CSIC, 1983. 1277-88. [The writer cites his dissertation in support of the following hypothesis: "Por la semejanza que a su vez guardan estas escenas (*A secreto agravio, secreta venganza,* II. 460ff y *The Two Gentlemen of Verona,* I. ii) con otra de la *Diana* de Montemayor, es dable deducir que Calderón, lo mismo que Shakespeare, conocía la novela del escritor luso-español."] [D] *España en Shakespeare: Presencia de España y lo español en Shakespeare y su obra*. Bilbao: Universidad de Deusto, 1991. 427pp.

1123. ESQUERDO SIVERA, VICENTA. El teatro en Valencia en el siglo XVII. Un aspecto: Los contratos entre los cómicos y el Hospital. 2 vols. Valencia, 1973.
❖ [A] "Aportaciones al estudio del teatro en Valencia durante el siglo XVII: Actores que representaron y su contratación por el Hospital General." *BRAE* 55.206 (1975): 429-530. [B] "Indumentaria con la que los cómicos representaban en el siglo XVII." *BRAE* 58 (1978): 447-544. [C] "Posible autoría en las comedias representadas en Valencia entre 1601 y 1679." *RL* 41 (1979): 219-38. [D] "Acerca de *La confusa* de Cervantes." *Cervantes, su obra y su mundo: Actas del primer congreso internacional sobre Cervantes, Madrid, 1978*. Ed. Manuel Criado de Val. Madrid: EDI-6, 1981. 243-47. [Apropos a lost play mentioned in a document (1627) of the Archivo del Hospital General de Valencia.] [E] "Pedro de Ascanio, comédien et directeur de compagnie dramatique." *BH* 86 (1984): 179-200. [The article consists of 18 documents related to this actor in seventeenth-century Valencia.]

1124. FEIWEL, MARIE. De *Comedia Nueva:* Over de Lectuur van Tekst en Uitleg. (The *Comedia nueva:* On the Reading of the Text and Interpretation.) 346 pp. Leiden, 1981. *DAI-C* 44: 6.

❖ Title as is. Amsterdam: Universiteit van Amsterdam, 1980.

1125. Fernández y Velasco, Saturnino. Elementos que concurren a la formación del teatro español: Su carácter durante la Edad Media. Examen de las obras de Juan del Enzina, Lucas Fernández, Gil Vicente y otros escritores hasta Lope de Rueda. Complutense, 1865.

❖ Title as is. Madrid: Minuesa, 1866. 63 pp.

1126. Ferrer Valls, Teresa. Orígenes y desarrollo de la práctica escénica cortesana: Del fasto medieval al teatro áulico en el reinado de Felipe III. 805 pp. Valencia, 1987. *DAI-C* 50: 4.

❖ [A] Title as is. Valencia: Universitat de València, Servicio de Publicaciones, 1987. [B] *La práctica escénica cortesana: De la época del Emperador a la de Felipe III.* London: Tamesis, in collaboration with Institució Valenciana d'Estudis i Investigació, 1991. 206 pp. (Colección Támesis, serie A. Monografías 143.) Rev.: (a) M. Débax. *Criticón* 59 (1993): 173–75; (b) F. A. de Armas. *H* [AATSP] 76.2 (1993): 275–77; (c) A. Cortijo Ocaña. *RFE* 73.3–4 (1993): 464–65; (d) F. Serralta. *BHS* 71.2 (1994): 264–65; (e) J. M. Ruano de la Haza. *RCEH* 10.2 (1994): 346–48; (f) R. Hernández Pecoraro. *Gestos* 10.20 (1995): 184–85; (g) O. Rivera. *NRFH* 43.1 (1995): 212–20. [C] "El espectáculo profano en la Edad Media: Espacio escénico y escenografía." *Historias y ficciones: Coloquio sobre la literatura del siglo XV. Actas del coloquio internacional, Valencia, 1990.* Ed. Rafael Beltrán, José Luis Canet, and Josep Lluís Sirera. Valencia: Universitat de València, Departament de Filologia Espanyola, 1992. 307–22. [D] *Nobleza y espectáculo teatral (1535–1622): Estudio y documentos.* Valencia: Universitat de València, 1993. 392 pp. (Serie textos teatrales hispánicos del siglo XVI 1.) Rev.: (a) A. González. *NRFH* 42.2 (1994): 662–63; (b) J. E. Varey. *BHS* 72.4 (1995): 433–34; (c) A. Soons. *Ibero* 43 (1996): 150–52.

1127. Flecniakoska, Jean-Louis. La Formation de l'*auto* religieux en Espagne avant Calderón (1550–1635). Paris, 1962. (Thèse d'État)

❖ [A] Title as is. Montpellier: Déhan, 1961. 531 pp. Rev.: (a) E.

Cros. *BBMP* 38 (1962): 181–82; (b) E. Cros. *BH* 64.3–4 (1962): 285–87; (c) J. Ares Montes. *Ínsula* 186 (1962): 8; (d) R. Larrieu. *LanM* 56 (1962): 76–77; (e) E. Cros. *RLR* 75 (1962): 75–77; (f) D. Briesemeister. *Archiv* 200 (1963): 310–11; (g) N. D. Shergold. *HR* 31 (1963): 265–70; (h) R. Larrieu. *LLNL* 57 (1963): 95–96; (i) E. Juliá Martínez. *RL* 23 (1963): 277–81; (j) R. Benítez Claros *Atlántida* 2 (1964): 215–16; (k) A. A. Parker. *BHS* 42 (1965): 192–94; (l) E. Juliá Martínez. *Segismundo* 1 (1965): 143–47. [B] "Les Conflits tragiques dans l'auto religieux précaldéronien." *Le Théâtre tragique*. Ed. J. Jacquot. Paris: CNRS, 1962. 107–17. [C] "Les Rôles de Satan dans les pièces du *Códice de autos viejos*." *RLR* 75 (1963): 195–207. [D] "Les Rôles de Satan dans les *autos* de Lope de Vega." *BH* 66 (1964): 30–44. [E] Valdivielso, J. de. El hospital de los locos *y* La serrana de Plasencia *(autos sacramentales)*. Ed. J. L. Flecniakoska. Salamanca: Anaya, 1971. (Biblioteca Anaya 20.) [F] "Las figuras de herejía y demonio al servicio de la propaganda política en los autos de Mira de Amescua." *BBMP* 52 (1976): 203–22. [For a more complete list of this scholar's publications, see *Hommage à Jean-Louis Flecniakoska par ses collègues, amis et élèves des Universités de Montpellier, Avignon et Perpignan*, 2 vols. (Montpellier: Université Paul Valéry, 1980) 1: 15–25.]

1128. Fothergill Payne-Guépin, Louise Wilhelmina. La alegoría en los autos y farsas anteriores a Calderón. 265 pp. Groningen, 1976.

❖ [A] Title as is. London: Tamesis, 1977. 223 pp. (Colección Támesis, serie A. Monografías 66.) Rev.: (a) S. Neumeister. *RJ* 29 (1978): 371–73; (b) W. F. Hunter. *BHS* 56 (1979): 252–53; (c) J. A. Parr. *H* [AATSP] 62 (1979): 729–30; (d) N. Griffin. *MLR* 74 (1979): 726–27; (e) J. H. Parker. *RCEH* 3 (1979): 197–98; (f) I. Villalobos Racionero. *RFE* 59 (1979 for 1977): 322–27; (g) H. T. Young. *Symposium* 33 (1979): 371–73; (h) I. L. McClelland. *ThR* 4 (1979): 150–51; (i) H. Bergman. *MP* 77 (1980): 411–13; (j) C. Stern. *RPh* 34 (1980): 273–76. [B] "La doble historia de la alegoría (unas observaciones generales sobre el modo alegórico en la literatura del Siglo de Oro)." *Actas del sexto congreso internacional de hispanistas, Toronto, 1977*. Ed. Alan M. Gordon and

Evelyn Rugg. Toronto: Univ. of Toronto, 1980. 261-64. [C] "The World Picture in Calderón's *Autos Sacramentales.*" *Calderón and the Baroque Tradition.* Ed. Kurt Levy, Jesús Ara, and Gethin Hughes. Waterloo: Wilfrid Laurier UP, 1985. 33-40.

1129. García Sanz, Luis. Los caracteres del teatro antiguo español. Complutense, 1852.

❖ [A] Title as is. Madrid: Rodríguez, 1852. 26 pp. [B] *Discurso sobre los caracteres del teatro antiguo español.* Madrid: Palacios, 1861. 24 pp.

1130. Garriga y Nogués, Ramón. La comedia y sus orígenes. Complutense, 1862.

❖ Title as is. Madrid: Martínez García, 1863. 58 pp. [A discussion of the origins and types of *comedia.*]

1131. Garrot, Juan Carlos. Le Thème juif et "converso" dans le théâtre religieux espagnol, notamment dans celui de Calderón (fin XVème siècle-XVIIème siècle). 679 pp. Paris/III, 1992.

[For the complete entry, see no. 1264.]

1132. Gewecke, Frauke. Thematische Untersuchungen zu dem vorcalderonianischen *Auto sacramental.* Hamburg, 1971.

❖ Title as is. Genève: Droz, 1974. 357 pp. (Kölner romanistische Arbeiten ns 42.) Rev.: (a) S. Neumeister. *RF* 88 (1976): 485-86; (b) D. Briesemeister. *Archiv* 214 (1977): 453-55; (c) N. Griffin. *MLR* 72 (1977): 220-22.

1133. Griffin, Nigel H. Some Aspects of Jesuit School Drama, 1550-1600, with Special Reference to Spain and Portugal. 2 vols. (552 pp.) Oxford, 1976.

❖ [A] "Some Jesuit Theatre Manuscripts." *HumC* 23-24 (1971-72): 427-34. [B] "Miguel Venegas and the Sixteenth-Century Jesuit School-Drama" *MLR* 68 (1973): 796-806. [C] "El teatro de los jesuitas: Algunas sugerencias para su investigación." *FMod* 54 (1975): 407-13. [D] *Jesuit School Drama: A Checklist of Critical Literature.* London: Grant and Cutler, 1976. 54 pp. (Research Bibliographies and Checklists 12.) Rev.: T. O'Reilly. *BHS* 55 (1978): 157-58. [E] *Two Jesuit Ahab Dramas:* Tragoedia cui nomen inditum Achabus *by Miguel Venegas and* Tragoedia Jezabelis *(Anonymous).* Ed. N. H. Griffin. Exeter: Univ. of Exeter, 1976. 171 pp. (Exeter Hispanic Texts 13.) Rev.: (a) L. Bradner. *JHP* 2

(1977): 70–71; (b) T. O'Reilly. *BHS* 55 (1978): 157–58. [F] "A Portuguese Jesuit Play in Seventeenth-Century Cologne." *Folio* 12 (1980): 46–69. [G] "Lewin Brecht, Miguel Venegas, and the School Drama: Some Further Observations." *HumC* 35–36 (1983–84): 19–86. [H] *Jesuit School Drama: A Checklist of Critical Literature.* Supp. 1. London: Grant and Cutler, 1986. 219 pp. (Research Bibliographies and Checklists 12.)

1134. GROSSMANN, RUDOLF. Spanien und das elisabethanische Drama. Leipzig, 1920. Abstract. *Jahrbuch der Philosophischen Fakultät Leipzig* 1 (1920): 10–12.

❖ Title as is. Hamburg: Friederichsen, 1920. 138 pp. (Hamburgische Universitäts-Abhandlungen aus dem Gebiet der Auslandskunde 4, Reihe B. Völkerkunde, Kulturgeschichte und Sprachen 3.) [The only Spanish "dramatic" work discussed is *La Celestina.*] Rev.: (a) M. A. *BBMP* 2 (1920): 324–25; (b) A. Brandl. *Archiv* 141 (1921): 310; (c) F. Krüger. *RFE* 8 (1921): 184–85; (d) F. C. D. *RG* 12 (1921): 434–35; (e) L. Pfandl. *Archiv* 143 (1922): 159–61; (f) E. Eckhardt. *EnSt* 56 (1922): 425–26; (g) W. F. Schirmer *NS* 30 (1922): 186–87; (h) V. Tarkiainen. *Neuphilologische Mitteilungen* 23 (1922): 166; (i) W. von Wurzbach. *ZRP* 42 (1922): 252–54; (j) L. Pfandl. *LGRP* 44 (1923): 351–54. [For a more complete list of this scholar's publications, see E. Lorenz and H. Schneider, "Verzeichnis der Schriften Rudolf Grossmanns (zu seinem 75. Geburtstag)," *RJ* 17 (1966): 231–41; also *Homenaje a Rodolfo Grossmann: Festschrift zu seinem 85. Geburtstag,* ed. S. Horl, J. M. Navarro de Adriaensens, H.-K. Schneider, and E. Lorenz (Frankfurt: Peter Lang, 1977) xiii–xxvi.]

1135. HACHTMANN, OTTO WILHELM. Graf Julius Heinrich von Soden als Dramatiker. Göttingen, 1902.

❖ Title as is. Göttingen: Kaestner, 1902. 160 pp. [The writer examines Soden's adaptation of Calderón's *La vida es sueño,* as well as several plays on Iberian themes—e.g., *Ignez de Castro.*]

1136. HÄMEL, ADALBERT. Der Cid im spanischen Drama des XVI. und XVII. Jahrhunderts. Würzburg, 1910.

❖ [A] Excerpt. Title as is. Halle: Karras, 1910. 104 pp. [B] Title as is. Halle: Niemeyer, 1910. 169 pp. (Zeitschrift für romanische Philologie, Beiheft 25.) Rev.: (a) L. Pfandl. *Archiv* 126 (1911):

473–75; (b) E. Mérimée. *BH* 13.2 (1911): 240–47. [C] "Las hazañas del Cid." *ZRP* 40 (1919–20): 623. [For a more complete list of this scholar's publications, see H. Stark, "Bibliographie der Veröffentlichungen A. Hämels (unter Ausschluss der Rezensionen)," *RJ* 5 (1952): 49–51.]

1137. HECKMANN, THEODOR. Massinger's *The Renegado* und seine spanischen Quellen. 66 pp. Halle, 1905.

❖ Title as is. Halle: Kaemmerer, 1905. [The writer examines, inter alia, the relationship between Massinger's play and Cervantes's *comedia* entitled *Los baños de Argel*.]

1138. HEIDENREICH, HELMUT. Figuren und Komik in den spanischen *Entremeses* des goldenen Zeitalters. 221 pp. Munich, 1962. // Rev.: (a) V. F. Dixon. *BHS* 40 (1963): 202–03; (b) J. M. Díez Taboada. *RL* 27 (1965): 228–29; (c) O. T. Myers. *RPh* 18.4 (1965): 520; (d) J. M. Díez Taboada. *Segismundo* 1 (1965): 150–52;

1139. HEINE, CARL. Johannes Velten: Ein Beitrag zur Geschichte des deutschen Theaters im XVII. Jahrhundert. Halle, 1887.

[Velten's strolling company included at least six plays of Calderón in its repertory.]

❖ [A] Title as is. Halle: Karras, 1887. 63 pp. [B] "Calderón im Spielverzeichnisse der deutschen Wandertruppen." *ZVL* ns 2 (1889): 165–75, 395–403. [C] *Das Schauspiel der deutschen Wanderbühne vor Gottsched*. Halle: Niemeyer, 1889. [D] "Die ausländischen Dramen im Spielplan des Weimarischen Theaters unter Goethes Leitung." *ZVL* ns 4 (1891): 313–21.

1140. HERMENEGILDO FERNÁNDEZ, ALFREDO. La tragedia en España en el siglo XVI. [4]+635 pp. Complutense, 1960. Abstract in *RUM* 9.36 (1960): 905–06.

❖ [A] *Los trágicos españoles del siglo XVI*. Madrid: Fundación Universitaria Española, 1961. 617 pp. Rev.: (a) C. Murciano. *PEsp* 76–77 (1962): 118; (b) J. Montero Padilla. *RFE* 45 (1962): 331–33; (c) E. Juliá Martínez. *RL* 23 (1963): 277–81. [B] "Nueva interpretación de un primitivo: Lucas Fernández." *Segismundo* 2.3 (1966): 9–43. [C] "Sobre la dimensión social del teatro primitivo español." *Prohemio* 2 (1971): 25–50. [D] *La tragedia en el Renacimiento español*. Barcelona: Planeta, 1973. 603 pp. [This is an extensively revised and expanded version of publication A.]

Rev.: (a) R. R. MacCurdy. *BCom* 27.2 (1975): 130–36; (b) A. Cioranescu. *RLC* 49.2 (1975): 316. [E] *Renacimiento, teatro y sociedad.* Madrid: Cincel, 1975. 256 pp. [F] "La imagen del rey y el teatro de la España clásica." *Segismundo* 12.23–24 (1976): 53–86. [G] "Adulación, ambición e intriga: Los cortesanos de la primitiva tragedia española." *Segismundo* 13.25–26 (1977): 43–87. [H] *Teatro español del siglo XVI.* Ed. A. Hermenegildo. Madrid: SGEL, 1982. 278 pp. [Contains *El auto de la Pasión* (Lucas Fernández), *Comedia Himenea* (Bartolomé Torres Naharro), *Tragicomedia de don Duardos* (Gil Vicente), *Tragedia de la destrucción de Numancia* (Cervantes).] [I] *Teatro español renacentista.* Ed. A. Hermenegildo. Madrid: Espasa Calpe, 1990. 306 pp. (Colección Austral 171.) [Contains *Égloga de Cristino y Febea* (Juan del Encina), *Égloga interlocutoria* (Diego de Ávila), *Égloga o Farsa del Nascimento de Nuestro Redemptor Jesucristo* (Lucas Fernández), *Comedia soldadesca* (Bartolomé Torres Naharro), *Tragedia de don Duardos* (Gil Vicente).] [J] "Experiencias dramáticas y públicos teatrales: La tragedia española del Renacimiento." *Nascita della tragedia di poesia nei paesi europei, Vicenza, 1990.* Ed. Myriam Chiabò and Federico Doglio. Vicenza: Centro Studi sul Teatro Medioevale e Rinascimentale, 1991. 261–82. [K] "Provisiones de enunciación y motricidad en la *Nise laureada* de Jerónimo Bermúdez." *Hispanic Essays in Honor of Frank P. Casa.* Ed. A. Robert Lauer and Henry W. Sullivan. New York: Peter Lang, 1997. 10–25.

1141. Hess, Rainer. Komische Elemente im romanischen geistlichen Schauspiel des 15. und 16. Jahrhunderts. 247 pp. Freiburg, 1961.

❖ [A] "Die Naturauffassung Gil Vicentes." *APK* 5 (1965): 1–64. [B] *Das romanische geistliche Schauspiel als profane und religiöse Komödie. 15. und 16. Jahrhundert.* München: Fink, 1965. 198 pp. (Freiburger Schriften zur romanischen Philologie 4.) [Frequent references to Lucas Fernández, Bartolomé Palau, Diego Sánchez de Badajoz, Bartolomé Torres Naharro, Gil Vicente, etc.] Rev.: (a) H. Th. Oostendorp. *Neophilologus* 50 (1966): 465; (b) M. Nerlich. *RF* 78 (1966): 582–86; (c) W. Engler. *ZFSL* 76 (1966): 381–83; (d) L. J. Friedman. *RPh* 21.1 (1967): 139–40; (e) R.

Warning. *Archiv* 205 (1968): 245–48; (f) W. Noomen. *RBPH* 46 (1968): 1036–37. [C] *El drama religioso románico como comedia religiosa y profana. (Siglos XV y XVI).* Trans. Rafael de la Vega. Madrid: Gredos, 1976. 333 pp. (BRH. II. Estudios y ensayos 252.) Rev.: (a) J. A. Míguez. *Arbor* 97 (1977): 141–43; (b) N. Griffin. *BHS* 55 (1978): 147–48.

1142. HORSTMEYER, GABRIELE. Die Kupplerin: Studien zur Typologie im dramatischen Schriftum Europas von den Griechen bis zur Französischen Revolution. 141 pp. Cologne, 1972.

[The *Celestina* is the only Spanish work discussed.]

1143. HOUSMAN, JOHN ERNEST. Parallel Plots in English and Spanish Drama of the Early Seventeenth Century. [3]+691 pp. London/External Degree, 1951.

1144. HUERTA CALVO, JAVIER. Introducción al teatro menor del Siglo de Oro: Gil López de Armesto. 2 vols. (511, 438 pp.) Complutense, 1983.

❖ [A] "Para una poética de la representación en el Siglo de Oro: Función de las piezas menores." *1616* 3 (1980): 69–81. [B] "Cómico y femenil bureo: Del amor y las mujeres en los entremeses del Siglo de Oro." *Criticón* 24 (1983): 5–68. [C] "Los géneros teatrales menores en el Siglo de Oro: Status y prospectiva de la investigación." *El teatro menor en España a partir del siglo XVI: Actas del coloquio, Madrid, 1982.* Ed. Luciano García Lorenzo. Madrid: CSIC, 1983. 23–62. [D] *Teatro breve de los siglos XVI y XVII: Entremeses, loas, bailes, jácaras y mojigangas.* Ed. J. Huerta Calvo. Madrid: Taurus, 1985. 410 pp. (Colección temas de España 148.) [E] *El nuevo mundo de la risa: Estudio sobre el teatro breve y la comicidad en los Siglos de Oro.* Palma de Mallorca: Olañeta, 1995. 185 pp. (Oro viejo 3.)

1145. ÍÑIGUEZ BARRENA, MARÍA FRANCISCA. Introducción al estudio de la parodia teatral. Barcelona, 1981.

❖ Excerpt. Title as is. Barcelona: Universitat de Barcelona, Centre de Publicacions, 1981. 17 pp.

1146. IZQUIERDO Y MARTÍNEZ, JOSÉ MARÍA. El derecho en el teatro español: Apuntes para una antología jurídica de las comedias del Siglo de Oro. Introducción, índice, programa y apéndice. Complutense, 1913(?).

❖ [A] "El derecho y el arte: Introducción a un estudio sobre 'El derecho en el teatro español.'" *La Lectura* 13 (1913): 117-34. [B] Title as is. Sevilla: Saavedra, 1914. 47 pp. [C] Also: Sevilla: Zarzuela, 1924. 374 pp. (Vol. 4 of *Obras completas.*)

1147. JONES, MELVEENA CHRISTINE. The *Mujer Varonil* in the Drama of the Golden Age: A Social and Literary Study of a Dramatic Type. Cambridge, 1967.

❖ [A] "The *Bandolera* of Golden-Age Drama: A Symbol of Feminist Revolt." *BHS* 46 (1969): 1-20. [B] "The 'Mujer Esquiva'—a Measure of the Feminist Sympathies of the Seventeenth-Century Spanish Dramatists." *HR* 40 (1972): 162-97. [C] McKendrick, Melveena C. *Woman and Society in the Spanish Drama of the Golden Age: A Study of the* Mujer Varonil. London: Cambridge UP, 1974. 346 pp. Rev.: (a) J. G. Weiger. *BCom* 27 (1975): 141-46; (b) A. V. Ebersole. *H* [AATSP] 58 (1975): 979-80; (c) R. R. MacCurdy. *RenQ* 28.2 (1975): 256-58; (d) J. T. Brotherton. *AUMLA* 45 (1976): 136-37; (e) E. Canito. *Ínsula* 354 (1976): 8-9; (f) D. Rogers. *MLR* 71 (1976): 447-48; (g) F. Weber de Kurlat. *BHS* 54 (1977): 61-63; (h) D. H. Darst. *RR* 69 (1978): 256-57.

1148. JOSÉ PRADES, JUANA DE. Aportación al estudio de la teoría literaria y bibliografía de los dramaturgos menores pertenecientes al ciclo dramático de Lope de Vega. vii+400 pp. Complutense, 1960. Abstract in *RUM* 10.40 (1961): 852.

[Includes works by Jerónimo de Villaizán, Julián de Armendáriz, Miguel Sánchez, Jerónimo de la Fuente, Gaspar de Ávila.]

❖ [A] *La teoría literaria (Retóricas, poéticas, preceptivas, etc.)*. Madrid: CSIC, Instituto de Estudios Madrileños, 1954. (Monografías bibliográficas 3. Literatura 1.) [B] "Hernán Cortés en *La sentencia sin firma* [of Gaspar de Ávila]." *RL* 19 (1961): 39-54. [C] *Teoría sobre los personajes de la comedia nueva en cinco dramaturgos.* Madrid: CSIC, 1963. 337 pp. Rev.: (a) J. M. Lope Toledo. *Berceo* 18.65 (1963): 108; (b) C. R. S. M. *NT* 21.113 (1963): 605; (c) J. M. Díez Taboada. *RFE* 46 (1963): 480-82; (d) F. Herrero. *RL* 23 (1963): 281-83; (e) A. Porqueras Mayo *RHM* 30 (1964): 145-46; (f) J. A. van Praag. *Neophilologus* 49 (1965): 181; (g) R. Esquer Torres. *Segismundo* 1 (1965): 147-49.

1149. KOHLER, EUGEN [EUGÈNE]. Sieben spanische dramatische

Eklogen mit einer Einleitung über die Anfänge der spanischen Dramas. Strasbourg, 1910.

❖ [A] Excerpt. Halle: Waisenhaus, 1911. 138 pp. [B] Title as is. Dresden: Printed for the Gesellschaft für romanische Literatur 27. Halle: Niemeyer, 1911. 365 pp. [In addition to one anonymous play, there are works by Diego (Guillén) de Ávila, Fernando Díaz, Diego Durán, Hernán López de Yanguas, Juan de París, and (Fernando del Prado) el Bachiller de la Pradilla.] Rev.: (a) M. A. Buchanan. *MLN* 27 (1912): 200; (b) A. Hämel. *LGRP* 34 (1913): col. 32–34; (c) M. A. Buchanan. *ZRP* 37 (1913): 503–05. [C] *Representaciones de Juan del Encina.* Strasbourg: Heitz; New York: Stechert, 1914(?).

1150. Köhler, Gerhard. Adolf Wilbrandts Dramen am Burgtheater. xiii+352 pp. Vienna, 1970.

[Wilbrandt produced plays by Calderón and other Spanish dramatists.]

1151. Konan, Jean. L'Écho dramatique des controverses théologiques suscitées par le problème de la grâce et de la liberté dans le théâtre religieux, de Cervantes à Calderón. 251 pp. Nantes, 1969.

❖ [A] "L'Aspect humain ou traditionnel du *Condenado por desconfiado.*" *AdUA* 5 (1972): 151–65. [B] "L'Aspect divin ou surnaturel du *Condenado por desconfiado.*" *AdUA* 7 (1974): 149–67. [C] "La Foi, comme phénomène psychologique dans *El condenado por desconfiado.*" *AdUA* 7 (1974): 139–47. [D] "Le Conflit entre la prédestination et la liberté dans *El esclavo del demonio.*" *AdUA* 8 (1975): 217–28. [E] "Le Péché originel et la grâce dans *El rufián dichoso.*" *AdUA* 8 (1975): 203–16. [F] "Gabriel Téllez: L'homme et l'auteur." *AdUA* 9 (1976): 285–93. [G] "*Ninfa del cielo* et les controverses théologiques." *AdUA* 9 (1976): 297–303. [H] "Origines des querelles *de auxiliis* dans 'las comedias' de Tirso de Molina, et dans le théâtre religieux de l'Espagne du Siècle d'Or en général." *AdUA* 9 (1976): 253–64. [I] "Prédestination et libre arbitre dans les 'autos' et 'comedias de santos' de Tirso de Molina." *AdUA* 9 (1976): 267–82.

1152. Laroche, Maximilien. Le Personnage du roi dans l'imitation des espagnols chez Corneille et Rotrou. vi+203 pp. Toulouse/II, 1971. (Thèse de 3e cycle)

1153. Latorre y Badillo, Manuel. Representación de los autos sacramentales en el período de su mayor florecimiento (1620-1681). Two handwritten versions, 270 pp. and 320 pp. Complutense, 1905.

❖ Title as is. *RABM* 25 (1911): 189-211, 342-67; 26 (1912): 72-89, 236-62.

1154. Ley, Charles David. El gracioso en el teatro peninsular. Complutense, 1950.

❖ [A] *El gracioso en el teatro de la península, siglos XVI-XVII.* Madrid: Revista de Occidente, 1954. 263 pp. Rev.: (a) C. Bravo Villasante. *Clavileño* 6.31 (1955): 73; (b) A. Zamora Vicente. *Ínsula* 10 (1955): 6-7; (c) J. Barceló. *AUMur* 14 (1955-56): 462-64; (d) M. Wilson. *BHS* 33.3 (1956): 171-72; (e) N. E. Zingoni. *RdE* 1 (1956): 226-28. [B] Rpt. Ann Arbor: Xerox Univ. Microfilms, 1975. 263 pp.

1155. Marín Casanova, José. Lo regional en el teatro de los dramáticos valencianos contemporáneos de Lope. 352 pp. Valencia, 1957.

1156. Martinenche, Ernest. La *Comedia* espagnole en France de Hardy à Racine. Paris, 1900. (Thèse d'État)

❖ [A] Title as is. Paris: Hachette, 1900. 434 pp. Rev.: (a) G. Le Gentil. *BH* 3.2 (1901): 174-78; (b) F. Brunetière. *RDM* 13 (1 Jan. 1903): 211-16. [B] "Les Sources espagnoles d'*Horace* et d'*Héraclius*." *RLR* 44 (1900): 262-68. [The two plays are by Pierre Corneille.] [C] *Molière et le théâtre espagnol.* Paris: Hachette, 1906. 273 pp. [D] "Über Jean Rotrou's spanische Quellen." *ZFSL* 29 (1906): 19-40. [E] Rpt. of publication A. Genève: Slatkine, 1970. 438 pp.

1157. Martinenche, Ernest. Quatenus Tragicomoedia *de Calisto y Melibea* vulgo *Celestina* dicta ad informandum hispaniense theatrum valuerit. Paris, 1900-01. (Thèse complémentaire)

❖ Title as is. Nîmes: Coopérative la Laborieuse, 1900. 123 pp. [The writer examines the role that the *Celestina* played in the origins of the Spanish theater.]

1158. McCabe, William Hugh. An Introduction to the Jesuit Theatre. Cambridge, 1929. Cambridge *Abstracts* (1928-29): 74-75.

❖ [A] "Music and Dance on a 17th-Century College Stage." *MQ* 24 (1938): 313-22. [B] Title as is. *A Posthumous Work*. Ed.

Louis J. Oldani, SJ. Saint Louis: Inst. of Jesuit Sources, 1983. 346 pp. [Very few specific references to Spain.] Rev.: (a) R. Engle. *TJ* 36 (1984): 431–32; (b) S. Gossett. *RenQ* 38 (1985): 160–64; (c) J. Hilton. *TLS* 22 Feb. 1985: 208.

1159. MENDIOLA QUEREJETA, ANTOLÍN. La tragedia clásica en el teatro español. 128 pp. Complutense, 1913.

1160. MENÉNDEZ AYUSO, EMILIO. La comedia, espejo de frustración. 358 pp. Complutense, 1974. Abstract in *RUCM* 23.94-2 (1974): 84.
[Deals with the Golden Age *comedia* as a reflection of the frustration of minorities.]

1161. MÉRIMÉE, HENRI-ERNEST-GUSTAVE. L'Art dramatique à Valencia depuis les origines jusqu'au commencement du XVIIe siècle. Paris, 1913. (Thèse d'État)
❖ [A] Title as is. Toulouse: Privat, 1913. 734 pp. (Bibliothèque méridionale 2e série, 16.) Rev.: (a) C. Déjob. *RCHLP* ns 77 (1914): 34–36; (b) Anon. *RFE* 1 (1914): 347–51; (c) M. A. Buchanan. *MLR* 11 (1916): 104–06. [B] *Théâtre espagnol.* Vol. 1: Encina, Torres Naharro, Lope de Rueda, Lope de Vega. Paris: Renaissance du Livre, 1925. Rev: (a) G. Cirot. *BH* 27 (1925): 366; (b) C. Pitollet. *RLR* 63 (1926): 349–68. [C] *El arte dramático en Valencia desde los orígenes hasta principios del siglo XVII.* Trans. Octavio Pellissa Safont. 2nd ed. 2 vols. Valencia: Institució Alfons el Magnànim-Institució Valenciana d'Estudis i Investigació, 1985. Rev.: C. Faliu-Lacourt. *BCom* 38 (1986): 262–63.

1162. MÉRIMÉE, HENRI-ERNEST-GUSTAVE. Spectacles et comédiens à Valencia (1580–1630). Paris, 1913. (Thèse complémentaire)
❖ Title as is. Toulouse: Privat, 1913. 267 pp. Rev.: (a) C. Déjob. *RCHLP* ns 77 (1914): 36–37; (b) M. A. Buchanan. *MLR* 11 (1916): 106–07.

1163. MÉRIMÉE, PAUL. L'Art dramatique en Espagne dans la première moitié du XVIIIe siècle (la *comedia,* les théoriciens). 2 vols. (637, 397 pp.) Paris, 1955. (Thèse d'État)
❖ [A] Abridged version of 1955 dissertation in offset. Toulouse, 1975. [B] Title as is. 2nd. ed. Toulouse: France-Ibérie Recherche, 1983. 540 pp. Rev.: (a) E. Arnaud. *CMHLB* 45 (1985): 149–54; (b) F. López. *BH* 88.3-4 (1986): 477–82.

1164. MERINO QUIJANO, GASPAR. Los bailes dramáticos del siglo XVII. 2 vols. Complutense, 1980.

❖ [A] Title as is. Madrid: Editorial de la Universidad Complutense, 1981. 2 vols. (766, 372 pp.) (Servicio de Reprografía de la Universidad Complutense.) [B] "El baile dramático: Sus cuatro integrantes." *Segismundo* 18.39-40 (1984): 51-72.

1165. MICHAELIS, GEORG. Die sogenannten *Comédies espagnoles* des Thomas Corneille, ihr Verhältnis zu den spanischen Vorlagen und ihre eventuellen weiteren Schicksale in dem Schrifttum anderer Nationen: Ein Beitrag zur vergleichenden Literaturforschung. 467 pp. Erlangen, 1913.

[In the dissertation, 12 French plays are analyzed in relation to *comedias* by such dramatists as Alarcón, Calderón, Cubillo, D. Figueroa and J. Figueroa, Lope, Moreto, Solís, and Tirso.]

❖ Title as is. Berlin: Ebering, 1914. 470 pp. [Of the original study, this printed version includes only ch. 10, which deals with Thomas Corneille's *Le Galant doublé* and its relationship to Calderón's *Hombre pobre todo es trazas* and Tirso's *La celosa de sí misma.*] Rev.: W. Mulertt. *LGRP* 41 (1920): col. 192.

1166. MIRATS BABA-MOUSSA, CHRISTINE. Le Manuscript 4,123 de la Biblioteca Nacional de Madrid: Édition critique, introduction et notes. 404 pp. Toulouse/II, 1988. (Thèse de 3e cycle)

["Le manuscript 4,123 de la Biblioteca Nacional de Madrid est composé de 66 bailes. . . . Avant d'être un genre théâtral le *baile* est, et continue à être jusqu'à nos jours une danse, tout simplement." (Diss.)]

❖ "Cinco bailes teatrales: Edición y notas." *Criticón* 41 (1988): 103-37.

1167. MITTERER, RICHARD. Die Sage von Bernardo del Carpio im spanischen Drama des 16. und 17. Jahrhunderts. Würzburg, 1930.

❖ Title as is. Würzburg: Graßer, 1930. 95 pp.

1168. MÜLLER, HANS-JOACHIM. "Disimular" und "fingir" oder die listige Verstellung auf dem spanischen Theater des "Siglo de Oro." 122 pp. Innsbruck, 1971.

❖ [A] Spanish translation of dissertation. Madrid: Anejos de la Revista Segismundo, 1974. [B] *Das spanische Theater im 17. Jahrhundert oder zwischen göttlicher Gnade und menschlicher List.*

Berlin: Schmidt, 1977. 169 pp. (Studienreihe Romania 2.) [C] "Das spanische Theater des *Siglo de Oro* und die Kasuistik." *MuK* 24.4 (1978): 295-305. [D] "Calderón und die Kasuistik." *Pedro Calderón de la Barca: Vorträge anläßlich der Jahrestagung der Görres-Gesellschaft 1978*. Ed. Theodor Berchem and Siegfried Sudhof. Berlin: Schmidt, 1983. 92-103.

1169. NALEPPA, GÖTZ. Frühformen des religiösen Theaters in Spanien: Ihre Entwicklung und Überreste in der Gegenwart (die *Loa* von La Alberca). 163 pp. Berlin/FU, 1970.

[The *loa* of La Alberca refers to the sixteenth-century *Loa a Nuestra Señora de la Asunción,* performed each year in the town of La Alberca, 48 miles south of Salamanca.]

1170. NEWELS, MARGARETE. Die dramatischen Gattungen in den Poetiken des *Siglo de Oro:* Eine einleitende Studie zum Thema der Dramentheorie im Goldenen Zeitalter. Cologne, 1959.

❖ [A] Title as is. Wiesbaden: Steiner, 1959. 192 pp. (Untersuchungen zur Sprach- und Literaturgeschichte der romanischen Völker 2.) Rev.: A. Soons. *NRFH* 17 (1963-64): 386-88. [B] Spanish version: *Los géneros dramáticos en las poéticas del Siglo de Oro: Investigación preliminar al estudio de la teoría dramática en el Siglo de Oro.* Trans. Amadeo Solé-Leris. London: Tamesis, 1974. 223 pp. (Colección Támesis, serie A. Monografías 35.)

1171. ÖHRLEIN, JOSEF. Der Schauspieler im spanischen Theater des Siglo de Oro (1600-1681): Untersuchungen zu Berufsbild und Rolle in der Gesellschaft. Heidelberg, 1986.

❖ [A] Title as is. Frankfurt: Vervuert, 1986. 269 pp. + illus. [B] "El actor en el Siglo de Oro: Imagen de la profesión y reputación social." *Actor y técnica de representación del teatro clásico español, Madrid, 1988.* Ed. José María Díez Borque. London: Tamesis, 1989. 17-33. (Colección Támesis, serie A. Monografías 140.) [C] *El actor en el teatro español del Siglo de Oro.* Trans. M. A. Vega. Madrid: Castalia, 1992. 356 pp. Rev.: (a) I. J. Miguel Gallo. *Criticón* 62 (1994): 147-50; (b) S. Thies. *Notas* 3 (1994): 48.

1172. OLDENGOTT, PAULA. Philipp II. im Drama der romanischen Literaturen (16. und 17. Jahrhundert). Münster, 1937.

❖ Title as is. Lengerich: Lengericher Handelsdruck, 1938. 157 pp. [The writer examines some 40 Spanish plays.]

1173. Ortiz Bordallo, María Concepción. Argel en el teatro español del Siglo de Oro. 761 pp. Complutense, 1986.

❖ Title as is. Madrid: Universidad Complutense, 1987. 761 pp. (Colección tesis doctorales no. 30/87.)

1174. Peters, (Ludwig Karl Friedrich) Robert. Über den Einfluß der spanischen Literatur auf das französische Drama [des XVII. Jahrhunderts]. Munich, 1893.

[The French dramatists discussed are Hardy, Rotrou, P. Corneille, Molière, and especially Scarron.]

❖ [A] Excerpt. Title as is. Naumburg: Lippert, 1893. 34 pp. [B] *Paul Scarron's* Jodelet duelliste *und seine spanischen Quellen (mit einer Einleitung: Die Resultate der bisherigen Forschungen über den spanischen Einfluß auf das französische Drama des XVII. Jahrhunderts).* Erlangen and Leipzig: Deichert, 1893. 102 pp. (Münchener Beiträge zur romanischen und englischen Philologie 6.) Rev.: (a) W. Cloëtta. *Archiv* 96 (1896): 222, 229–30; (b) A. L. Stiefel. *LGRP* 17 (1896): 271–75; (c) part 2, A. L. Stiefel. *ZFSL* 18 (1896): 94–102.

1175. Praag, Jonas Andries van. La *Comedia* espagnole aux Pays-Bas au XVIIe et au XVIIIe siècle. Amsterdam, 1922. Summary in "Notas bibliográficas," *BRAE* 11 (1924): 96.

❖ [A] Title as is. Amsterdam: H. J. Paris, A. H. Kruyt, 1922. 292 pp. Rev.: (a) C. Pitollet. *Renaissance d'Occident* 7 (1923): 1293–1307; (b) W. J. Entwistle. *MLR* 20 (1925): 233–34. [B] "Lope y los Países Bajos." *BSCC* 16 (1935): 424–31. [For a more complete list of this scholar's publications, see "Writings of J. A. van Praag," *Homenaje a J. A. van Praag, catedrático de la Universidad de Amsterdam, 1930–1955* (Amsterdam: Veen, 1957) 8–11.]

1176. Purcell, Hugh Dominic. Spanish Literary Influence on the English Drama to 1625. Cambridge, 1967.

1177. Ramírez y la Guardia, Luis. Causas fundamentales que determinan la existencia del teatro español: Desenvolvimiento del mismo durante el siglo XVI, y significación de Lope de Vega. Complutense, 1867.

[For the complete entry, see no. 1578.]

1178. Recoules, Henri. Les Intermèdes des collections imprimées:

Vision caricaturale de la société espagnole au XVIIe siècle. 1274 pp. Montpellier, 1969.

❖ [A] "Les Personnages des intermèdes de Cervantes." *ACer* 10 (1971): 51-168. [B] "Cervantes y Timoneda y los entremeses del siglo XVII." *BBMP* 48 (1972): 231-91. [C] Title as is. Lille: Université de Lille, Service de Reproduction des Thèses, 1973. 2 vols. (1,272 pp.) [D] "En busca del pasado con los *entremeses* de Cervantes." *ACer* 12 (1973): 39-72. [E] "Las cadenas del vizcaíno fingido." *ACer* 15 (1976): 249-56. [Apropos Cervantes's *entremés El vizcaíno fingido*.] [F] "Una colección facticia de piezas intermedias sueltas: El libro núm. V 11.293 de la Biblioteca Municipal de Montpellier." *BRAE* 56 (1976): 83-115. [G] "Los rábanos y la fiesta de toros. (En torno al tema del *Retablo de las maravillas* de Cervantes.)" *ACer* 15 (1976): 294-302.

1179. Recoules, Henri. *Ramillete gracioso* (Valencia, 1643): Introduction, édition et notes. 3 vols. (564 pp.) Montpellier, 1967. (Thèse de 3e cycle)

[This dissertation is an edition of Ramillete gracioso: *Compuesto de entremeses famosos, y bailes entremesados. Por diferentes ingenios*. Valencia: Esparsa, 1643. 239 pp.]

1180. Reyes Peña, Mercedes de los. El *Códice de autos viejos:* Un estudio de historia literaria. 3 vols. (1,493 pp.) Seville, 1983. Universidad de Sevilla, *Resúmenes 82/83* (1984): 89-97.

❖ [A] "Edición del acto del *Santísimo Sacramento, hecho en Andújar, año 1575,* y estudio comparativo con la *Farsa sacramental del desafío del hombre.*" *ArH* 205 (1984): 105-45. [The *Farsa sacramental del desafío del hombre* is in the *Códice de autos viejos*.] [B] "Algunos reflejos de la sociedad española del siglo XVI en el *Códice de autos viejos*." *Ceti sociali et ambienti urbani nel teatro religioso europeo del '300 e del '400: Atti del colloquio, Viterbo, 1985*. Ed. Myriam Chiabò and Federico Doglio. Viterbo: Centro Studi sul Teatro Medioevale e Rinascimentale; Union Editrice, 1986. 295-311. [C] Title as is. Sevilla: Alfar, 1988. [3 volumes, with the same distribution and pagination as the original, "para facilitar la localización de las referencias intertextuales," pero ampliada la edición con un prólogo de Francisco López Estrada y un anexo bibliográfico.] Rev.: F. Cazal. *Criticón* 50 (1990): 189-91. [D] "La figura del pastor en el *Códice de autos viejos.*" *Arcadia: Estudios y textos dedicados a Francisco López Estrada.* Ed. Ángel Gómez Moreno, Javier Huerta Calvo, and Víctor Infantes. 2 vols. Madrid: Universidad Complutense, 1990. 1: 429–42. [E] "Edición de unos 'Papeles sueltos' pertenecientes a dos autos del Siglo XVI sobre *La degollación de San Juan.*" *Crítica textual y anotación filológica en obras del Siglo de Oro: Actas del seminario internacional para la edición y anotación de textos del Siglo de Oro, Pamplona, 1990.* Ed. Ignacio Arellano and Jesús Cañedo. Madrid: Castalia, 1991. 431–57. [F] "Sobre acotaciones en el *Códice de autos viejos.*" *Comedias y comediantes: Estudios sobre el teatro clásico español. Actas del congreso internacional sobre teatro y prácticas escénicas en los siglos XVI y XVII, València, 1989.* Ed. Manuel V. Diago and Teresa Ferrer. Valencia: Universitat de València, 1991. 13–35.

1181. Riaño Rodríguez, Timoteo. La rebeldía en las comedias religiosas del Barroco. xxix+493+34 pp. Murcia, 1963.

1182. Rodríguez Rodríguez, José Javier. La comedia pastoril española del siglo XVI. 4 vols. (1,543 pp.) Complutense, 1990.

❖ [A] "Notas en torno a 'Cuando las madejas de oro,' un romance pastoril inédito con complemento lírico en octavas." *CILH* 11 (1989): 203–15. [B] "Literatura pastoril del s. XVI: Acercamiento a su lengua poética." *CILH* 13 (1990): 107–22. [C] "La imitación de *Il pastor fido* en la *Comedia de Diana y Silvestro* (el valor histórico de un texto olvidado)." *Sviluppi della drammaturgia pastorale nell'Europa del cinque-seicento (XV convegno, Roma, 1990).* Ed. Myriam Chiabò and Federico Doglio. [Viterbo]: Centro Studi sul Teatro Medioevale e Rinascimentale, 1991. 201–34. [D] "La función del componente lírico en la *Comedia a lo pastoril* para la noche de Navidad (1550–1575)." *CILH* 15 (1992): 113–27.

1183. Roux, Lucette Elyane. Du Logos à la scène, éthique et esthétique, la dramaturgie de la comédie de saints dans l'Espagne du Siècle d'Or, 1580–1635. Nice, 1974. (Thèse d'État)

❖ [A] "Quelques aperçus sur la mise en scène de la *comedia de santos* au XVIIème siècle." *Le Lieu théâtral à la Renaissance.* Ed. Jean Jacquot. Paris: CNRS, 1964. 235–52. [B] Title as is. Lille: Université de Lille, Service de Reproduction des Thèses, 1975. 4 vols. (471, 592, 510, 527 pp.)

1184. SÁEZ PÉREZ, ISIDRO EMILIO. Aportaciones a la historia del teatro en Granada. 900 pp. Granada, 1985.

❖ [A] "Notas sobre historia del teatro en Granada." *Estudios sobre literatura y arte dedicados al profesor Emilio Orozco Díaz*. Ed. Antonio Gallego Morell, Andrés Soria, and Nicolás Marín. 3 vols. Granada: Universidad de Granada, 1979. 3: 239-44. [B] "Un aspecto de la historia del teatro en Granada: Las compañías de cómicos." *Angélica* 3 (1992): 67-92. [C] "El teatro andaluz en el siglo XVIII: Granada." *BH* 94.1 (1992): 141-67. [The article includes information on productions of Siglo de Oro *comedias*.]

1185. SÁNCHEZ CASTAÑER Y MENA, FRANCISCO. La pecadora penitente en el teatro español: Sus fuentes y evolución. 4 vols. Complutense, 1941. Abstract in *Sumarios y extractos, Historia* (1939-44): 193-201.

❖ [A] "Alusiones teatrales en *La pícara Justina*." *RFE* 25 (1941): 225-44. [The writer examines, inter alia, two plays about *pecadoras penitentes*.] [B] "Aportación española a una leyenda universal." *Estudios románicos dedicados al profesor Andrés Soria Ortega en el XXV aniversario de la Cátedra de Literaturas Románicas.* Ed. Jesús Montoya Martínez and Juan Paredes Núñez. 2 vols. Granada: Universidad de Granada, 1985. 2: 485-92. [The legend is known as *la légende de la sacristine* or *la leyenda de Sor Beatriz*. Apropos the anonymous *auto,* entitled *Nuestra Señora del Rosario, de la Abadesa del Cielo* and Luis Vélez de Guevara's *auto,* entitled *La abadesa del cielo*.] [For a more complete list of this scholar's publications, see "Curriculum vitae del Dr. F. Sánchez-Castañer: Publicaciones," *ALH* 7 (1978): 21-26. Special issue entitled *Homenaje a F. Sánchez-Castañer.*]

1186. SCHLENKER, WILLI. Die iberische Geschichte im dramatischen Werk von Henry de Montherlant. Tübingen, 1966.

❖ Title as is. Tübingen: Präzis, 1966. 186 pp.+4 pl. [The dissertation examines three plays: *La Reine morte* (1942), *Le Maître de Santiago* (1947), and *Le Cardinal d'Espagne* (1960). The first work shows the influence of plays by Bermúdez, Mejía de la Cerda, and Vélez de Guevara.]

1187. SCHMIDT, ERICH. Die Darstellung des spanischen Dramas vor Lope de Rueda. Berlin, 1935.

❖ Title as is. Berlin: Michel, 1935. 90 pp. Rev.: (a) W. H. Shoemaker. *HR* 6 (1938): 84–87; (b) E. Glässer. *LGRP* 59 (1938): col. 337–40.

1188. SCHNEIDER, HERMANN. Friedrich Halm und das spanische Drama. Chs. 1-3. 78 pp. Berlin, 1909.

[Friedrich Halm is the pseudonym of Eligius Freiherr von Münch-Bellinghausen (1806–71). He translated *El alcalde de Zalamea,* among other works, and wrote about the *comedia* collection of the Austrian National Library (then Wiener Kaiserliche Hofbibliothek).]

❖ [A] Title as is. Berlin: Mayer & Müller, 1909. 78 pp. [B] *Friedrich Halm und das spanische Drama*. Berlin: Mayer & Müller, 1909. 258 pp. (Palaestra 28.) Rev.: (a) Ph. A. Becker. *DLZ* 31 (1910): col. 871–72; (b) W. von Wurzbach. *LitEcho* 12 (1910): col. 1613–15; (c) M.K. *LitZent* 61 (1910): col. 1388.

1189. SCHNEIDER, JOHANN FRIEDRICH. Simulthetik als dramatologisches Integrum in Schauspielen des *Siglo de Oro:* Versuch eines Beitrags zur Lösung des Problems "Hie Dichtung! Hie Bühne!" 248 pp. Hamburg, 1961.

[The writer studies *apartes* and *acotaciones* as a contribution to solving the problem of drama as literary text versus drama as performance.]

1190. SCHWEINHAMMER, KARL. Der spanische Einfluß im deutschen Drama der Romantik und Nachromantik. iv+166 pp. Vienna, 1933.

1191. SENTAURENS, JEAN. Séville et le théâtre: De la fin du Moyen Âge à la fin du XVIIe siècle. 5 vols. (1359 pp.) Bordeaux/III, 1979.

❖ [A] "Le Problème du public de la *comedia* au Siècle d'Or: L'Exemple de Séville." *TS* 4 (1983?): 103–18. [B] Title as is. Talence: Presses Universitaires de Bordeaux, 1984. 2 vols. Rev.: (a) J. M. Pelorson. *BHS* 62 (1985): 200–03; (b) J. M. Díez Borque. *Criticón* 31 (1985): 153–63. [C] "Los corrales de comedias de Sevilla." *CTC* 6 (1991): 69–89. [D] "La Edad de Oro de la comedia en Sevilla: Los malogrados caminos de una modernidad temprana." *La comedia: Seminario hispano-francés organizado por la Casa de Velázquez, Madrid, 1991–1992.* Ed. Jean Canavaggio. Madrid: Casa de Velázquez, 1995. 145–53. (Collection de la Casa de Velázquez 48.).

1192. Shergold, Norman David. The Staging of Secular Drama in Spain: 1550-1700. Cambridge, 1954. Cambridge *Abstracts* (1953-54): 180-81.

❖ [A] "Nuevos documentos sobre los corrales de comedias de Madrid en el siglo XVII." *RBAM* 20 (1951): 391-445. [B] "Calderón y Vera Tassis." *HR* 23 (1955): 212-18. [C] "Juan de la Cueva and the Early Theatres of Seville." *BHS* 32 (1955): 1-7. [D] "Ganassa and the *Commedia dell'Arte* in Sixteenth-Century Spain." *MLR* 51 (1956): 359-68. [E] "Juan de la Cueva y los primeros teatros de Sevilla." *ArH* 24 (1956): 57-64. [F] "The First Performance of Calderón's *El mayor encanto amor.*" *BHS* 35 (1958): 24-27. [G] "Nuevos documentos sobre los corrales de comedias de Madrid, 1652-1700." *BBMP* 35 (1959): 209-346. [H] *A History of the Spanish Stage: From Medieval Times until the End of the Seventeenth Century.* Oxford: Clarendon, 1967. 624 pp. Rev.: (a) G. Jackson. *AHR* 73 (1967): 501; (b) Anon. *TLS* (19 Oct. 1967): 986; (c) Anon. *Choice* 4 (1967-68): 1131; (d) J. A. Byrnes. *SCN* 26 (1968): 16; (e) A. A. Parker. *BHS* 46 (1969): 57-60; (f) C. A. Jones. *MLR* 64 (1969): 685-86; (g) C. Tindemans. *RBPH* 47 (1969): 686-87; (h) W. Mettmann. *ZRP* 85 (1969): 480. [I] "*El gran teatro del mundo* y sus problemas escenográficos." *Hacia Calderón:* [Primer] coloquio anglogermano, Exeter, 1969. Ed. Hans Flasche. Berlin: de Gruyter, 1970. 77-84. [J] "Dos documentos teatrales inéditos, de 1634." *Homenaje a William L. Fichter: Estudios sobre el teatro antiguo hispánico y otros ensayos.* Ed. A. David Kossoff and José Amor y Vázquez. Madrid: Castalia, 1971. 687-92. [On Madrid theaters.] [K] "Lope de Vega and the Other *Caballero de Olmedo.*" *Studies in Spanish Literature of the Golden Age Presented to Edward M. Wilson.* Ed. R. O. Jones. London: Tamesis, 1973. 267-81. (Colección Támesis, serie A. Monografías 30.) [For this scholar's publications in collaboration with John E. Varey, see the entry under the latter's name, at no. 1204.]

1193. Sirera Turó, José Luis [Josep Lluís]. El teatro en Valencia durante los siglos XVI y XVII: La producción dramática valenciana en los orígenes de la comedia barroca. 4 vols. Valencia, 1981.

❖ [A] *El fet teatral dins la societat valenciana.* Valencia: Lindes, 1979. [B] *Passat, present i futur del teatre Valencià.* Valencia: Institució Alfons el Magnànim, 1981. 94 pp. [C] "La evolución del espectáculo dramático en los autores valencianos del XVI, desde el punto de vista de la técnica teatral." *BCom* 34.2 (1982): 173-87. [D] "Panorama crítico de los estudios sobre la historia del teatro valenciano (siglos XIII al XVII)." *Teatro y prácticas escénicas 1: El quinientos valenciano.* Ed. Manuel V. Diago Moncholí. Valencia: Institució Alfons el Magnànim, 1984. 43-60. [E] "El teatro en la corte de los duques de Calabria." *Teatro y prácticas escénicas 1. El quinientos valenciano.* Ed. Manuel V. Diago Moncholí. Valencia: Institució Alfons el Magnànim, 1984. 259-79. [F] "El teatro medieval valenciano." *Teatro y prácticas escénicas 1: El quinientos valenciano.* Ed. Manuel V. Diago Moncholí. Valencia: Institució Alfons el Magnànim, 1984. 87-107. [G] "Las 'comedias de santos' en los autores valencianos: Notas para su estudio." *Teatro y prácticas escénicas 2: La comedia.* Ed. José Luis Canet Vallés. London: Tamesis, 1986. 187-228. (Colección Támesis, serie A. Monografías 123.) [H] "Espectáculo y teatralidad en la Valencia del Renacimiento." *EdO* 5 (1986): 247-70. [I] "La infraestructura teatral valenciana." *Teatro y prácticas escénicas 2: La comedia.* Ed. José Luis Canet Vallés. London: Tamesis, 1986. 26-49. (Colección Támesis, serie A. Monografías 123.) [J] "Rey de Artieda y Virués: La tragedia valenciana del quinientos." *Teatro y prácticas escénicas 2: La comedia.* Ed. José Luis Canet Vallés. London: Tamesis, 1986. 69-101. (Colección Támesis, serie A. Monografías 123.) [K] *El teatre Principal de València: Aproximació a la seua història.* Valencia: Institució Alfons el Magnànim, 1986. 412 pp.

1194. STAHL, AUGUSTA ELAINE. Die spanischen Habsburger im spanischen Drama. 294 pp. Vienna, 1953.

1195. SUREDA, FRANÇOIS [FRANCIS]. Théâtre et société à Valencia au XVIIIe siècle (1700-1779). 751 pp. Perpignan, 1987. (Thèse d'État)

❖ [A] "Algunas tragedias del Siglo de Oro ante el público valenciano del siglo XVIII." *Horror y tragedia en el teatro del Siglo de Oro: Actas del cuarto coloquio del GESTE, Toulouse, 1983. Criticón* 23 (1983): 117-32. [B] "Physionomie du public valencien de

1700 à 1712: Limites d'une approche socio-économique." *TS* 4 (1983?): 119-39. [C] "La Transgression dans les *comedias* répresentées sur la scène des théâtres valenciens au XVIIIe siècle." *Critique sociale et conventions théâtrales (domaine ibérique): Colloque international de Pau, 1988.* Pau: Université de Pau et des Pays de l'Adour, 1989. 105-16. (Cahiers de l'Université ns 20.) [D] "*El tejedor de Segovia* de Juan Ruiz de Alarcón: Su acogida por el público de los corrales valencianos del siglo XVIII." *El teatro mexicano visto desde Europa: Actes des premières journées internationales sur le théâtre mexicain en France, Perpignan, 1993.* Ed. Daniel Meyran and Alejandro Ortiz. Perpignan: Presses Universitaires de Perpignan, 1994. 55-64.

1196. TAYLER, NEALE HAMILTON. The Influence of the Spanish and Other European Theatres on Tamayo y Baus. 20+283 pp. Toronto, 1948.

❖ *Las fuentes del teatro de Tamayo y Baus: Originalidad e influencias.* Madrid: Uguina, 1959. 211 pp. ". . . todos los dramas en que colaboró Tamayo con estos hombres [Aureliano and Luis Fernández-Guerra and Manuel Cañete] demuestran la influencia perceptible del Siglo de Oro. Puesto que hay trece comedias que exhiben los rasgos característicos del teatro tradicional español, no se puede menospreciar la importancia de esta influencia en el teatro de Tamayo." (Prt. Diss.) Rev.: R. Esquer Torres. *RL* 15.29-30 (1959): 140-42.

1197. TENNER, FRITZ. François le Metel de Boisrobert als Dramatiker und Nachahmer des spanischen Dramas. 1: Die Tragikomödien. [2. Die Tragödie *Didon la chaste.*] Leipzig, 1907.

[Boisrobert translated and adapted Calderón's *La vida es sueño, Peor está que estaba,* and *Lances de amor y fortuna* as well as other Spanish plays.]

❖ [A] Title as is. Schkeuditz and Leipzig: Wachsmuth, 1907. 178 pp. [B] *François le Metel de Boisrobert als Lustspieldichter und Vorläufer Molières.* Gera, 1912. 31 pp.

1198. TIEMANN, HERMANN. Studien zur spanischen Dramatik in Flandern (Diego Muxet de Solís, D. Jacinto de Herrera y Sotomayor, D. Miguel de Barrios). 167 pp. Göttingen, 1924. Abstract. *Jahrbuch der Philosophischen Fakultät Göttingen* (1924): 40-42.

❖ "Gilles van Staveren als Übersetzer spanischer *comedias*." *Neophilologus* 18.1-4 (1933): 166-75. [For a more complete list of this scholar's publications, see Werner Kayser, "Verzeichnis der Schriften von Hermann Tiemann 1923-1974," *HermannTiemann: Essays, Vorträge und Aufsätze aus vier Jahrzehnten: Mit einem Vorwort von Fritz Schalk und einem Verzeichnis der wichtigsten Schriften des Verfassers,* ed. Christian Voigt. (For the Maximilian Society in Hamburg.) N.p.: n.p., 1973? 256-62. (Jahresgabe—Maximilian-Gesellschaft, 1973.)]

1199. TORDERA SÁEZ, ANTONIO. Texto y representación: Historia crítica de la semiótica teatral. 2 vols. Valencia, 1979.

❖ [A] "Actor, espacio, espectador: El teatro." *CdF* 1.1 (1979): 143-58. [B] Tordera Sáez, Antonio, and Evangelina Rodríguez. *La escritura como espejo de palacio:* El toreador *de Calderón.* Kassel: Reichenberger, 1985. 87 pp. (Problemata semiótica 4.) [C] "Historia y mojiganga del teatro." *Actas de las jornadas sobre teatro popular en España.* Coord. Joaquín Álvarez Barrientos and Antonio Cea Gutiérrez. Madrid: CSIC, 1987. 249-87. [". . . el teatro puede ser visto como un proteico conjunto de signos que son utilizados por los hombres con múltiples usos."]

1200. TORRE SEQUERA, VICENTE DE LA. Poesía dramática y sus especies. [39] pp., handwritten. Complutense, 1880.

1201. TORRES MONREAL, FRANCISCO. El teatro español en Francia 1935-1973: Análisis de la penetración y de sus mediaciones. 2 vols. (1-435, 436-833 pp.) Murcia, 1974.

❖ [A] Title as is. Madrid: Fundación Juan March, 1976. 50 pp. (Serie universitaria 10.) [On pp. 21-31 the writer describes performances of plays by Cervantes, Lope, Calderón, and Tirso.] Rev.: Anon. *L/F* 46 (1977): 1-3. [B] "Cervantes en el teatro francés, 1935-1965." *Cervantes: Estudios en la víspera de su centenario.* Ed. Kurt Reichenberger. 2 vols. Kassel: Reichenberger, 1994. 2: 605-46.

1202. URDIN, M. B. Les Itinéraires des troupes de théâtre en Espagne au XVIe et au XVIIe siècles. Paris/IV, 1977.

1203. VALLE ABAD, FEDERICO DEL. Juan Rotrou (1609-1650) y la influencia de la literatura española sobre el teatro francés del siglo XVII. 365 pp. Complutense, 1940.

❖ [A] "Influencia española sobre la literatura francesa, Pedro Corneille, 1606-1684: Ensayo crítico." *BUG* 17 (1945): 137-241. [B] *Influencia española sobre la literatura francesa: Juan Rotrou (1609-1650), ensayo crítico.* Ávila: Senén Martín, 1946. 260 pp. Rev.: G. Hainsworth. *FS* 5.1 (1951): 71-73.

1204. VAREY, JOHN EARL. Minor Dramatic Forms in Spain, with Special Reference to Puppets. 2 vols. Cambridge, 1951. Cambridge *Abstracts* (1950-51): 150-51.

❖ [A] "Titiriteros y volatines en Valencia: 1585-1785." *RVF* 3 (1953): 215-76. [B] "Representaciones de títeres en teatros públicos y palaciegos, 1211-1760." *RFE* 38 (1954): 170-211. [C] *Historia de los títeres en España (desde sus orígenes hasta mediados del siglo XVIII).* Madrid: Revista de Occidente, 1957. 493 pp. Rev.: M. Wilson. *BHS* 35.3 (1958): 179-80. [D] *Títeres, marionetas y otras diversiones populares de 1758 a 1859.* Madrid: Ayuntamiento, 1959. 290 pp. [E] *Los títeres y otras diversiones populares de Madrid, 1758-1840: Estudio y documentos.* London: Tamesis, 1972. 291 pp. (Colección Támesis, serie C. Fuentes para la historia del teatro en España 7.) [F] *Cartelera de los títeres y otras diversiones populares de Madrid, 1758-1840: Estudio y documentos.* London: Tamesis, 1995. 491 pp. (Colección Támesis, serie C. Fuentes para la historia del teatro en España 8.) [For a more complete list of this scholar's publications, see *El mundo del teatro español en su Siglo de Oro: Ensayos dedicados a John E. Varey,* ed. José María Ruano de la Haza (Ottawa: Dovehouse, 1989) 15-20. (Ottawa Hispanic Studies 3.)]

1205. VENTURA CRESPO, CONCHA MARÍA. La figura del Cid en el teatro español. 2 vols. ([3]+773+[2], 774-1,324 pp.) Salamanca, 1986.

1206. VITREY, ANNE. Le Théâtre des Jésuites dans leur collège de Luxembourg pendant l'occupation espagnole au XVIIe siècle. Paris/IV, 1980.

1207. VITSE, MARC. Éléments pour une histoire du théâtre espagnol du XVIIe siècle. 717 pp. Toulouse/II, 1987. (Thèse d'État) // Rev.: J. M. Díez Borque. *Ínsula* 527 (1990): 3.

❖ *Éléments pour une théorie du théâtre espagnol du XVIIe siècle.* Toulouse: France-Ibérie Recherche, 1988. 719 pp.; 2nd ed. Toulouse: France-Ibérie Recherche et Presses Universitaires du Mirail, 1990. 719 pp. (Thèses et recherches 17.) Rev.: (a) M. J. Martínez López. *RILCE* 5.1 (1989): 170–73; (b) A. Hermenegildo. *BHS* 67.4 (1990): 420–21; (c) A. Poses Sobral. *RL* 52.103 (1990): 232–38; (d) L. Luna. *EdO* 10 (1991): 215–20; (e) J. L. Sirera. *Ínsula* 535 (1991): 4–5; (f) R. ter Horst. *MLN* 106.2 (1991): 448–50; (g) T. A. O'Connor. *BCom* 44.1 (1992): 172–74.

1208. VOCKRODT, EBBA SÜCHTING. Der König D. Pedro I. de Castilla in der spanischen *Comedia* der Blütezeit unter besonderer Berücksichtigung des Verhältnisses der dichterischen Darstellung zur Geschichte. 215 pp. Göttingen, 1948.

[The writer examines sixteen plays that deal with Pedro I.]

1209. VOIGT, JOACHIM. Das Spiel im Spiel: Versuch einer Formbestimmung an Beispielen aus dem deutschen, englischen und spanischen Drama. 179 pp. Göttingen, 1955.

[The writer discusses two Spanish plays: *El gran teatro del mundo* (Calderón) and *Lo fingido verdadero* (Lope de Vega).]

1210. WALTHAUS, RINA. "La nieve que arde o abrasa": Dido en Lucretia in het Spaanse drama van de 16de en 17de eeuw. Con un resumen en español, with an English summary. 357 pp. Leiden, 1988.

❖ [A] "*Elisa Dido* y el *contemptus mundi* postridentino: Simbolismo y moraleja en un drama de Cristóbal de Virués." *BCom* 37.2 (1985): 191–208. [B] "Imágenes y simbolismo en *Dido y Eneas* de Guillén de Castro." *Neophilologus* 69.1 (1985): 75–89. [C] Title as is. Leiden: Reprodienst Faculteit Sociale Wetenschappen, 1988. 357 pp. Rev.: (a) A. L. Mackenzie. *BHS* 68.2 (1991): 332–33; (b) H.-J. Lope. *RF* 104.1–2 (1992): 256–57. [D] "Dido en el teatro español de fines del siglo XVII: *Destinos vencen finezas* y finezas vencen destinos." *Teatro español a fines del siglo XVII: Historia, cultura y teatro en la España de Carlos II.* Ed. Javier Huerta Calvo, Harm den Boer, and Fermín Sierra Martínez. 3 vols. Amsterdam: Rodopi, 1989. 2: 369–81. [This play is by Lorenzo de las Llamosas, Peruvian dramatist (1665?–1705).] [E] "Entre Diana y Venus: Mujeres castas y mujeres fatales en el teatro de Juan de la Cueva y Cristóbal de Virués." *Foro Hispánico* 5 (1993): 71–90. [F] "La fortuna de Dido en la literatura española medieval (desde las crónicas alfonsíes a la tragedia renacentista de Juan Cirne)." *Actas del tercer congreso de la Asociación Hispánica de Literatura Medieval, Salamanca, 1989*. Ed. María Isabel Toro Pascua. Salamanca: Biblioteca Española del Siglo XVI-Departamento de Literatura Española e Hispanoamericana, 1994. 1171-81.

1211. YOUNG, RICHARD ALAN. The Pastoral Mode in Spanish Drama before 1520. 634 pp. Alberta, 1970.

❖ [A] "Gil Vicente's Castilian Debut." *Segismundo* 8.15-16 (1972): 25-50. [B] "The *Farsa del mundo y moral* of Fernán López de Yanguas and the *auto sacramental*." *Segismundo* 10.19-20 (1974): 9-16. [The writer sees evidence of the pastoral tradition in the figure of *Apetito,* who "se ha de vestir . . . como pastor."]

1212. ZAGLER, S. Das auto sacramental: Eine dramatische Gattung und ihre Nachwirkung. (The *Auto Sacramental:* The Religious Play in the *Siglo de Oro* and in the 20th Century.) 218 pp. Vienna, 1982. *DAI-C* 45: 633. Summary in *Sprachkunst* 14 (1983): 203.

AGUILAR, GASPAR DE (1561-1623)

1213. CAÑAS MURILLO, JESÚS. El teatro de Gaspar Aguilar. 508 pp. Madrid/Autónoma, 1978. Abstract in *MEC.* Tesis doctorales 106 (1977-78): 57-58.

❖ [A] "Gaspar de Aguilar: Estado actual de sus estudios." *AEFil* 3 (1980): 31-49. [B] "Personajes tipo y tipo de personajes en el teatro de Gaspar de Aguilar." *AEFil* 6 (1983): 35-56. [C] "Recursos de composición en la obra dramática de Gaspar de Aguilar." *AEFil* 8 (1985): 49-59. [D] "Problemas de composición en el teatro de Gaspar de Aguilar: El trazado de la acción." *AEFil* 9 (1986): 55-74. [E] "El tema y los temas en el teatro de Gaspar de Aguilar." *AEFil* 12 (1989): 7-23.

1214. VALLADARES DEL REGUERO, AURELIO. Vida y obra de Gaspar Aguilar. Complutense, 1980.

❖ [A] Title as is. Madrid: Editorial de la Universidad Complutense, 1981. 616 pp. [B] "San Luis Bertrán: Una comedia de Aguilar refundida por Moreto." *Calderón: Actas del congreso internacional sobre Calderón y el teatro español del Siglo de Oro, Madrid,*

1981. Ed. Luciano García Lorenzo. 3 vols. Madrid: CSIC, 1983. 3: 1747–55.

Anonymous

1215. Alonso Asenjo, Julio. *La comedia de Sepúlveda:* Una comedia erudita española. 965 pp. Valencia, 1987. *DAI-C* 50: 405.
❖ [A] "La *Comedia de Sepúlveda* y los intentos de comedia erudita." *Teatro y prácticas escénicas 1: El quinientos valenciano*. Ed. Manuel V. Diago Moncholí. Valencia: Institució Alfons el Magnànim, 1984. 301–28. [B] Title as is. Valencia: Universitat de València, Servicio de Publicaciones, 1987. [C] *La comedia erudita de Sepúlveda: Estudio y texto paleográficocrítico anotado*. Ed. J. Alonso Asenjo. London: Tamesis, 1990. 251 pp. (Colección Támesis, serie B. Textos 33.) Rev.: (a) R. E. Surtz. *BHS* 70.3 (1993): 370; (b) M. Ihrie. *H*[AATSP] 76.3 (1993): 470–71; (c) A. Gier. *ZRP* 110.3–4 (1994): 621–22.

1216. Canet Vallés, José Luis (Josep Lluís). *La Comedia Thebayda, Ypolita y Seraphina:* Edición crítica. 2 vols. (1,035 pp.) Valencia, 1985.
[The earliest known printing of these three anonymous plays is Valencia, 1521.]
❖ [A] "La *Thebayda* y la *Serafina*." *Teatro y prácticas escénicas 1: El quinientos valenciano*. Ed. Manuel V. Diago Moncholí. Valencia: Institució Alfons el Magnànim, 1984. 283–300. [B] Tárrega, F. A. *El Prado de Valencia*. Ed. J. L. Canet Vallés. London: Tamesis, 1985. 210 pp. (Colección Támesis, serie B. Textos 26.) [C] "La *Comedia Thebayda:* Una reprobatio amoris." *Celestinesca* 10.2 (1986): 3–15. [D] "Algunos datos más para la fecha de edición de la *Comedia Thebayda*." *Varia bibliographica: Homenaje a José Simón Díaz*. Kassel: Reichenberger, 1987. 137–43. [E] "La *Comedia Thebayda:* ¿Una comedia humanística especial?" *Literatura Hispánica; Reyes Católicos; Descubrimiento*. Ed. Manuel Criado de Val. Barcelona: PPU, 1989. 331–36. [F] Rueda, L. de. *Pasos*. Ed. J. L. Canet Vallés. Madrid: Castalia, 1992. 324 pp. (Clásicos Castalia 196.) [The base texts are Valencia, 1567 and 1570.] [G] *De la comedia humanística al teatro*

representable (Égloga de la Tragicomedia de Calisto y Melibea, Penitencia de amor, Comedia Thebayda, Comedia Hipólita, Comedia Serafina). Valencia: UNED, Universidad de Sevilla, Universitat de València, 1993. 398 pp. (Serie textos teatrales hispánicos del siglo XVI 2.) Rev.: (a) C. F. Fraker. *BCom* 46.2 (1994): 275–77; (b) M. L. Cuesta Torre. *La Corónica* 24.2 (1996): 208–11. [H] "La comedia humanística y la ética." *Los albores del teatro español: Actas de las XVII jornadas de teatro clásico, Almagro, 1994*. Ed. Felipe B. Pedraza Jiménez and Rafael González Cañal. Almagro: Universidad de Castilla-La Mancha, 1995. 173–87. [I] "Los penitenciales: Posible fuente de las primitivas comedias en vulgar." *Celestinesca* 20.1–2 (1996): 3–19.

1217. Ferbal y Campos, Luis. La lengua castellana en el fragmento del *Auto de los Reyes Magos*. 102 pp. Complutense, 1910.

1218. Granja López, Agustín de la. Una comedia jesuítica del Siglo de Oro: Estudio y edición de *La vida de San Eustaquio*. 3 vols. (353, 375, 367 pp.) Granada, 1980.

❖ [A] "Aportación al estudio del teatro jesuítico: Los *Juegos de Fe y Amor* del padre Valentín de Céspedes (1595–1668)." Universidad de Granada, Memoria de licenciatura, 1977. [B] "Hacia una revalorización del teatro jesuítico en la Edad de Oro: Notas sobre el P. Valentín de Céspedes." *Estudios sobre literatura y arte dedicados al profesor Emilio Orozco Díaz*. Ed. Antonio Gallego Morell, Andrés Soria, and Nicolás Marín. 3 vols. Granada: Universidad de Granada, 1979. 2: 145–59. [C] "Un documento inédito contra las comedias en el siglo XVI: Los *Fundamentos* del P. Pedro de Fonseca." *Homenaje a Camoens: Estudios y ensayos hispano-portugueses*. Ed. Nicolás Extremera Tapia and Manuel Correia Fernández. Granada: Universidad de Granada, 1980. 173–94. [D] La vida de San Eustaquio: *Comedia jesuítica del Siglo de Oro.* Granada: Universidad de Granada, 1982. 608 pp. (Colección filológica 30.) Rev.: M. Batllori. *AHSI* 52 (1983): 177–78. [E] "El templo disfrazado: Espacios escénicos, textos, actores y público a la luz de varias crónicas inéditas." *Espacios teatrales del Barroco español: Calle, iglesia, palacio, universidad. XIII jornadas de teatro clásico, Almagro, 1990*. Ed. José María Díez Borque. Kassel: Reichenberger, 1991. 121–47. [All the *crónicas* deal with Jesuit theater.]

1219. HARTMANN, KARL AUGUST MARTIN. Über das altspanische Dreikönigsspiel, nebst einem Anhang enthaltend ein bisher ungedrucktes lateinisches Dreikönigsspiel, einen Wiederabdruck des altspanischen Stückes, sowie einen Excurs über die Namen der drei Königs Caspar, Melchior, Baltasar. 50 pp. Leipzig, 1879.
❖ Title as is. Bautzen: Kayser, 1879, 94 pp. [Apropos *El auto de los Reyes Magos*.] Rev.: (a) V. E. Lidforss. *LGRP* 1 (1880): 461–65; (b) A. Morel-Fatio. *Romania* 9 (1880): 464–69; (c) G. Baist. *ZRP* 4 (1880): 443–55.

1220. KOHLER, EUGEN [EUGÈNE]. Sieben spanische dramatische Eklogen mit einer Einleitung über die Anfänge der spanischen Dramas. Strasbourg, 1910.
[For the complete entry, see no. 1149. The fourth reprinted play is an anonymous *Égloga pastoril*.]

ARMENDÁRIZ, JULIÁN DE (1585?–1614)

1221. JOSÉ PRADES, JUANA DE. Aportación al estudio de la teoría literaria y bibliografía de los dramaturgos menores pertenecientes al ciclo dramático de Lope de Vega. vii+400 pp. Complutense, 1960. Abstract in *RUM* 10.40 (1961): 852.
[For the complete entry, see no. 1148.]

AVENDAÑO, FRANCISCO DE (FL. 1551)

1222. BENAVIDES LILLO, RICARDO. Francisco de Avendaño: *Comedia Florisea*. 86 pp. Complutense, 1954.
[The base text of the dissertation is the *princeps* (n.p., 1551).]
❖ "Francisco de Avendaño y el teatro renacentista español." *BFC* 12 (1960): 51–164.

ÁVILA, DIEGO GUILLÉN DE (16TH C.)

1223. KOHLER, EUGEN [EUGÈNE]. Sieben spanische dramatische

Eklogen mit einer Einleitung über die Anfänge der spanischen Dramas. Strasbourg, 1910.

[For the complete entry, see no. 1149. The third reprinted play is the *Égloga interlocutoria* of Diego Guillén de Ávila.]

Ávila, Gaspar de (?–after 1645)

1224. José Prades, Juana de. Aportación al estudio de la teoría literaria y bibliografía de los dramaturgos menores pertenecientes al ciclo dramático de Lope de Vega. vii+400 pp. Complutense, 1960. Abstract in *RUM* 10.40 (1961): 852.

[For the complete entry, see no. 1148.]

Bances Candamo, Francisco Antonio de (1662–1709)

1225. Behnam, John Abdul Ahed. Contribución al estudio literario de Bances Candamo. Complutense, 1963.

1226. Cuervo-Arango y González-Carvajal, Francisco. Don Francisco Antonio de Bances y López Candamo: Estudio bio-bibliográfico y crítico. 300 pp. + 3 pp. of music. Complutense, 1915.
❖ Title as is. Madrid: Hernández, 1916. 223 pp.

1227. Pérez Feliú, José Jorge. Los autos sacramentales de Bances Candamo. Complutense, 1969. Abstract in *RUM* 18.72 (1969): 44–45.
❖ [A] "La métrica en los autos sacramentales de Bances Candamo." *RFE* 57 (1974–75): 127–57. [B] *Autos sacramentales de Fco. Bances Candamo.* Oviedo: Diputación de Oviedo, Instituto de Estudios Asturianos, 1975. 192 pp.

Barrios, Miguel de (1625?–1701)
(Daniel Leví de Barrios)

1228. Tiemann, Hermann. Studien zur spanischen Dramatik in Flandern (Diego Muxet de Solís, D. Jacinto de Herrera y Sotomayor, D. Miguel de Barrios). 167 pp. Göttingen, 1924. Abstract in *Jahrbuch der Philosophischen Fakultät Göttingen* (1924): 40–42.

[For the complete entry, see no. 1198.]

Basurto, Fernando (fl. 1530–1542)

1229. Río Nogueras, Alberto del. La obra literaria de Fernando Basurto. 4 vols. (11+1,705 pp.) Zaragoza, 1988. // Rev.: Anon., *Ínsula* 495 (1988): 2.

[Only one dramatic work by Basurto is extant: The *entremés Martirio de Santa Engracia,* an edition of which is included in this dissertation.]

❖ [A] "Dos recibimientos triunfales en un libro de caballerías del siglo XVI." *Homenaje a José Manuel Blecua.* Ed. María Luisa Atares et al. Huesca: Instituto de Estudios Altoaragoneses, 1986. 19–30. [B] *Teatro y entrada triunfal en la Zaragoza del Renacimiento: Estudio de la* Representación del Martirio de Santa Engracia *de Fernando Basurto en su marco festivo.* Zaragoza: Ayuntamiento, 1988. 96 pp. Rev.: A. Soons. *Criticón* 49 (1990): 106–08. [C] "Una trayectoria caballeresca singular: El *Don Florindo* de Fernando Basurto." *JHP* 12.3 (1988): 191–205.

Belmonte Bermúdez, Luis de (1587?–1650?)

1230. Piñero Ramírez, Pedro Manuel. Luis de Belmonte Bermúdez: Estudio de *La Hispálica.* 620 pp. Seville, 1971.

❖ [A] "Estudio de la comedia *El cerco de Sevilla por el rey don Fernando* de Luis de Belmonte Bermúdez." *Homenaje al profesor [Juan de Mata] Carriazo.* Ed. L. Núñez Contreras. Sevilla: Universidad de Sevilla, Facultad de Filosofía y Letras, 1973. 3: 255–78. [B] Belmonte Bermúdez, L. de. *La Hispálica.* Ed. P. M. Piñero Ramírez. Sevilla: Universidad de Sevilla, 1974. [C] Title as is. Sevilla: Diputación Provincial, 1976. 372 pp. (Publicaciones de la Excma. Diputación Provincial de Sevilla. Sección literatura, serie 1, no. 5.) The printed dissertation (1976) on Belmonte's epic poem *La Hispálica* includes a chapter on his life and works, pp. 7–39, and a chapter entitled "Fernando III y la conquista de Sevilla en la literatura" (including the theater), pp. 75–93.

Bermúdez, Jerónimo (1530?–1590?)

1231. Alonso y Linares, Ignacio. Tragedias de Jerónimo Bermúdez. [2]+87 pp., handwritten. Complutense, 1901.

Bocángel y Unzueta, Gabriel (1603–1658)

1232. Benítez Claros, Rafael. Vida y escritos de don Gabriel Bocángel y Unzueta. 327 pp. Complutense, 1945.
❖ [A] *Obras de don Gabriel Bocángel y Unzueta.* Ed. R. Benítez Claros. 2 vols. Madrid: CSIC, 1946. (Biblioteca de antiguos libros hispánicos, serie B, vols. 1 and 2.) [See vol. 2 for the text of the *representación real y festiva máscara* entitled *El nuevo Olimpo* (pp. 141–217) and the text of the *comedia El emperador fingido* (pp. 371–443)]. [B] *Vida y poesía de Bocángel.* Madrid: CSIC, 1950. 459 pp. [On Bocángel's "Obras teatrales," see pp. 407–21.]

1233. Dadson, Trevor John. The Poetry of Don Gabriel Bocángel y Unzueta (1603–1658). viii+291 pp. Cambridge, 1974.
❖ [A] *The Genoese in Spain: Gabriel Bocángel y Unzueta (1603–1658), a Biography.* London: Tamesis, 1983. 192 pp. (Colección Támesis, serie A. Monografías 97.) Rev.: (a) A. MacKay. *MLR* 81.4 (1986): 1020–21; (b) W. F. King. *MP* 83.3 (1986): 310–13. [B] "Guía bibliográfica y crítica de y sobre las obras de Gabriel Bocángel y Unzueta." *Censo de escritores al servicio de los Austrias y otros estudios bibliográficos*. Madrid: CSIC, 1983. 67–97. [On Bocángel's only known *comedia, El emperador fingido,* see numbers 40–42 in ch. 2.] [C] Bocángel, G. *La lira de las musas.* Ed. T. J. Dadson. Madrid: Cátedra, 1985. 504 pp. + unnumbered index of first lines. [D] "Documentos inéditos para la biografía de la familia hispano-genovesa de Gabriel Bocángel y Unzueta." *AIEM* 22 (1985): 415–52. [E] "A Genoese Family in Sixteenth-Century Toledo." *A*

Face Not Turned to the Wall: Essays on Hispanic Themes for Gareth Alban Davies. Ed. C. A. Longhurst. Leeds: Univ. of Leeds, Dept. of Spanish and Portuguese, 1987. 27–49. [F] "Una comedia problemática: *El emperador fingido* de Gabriel Bocángel." *Criticón* 42 (1988): 53–64. [G] *La casa bocangelina: Una familia hispano-genovesa en la España del Siglo de Oro.* Pamplona: Universidad de Navarra, 1991. 240+229 [documents] pp.

Calderón de la Barca, Pedro (1600–1681)

1234. Ahmed, Uta. Form und Funktion der *Cuentos* in den *Comedias* Calderóns. Hamburg, 1971.
❖ [A] "La función del cuento en las comedias de Calderón." *Hacia Calderón: Segundo coloquio anglogermano, Hamburgo, 1970.* Ed. Hans Flasche. Berlin: de Gruyter, 1973. 71–77. [B] Title as is. Berlin: de Gruyter, 1974. 172 pp. (Hamburger romanistische Studien B. Ibero-amerikanische Reihe 37. Calderoniana 8.)

1235. Arango y del Valle, Mercedes de. Edición crítica del auto de Calderón, *Sueños hay que verdad son.* Complutense, 1948.

1236. Arnold, Ernst. Die Darstellung der Liebe in den Dramen von Calderón. 190 pp. Munich, 1958.

1237. Bainton, Cecilia Christine Diana. A Critical Edition, with Introduction and Notes, of *El monstruo de los jardines* by Don Pedro Calderón de la Barca. vii+323 pp. Cambridge, 1977.

1238. Ballesteros Barahona, Pedro. Calderóns erste Fassung von *El mágico prodigioso* und das Doktor-Faustus-Spiel der englischen Komödianten. 175 pp. Berlin/FU, 1972. *DAI-C* 42: 699.

1239. Battilana, Carlos. Vorarbeit zu einer kritischen Edition des calderonianischen Schauspiels *La devoción de la misa.* Hamburg, 1975.
❖ Title as is. Frankfurt: Peter Lang, 1978. 190 pp. (Europäische Hochschulschriften, Reihe 24. Ibero-romanische Sprachen und Literaturen 7.)
[The base text is the autograph MS in the Biblioteca Municipal of Madrid.]

1240. Bauer, Helga. Der Index Pictorius Calderóns: Untersuchungen zu seiner Malermetaphorik. Hamburg, 1970.

❖ Title as is. Hamburg: Cram; de Gruyter, 1969. 267 pp. (Hamburger romanistische Studien B. Ibero-amerikanische Reihe 32. Calderoniana 3.) Rev.: (a) R. Sánchez Mariño. *Arbor* 78.301 (1971): 139–43; (b) A. L. Mackenzie. *BHS* 49 (1972): 78–79.

1241. BAUER, HERMINE. Zacharias Werners Beziehungen zu Calderón. 156+[3] pp. Vienna, 1928.

1242. BERENS, PETER. Calderóns Schicksalstragödien. Bonn, 1921.
❖ Title as is. *RF* 39 (1926): 1–66.

1243. BEYSCHLAG, WILLIBOLD. De Cypriano mago et martyre calderonicae tragoediae persona primaria dissertatio. 18 pp. Halle, 1866.
❖ Title as is. Halis (Halle): Formis Hendeliis, 1866. 18 pp. [Apropos Calderón's *El mágico prodigioso*.] Rev.: Anon. *Archiv* 39 (1866): 471–72.

1244. BRANSCHEID, WALTRAUD. Grillparzer und Calderón. Cologne, 1963.
❖ Title as is. Düsseldorf: Zentral-Verlag für Dissertationen Triltsch, 1963. 110 pp.

1245. BRYANS, JOHN V. M. Imagery, Rhetoric and Drama in Some *Comedias* of Don Pedro Calderón de la Barca. vi+xxv+361 pp. Oxford, 1974.
❖ *Calderón de la Barca: Imagery, Rhetoric and Drama*. London: Tamesis, 1977. 207 pp. (Colección Támesis, serie A. Monografías 64.) Rev.: (a) J. H. Parker. *Symposium* 32 (1978): 365–66; (b) T. R. A. Mason. *BHS* 56 (1979): 254–55; (c) W. M. Whitby. *H*[AATSP] 62 (1979): 730; (d) A. Soons. *JHP* 3 (1979): 187–90; (e) C. Bainton. *MLR* 74 (1979): 478–79; (f) E. Rull. *RFE* 59 (1979 for 1977): 319–22; (g) A. García Cruz. *RJ* 31 (1980): 429–31.

1246. BUTLER, FRED ALLEN. El existencialismo y la problemática de la vida en algunas obras de Calderón de la Barca. 98 pp. Complutense, 1967.

1247. CHARLIER, ALFRED. Contribution à l'étude sur l'influence du théâtre de Calderón en France (Th. Corneille à Scarron). Brussels, 1930–31.

1248. CHERKAOUI, OUM KELTOUM. Pedro Calderón de la Barca. *El gran príncipe de Fez:* Éd. critique. 383 pp. Aix-en-Provence, 1981.

1249. CLIFFORD, JOHN. Calderón's "arte nuevo" in the First Act of *El médico de su honra.* [4]+294 pp. St. Andrews, 1982. (Abstract available on fiche) [Listed as PhD dissertation in *Aslib* 32.2 (1983): 201, but 1995 correspondence from St. Andrews to the compilers of this volume identifies it as MPhil.]

1250. CONSTANDSE, ANTON LEVIEN. Le Baroque espagnol et Calderón de la Barca. Amsterdam, 1951.
❖ Title as is. Amsterdam: Van Campen, 1951. 144 pp. Rev.: (a) Ch. V. Aubrun. *BH* 54.2 (1952): 230; (b) A. Valbuena Prat. *Clavileño* 3.14 (1952): 77–78; (c) Ch. V. Aubrun. *BH* 57.4 (1955): 463–65; (d) B. W. Wardropper. *HR* 23 (1955): 140–43.

1251. CRUICKSHANK, DON WILLIAM. A Critical Edition and Study of Calderón's *En la vida todo es verdad y todo mentira.* vii+406 pp. Cambridge, 1969.
❖ [A] "Calderón's Handwriting." *MLR* 65 (1970): 65–77. [B] Calderón de la Barca, P. *En la vida todo es verdad y todo mentira.* Ed. D. W. Cruickshank. London: Tamesis, 1971. cxxxix+255 pp. (Colección Támesis, serie B. Textos 10.) Rev.: (a) C. F. Smith. *H* [AATSP] 56 (1973): 1118–19; (b) G. Edwards. *MLR* 68 (1973): 673–75; (c) M. Engelbert. *RJ* 25 (1974): 374–77. [C] "Some Uses of Palaeographic and Orthographical Evidence in *Comedia* Editing." *BCom* 24.2 (1972): 40–45. [D] Calderón de la Barca, P. Comedias*: A Facsimile Edition, with Textual and Critical Studies.* Prepared by D. W. C. and J. E. Varey. 19 vols. Westmead, Eng.: Gregg; London: Tamesis, 1973. [Vol. 1 includes the following pertinent studies by D. W. C.: "The Textual Criticism of Calderón's *Comedias:* A Survey," pp. 1–35; "A Census of Rare *Partes,*" pp. 37–53; "The Text of *La vida es sueño,*" pp. 79–94; "The Printing of Calderón's *Tercera parte,*" pp. 117–41; "Calderón's *Primera* and *Tercera partes:* The Reprints of '1640' and '1664,'" pp. 143–60; "The Two Editions of Calderón's *Quinta parte* (1677)," pp. 201–10.] [E] "The Editing of Spanish Golden-Age Plays from Early Printed Versions." *Editing the* Comedia. Ed. Frank P. Casa and Michael D. McGaha. Ann Arbor: Univ. of Michigan, Dept. of Romance Languages, 1985. 52–103. (Michigan Romance Studies 5.) [F] "Some Problems Posed by *Suelta* Editions of Plays." *Editing the* Comedia II. Ed. Michael McGaha and Frank P. Casa. Ann Arbor: Univ. of Michigan, Dept. of

Romance Languages, 1991. 97–123. (Michigan Romance Studies 11.)

1252. DOMMEL, HERMANN. Die gedankliche und dramatische Struktur von Calderóns Drama *La vida es sueño.* 436 pp. Würzburg, 1972.

1253. EDER, HARALD. Eichendorff als Übersetzer spanischer Literatur mit besonderer Berücksichtigung der Übersetzung der Fronleichnamsspiele Calderóns. vii+129 pp. Mainz, 1956.

1254. EDWARDS, GWYNNE. Calderón's *La hija del aire:* A Critical Annotated Edition of the *Primera parte,* with a Study of the Semiramis Legend and Its Dramatic Treatment by Calderón in Relation to Earlier Dramatisations of the Theme. [4]+ii+435 pp. London/King's College, 1961.

❖ [A] "Calderón's *La hija del aire* in the Light of His Sources." *BHS* 43 (1966): 177–96. [B] "Calderón's *La hija del aire* and the Classical Type of Tragedy." *BHS* 44 (1967): 161–94. [C] Calderón de la Barca, P. La hija del aire: *Edición crítica.* Ed. G. Edwards. London: Tamesis, 1970. lxxxiii+298 pp. (Colección Támesis, serie B. Textos 9.) Rev.: (a) H.-J. Lope. *RF* 83 (1971): 659–61; (b) M. Wilson. *BHS* 49 (1972): 187–89; (c) P. Dunn. *HR* 41 (1973): 567–70; (d) A. K. G. Paterson. *MLR* 68 (1973): 203–06; (e) M. Engelbert. *RJ* 25 (1974): 374–77; (f) M. S. *Brotéria* 114.1 (1982): 107–08. [D] *The Prison and the Labyrinth: Studies in Calderonian Tragedy.* Cardiff: U of Wales P, 1978. 197 pp. [Ch. 2, pp. 28–59, is entitled *"La hija del aire."*]

1255. EGERER, EDDA. Don Pedro Calderón de la Barca und das Wiener Burgtheater: Die Stellung des spanischen Dichters an dieser Bühne bis 1900 mit einem kurzen Überblick über die bisherige Entwicklung im 20. Jahrhundert. 222 pp. Vienna, 1963.

1256. EHRGOTT, ULRIKE. Das Schicksal Calderóns in Deutschland unter besonderer Berücksichtigung der Übersetzungen von *La vida es sueño.* 309 pp. Innsbruck, 1964. Microfilmed, 1964.

1257. ENEBRAL CASARES, ANA MARÍA. Aspectos semánticos en la obra de Calderón. La Laguna, 1990. Summary in Universidad de La Laguna, *Serie: Resúmenes de tesis,* 1990. 57 pp.

❖ "Argumentos en pro de una reinterpretación de *La vida es sueño.*" *Hacia Calderón: Décimo coloquio anglogermano, Passau, 1993.*

Ed. Hans Flasche. Stuttgart: Steiner, 1994. 223–42. (Archivum Calderonianum 7.)

1258. ENGELBERT, MANFRED. *Auto sacramental del pleito matrimonial del cverpo y el alma* de Don Pedro Calderón de la Barca: Kritische Ausgabe und Kommentar. Hamburg, 1969.

❖ [A] Calderón de la Barca, P. *El pleito matrimonial del cuerpo y el alma.* Critical ed. and commentary by M. Engelbert. Hamburg: Cram; de Gruyter, 1969. 320 pp. (Hamburger romanistische Studien B. Ibero-amerikanische Reihe 31. Calderoniana 2.) [The base text is the *princeps,* Madrid: María de Quiñones, 1655.] Rev.: (a) S. Neumeister. *Archiv* 207 (1970): 76–80; (b) U. Knoke. *Ibero* 2 (1970): 162–66; (c) J. F. Elvira-Hernández. *RF* 82 (1970): 448–52; (d) J. Hahn. *MLN* 86 (1971): 305–06; (e) C. Valderrama Andrade. *Thesaurus* 26 (1971): 637; (f) A. A. Parker. *BHS* 52 (1975): 409–12. [B] "Zur Sprache Calderóns: Das Diminutiv." *RJ* 20 (1969): 290–303. [C] "Etimologías calderonianas." *Hacia Calderón: [Primer] coloquio anglogermano, Exeter, 1969.* Ed. Hans Flasche. Berlin: de Gruyter, 1970. 113–22. [D] "Wie ediert man Dramen?" *Texte und Varianten.* Ed. Gunter Martens and Hans Zeller. München: Beck, 1971. 355–69. [E] "Las formas de tratamiento en el teatro de Calderón." *Hacia Calderón: Segundo coloquio anglogermano, Hamburgo, 1970.* Ed. Hans Flasche. Berlin: de Gruyter, 1973. 191–200.

1259. ENGLING, EZRA SAMUEL. A Critical Edition and Study of Pedro Calderón de la Barca's *La aurora en Copacabana.* cxxxi+147 pp. Jamaica, 1986.

❖ [A] "*La aurora en Copacabana:* A Calderonian Tapestry." *BCom* 43.1 (1991): 133–45. [B] Calderón de la Barca, P. *La aurora en Copacabana.* Ed., with introd. and notes, by E. S. Engling. London: Tamesis, 1994. 264 pp. (Colección Támesis, serie B. Textos 36.) Rev.: R. M. Shannon. *REHb* 31.1 (1997): 130–32.

1260. FERDINANDY, MAGDALENA DE. Sprache und Gebärde: Untersuchungen zur mimischen Interpretation Calderóns und seiner deutschen Übersetzer. 119 pp. Berlin/FU, 1965.

❖ Title as is. München: n.p., 1966. 119 pp. [This study is based on *La vida es sueño, El alcalde de Zalamea,* and *La dama duende.*] Rev.: J. M. Díez Taboada. *Segismundo* 3.5–6 (1967): 414–17.

1261. Fernández Giner, Manuel. Calderón y su teatro. [79] pp., handwritten. Complutense, 1877.

1262. Frutos Cortés, Eugenio. Las ideas filosóficas de Calderón como signo de su época. 757 pp. Complutense, 1946. Abstract in *Sumarios y extractos, Historia* (1944–47): 129–36.

❖ [A] "Origen, naturaleza y destino del hombre en los autos sacramentales de Calderón." *RdF* 4 (1945): 525–58. [B] "La voluntad y el libre albedrío en los autos sacramentales de Calderón." *Universidad* (Zaragoza) 25 (1948): 3–26. [C] "La filosofía del Barroco y el pensamiento de Calderón." *RUBA* 5.20 (1951): 172–230. [D] *La filosofía de Calderón en sus autos sacramentales.* Zaragoza: CSIC, Institución Fernando el Católico, 1952, 1981. 345 pp. Rev.: (a) A. Valbuena Prat. *Clavileño* 4.22 (1953): 77–78; (b) R. de Garciasol. *Ínsula* 90 (1953): 6; (c) G. Bravo. *Pensamiento* 10 (1953): 504–06; (d) C. Láscaris Comneno. *RIE* 11 (1953): 90–93. [E] "La filosofía de Calderón en sus autos sacramentales: Las potencias del alma y el libre albedrío." *Calderón y la crítica: Historia y antología.* Ed. Manuel Durán and Roberto González Echevarría. 2 vols. Madrid: Gredos, 1976. 481–540.

1263. García Solalinde, Antonio. La primera versión española de *El purgatorio de San Patricio* y la difusión de esta leyenda en España. 41 pp. Complutense, 1924.

[For the complete entry, see no. 1038.]

1264. Garrot, Juan Carlos. Le Thème juif et "converso" dans le théâtre religieux espagnol, notamment dans celui de Calderón (fin XVème siècle–XVIIème siècle). 679 pp. Paris/III, 1992.

["... lo fundamental de mi estudio gira en torno al auto sacramental sobre todo en lo que concierne a Calderón, autor que ocupa el segundo volumen de la tesis." (Personal letter from writer)]

❖ [A] "Sinagoga abandonada: Celos a lo divino en algunos autos calderonianos." *Relations entre hommes et femmes en Espagne aux 16e et 17e siècles: Réalités et fictions.* Ed. Augustin Redondo. Paris: Presses de la Sorbonne Nouvelle, 1995. 199–206. [B] "El problema converso en la *Recopilación en metro.*" *Criticón* 66–67 (1996): 179–94.

1265. González Velasco, Manuela María del Pilar. Temas y situaciones de Segismundo en la obra de Calderón de la Barca. 2 vols. ([3]+408+[5], 409-673 pp.) Salamanca, 1987. Summary in Universidad de Salamanca, *Serie: Resúmenes de tesis doctorales,* 1987. 36 pp.

❖ [A] Title as is. Salamanca: Universidad de Salamanca, 1987. [B] *Variaciones de Segismundo en la obra de Calderón*. Salamanca: Universidad de Salamanca, 1989. 225 pp. (Acta Salmanticensia. Estudios filológicos 215.)

1266. GOTTSCHALK, KLAUS-DIETER. Untersuchungen zur Frage der Passiversatzformen im Romanischen: Eine Studie am Werk von Pedro Calderón de la Barca, unter besonderer Beachtung der französischen, italienischen und spanischen Grammatik. 399 pp. Marburg, 1962.

1267. HAAS, HELMUTH DE. Hofmannsthals Weg zu Calderón. 490 pp. Munich, 1955.

1268. HARDY, SWANA L. Goethe, Calderón und die romantische Theorie des Dramas. Heidelberg, 1962.

❖ Title as is. Heidelberg: Winter, 1965. 200 pp. (Heidelberger Forschungen 10.) Rev.: (a) M. Franzbach. *GRM* 16 (1966): 437-38; (b) P. Pfaff. *RC* 40 (1966): 462; (c) R. Ayrault. *ÉG* 22 (1967): 287-88; (d) H. Steinmetz. *Neophilologus* 51 (1967): 308-09; (e) J. M. Díez Taboada. *Segismundo* 3.5-6 (1967): 417-18.

1269. HAVERBECK OJEDA, NORMAN ERWIN. El tema mitológico en el teatro de Calderón. 596 pp. Complutense, 1972. Abstract in *RUCM* 21.84-2 (Oct.-Dec. 1972): 116-17.

❖ [A] "La comedia mitológica calderoniana: Soberbia y castigo." *RFE* 56 (1973): 69-74. [B] Title as is. Valdivia: Universidad Austral de Chile, Área de Estudios Filológicos, Facultad de Letras y Educación, 1975. 188 pp.

1270. HEIBERG, JOHAN LUDVIG. De Poëseos dramaticae genere hispanico, et praesertim de Petro Calderone de la Barca, principe dramaticorum. Copenhagen, 1817. (Madsen 115)

❖ Title as is. København: Gyldendal, 1817. 158 pp.

1271. HILBORN, HARRY WARREN. A Chronology of the Plays of Don Pedro Calderón de la Barca. 250 pp. Toronto, 1935. Programme, Jan. 1935.

[The chronology is based on analysis of versification.]

❖ [A] Title as is. Toronto: U of Toronto P, 1938. 119 pp. Rev.: (a) C. Bruerton. *HR* 8 (1940): 267-72; (b) E. Juliá Martínez. *RFE* 26 (1942): 112-16. [B] "The Versification of *La selva confusa*." *MLN* 53 (1938): 193-94. [C] "Calderón's *Agudos* in Italianate Verse." *HR* 10 (1942): 157-59. [D] "Calderón's *Silvas*." *PMLA* 58 (1943): 122-48. [E] "Calderón's *Quintillas*." *HR* 16 (1948): 301-10.

1272. HOFMANN, FRIEDRICH. J. D. Gries als Übersetzer. 258 pp. Frankfurt, 1925.

❖ Title as is. Extract. Frankfurt: Englert & Schlosser, 1925. 2 pp. [This poet was especially famous for his 8-volume translation of Calderón's plays (1815-42).]

1273. HOFMANN, GERD. Pedro Calderón de la Barca, *La cena del rey Baltasar.* Kritische Ausgabe und Kommentar. Hamburg, 1971.

❖ Title as is. Berlin: de Gruyter, 1971. 238 pp. (Hamburger romanistische Studien B. Ibero-amerikanische Reihe 34. Calderoniana 5.) [The base text for this edition is the *princeps* (Madrid, 1644).] Rev.: (a) L. López Molina. *ZRP* 89 (1973): 383-85; (b) W. F. Hunter. *BHS* 51 (1974): 294-96; (c) J. Horrent. *RLV* 40 (1975): 416.

1274. HORST, KARL-AUGUST. Die Metapher in Calderóns *Comedias.* 132 pp. Bonn, 1947.

1275. HORSTHEMKE, JOHANNES. Melchior von Diepenbrock als Übersetzer spanischer Dichtungen. Münster, 1916.

❖ Title as is. Münster: Westfälische Vereinsdruckerei, 1915. 102 pp. [This analysis centers on von Diepenbrock's translation of Calderón's *auto La vida es sueño.*]

1276. HUNTER, WILLIAM FIDDES. A Critical Edition of Calderón's *La inmunidad del sagrado.* vi+404 pp. Cambridge, 1972.

❖ [A] "Métodos de crítica textual." *Hacia Calderón: [Primer] coloquio anglogermano, Exeter, 1969.* Ed. Hans Flasche. Berlin: de Gruyter, 1970. 13-28. [B] Hunter, William F., and Don W. Cruickshank. "Notes on the Text of Calderón's *Psiquis y Cupido para Toledo.*" *Ibero* 2.4 (1970): 282-89. [C] Calderón, P. *El Auto Sacramental de la Universal Redempción.* Ed. W. F. Hunter. Exeter: Univ of Exeter, 1976. (Exeter Hispanic Texts 10.) [The writer rejects attribution to Calderón.] [D] "Editing Texts in Multiple

Versions." *Editing the* Comedia. Ed. Frank P. Casa and Michael D. McGaha. Ann Arbor: Univ. of Michigan, Dept. of Romance Languages, 1985. 24–51. (Michigan Romance Studies 5.)

1277. ISBERT Y CUYÁS, BENITO. Carácter del teatro de Shakespeare comparado con el de Calderón. [64] pp., handwritten. Complutense, 1880.

❖ "Paralelo entre Calderón y Shakespeare." *IEA* 25.19 (1881): 335.

1278. JAMES, NICHOLAS JOHN. A Critical Edition of *Ni amor se libra de amor* by Don Pedro Calderón de la Barca, with Music by Juan Hidalgo. ix+452 pp. Southampton, 1981. *DAI-C* 44: 468.

1279. JONES, CYRIL ALBERT. The Code of Honour in the Spanish Drama of the Golden Age, with Special Reference to Calderón. xvii+338 pp. Oxford, 1955.

❖ [A] "Honor in *El alcalde de Zalamea*." *MLR* 50 (1955): 444–49. [B] "Honor in Spanish Golden Age Drama: Its Relation to Real Life and to Morals." *BHS* 35 (1958): 199–210. [C] Calderón, P. *El médico de su honra*. Ed. C. A. Jones. Oxford: Oxford UP, 1961. xxvi+111 pp. [D] "Spanish Honour as Historical Phenomenon, Convention and Artistic Motive." *HR* 33 (1965): 32–39. [E] Rpt. of publication C. Oxford: Dolphin, 1976. 140 pp.

1280. KAHOFER, GERTRUDE. Hugo von Hofmannsthals Beziehungen zu den Vorlagen seiner Dramen: *Jedermann, Das Salzburger grosse Welttheater, Der Turm*. 97 pp. Vienna, 1950.

[The "models" for *Das Salzburger grosse Welttheater* (1922) and *Der Turm* (1925) were Calderón's *El gran teatro del mundo* and *La vida es sueño,* respectively.]

1281. KAUFMANN, BRIGITTE. Die *Comedia* Calderóns: Studien zur Interdependenz von Autor, Publikum und Bühne. Heidelberg, 1975.

❖ Title as is. Bern: Herbert Lang; Frankfurt: Peter Lang, 1976. 328 pp.+lv (bibliography). (Heidelberger Beiträge zur Romanistik 10.)

1282. KEIDITSCH, OTTO. Der Monolog bei Calderón. Munich, 1911.

❖ Title as is. Jena: Vopelius, 1911. 111 pp. Rev.: A. Hämel. *LGRP* 34 (1913): col. 292–93.

1283. KELLENBERGER, JAKOB. Calderón de la Barca und das Komische, unter besonderer Berücksichtigung der ernsten Schauspiele. Zürich, 1975.

❖ Title as is. Bern: Herbert Lang; Frankfurt: Peter Lang, 1975. 211 pp. (Europäische Hochschulschriften, Reihe 24. Iberoromanische Sprachen und Literaturen 5.) [Includes all the plays except *comedias de capa y espada*. Chapter titles (in English translation): "The *Gracioso*," "Analysis of Language *(Moriscos, Villanos)*, Puns, Metaphors, *Refranes*," "Satire and Irony."]

1284. Kelly, Mary Catherine. Edición y estudio de los dos autos sacramentales: *El Santo Rey Don Fernando, primera y segunda parte,* de Don Pedro Calderón de la Barca. 284 pp. Complutense, 1965. Abstract in *RUM* 15.57-60 (1966): 53-54.

1285. Kergel, Willi. Die Calderónübersetzung von Ernst Friedrich Georg Otto von der Malsburg. 55 pp. Breslau, 1921. Abstract, Breslau: Hochschulverlag, 1921. 3 pp.

1286. Kern, Hanspeter. Ludwig Tiecks Calderonismus. 168 pp. Freiburg, 1966.

❖ [A] Title as is. *SFG* 1.23 (1967): 189-356. [B] "Calderon und Tiecks Weltbild." *SFG* 1.24 (1968): 337-96.

1287. Körner, Karl-Hermann. Die "Aktionsgemeinschaft finites Verb + Infinitiv" im spanischen Formensystem: Vorstudie zu einer Untersuchung der Sprache P. C. de la Barcas. Hamburg, 1968.

❖ [A] Title as is. Hamburg: Cram; de Gruyter, 1968. 149 pp. (Hamburger romanistische Studien B. Ibero-amerikanische Reihe 30. Calderoniana 1.) Rev.: (a) A. L. Mackenzie. *BHS* 46 (1969): 274-75; (b) P. Wunderli. *RF* 81 (1969): 480-85; (c) J. J. Montes Giraldo. *Thesaurus* 24 (1969): 312-13; (d) M. M. G. Sandmann. *RPh* 23.3 (1970): 364. [B] "El uso de los tiempos verbales en *La vida es sueño* (auto)." *Hacia Calderón: [Primer] coloquio anglogermano, Exeter, 1969*. Ed. Hans Flasche. Berlin: de Gruyter, 1970. 105-12. [C] "El comienzo de los textos en el teatro de Calderón (Contribución al estudio del imperativo en la lengua literaria)." *Hacia Calderón: Segundo coloquio anglogermano, Hamburgo, 1970*. Ed. Hans Flasche. Berlin: de Gruyter, 1973. 181-90. [D] "El futuro 'performativo' y el teatro (Contribución al estudio de la lengua calderoniana)." *Hacia Calderón: Tercer coloquio anglogermano, Londres, 1973*. Ed. Hans Flasche. Berlin: de Gruyter, 1976. 233-39. [E] "Überlegungen zur sprachlichen Konstitution von Calderóns Auto sacramental." *Wolfenbütteler Forschungen* 13 (1981): 75-98. [Linguistic study of such constructions as *quiere venir.*] [F] "La función atenuadora de 'en fin' en los textos calderonianos." *Hacia Calderón: Noveno coloquio anglogermano, Liverpool, 1990.* Ed. Hans Flasche. Stuttgart: Steiner, 1991. 9–14. (Archivum Calderonianum 6).

1288. Lewis, Christopher Ian. A Study of the Relationship between the Themes of Love, Honour and Jealousy in Calderón's *comedias de capa y espada.* v+218 pp. Cambridge, 1982. Abstract available on fiche.

1289. Lindner, Ernst. Die poetische Personifikation in den Jugendschauspielen Calderóns: Ein Beitrag zu Studien über Stil und Sprache des Dichters. 32 pp. Munich, 1904.

❖ Title as is. Leipzig: Deichert Nachf. 1904. 150 pp. (Münchener Beiträge zur romanischen und englischen Philologie 32.) [This study, based on twenty-eight plays, consists of four chapters: "Personifikationen aus dem Gebiete der Natur," "Die Personifikation von Teilen des menschlichen Körpers, sowie von Äusserungen und Zuständen seiner sinnlichen und seelischen Existenz," "Die Personifikation von Abstrakten Begriffen," "Die Personifikation von Gebäuden und Geräten."] Rev.: (a) Ph. A. Becker. *DLZ* 25 (1904): 2678–79; (b) G. Carel. *Archiv* 116 (1906) 465–69.

1290. Lobato, María-Luisa. Edición y estudio del teatro cómico breve de Calderón. [1]+549 pp. Salamanca, 1985.

❖ [A] "Segunda parte inédita del entremés *Las jácaras* atribuido a Calderón." *RILCE* 2.1 (1986): 119–40. [B] "Un códice de teatro desconocido del siglo XVII: Edición de la mojiganga *La pandera* de Calderón." *Criticón* 37 (1987): 169–201. [C] "*El escolar y el soldado:* Entremés inédito de Calderón para el auto *¿Quién hallará mujer fuerte?*" *Castilla* 13 (1988): 61–78. [D] "Métrica del teatro cómico breve de Calderón." *Canente* 3 (1988): 68–92. [E] "Una mojiganga inédita de Calderón: *El Parnaso.* Segunda parte de *La rabia.*" *Estudios sobre Calderón: Actas del coloquio calderoniano, Salamanca, 1985.* Salamanca: Universidad de Salmanca, 1988. 71–90. [F] Calderón, P. *Teatro cómico breve.* Ed. M. L. Lobato. Kassel: Reichenberger, 1989. 748 pp. (Teatro del Siglo de Oro. Ediciones críticas 17.) Rev.: (a) S. Tarzibachi. *Incipit* 9 (1989): 215–16; (b) L. Vázquez. *EstM* 48.176 (1992): 189. [Includes forty-one works: *entremeses, jácaras, bailes,* and *mojigangas.*]

[G] "Tres calas en la métrica del teatro breve español del Siglo de Oro: Quiñones de Benavente, Calderón y Moreto." *Homenaje a Hans Flasche*. Ed. Karl-Hermann Körner and Gunther Zimmermann. Stuttgart: Steiner, 1991. 113–54.

1291. López de Alda, Andrés. La teología de la muerte en Calderón de la Barca, teólogo popular español del siglo XVII. Louvain-la-Neuve, 1978.

1292. Losada Diéguez, Antonio. Simbólica e ideas filosóficas contenidas en *La vida es sueño,* drama en tres jornadas y verso de D. Pedro Calderón de la Barca. Two handwritten versions, 131 pp. and 136 pp. Each has an additional 3 pp. of notes. Complutense, 1905. ❖ Title as is. Santiago: Balado, 1910. 52 pp.

1293. Macau Matas, Montserrat. Influjo y evolución de los temas calderonianos en la obra de Hugo von Hofmannsthal. 195 pp. Complutense, 1957.

1294. Maestre Payá, Rafael. Gramática escénica de Calderón de la Barca. 427 pp. Murcia, 1987.

❖ [A] "Humanismo, historia y teatro en el Renacimiento: El fenómeno italiano." *RdHM* 5 (1985): 196–207. [B] "El espejo cóncavo en Calderón de la Barca y Valle-Inclán." *CH* 8.1 (1986): 37–51. [C] "La gran maquinaria en comedias mitológicas de Calderón de la Barca." *El mito en el teatro clásico español: Ponencias y debates de las séptimas jornadas de teatro clásico español, Almagro, 1984.* Ed. Francisco Ruiz Ramón and César Oliva. Madrid: Taurus, 1988. 55–81. [D] "El actor calderoniano en el escenario palaciego." *Actor y técnica de representación del teatro clásico español, Madrid, 1988.* Ed. José María Díez Borque. London: Tamesis, 1989. 177–93. (Colección Támesis, serie A. Monografías 140.) [E] *Escenotecnia del Barroco: El error de Gomar y Bayuca.* Murcia: Universidad de Murcia, 1989. 220 pp. (Colección maior 19.) [Jusepe Gomar and Bautista Bayuca were pupils of the Valencian architect and scene designer José Caudi (d. 1696).] [F] "Escenotecnia de los Salones Dorados: El del Alcázar, el del Palacio del Buen Retiro." *Espacios teatrales del Barroco español: Calle, iglesia, palacio, universidad. XIII jornadas de teatro clásico, Almagro, 1990.* Ed. José María Díez Borque. Kassel: Reichenberger, 1991. 185–97. [G] "Calderón de la Barca-Baccio del Bianco: Un binomio escénico." *RdHM* 11 (1992): 239–50. [H]

Vega, Lope de. *El caballero de Olmedo.* Ed. R. Maestre. Alicante: Aguaclara, 1992. 132 pp. [I] Maestre Payá, R., and César Oliva. "Espacio y espectáculo en la comedia de magia de mediados del siglo XIX." *La comedia de magia y de santos.* Ed. Francisco Javier Blasco et al. Madrid: Júcar, 1992. 421-31. [J] Maestre Payá, R., and César Oliva. "Ideas de teatro en la Edad Media." *Teatro y espectáculo en la Edad Media.* Ed. Lluís Quirante Santacruz. Alicante: Diputación de Alicante, 1992. 177-87. [K] Calderón, P. *Andrómeda y Perseo.* Philological, critical, and staging ed. by R. Maestre. Madrid: Ministerio de Cultura, Museo Nacional del Teatro, 1994. 267 pp. [L] "Baccio del Bianco: Aportaciones a la escena áurea española." *En torno al teatro del Siglo de Oro: Actas de las jornadas IX-X celebradas en Almería.* Ed. Heraclia Castellón, Agustín de la Granja, and Antonio Serrano. Almería: Instituto de Estudios Almerienses, 1995. 53-59. (Colección Actas 17.)

1295. MALEY, UTA. Schreyvogel und Calderón: Ein Beitrag zur Erforschung der österreichischen Calderónrezeption im 19. Jahrhundert. 255 pp. Innsbruck, 1976.

❖ "Josef Schreyvogel und die spanische Dramatik des Siglo de Oro (Dargestellt am Beispiel seiner Bearbeitung von Calderóns *comedia simbólica La vida es sueño*)." *MuK* 24.4 (1978): 358-70.

1296. MARCOS VILLANUEVA, BALBINO. La ascética de los Jesuitas en los autos sacramentales de Calderón. 394 pp. Complutense, 1971. Abstract in *RUCM* 21.84-2 (Oct.-Dec. 1972): 17-28.

❖ Title as is. Bilbao: Universidad de Deusto, Departamento de Publicaciones, 1973. 311 pp.

1297. MARGRAFF, NICOLAUS. Der Mensch und sein Seelenleben in den *Autos sacramentales* des Don Pedro Calderón de la Barca. Bonn, 1912.

❖ Title as is. Bonn: Ludwig, 1912. 114 pp.

1298. MATOS HERNÁNDEZ, VÍCTOR. Proyecciones de la obra de Calderón en el mundo poético de Shelley. Complutense, 1971. Abstract in *RUM* 20.80 (1971): 51-52.

1299. MATTHEWS, DOROTHY JOAN. A Critical Edition of *El gran príncipe de Fez* by Calderón de la Barca (Prepared from the Autograph Manuscript and with a Critical and Historical Study of the Play and Its Sources). 305 pp. London/Birkbeck College, 1968.

1300. MEHRHOFF, HERBERT. Die Calderón-Übersetzungen Edward FitzGeralds dargestellt an *The Painter of His Own Dishonour* und *Such Stuff as Dreams Are Made Of.* xii+136+53 pp. Marburg, 1952.

1301. MICHELS, WILHELM. Barockstil bei Shakespeare und Calderón. 89 pp. Frankfurt, 1929.
❖ Title as is. *RH* 75 (1929): 370–458. Rev.: (a) H. Hatzfeld. *DLZ* 51 (1930): col. 793–95; (b) A. Hämel. *LGRP* 52 (1931): col. 452–53.

1302. MIGUEL, FELIPE DE. La Philosophie "implicite" de la vie dans les *autos sacramentales* de Pedro Calderón de la Barca. 435 pp. Bordeaux/III, 1977. (Thèse de 3e cycle)

1303. MÜNNIG, ELISABETH. Calderón und A. W. Schlegel. 41 pp. Munich, 1912.
❖ [A] Title as is. Berlin: Berliner Buch- und Kunstdruckerei, 1912. 41 pp. [B] *Calderón und die ältere deutsche Romantik.* Berlin: Mayer & Müller, 1912. 88 pp. Rev.: M. M. *EstudB* 6 (1914): 358–59.

1304. MUNTADAS, JUAN FEDERICO. Discurso sobre Shakespeare y Calderón. Complutense, 1849.
❖ Title as is. Madrid: Imprenta de la Publicidad, 1849. 32 pp.

1305. NARINESINGH, LAL. A Critical Edition and Study of Calderón's *Apolo y Climene.* clxi+143 pp. Cambridge, 1968.

1306. NIEMEYER, HELGA. *El alcalde de Zalamea,* oder die Kunst der *Comedia:* Untersuchungen zu Lope de Vegas Theaterstück und vergleichende Betrachtung der Calderónschen *Alcalde*-Version. Paderborn, 1990(?).
❖ Title as is. Aachen: Alano Rader, 1991. 266 pp. Rev.: (a) G. Wogatzke Luckow. *RJ* 43 (1992): 352–56; (b) F. Leinen. *ZRP* 111.1 (1995): 136–37.

1307. OCHSE, HORST. Studien zur Metaphorik Calderóns. 161 pp. Freiburg, 1959.
❖ Title as is. München: Fink, 1967. 127 pp. (Freiburger Schriften zur romanischen Philologie 1.) Rev.: (a) S. Jauernick. *NS* 67 (1968): 413–14; (b) E. Glaser. *RF* 80 (1968): 606–10 (i.e., 706–10).

1308. ORTIZ, GEORG. Die Weltanschauung Calderóns. Bern, 1897.
❖ Title as is. Bern: Steiger, 1897. 67 pp. (Berner Studien zur Philosophie und ihrer Geschichte 5.)

1309. PAILLER, CLAIRE. Questions d'amour dans les *comedias* de Calderón de la Barca. Besançon, 1972. (Thèse de 3e cycle)

❖ [A] *La Question d'amour dans les "comedias" de Calderón de la Barca.* Paris: Belles Lettres, 1974. 177 pp. (Annales littéraires de l'Université de Besançon 165.) Rev.: (a) M. Vitse. *CMHLB* 25 (1975): 205-07; (b) J. M. Díez Borque. *CHA* 349 (1979): 217-19. [B] "El gracioso y los 'guiños' de Calderón: Apuntes sobre 'autoburla' e ironía crítica." *Risa y sociedad en el teatro español del Siglo de Oro: Actes du troisième colloque du GESTE, Toulouse, 1980.* Ed. Yves-René Fonquerne. Paris: CNRS, 1980. 33-50. Regarding her classification of Calderón's plays, the writer refers the reader to her printed dissertation. She concludes her analysis as follows: "La coincidencia entre la distanciación frente a la obra dramática (es decir la afirmación de que la creación es juego libremente regulado), y la expresión máxima del juego del espíritu que es la *cuestión de amor* nos parece presentar una coherencia dentro del sistema dramático calderoniano."

1310. PITOLLET, LÉON-ALEXANDRE-CAMILLE. La Querelle caldéronienne de Johan Nikolas Böhl von Faber et José Joaquín de Mora reconstituée d'aprés les documents originaux. Toulouse, 1909. (Thèse complémentaire)

❖ Title as is. Paris: Alcan, 1909. lv+272 pp. Rev.: (a) A. Ludwig. *Archiv* 125 (1910): 227-28; (b) F. Baldensperger. *RCHLP* ns 69 (1910): 132-33; (c) P. van Tieghem. *RSH* 21 (1910): 213-24; (d) B. Sanvisenti. *StudFilMod* 4 (1911): 135-37; (e) L. P. Thomas. *ZFSL* 37 (1911): 39-41; (f) A. L. Stiefel. *LGRP* 35 (1914): col. 291-300.

1311. POTTHOFF, ADOLF. Eichendorff als Calderón-Übersetzer. 256 pp. Münster, 1920.

❖ [A] Calderón de la Barca, P. *Der wundertätige Magier.* New trans. A. Potthoff. München: Müncherner Drucke, 1925. 163 pp. [B] Calderón de la Barca, P. Das Leben ein Traum: *Schauspiel in drei Aufzügen.* Trans. A. Potthoff. Hildesheim: Borgmeyer, 1931. 104 pp.

1312. RIZZI, ELEONORE. Nicholas Linguets Bearbeitungen Calderonscher Schauspiele: Ein Beitrag zur französischen Übersetzungsliteratur des 18. Jahrhunderts. 123 pp. Vienna, 1933.

1313. ROZIK, ELYAHU. Figurative Elements in the Spanish Poetic Drama of Lope de Vega, Calderón, [and] Federico García Lorca. [Text in Hebrew.] 470 pp. Jerusalem, 1973.

1314. RUANO DE LA HAZA, JOSÉ MARÍA. A Critical Edition of *Cada uno para sí* by D. Pedro Calderón de la Barca. 643 pp. London/Westfield College, 1975.

❖ [A] Calderón, P. Cada uno para sí: *A Critical Edition, with Introduction, Including a Study of the Transmission of the Text, and Notes.* Ed. J. M. Ruano de la Haza. Kassel: Reichenberger, 1982. 403 pp. (Teatro del Siglo de Oro. Ediciones críticas 1.) Rev.: (a) J. Caminero. *LdD* 13.27 (1983): 195; (b) M. Vitse. *Criticón* 27 (1984): 109–28; (c) D. L. Smith. *RCEH* 10 (1985): 330–31; (d) M. McKendrick. *BHS* 63 (1986): 170; (e) D. Altamiranda. *Incipit* 6 (1986): 226–27; (f) M. C. Quintero. *KRQ* 33.4 (1986): 505–06; (g) R. ter Horst. *MLN* 101 (1986): 440–43; (h) W. F. Hunter. *MLR* 81 (1986): 770–71. [B] "Editing the Seventeenth-Century Dramatic Text: The Eclectic Method." *Editing the* Comedia II. Ed. Michael McGaha and Frank P. Casa. Ann Arbor: Univ. of Michigan, Dept. of Romance Languages, 1991. 39–65. (Michigan Romance Studies 11.)

1315. RUIZ LAGOS, MANUEL. Estética de la pintura en el teatro de Calderón. 2 vols. (407, 394 pp.) Granada, 1966.

❖ [A] "Las alegorías inanimadas, como técnica escenográfica en el teatro simbólico de Calderón." *AO* 15 (1965): 256–74. [B] "Una técnica dramática de Calderón: La pintura y el centro escénico." *Segismundo* 2.3 (1966): 91–104. [C] "Algunas relaciones pictóricas y literarias en el teatro alegórico de Calderón." *CAL* 1 (1967): 21–71 + 4 pl. [D] Title as is. Extract. Granada: Universidad de Granada, Facultad de Filosofía y Letras, 1969. 73 pp. Rev.: C. Cuevas García. *RL* 35.69–70 (1969): 118–19. [E] "Apuntes sobre acotaciones musicales en los autos de Calderón." *AIEM* 6 (1970): 63–77. [F] "Estudio y catálogo del vestuario escénico en las personas dramáticas de Calderón." *AIEM* 7 (1971): 181–214. [G] "Interrelación pintura/poesía en el drama alegórico calderoniano: El caso imitativo de la iconología de C. Ripa." *Goya* 161–62 (1981): 282–89. [H] Ruiz Lagos, M., and María de los Ángeles Campos Blasco. "Idea e imagen pictórica en el teatro alegórico de Calderón." *Cauce* 4 (1981): 77-130.

1316. Sanz y Villanueva, María de la Consolación. Pedro Crespo, alcalde de Zalamea. 54 pp. Complutense, 1925.

1317. Schmitt, Hermann. Edward FitzGeralds Calderón-Übersetzung von 1853. 163 pp. Würzburg, 1922.

1318. Schramm, Edmund. Corneilles *Héraclius* und Calderóns *En esta vida todo es verdad y todo mentira:* Ein Beitrag zur Geschichte der literarischen Beziehungen zwischen Frankreich und Spanien im 17. Jahrhundert. Würzburg, 1927.

❖ Title as is. *RH* 71 (1927): 225-308. Rev.: (a) W. von Wurzbach. *LGRP* 50 (1929): col. 267-68; (b) A. Hämel. *ZRP* 54 (1934): 345-46. [For a more complete list of this scholar's publications, see *Edmund Schramm (1902-1975): Würdigung bei der Gedächtnisfeier des Fachbereichs 15 (Philologie III) der Johannes-Gutenberg-Universität Mainz am 27. November 1975* (Mainz: Johannes-Gutenberg-Universität, 1976) 34 pp. Bibliography not paginated.]

1319. Schrek, Johanna Rudolphine. Calderón de la Barca, Pedro: *El sitio de Bredá,* comedia. Edición crítica con introducción y notas. Utrecht, 1957.

❖ Title as is. El Haya: van Goor Zonen, 1957. 259 pp. (Publicaciones del Instituto de Estudios Hispánicos, Portugueses e Iberoamericanos de la Universidad Estatal de Utrecht 1.) [The base text is BNM MS 14.952.] Rev.: (a) F. López Estrada. *ArH* 84-85 (1957): 97-99; (b) E. M. Wilson. *BHS* 34 (1957): 227-29; (c) P. Groult. *LR* 14 (1960): 285-87.

1320. Schukowitz, Johann. Don Pedro Calderón de la Barca und die deutschen Romantiker: Eine literarhistorische Untersuchung. Vienna, 1893.

1321. Schulte, Irmhild. Buch- und Schriftwesen in Calderóns weltlichem Theater. Bonn, 1938.

❖ Title as is. Bochum-Langendreer: Pöppinghaus, 1938. 116 pp. ["Estudio de palabras, metáforas, juegos de palabras, etc., pertenecientes al arte del libro y la escritura" (McCready, no. 2332).] Rev.: F. Weber. *RFH* 5 (1943): 182-83.

1322. Serrano Mañes, Montserrat. El teatro de Thomas Corneille:

Estudio estructural y comparativo de las comedias inspiradas en Calderón. 818 pp. Granada, 1988.

❖ Title as is. Granada: Universidad de Granada, 1989. 12 microfiches.

1323. SLOMAN, ALBERT EDWARD. The Sources of Calderón's *Príncipe constante:* With a Critical Edition of Its Immediate Source, *La fortuna adversa del infante don Fernando de Portugal* (a Play Attributed to Lope de Vega) and a Study of Moorish Jargon. xv+144+24+13 pp. Oxford, 1948.

❖ [A] "The Phonology of Moorish Jargon in the Works of Early Spanish Dramatists and Lope de Vega." *MLR* 44.2 (1949): 207–17. [B] *The Sources of Calderón's* El príncipe constante, *with a Critical Edition of Its Immediate Source,* La fortuna adversa del infante don Fernando de Portugal *(a Play Attributed to Lope de Vega).* Oxford: Blackwell, 1950. 228 pp. Rev.: (a) E. A. Peers. *BSS* 28 (1951): 222–23; (b) A. del Hoyo. *Ínsula* 6.72 (1951): 5; (c) A. Valbuena Prat. *Clavileño* 3.14 (1952): 77; (d) E. W. Hesse. *HR* 20 (1952): 261–63; (e) A. A. Parker. *MLR* 47.2 (1952): 254–56; (f) C. Bruerton. *Symposium* 6 (1952): 213–15; (g) A. Rey. *MP* 50 (1953): 278–80; (h) W. Mettmann. *RF* 65.1–2 (1953): 197–99. [C] *The Dramatic Craftmanship of Calderón: His Use of Earlier Plays.* Oxford: Dolphin, 1958. 327 pp. [In addition to *El príncipe constante,* this book studies the following plays: *El médico de su honra, Las armas de la hermosura, Los cabellos de Absalón, El mayor encanto amor, La niña de Gómez Arias, El alcalde de Zalamea,* and *La vida es sueño.*] Rev.: (a) L. J. MacLennan. *Arbor* 163–64 (1959): 478–79; (b) J. H. Silverman. *BAbr* 33 (1959): 354; (c) N. Salomon. *BH* 61 (1959): 452–54; (d) A. A. Parker. *BHS* 36.3 (1959): 182–84; (e) E. S. Ch. *Cuadernos* 38 (1959): 111–12; (f) E. W. Hesse. *H*[AATSP] 42 (1959): 287–88; (g) R. Hilton. *HAR* 12 (1959): 63–64; (h) R. D. Pring-Mill. *RJ* 10 (1959): 383–86; (i) R. R. MacCurdy. *Symposium* 13 (1959): 350–53; (j) E. M. Wilson. *MLR* 55 (1960): 124–25; (k) A. M. Pollin. *RHM* 26 (1960): 135; (l) W. M. Whitby. *RR* 51 (1960): 281–83; (m) A. Zamora Vicente. *ZRP* 76 (1960): 169–71; (n) A. G. Reichenberger. *HR* 29 (1961): 254–56; (o) P. Groult. *LR* 15 (1961): 177–80; (p) P. Cabañas. *RFE* 44 (1961): 451–54 (q) J. de José Prades. *RL* 21. 41–42 (1962): 194–95.

1324. SOUILLER, DIDIER. La Dialectique de l'ordre et de l'anarchie dans les œuvres de Shakespeare et de Calderón. Paris/IV, 1983.
❖ [A] Title as is. Berne: Peter Lang, 1985. 367 pp. (Publications universitaires européennes, ser. 18. Littérature comparée 42.) Rev.: J.-P. Leroy. *RLC* 63.3 (1989): 408–11. [B] *Calderón de la Barca et le grand théâtre du monde.* Paris: Presses Universitaires de France, 1992. 390 pp. [C] "*Le Grand théâtre du monde,* de Calderón: Signification philosophique et ambiguïté." *Littératures* 26 (1992): 102–14.

1325. SPECHT, GERTRAUD. Die Darstellung der Familie in den Dramen von Lope de Vega und Calderón. 134 pp. Munich, 1957.

1326. SZYNALIK-DOBROWOLSKY, JULIÁN. Calderón en Polonia. 226 pp. Complutense, 1967. Abstract in *RUM* 16.61–64 (1967): 47–48.

1327. TEJADA CORPAS, AMELIA. Untersuchungen zum Humor in den *Comedias* Calderóns unter Ausschluß der *Gracioso*-Gestalten. Hamburg, 1974.
❖ Title as is. Berlin: de Gruyter, 1974. 365 pp. (Hamburger romanistische Studien B. Ibero-amerikanische Reihe 38. Calderoniana 9.) Rev.: T. R. A. Mason. *BHS* 53 (1976): 248–49.

1328. ULBRICH, HUGO. Quaestiones Calderonianae: Dissertatio philologica. Bonn, 1865.
❖ [A] *Ueber Calderon's Schauspiel* Die Kirchenspaltung von England *mit der deutschen Uebersetzung des ersten Actes in den Versmaassen und Reimweisen des Originals.* Crefeld: Kühler, 1863. 45 pp. (Wissenschaftliche Beilage zum Programm der Städtischen Realschule zu Crefeld.) [B] Title as is. Bonnae: form. Carthusianis, 1865. 28 pp.

1329. UPPENDAHL, KLAUS. Calderón de la Barca, Pedro. *Mística y real Babilonia:* Kritische Ausgabe und Kommentar. Hamburg, 1978.
❖ Title as is. Berlin: de Gruyter, 1979. 726 pp. (Hamburger romanistische Studien B. Ibero-amerikanische Reihe 40. Calderoniana 11.) [The base text is the autograph MS.] Rev.: D. W. Cruickshank. *BHS* 58 (1981): 84–85.

1330. VALBUENA PRAT, ÁNGEL. Los autos sacramentales de Calderón. 2 vols. Complutense, 1924.
❖ [A] "Los autos sacramentales de Calderón: Clasificación y

análisis." *RH* 61 (1924): 1-302. [B] Calderón, P. *Autos sacramentales.* Ed. A. Valbuena Prat. 2 vols. 1st ed. Madrid: Espasa Calpe, Vol. 1: (1926) lix+197 pp. (Clásicos castellanos 69.) Vol. 2: (1927) lxxii+213 pp. (Clásicos castellanos 74.) [The prologue of vol. 1 includes Valbuena Prat's classification of Calderón's *autos.*] [C] "Los autógrafos de los autos de Calderón." *RBAM* 4 (1927): 484-86. [D] "Los autos del 'Año Santo' de Calderón." *RBAM* 5 (1928): 60-73. [E] "Una representación de *El gran teatro del mundo:* La fuente de este auto." *RBAM* 5 (1928): 79-83. [F] *Literatura dramática española.* Barcelona: Labor, 1930. 336 pp. [G] *Calderón, su personalidad, su arte dramático, su estilo y sus obras.* Barcelona: Juventud, 1941. 215 pp. [H] *De la imaginería sacra de Lope de Vega a la teología sistemática de Calderón: Dos momentos del teatro nacional.* Murcia: Universidad de Murcia, 1945. 48 pp. [I] "Calderón y el Año Santo de 1650." *Clavileño* 1.1 (1950): 27-36. [J] "Los autos calderonianos en el ambiente teológico español." *Clavileño* 3.15 (1952): 33-35. [K] Calderón, P. *Obras completas.* Vol. 3: *Autos sacramentales.* Comp., prologue, and notes by A. Valbuena Prat. 1st ed. Madrid: Aguilar, 1952. 1,915 pp. [The prologue includes A. V. P.'s "Clasificación de los autos."] [L] *Historia del teatro español.* Barcelona: Noguer, 1956. 703 pp. [M] *El teatro español en su siglo de oro.* Barcelona: Planeta, 1969. 402 pp. [For a more complete list of this scholar's publications, see Francisco Javier Díez de Revenga, "Recuerdo bibliográfico de Ángel Valbuena Prat," *Monteagudo* 57 (1977): 39-43.]

1331. WILLE, JUTTA. Calderóns Spiel der Erlösung: Eine spanische Bilderbibel des 17. Jahrhunderts. 91 pp. Zürich, 1932.

❖ [A] "Calderón und die spanischen Fronleichnamsspiele." *Theaterkultur* 3 (1931): 19-25. [B] Title as is. München: Kaiser, 1932. 259 pp. [This is a study of Calderón's *autos sacramentales.*] Rev.: (a) E. Seifert. *ARom* 16 (1932): 465-66; (b) F. Finger. *BBGE* 5 (1932): 77-78; (c) A. Hämel. *ZRP* 54 (1934): 347-48.

1332. WILSON, EDWARD MERYON. Culteranism in the Spanish Drama of the Seventeenth Century, with Particular Reference to the *Comedias* of Pedro Calderón de la Barca. Cambridge, 1933. Cambridge *Abstracts* (1932-33): 86-87.

❖ [A] "The Four Elements in the Imagery of Calderón." *MLR*

31 (1936): 34–47. [B] *Spanish and English Literatures of the 16th and 17th Centuries: Studies in Discretion, Illusion and Mutability*. Ed. Don W. Cruickshank. Cambridge: Cambridge UP, 1980. 281 pp. [For a more complete list of this scholar's publications, see publication B, "A List of the Publications of Edward M. Wilson," pp. xiii–xix.]

1333. Winkler, André. *La vida es sueño* de Pedro Calderón de la Barca: Imagerie et structure dialectique. 59 pp. Zürich, 1963.
❖ Title as is. Zürich: n.p., 1963.

1334. Wulf, Gerhard. Studien zur Schlegelschen Calderón-Übersetzung. 84 pp. Münster, 1926. Abstract, Münster: Höing, 1913. 6 pp.

Camões, Luís de (Portugal. 1524/25–1580)

1335. Wilmsmeier, Wilhelm. Camoens in der deutschen Dichtung des 19. Jahrhunderts: Ein Beitrag zum Künstler-Drama. Münster, 1913.
❖ Title as is. Erfurt: Ohlenroth, 1913. 132 pp.

Cañizares, José de (1676–1750)

1336. Onrubia de Mendoza, José. El teatro de José de Cañizares. 337 pp. Barcelona, 1964. Resumen 212. Barcelona: Universidad de Barcelona, 1965. 22 pp.

Caro y Mallén, Ana (fl. 1653)

1337. Luna, Lola. Ana Caro, una escritora "profesional" del Siglo de Oro: Vida y obra. 2 vols. (1–439, 440–717 pp.) Seville, 1992.
❖ [A] Caro, A. *El conde Partinuplés*. Ed., introd. and notes by L. Luna. Kassel: Reichenberger, 1993. 186 pp. (Teatro del Siglo de Oro. Ediciones críticas 45.) [B] Caro, A. *Valor, agravio y mujer*. Ed., introd. and notes by L. Luna. Madrid: Castalia, 1993. 185 pp. Rev.: F. López Estrada. *ArH* 76.233 (1993, pub. 1975): 75–82.

[C] "Ana Caro, una escritora 'de oficio' del Siglo de Oro." *BHS* 72.1 (1995): 11-26. [For a more complete list of this scholar's publications, see Francisco López Estrada, "Bibliografía de Lola Luna," *ArH* 76.233 (1993, pub. 1995): 80-82.]

Castillo Solórzano, Alonso de (1584-1648)

Regarding this author's inclusion of plays in his prose works, see editorial note preceding United States item no. 360.

1338. Ba, Tamsir. L'œuvre de Alonso de Castillo Solórzano: L'Espace et le temps, les personnages, le ludisme. Recherches de sociologie romanesque. Paris/IV, 1991.

1339. Velasco Kindelán, Magdalena. La obra literaria de Alonso Castillo Solórzano. iv + 223 pp. Complutense, 1976. Resumen de tesis doctoral, in *RUCM* 25.106-2 (1976): 156-57.
❖ La novela cortesana y picaresca de Castillo Solórzano. Valladolid: Servicio de Publicaciones de la Diputación Provincial, 1983. 138 pp. [Ch. 2, sec. 3, pp. 39-41, is entitled "El teatro."]

Castro y Bellvís, Guillén de (1569-1631)

1340. Arens, Arnold. Zur Tradition und Gestaltung des Cid-Stoffes. 437 pp. Münster, 1971.
❖ Title as is. Frankfurt: Akademische, 1975. 437 pp. (Studien zur Romanistik. Studienreihe Humanitas.) [Part 1 of this dissertation deals with Guillén de Castro's *Las mocedades del Cid* and its sources. Parts 2 and 3 compare Castro's play and Corneille's *Le Cid*.]

1341. Faliu-Lacourt, Christiane. Guillén de Castro. 3 vols. (792 pp.) Toulouse/II, 1984. (Thèse d'État) // Rev.: E. Arnaud. *BH* 88.1-2 (1986): 271-73.
❖ [A] "Sacrificios y rendición, o de la fatalidad al libre albedrío en el teatro del Siglo de Oro." *Criticón* 23 (1983): 49-63. [Apropos Castro's *Progne y Filomena* and his *Curioso impertinente*.] [B] Title as is. Lille: Université de Lille III, ANRT, 1984. 792 pp.

Rev.: (a) A. Rodríguez López-Vázquez. *Castilla* 9-10 (1985): 179-82; (b) A. Rodríguez López-Vázquez. *RL* 94 (1985): 296-99; (c) J. M. Díez Borque. *Ínsula* 475 (1986): 18; (d) M. S. Carrasco Urgoiti. *RFE* 67.3-4 (1987): 392-95. [C] Las mocedades del Cid *de Guillén de Castro: Estudio preliminar, edición, y notas de C. Faliu-Lacourt*. Madrid: Taurus, 1987. 162 pp. (Temas de España 180.) [D] *Un Dramaturge espagnol du Siècle d'Or: Guillén de Castro.* Toulouse: Université de Toulouse-Le Mirail, France-Ibérie Recherche, 1989. 792 pp. [This seems to be the printed version of publication B.] [E] Castro, G. de. *El curioso impertinente.* Critical ed. C. Faliu-Lacourt and M. L. Lobato. Kassel: Reichenberger, 1991. 201 pp. (Teatro del Siglo de Oro. Ediciones críticas 31.) [For a more complete list of this scholar's publications, see "Bibliografía de C. Faliu-Lacourt," *Del horror a la risa: Los géneros dramáticos clásicos. Homenaje a Christiane Faliu-Lacourt,* ed. Ignacio Arellano, Víctor García Ruiz, and Marc Vitse (Kassel: Reichenberger, 1994) 4-8.]

1342. Floeck, Wilfried. *Las mocedades del Cid* von Guillén de Castro und *Le Cid* von Pierre Corneille: Ein neuer Versuch. Bonn, 1968. ❖ Title as is. Bonn: Romanisches Seminar der Universität, 1969. 234 pp. (Romanistische Versuche und Vorarbeiten 26.) Rev.: (a) J. Cantera. *FMod* 9.33-34 (1969): 160-61; (b) R. Pageard. *BH* 72 (1970): 222-24; (c) A. L. Mackenzie. *BHS* 47 (1970): 258-60; (d) K. A. Ott. *Archiv* 208 (1971): 230-34; (e) M. Burrio. *NS* (1973): 624.

1343. Rakotomalala, Gérard. Le Vocabulaire de l'amour dans le théâtre de Guillén de Castro: *Comedias de enredo.* 389 pp. Toulouse/II, 1984.

1344. Rodríguez García Vao, Antonio. Guillem de Castro y Belvis: Su vida. Carácter de su teatro. *Las mocedades.* 100 pp., handwritten. Complutense, 1885.

Catalan Theater

1345. Cenoz del Águila, Guillermina. El teatro navideño catalán de técnica medieval. 2 vols. (595 pp.) Barcelona/Autònoma,

1977. Abstract in *MEC. Tesis doctorales* 9 (anexo 1976–77): 4–5. Resumen de tesis doctoral. Barcelona: Universitat Autònoma de Barcelona, 1977. 19 pp.

1346. HUERTA VIÑAS, FERNANDO. Teatro religioso medieval catalán: Las seis "consuetas" basadas en el antiguo testamento pertenecientes al MS 1139 de la Biblioteca de la Diputación de Barcelona. Barcelona, 1967. Resumen no. 652. Barcelona: Universidad de Barcelona, 1975. 12 pp.

❖ [A] Title as is. Barcelona: Universidad de Barcelona, Secretariado de Publicaciones, 1975. [B] *Teatre bíblic: Antic Testament.* Barcelona: Barcino, 1976. 314 pp. [C] Cenoz i del Águila, G., and F. Huerta i Viñas. "La *consueta del fill pròdich,* peça núm. 13 del Ms. 1139 de la Biblioteca de Catalunya." *Estudis de literatura catalana en honor de Josep Romeu i Figueras.* Ed. Lola Badia and Josep Massot i Muntaner. Barcelona: Associació Internacional de Llengua i Literatura Catalanes, 1986. 1: 259–88. [D] "Els drames de Nadal al teatre medieval català i les tradicions llegendàries [s. XV]." *El teatre durant l'Edat Mitjana i el Renaixement: Actes del primer simposi internacional d'història del teatre, Sitges, 1983.* Ed. Ricard Salvat. Barcelona: Universitat de Barcelona, 1986. 39–47. [E] "Un ejemplo de representación del mal en el teatro religioso del XVI: Los dramas catalanes de los ciclos navideño y neotestamentario." *Comedias y comediantes: Estudios sobre el teatro clásico español. Actas del congreso internacional sobre teatro y prácticas escénicas en los siglos XVI y XVII, València, 1989.* Ed. Manuel V. Diago and Teresa Ferrer. Valencia: Universitat de València, 1991. 37–45.

1347. PONS, JOSEPH SÉBASTIEN. La Littérature catalane en Roussillon au XVIIe siècle et au XVIIIe siècle: L'Esprit provincial. Les Mystiques. Les *Goigs* et le théâtre religieux. Toulouse, 1929. (Thèse d'État)

❖ [A] Title as is. Toulouse: Privat; Paris: Didier. 1929. 399 pp. Rev.: (a) M. Bataillon. *RHistM* 5 (1930): 461–63; (b) G. Cirot. *BH* 33.3 (1931): 262–64. [B] "Note sur la *Passion Provençale* du manuscrit Didot et la *Passion Catalane.*" *BH* 37 (1935): 390–92.

1348. PONS, JOSEPH SÉBASTIEN. La Littérature catalane en Roussillon (1600–1800): Bibliographie. Toulouse, 1929. (Thèse complémentaire)

❖ Title as is. Toulouse: Privat; Paris: Didier, 1929. 108 pp.

Cervantes, Miguel de (1547–1616)

1349. Agostini Bonelli del Río, Amelia. El teatro cómico de Cervantes. 280+[2] pp. Complutense, 1958.
❖ [A] "Vida, sociedad y arte en el teatro cómico de Cervantes." *ACer* 8 (1959–60): 51–73. [B] "El teatro cómico de Cervantes." *BRAE* 44 (1964): 223–307, 475–539; 45 (1965): 65–116. [C] Title as is. Madrid: Aguirre, 1965. 207 pp.

1350. Anderson, Ellen Marie. Role-Playing and Role-Changing as Means of Self-Discovery in Selected Works of Cervantes. 2 vols. (1–304, 305–682 pp.) Toronto, 1986. *DAI* 47A: 4403.
❖ [A] Title as is. Canadian Theses Service-Services des Thèses Canadiennes, 1986(?). 8 microfiches (706 frames). [The pertinent works analyzed are the Algerine plays as well as *El rufián dichoso* and *Pedro de Urdemalas*.] [B] "Playing at Moslem and Christian: The Construction of Gender and the Representation of Faith in Cervantes' Captivity Plays." *Cervantes* 13.2 (1993): 37–59. [C] "Articulate Characters: Gender, Genre, and Genius in Cervantes's *El coloquio de los perros* and *Pedro de Urdemalas*." *RLAn* 5 (1994): 349–55. [D] "Refashioning the Maze: The Interplay of Gender and Rank in Cervantes's *El laberinto de amor*." *BCom* 46.2 (1994):165–85.

1351. Canavaggio, Jean. Recherches sur le théâtre de Cervantès. 3 vols. (750 pp.) Paris/III, 1975. (Thèse d'État)
❖ [A] *Cervantès dramaturge: Un théâtre à naître.* Paris: Presses Universitaires de France, 1977. 506 pp. Rev.: (a) A. Sánchez. *ACer* 16 (1977): 268–77; (b) E. H. Friedman. *BCom* 31 (1979): 145–47; (c) J. B. Avalle-Arce. *MLN* 94 (1979): 413–15; (d) M. Joly. *NRFH* 28 (1979): 418–25; (e) J. Huerta Calvo. *RL* 41.82 (1979): 193–210; (f) F. Márquez Villanueva. *BH* 82 (1980): 500–04. [B] "Le Dénouement de *Numance:* Jalons d'une tradition." *Les Cultures ibériques en devenir: Essais publiés en hommage à la mémoire de Marcel Bataillon, 1895–1977.* Paris: Fondation Singer-Polignac, 1979. 647–57. [C] "Las figuras del donaire en las comedias de Cervantes."

Risa y sociedad en el teatro español del Siglo de Oro: Actes du troisième colloque du GESTE, Toulouse, 1980. Ed. Yves-René Fonquerne. Paris: CNRS, 1980. 51-67. [D] "Brecht, lector de los entremeses cervantinos: La huella de Cervantes en los *Einakter.*" *Cervantes, su obra y su mundo: Actas del primer congreso internacional sobre Cervantes, Madrid, 1978.* Ed. Manuel Criado de Val. Madrid: EDI-6, 1981. 1023-30. [E] Cervantes, M. de. *Entremeses.* Ed. J. Canavaggio. Madrid: Taurus, 1982. 173 pp. [F] "García Lorca ante el entremés cervantino: El telar de *La zapatera prodigiosa.*" *El teatro menor en España a partir del siglo XVI: Actas del coloquio, Madrid, 1982.* Ed. Luciano García Lorenzo. Madrid: CSIC, 1983. 141-53. [G] "Los pastores del teatro cervantino: Tres avatares de una Arcadia precaria." La Galatea *de Cervantes-cuatrocientos años después (Cervantes y lo pastoril).* Ed. Juan Bautista Avalle-Arce. Newark: Juan de la Cuesta, 1985. 37-52. [H] "Sobre lo cómico en el teatro cervantino: Tristán y Madrigal, bufones *in partibus.*" *NRFH* 34.2 (1985-86): 538-47. [I] "Pedro de Urdemalas, montañés famoso." *ACer* 25-26 (1988): 117-19. [J] "Una huella probable del *Conde Lucanor* en el teatro de Cervantes." *Teatro del Siglo de Oro: Homenaje a Alberto Navarro González.* Ed. Víctor García de la Huerta, Jean Canavaggio, and Theodor Berchem. Kassel: Reichenberger, 1990. 87-93. [K] "'Madre, la mi madre': Textes et contextes." *BH* 92.1 (1990): 111-23. [Apropos this *cantar* in *El celoso extremeño* and *La entretenida.*] [L] "Para la génesis del *Rufián dichoso:* El *Consuelo de penitentes* de Fray Alonso de San Román." *NRFH* 38.2 (1990): 461-76. [M] "La conversión del rufián dichoso: Fuentes y recreación." *On Cervantes: Essays for L. A. Murillo.* Ed. James A. Parr. Newark: Juan de la Cuesta, 1991. 11-19. [N] Cervantes, M. de. *Los baños de Argel. Pedro de Urdemalas.* Ed. J. Canavaggio. Madrid: Taurus, 1992. 378 pp. (Clásicos Taurus 17.)

1352. Castro Madinaveitia, Carmen. Los personajes femeninos de Cervantes. 265 pp. Complutense, 1953.

1353. García de la Torre, Moisés. Un aspecto histórico y literario en la Edad de Oro: Arrieros, mozos de mulas y su mundo. 349 pp. Complutense, 1977. Abstract in *UCM. Tesis doctorales* 1 (1976-77): 140-41.

[Includes dramatic works.]

❖ [A] *Las mulas en la época de Cervantes y en su obra: Realidad histórica y ficción literaria.* Alcalá de Henares: Ayuntamiento, 1978. [B] "Historia y literatura de arrieros, mozos de mulas y su mundo: Perspectivas de investigación." *I Jornadas de estudios sobre la provincia de Madrid.* Madrid: Diputación Provincial, 1979. 761-68. [C] "Las ventas en la España del Antiguo Régimen." *HispM* 39 (1979): 397-453. [D] "Realidad histórica y ficción literaria: El mundo de los caminos en Cervantes y su época." *ACer* 20 (1982): 113-23. [E] "Diversos aspectos de un grupo social marginado: Los arrieros en la España de los Austrias." *RIS* 41.48 (1983): 639-62.

1354. García Martín, Manuel. Cervantes y la comedia española en el siglo XVII. 676 pp. Salamanca, 1977.

❖ [A] Extracto de tesis doctoral, T-L-204. Salamanca: Universidad de Salamanca, Facultad de Filosofía y Letras, 1977. 19 pp. [B] "Dos modelos cervantinos en Tirso de Molina." *ACer* 17 (1978): 137-46. [" . . . compuso Tirso dos comedias, *Palabras y plumas* y *Quien da luego da dos veces* . . . que guardan estrechísima afinidad con las dos novelas ejemplares que Cervantes sitúa en ambiente italiano: *El amante liberal* y *La señora Cornelia*."] [C] Title as is. Salamanca: Universidad de Salamanca, 1980. 271 pp. (Acta Salmanticensia. Filosofía y Letras 117.) ["El propósito del presente trabajo es ofrecer un compendio bibliográfico que refleje la significación cervantina en el teatro áureo español. En este sentido, se incluyen cincuenta y nueve piezas dramáticas de la época relacionadas, por unas u otras motivaciones, con la producción del insigne escritor." (Prt. Diss.)] Rev.: M. F. Vilches de Frutos. *ACer* 20 (1982): 229-31. [D] Matos Fragoso, J. de, Diamante, J. B., Vélez de Guevara, J. *El Hidalgo de la Mancha.* Ed. Manuel García Martín. Salamanca: Universidad de Salamanca, 1982. 149 pp. (Acta Salmanticensia. Serie varia. Temas científicos y literarios 40.)

1355. Garrote Pérez, Francisco. El concepto de la naturaleza en Cervantes. 2 vols. ([1]+264, 265-673 pp.) Salamanca, 1974.

❖ [A] Extracto de tesis doctoral, T-L-129. Salamanca: Universidad de Salamanca, 1974. 18 pp. [B] "Cervantes y la cosmovisión de su época." *ACer* 15 (1976): 181-98. ["El presente artículo no es más que un avance de un aspecto de mi tesis doctoral."] [C] *La naturaleza en el pensamiento de Cervantes.*

Salamanca: Universidad de Salamanca, 1979. 170 pp. (Acta Salmanticensia. Serie varia 23.) "Fácilmente se desprende de lo dicho que eclecticismo y fideísmo son las constantes en el pensamiento natural cervantino. Si el eclecticismo peculiariza el universo ideológico de Cervantes, también lo singulariza su fideísmo, que lleva a todas sus concepciones naturales y existenciales a conectar continuamente con lo sobrenatural, como veremos a lo largo de nuestro trabajo. Así entendemos a Cervantes, éste es nuestro punto de partida y los límites dentro de los cuales nos movemos a lo largo de nuestro estudio." (Prt. Diss.) Rev.: A. Sánchez. *ACer* 20 (1982): 226–29. [D] *Naturaleza y pensamiento en España en los siglos XVI y XVII*. Salamanca: Universidad de Salamanca, 1981. 172 pp. ["Es evidente que las conclusiones de este estudio se pueden aplicar a cualquier obra o autor de aquella etapa importante de la literatura española. Nosotros ya lo hemos hecho con la obra cervantina en el libro *El concepto de naturaleza en Cervantes*."] [E] "Universo supersticioso cervantino: Su materialización y función poética." *Cervantes, su obra y su mundo: Actas del primer congreso internacional sobre Cervantes, Madrid, 1978*. Ed. Manuel Criado de Val. Madrid: EDI-6, 1981. 59–74. [F] "Algunas cuestiones cervantinas: Una vía clarificadora de su pensamiento." *ACer* 20 (1982): 59–92.

1356. GEISSLER, RUTH. Torheit und Narrheit bei Cervantes. 101 pp. Freiburg, 1950.

1357. JACQMIN, ALPHONSE. Les Unités en Espagne avant le triomphe de la *comedia* (Cervantes dramaturge et les règles). Brussels, 1924–25.

1358. LEWIS-SMITH, PAUL. Cervantes and the *Comedia:* A Study of the Dramatic Criticism and Practice of Miguel de Cervantes. Cambridge, 1982. Abstract available on fiche.

❖ [A] Smith, P. Lewis [sic]. "*La gran sultana doña Catalina de Oviedo:* A Cervantes Practical Joke." *FMLS* 17.1 (1981): 68–82. [B] "Cervantes' *Numancia* as Tragedy and as Tragi-comedy." *BHS* 64.1 (1987): 15-26. [C] "Cervantes and Inverisimilar Fiction: Reconsidering *La casa de los celos y selvas de Ardenia*." *Golden Age Spanish Literature: Studies in Honour of John Varey by His Colleagues and Pupils*. Ed. Charles Davis and Alan Deyermond. London: Westfield Coll., 1991. 127–36. [D] "Cervantes on Human Absurdity: The Unifying Theme of *La casa de los celos y selvas de Ardenia.*" *Cervantes* 12.2 (1992): 93–103.

1359. MAC EÓIN, GEARÓID ANTON. The Religious and Moral Attitudes and Outlook of Miguel de Cervantes. 290 pp. Dublin, 1951. ❖ *Cervantes.* Milwaukee: Bruce, 1950. 223 pp. Rev.: J. O. Swain. *MLJ* 35.8 (1951): 653–55.

1360. MEDRANO VICARIO, ISABEL. Integración de épica y comedia en la narrativa de Fielding y Cervantes. 552 pp. Complutense, 1988. ❖ Title as is. Madrid: Editorial de la Universidad Complutense, 1988.

1361. MONER, MICHEL. Cervantès conteur: Poétique et idéologie. 353 pp. Grenoble/III, 1985. (Thèse d'État)
The dissertation includes the dramatic works.
❖ [A] *Cervantès: Deux thèmes majeurs (l'amour—les armes et les lettres).* Toulouse: Université de Toulouse-Le Mirail, France-Ibérie Recherche, 1986. 151 pp. (Thèses et recherches 15.) Rev.: (a) A. Sánchez. *ACer* 24 (1986): 243–46; (b) M. McKendrick. *BHS* 66 (1989): 379–80. [B] *Cervantès conteur: Écrits et paroles.* Madrid: Casa de Velázquez, 1989. 353 pp. Rev.: (a) Y. Jehenson. *JHP* 14.1 (1989): 107–09; (b) O. Barrero Pérez. *EdO* 9 (1990): 335–38; (c) H. Merkl. *Ibero* 32 (1990): 128–30; (d) M. S. Arredondo. *Criticón* 51 (1991): 151–53; (e) T. Hart. *HR* 59.1 (1991): 91–93; (f) M. S. Carrasco Urgoiti. "Nueva perspectiva cervantina: *Cervantès conteur* de Michel Moner." *RFE* 72.1-2 (1992): 167–76.

1362. NEUMANN, MAX-HELLMUT. Cervantes in Frankreich (1582–1910). Freiburg, 1916.
❖ Title as is. *RH* 78 (1930): 1–309. [On theater, see pp. 66, 171, and 225.]

1363. ODOUL, PIERRE. Sur quelques aspects de *Don Quichotte* concernant la polémique Lope de Vega-Cervantes. 513 pp. Montpellier/III, 1983. (Thèse de 3e cycle) // Rev.: A. Sánchez. *ACer* 23 (1985): 263–64.

1364. POINTON, ROSE BRESNAN. Contribución al estudio lingüístico de la obra de Cervantes. 333 pp. Complutense, 1962. Abstract in *RUM* 11.44 (1962): 636–37.

1365. RAMÍREZ Y DORESTE, JUAN EVANGELISTA. Miguel de Cervantes como dramático. 73 pp., handwritten. Complutense, 1882.

1366. RÍOS VICENTE, ENRIQUE. La ética en la obra de Cervantes. Complutense, 1987.

❖ Title as is. Madrid: Universidad Complutense, 1988. 887 pp. (Colección tesis doctorales no. 417/88.)

1367. STAPP MOODY, WILLIAM A. Técnica e idea de la comedia cervantina. 387 pp. Complutense, 1979.

❖ [A] "*El gallardo español:* La fama como arbitrio de la realidad." *ACer* 17 (1978): 123-36. [B] "*El gallardo español:* La fama como arbitrio de la realidad." *Cervantes, su obra y su mundo: Actas del primer congreso internacional sobre Cervantes, Madrid, 1978.* Ed. Manuel Criado de Val. Madrid: EDI-6, 1981. 261-72. [C] Title as is. Madrid: Editorial de la Universidad Complutense, 1981. 387 pp. [D] "Dichoso por confiado." *ACer* 25-26 (1987-88): 413-52. [Apropos *El rufián dichoso.*]

1368. THOMPSON, JENNIFER. An Examination of the Treatment of Love and Related Themes in the Works of Cervantes. 395 pp. London/Westfield College, 1962-63.

[Ch. 4 (pp. 240-314) treats the *comedias.*]

1369. ZMANTAR, M.-FRANÇOISE. *El trato de Argel,* Miguel de Cervantes Saavedra: Édition critique. 3 vols. (270, 155, 155 pp.) Clermont-Ferrand/II, 1978. (Thèse de 3ᵉ cycle.)

❖ [A] "Saavedra et les captifs du *Trato de Argel* de Miguel de Cervantes Saavedra." *L'Autobiographie dans le monde hispanique: Actes du colloque international de la Baume-les-Aix, 1979.* Aix-en-Provence: Université de Provence, 1980. 185-203. [B] "Miguel de Cervantes y sus fantasmas de Argel." *Quimera* 2 (1980): 31-37.

CLARAMONTE, ANDRÉS DE (DIED 1621?)

1370. ORTIZ DE VILLAJOS, CARMEN. Andrés de Claramonte y sus obras. Complutense? 1954.

CORDEIRO [CORDERO], JACINTO (PORTUGAL. 1606-1646)

1371. GONZÁLEZ CHRISTOPHE. Le Dramaturge Jacinto Cordeiro et son temps. 705 pp. Aix-en-Provence, 1987.

❖ [A] "Le Thème d'Inès de Castro dans le théâtre de Jacinto Cordeiro." *Quadrant* (1988): 25–40. [B] "Notes sur quelques échos de Cervantès et de Gongora dans le théâtre de Jacinto Cordeiro." *Hommage à Robert Jammes*. Ed. Francis Cerdan. 3 vols. Toulouse: Presses Universitaires du Mirail, 1994. 2: 473–79.

Cubillo de Aragón, Álvaro (1596?–1661)

1372. Schmidt, Marie-France. Cubillo de Aragón, Álvaro: *Auto sacramental de la muerte de Frislán*. Édition commentée d'un manuscrit inédit. 307 pp. Nice, 1974. (Thèse de 3e cycle)
❖ [A] Cubillo de Aragón, A. *Auto sacramental de la muerte de Frislán*. Introd., text, and notes by M.-F. Schmidt. Paris: Reder, 1980. 307 pp. facsimile. [B] Cubillo de Aragón, A. *Auto sacramental de la muerte de Frislán*. Introd., text, and notes by M.-F. Schmidt. Preface by Bernard Sesé. Kassel: Reichenberger, 1984. 210 pp. (Teatro del Siglo de Oro. Ediciones críticas 4.) Rev.: (a) C. Morón Arroyo. *BBMP* 61 (1985): 365-69; (b) A. Maggio. *Incipit* 6 (1986): 230–33; (c) J. Marey. *LLNL* 81.1 (1987): 188–89; (d) A. A. Heathcote. *MLR* 82.1 (1987): 223.

Cueva, Juan de la (1543–1610)

1373. Closset, Adelin. Juan de la Cueva et son système dramatique. Brussels, 1926–27.
1374. Watson, Anthony I. The Political Implications of the Drama of Juan de la Cueva. (4)+ii+377 pp. London/External Degree, 1956.
❖ [A] *Juan de la Cueva and the Portuguese Succession*. London: Tamesis, 1971. 280 pp. (Colección Támesis, serie A. Monografías 10.) Rev.: (a) W. Krauss. *RF* 84 (1972): 641–42; (b) A. A. Heathcote. *MLR* 68 (1973): 428–29; (c) W. Mettmann. *ZRP* 90 (1974): 644; (d) R. ter Horst. *RR* 66 (1975): 244–45. [B] Cueva, J. de la. *Bernardo del Carpio*. Ed. A. Watson. Exeter: Univ. of Exeter, 1974. Rev.: A. L. Mackenzie. *BHS* 53 (1976): 277.

Diamante, Juan Bautista (1625–1687)

1375. Habicht, Joachim. Die Dramen des Don Juan Bautista Diamante: Ein Beitrag zur Spät-*Comedia.* 183 pp. Cologne, 1971.
1376. Wisleitner, Raimund. Die Komödien Juan Bautista Diamantes. 201 pp. Vienna, 1949.

Dias, Baltasar (Portugal. 16th c.)

1377. Espadinha, Maria Antónia Nicolau. O *Auto de Santo Aleixo* de Baltasar Dias: Subsidios para o estudo de uma obra do repertório de teatro popular. 141 pp. Salzburg, 1976. Summary in *Sprachkunst* 8 (1977): 123.
1378. Fonseca, Edmée. Le Théâtre de Baltasar Dias. Paris/IV, 1984.

Díaz, Fernando (16th c.)

1379. Kohler, Eugen [Eugène]. Sieben spanische dramatische Eklogen mit einer Einleitung über die Anfänge der spanischen Dramas. Strasbourg, 1910.

[For the complete entry, see no. 1149. The sixth reprinted play is *Farsa nuevamente trobada* of Fernando Díaz.]

Don Juan Theme

1380. Barfoed, Niels. Don Juan: En studie i dansk litteratur. Copenhagen, 1978.

❖ [A] Title as is. København: Gyldendal, 1978. 358 pp. [B] "Don Juan forenet med loven: Tilegnet Aage Henriksen pa 60-arsdagen 25.4.1981." *Frigørelse: Humaniora, digtning og sprog.* Ed. Lisbet Holst et al. Kongerslev: GMT, 1981. 275–80.
1381. Barkley, Pilar. Main Themes in the Spanish Drama of Franco's Rule: 1940–1975. 2 vols. (ix+422, 423–600 pp.) Toronto, 1982. *DAI* 44A: 183.

["... amongst the themes surveyed there [is] ... the development—during the period studied—of two classic themes: 'honour' and 'donjuanismo.'" (Abs.)]

1382. Bremond Ranocchia, Lydie. Don Juan dans la littérature du XXe siècle. Aix-en-Provence, 1985.

1383. Butt, Khalid. De Shaw à Lenormand, le thème de Don Juan dans le théâtre anglais et français. 365 pp. Paris, 1966.

1384. Draeger, Richard. Molière's *Dom Juan* historisch-genetisch neu beleuchtet. Halle, 1899.

❖ Title as is. Halle: Schlesinger, 1899. 35 pp.

1385. Gendarme de Bévotte, Georges. La Légende de Don Juan: Son évolution dans la littérature, des origines au romantisme. Paris, 1907. (Thèse d'État)

❖ [A] Title as is. Paris: Hachette, 1906. 547 pp. Rev.: (a) R. Menéndez Pidal. *Cultura Española* (Madrid) 7 (1907): 807–08; (b) G. Audiat. *Polybiblion* 2nd ser. 66 (1907): 529–31; (c) F. Baldensperger. *RCHLP* ns 64 (1907): 394–96; (d) L. Maury. *RB* 46th year, 5th ser. 10 (1908): 505–08. [B] *La Légende de Don Juan.* 2 vols. [vol. 1: Title as in dissertation; vol. 2: *Son évolution dans la littérature du romantisme à l'époque contemporaine.*] Paris: Hachette, 1911. Rev.: (a) G. Audiat. *Polybiblion* 2nd ser. 74 (1911): 323–24; (b) E. Rigal. *RLR* 54 (1911): 522–23; (c) M. J. Wolff. *Archiv* 128 (1912): 406–08. [C] 2nd ed. of item B. Paris: Hachette, 1929. [D] Rpt. of work originally published in Paris, 1906. Genève: Slatkine, 1970. xx+549 pp. [For an update of this work, see United States dissertation no. 446 by Martin Nozick.]

1386. Gnüg, Hiltrud. Die dramatische Intentionalität des Don Juan-Typs. Cologne, 1973.

[Chapter 2 of the dissertation deals with Tirso.]

❖ [A] *Don Juans theatralische Existenz: Typ und Gattung.* München: Fink, 1974. 260 pp. Rev.: (a) A. E. Singer. *Erasmus* 27 (1975): 410–14; (b) R. Peacock. *MLR* 72 (1977): 880–81. [B] "Dandy und Don-Juan-Typ." *Arcadia* 22.2 (1987): 164–79. [C] *Kult der Kälte: Der klassische Dandy im Spiegel der Weltliteratur.* Stuttgart: Metzler, 1988. 348 pp. [See pp. 178–234, "Die dandystische Inszenierung Don Juans."] [D] *Don Juan: Eine Einführung.* München: Artemis, 1989. 164 p. [E] "Don Juan und Faust: Christian

Dietrich Grabbe *Don Juan und Faust*—Théophile Gautier *La comédie de la mort*." *Grabbe und die Dramatiker seiner Zeit: Beiträge zum II. internationalen Grabbe-Symposium 1989*. Ed. Detlev Kopp and Michael Vogt, with the assistance of Werner Broer. Tübingen: Niemeyer, 1990. 232-44.

1387. GOUDSCHAAL, JÜRGEN. Studien zur spanischen Don Juan-Dichtung. ix+160 pp. Marburg, 1952.

1388. HECKEL, HANS. Das Don Juan-Problem in der neuren Dichtung. Breslau, 1915.

❖ [A] Extract. Stuttgart: Metzler, 1915. 39 pp. [B] Title as is. Stuttgart: Metzler, 1915. 172 pp. (Breslauer Beiträge zur Literaturgeschichte ns 47.) [Includes brief mention of *El burlador*.] Rev.: (a) E. Metis. *LitZent* 67.8 (1916): col. 220-21; (b) W. Davids. *Neophilologus* 2 (1916): 151-54.

1389. JACOBS, HANS J. Don Juan—heute: Die "Don-Juan-Figur" im Drama des zwanzigsten Jahrhunderts. Mythos und Konfiguration. Bonn, 1989.

❖ Title as is. Rheinbach-Merzbach: CMZ, 1989. 371 pp. (Bonner Untersuchungen zur vergleichenden Literaturwissenschaft 4.)

1390. KARPIAK, ROBERT IGOR. Don Juan in Slavic Drama. xxvii+384 pp. Ottawa, 1977.

❖ [A] "Don Juan: A Universal Theme in Ukrainian Drama." *CSP* 24.1 (1982): 25-31. [B] "The Crisis of Idealism: E. T. A. Hoffmann and the Russian Tradition of Don Juan." *Crisis and Commitment: Studies in German and Russian Literature in Honour of J. W. Dyck*. Ed. John Whiton and Harry Loewen. Waterloo: U of Waterloo P, 1983. 127-39.

1391. KREFT, JÜRGEN. Hamlet-Don Juan-Faustus (Vaterflucht-Mutterbindung-Disintegration): Interpretationen dreier moderner Romane (zugleich Versuch eines Beitrages zum Problem des modernen Romans). iii+267+[6] pp. Bonn, 1955.

[The "Don Juan" of the dissertation title refers to a seducer in *Die Schuldlosen* (1950) by the Austrian novelist Hermann Broch (1886-1951). The character bears the anagrammatic name Herr von Juna.]

1392. ROUSSEL, MADELEINE. Edmond Rostand, *La Dernière Nuit de Don Juan:* Étude littéraire. 289 pp. Montpellier, 1970.

1393. SCHRÖDER, THEODOR AUGUST EMIL. Die Quellen des *Dom Juan* von Molière. xii+32 pp. Kiel, 1911.
❖ [A] Title as is. Halle: Karras, 1911. 32 pp. [B] *Die dramatischen Bearbeitungen der Don Juan-Sage in Spanien, Italien und Frankreich bis auf Molière einschliesslich.* Halle: Niemeyer, 1912. 215 pp. (Zeitschrift für romanische Philologie, Beiheft 36.) Rev.: (a) L. Roustan. *RCHLP* ns 74 (1912): 133–35; (b) A. Farinelli. *DLZ* 34 (1913): col. 2215–17; (c) M. K. *LitZent* 64 (1913): 16; (d) P. A. Becker. *ZFSL* 41 (1913): 52–54; (e) M. J. Wolff. *Archiv* 132 (1914): 190–91; (f) A. C. *RFE* 1 (1914): 410–11; (g) A. Hämel. *LGRP* 36 (1915): 227–29.

1394. SCILLETTA, CATHERINE. La Figure du commandeur dans le mythe de Don Juan. Paris/X, 1986.

1395. STEIGER, AUGUST. Thomas Shadwell's *Libertine:* A Complementary Study to the Don Juan Literature. Bern, 1903.
❖ [A] Title as is. Berne: Büchler, 1904. 66 pp. [B] Title as is. Berne: Francke, 1904. (Untersuchungen zur neueren Sprach- und Literaturgeschichte 5.)

1396. TAN, HAUW GIE. La Matière de Don Juan et les genres littéraires. 152 pp. Leiden, 1974.
❖ Title as is. Leyde: Presse Universitaire de Leyde, 1974. 148 pp. (Publications romanes de l'Université de Leyde 20.) Rev.: R. Trousson. *CRCL* 5 (1978): 369.

1397. WITOCHYNSKY, OLHA. Deux Don Juan, français et ukranien, suivi de la traduction de l'*Amphitryon de pierre,* de Lessia Oukrainka. 127+46+11 pp. Paris/III, 1976.

DURÁN, DIEGO (DIED 1588?)

1398. KOHLER, EUGEN [EUGÈNE]. Sieben spanische dramatische Eklogen mit einer Einleitung über die Anfänge der spanischen Dramas. Strasbourg, 1910.
[For the complete entry, see no. 1149. The fifth reprinted play is the *Égloga nueva* of Diego Durán.]

ENCINA, JUAN DEL (1468?-1529?)

1399. LÓPEZ MORALES, HUMBERTO. Estudio lingüístico de la obra dramática de Juan del Enzina. 165+44+17 pp. Complutense, 1961. Abstract in *RUM* 11.44 (1962): 628-29.
❖ [A] Enzina, J. del. *Églogas de Juan del Encina*. Vol. 1: *Textos*. Ed., prologue and notes by H. López Morales. Madrid: Escelicer; New York: Las Americas, 1963. 313 pp. Rev.: (a) O. T. Myers. *RPh* 18.4 (1965): 519-20; (b) C. Stern. *HR* 34 (1966): 366-70; (c) P. Heugas. *BH* 69 (1967): 528-29. [B] "Elementos leoneses en la lengua del teatro pastoril de los siglos XV y XVI." *Actas del segundo congreso internacional de hispanistas, Nijmegen, 1965*. Ed. Jaime Sánchez Romeralo and Norbert Poulussen. Nijmegen, Netherlands: Univ. Nijmegen, 1967. 411-19. [C] Encina, J. del. *Églogas completas*. Rev. ed. H. López Morales. Madrid: Escelicer; New York: Las Americas, 1968. 391 pp. [D] *Tradición y creación en los orígenes del teatro castellano*. Madrid: Alcalá, 1968. 259 pp. [See esp. "La lengua de los pastores," pp. 172-90.] Rev.: (a) L. A. Castellanos. *Universidad* 76 (1968): 278-82. (b) J. H. Parker. *H* [AATSP] 52.4 (1969): 958-59; (c) L. L. Barrett. *MLQ* 30.3 (1969): 446-48; (d) R. Oroz. *BFC* 21 (1970): 339-40; (e) E. J. Webber. *MP* 67.4 (1970): 373-76; (f) M. J. Ruggerio. *RPh* 24.3 (1970-71): 541-45; (g) D. Hershberg *REHb* 6.2 (1972): 320-21. [E] "Nueva hipótesis sobre el teatro medieval castellano." *REHc* 2.1-4 (1972): 7-19. [F] "Sobre el teatro medieval castellano: *Status quaestionis*." *BAPLE* 14.1 (1986): 99-122. [G] "Alfonso X y el teatro medieval castellano." *RFE* 71 (1991): 227-52. [H] "La *Pastorada* leonesa y el teatro de Encina y Lucas Fernández." *Ex libris: Homenaje a José Fradejas Lebrero*. Ed. José Romera Castillo, Ana Freire López, and Antonio Lorente López. 2 vols. Madrid: UNED, 1993. 1: 163-71. [For a more complete list of this scholar's publications, see *Homenaje a Humberto López Morales,* ed. María Vaquero and Amparo Morales (Madrid: Arco-Libros, 1992) 25-32.]
1400. MAURIZI, FRANÇOISE. Théâtre et tradition populaires chez Juan del Encina et Lucas Fernández. Aix-en-Provence, 1991. (Doctorat de Nouveau Régime)

❖ [A] "Le Pouvoir et l'écriture théâtrale à la fin du Moyen Âge: Juan del Encina et Lucas Fernández." *Écrire à la fin du Moyen Âge: Le Pouvoir et l'écriture en Espagne et en Italie (1450–1530). Colloque international France-Espagne-Italie, Aix-en-Provence, 1988.* Ed. Jeanne Battesti-Pelegrin and Georges Ulysse. Aix-en-Provence: Université de Provence Aix-Marseille/I, 1990. 227-39. (Études hispano-italiennes, 4.) [B] Title as is. Aix-en-Provence: Publications de l'Université de Provence, 1994. 406 pp. (Études hispaniques 21.) Rev.: C. Stern. *La Corónica* 24.2 (1996): 216-17. [C] "La teatralización del soldado a fines del siglo XV en Lucas Fernández. *Criticón* 66-67 (1966): 287-305.

Enríquez Gómez, Antonio (1600/02-1663?)
(Fernando de Zárate y Castronovo)

1401. Oelman, Timothy. Two Poems by Antonio Enríquez Gómez: "Romance al Divín Mártir, Judá Creyente" and "Sansón Nazareno" (with Introduction and Notes). 2 vols. (755 pp.) London/King's College, 1976.

❖ [A] "Antonio Enríquez Gómez's 'Romance al Divín Mártir, Judá Creyente': Edited Text with Introduction." *JJS* 26 (1975): 112-31. [B] "Tres poetas marranos." *NRFH* 30 (1981): 184-206. [C] *Marrano Poets of the Seventeenth Century: An Anthology of the Poetry of Joâo Pinto Delgado, Antonio Enríquez Gómez, and Miguel de Barrios.* Ed. and trans. T. Oelman. Rutherford: Fairleigh Dickinson UP; London: Assoc. UPs, 1982. [D] "The Religious Views of Antonio Enríquez Gómez: A Profile of a Marrano." *BHS* 60 (1983): 201-09. [E] Enríquez Gómez, A. Romance al divín mártir, Judá Creyente [don Lope de Vera y Alarcón] martirizado en Valladolid por la Inquisición: *A Critical Edition from Original Manuscript Sources.* Transcribed and ed. T. Oelman. Rutherford: Fairleigh Dickinson UP; London: Assoc. UPs, 1986. [". . . this study is based principally on the work carried out in connection with my doctoral thesis." Included are a chapter on A. E. G.'s biography and another on his religious views.] [F] Enríquez Gómez, A. Loa sacramental de los siete planetas: *A Critical Edition from the Manuscript*. Ed. C. H. Rose with T. Oelman. Exeter: Univ. of Exeter, 1987.

Fajardo y Acevedo, Antonio (1630?–1700?)

1402. Buey Pérez, Félix del. *La estrella de Europa y Fénix de África:* Comedia inédita del maestro Antonio Fajardo y Acevedo. Edición y estudio. 2 vols. (pp. 1–176: transcription of the text; pp. 177–565: study) Granada, 1986–87.

❖ Title as is. With subtitle: *La leyenda de la Virgen de Regla en el teatro barroco*. Granada: Provincia Franciscana de Granada, 1989. 514 pp. [Included as an appendix, pp. 435–512: "*Nuestra Señora de la Regla, la milagrosa africana:* Comedia famosa de Ambrosio de Cuenca, transcripción modernizada de la edición única, Madrid, 1667."]

Fernández, Lucas (1474?–1542)

1403. Maurizi, Françoise. Théâtre et tradition populaires chez Juan del Encina et Lucas Fernández. Aix-en-Provence, 1991. (Doctorat de Nouveau Régime)

[For the complete entry, see no. 1400.]

Fernández, Sebastián (fl. 1547)

1404. Esteban Martín, Luis Mariano. Edición y estudio de la *Tragedia Policiana* de Sebastián Fernández. 367 pp. Complutense, 1992.

❖ Title as is. Madrid: Editorial de la Universidad Complutense, 1992. 367 pp. (Colección tesis doctorales no. 388/92.)

1405. Mörtinger-Grohmann, Gertrud. *Tragedia Policiana* von Sebastián Fernández: Untersuchung einer der spanischen Imitationen der *Celestina*. iii+135 pp. Salzburg, 1979.

Ferreira, António (Portugal. 1528–1569)

1406. Roig, Adrien. Études sur l'œuvre d'António Ferreira. 4 books in 5 vols. Montpellier, 1969. (Thèse d'État)
❖ [A] *António Ferreira: Études sur sa vie et son œuvre, 1528–1569.* Paris: Fundaçâo Calouste Gulbenkian, Centro Cultural Português, 1970. 216 pp. (Série histórica e literária 2.) Rev.: J. Ares Montes. *RFE* 55.1–2 (1972): 72–74. [B] *La Tragédie* Castro *d'António Ferreira: Établissement du texte des éditions de 1587 et 1598, suivi de la traduction française.* Paris: Fundaçâo Calouste Gulbenkian, Centro Cultural Português, 1971. 399 pp. (Série histórica e literária, 8.) [C] Ferreira, A. La Comédie de Bristo, ou l'Entremetteur (Comédia do Fanchono, ou de Bristo), *d'António Ferreira (1562).* Study and lexical analysis, critical ed., and trans. by A. Roig. Paris: Presses Universitaires de France, 1973. 555 pp. Rev.: (a) J. Roche. *LLNL* 208 (1974): 126–28; (b) J. Ares Montes. *RFE* 57 (1974–75): 341–45; (c) Y. David-Peyre. *BH* 77.3–4 (1975): 445–48. [D] "La *Castro* d'António Ferreira tragédie du sang." *Mélanges à la mémoire de Louis Michel.* Montpellier: Université Paul-Valéry, 1979. 423–48. [E] "Le Personnage du Roi dans la tragédie *Castro* d'António Ferreira." *Estudos portugueses: Homenagem a Luciana Stegnano Picchio.* Lisboa: Difusâo Editorial, Lda. (DIFEL), 1991. 411–59. [F] "Inès dans la tragédie *Castro* d'António Ferreira." *De la Péninsule Ibérique à l'Amérique Latine: Mélanges en l'honneur de Jean Subirats.* Ed. Marie Roig Miranda. Nancy: Presses Universitaires de Nancy, 1992. 41–58. [For a more complete list of this scholar's publications, see "Travaux et publications," *Arquivos* 31 (1992): 5–14. Special issue entitled *Hommage au professeur Adrien Roig.*]

Folch Cardona, Antonio (1623–1694)

1407. Sarrió Rubio, Pilar. Los postnocturnos y la teatralidad valenciana: Catálogo y calendario. El caso de Antonio Folch Cardona. 1,091 pp. Valencia, 1989. *DAI-C* 52: 5.
❖ [A] Title as is. Valencia: Universitat de València, Servicio de

Publicaciones, 1989(?). [B] "Folch Cardona en el teatro valenciano del siglo XVII: Influencias e innovaciones." *Estado actual de los estudios sobre el Siglo de Oro: Actas del segundo congreso internacional de hispanistas del Siglo de Oro, Salamanca y Valladolid, 1990.* Ed. Manuel García Martín, Ignacio Arellano, Javier Blasco, and Marc Vitse. 2 vols. Salamanca: Universidad de Salamanca, 1993. 2: 967-75. [C] "*Lo mejor es lo mejor:* Una comedia espectáculo de Antonio Folch de Cardona." *QFEL* 1.2 (1995): 773-97.

Fuente, Jerónimo de la (late 16th c.-early 17th c.)

1408. José Prades, Juana de. Aportación al estudio de la teoría literaria y bibliografía de los dramaturgos menores pertenecientes al ciclo dramático de Lope de Vega. vii+400 pp. Complutense, 1960. Abstract in *RUM* 10.40 (1961): 852.

[For the complete entry, see no. 1148.]

Godínez, Felipe (1588-1639?)

1409. Bolaños Donoso, Piedad. La obra dramática de Felipe Godínez. (Trayectoria de un dramaturgo marginado.) 2 vols. (1-679, 681-1343 pp.) Seville, 1981-82.

❖ [A] Title as is. Sevilla: Excma. Diputación Provincial de Sevilla, 1983. 741 pp. Rev.: (a) A. Torés García. *AnMal* 7 (1984): 342-43; (b) B. López Bueno. *ArH* 205 (1984): 205-07; (c) C. Menéndez Onrubia. *Segismundo* 17.37-38 (1984): 279-81; (d) H. W. Sullivan. *HR* 54 (1986): 222-23. [B] Godínez, F. *Aun de noche alumbra el sol; Los trabajos de Job.* Ed., introd. and notes by P. Bolaños Donoso and P. M. Piñero Ramírez. Kassel: Reichenberger, 1991. 243 pp.

1410. Vega García-Luengos, Germán. El teatro de Felipe Godínez: Estudio y edición [*La reina Ester* y *Ludovico el piadoso*]. Valladolid, 1983-84.

❖ [A] "El *Libro de Ester* en las versiones dramáticas de Lope de Vega y Felipe Godínez." *Castilla* 2-3 (1981): 1-39. [B] "Notas para una bibliografía de Felipe Godínez." *Castilla* 8 (1984): 127-39. [C] *Problemas de un dramaturgo del Siglo de Oro: Estudios sobre Felipe Godínez. Con dos comedias inéditas:* La reina Ester *y* Ludovico el piadoso. Valladolid: Universidad de Valladolid, Secretariado de Publicaciones; Salamanca: Caja de Ahorros y Monte de Piedad de Salamanca, 1986. 430 pp. Rev.: (a) L. Rubio González. *Castilla* 13 (1988): 214-15; (b) P. Bolaños Donoso. *HR* 57 (1989) 99-101; (c) J. Ávila Arellano. *Ínsula* 508 (1989): 6. [D] "Una edición crítica para *Las lágrimas de David,* la comedia más difundida de Felipe Godínez." *La edición de textos: Actas del primer congreso internacional de hispanistas del Siglo de Oro, 1987.* Ed. Pablo Jauralde, Dolores Noguera, and Alfonso Rey. London: Tamesis, 1990. 483-91. (Colección Támesis, serie A. Monografías 139.)

Góngora, Luis de (1561-1627)

1411. Alonso y Fernández de las Redondas, Dámaso.
Evolución de la sintaxis de Góngora. 168 pp. Complutense, 1928.
❖ [A] *La lengua poética de Góngora.* Primera parte. Madrid: 1935, 230 pp. (Anejo de la *Revista de Filología Española* 20); 2nd ed., corrected. Madrid: CSIC, 1950. 230 pp.; 3rd ed., corrected. Madrid: CSIC, 1961. 230 pp. [In *Dámaso Alonso* (New York: Twayne, 1970; TWAS 126) p. 152, Andrew P. Debicki points out that the writer's *Evolución de la sintaxis de Góngora* is "included" in the above publication. In the latter work, Alonso footnotes the following statement: "He esquivado, pues (casi siempre), el aducir ejemplos tomados de esta comedia, aunque ellos hubieran sido un buen apoyo de mis argumentos." The *comedia* is *Las firmezas de Isabela.*] Rev.: (a) H. Hatzfeld. *Volkstum und Kultur der Romanen* 8 (1936): 362-64; (b) G. Cirot. *BH* 39 (1937): 65-68; (c) H. Keniston. *HR* 5 (1937): 353-56; (d) W. J. Entwistle. *MLR* 32 (1937): 116-19; (e) Á. del Río. *RR* 28 (1937): 276-80; (f) E. Orozco Díaz. *Arbor* 6 (1950): 312-13; (g) posthumous review article by J. F. Montesinos *RL* 46.91 (1984): 21-42. [B] *La poesía*

dramática en el Don Duardos *de Gil Vicente.* Valencia: Facultad de Filosofía y Letras, 1939. 33 pp. [This essay is included in publication C.] [C] Vicente, G. *Tragicomedia de Don Duardos*. Ed. D. Alonso. Vol. 1: Text, studies, and notes. Madrid: CSIC, 1942. 326 pp. [D] *Estudios y ensayos gongorinos*. Madrid: Gredos, 1955; 2nd ed. 1960. 623 pp. [For a more complete list of this scholar's publications, see Fernando Huarte Morton, "Bibliografía de Dámaso Alonso," *Homenaje universitario a Dámaso Alonso reunido por los estudiantes de filología románica, curso 1968-1969* (Madrid: Gredos, 1970) 295-332.]

1412. Hoyo-Rodríguez, María Refugio. Critical Edition of the Theatrical Works of Góngora. 5 microfiches, 478 frames. Alberta, 1987.

1413. Jammes, Robert. Études sur l'œuvre poétique de Don Luis de Góngora y Argote. Bordeaux, 1967. (Thèse d'État)

❖ [A] Title as is. Bordeaux: Institut d'Études Ibériques et Ibéro-Américaines, 1967. 701 pp. Rpt. 1983. [B] Title as is. Bordeaux: Féret, 1967. 701 pp. (Bibliothèque de l'École des Hautes Études Hispaniques 40.) [Third part, ch. 3, pp. 467-531, "Le Théâtre."] Rev.: (a) S. Sarduy. *QL,* no. 49 (15-30 Apr., 1968): 12-13; (b) R. O. Jones *BHS* 47 (1970): 358-60. [C] "*La destruyción de Troya,* entremés attribué a Góngora." *Criticón* 5 (1978): 31-52. [D] Góngora, L. de. *Las firmezas de Isabela*. Ed., introd. and notes by R. Jammes. Madrid: Castalia, 1984. 305 pp. (Clásicos Castalia 137.) [E] *La obra poética de Don Luis de Góngora y Argote*. Trans. Manuel Moya. Madrid: Castalia, 1987. 573 pp. [Third part, ch. 3, pp. 393-447, "El teatro."] Rev.: (a) A. Carreira. *Ínsula* 496 (1988): 8; (b) F. Villamía Ugarte. *RL* 99-100 (1988): 591-94. [F] "Las didascalias en el teatro de Góngora." *Le Livre et l'édition dans le monde hispanique, XVIe-XXe siècles: Pratiques et discours paratextuels.* Ed. Michel Moner and Michel Lafon. Grenoble: Cerhius, 1992. 143-59. [For a more complete list of this scholar's publications, see Odette Gorsse, "R. Jammes: Bibliographie," *Hommage à Robert Jammes,* ed. Francis Cerdan, 3 vols. (Toulouse: Presses Universitaires du Mirail, 1994) 1: xv-xx.]

Herrera y Sotomayor, Jacinto de (?-1641)

1414. Tiemann, Hermann. Studien zur spanischen Dramatik in Flandern (Diego Muxet de Solís, D. Jacinto de Herrera y Sotomayor, D. Miguel de Barrios). 167 pp. Göttingen, 1924. Abstract. *Jahrbuch der Philosophischen Fakultät Göttingen* (1924): 40-42.
   [For the complete entry, see no. 1198.]

Hoz y Mota, Juan de la (1622-1714)

1415. Domínguez de Paz, Elisa María. La obra dramática de Juan de la Hoz y Mota. 176 pp. Valladolid, 1984.
   ❖ [A] "Un aspecto del feminismo en las comedias de capa y espada de Juan de la Hoz y Mota." *Castilla* 9-10 (1985): 9-13. [B] Title as is. Valladolid: Universidad de Valladolid, Secretariado de Publicaciones, 1986. 176 pp. Rev.: (a) V. Arizpe. *HR* 57.2 (1989): 238-40; (b) A. J. Farrell. *RL* 53.106 (1991): 743-45. [C] "*El invisible,* un entremés inédito de Juan de la Hoz y Mota: Estudio y edición." *Canente* 1-2.1 (1987): 99-116. [D] Domínguez, E., and Pablo Carrascosa. "Aproximación a algunos problemas de técnica dramática en *El niño inocente de la Guardia* de Lope y *La viva imagen de Cristo* de Hoz y Cañizares." *Canente* 5 (1989): 25-38. [E] Domínguez de Paz, E., and Pablo Carrascosa Miguel. "*El niño inocente de la Guardia,* de Lope, y *La viva imagen de Cristo,* de Hoz y Cañizares: Semejanzas y diferencias." *Teatro español a fines del siglo XVII: Historia, cultura y teatro en la España de Carlos II.* Ed. Javier Huerta Calvo, Harm den Boer, and Fermín Sierra Martínez. 3 vols. Amsterdam: Rodopi, 1989. 2: 343-57. [F] Hoz y Mota, J. de la. *El encanto del olvido.* Critical ed. E. Domínguez de Paz. Valladolid: Universidad de Valladolid, Secretariado de Publicaciones, 1991. 158 pp. (Literatura 18.) [G] "Problemas documentales para el estudio de la vida y de la obra de Juan de la Hoz y Mota." *Teatros y vida teatral en el Siglo de Oro a través de las fuentes documentales.* Ed. Luciano García Lorenzo and John E. Varey. London: Tamesis, 1991. 317-26. (Colección Támesis, serie A. Monografías 145.) [H] "Algunos

aspectos técnico-dramáticos de *El encanto del olvido* de Juan de la Hoz y Mota." *Actas del décimo congreso de la Asociación Internacional de Hispanistas, Barcelona, 1989*. Ed. Antonio Vilanova. 4 vols. Barcelona: PPU, 1992. 1: 893-904. [I] "Reflexiones en torno al feminismo en la obra dramática de Juan de la Hoz y Mota: *La más valiente guerrera*." *Studia aurea: Actas del tercer congreso de la AISO, Toulouse, 1993*. 3 vols. Toulouse-Pamplona: GRISO-LEMSO, 1996. Vol 2. *Teatro*. Ed. Ignacio Arellano, María del Carmen Pinillos, Frédéric Serralta, and Marc Vitse. 2: 129-39.

Hurtado de Mendoza, Antonio (1586-1644)

1416. Davies, Gareth Alban. The Life and Works of Don Antonio Hurtado de Mendoza (1586-1644). xviii+404 p. Oxford, 1955-56. ❖ [A] "Antonio Hurtado de Mendoza: Biographical Notes." *BHS* 34 (1957): 79-88. [B] "Una carta inédita de Antonio Hurtado de Mendoza al Conde Duque de Olivares." *HispM* 19 (1959): 82-91. [C] "A Chronology of Antonio de Mendoza's Plays." *BHS* 48 (1971): 97-110. [D] *A Poet at Court: Antonio Hurtado de Mendoza (1586-1644)*. Oxford: Dolphin, 1971. 367 pp. [The writer deals with Mendoza's theater in chs. 9-12 and appendixes 2 and 5.] Rev.: (a) G. Hughes. *Ren&R* 11 (1973): 140-41; (b) A. A. Parker. *MLR* 71 (1976): 196-97; (c) B. W. Wardropper. *RR* 67 (1976): 79-81. [E] "The Country Cousin at Court: A Study of Antonio de Mendoza's *Cada loco con su tema* and Manuel Bretón de los Herreros' *El pelo de la dehesa*." *Leeds Papers on Hispanic Drama*. Ed. Margaret A. Rees. Leeds: Trinity and All Saints Coll., 1991. 43-60.

1417. Guérin-Saumade, Christiane. Le Théâtre d'Antonio Hurtado de Mendoza. 318 pp. Paris, 1963. (Thèse de 3e cycle) Abstract in *Positions* (1963): 123-24.

Inés de Castro (1320?-1355) Theme

1418. Apraiz y Buesa, Ángel. Doña Inés de Castro en el teatro castellano. 125+xxii pp. Complutense, 1905.

❖ Title as is. Vitoria: Sar, 1911. 82 pp. [For a commentary, see Hauer, Vélez de Guevara, no. 15.]

1419. CORNIL, SUZANNE. Inès de Castro: Contribution à l'étude du thème dans les littératures romanes. De l'histoire à la légende et de la légende à la littérature. Brussels, 1946-47.
❖ [A] *Inès de Castro: Contribution à l'étude du développement littéraire du thème dans les littératures romanes. De l'histoire à la légende et de la légende à la littérature.* Bruxelles: Académie Royale de Belgique, 1952. 154 pp. (Classe des lettres et des sciences morales et politiques. Mémoires 47.2.) Rev.: P. van Bever. *RLMC* 4 (1953): 310-12. [B] "Le Thème d'Inès de Castro et Montherlant." *Les Rapports culturels et littéraires entre le Portugal et la France: Actes du colloque, Paris, 1982.* Ed. Luis de Albuquerque. Paris: Fondation Calouste Gulbenkian, Centre Culturel Portugais, 1983. 599-604.

1420. HEINERMANN, HEINRICH THEODOR. Ignez de Castro: Die dramatischen Behandlungen der Sage in den romanischen Literaturen: Ein Beitrag zur vergleichenden Literaturgeschichte. Münster, 1915.
❖ [A] Title as is. Borna and Leipzig: Noske, 1914. 112 pp. Rev.: (a) A. Hämel. *LGRP* 37 (1916): col. 303-06; (b) J. F. Montesinos. *RFE* 8 (1921): 82-83. [B] Title as is. *Die Schaubühne* 33 (München, 1940).

1421. SITO ALBA, MANUEL. Lo hispánico en *La Reine morte,* de Henry de Montherlant: Análisis comparado con *Reinar después de morir,* de Vélez de Guevara. 3 vols. (1,005 pp.) Complutense, 1973. Abstract in *RUCM* 22.88-2 (1973): 102-03.
[For the complete entry, see no. 1603.]

JIMÉNEZ DE ENCISO, DIEGO (1585-1634)

1422. BEHNKE, FRITZ. Diego Ximénez de Encisos *Los Médicis de Florencia,* Giovanni Rosinis *Luisa Strozzi* und Alfred de Mussets *Lorenzaccio* in ihrem Verhältnis zur Geschichte. Berlin, 1910.
❖ Title as is. Berlin: Trenkel, 1910. 147 pp. Rev.: A. Hämel. *LGRP* 34 (1913): col. 153.

1423. MARÍN OCETE, ANTONIO. El negro Juan Latino: Ensayo de un estudio biográfico y crítico. 177 pp. Complutense, 1923.

❖ [A] Title as is. *Revista del Centro de Estudios Históricos de Granada* 13 (1923): 97–120. [B] *El negro Juan Latino: Ensayo biográfico y crítico.* Granada: Librería Guevara, 1925. 94 pp. [The writer quotes from Jiménez de Enciso's *Comedia de Juan Latino* on pp. 7, 19, and 76–78. Regarding the first quotation, in which the character Juan Latino says that he was born in Baena, Marín Ocete observes, "Contra lo que parezca, el testimonio no es de gran valor. Ximénez de Enciso es más que nada un literato que no andaría muy preocupado con detalles semejantes. Errores que iremos haciendo notar, es verdad que mezclados con notas indudablemente históricas, en toda la comedia y aun en el mismo soneto copiado, nos hacen desconfiar de su veracidad. Y sobre todo hay que tener en cuenta que la fama de Juan Latino llegaría a él alterada y mezclada con mil leyendas." There is a summary of the *comedia* on pp. 64–65.] Rev.: (a) V. R. *CdD* 143 (1925): 301; (b) U. G. de la C. *RFE* 14 (1927): 297–98.

Juana Inés de la Cruz (Mexico. 1648/51–1695)

1424. Bénassy, Marie-Cécile. Humanisme et religion chez Sor Juana Inés de la Cruz: La Femme et la culture au XVIIème siècle. 2 vols. (750 pp.) Paris/III, 1979. (Thèse d'État)

❖ [A] Bénassy-Berling, Marie-Cécile. Title as is. Paris: Éditions Hispaniques, 1982. 510 pp. (Collection "Thèses, mémoires et travaux.") [B] *Humanismo y religión en Sor Juana Inés de la Cruz.* México: Universidad Autónoma de México, 1983. 532 pp. [The "sexta parte" is entitled "Lo profano y lo sagrado: *El divino Narciso* y su simbolismo," pp. 359–95.]

López de Yanguas, Hernán (early 16th c.)

1425. Kohler, Eugen [Eugène]. Sieben spanische dramatische Eklogen mit einer Einleitung über die Anfänge der spanischen Dramas. Strasbourg, 1910.

[For the complete entry, see no. 1149. The first reprinted play is the *Égloga de la Natividad de Nuestro Señor* by López de Yanguas.]

Machado, Simão (Portugal. 1557?–1634?)

1426. Marcos de Dios Dubroca, Danielle. *Comédia da Pastora Alfea* de Simão Machado. Paris/IV, 1983.

Matos Fragoso, Juan de (1608–1689)

1427. Santo Rossi, Elsa Leonor di. Vida y obra de Juan de Matos Fragoso, poeta y dramaturgo del siglo XVII: Estudio de sus comedias originales, con especial referencia al *Traidor contra su sangre.* Complutense, 1979. Abstract in *UCM. Tesis doctorales* 3 (1978–79): 97; *MEC. Tesis doctorales* 421 (1978–79): 211.
❖ "Noticias sobre la vida de Juan de Matos Fragoso." *Segismundo* 14.27–32 (1978–80): 217–31.

Mira de Amescua, Antonio (1574?–1644)

1428. Ahrens, Theodor G[eorg]. Zur Charakteristik des spanischen Dramas im Anfang des XVII. Jahrhunderts. (Luis Vélez de Guevara und Mira de Mescua.) Halle, 1911.
❖ Title as is. Halle: Waisenhaus, 1911. 106 pp. Rev.: A. Hämel. *LGRP* 34 (1913): col. 154.

1429. Dietz, Rolf. Antonio Mira de Amescua: Studien zum Werk eines spanischen Dichters des *Siglo de Oro*. Cologne, 1974.
❖ Title as is. Bern: Herbert Lang; Frankfurt: Peter Lang, 1974. 332 pp. (Europäische Hochschulschriften, Reihe 24. Iberoromanische Sprachen und Literaturen 4.) Rev.: (a) P. Cabañas. *BHS* 54 (1977): 344–46; (b) A. L. Mackenzie. *MLR* 72 (1977): 225–26.

1430. González Dengra, Miguel. *El mártir de Madrid,* de Mira de Amescua: Estudio crítico y edición. 424 pp. Granada, 1991.

❖ [A] "Las relaciones amorosas en *El mártir de Madrid*." *RILCE* 7.2 (1991): 351–61. [B] "La escenografía en las comedias de santos de Antonio Mira de Amescua." *Texto y espectáculo: Selected Proceedings of the Fifteenth Golden Age Spanish Theatre Symposium, El Paso, 1995*. Ed. José Luis Suárez García. York: Spanish Literature Publications, 1996. 1–33.

1431. LEBERMANN, NAPHTALI. Belisar in der Litteratur der romanischen und germanischen Nationen. Heidelberg, 1899.

❖ Title as is. Nürnberg: Gutmann, 1899. 118 pp. [The writer discusses Mira's *El ejemplo mayor de la desdicha y Capitán Belisario,* which he wrongly attributes to Lope.] Rev.: A. L. Stiefel. *SvglL* 1 (1901): 136+.

1432. LUGO APONTE DE LUIS, ELBA MILAGROS. Contribución al estudio del teatro de Antonio Mira de Amescua: Los autos sacramentales. 2 vols. Complutense, 1963. Abstract in *RUM* 12.48 (1963): 765–66.

1433. PIETRYGA, JOHANNES. *El rico avariento.* Zwei *Autos sacramentales,* bisher zugeschrieben Francisco de Rojas Zorrilla. 162 pp. Cologne, 1958.

[A study and edition of the two *autos* entitled *El rico avariento,* both hitherto attributed to Rojas Zorrilla: (1) BNM MS 15.150 and (2) BNM MS 15.266. The writer argues that only (1) is by Rojas and that (2) is the work of Mira de Amescua. Regarding the MS *auto* of the same title in the Palatine Library of Parma, he concludes: "Es muss weiterhin als anonym gelten. Für uns bleibt das Auto ohne weitere Bedeutung."]

[For the complete entry, see no. 1464.]

1434. SMITH, CLIFFORD. El doctor Mira de Amescua: An Examination of His Plays with an Introductory Biographical Study. vii+331 pp. British Columbia, 1976. *DAI* 37A: 4405.

❖ "Authorship of the *Don Álvaro de Luna* Plays" (Letter to the Editor). *H* [AATSP] 59 (1976): 289–90. [Apropos S. L. Brown's article "A Reconsideration of the Authorship of the *Don Álvaro de Luna* Plays." See S. L. Brown entry no. 608 under Téllez in the United States section.]

1435. VILLANUEVA FERNÁNDEZ, JUAN MANUEL. Vida y obra de Antonio Mira de Amescua. (Hacia una tipología de sus comedias.) 3

vols. (xiv+1-527, 528-707, 708-914; appendix to vol. 2: 1-404 pp.) Alicante, 1986.

Monroy y Silva, Cristóbal de (1612-1649)

1436. Barbe, Louis. Contribution à l'étude du règne de Philippe Trois: Don Pedro Téllez Girón, duc d'Osuna, vice-roi de Sicile (1610-1616). 716 pp. Grenoble/III, 1986.
[A study of Pedro de Alcántara Téllez Girón y Guzmán, third duke of Osuna, "el Grande" (1574-1624). Son of Juan Téllez Girón, second duke of Osuna (1554-1600), the third duke was the subject of Cristóbal de Monroy y Silva's *comedia* entitled *Las mocedades del duque de Osuna.* Moreover, F. J. Bianco believes that Luis Vélez de Guevara's *Más pesa el rey que la sangre* (see no. 810) "is a direct reflection of the events in the life of Don Pedro Téllez-Girón, Grand Duke of Osuna." According to the controversial hypothesis of Doña Blanca de los Ríos, Gabriel Téllez (Tirso de Molina) was the illegitimate son of Don Juan Téllez-Girón and the younger brother of Don Pedro.]
❖ *Don Pedro Téllez Girón, duc d'Osuna, vice-roi de Sicile 1610-1616. Contribution à l'étude du règne de Philippe III.* Grenoble: Ellug; Université Stendhal, 1992. 299 pp.

1437. Bem Barroca, Manuel R. Vida y obra de Monroy. 2 vols. (1-437, 438-928 pp.) Seville, 1967.
❖ *Dos comedias inéditas de don Cristóbal Monroy y Silva* [No hay más saber que saber salvarse *y* No hay amor donde no hay celos.] Chapel Hill: Univ. of North Carolina, Dept. of Romance Languages, 1976. 210 pp. (Estudios hispánicos 41.) Rev.: C. Romero Muñoz. *RIber* 8 (1980): 61-65.

Monteser, Francisco Antonio de (1620?-1668)

1438. Serralta, Frédéric. Une Tradition littéraire: *La renegada de Valladolid.* Étude et édition critique de la *comedia* burlesque de Monteser, Solís, et Silva. 238 pp. Toulouse, 1968.

❖ [A] "Sur une *comedia* inconnue de Monteser, Solís et Silva: Tentative d'identification." *Études ibériques et latino-américaines: Quatrième congrès des hispanistes français, Poitiers, 1967.* Paris: Presses Univeritaires de France, 1968. 97–104. [*La restauración de España,* cited by Barrionuevo, is the same play as *La renegada de Valladolid.*] [B] *La renegada de Valladolid: Trayectoria dramática de un tema popular.* Toulouse: France-Ibérie Recherche, Institut d'Études Hispaniques, Hispano-Américaines et Luso-Brésiliennes, 1970. 87 pp. Rev.: (a) Anon. *Ínsula* 292 (1971): 18; (b) J. R. Outin. *LLNL* 65.196 (1971): 81–82; (c) M. McKendrick. *BHS* 49 (1972): 303–05. [C] "La comedia burlesca: Datos y orientaciones." *Risa y sociedad en el teatro español del Siglo de Oro: Actes du troisième colloque du GESTE, Toulouse, 1980.* Ed. Yves-René Fonquerne. Paris: CNRS, 1980. 99–129. [D] "Otra adaptación teatral de *La renegada de Valladolid.*" *Criticón* 44 (1988): 135–40. [The adaptation is by F. Bernardo de Quirós.]

Morales, Alonso de (1560?–1613?)

1439. Canavaggio, Jean. Morales, *Comedia de los amores y locuras del conde loco:* Édition commentée d'un manuscrit inédit. xci+132 pp. + illus. Paris, 1967. Abstract in *Positions* (1967): 295–96. (Thèse de 3e cycle)

❖ [A] Title as is. Paris: Centre de Recherches Hispaniques, Institut d'Études Hispaniques, 1969. 192 pp. (Thèses, mémoires et travaux 11.) [B] "Teatro y comediantes en el Siglo de Oro: Algunos datos inéditos [sacados de la *Comedia de los naufragios de Leopoldo,* de Morales (1594)]." *Segismundo* 12.23–24 (1976): 27–51.

Moreto, Agustín (1618–1669)

1440. Balbín de Lucas, Rafael. Teatro menor profano de Moreto. 2 vols. Complutense, 1942. Abstract in *Sumarios y extractos, Historia* (1939–44): 267–73.

❖ [A] "Tres piezas menores de Moreto inéditas." *RBN* 3 (1942): 80–116. [*Baile del Conde Claros; Baile de Lucrecia y Tarquino; Entremés famoso del vestuario.*] [B] "Notas sobre el teatro menor de Moreto." *Homenaje a Fritz Krüger.* Ed. T. M. Lucero and A. Dornheim. Mendoza, Arg.: Universidad Nacional de Cuyo, 1952–54. Vol. 2 (1954): 601–12. Rev.: R. Fernández Pousa. *RABM* 61.2 (1955): 685–89 [comment on the article.] [C] "*El entremés de doña Esquina,* de Agustín Moreto." *Segismundo* 1 (1965): 95–100. [For a more complete list of this scholar's publications, see M. A. Garrido Gallardo, "Rafael de Balbín (5-III-1910/27-I-1978)," *RFE* 60.1-4 (1978–80): 345–53, esp. pp. 347–53.]

1441. Bennholdt-Thomsen, Uwe Carl. Das idealisierte Weltbild des Theaters im *Siglo de Oro:* Eine Studie zum dramatischen Werk Moretos. 241 pp. Cologne, 1966. // Rev.: W. Floeck. *RJ* 20 (1969): 379–85 (pp. 384–85 are pertinent).

1442. Kirchgässner, Wihelmine. Moretos Charakterlustspiel *El desdén con el desdén.* 217 pp. Graz, 1918.

1443. Nohel, Paul. Das spanische Lustspiel *El desdén con el desdén* von Moreto und seine Bearbeitungen bei Molière und Carlo Gozzi. Vienna, 1909.

1444. Ríos, Diego Manuel de los. Antiguo teatro español: Moreto, Rojas, Alarcón. Sus principales obras. Complutense, 1857.

Muñón, Sancho de (fl. 1549)

1445. Goddard, Vladimir Cyril. Sancho de Muñón: A Background Study and a Critical Edition of His *Tragicomedia de Lysandro y Roselia.* 825 pp. London/Birkbeck College, 1978.

Muxet de Solís, Diego (fl. early 17th c.)

1446. Tiemann, Hermann. Studien zur spanischen Dramatik in Flandern (Diego Muxet de Solís, D. Jacinto de Herrera y Sotomayor, D. Miguel de Barrios). 167 pp. Göttingen, 1924. Abstract in *Jahrbuch der Philosophischen Fakultät Göttingen* (1924): 40–42.

[For the complete entry, see no. 1198.]

PALMIRENO, JUAN LORENZO (1524-1579)

1447. ARTIGAS Y FERNANDO, MIGUEL. Estudio biográfico-bibliográfico-crítico de Juan Lorenzo Palmireno y sus obras. 120 pp. Complutense, 1910.
[For a list of this scholar's publications, see *BBMP,* special issue in homage to D. Miguel Artigas, 2 vols. Santander, 1931-32. 1: xiii-xvi.]

1448. GALLEGO BARNÉS, ANDRÉS. Juan Lorenzo Palmireno: Contribution à l'histoire de l'Université de Valence. 4 vols. (1,071 pp.) Toulouse, 1980. (Thèse d'État)
❖ [A] *Les "Refranes" de Juan Lorenzo Palmireno.* Toulouse. 1969. 317 pp. (Thèse de 3e cycle). [B] "La risa en el teatro escolar de Juan Lorenzo Palmireno." *Risa y sociedad en el teatro español del Siglo de Oro: Actes du troisième colloque du GESTE, Toulouse, 1980.* Ed. Yves-René Fonquerne. Paris: CNRS, 1980. 187-96. [C] *Juan Lorenzo Palmireno (1524-1579): Un humanista aragonés en el Studi General de Valencia.* Zaragoza: Institución Fernando el Católico, 1982. 307 pp. [Abridged version of dissertation.] Rev.: M. Peset. *CHA* 407 (1984): 164-67.

PARÍS, JUAN DE (16TH C.)

1449. KOHLER, EUGEN [EUGÈNE]. Sieben spanische dramatische Eklogen mit einer Einleitung über die Anfänge der spanischen Dramas. Strasbourg, 1910.
[For the complete entry, see no. 1149. The seventh reprinted play is the *Égloga* of Juan de París.]

PÉREZ DE MONTALBÁN, JUAN (1602-1638)

1450. DIXON, VICTOR FREDERICK. The Life and Works of Juan Pérez de Montalbán, with Special Reference to His Plays. 22+372+18 pp. Cambridge, 1959.
❖ [A] "Juan Pérez de Montalbán's *Segundo tomo de las comedias.*" *HR*

29 (1961): 91–109. [B] "A Note on *Diferentes 30*." *BHS* 39 (1962): 92–96. [This *parte* includes three *comedias* of Juan Pérez de Montalbán.] [C] "Juan Pérez de Montalbán's *Para Todos*." *HR* 32 (1964): 35–59. [This collection contains six dramatic works.] [D] "Montalbán's *Vida y purgatorio de San Patricio:* Its Early Textual History." *BHS* 52 (1975): 227–34. [E] "Saint Patrick of Ireland and the Dramatists of Golden-Age Spain." *Hermathena* 121 (1976): 142–58. [Pérez de Montalbán's treatise entitled *Vida y purgatorio de San Patricio* (1628) inspired Calderón's *comedia El purgatorio de San Patricio.*]

1451. Parker, Jack Horace. *La gitanilla* (Attributed to Juan Pérez de Montalván) by Antonio de Solís y Rivadeneyra, Edited, with Introduction and Notes, Together with a Study of the Versification of the Plays of Solís and Montalván. lvi+181 pp. Toronto, 1941. Programme, May 1941. [See also no. 1491.]

❖ [A] "A Possible Source of a *jeu de scène* in Molière's *École des maris*." *MLN* 55 (1940): 453–54. [The possible source is Pérez de Montalbán's *No hay vida como la honra*.] [B] "The Chronology of the Plays of Juan Pérez de Montalván." *PMLA* 67.2 (1952): 186–210. Rev.: Ch. V. Aubrun. *BH* 54.3–4 (1952): 442–43. [C] "*La Gitanilla* de Montalván: Enigma literario del siglo XVII." *Actas del primer congreso internacional de hispanistas, Oxford, 1962*. Ed. Frank Pierce and Cyril A. Jones. Oxford: Dolphin, 1964. 409–14. [D] "*La monja alférez* de Juan Pérez de Montalván: Comedia americana del siglo XVII." *Actas del tercer congreso internacional de hispanistas, México, 1968*. Ed. Carlos H. Magis. México: Colegio de México, 1970. 665–71. [Apropos Montalbán's *comedia* dealing with Catalina de Erauso, "la monja alférez," in a mainly Peruvian setting.] [E] *Juan Pérez de Montalbán*. Boston: Twayne, 1975. 168 pp. (TWAS 352.)

1452. Tena, Jean. Les Noms de personnages dans les *comedias* de Juan Pérez de Montalbán. xxix+216 pp. Montpellier, 1970. (Thèse de 3e cycle)

Portuguese Theater

1453. Frèches, Claude-Henri. Le Théâtre néo-latin au Portugal (1550–1745). Paris, 1964. (Thèse d'État)

❖ [A] Title as is. Paris: Nizet; Lisboa: Bertrand, 1964. 586 pp. [Includes "Origines et tendances du théâtre de Gil Vicente," pp. 24-50.] Rev.: (a) L. Stegagno Picchio. *CN* 24 (1964): 289-94; (b) P. Le Gentil. *BÉP* ns 26 (1965): 250-53; (c) M. Martins. *Brotéria* 80 (1965): 261-63; (d) A. da Costa Ramalho. *HumC* 17-18 (1965-66): 361-63; (e) R. Hess. *RF* 78 (1966): 618-19; (f) J.-M. Massa. *RHT* 18 (1966): 236-38; (g) M. Scaduto. *AHSI* 36 (1967): 194-200; (h) J. L. de Carvalho. *Euphrosyne* ns 1 (1967): 291-92. [B] "Quelques aspects du drame néo-latin au Portugal." *Colóquio* 36 (1965): 56-58. [C] "Le Théâtre néo-latin au Portugal: *La Tragicomédie de Dom Manuel*." *APK* 5 (1965): 106-48. [D] "Le Théâtre néo-latin au Portugal: Histoire et actualité dans les tragicomédies du XVIIe siècle." *Euphrosyne* ns 2 (1968): 87-131. [E] "Le Personnage d'Inês de Castro chez Ferreira, Vélez de Guevara et Montherlant." *Arquivos* 3 (1971): 253-71.

Prado, Fernando (del) (1461?-after 1518)
(El Bachiller de la Pradilla)

1454. Kohler, Eugen [Eugène]. Sieben spanische dramatische Eklogen mit einer Einleitung über die Anfänge der spanischen Dramas. Strasbourg, 1910.

[For the complete entry, see no. 1149. The second reprinted play is the *Égloga Real* by the Bachiller de la Pradilla.]

Prestes, António (Portugal. 16th c.)

1455. Ribet, Simone. Édition critique et analyse de la pièce de António Prestes intitulée *O Auto da Ave Maria.* 4+cv+162 pp. Bordeaux, 1961. (Thèse de 3e cycle)

Quevedo, Francisco de (1580-1645)

1456. Mérimée, Ernest. Essai sur la vie et les œuvres de Francisco de Quevedo (1580-1645). Paris, 1886.

❖ Title as is. Paris: Picard, 1886. 466 pp. [A portion of ch. 6, "Les poésies," deals with "Poésies de théâtre: Comédies, Loas, Bailes, Jácaras, Entremeses—leur authenticité." (Prt. diss.)] Rev.: E. Pardo Bazán. *Nuevo Teatro Crítico* 18 (1892): 20-59; 19 (1892): 20-51; 23 (1892): 19-60. [For a more complete list of this scholar's publications, see "Bibliographie des travaux de Ernest Mérimée," *BH* 27.1 (1925): 79-87.]

1457. VILLEGAS, JEAN-CLAUDE. Le "Matasanos," tradition burlesque et invention au Siècle d'Or: Étude du médecin chez Quevedo et Lope de Vega. Bordeaux/III, 1982.

Editorial note: James Crosby's Quevedo bibliographies (1976, 1982, and 1993) include some twenty-four other non-United States dissertations on Don Francisco. Although several make sporadic references to his plays and all contribute to our knowledge of the great *polígrafo,* none deals exclusively or extensively with his theater and therefore they have not been listed here.

One example of a valuable linguistic and interpretative contribution that does not deal directly with theater is the 1983 dissertation by Ignacio Arellano Ayuso. It was partially published under the title *Poesía satírico-burlesca de Quevedo: Estudio y anotación filológica de los sonetos* (Pamplona: Universidad de Navarra, 1984. 577 pp.) In this book Arellano describes "los entremeses quevedianos" as "género en tantos aspectos . . . cercano a este tipo de poesía." Elsewhere, in reference to such statements of Eugenio Asensio as "las isoglosas de un género literario como el entremés penetran hondamente en los géneros vecinos," Arellano remarks that "las afirmaciones de Eugenio Asensio sobre el entremés son perfectamente aplicables a la poesía satírica." Arellano cites Asensio's study *Itinerario del entremés* (Madrid: Gredos, 1965) at least 27 times and the *entremeses* of Quevedo at least 17 times.

QUIÑONES DE BENAVENTE, LUIS (1589?-1651)

1458. SCHURACK, MARIANNE. Zeitbeständige Mimustypen bei Quiñones de Benavente unter Berücksichtigung ihrer Entwicklungsgeschichte. 198 pp. Hamburg, 1952.

[*Mimus* was the Latin term for "farce."]

Rebolledo, Conde de, o Rebolledo, Bernardino de (1597–1676)

1459. Gigas, Emil Leopold. Grev Bernardino de Rebolledo, spansk gesandt i Kjøbenhavn 1648-1659. Copenhagen, 1883.
[Rebolledo was the Spanish envoy in Copenhagen from 1648 to 1659.] (Madsen 115)
❖ [A] Title as is. København: Schubothe, 1883. 413 pp. [B] "En spansk Marsk Stig [*El príncipe despeñado* of Lope de Vega]" and "J. L. Heiberg og den spanske litteratur [with special reference to Calderón]" in vol. 1 of the writer's *Litteratur og historie: Studier og essays* (København, 1898-1902).

1460. Rengifo de la Vega, Josefina. Don Bernardino de Rebolledo y su obra poética. 70 pp. Complutense, 1955. Abstract in *RUM* 4.14 (1955): 264-65. [Concerning Rebolledo, see Rafael González Cañal, *La obra dramática del Conde de Rebolledo* (León: Diputación Provincial, 1988). 391 pp. This is a published version of his "memoria de licenciatura," Universidad Autónoma de Madrid, 1985.]

Remón, Fray Alonso (1561-1632)

1461. Fernández Nieto, Manuel. Vida y obra de Alonso Remón. 453 pp. Complutense, 1972. Abstract in *RUCM* 21.84-2 (Oct.-Dec. 1972): 90-91.
❖ *Investigaciones sobre Alonso Remón, dramaturgo desconocido del siglo XVII con dos comedias inéditas.* Madrid: Retorno-Istmo, 1974. 306 pp. [*Auto* of *El hijo pródigo* and *comedia* of *Las tres mujeres en una.*] Rev.: M. D. Echeverría. *Segismundo* 10.19-20 (1974): 378-79.

1462. López Tascón, José. Fray Alonso Remón, mercedario (1561-1632): Estudio biobibliográfico. 378 pp. Complutense, 1932.
❖ [A] "*El condenado por desconfiado* y fray Alonso Remón." *BBMP* 16 (1934): 533-46; 17 (1935): 14-29, 144-71, 274-93; 18-20 (1936-38): 35-82, 133-82. [B] "Colaboradores dramáticos de Lope de Vega." *BBMP* 17.4 (1935): 343-66. [The writer regards Remón as a collaborator of Lope in *¿De cuándo acá nos vino?* and *La ventura*

en el engaño.] [C] "En torno de algunos grandes dramas lopistas: Relaciones de los mismos con *El tejedor de Segovia* (primera parte) y con el doctor Remón." *CT* 53 (1935): 61-76, 291-308; 54 (1936): 32-47, 193-233.

Rojas Zorrilla, Francisco de (1607-1648)

1463. Kropatschek, Gertrude. Don Francisco de Rojas Zorrilla: Sein Leben und seine Werke. 141 pp. Vienna, 1949.

1464. Pietryga, Johannes. *El rico avariento:* Zwei *Autos sacramentales,* bisher zugeschrieben Francisco de Rojas Zorrilla. 162 pp. Cologne, 1958.

[A study and edition of the two *autos* entitled *El rico avariento,* both hitherto attributed to Rojas Zorrilla: (1) BNM MS 15.150 and (2) BNM MS 15.266. The writer argues that only (1) is by Rojas and that (2) is the work of Mira de Amescua. Regarding the MS *auto* of the same title in the Palatine Library of Parma, he concludes: "Es muss weiterhin als anonym gelten. Für uns bleibt das Auto ohne weitere Bedeutung."]

❖ Title as is. Köln: Photostelle der Universität zu Köln, [1958].

1465. Ríos, Diego Manuel de los. Antiguo teatro español: Moreto, Rojas, Alarcón. Sus principales obras. Complutense, 1857.

1466. Schmidt, Gisela Eva. Studien zu den Komödien des Don Francisco de Rojas Zorrilla. 240 pp. Cologne, 1959. // Rev.: A. G. Reichenberger. *HR* 32 (1964): 357-59.

1467. Wittmann, Brigitte. *Donde ay agravios no ay zelos* von Francisco de Rojas Zorrilla: Textausgabe und Kommentar. Cologne, 1963.

❖ [A] Title as is. Genève: Droz; Paris: Minard, 1962. 268 pp. (Kölner romanistische Arbeiten ns 26.) [The base text is the *princeps* (Madrid, 1640).] Rev.: (a) J. T. Boorman. *BHS* 41 (1964): 69-70; (b) A. G. Reichenberger. *HR* 32 (1964): 355-57; (c) P. Groult. *LR* 19 (1965): 268-70; (d) J. M. Díez Taboada. *Segismundo* 1 (1965): 168-70. [B] "Falscher Zorbeer für Rojas Zorrilla?" *Ibero* 1 (1969): 261-68. [The writer has reservations about attributing *Del rey abajo ninguno* to Rojas Zorrilla.] [C] Rojas Zorrilla, F. *Del rey abajo, ninguno, o El labrador más honrado,*

García del Castañar. Ed. B. Wittmann. Salamanca: Anaya, 1970. (Biblioteca Anaya 15.) Rev. ed. Madrid: Cátedra, 1980. (Letras hispánicas 132.)

RUEDA, LOPE DE (?–1565)

1468. FELIPE DE LA TORRE, E. El personaje negro en las obras de Lope de Rueda y Lope de Vega. Murcia, 1961.

1469. JASIMEZYK JABLONSKA, WANDA. Der verkürzte Satz bei Lope de Rueda. Vienna, 1918.

1470. SÁEZ GODOY, LEOPOLDO. El léxico de Lope de Rueda: Clasificaciones conceptual y estadística. 415 pp. Bonn, 1967.
❖ [A] Title as is. Bonn: Rheinische Friedrich-Wilhelms-Universität, 1968. Rev.: G. de Granda. *Thesaurus* 24 (1969): 115–16. [B] "Las leyes de Estoup-Zipf y el vocabulario de Lope de Rueda." *BFC* 20 (1968): 313–27.

1471. SCHMIDT, ERICH. Die Darstellung des spanischen Dramas vor Lope de Rueda. Berlin, 1935.
[For the complete entry, see no. 1187.]

1472. SCHÖNY, URSULA. Der dramatische Mensch auf der Bühne Lope de Ruedas. 94 pp. Heidelberg, 1944.

RUIZ DE ALARCÓN Y MENDOZA, JUAN (MEXICO. 1581?–1639)

1473. DENIS, SERGE. La Langue de Juan Ruiz de Alarcón: Contribution à l'étude du langage dramatique de la *comedia* espagnole. Paris, 1945. (Thèse d'État)
[Continuation of *Lexique* . . . (see no. 1474).]
❖ Title as is. Paris: Droz, 1943. 370 pp. Rev.: J. Villégier. *LanM* 40 (1946): 115–17.

1474. DENIS, SERGE. Lexique du théâtre de Juan Ruiz de Alarcón. Paris, 1945. (Thèse complémentaire)
❖ Title as is. Paris: Droz, 1943. 707 pp. Rev.: J. Villégier. *LanM* 40 (1946): 115–17.

1475. GILMOUR, JOHN WILLIAM. Political Themes in the Plays of Juan Ruiz de Alarcón. Cardiff, 1971.
❖ "Ruiz de Alarcón's Treatment of the King Peter Theme." *RJ* 24 (1973): 294–302.

1476. MUSSA Y BATTAL, MOISÉS. *La verdad sospechosa* y *Le Menteur:* Contribución a su estudio crítico-comparativo. 123 pp. Complutense, 1928.
[*Le Menteur* was written by Pierre Corneille.]

1477. RÍOS, DIEGO MANUEL DE LOS. Antiguo teatro español: Moreto, Rojas, Alarcón. Sus principales obras. Complutense, 1857.

1478. SACKHEIM, MUSSIA. Die Lebensphilosophie des Dichters Don Juan Ruiz de Alarcón y Mendoza. Berlin, 1936.
❖ Title as is. Berlin: Triltsch & Huther, 1936. 155 pp.

SALAS BARBADILLO, ALONSO JERÓNIMO DE (1581–1635)

1479. ARNAUD, ÉMILE. La Vie et l'œuvre d'Alonso Jerónimo de Salas Barbadillo: Contribution à l'étude du roman en Espagne au début du XVIIème siècle. 853 pp. Toulouse/II, 1979.
[Concerning Salas's theater, see Part 4, pp. 551–626.]
// Review article: Marc Vitse. "Salas Barbadillo y Góngora: Burla e ideario de la Castilla de Felipe III." *Criticón* 11 (1980): 5–142.

SALUCIO DEL POYO, DAMIÁN (1550?–1614)

1480. TOLL, KLAUS. Damián Salucio del Poyo, *El rey perseguido y corona pretendida (comedia):* Mit einer biographisch-kritischen Einführung. Jena, 1937.
❖ [A] Title as is. Borna and Leipzig: Noske; Paris: Droz, 1937. 188 pp. (Leipziger romanistische Studien 2. Literaturwissenschaftliche Reihe 6.) [The base text for this edition is BNM MS 14.960.] Rev.: (a) A. Hämel. *DLZ* 59 (1938): col. 805–06; (b) P. Weinmann. *NS* 47 (1939): 170; (c) H. Rheinfelder. *LGRP* 65–66 (1944): col. 94–95. [B] "Die spanische *comedia* im Unterricht der höheren Schule." *NS* 46 (1938): 418–24.

Sánchez, Miguel (1545–1630)

1481. José Prades, Juana de. Aportación al estudio de la teoría literaria y bibliografía de los dramaturgos menores pertenecientes al ciclo dramático de Lope de Vega. vii+400 pp. Complutense, 1960. Abstract in *RUM* 10.40 (1961): 852.
[For the complete entry, see no. 1148.]

Sánchez de Badajoz, Diego (16th c.)

1482. Fluegge, Gladstone R. Four *Farsas* by Diego Sánchez de Badajoz *(Farsa del matrimonio, Farsa de Santa Susana, Farsa de la hechicera, Farsa de la ventera):* Edited with Introduction and Notes. 270 pp. Toronto, 1953.

1483. Núñez de Cela, Manuel. Three *Farsas* by Diego Sánchez de Badajoz: *Farsa militar, Farsa moral, Farsa del juego de cañas.* A Critical Edition with Introduction and Notes. 387 pp. Toronto, 1974. *DAI* 38A: 3534-35.

1484. Pérez Priego, Miguel Ángel. El teatro de Diego Sánchez de Badajoz. 293 pp. Madrid/Autónoma, 1974.
❖ [A] Title as is. Cáceres: Universidad de Extremadura, 1982. 293 pp. Rev.: (a) J. E. Mateo Rodríguez. *RL* 45.90 (1983): 195-99; (b) J. Rubio Tovar. *CHA* 424 (1985): 187-89; (c) J. M. Marín Martínez. *Segismundo* 19.41-42 (1985): 291-94. [B] Sánchez de Badajoz, D. *Farsas.* Ed. M. A. Pérez Priego. Madrid: Cátedra, 1985. Rev.: C. Fernández-Daza Álvarez. *REE* 46.3 (1990): 767-68. [C] *Teatro renacentista.* Ed. M. A. Pérez Priego. Barcelona: Plaza y Janés, 1987. 343 pp. (Clásicos Plaza y Janés 58.)

Sepúlveda, Lorenzo de (fl. mid-16th c.)

1485. Alonso Asenjo, Julio. *La comedia de Sepúlveda:* Una comedia erudita española. 965 pp. Valencia, 1987. *DAI-C* 50: 405.
[For the complete entry, see no. 1215.]

Silva, António José da (Portugal. 1705–1739)

1486. Frèches, Claude-Henri. *El prodigio de Amarante (S. Gonçalo)* del Doctor António José da Silva: Introduction, Édition critique, notes et glossaire. Paris, 1964. (Thèse complémentaire)
❖ Silva, António José da. *El prodigio de Amarante, comedia famosa.* Critical ed., introd., notes, and glossary by C.-H. Frèches. Lisboa: Bertrand; Paris: Belles Lettres, 1967. 263 pp. ["*El Prodigio de Amarante* (written in Spanish) est une 'comédia de santo,' comme il s'en est encore publié au XVIIIème siècle. . . . Soit qu'il veuille pasticher ou parodier le langage de la 'comedia famosa,' soit qu'il veuille simplement adapter son style à ce genre théâtral, António José da Silva utilise abondamment le vocabulaire et les constructions de Calderón." (Prt. Diss.)]

1487. Nesswetha, Willy. Die Konstituenten der Komik in den *óperas* des António José da Silva (o Judeu). 147 pp. Graz, 1981. Short summary in *Sprachkunst* 13 (1982): 179.

Silva, Diego de (1621?–after 1685)

1488. Serralta, Frédéric. Une Tradition littéraire: *La renegada de Valladolid.* Étude et édition critique de la *comedia* burlesque de Monteser, Solís, et Silva. 238 pp. Toulouse, 1968.
[For the complete entry, see no. 1438.]

Silva, Feliciano de (16th c.)

1489. Baranda Leturio, Consolación. Feliciano de Silva y la *Segunda Celestina.* Complutense, 1988.
❖ [A] Title as is. Madrid: Editorial de la Universidad Complutense, 1988. 2 vols. (173, 203 pp.) (Colección tesis doctorales no. 286/88.) Rev.: J. Sepúlveda. *RIber* 35 (1989): 31–32. [B] Silva, F. de. *Segunda Celestina.* Ed. C. Baranda. Prologue by Fernando Arrabal. Madrid: Cátedra, 1988. 583 pp. [C] "De *Celestinas:* Problemas metodológicos." *Celestinesca* 16.2 (1992): 3–32.

1490. MONK, ISOBEL ANN. The *Segunda Celestina* of Feliciano de Silva: A Study and an Edition. 2 vols. (iv+155, vii+361 pp.) Exeter, 1973.

SOLÍS Y RIVADENEYRA, ANTONIO DE (1610–1686)

1491. PARKER, JACK HORACE. *La gitanilla* (Attributed to Juan Pérez de Montalván) by Antonio de Solís y Rivadeneyra, Edited, with Introduction and Notes, Together with a Study of the Versification of the Plays of Solís and Montalván. lvi+181 pp. Toronto, 1941. Programme, May 1941. [See also no. 1451.]

❖ [A] "The Versification of the *Comedias* of Antonio de Solís y Rivadeneyra." *HR* (1949): 308–15. [B] "The Chronology of the Plays of Juan Pérez de Montalván." *PMLA* 67.2 (1952): 186–210. Rev.: Ch. V. Aubrun. *BH* 54.3–4 (1952): 442–43. [C] "*La Gitanilla* de Montalván: Enigma literario del siglo XVII." *Actas del primer congreso internacional de hispanistas, Oxford, 1962.* Ed. Frank Pierce and Cyril A. Jones. Oxford: Dolphin, 1964. 409–14.

1492. SERRALTA, FRÉDÉRIC. Une Tradition littéraire: *La renegada de Valladolid*. Étude et édition critique de la *comedia* burlesque de Monteser, Solís, et Silva. 238 pp. Toulouse, 1968.

[For the complete entry, see no. 1438.]

1493. SERRALTA, FRÉDÉRIC. Antonio de Solís et son théâtre. Toulouse/II, 1987. (Thèse d'État)

❖ [A] "Sobre el origen de la atribución errónea de *La gitanilla* a Juan Pérez de Montalbán." *BCom* 29.2 (1977): 118–19. [B] "*Amor al uso* y protagonismo femenino." *La mujer en el teatro y la novela del siglo XVII: Actas del segundo coloquio del GESTE, Toulouse, 1978.* Toulouse: Université de Toulouse-Le Mirail, 1979. 97–109. [C] "El testamento de Antonio de Solís y otros documentos biográficos." *Criticón* 7 (1979): 1–57. [D] "Antonio de Solís y el teatro menor en palacio." *El teatro menor en España a partir del siglo XVI: Actas del coloquio, Madrid, 1982.* Ed. Luciano García Lorenzo. Madrid: CSIC, 1983. 155–72. [E] "Las comedias de Antonio de Solís: Reflexiones sobre la edición de un texto del Siglo de Oro." *Criticón* 34 (1986): 159–74. [F] "Nueva biografía de Antonio de Solís y Rivadeneyra." *Criticón* 34 (1986):

51-157. [G] *Antonio de Solís et la* comedia *d'intrigue*. Toulouse: France-Ibérie Recherche, 1987. 470 pp. (Collection "Thèses et recherches" 16.) Rev.: J. H. Parker. *BCom* 40.2 (1988): 252-54. [H] "La doble visión de los gitanos en las *Gitanillas* de Antonio de Solís." *Critique sociale et théâtre: Domaine ibérique. Table ronde du Centre de Recherche Pyrenaica, 1987*. Pau: Université de Pau, 1988. 37-48. [I] "El enredo y la comedia: Deslinde preliminar." *Criticón* 42 (1988): 125-37. [J] "Donjuanismo, feminismo, decoro y modernidad: *El amor al uso* de Antonio de Solís." *El redescubrimiento de los clásicos: Actas de las XV jornadas de teatro clásico, Almagro, 1992*. Ed. Felipe B. Pedraza Jiménez. Castilla-La Mancha: Universidad de Castilla-La Mancha, 1993. 91-101.

Suárez de Deza, Vicente (fl. mid-17th c.)

1494. Crespo Matellán, Salvador. La parodia dramática en la literatura española: Esbozo de una historia y análisis de *Los amantes de Teruel,* comedia burlesca de Vicente Suárez de Deza. 2 vols. (357, 355+[1] pp.) Salamanca, 1973.
❖ [A] Extracto de tesis doctoral, T-L-104. Salamanca: Europa, 1973. 14 pp. [B] *La parodia dramática en la literatura española: Esbozo de una historia de la parodia dramática en la literatura española y análisis de* Los amantes de Teruel, *comedia burlesca de Vicente Suárez de Deza.* Salamanca: Universidad de Salamanca, 1979. 216 pp. (Acta Salmanticensia. Filosofía y Letras 107.) [Includes a facsimile edition of Suárez de Deza's *comedia* (1663).] Rev.: F. Serralta. *Criticón* 10 (1980): 103-08. [C] "La construcción de los personajes en la parodia dramática: El Tenorio modernista." *Actas del segundo simposio internacional de semiótica, Oviedo, 1986*. Vol. 2: *Lo teatral y lo cotidiano*. Ed. Asociación Española de Semiótica. Oviedo: Universidad de Oviedo, 1988. 153-68.

Suárez de Figueroa, Cristóbal (1571?-1639?)

1495. Arce Menéndez, Ángeles. Cristóbal Suárez de Figueroa:

Nuevas perspectivas de su obra. 871 pp. Complutense, 1978. Abstract in *UCM. Tesis doctorales* 2 (1977-78): 92-93; *MEC. Tesis doctorales* 255 (1977-78): 133-34.

❖ La *Piazza universale* de Tommaso Garzoni y la *Plaza universal* de Cristóbal Suárez de Figueroa. Complutense, 1971. Tesis de licenciatura inédita.

1496. ENTRAMBASAGUAS Y PEÑA, JOAQUÍN DE. Una guerra literaria del Siglo de Oro (Lope de Vega, Torres Rámila, López de Aguilar, Suárez de Figueroa, Tamayo de Vargas, etc.). 446 pp. Complutense, 1929.

[For the complete entry, see no. 1548.]

1497. KIMMEL, LORE. *La piazza universale di tutte le professioni del mondo* (1585) von Thomaso Garzoni und die spanische Übersetzung und Umarbeitung in *Plaza universal de todas ciencias y artes* (1615) von Cristóbal Suárez de Figueroa. 281 pp. Munich, 1969.

["The *Plaza universal* (completed 1612; published 1615) is best known to students of Spanish literature in connection with the history of the stage. The list of actors and actresses which he gives, is an important document for the history of the *comediantes*. Already in 1612, Figueroa was bitterly opposed to the Spanish national theater, and in his works he strongly censured the immorality of the stage." J. P. W. Crawford, *The Life and Works of Cristóbal Suárez de Figueroa* (Philadelphia; Univ. of Pennsylvania, 1907) 54-55.]

1498. NOUGUÉ, MARIE-GENEVIÈVE. Le Vocabulaire technique de la *Plaza universal* de Cristóbal Suárez de Figueroa: Introduction, glossaire, index. 744 pp. Toulouse, 1969. (Thèse de 3e cycle)

[See note at 1497.]

TÉLLEZ, FRAY GABRIEL (1583?-1648)
(Tirso de Molina)

1499. ARBONA PIZÁ, MIGUEL, SI. Estudio crítico en torno a *El Aquiles.* 2 vols. Barcelona, 1965. *El Aquiles: Comedia mitológica de Tirso de Molina. Resumen* 421. Barcelona: Universidad de Barcelona, 1971. 11 pp.

1500. Arquimbau Amblat, Paul. *En Madrid y en una casa, comedia* attribuée à Tirso de Molina: Essai d'édition critique (introduction, texte, notes et variantes). 158 pp. Poitiers, 1978. (Thèse de 3e cycle)

1501. Barrera García, Consuelo. *La Santa Juana* de Tirso de Molina. Edición crítica, estudio y notas. 2 vols. (489, 588 pp.) Navarre, 1982.
❖ "Estructura del refrán en tres comedias del Siglo de Oro." *EstM* 46.170 (1990): 37–64. [Téllez, *Santa Juana;* Calderón, *Dar tiempo al tiempo;* Vega Carpio, *Las bizarrías de Belisa.*]

1502. Bogner, Irene Wieland. *El burlador de Sevilla y convidado de piedra* von Tirso de Molina als Kunstwerk. Würzburg, 1970.
❖ Title as is. München: UNI-Druck, 1969. 413 pp. Rev.: G. Schüler. *RJ* 22 (1971): 392–93.

1503. Bonifaci, Sol [Bonifaci de la Torre, Consolación]. ×Tirso o Téllez? Neuchâtel, 1979.
❖ [A] Title as is. *EstM* 35.124 (1979): 3–277 (spec. issue). [B] Offprint. Title as is. Madrid: Revista "Estudios," 1979. 277 pp. [C] "Después de una tesis." *EstM* 36.128 (1980): 71–86.

1504. Cámara, Nahiye León. Dieu et l'homme dans *El condenado por desconfiado* de Tirso de Molina. Montpellier/III, 1984. (Thèse de 3e cycle)

1505. Cazottes, Gisèle. *Los balcones de Madrid,* de Tirso de Molina: Édition critique, introduction, texte, notes et variantes. lxviii+397 pp. Toulouse, 1970. (Thèse de 3e cycle)
❖ [A] "A propósito de dos refundiciones tirsianas: *Amor no teme peligros* y *Los balcones de Madrid.*" *EstM* 37.136 (1982): 5–13. [B] Téllez, Gabriel. *Los balcones de Madrid.* Ed. G. Cazottes. Madrid: Ayuntamiento, 1982. Rev.: G. E. Wade. *H* [AATSP] 66 (1983): 634.

1506. Evans, Peter William. Unifying Images of Love in the Comedies of Tirso de Molina. Cambridge, 1975.
❖ [A] "Language and Structure in *La villana de Vallecas.*" *FMLS* 14 (1978): 32–41. [B] "The Call of the Siren: Tirso's Women in *El castigo del penséque.*" *FMLS* 18 (1982): 351–62. [C] "The Roots of Desire in *El burlador de Sevilla.*" *FMLS* 22 (1986): 232–47. [D] "Sexo y cultura en *El pretendiente al revés* de Tirso de Molina." *El mundo del teatro español en su Siglo de Oro: Ensayos dedicados a*

John E. Varey. Ed. José María Ruano de la Haza. Ottawa: Dovehouse, 1989. 267–74. (Ottawa Hispanic Studies 3.)

1507. Florit Durán, Francisco. La poética dramática de Tirso de Molina. Murcia, 1984.

❖ [A] "Tirso de Molina y el uso teatral del refranero." *Monteagudo* 84 (1984): 21–27. [B] "Sobre la finalidad del arte literario en Tirso de Molina." *EstM* 41.148 (1985): 51–60. [C] "Tirso de Molina ante la Comedia Nueva: Aproximación a una poética." *EstM* 42.155 (1986): 186 pp. (spec. issue). Rev.: (a) I. Arellano. *Criticón* 40 (1987): 167–70; (b) A. A. Heathcote. *BHS* 66.2 (1989): 182–83. [D] "Variedad escénica y heterogeneidad del público en el teatro de Tirso de Molina." *Tirso de Molina: Vida y obra. Actas del primer simposio internacional sobre Tirso, Washington, 1984* (error for 1985). Ed. Josep M. Solà-Solé and Luis Vázquez Fernández. Madrid: Revista "Estudios," 1987. 211–18.

1508. Gijón Zapata, Esmeralda. El humor en Tirso de Molina. 366 pp. Complutense, 1948.

❖ [A] Title as is. Madrid: Guardia Civil, 1959. 235 pp. [B] Title as is. *EstM* 15.47 (1959): 523–749.

1509. Halkhoree, Premraj Radhe Krishna. Social and Literary Satire in the Comedies of Tirso de Molina. 606 pp. Edinburgh, 1969.

❖ [A] "Satire and Symbolism in the Structure of Tirso de Molina's *Por el sótano y el torno.*" *FMLS* 4 (1968): 374–86. [B] "The Foundation of Nobility: An Interpretation of Tirso de Molina's *Ventura te dé Dios, hijo.*" *FMLS* 9 (1973): 379–402. [C] "La experimentación dramática de Tirso de Molina." *Actas del sexto congreso internacional de hispanistas, Toronto, 1977.* Ed. Alan M. Gordon and Evelyn Rugg. Toronto: Univ. of Toronto, 1980. 368–72. [Apropos *Don Gil de las calzas verdes; Por el sótano y el torno; Ventura te dé Dios, hijo.*] [D] Title as is. Ed. José María Ruano de la Haza and Henry W. Sullivan. Ottawa: Dovehouse, 1989. 293 pp. (Ottawa Hispanic Studies 5.) Rev.: (a) R. Conlon. *BCom* 43.1 (1991): 177–78; (b) M. Delgado-Morales. *H* [AATSP] 74.2 (1991): 311–12; (c) D. Smith. *RCEH* 15 (1991): 352–53; (d) E. S. Engling. *RomQ* 38.1 (1991): 116–17. [E] "The 'Context of Situation' in Tirso's *La mujer por fuerza.*" *BCom* 43.2 (1991): 259–73. [This study was an appendix to the writer's dissertation.]

1510. HORL, SABINE. Leidenschaften und Affekte im dramatischen Werk Tirso de Molinas. Hamburg, 1970.

❖ Title as is. Hamburg: Romanisches Seminar der Universität, 1969. 190 pp. (Hamburger romanistische Dissertationen 7.) Rev.: A. L. Mackenzie. *BHS* 49 (1972): 72–78 (esp. pp. 76–78).

1511. JAESCHKE, SIGRID WEIDEMANN. Grenzen der Charakterdarstellung bei Tirso de Molina. 216 pp. Berlin/FU, 1970.

❖ Title as is. Berlin: Dissertationsdruckstelle, 1970. 216 pp.

1512. KREIS, KARL-WILHELM. Studien zur Liebesmetaphorik im Theater Tirso de Molinas. 495 pp. Göttingen, 1971. *DAI-C* 39: 194. // Rev.: S. Horl. *RJ* 23 (1972): 382–83.

❖ "Das Renaissance-Ideal *armas y letras* im Theater Tirso de Molinas." *RJ* 29 (1978): 270–302.

1513. LABARRE, FRANÇOISE MELLE. *El vergonzoso en palacio,* édition critique et traduction. 2 vols. (236, 279 pp.) Paris/III, 1974. (Thèse de 3e cycle)

❖ [A] Labarre, F., and Roland Labarre. "En torno a la fecha de *El vergonzoso en palacio,* y algunas otras comedias de Tirso de Molina." *Criticón* 16 (1981): 47–64. [B] Téllez, G. *Le Timide à la Cour.* Critical ed. and trans. F. Labarre and Roland Labarre. Paris: Aubier, 1983. 373 pp. Rev.: J. Canavaggio. *XVIIe Siècle* 144 (1984): 281–82. [C] "*Le Timide à la Cour:* Fantaisie et jeu." *LLNL* 78.248 (1984): 21–33.

1514. LAJOIE, RAYMOND-GÉRIN. Tirso de Molina (Gabriel Téllez), *El condenado por desconfiado:* Établissement d'un texte d'après la princeps de 1635, précédé d'une introduction critique, historique, doctrinale. 620 pp. Paris, 1956. (Doctorat d'Université)

❖ "La singularidad de los dos errores de la *Segunda parte* de las comedias del maestro Tirso de Molina, 1635." *BH* 57 (1955): 417–20. [Apropos the text of *El condenado por desconfiado.*]

1515. MAUREL, SERGE. L'Univers dramatique de Tirso de Molina. Paris, 1970. (Thèse d'État)

❖ [A] Title as is. Poitiers: Université de Poitiers, 1971. 623 pp. Rev.: (a) A. Nougué. *RABM* 76 (1973): 149–64; (b) M. Wilson. *BHS* 51 (1974): 291–93; (c) J. Canavaggio. *HR* 42 (1974): 346–49;

(d) A. Cioranescu. *RLC* 49.3 (1975): 514-15; (e) F. Schalk. *RF* 88.1 (1976): 140-42. [B] "Le Monde paysan et sa fonction de marque dans le théâtre de Tirso de Molina." *BH* 79 (1977): 329-45. [C] "Le Public de *Burlador* de Séville: Essai d'identification." *LLNL* 71.223 (1977): 18-32. [D] Molina, T. de. *La celosa de sí misma./La jalousie d'elle-même.* Ed., introd., trans., and notes by S. Maurel. Poitiers: S. Maurel, 1981. [E] "Le Public du *Burlador* de Séville: Essai d'identification." *TS* 4 (1983?): 75-86. [F] "Le Rire et son effet de distanciation dans *El condenado por desconfiado (Le damné pour manque de foi)* de Tirso de Molina." *La Licorne* 7 (1983): 11-23.

1516. Mettmann, Walter. Studien zum religiösen Theater Tirso de Molinas. 184 pp. Cologne, 1951.

❖ Title as is. Köln: Romanisches Seminar, 1954. 102 pp. (Kölner romanistische Arbeiten ns 1.) Rev.: (a) G. Sobejano. *RFE* 38.1-4 (1954): 347-51; (b) K. Maurer. *Archiv* 192.2-3 (1955): 244-45; (c) Ch. V. Aubrun. *BH* 57.1-2 (1955): 190-91; (d) A. Porqueras-Mayo. *RL* 8.13-14 (1955): 245-46; (e) H. Bihler. *RF* 67.3-4 (1956): 443-45; (f) C. Combe. *BH* 59.3 (1957): 343-44.

1517. Milke Molina, Marguerite. Elementos barrocos en Tirso de Molina. 303 pp. Complutense, 1967. Abstract in *RUM* 16.61-64 (1967): 32-33.

1518. Millán, Émile. Recherches sur le Couvent de Nuestra Señora del Olivar en liaison avec l'œuvre de Tirso de Molina: Contribution à l'histoire aragonaise. 217 pp. Poitiers, 1979. (Thèse de 3e cycle)

[Apropos Tirso's play *La dama del Olivar.*]

❖ "Investigaciones sobre el convento de Ntra. Sra. del Olivar en conexión con la obra de Tirso de Molina (contribución a la historia de Aragón)." *Homenaje a Tirso.* Madrid: Revista "Estudios," 1981. 37-118.

1519. Nougué, Marcel-André-Pierre. L'Œuvre en prose de Tirso de Molina: *Los Cigarrales de Toledo* et *Deleytar aprovechando.* Toulouse, 1961. (Thèse d'État)

❖ [A] Title as is. Paris: Centre de Recherches de l'Institut d'Études Hispaniques, 1962. 497 pp. [See esp. pp. 347-60: "Le dramaturge: Théories et réalisations."] Rev.: (a) G. Placer López. *EstM* 58 (1962): 555-57; (b) M. Wilson. *BHS* 40 (1963): 189-90; (c) G.

E. Wade. *H* [AATSP] 46 (1963): 664; (d) J. Ares Montes. *Ínsula* 203 (1963): 10; (e) L. Roux. *RLR* 75 (1963): 212-14; (f) G. Larrieu. *BH* 66 (1964): 422-26; (g) J. Cañedo. *RL* 28 (1965): 275-80; (h) A. Amorós. *CHA* 65 (1966): 362-64. [B] "*El laberinto de Creta* de Tirso de Molina (Essai de datation)." *BH* 79 (1977): 395-99. [C] Téllez, G. El bandolero, *de Tirso de Molina.* Ed. A. Nougué. Madrid: Castalia, 1979. 394 pp.

1520. NOUGUÉ, MARCEL-ANDRÉ-PIERRE. Tirso de Molina: *La patrona de las Musas* et *Los triunfos de la verdad*. Toulouse, 1961. (Thèse complémentaire)

1521. PALOMO VÁZQUEZ, MARÍA DEL PILAR. El teatro de Tirso de Molina: Comedias cortesanas. 266 pp. Complutense, 1959. Abstract in *RUM* 9.36 (1960): 911-12.

[The *comedias cortesanas* are *Don Gil de las calzas verdes, Marta la piadosa, El amor médico,* and *Por el sótano y el torno.*]

❖ [A] Portugal en la obra de Tirso de Molina. Complutense, 1956. Tesis de licenciatura. [B] "La creación dramática de Tirso de Molina." In her edition of *Tirso de Molina: Obras*. Barcelona: Vergara, 1968. 9-125. [C] "Estudio preliminar: Fray Gabriel Téllez, un español del Barroco." In her edition of *Obras de Tirso de Molina*. Madrid: Atlas, 1970. i-lxxix. (BAE 236).

1522. PATERSON, ALAN KEITH GORDON. Tirso de Molina: An Edition of *La venganza de Tamar,* with Bibliographical, Textual and Literary Criticism. Cambridge, 1966.

❖ [A] "Tirso de Molina: Two Bibliographical Studies." *HR* 35 (1967): 43-68. [B] "The Textual History of Tirso's *La venganza de Tamar*." *MLR* 63 (1968): 381-91. [C] Téllez, G. *La venganza de Tamar.* Ed. A. K. G. Paterson. London: Cambridge UP, 1969. 150 pp. Rev.: (a) M. Wilson. *BHS* 47 (1970): 164-65; (b) A. Nougué. *BH* 73 (1971): 104-24; (c) D. Rogers. *MLR* 67 (1972): 197-98; (d) J. Asensio. *Reflexión2* ns 1.1 (1972): 179-80.

1523. PIELTÁIN Y BARTOLI, JOSÉ MARÍA. Exposición histórica del teatro de Tirso de Molina. 77 pp., handwritten. Complutense, 1883.

1524. RABATE, JEAN-CLAUDE. *La dama del Olivar* de Tirso de Molina et sa descendance au XIXe et au XXe siècle: Une Comédie édifiante et ses publics successifs. 208 p. Poitiers, 1980.

1525. Smith, Dawn L. E. A. A Critical Edition of Tirso de Molina's Play *La mujer que manda en casa.* xiv+564 pp. Oxford, 1975.

❖ [A] "Stagecraft, Theme and Structure in Tirso's *La mujer que manda en casa.*" *RCEH* 3 (1979): 137-60. [B] Molina, T. de. *La mujer que manda en casa.* Ed. D. L. Smith. London: Tamesis, 1984. 180 pp. Rev.: (a) M. Wilson. *BHS* 64.4 (1987): 374-75; (b) M. McKendrick. *MLR* 83.2 (1988): 490-91. [C] "*La mujer que manda en casa:* Una versión refundida para el público del siglo XVIII." *Tirso de Molina: Del Siglo de Oro al siglo XX. Actas del coloquio internacional, Pamplona, 1994.* Ed. Ignacio Arellano, María del Carmen Pinillos, and Miguel Zugasti. Madrid: Revista "Estudios," 1995; also in *EstM* 51. 189-90 (1995): 323-36.

1526. Torre Temprano, María. Cuestiones de métrica y de datación en las comedias de Tirso de Molina. Navarre, 1976. Abstract in *MEC. Tesis doctorales* 509 (anexo 1976-77): 210.

1527. Zugasti, Miguel. La "Trilogía de los Pizarros" de Tirso de Molina: *Todo es dar en una cosa, Amazonas en las Indias* y *La lealtad contra la envidia.* Edición crítica y estudio. 903 pp. Navarre, 1992. *DAI-C* 54: 991.

❖ [A] "La imagen de Francisco Pizarro en el teatro áureo: Tirso, Vélez de Guevara, Calderón." *Las Indias (América) en la literatura del Siglo de Oro: Actas del congreso internacional.* Ed. Ignacio Arellano. Kassel: Reichenberger, 1992. 127-44. [B] La Trilogía de los Pizarros *de Tirso de Molina. Vol. 1: Estudio crítico.* Critical ed., bibliog. and notes by M. Zugasti. Kassel: Reichenberger; Trujillo: Obra Pía de los Pizarro, 1993. 220 pp. [C] *Trilogía de los Pizarros. Vol. 2:* Todo es dar en una cosa, *de Tirso de Molina.* Critical ed., bibliog. and notes by M. Zugasti. Kassel: Reichenberger; Trujillo: Obra Pía de los Pizarro, 1993. 254 pp. [D] *Trilogía de los Pizarros. Vol. 3:* Amazonas en las Indias, *de Tirso de Molina.* Critical ed., bibliog., and notes by M. Zugasti. Kassel: Reichenberger; Trujillo: Obra Pía de los Pizarro, 1993. 220 pp. [E] *Trilogía de los Pizarros. Vol. 4:* La lealtad contra la envidia, *de Tirso de Molina.* Critical ed., bibliog. and notes by M. Zugasti. Kassel: Reichenberger; Trujillo: Obra Pía de los Pizarro, 1993. 242 pp. Rev.: publications B-E: (a) L. Vázquez. *EstM* 49.183 (1993): 155-60; (b) C. B. Weimer. *H* [AATSP]

77.3 (1994): 431-32; (c) J. Horno García. *RILCE* 11.1 (1995): 185-88. [F] "Notas para un repertorio de comedias indianas del Siglo de Oro." *Studia aurea: Actas del tercer congreso de la AISO, Toulouse, 1993.* 3 vols. Toulouse-Pamplona: GRISO-LEMSO, 1996. Vol. 2 *Teatro.* Ed. Ignacio Arellano, María del Carmen Pinillos, Frédéric Serralta, and Marc Vitse. 2: 429-42. [G] "*Las palabras a los reyes y gloria de los Pizarros,* comedia olvidada, que no perdida, de Luis Vélez de Guevara." *Luis Vélez de Guevara y su época: Cuarto congreso de historia de Écija, Écija, 1994.* Ed. Piedad Bolaños Donoso and M. Martín Ojeda. Sevilla: Excmo. Ayuntamiento de Écija and Fundación El Monte, 1996. 299-311. [H] "Propaganda y mecenazgo literario: *La familia de los Pizarro,* Tirso de Molina y Vélez de Guevara." *Teatro, historia y sociedad. (Seminario internacional sobre teatro del Siglo de Oro español.) Asociación Internacional de Teatro Español y Novohispano del Siglo de Oro, Murcia, 1994.* Ed. Carmen Hernández Valcárcel. Murcia: Universidad de Murcia; Ciudad Juárez: Universidad Autónoma de Ciudad Juárez, 1996. 35-52.

Timoneda, Juan (?-1583)

1528. Diago Moncholí, Manuel V. *Amphitrión, Los Menennos, Carmelia.* Las tres comedias de Juan Timoneda. [Edición.] 624 pp. Valencia, 1987.

❖ [A] "La *Comedia llamada Aurelia* de Joan Timoneda: Una pieza clave del teatro prelopista." *Quaderns de Filologia, Miscel·lània Sanchis Guarner* 2 (1984): 99-103. [B] "Reflexiones en torno a los autos en catalán de Joan Timoneda: Fuentes, lengua, público." *Comedias y comediantes: Estudios sobre el teatro clásico español. Actas del congreso internacional sobre teatro y prácticas escénicas en los siglos XVI y XVII, València, 1989.* Ed. Manuel V. Diago and Teresa Ferrer. Valencia: Universitat de València, 1991. 47-53. [C] "Una adaptación española de *Il negromante* de Ariosto: *La comedia llamada Carmelia* de Joan Timoneda." *Origini della commedia nell'Europa del cinquecento (XVII convegno, Roma, 1993).* Ed. Myriam Chiabò and Federico Doglio.

[Viterbo]: Ministero di Turismo e Spettacolo, Centro Studi sul Teatro Medioevale e Rinascimentale, 1994. 161–76. [D] "La mujer en el teatro profesional del Renacimiento: Entre la sumisión y la astucia. (A propósito de *Las tres Comedias* de Joan Timoneda.)" *Criticón* 63 (1995): 103–17.

1529. PETERSON, HOLLAND. *Amphitrión* and *Los Menemnos:* An Edition of the First Two Plays of Juan Timoneda's *Las tres comedias,* with an Introduction on Plautine Influences. 380 p. Toronto, 1961.

TORQUEMADA, ANTONIO DE (1530?–1590)

1530. RODRÍGUEZ CACHO, LINA. Los *Coloquios satíricos con un coloquio pastoril* (1553) de Antonio de Torquemeda. Edición y estudio. 3 vols. (1–429, 430–764, 765–1319 pp.) Madrid/Autónoma, 1987–88. [The additional "pastoral colloquy" of the title refers to "*colloquio pastoril,* en que se tratan los amores de un pastor llamado Torcato, con una pastora llamada Belissia; el qual da cuenta dellos a otros dos pastores llamados Filonio y Grisaldo, quexándose del agravio que recibió de su amiga." (See La Barrera, *Catálogo* 398, who describes this work as "de formas dramáticas y propio para ser representado.)]

❖ [A] *Pecados sociales y literatura satírica en el siglo XVI: Los "Coloquios" de Torquemada.* Madrid: Universidad Autónoma de Madrid, 1989. 276 pp. (Colección de estudios 24.) [This study excludes the *coloquio pastoril.*] Rev.: (a) A. Soons. *Criticón* 55 (1992): 167–68; (b) D. J. Hildner. *HR* 60 (1992): 474–76. [B] Title as is. Madrid: Ediciones de la Universidad Autónoma de Madrid, 1990. 15 microfiches. [C] Torquemada, A. de. *Obras completas.* Vol. 1: *Manual de escribientes, Coloquios satíricos, Jardín de flores curiosas.* Ed. L. Rodríguez Cacho. Madrid: Turner, 1994. 904 pp.

TORRES NAHARRO, BARTOLOMÉ DE (?–1524?)

1531. DEPTA, MAX VIKTOR. Die *Celestina* in ihrem Verhältnis zu den novellistischen Komödien der *Propaladia* des Torres Naharro. 139

pp. Breslau, 1920. Abstract, Breslau: Hochschulverlag, 1920. 2 pp.

1532. GIORDANO GRAMEGNA, ANNA LUCIA. La influencia del primer teatro renacentista italiano en las comedias de Bartolomé Torres Naharro. 756 pp. Valencia, 1986. *DAI-C* 50: 171.

❖ [A] Title as is. Valencia: Universitat de València, Servicio de Publicaciones, 1986. [B] "Influencia italiana en Bartolomé Torres Naharro." *Teatro y prácticas escénicas 2: La comedia.* Ed José Luis Canet Vallés. London: Tamesis, 1986. 11–25. (Colección Támesis, serie A. Monografías 123.)

VALDIVIELSO, JOSÉ DE (1560?–1638)

1533. FLECNIAKOSKA, JEAN-LOUIS. Valdivielso, Joseph de: *Auto sacramental del Caballero de la ardiente espada,* ou *El fénix de Amor.* Édition synoptique et critique, introduction et notes. 203 pp. Paris, 1962. (Thèse complémentaire)

1534. SÁNCHEZ ROMERALO, JAIME. Estudio biográfico: El maestro José de Valdivielso. Nuevos datos acerca de su vida. 2 vols. Complutense, 1967.

VASCONCELOS, JORGE FERREIRA DE (PORTUGAL. 1527–1584/85)

1535. SUBIRATS, JEAN. Les Comédies et l'épître de Jorge Ferreira de Vasconcelos: Contribution à l'étude socio-littéraire du XVIe siècle portugais. 2 vols. (798 pp.) Montpellier/III, 1975. *DAI-C* 38: 361. (Thèse d'État)

❖ [A] Title as is. Lille: Université de Lille, Service de Reproduction des Thèses, 1976. 2 vols. (798 pp.) Rev.: M. de Lourdes Belchior. *TILAS* 16–17 (1976–77): 238–41. [B] "L'Oiseau dans le théâtre de Jorge Ferreira de Vasconcelos." *Hommage des hispanistes français à Noël Salomon: Publié par les soins de la Société des Hispanistes Français.* Barcelona: Laia, 1979. 793–805. [C] *Jorge Ferreira de Vasconcelos: Visages de son œuvre et de son temps.*

2 vols. Coimbra: Universidade de Coimbra, 1982. [D] "L'Outremer dans le théâtre de Jorge Ferreira de Vasconcelos: Donnée dramatique et équation personnelle." *L'Humanisme portugais et l'Europe: Actes du XXI*[ème] *colloque international d'études humanistes, Tours, 1978.* Ed. Luis de Albuquerque. Paris: Fondation C. Gulbenkian, 1984. 735–46. [E] "*Parvo* et *parvoice* chez Jorge Ferreira de Vasconcelos." *Arquivos* 23 (1987): 585–604. [F] "A propos de Parasito, le parasite de Jorge Ferreira de Vasconcelos." *Arquivos* 31 (1992): 907–15. Special issue entitled *Hommage au professeur Adrien Roig.* [For a more complete list of this scholar's publications, see "Bibliographie des travaux publiés par J. Subirats," *De la Péninsule Ibérique à l'Amérique Latine: Mélanges en l'honneur de Jean Subirats,* ed. Marie Roig Miranda (Nancy: Presses Universitaires de Nancy, 1992) 8.]

Vega Carpio, Lope Félix de (1562–1635)

1536. Adams, Carole. A Study of Certain Early Plays by Lope de Vega. 254 pp. Cambridge, 1972.

"The starting point of the thesis is a detailed analysis of one play which seems representative of virtually all seventy, that is of *El mármol de Felisardo*." (Diss.)

1537. Albarracín Teulón, Agustín. La medicina en el teatro de Lope de Vega. 272 pp. Complutense, 1952.

❖ [A] "La naturaleza humana en el teatro de Lope de Vega." *AIHM* 3 (1951): 475–517. [B] "La patología en el teatro de Lope de Vega." *AIHM* 4 (1952): 407–535. [C] Title as is. Madrid: CSIC, Instituto Arnaldo de Vilanova, 1954. 382 pp. Rev.: K. M. Parker. *BAbr* 30 (1956): 72. [D] "Teatro, sociedad y medicina: La medicina en la obra de Lope de Vega." *BSEHM* 2.3 (1962): [5–11]. [E] "Lope de Vega y el hombre enfermo." *CHA* 54.161–62 (1963): 435–535.

1538. Andrés, Christian. Connaissances et croyances au Siècle d'Or d'après l'œuvre théâtrale de Lope de Vega. xlii+1,724 pp. Paris/X, 1987. (Thèse d'État)

["Es un análisis de la mentalidad y cultura de Lope de Vega, y de su tiempo, en los campos de la medicina, la filosofía y varias creencias, a partir del examen de casi 200 comedias."]

❖ [A] Title as is. Lille: Université de Lille, Service de Reproduction des Thèses, 1987. [B] "Quelques figures d'un bestiaire igné dans la *comedia* de Lope de Vega." *Eidôlon* (Bordeaux) 35 (1988): 155-68. [C] "La Nature de la femme: Aristote, Thomas d'Aquin et l'influence du *Cortesano* dans la *comedia* lopesque." *BH* 91 (1989): 255-77. [The writer cites his dissertation on p. 255, n. 1, and elsewhere.] [D] "Juegos mitológicos y amorosos en el teatro de Lope de Vega." *Crisol* 11 (1990): 13-22. [E] "Grandes mitos clásicos y utilización dramática en el teatro de Lope de Vega." *BCom* 43.1 (1991): 31-49. [F] "Lope de Vega et l'absolutisme royal: Mythe et réalité." *L'Imaginaire de la nation, 1792-1992*. Ed. Claude-Gilbert Dubois. Talence: Presses Universitaires de Bordeaux, 1991. 263-76. [G] "Éléments d'une vision de l'Indien dans le théâtre de Lope de Vega." *Crisol* 16 (1992): 61-68. [H] "Nota sobre lo cómico médico en el teatro de Lope de Vega y de Molière (algunos aspectos comparativos y problema de la fuente)." *Estudios de Investigación Franco-Española* 6 (1992): 91-104. [I] "Aspects du Nouveau Monde dans l'œuvre théâtrale de Lope de Vega et de Tirso de Molina." *Théâtres du Monde: Revue Interdisciplinaire de l'Institut de Recherches Internationales sur les Arts du Spectacle de l'Université d'Avignon* 3 (1993): 23-34. [J] "Aspectos astrológicos en el teatro de Cervantes y Lope de Vega." *Studia aurea: Actas del tercer congreso de la AISO, Toulouse, 1993*. 3 vols. Toulouse-Pamplona: GRISO-LEMSO, 1996. Vol. 2. *Teatro*. Ed. Ignacio Arellano, María del Carmen Pinillos, Frédéric Serralta, and Marc Vitse. 2: 23-31.

1539. Bastianutti, Diego Louis. A Critical Edition of Lope de Vega's *La niñez del Padre Roxas*. 459 pp. Toronto, 1974. *DAI* 37A: 6525-26.

❖ [A] "Autobiographical Elements in Lope de Vega's *La niñez del Padre Roxas*." *BCom* 28 (1976): 43-49. [B] Vega, L. de. *La niñez del Padre Roxas*. Ed. from autograph MS by D. L. Bastianutti. New York: Peter Lang, 1988. 274 pp. (American University Studies 2: Romance Languages and Literature 54.) Rev.: M. McKendrick. *MLR* 86.2 (1991): 495.

1540. BOCSI, JOSEPH PETER. Hungría en el teatro de Lope de Vega. 547 pp. Complutense, 1963.

❖ [A] "Hungría en el teatro de Lope de Vega." *RL* 31.61-62 (1967): 95-103. [B] "Hungría en el teatro de Lope de Vega." *Segismundo* 11.21-22 (1975): 49-60.

1541. BORAO Y CLEMENTE, GERÓNIMO. El amor en el teatro de Lope. Complutense, 1868.

❖ Title as is. Madrid: Rojas, 1868. 57 pp.

1542. BRADBURY, GAIL. A Study and Edition of Lope de Vega's *El mayordomo de la Duquesa de Amalfi.* 329 pp. London/King's College, 1978.

❖ [A] "Lope Plays of Bandello Origin." *FMLS* 16 (1980): 53-65. [*El mayordomo de la Duquesa de Amalfi* is of Bandellian origin.] [B] "Tragedy and Tragicomedy in the Theatre of Lope de Vega." *BHS* 68 (1981): 103-11. [One of the plays studied is *El mayordomo de la Duquesa de Amalfi.*]

1543. BRAUN, DIETER. Die Situationsfunktionen als Elemente der dramatischen Struktur in Lope de Vegas *Fuenteovejuna.* 178 pp. Münster, 1967.

1544. CANONICA DE ROCHEMONTEIX, ELVEZIO. El poliglotismo en el teatro de Lope de Vega. 402 pp. Fribourg, 1991. // Rev.: M. Presotto. *Anuario Lope de Vega* 1 (1995): 248-50.

❖ [A] "Lo spagnolo degli italiani e l'italiano degli spagnoli in alcune commedie del XVI e del XVII secolo." *Nuova Secondaria* 3 (1988): 68-73. [B] "Lenguas en la escena: En torno al poliglotismo en el teatro de Lope de Vega." *Boletín de la Sociedad Suiza de Estudios Hispánicos* 36 (1990): 3-13. [C] Title as is. Kassel: Reichenberger, 1991. 617 pp. (Teatro del Siglo de Oro. Estudios de literatura 11.) Rev.: (a) F. Cazal. *Criticón* 55 (1992): 170-72; (b) L. Vázquez. *EstM* 48.177 (1992): 207; (c) B. Fra-Molinero. *JHP* 16.3 (1992): 341-42; (d) J. Lihani. *BCom* 45.1 (1993): 163-65; (e) J. M. López de Abiada. *Ibero* 38 (1993): 120-22; (f) M. G. Profeti. *RIber* 49 (1994): 52-54; (g) S. B. Whitaker. *Hispanófila* 116 (1996): 97-98. [D] "Del plurilingüismo al bilingüismo: El camino hacia la verosimilitud en las comedias de Torres Naharro." *Estudios de literatura y lingüística españolas: Miscelánea en honor de Luis López Molina.* Ed. Irène Andrés-Suárez, G. Colón

Doménech, A. Lara Pozuelo, and R. Sugranyes de Franch. Lausanne: Sociedad Suiza de Estudios Hispánicos, 1992. 115–29. (Hispanica Helvetica 4.) [E] "Del pecado plurilingüe a la absolución monolingüe: *La farsa del Sacramento, llamada de los lenguajes.*" *Criticón* 66–67 (1996): 369–82. [F] "Lenguas en la escena: El plurilingüismo en el teatro prelopesco." *Studia aurea: Actas del tercer congreso de la AISO, Toulouse, 1993.* 3 vols. Toulouse-Pamplona: GRISO-LEMSO, 1996. Vol. 2. *Teatro.* Ed. Ignacio Arellano, María del Carmen Pinillos, Frédéric Serralta, and Marc Vitse. 2: 109–17.

1545. David, Marcel. Contribution à l'étude du vocabulaire de Lope de Vega. 136 pp. Innsbruck, 1945.

1546. Didier, André. La Légende de Barlaam et Josaphat: Importance historique du thème et la *comedia* de Lope de Vega *Barlaan y Josafat.* 2 vols. (644 pp.) Strasbourg, 1964. (Doctorat d'Université)

1547. Díez Borque, José María. Teatro y sociedad en el siglo XVII: A propósito de la comedia de Lope de Vega. Complutense, 1974. Abstract in *RUCM* 24.100–2 (1975): 66–67.

❖ [A] *Sociología de la comedia española del siglo XVII.* Madrid: Cátedra, 1976. 369 pp. ["Mi estudio está basado en la producción dramática de Lope de Vega, de 1621 a 1635, contando con su teatro anterior. A partir de esta amplia muestra, en el período del reinado de Felipe IV, se generaliza—con las necesarias limitaciones—habida cuenta de que Lope de Vega es el creador de un *modelo* y el dramaturgo que llena los corrales y marca los rumbos de la comedia nacional hasta Calderón."] [B] *Estructura social del Madrid de Lope de Vega.* Madrid: Artes Gráficas Municipales, 1977. 31 pp. [C] *Sociedad y teatro en la España de Lope de Vega.* Barcelona: Bosch, 1978. 304 pp. Rev.: (a) J. Huerta Calvo. *CHA* 350 (1979): 449–54; (b) S. Alonso. *NE* 8 (1979): 96–97; (c) M. G. Profeti. *RIber* 6 (1979): 63–66; (d) A. Porqueras-Mayo. *HR* 48 (1980): 493–96; (e) N. D. Shergold. *MLR* 75 (1980): 427. [D] Vega, L. de. *La villana de Getafe.* Ed. J. M. Díez Borque. Madrid: Orígenes, 1990. 227 pp. + illus.

1548. Entrambasaguas y Peña, Joaquín de. Una guerra literaria del Siglo de Oro (Lope de Vega, Torres Rámila, López de Aguilar,

Suárez de Figueroa, Tamayo de Vargas, etc.). 446 pp. Complutense, 1929.

❖ [A] *Una guerra literaria del Siglo de Oro: Lope de Vega y los preceptistas aristotélicos.* Madrid: Archivos, 1932. 426 pp. Rev.: (a) A. Baig-Baños. *ErudIU* 3 (1932): 657-62; (b) F. C. Sainz de Robles. *RBAM* 9 (1932): 462-64; (c) J. Millé y Giménez. *AUM* 2 (1933): 239-40; (d) E. Buceta. *BAbr* 7 (1933): 481-82. [B] Rpt. in *BRAE* 19-21 (1932-34), various pages. [C] Rpt. with same title, in his *Estudios sobre Lope de Vega.* Madrid: CSIC, 1947. 2 vols; 2nd ed., corrected and expanded. Madrid: CSIC, 1967. [For a more complete list of this scholar's publications, see Joaquín de Entrambasaguas, *Biobibliografía de Joaquín Entrambasaguas y Peña* (Madrid: J. de Entrambasaguas, 1983) 90 pp.]

1549. Felipe de la Torre, E. El personaje negro en las obras de Lope de Rueda y Lope de Vega. Murcia, 1961.

1550. Fernández López, Jaime. Filosofía del honor en el pueblo según los teatros de Lope de Vega y Monzaemon Chikamatsu. 3 vols. Complutense, 1984.

❖ [A] "El honor según la contraposición 'noble-villano' en el teatro de Lope de Vega." *BFFLS* (Sophia University, Tokyo) 19 (1985): 143-72. [B] "Tensión y valores (honor-riqueza) en *La prueba de los amigos* de Lope de Vega." *ALE* 5 (1986-87): 5-112. [C] "Carencia de discreción, causa de deshonra: *El cuerdo en su casa* de Lope de Vega." *Varia hispanica: Homenaje a Alberto Porqueras-Mayo.* Ed. Joseph L. Laurenti and Vern G. Williamsen. Kassel: Reichenberger, 1989. 17-26. (Teatro del Siglo de Oro. Estudios de literatura 5.) [D] "El individualismo como causa de deshonra: *La necedad del discreto* de Lope de Vega." *Actas del décimo congreso de la Asociación Internacional de Hispanistas, Barcelona, 1989.* Ed. Antonio Vilanova. 4 vols. Barcelona: PPU, 1992. 2: 931-37.

1551. Forastieri-Braschi, Eduardo. Aproximación estructural al teatro de Lope de Vega (La honra de los villanos: 1610-1615). 118 pp. San Juan (Puerto Rico), 1975.

❖ [A] "*Fuenteovejuna* y la justificación." *REHc* 2.1-4 (1972): 89-99. [B] Title as is. Madrid: Hispanova, 1976. 188 pp. Rev.: (a) C. Chauchadis. *CMHLB* 30 (1978): 188-91; (b) W. R. Blue. *JHP* 3 (1978): 94-96; (c) S. Ghertman. *BCom* 31 (1979): 77-79.

1552. FOX, ARTHUR MEREDITH. A Critical Edition of the Autograph Manuscript of *El poder en el discreto* by Lope de Vega Carpio, Together with a Subject Index of Illustrative Anecdotes in His *Comedias Novelescas y Costumbristas.* ix+270 pp. Toronto, 1961. Programme, 31 Oct., 1961.

1553. FRÍAS TOMERO, MARÍA DEL CARMEN DE. Los elementos autobiográficos en las comedias de Lope de Vega. 674 pp. Complutense, 1976. Abstract in *RUCM* 25.106-2 (Nov.-Dec. 1976): 171-73; *MEC. Tesis doctorales* 290 (anexo 1976-77): 114.

1554. GARCÍA SÁNCHEZ, MARÍA CONCEPCIÓN. Edición y estudio de *Carlos el perseguido,* de Lope de Vega. 434 pp. Granada, 1989.

❖ [A] Carlos el perseguido *de Lope de Vega: Estudio y edición.* Granada: Universidad de Granada, Servicio de Publicaciones, 1990. 7 microfiches. [B] "Antecedentes de *Carlos el perseguido,* comedia de Lope de Vega." *RILCE* 7 (1991): 50-61.

1555. HAMILTON, JOHN WARD. Lope de Vega: Dos obras de tema americano. [1]+liii+220 pp. Salamanca, 1960.

[The two plays are *El Brasil restituido* and *La Araucana.*]

❖ [A] "América en las obras de Calderón de la Barca." *ALM* 6 (1966-67): 213-15. [B] "Las relaciones personales de Lope de Vega con el Nuevo Mundo." *RomN* 8.2 (1967): 260-65. [C] Title as is. Auburn: Auburn Univ., 1968. 178 pp.

1556. HENNIGS, JOHANN AUGUST JULIUS WILHELM. Studien zu Lope de Vega Carpio: Eine Klassifikation seiner *Comedias.* Göttingen, 1890.

❖ [A] Title as is. Göttingen: Dieterich, 1891. 105 pp. [B] Title as is. Göttingen: Vandenhoeck und Ruprecht, 1891. 105 pp. Rev.: (a) Anon. *DLZ* 13 (1891): 662-63; (b) A. L. Stiefel. *LGRP* 12 (1891): 277-79; (c) H. A. Rennert. *MLN* 6 (1891): col. 433-35; (d) G. Steffens. *RCHLP* ns 32 (1891): 83-84.

1557. HESELER, MARIA. Studien zur Figur des *Gracioso* bei Lope de Vega und Vorgängern. Göttingen, 1934.

❖ Title as is. Hildesheim: Borgmeyer, 1933. 132 pp. [The predecessors studied are Plautus, Terence, Ariosto, and Aretino.] Rev.: (a) G. Cirot. *BH* 37.3 (1935): 410-11; (b) W. C. Atkinson. *MLR* 30 (1935): 560-61; (c) E. Glässer. *LGRP* 57 (1936): col. 340-44; (d) E. Seifert. *ZRP* 59 (1939): 124-25.

1558. Hoock, Helga. Lope de Vegas *Fuente Ovejuna* als Kunstwerk. 225 pp. Würzburg, 1963.

1559. Jörder, Otto. Die Formen des Sonetts bei Lope de Vega. x+ 372 pp. Freiburg, 1936.

❖ Title as is. Halle: Niemeyer, 1936. 372 pp. (Zeitschrift für romanische Philologie, Beiheft 86.) [The writer includes sonnets from Lope's plays. There is an index of 1,587 *sonetos*.] Rev.: G. Cirot. *BH* 39.3 (1937): 276-77.

1560. Klausner, Gertrud. *Die drei Diamanten* des Lope de Vega und die Magelonen Sage. Berlin, 1907.

❖ [A] Title as is. Dessau: Gutenberg, 1907. 178 pp. [B] *Die drei Diamanten* des Lope de Vega und die schöne Magelone. Berlin: Felber, 1909. 178 pp. (Literarhistorische Forschungen 39) Rev.: (a) A. Ludwig. *Archiv* 123 (1909): 220-22; (b) W. von Wurzbach. *LGRP* 30 (1909): col. 237-39; (c) Anon. *KJrP* 12 (1909-10): part 2, p. 366; (d) P. A. Becker. *DLZ* 31 (1910): col. 2666-67. [C] Rpt. Nendeln, Liechtenstein: Kraus, 1977.

1561. Kouassi, Gogo. La Pureté de sang dans la *comedia* lopesque. 332 pp. Montpellier/III, 1979. (Thèse de 3e cycle)

1562. Labib, Gisela Reupcke. Der Maure in dem dramatischen Werk Lope de Vega's. Ein Beitrag zu dem Problem: Der Maure, eine literarisch stilisierte Fiktion oder historische Wirklichkeit? Hamburg, 1962.

❖ Title as is. Hamburg: n.p., 1961. 334 pp. [The index lists some 320 *comedias* of Lope.] Rev.: (a) J. M. Díez Taboada. *RL* 25 (1964): 228; (b) J. M. Díez Taboada. *Segismundo* 1 (1965): 155-57.

1563. León, Isidoro M. La leyenda de Bernardo del Carpio en el teatro de Lope de Vega. 328 pp. Complutense, 1932. [H. Serís lists this dissertation in his *Manual de bibliografía de la literatura española* under the name I. M. Levy; see Serís no. 3353.]

1564. Ludwig, (Karl) Albert. Lope de Vegas Dramen aus dem karolingischen Sagenkreise. 60 pp. Berlin, 1898.

❖ [A] Title as is. Berlin: Mayer & Müller, 1898. 155 pp. [The writer examines the following plays: *Los palacios de Galiana, La mocedad de Roldán, Las pobrezas de Reinaldos, Angélica en el Catay, El marqués de Mantua, El casamiento en la muerte,* and *Melisendra*.] Rev.:

(a) Anon. *LitZent* 49 (1898): 910-11; (b) G. Paris. *Romania* 27 (1898): 524-25; (c) A. Farinelli. *Archiv* 102 (1899): 446-60; (d) W. von Wurzbach. *ZVL* 13 (1899): 408-10; (e) Anon. *RCHLP* ns 51 (1901): 36-37. [B] "Lope de Vega als Schüler Ariosts." *Festschrift Adolf Tobler zum siebzigste Geburtstage dargebracht von der Berliner Gesellschaft für das Studium der neueren Sprachen*. Braunschweig: Westermann, 1905. 241-62. Festschrift rpt. Genève: Slatkine, 1978. [Apropos two of Lope's "Carolingian" *comedias: Los celos de Rodamonte* and *El premio de la hermosura*.]

1565. LY, NADINE. L'Affrontement interlocutif dans le théâtre de Lope de Vega: Systèmes internes et contraintes socio-linguistiques et littéraires. 2 vols. (712 pp.) Bordeaux/III, 1978. (Thèse d'État)

❖ [A] Title as is. Lille: Université de Lille, Service de Reproduction des Thèses, 1981. 712 pp. Rev.: E. Arnaud. *Criticón* 18 (1982): 109-16. [B] *La Poétique de l'interlocution dans le théâtre de Lope de Vega*. Bordeaux: Université de Bordeaux, 1982. 363 pp. [Abbreviated version of dissertation.] [C] "Le Rapport interlocutif à l'interieur de la *comedia* de Lope de Vega: Ses implications sociologiques et idéologiques." *L'Idéologique dans le texte (textes hispaniques)*. Toulouse: Université de Toulouse-Le Mirail, 1984. 25-33. [D] "La Diction de l'amour dans la *comedia El perro del hortelano* de Lope de Vega." *BH* 92.1 (1990): 493-547.

1566. MACARTHUR, DONALD EDWIN. A Critical Edition with Introduction and Notes of Lope de Vega's *Castelvines y Monteses*. Cambridge, 1978.

1567. MCARDLE LANAHAN, KATHRYN MARY. El elemento religioso en la obra dramática profana de Lope de Vega. 555 pp. Complutense, 1967. Abstract in *RUM* 17.65-68 (1968): 39-40.

1568. MOLINA MARÍN, DIEGO. La intriga secundaria en la técnica dramática de Lope de Vega. 265 pp. Toronto, 1956.

❖ [A] "Técnica de la intriga secundaria en Lope de Vega." *H*[AATSP] 38 (1955): 272-75. [B] "Carácter y función de la intriga secundaria en el teatro de Lope de Vega." *Hispanófila* 1 (1957): 41-51. [C] *La intriga secundaria en el teatro de Lope de Vega*. México: De Andrea; Toronto: U of Toronto P, 1958. 197 pp. (Colección Studium 22.) Rev.: (a) E. Segura Covarsí. *Arbor* 165-66 (1959): 608-10; (b) R. Minian de Alfié. *Filología* 6 (1960):

129-31; (c) R. M. Hornedo. *RyF* 758 (1961): 324-25; (d) J. E. Varey. *BHS* 44 (1967): 61-65. [D] "On the Dramatic Function of Versification in Lope de Vega." *TA* 19 (1962): 27-42. [E] *Uso y función de la versificación dramática en Lope de Vega.* Valencia: Castalia, 1962. 120 pp. (Estudios de Hispanófila 2.) [F] 2nd ed. Garden City: Adelphi Univ., 1968. 120 pp. (Estudios de Hispanófila 2.)

1569. MONGE CASAO, TADEO FÉLIX. Estudios sobre sintaxis y estilística del Siglo de Oro: Determinación lingüística y literaria de la *Dorotea.* 378 pp. Complutense, 1949.

❖ [A] "*La Dorotea* de Lope de Vega." *VR* 16 (1957): 60-145. [B] "Celestina: La seducción y el lenguaje." *Orbis Mediaevalis: Mélanges de langue et de littérature médiévales offerts à Reto Raduolf Bezzola à l'occasion de son quatre-vingtième anniversaire.* Ed. Georges Güntert, Marc-René Jung, and Kurt Ringger. Bern: Francke, 1978. 269-80. [Compares Celestina and Lope's Gerarda.] [C] "'Literatura' y erudición en *La Dorotea.*" *Homenaje a José Manuel Blecua, ofrecido por sus discípulos, colegas y amigos.* Madrid: Gredos, 1983. 449-63. [D] El tipo celestinesco en la literatura clásica española: Discurso de ingreso leído por el académico electo M. I. Sr. D. Félix Monge Casao en su recepción académica y contestación al mismo por la académica numeraria M. I. Sra. Dña. Aurora Egido Martínez. Zaragoza: Real Academia de Nobles y Bellas Artes de San Luis, 1993. 38 pp. [Gerarda in *La Dorotea* is a famous Celestinesque type.] [For a more complete list of this scholar's publications, see "Bibliografía de Félix Monge," *Homenaje a Félix Monge: Estudios de lingüística hispánica* (Madrid: Gredos, 1995) 17-20.]

1570. MORAGÓN Y MAESTRE, MANUEL. La mitología en la obra de Lope de Vega. 408 pp. Complutense, 1948.

1571. MÜLLER, GERD F. Studien zum hagiographischen Theater Lope de Vegas: Exemplarische Interpretation von sechs *Comedias de Vidas de Santos.* 178 pp. Cologne, 1970.

[The six plays are: *La niñez del Padre Rojas, El Cardenal de Belén, Lo fingido verdadero, La gran columna fogosa: San Basilio Magno, El Hamete de Toledo,* and *San Isidro Labrador de Madrid.*]

❖ "*Sabiduría,* heilsgeschichtliche Metaphorik und Mariologie in einer *Comedia* von Lope de Vega." *Ibero* ns 1 (1974): 81-93. [In *La niñez del Padre Rojas*.]

1572. NIEMEYER, HELGA. *El alcalde de Zalamea,* oder die Kunst der *Comedia:* Untersuchungen zu Lope de Vegas Theaterstück und vergleichende Betrachtung der Calderónschen *Alcalde*-Version. Paderborn, 1990(?).

   [For the complete entry, see no. 1306.]

1573. NOGUER, VICTOR JAMES H. F. La valoración estética y literaria del teatro de Lope de Vega. Complutense, 1966. Abstract in *RUM* 15.57-60 (1966): 58-59.

1574. ODOUL, PIERRE. Sur quelques aspects de *Don Quichotte* concernant la polémique Lope de Vega-Cervantes. 513 pp. Montpellier/III, 1983. (Thèse de 3e cycle) // Rev.: A. Sánchez. *ACer* 23 (1985): 263-64.

1575. OPPENHEIMER, RUTH ANNELISE. *Santiago el Verde,* eine *Comedia* von Lope de Vega Carpio, zum ersten Mal nach der Handschrift des Britischen Museums kritisch herausgegeben mit einer Studie und Anmerkungen. Hamburg, 1938.

   ❖ [A] Title as is. Hamburg: Preilipper, 1938. 198 pp. Rev.: (a) W. L. Fichter. *HR* 7 (1939): 357-59; (b) J. A. Tamayo. *RFE* 24 (1940 for 1937): 414-18. [B] 2nd ed. Madrid: CSIC, 1940. 220 pp. (Teatro Antiguo Español 9.) Rev.: (a) J. A. Tamayo. *RBAM* 13 (1944): 231-33; (b) W. L. Fichter. *HR* 12 (1944): 273-74.

1576. PÉREZ, MARCEL GÉRARD. *El arenal de Sevilla:* Édition critique avec introduction et notes. 240 pp. Paris/X, 1973. (Thèse de 3e cycle)

1577. RAMÍREZ DE ARELLANO RECHANI, DIANA. La comedia genealógica en Lope de Vega: Edición crítica de *Los Ramírez de Arellano.* 462 pp. Complutense, 1952. Abstract in *RUM* 1.2 (1952): 310-11.

   ❖ Vega L. de. Los Ramírez de Arellano *de Lope de Vega: Contribución al estudio de las comedias genealógicas de Lope de Vega.* Ed. D. Ramírez de Arellano. Madrid: CSIC, Instituto de Estudios Madrileños, 1954. 298 pp. Rev.: (a) E. Catena de Vindel. *RL* 6.11-12 (1954): 419-21; (b) A. Carballo Picazo. *Clavileño* 6.32 (1955): 73-74.

1578. RAMÍREZ Y LA GUARDIA, LUIS. Causas fundamentales que determinan la existencia del teatro español: Desenvolvimiento del mismo durante el siglo XVI, y significación de Lope de Vega. Complutense, 1867.

❖ Title as is. Madrid: Rivadeneyra, 1868. 64 pp.

1579. RIVAS ESQUIVEL, MARÍA ARANDA. Recherches sur la dramaturgie de Lope de Vega: Approche théorique de la *comedia* lopesque dans ses figures permanentes et ses structures variables. Paris/IV, 1988. (Thèse d'État)

❖ [A] "Faveur et disgrâce dans *El perro del hortelano* de Lope de Vega." *Mélanges offerts à Maurice Molho.* Ed. Jean Claude Chevalier and M.-F. Delport. 3 vols. Paris: Éditions Hispaniques, [1987]-1988. 1: 527-36. [B] "*El perro del hortelano* ou Tristan l'enfanteur." *LLNL* 275 (1990): 23-36. [C] Aranda, María. *Le Galant et son double: Approche théorique du théâtre de Lope de Vega dans ses figures permanentes et ses structures variables.* Toulouse: Presses Universitaires du Mirail, 1995. 290 pp.

1580. RIVAS ESQUIVEL, MARÍA ARANDA. Recherches sur la structure de trois *comedias* de Lope de Vega: *El castigo sin venganza, El duque de Viseo,* et *El caballero de Olmedo.* 257 p. Paris/IV, 1981. (Thèse de 3e cycle)

1581. RODRÍGUEZ BALTANÁS, ENRIQUE J. Lope de Vega y el problema de la tragedia en el teatro español del Siglo de Oro. 2 vols. (1-450, 452-1,001 pp.) Seville, 1986.

❖ [A] Vega, L. de. *Fuente Ovejuna.* Barcelona: Laia, 1984. 117 pp. (Guías Laia de literatura 9.) [See "*Fuente Ovejuna,* tragedia," pp. 92-95.] [B] "Amor, honor y poder: Tres valores renacentistas en el teatro trágico de Lope de Vega." *BCom* 43.1 (1991): 51-69.

1582. ROSADO GIL, GABRIEL. La fábula de tipo esópico en el teatro de Lope de Vega: Estudio de un aspecto de su técnica dramática. 531 pp. Salamanca, 1969.

❖ "Observaciones sobre las fuentes de dos comedias de Lope de Vega: *El esclavo de Roma* y *Lo que ha de ser.*" *BCom* 24.2 (1972): 25-30. [The action of these two plays "está montada sobre sendas fábulas de tipo esópico."]

1583. ROZIK, ELYAHU. Figurative Elements in the Spanish Poetic Drama of Lope de Vega, Calderón, [and] Federico García Lorca. [Text in Hebrew.] 470 pp. Jerusalem, 1973.

1584. Ruser, Wilhelm. *Roma abrasada*—ein echtes Jugenddrama. Würzburg, 1928.

❖ "*Roma abrasada*—ein echtes Jugenddrama: Eine Studie zu Lope de Vega." *RH* 72 (1928): 325-411.

1585. Sales de Expósito, Louise. El religioso, personaje del teatro de Lope de Vega y su escuela. 711 pp. Complutense, 1975. Abstract in *RUCM* 24.100-2 (Nov.-Dec. 1975): 79-80.

1586. Salomon, Noël. Recherches sur le thème paysan dans la *comedia* au temps de Lope de Vega. Paris, 1959. (Thèse d'État)

❖ [A] Title as is. Bordeaux: Université de Bordeaux, Institut d'Études Ibériques et Ibéro-Américaines; Féret, 1965. 946 pp. Rev.: (a) J. Rodríguez Puértolas. *Atenea* (Chile) 44.417 (1967): 215-24; (b) M. Tuñón de Lara. *CA* 26.2 (1967): 156-77; (c) A. Gil Novales. *CHA* 72 (1967): 226-33; (d) F. López Estrada. *RFE* 49 (1968 for 1964): 365-85; (e) J. Pérez. *BH* 70 (1968): 458-67; (f) M. Horányi. *ALitASH* 11 (1969): 427-29; (g) J. Rodríguez Puértolas. *EEsc* 13 (1969): 35-57; (h) E. Müller-Bochat. *RJ* 20 (1969): 371-76; (i) P. Ponsot. *AÉSC* 25 (1970): 1400-02; (j) S. Maurel. *NRFH* 19 (1970): 160-64. [B] "Pour une sociologie de la 'comedia' lopesque: Recherche d'un 'modele.'" *TS* 4 (1983?): 41-59. [C] Versión española: *Lo villano en el teatro del Siglo de Oro.* Trans. Beatriz Chenot. Madrid: Castalia, 1985. 773 pp. Rev.: (a) Anon. *LSECL* 40 (1985): 28; (b) J. B. Spieker. *HisJ* 8.1 (1986): 194-95; (c) D. Altamiranda. *Incipit* 6 (1986): 220-22. [For a more complete list of this scholar's publications, see *Hommage des hispanistes français à Noël Salomon: Publié par les soins de la Société des Hispanistes Français* (Barcelona: Laia, 1979) 7-9.]

1587. Sánchez Mariño, Rafael. Alonso Pérez de Montalbán y su importancia en el círculo literario de Lope de Vega. 243 pp. Complutense, 1955.

[Father of Juan Pérez de Montalbán.]

❖ "Sobre Alonso Pérez de Montalbán y el falso *Quijote.*" *ACer* 5 (1955-56): 274-75. [". . . doy aquí algunas notas sacadas de mi . . . tesis doctoral leída en el año 1955."]

1588. Scheid, Sibylle. Petrarkismus in Lope de Vegas Sonetten. Cologne, 1966.

❖ Title as is. Wiesbaden: Steiner, 1965. 123 pp. (Untersuchungen zur Sprach- und Literaturgeschichte der romanischen Völker 4.) [Lope's theater is included in the writer's analysis.] Rev.: (a) H. Gillessen. *RF* 78 (1966): 493–94; (b) L. Abicht. *Erasmus* 19 (1967): 660–61; (c) B. König. *RJ* 18 (1967): 374–77; (d) M. Franzbach. *Arcadia* 3 (1968): 205–07.

1589. SCHÜLER, GERDA. Die Rezeption der spanischen *Comedia* in Frankreich in der ersten Hälfte des 17. Jahrhunderts: Lope de Vega und Jean Rotrou. 151 pp. Cologne, 1966.

❖ "L'Honneur de Dom Juan." *Estudios de literatura española y francesa: Siglos XVI y XVII. Homenaje a Horst Baader.* Ed. Frauke Gewecke. Barcelona: Hogar del Libro, 1984. 123–30.

1590. SCHULTE-HERBRÜGGEN, HEINZ. Studien zu Lope de Vega's Gotendramen. 119 pp. Würzburg, 1943.

[Apropos *El último godo* and *El rey Bamba.*]

❖ "El arte dramático de Lope de Vega: Estudios críticos." *AUC* 108.80 (1950): 5–94.

1591. SLOMAN, ALBERT EDWARD. The Sources of Calderón's *Príncipe constante:* With a Critical Edition of Its Immediate Source, *La fortuna adversa del infante don Fernando de Portugal* (a Play Attributed to Lope de Vega) and a Study of Moorish Jargon. xv+144+ 24+13 pp. Oxford, 1948.

[For the complete entry, see no. 1323. Of the eight source plays discussed in the writer's *The Dramatic Craftmanship of Calderón: His Use of Earlier Plays* (Oxford: Dolphin, 1958; rpt. 1968), three are attributed to Lope de Vega: *El médico de su honra, El alcalde de Zalamea,* and *La fortuna adversa del infante don Fernando de Portugal.*]

1592. SPECHT, GERTRAUD. Die Darstellung der Familie in den Dramen von Lope de Vega und Calderón. 134 pp. Munich, 1957.

1593. STEFFENS, GEORG FERDINAND RICHARD. Rotrou-Studien. Vol. 1: Jean de Rotrou als Nachahmer Lope de Vega's. Göttingen, 1890.

❖ Title as is. Oppeln: Franck, 1891. 104 pp. Rev.: (a) H. A. Rennert. *MLN* 8 (1893): col. 305–08; (b) A. L. Stiefel. *ZFSL* 15 (1893): Zweite Hälfte, Referate und Rezensionen, 35–40;

1594. TIETZE, MARIA. Lope de Vega und Amarilis. Würzburg, 1926.

❖ [A] Title as is. Halle: Karras, Kröber, Nietschmann, 1926. 46 pp. [B] *ZRP* 46 (1926): 165–210.

[Amarilis was Marta de Nevares (d. 1632), "the last great love" of Lope.]

1595. Villegas, Jean-Claude. Le "Matasanos," tradition burlesque et invention au Siècle d'Or: Étude du médecin chez Quevedo et Lope de Vega. Bordeaux/III, 1982.

1596. Wagner, Klaus. Lope de Vega Carpio. *Comedia famosa de dineros son calidad:* Textkritische und literarhistorische Untersuchungen. 272 pp. Mainz, 1964.

[In the dissertation the writer offers a parallel edition of BNM MS 16.924 and the text in *Parte 24* (Zaragoza, 1633) with variants from other sources.]

❖ Title as is. Wiesbaden: Steiner, 1966. 272 pp. (Mainzer romanistische Arbeiten 5.) Rev.: (a) O. T. Myers. *Erasmus* 20 (1968): 415–17; (b) M. Engelbert. *RJ* 19 (1968): 356–64.

1597. Wehmeyer, Maria-Ingeborg. Studien zum spanischen Volkscharakter nach Lope de Vega. 128 pp. Hamburg, 1962.

1598. Zabala López, Arturo. Valencia en la vida y en la obra de Lope de Vega. 429 pp. Complutense, 1944. Abstract in *Sumarios y extractos, Historia* (1939–44): 331–36.

❖ [A] "Rastros léxicos del valenciano en la obra de Lope de Vega." [In *El bobo del colegio* and *El hijo pródigo*.] *Mediterráneo* 5 (1944): 37–48. [B] "Alusión de Lope de Vega a unos supuestos amores valencianos." *Estudios dedicados a Menéndez Pidal.* Ed. Rafael de Balbín Lucas. 7 vols in 8. Madrid: CSIC, 1950–62. (1956) 6: 591–609. [C] "Lope de Vega y Valencia." *ABC,* 8 Apr. 1962, unnumbered. (See special issue of *ABC* of the same date, dedicated to Lope de Vega.) [D] "Sobre la primitiva Casa de la Olivera (dos documentos para la historia del teatro en Valencia)." *Homenaje al Dr. Juan Reglá Campistol.* 2 vols. Valencia: Universidad de Valencia, 1975. 1: 427–35. [E] *El teatro en la Valencia de finales del siglo XVIII.* Madrid: CSIC, 1982. 472 pp. (Estudios universitarios 7.) [F] "El decorado verbal y otras observaciones en y sobre las comedias valencianas de Lope de Vega." *Comedias y comediantes: Estudios sobre el teatro clásico español. Actas del congreso internacional sobre teatro y prácticas escénicas en los siglos XVI y XVII, Valencia, 1989.* Ed. Manuel V. Diago and Teresa Ferrer. Valencia: Universitat de València, 1991. 143–61.

Vélez de Guevara, Luis (1579–1644)

1599. Ahrens, Theodor G[eorge]. Zur Charakteristik des spanischen Dramas im Anfang des XVII. Jahrhunderts. (Luis Vélez de Guevara und Mira de Mescua.) Halle, 1911.

[For the complete entry, see no. 1428.]

1600. Herzog, Werner. Vélez de Guevara: *Comedia famosa del Rey don Sebastián.* Zürich, 1971.

❖ Title as is. Madrid: Real Academia Española, 1972. 169 pp.

[The critical edition is based on BNM MS 15.291 and the printed text in Adolph Schaeffer's *tomo antiguo.* For commentaries, see M. G. Profeti, "L. Vélez de Guevara e l'esercizio ecdotico," *QLL* 5 (1980): 49–94 (specifically pp. 63–70); and Hauer, "Addendum," no. 29.]

1601. Monahan, Caroline. A Critical Edition of Luis Vélez de Guevara's *Los hijos de la barbuda.* 271 pp. London/Westfield College, 1974. For commentaries, see M. G. Profeti, "L. Vélez de Guevara e l'esercizio ecdotico," *QLL* 5 (1980): 49–94 [specifically pp. 88–89]; and Hauer, "Addendum," no. 43.

❖ "The Transmission of the Text of Luis Vélez' *Los hijos de la Barbuda.*" *Library* 33.2 (1978): 153–57.

1602. Rodríguez Cepeda, Enrique. *La serrana de la Vera* y Luis Vélez de Guevara. 13+270+[8] pp. Complutense, 1967. Abstract in *RUM* 16.61-64 (1967): 44.

❖ [A] Vélez de Guevara, L. *La serrana de la Vera.* Study and ed. by E. Rodríguez Cepeda. Madrid: Alcalá, 1966. 165 pp. (Colección Aula Magna 9.) [This edition is based on that of Ramón Menéndez Pidal and María Goyri de Menéndez Pidal (Madrid, 1916).] Rev.: E. Rull. *Segismundo* 2.4 (1966): 390–92. [B] "Sentido de los personajes en *La serrana de la Vera.*" *Segismundo* 9.17–18 (1973): 165–96. [C] "Fuentes y relaciones de *La serrana de la Vera.*" *NRFH* 23 (1974): 100–101. [D] "Consideraciones sobre Vélez de Guevara." *Mester* 5.2 (1975): 112–22. [E] "Para la fecha de *La serrana de la Vera.*" *BCom* 27.1 (1975): 19–26. [F] "Temática y pueblo en *La serrana de la Vera.*" *ExTL* 4 (1975–76): 169–75. [G] Rev. ed. of *La serrana.* Madrid: Cátedra, 1982. 205 pp. (Letras hispánicas 166.) Rev.: J. M. Ruano. *RCEH* 9 (1985): 295–96.

1603. SITO ALBA, MANUEL. Lo hispánico en *La Reine morte,* de Henry de Montherlant: Análisis comparado con *Reinar después de morir,* de Vélez de Guevara. 3 vols. (1,005 pp.) Complutense, 1973. Abstract in *RUCM* 22.88-2 (1973): 102-03.

[The person who will reign after death is Inés de Castro.]

❖ [A] "Notas metodológicas sobre la leyenda de Pedro e Inés de Castro." *Arbor* 98.383 (1977): 185-98. [B] "Diatopía y diacronía de un título teatral: De la *Castro* de Ferreira a *La Reine morte* de Montherlant." *SpM* 9 (1978): 18-34. [C] *Montherlant et l'Espagne: Les sources hispaniques de* La Reine morte. Paris: Klincksieck, 1978. 179 pp. Rev.: (a) L. A. Cuenca. *Gaceta* 342 (1978): 652-56; (b) J. Casalduero. *Ínsula* 383 (1978): 4; (c) F. Meregalli. *RIber* 3 (1978): 55-56; (d) P. Vecchi. *SpM* 9 (1978): 199-200; (e) L. Fiorentino. *Ausonia* 34 (1979): 87-88; (f) M. Villar. *NE* 9-10 (1979): 125; (g) J. M. Díez Borque. *CILH* 2-3 (1980): 520-22; (h) F. P. Bowman. *HR* 48 (1980): 254-55; (i) M. García de la Torre. *RL* 42.83 (1980): 244-45; (j) E. Aragone Terni. *RLMC* 33 (1980): 318-19; (k) T. Stefanovics. *Ibero* 13 (1981): 117-18. [D] "El monarca ideal y real a través de una doble lectura de *Reinar después de morir.*" *Actas del coloquio (Roma, 1978): Teoría y realidad en el teatro español del siglo XVII. La influencia italiana.* Roma: Instituto Español de Cultura y de Literatura, 1981. 147-70. [E] "Tiempo dramático/Tiempo real: Notas sobre la primera jornada de *Reinar después de morir.*" *Studia Philologica in Honorem M. Batllori.* Roma: Instituto Español de Cultura, 1984. 11-24; rpt. in M. Sito Alba. *Análisis de la semiótica teatral.* Madrid: UNED, 1987. 155-78.

1604. VASSEROT LIMINANA, NOELLE. Édition critique de *La mayor desgracia de Carlos V y jornada de Argel,* pièce attribuée à Luis Vélez de Guevara. Aix-en-Provence, 1986.

1605. ZEBINA, HÉCTOR. Trois *comedias* de Luis Vélez de Guevara: Édition critique, introduction et notes. cii+201 pp. Poitiers, 1971. (Thèse de 3e cycle)

VICENTE, GIL (PORTUGAL. 1460?-1536?)

1606. CORNIL, SUZANNE. C'est de *La Célestine* que s'est inspiré Gil

Vicente pour le personnage de Brigida Vas, dans l'*Auto da Barca do Inferno*. Brussels, 1946-47. (Thèse annexe)

1607. D'ANS, A. Contribution à la connaissance de l'œuvre théâtrale de Gil Vicente. Liège, 1960.

[Stathatos 56 (no. 248) lists this title with the notation "not seen." The Université de Liège "ne possède pas la thèse," according to a 1995 letter from that institution to the compilers of this volume.]

1608. KLEIMAN, OLINDA. Richesse et pauvreté dans l'œuvre de Gil Vicente: Expression et interpretation. Paris/IV, 1988. (Doctorat de Nouveau Régime)

1609. KÖHLER, RUDOLF. Der Einfluß Gil Vicentes auf das spanische Theater des Goldenen Zeitalters. 312 pp. Göttingen, 1968. // Rev.: C. Stern *HR* 40 (1972): 220-22.

1610. PECH, MARIE-CLAUDE. La Poésie lyrique castillane dans le théâtre de Gil Vicente. 119 pp. Toulouse, 1967.

[Stathatos 59 (no. 276) lists this "dissertation" with the notation "not seen." A 1995 letter from the Université de Toulouse to the compilers of this volume reports that the study is a "tesina de licenciatura."]

1611. SARAIVA, ANTÓNIO JOSÉ. Gil Vicente e o fim do teatro medieval. Lisbon, 1943.

❖ [A] Title as is. Lisboa: A. J. Saraiva, 1942. 134 pp. Rev.: (a) D. M. Gomes dos Santos. *Brotéria* 38 (1944): 308-18; (b) Ch. V. Aubrun. *BH* 49.3-4 (1947): 467-68; (c) M. Bataillon. *RLC* 22 (1948): 135-39. [B] "Gil Vicente, reflexo da crise." In his *História da cultura em Portugal.* Lisboa: Jornal do Fôro, 1953. 2: 231-368. [C] *Teatro de Gil Vicente.* Ed. A. J. Saraiva. Lisboa: Portugália, 1959. 396 pp. [Rpt. 1963, 1967, 1968.] Rev.: F. S. *Ocidente* 57 (1959): 223. [D] Title as is. 2nd ed. Lisboa: Europa-América, 1965. 213 pp. (Coleção estudos e documentos.) Rev.: (a) J. Mendes. *Brotéria* 82 (1966): 676-83; (b) G. M. Moser. *H* [AATSP] 49 (1966): 886; (c) O. Aguiar. *Rumo* 110 (1966): 314-15.] [E] Title as is. 3rd ed. Lisboa: Europa-América, 1970. 213 pp. [F] "Estética dos *autos de devoção.*" In his *Poesia e drama: Bernardim Ribeiro. Gil Vicente. Cantigas de Amigo.* Lisboa: Gradiva, 1990. 145-78. [This essay was originally published in *Revista da Facul-*

dade de Letras (Universidade de Lisboa) 5 (1938): 272–98.] [G] Title as is. 4th ed. Lisboa: Gradiva, 1992.

1612. Teyssier, Paul. Dictionnaire de la langue de Gil Vicente. 804 pp. Paris, 1956. (Thèse complémentaire)

1613. Teyssier, Paul. La Langue de Gil Vicente. Paris, 1956. (Thèse d'État)

❖ [A] Title as is. Paris: Klincksieck, 1959. 554 pp. Rev.: (a) L. Stegagno Picchio. *CN* 19 (1959): 265–74; (b) H. Kröll. *RJ* 11 (1960): 418–22; (c) T. P. Waldron. *BHS* 38 (1961): 247–49; (d) F. Weber de Kurlat. *Filología* 7 (1961): 211–18; (e) C. Stern. *HR* 29 (1961): 269–73; (f) T. R. Hart. *MLN* 76 (1961): 181–85; (g) P. Pohl. *RF* 73 (1961): 441–45; (h) A. J. da Costa Pimpâo. *RHLP* 1 (1962): 322–29; (i) L. Sletsjoe. *SN* 34 (1962): 187–92; (j) J. J. Montes G. *Thesaurus* 18 (1963): 511–15; (k) J. G. Herculano de Carvalho. *RPh* 17 (1963–64): 809–13. [B] *Romagem d'agravados.* Ed. P. Teyssier. Paris: Éditions Hispaniques, 1975. 147 pp. [C] *Gil Vicente—o autor e a obra.* Lisboa: ICALP, 1982. 177 pp. (Biblioteca breve 67.) [D] "Normes pour une édition critique des œuvres de Gil Vicente." *Actes du colloque international de critique textuelle portugaise, Paris, 1981.* Paris: Fondation Calouste Gulbenkian, Centre Culturel Portugais, 1986. 123–30. [E] "L'Envers de l'épopée." *Critique: Revue Générale des Publications Françaises et Étrangéres* 44.495–96 (1988): 676–83. [Apropos *Auto da India.*] [F] "A língua de Gil Vicente e os dicionários de Jerónimo Cardoso." *Memórias da Academia das Ciências de Lisboa: Classe de Letras* 27 (1988): 199–206. [For a more complete list of this scholar's publications, see *Arquivos* 23 (1987): xvii–xxi. Special issue entitled *Homenagem à Paul Teyssier.*]

Villaizán, Jerónimo de (1604–1633?)

1614. Inserni, Frank M. Vida y obra de Jerónimo de Villaizán y edición crítica y anotada de *A gran daño gran remedio.* xlviii+164 pp. Complutense, 1955.

❖ Title as is. Barcelona: Rumbos, 1960. 155 pp.

1615. José Prades, Juana de. Aportación al estudio de la teoría literaria y bibliografía de los dramaturgos menores pertenecientes al ciclo dramático de Lope de Vega. vii+400 pp. Complutense, 1960. Abstract in *RUM* 10.40 (1961): 852.

[For the complete entry, see no. 1148.]

Zamora, Antonio de (1664?–1728?)

1616. Manning, Margaret. Estudio biográfico y bibliográfico de D. Antonio de Zamora. 2 vols. (327, 328). Complutense, 1972. Listed in *RUM* 21.84-2 (1972): 111.

Index of Institutions
Índice de instituciones

Index of Dissertation Writers and Directors

Índice de autores y directores de tesis

Subject and Title Index

Índice de materias y títulos

Items in **boldface** type refer to major writers and themes under which the dissertations are grouped.

About the Authors

Acerca de los autores

John J. Reynolds received his BA, MA, and PhD degrees at the University of California, Berkeley. Following four years as a teaching assistant at Berkeley, he taught for ten years at the University of Arizona, Tucson. From 1960 until his retirement in 1989, Reynolds taught graduate and undergraduate courses at Saint John's University, New York. His area of expertise is Golden Age drama, and for over ten years he was cocompiler of the "Bibliography on the *Comedia*," which appears once a year in the *Bulletin of the Comediantes,* a journal devoted to this field. In addition, he has published studies and reviews, mainly on Peninsular Spanish literature of the sixteenth and seventeenth centuries, in the *Bulletin of the Comediantes, Estudios, Hispania, Hispanic Journal, Hispanófila, Journal of Hispanic Philology, Modern Language Notes, Modern Language Studies, Renaissance Quarterly,* and *Romance Notes.* Reynolds's book *Juan Timoneda* was published by G. K. Hall in 1975 in the Twayne's World Authors Series.

Szilvia E. Szmuk earned her PhD in Spanish literature at the Graduate Center, City University of New York, and a BA and MA in Spanish literature and a master's in library science at Queens College. Szmuk's special interests are eighteenth-century Spanish printing, specifically *comedias sueltas,* and descriptive bibliography. Since 1986 she has been collaborating in the annual "Bibliography on the *Comedia*" and has published several reviews in the *Bulletin of the Comediantes.* With Hannah Bergman she cocompiled *A Catalogue of* Comedias Sueltas *in the New York Public Library* (2 vols.), published by Grant and Cutler in 1980. At present, Szmuk is Special Collections Librarian at Saint John's University, New York, where she also teaches history of books and printing, as well as book preservation in the Division of Library and Information Science. She is a member of the Grolier Club.